RETHINKING METHODIST HISTORY
A Bicentennial Historical Consultation

Editors
Russell E. Richey   Kenneth E. Rowe

Papers given at Drew University, April 1983
in a Consultation on Methodism and Ministry: Historical Explorations
sponsored by Division of Ordained Ministry
of the General Board of Higher Education and Ministry
The United Methodist Church
The Theological and Graduate Schools, Drew University
General Commission on Archives and History,
The United Methodist Church

Kingswood Books
An Imprint of The United Methodist Publishing House
NASHVILLE

RETHINKING METHODIST HISTORY

ISBN 0-687-361702

CONTENTS

FOREWORD

The Bicentennial of United Methodism was observed by the Division of Ordained Ministry of the General Board of Higher Education and Ministry through a celebration of contemporary United Methodist scholarship. Four significant volumes were either published or encouraged by the division in a series entitled *An Informed Ministry: 200 Years of United Methodism*. They were: *Ministerial Education in the Methodist Movement* by Gerald O. McCulloh (1981); *A Source Book of American Methodism* by Frederick A. Norwood (1982); *Practical Divinity* by Thomas A. Langford (1983); *An Educated Ministry Among Us: United Methodist's Investment in Theological Education* by G. Melton Mobley (1984).

In addition to these publications, the celebration of scholarship continued with two outstanding consultations initiated and managed by the division. In April 1983, Drew University was the site for historians to gather under the theme of *Methodism and Ministry: Historical Explorations*. Emory University was the location in August of that year for the second consultation, *Wesleyan Theology in the Next Century*, at which theologians from across the church met to review our denomination's theological task for the next century.

These consultations constituted the largest and most representative scholarly events in the history of our denomination—an appropriate recognition of two centuries of commitment to scholarship in the Wesleyan tradition. Those privileged to attend the consultations were inspired and stimulated by the high quality of major addresses and workshop papers. The Division of Ordained Ministry applauds The United Methodist Publishing House in making many of the documents from both occasions available to a wide audience throughout the church. Superbly edited by Dr. Russell Richey of Drew University, assisted by Dr. Kenneth Rowe, and Dr. Theodore Runyon of Candler School of Theology, these volumes will be valuable resources in the continuing historical and theological exploration of our Wesleyan tradition.

May readers discover some of the excitement and inquiring spirit these papers reflected in their original presentation.

Donald H. Treese
Associate General Secretary
Division of Ordained Ministry
General Board of Higher
  Education and Ministry
The United Methodist Church

PREFACE

The Division of Ordained Ministry of the General Board of Higher Education and Ministry is pleased to share with The United Methodist Publishing House in this effort toward a renewal of historical and theological integrity within The United Methodist Church.

The Consultation from which these papers have been selected, entitled, "Methodism and Ministry: Historical Explorations," was held at Drew University, Madison, New Jersey, in the spring of 1983. As part of the Division of Ordained Ministry's program of Bicentennial Observances, the Consultation was co-sponsored by the Division, the Theological and Graduate Schools of Drew University, and the General Commission on Archives and History. We are indebted to Deans Thomas Ogletree and Bard Thompson of Drew University; Drs. Richard Heitzenrater, Charles Yrigoyen, and Louise Queen of the General Commission on Archives and History; Dr. David Giles of the Division of Ordained Ministry; and Drs. Russell Richey and Kenneth Rowe of the Drew faculty; each of whom served as members of the steering committee. This committee, ably chaired by Russell Richey, one of the editors of this volume, was assisted, in its on-site work, by Mr. Donald Thorsen, a Ph.D. candidate at Drew.

Our purpose was threefold: (a) to identify and feature the work of young scholars in the area of church history; (b) to undergird and strengthen the teaching of United Methodist Studies by providing an opportunity for teachers in this area to gather and share ideas and resources; and (c) to rediscover and reaffirm our own unique historical and theological Wesleyan heritage. This publication, and others which have grown out of the Consultation, demonstrate both the wisdom and success of each of these goals.

John L. Topolewski
Project Manager,
    Bicentennial Observances
Division of Ordained Ministry,
    General Board of Higher Education
    and Ministry

INTRODUCTION

Russell E. Richey

The essays of *Rethinking Methodist History* offer a fresh reading of important Methodist topics; revise major interpretations; model new approaches to the study of the several Methodisms; explore promising but largely uncharted terrain; project paradigms for further testing; offer schemes for inclusion—of women, blacks, native Americans, Asians in Methodism and of the several Methodisms in the Protestant and American experience; reach for controlling themes in Methodist experience; and bring both passion and moral judgment to scholarly assessment of Methodist dilemmas.

The twenty-three papers included were among fifty selected to be presented at a bicentennial Consultation on Methodism and ministry, held in April 1983, under the sponsorship of The Theological and Graduate Schools of Drew University and the Division of Ordained Ministry and the General Commission on Archives and History of the United Methodist Church. The consultation sought fresh appraisals by scholars actively engaged in examining the histories of the several denominations of the Methodist family. By purpose and design, both that consultation and this volume which issues from it, re-estimate the Methodist past. Taken collectively, these essays do not tell a sustained Methodist story. Collections rarely do. Rather, they move readers into the midst of the current historical enquiry, provide them access to the range of methods in use, open up debates, and invite them into the field.

Organization

The volume is structured so as to model three approaches to rethinking Methodist history (represented by the three sections). Within each section the essays follow roughly in chronological order. Persons wishing a broad overview might read the analyses of long-term trends by Rowe, Dunlap, and Schmidt and then see below for chronological ordering.

In I, **"Reappraisals,"** authors reassess central Methodist themes. While only three (Baker, Smith, Schmidt) self-consciously revise standard assumptions, all re-interpret the Methodist past in some fashion and all attend to general patterns. Even the apparently focused studies by Smith (on Bishop Coke) and Forbes (on native

American missions) reach for general conclusions. Not surprisingly, these essays rely on the approaches utilized for the big picture—intellectual history and the narrative form. Their "rethinking" derives from a fresh and imaginative reading of the data.

Surprises and insight result. Smith, for instance, transforms Coke from an occasional British visitor, an episcopal phantom, into the force that gave name, shape, tone, and direction to episcopal Methodism. Baker, in a kindred endeavor, shows developments that have been traditionally read as evidencing Americanization to be typical stages in the unfolding of (British) Methodism. In an act of unusual scholarly grace, Schmidt revises herself, notably her theory of a late 19th-century public party/private party Protestant schism. Methodism, she argues, boasted a succession of apostles who sustained the Wesleyan tension between piety and social mission. Rowe also charts a Methodist faithful, yet with more ironic result. Methodism's historians, though accenting their accounts differently, remained surprisingly committed to numerical expansion as the measure of Methodist fidelity. They failed to see, however, the diversity that the numbers represented.

Several papers rethink ministry. In succinct fashion Dunlap reviews another central aspect of Methodism—itineracy—charting its evolution and its relation to connectionalism. Forbes shows that an itineracy apparently so functional among white Americans proved disastrous when utilized cross-culturally for missions to native Americans. Jones tracks the careers of two successful itinerants, whose "call" to holiness itineracy brought them into conflict with the rules and rulers of Methodist itineracy. And Sledge usefully describes the modeling of ministry though the course of study, a remarkable device for holding together Methodist commitments to a mobile ministry and to education.

In II, **"New Approaches,"** the authors experiment with new methods, apply to religious history perspectives borrowed from other disciplines, draw upon innovative trends in American historiography. The essays reflect the resurgence of social history and its application to American history of theory, method, focus derived from the social sciences. Following the pattern of social historians, the authors borrow freely and diversely. Mathews and Williams employ anthropology; Carwardine, political science; Andrews, Marti, and Gillespie, sociology; Gravely and King, generalized social theory. The arguments are complex. As such, none readily yields one sentence summation. In general, these essays attempt to locate Methodist development in the rich texture of American life. Thereby, stale denominational terms, seemingly parochial conflict, tired generalizations recast themselves in vigorous imaginative fashion. These re-imagings bring into sharp relief the cleavages in Methodism—gentry and poor folk, white and black, men and women, clergy and laity, northerners and southerners. They also display the sheer power of the Methodist vision, which swept over these divisions to class, race, sex, region, nationality—to alter and be altered. In this section, the Methodist past is re-viewed, quite literally. Through new lenses, the familiar assumes different shape.

In III, **"Agenda,"** the authors point Methodist scholarship in new directions. They do so in various fashion. Some bring heightened sensitivity to the exploration of unused or underutilized materials. Zaragoza imaginatively probes the extensive spiritual manuscripts left by Catherine Garrettson, heretofore known primarily as the wife of a famous itinerant. Tholin reads the once immensely popular dialect humor of Marietta Holley in feminist perspective. McClain "investigates" the FBI with evidence released under the Freedom of Information Act.

Others enlarge the context within which Methodism is understood. Yrigoyen, for example, views Methodism through the eyes of major critics. Baldwin compares the black Methodisms. Kim juxtaposes Korean and Korean-American Methodist and Presbyterial polity. Still others bring national issues into case study. Lippy does so by exploring the quest for open itineracy and an inclusive church in South Carolina. Zaragoza and Tholin refract women's religious experience through a single person's writings. McClain raises general questions about restraints on social ministry by exposing the FBI's harassment of Harry F. Ward. Finally, Baldwin's essay self-consciously and other essays in this section indirectly call for the posing of new questions and the developments of new paradigms for gathering Methodist data.

The tidy classifying of essays into re-reading, re-viewing, re-directing perhaps puts far more order into the present scholarly ferment than either these essays or the new Methodist scholarship warrant. The editors concede that a number of the essays were candidates for more than one section. Further division of the essays would also serve to highlight other trends. The classifications were intended to open rather than close the question of "Whither Methodist history?" Fortunately, to that question the essays speak richly and diversely.

The Essays

In **"Counting the Converts: Progress Reports as Church History,"** Kenneth E. Rowe pursues as the theme of Methodist history the Wesleyan imperative to report membership numbers. He documents in five major interpreters from the Methodist Episcopal Church an unreflective reliance on religious body count as criterion of success, providential blessing, Americanization, progress, denominational legitimacy, and correct policy. The tone and purpose of the accounts differ. Jesse Lee's "honest," "undiplomatic," even "uncomplimentary" 1810 narrative of growth befits a reformer. Nathan Bangs took four volumes in 1838-41 to show expanding Methodist Episcopacy rather than the reformist movements to constitute faithfulness to Wesley. Also in four volumes (1864-67) and in various abridgments thereof, Abel Stevens portrayed a national Methodism as the providential agent of American civilization and progress. James M. Buckley saw decline rather than progress in Methodism's acculturation but fought with history (and other weapons) to defend her strength, polity. The great 20th century historian of Methodism, William Warren Sweet, made his Mississippi Valley frontier the test of American religions and pronounced Methodists (and Baptists) the typically American denominations on the strength of their numerical success there. Numbers were the measure of Methodism.

Like Rowe, E. Dale Dunlap traces a central feature of Methodism, **"The United Methodist System of Itinerant Ministry."** With Rowe, he is impressed by the pragmatic attitude and presumption of providence that permitted American Methodists to adapt and reshape this Wesleyan legacy. He devotes much of the essay to the "slow but steady change from radical itineracy to localism." Yet Dunlap insists upon continuity as well as change. He suggests three resilient essentials of itineracy: missional and strategic character; actualized in a covenant that bound congregation, clergy, and connection, sealed by an appointive power lodged in bishops; and exercised through the principle of mobility. Possessed of this basic integrity, conducive to connectionalism, yet adaptive and flexible, itineracy, according to Dunlap, retains the capacity to respond to challenges from within and without the system today.

Frank Baker dissents from the historiographical tradition described by Rowe which measures American Methodism for its "Americanness." When called upon to assess American Methodism, Baker has drawn upon his unparalleled acquaintance with the Wesleys to portray a continuing Wesleyan legacy.[1] In **"The Status of Methodist Preachers in America, 1769-1791,"** Baker extends that search for trans-Atlantic continuities by stretching not just Wesley but also the British connexion across the waters. He finds early American Methodist activities, ministerial careers, restiveness with the Wesleyan yoke, reaffirmation of loyalty, maturity and even independence to be *natural* within the Wesleyan economy and paralleled by the British experience. His discussion reassigns into the morphology of Wesleyanism those acts in the colonial and post-Revolutionary drama that have often been read as the Americanization of Methodism. Baker concedes that the Methodisms over time have come to differing nuances, but the concession only reinforces the conclusion that radical reassessment of early American Methodism is in order.

Like Baker, Warren Thomas Smith magnifies the British component in American Methodism. His title only hints at the claims for Coke's importance (**"Thomas Coke's Contribution to the Christmas Conference: A Study in Ecclesiology"**). Possible architect of the plan to transfer authority, Coke as Wesley's secretary/confidant, legal adviser, alter ego, and troubleshooter was the logical agent of its execution. He planned and presided over the organizing conference, planted the name, ordained, preached the ordination sermon, altered both the title of the presiding officer and part of the liturgy, published the latter (and, with Asbury, the *Discipline*), took over the plans for a school and the anti-slavery campaign, and left the missionary impulse as his monument. While cautious where evidence is thin, Smith thinks that Coke was the shaping force of the denomination.

"Methodist Mission Among the Dakotas: A Case Study of Difficulties," by Bruce David Forbes, compares the efforts of five mission programs, with the Methodists emerging a relative failure. In contrast to missionary boards which committed personnel to the Dakotas for the long haul and then resourced them, the Methodists experimented with enveloping the native Americans in the itinerant system. Among European peoples (and perhaps African?), itin-

eracy could elicit indigenous leadership, affirm community, draw upon the vernacular, accommodate varying Anglo-American authority systems, adapt in strategic fashion to adverse situations, and educate its ministerial leadership while in harness. It proved incapable on all those points in a cross-cultural situation. The Methodist missionaries failed the initial course, learning the language, the medium of meaningful communication. The mission was eventually thrust out. Much Methodist history, as Rowe has reminded us, all but apotheosized itineracy. Forbes' account suggests that we need to ask again how features of the Methodist system really worked. Studies of polity and of mission which have perhaps too long gone their separate ways may well provide answers. On this point see also the essay by Kim.

As Forbes shows connectional itineracy to be ineffectual when functionally closed to the community it sought to penetrate, so Charles Edwin Jones explores the disruption occasioned when itineracy surfaces within itineracy. In **"The Holiness Complaint with Late-Victorian Methodism,"** he compares two resolutions of that conflict, that of Henry Clay Morrison who stayed technically within episcopal Methodism by location and that of Phineas F. Bresee who withdrew to organize the Church of the Nazarene. Both had long and successful careers within the itinerant system until they began to itinerate for the holiness cause. Both experienced the church as opposed to holiness. In 1890 when Jones draws the comparison, Morrison was using the columns of his *Pentecostal Herald* to wonder about the sanctity of the Methodist system.

The courses of study were the reading/testing programs by which 19th century Methodism prepared its ministers and cultivated connectional unity and uniformity. In **"The Well-Furnished Minister: The Conference Course of Study in the M.E. Church, South, 1900-1939,"** Robert W. Sledge pursues the policy and procedure governing that course in the years of its decline. The course, he argues, reflected (and reinforced) important developments in the church as a whole—the drift from episcopal to commission authority, theological shifts, deliberate efforts to achieve unity, the inclusion of new theological disciplines, professionalization and centralization of instruction in a Vanderbilt-based correspondence school, the gradual valuation of training gained in colleges and seminaries. Sledge profiles the minister as the course would have "him." He also remarks on what the 20th century course lacked—anti-semitism, denominational polemics, discussion of the holiness issue, literature on race relations. Ministry he finds to have been a gentleman's pursuit.

" 'Reforming the Continent and Spreading Scriptural Holiness': Reexamining the Public/ Private Split" summarizes Jean Miller Schmidt's agenda. Fabricator of the thesis that late 19th century Protestantism divided into public and private parties, Schmidt asks herself whether it adequately explains Methodism. She answers in the negative. Within Methodism there existed a will to hold together the twin Wesleyan purposes (of her title). She discerns that will, however, on the boundaries—in reform and reformers. She selects four historical moments and a number of exemplary figures who combine deep personal piety with social vision and action. These include the abolitionist and Wesleyan Methodists, Orange Scott, La Roy Sunderland, and Luther Lee; the anti-segregationist bishop, Gilbert Haven; Frances Willard, Lucy Rider Meyer, and Belle Harris Bennett, generators of women's organizations and women's consciousness; and Bishops Reverdy Ransom (AME) and Francis McConnell (MEC), campaigners for social justice. Schmidt concludes by searching for historical understandings adequate to this tradition and by associating herself with it in a call for fidelity and renewal. Methodist history and historians, she suggests, must find ways to reflect (upon) the Wesleyan vision.

Donald G. Mathews has already earned acclaim for his re-creation of the evangelical world. In "Evangelical America—The Methodist Ideology," Mathews confines himself to Methodists and to the Revolutionary generation, 1770-1810. He functions as translator. He seeks fresh meaning for the words Methodists employed for religious experience. The watchwords—preaching, itinerancy, conversion, holiness, liberty, discipline, society, anti-slavery, camp meeting— shatter to disclose language that itself shattered conventions. The Methodist ideology countered the social and political meanings of gentility with visions of new community and new identity. Some who share Mathews' estimation of evangelicalism construe these psychological revolutions as preparatory of the Revolution or Republicanism. Wary of such excess, Mathews does regard the creation of the Methodist language as a political endeavor. He evokes the power of Methodist terms "for scrutinizing 'authority,' establishing 'legitimacy,' assuming 'personal responsibility,' and expressing 'liberty.' " Among blacks, he suggests, this language comes to highest fulfillment. Early black Methodism thus becomes Methodism's most adequate self-expression.

The essay by William Williams, "The Attraction of Methodism: The Delmarva Peninsula as a Case Study, 1769-1820," complements the essay by Mathews. Why by the end of the revolution were 20% of the adult population Methodists? Why was almost one-third of Methodism on the peninsula? What explains the Methodist appeal? Williams isolates five reasons: ethnicity—Methodism succeeded in Anglican/ English areas as a second English church; demography—it capitalized on country-town antipathies; efficiency—Methodism out-proselytized its competition; and the promise of salvation—a major factor in the universality of its appeal, according to Williams. But he devotes the bulk of the paper to a fifth factor—Methodism as "An Alternative Value System." Effecting a moral revolution, capitalizing on dis-ease in and with the dominant gentry culture, Methodism appealed in diverse fashion to various groups. Williams analyzes its attraction to "The Better Sort," "The Middling Sort," "Poor Whites," "White Women," and "Blacks."

In "African Methodisms and the Rise of Black Denominationalism," Will B. Gravely charts the step-by-step process by which blacks achieved religious independence. Comparing the sagas in Philadelphia, Baltimore, Wilmington, and New York, Gravely accents the spontaneous, communal initiatives which eventuated in the AME, African Union, and AME Zion denominations. Seeking congregational legitimacy and integrity, blacks resorted to independence only when denied enabling requests. "Their routes to congregational autonomy carried them through the processes of property ownership, church building and maintenance, black trusteeism, access to local preacher, exhorter and diaconal ranks of ministry, the control of congregational discipline and the question of denominational representation." When full ordination and representation were denied and independence was declared, separatism was complete. Black trusteeism looms particularly large, an interesting note given the theme's importance elsewhere in Methodism and in American life.

Mathews and Williams delineate a Methodist ideology counterpoised to gentility. Dee Andrews in "The People and the Preachers at St. George's: An Anatomy of a Methodism Schism" catches a community divided at that breakingpoint in the social spectrum. An early Philadelphia schism honored class lines. Comparing the membership and lay leadership of a party which withdrew to form a separate congregation with that left to face (but stave off) imminent financial ruin, she found the former to be primarily merchants and the latter artisans. She hypothesizes that religious life style and personality differences, largely class based, underlay the exercises in Methodist discipline/politics which the record shows. Differences and dissension derived from a late 1790s revival. Revival doubled both white and black membership. It also created clashing expectations for congregation and ministry. The dispute made interesting bedfellows. The cultured Ezekiel Cooper, who sized up the dispute much as has she, bedded down with the poorer sort. Bishop Asbury, who for the record worried over Methodism's inclusion of the wealthy, its toe-holds in the cities, and the dangers of schism and who waxed eloquent over Methodism and the poor, lay down with the better sort. In this dispute, Andrews finds that laity exercised power and influence not scripted by the *Discipline*.

In **"Methodist Ministers and the Second Party System,"** Richard Carwardine also investigates politics, outside rather than within the system. He treats Methodism's assumption of public responsibilities in keeping with her mid-century size and respectability. Abandoning older political inhibitions and sympathy for the Democrats largely reactive to the Federalist Calvinists, Methodists joined other evangelicals in defense of Christian America through the Whig party. Driven by fears (Romanism, Mormonism, freethinkers and apparent Democratic courtship thereof) and by hopes (represented in Whig manipulation of Christian symbols and policy on issues of anti-masonry, Indians, and partisanship), Methodist ministers in the 1840s across the nation experimented with a variety of political roles on Whig behalf. This common political cause with denominations which had once disdained them brought into the national political forum two issues which would shatter the second party system and the churches alike, slavery and nativism. By the mid-1850s, episcopal Methodism was several times divided. And Northern Methodists were finding a new home in the Republican party while their Southern counterparts were drifting into the Democratic fold of Fillmore's American party. Meddling in politics became a new ministerial fashion, "sin" according to the Southern lexicon. The effects, Carwardine argues, were not ministerial manipulation of congregations as critics charged but rather the political tutoring of Methodist folk and loosing in the political realm of an uncompromising moral rhetoric. They had "sounded forth the trumpet that shall never call retreat."

Astounded that an 1883 volume dedicated to *Methodism and Literature* could overlook a periodical which lasted 35 years and claimed a paid circulation of 40,000, Joanna Bowen Gillespie explores **"The Ladies Repository, 1841-1861: The Emerging Voice of The Methodist Woman."** Methodist (male) ministerial oversight in its senses of prescriptive care and of inattentive omission is the foil for Gillespie's narrative. Although male governed, the *Repository* served as a medium through which the educated, ambitious female leadership of Methodism gained a public voice on subjects once reserved to men. That voice became audible—despite the ministerial editors—through letters to the editor. These attained ever greater prominence until they became a regular column. Therein the "Ladies" nurtured one another into the religious maturity and independence that would eventually yield a new consciousness and varied forms of activism. When that occurred, they no longer needed the *Repository*. The magazine gave space and respectability to the concerns that weighed on women's spirits until they finally outgrew it. Through their letters, then, the readers had shaped their magazine and themselves.

Like Gillespie, Donald B. Marti employs a publication as a symbol system through which to re-enter the 19th century Methodist world. Marti's topic, however, is men, **"Rich Methodists: The Rise and Consequence of Lay Philanthropy in the Mid-19th Century."** And his publication is Bishop Matthew Simpson's *Cyclopaedia of Methodism*. Singularly adroit at garnering the support of rich laity for his causes, Simpson celebrated these ornaments of Methodism in his *Cyclopaedia*. Of its 1600 biographical entries, 347 described MEC laity. That professional and commercial elite exercised through philanthropy "a new kind of lay participation in Methodist polity." Lay participation in governance came, Marti suggests, as ecclesiastical recognition of responsibility already assumed. Marti charts the substantial roles played by a cluster of wealthy Bostonians on the church's behalf and then the way in which the "substantial" character of advocates for lay representation earned support. The 129 men present during the 1872 General Conference were recognized as "men of note" in their respective localities. Simpson's *Cyclopaedia* featured 92 of them.

A further sign of Methodism's acculturation is to be found in its experimentation with inclusive, culture-affirming ministries. This William McGuire King explores in **"The Role of Auxiliary Ministries in Late Nineteenth-Century Methodism."** He focuses upon religious education represented in the Sunday Schools and Chautauqua; the Epworth League which brought youth into teaching, service, and church life generally; and the deaconness movement which afforded women vocational self-identification in service. King highlights the agency of Bishop John Heyl Vincent in these diverse experiments in lay service to the culture. In contrast with revivalism's denial of culture, the auxiliary ministries stressed education, professionalism, lay training, and service. So they prepared the church for two important 20th century trends—the social gospel and the culture of professionalism.

Mathews, Williams, and Andrews depict Methodism in social/ideological struggle with gentility. **"Lost in the Ocean of Love: The Spiritual Writings of Catherine Livingston Garrettson,"** by Diane Lobody Zaragoza probes that struggle as inner and spiritual. The soul in turmoil belonged to the elite Livingston family. A traumatic conversion altered her life-style, threw her with the despised Methodists and consummated in marriage to the itinerant, Freeborn Garrettson—all to her family's horror. Diaries, journals, and letters, some richly sexual, many highly mystical, all precisely introspective, chart the soul's progress. Are such mystical streaks typical or extraordinary? Inner battles pose interpretive problems as acute as the clash of class or ideology. With sensitivity, Zaragoza analyzes the extensive spiritual writings of Garrettson as inner dramas of women's spirituality, Methodist perfection, and Western mysticism.

His title, **"New Directions for the Study of Blacks in Methodism,"** only partially describes Lewis V. Baldwin's endeavor. In the process of proposing new problems and new paradigms, Baldwin surveys existing literature on blacks in Methodism. Both in its descriptive and prospective thrusts, the essay seeks to overcome the barriers that have segmented the study of blacks and Methodism. Baldwin demands scholarship surmounting the lines drawn by racism and denominationalism. That, in turn, will occasion rethinking many historical generalizations and attention to neglected topics. Among the former, he numbers judgments about the political-social activity of black Methodism before the civil rights movement. Among the latter he suggests John Wesley and Africa, black women, blacks, and ecumenism.

Methodism's mid-19th century strategic unity with other evangelical denominations and accession to social responsibility muted some opposition and criticism. But Methodist colabor for evangelical America earned the church new critics. Opponents of the evangelical cultural synthesis thought Methodism responsible for its most "objectionable" features. The romantically conservative movement in the German Reformed Church led by John Williamson Nevin and Philip Schaff construed Methodism the exemplar of un-Protestant, new measures revivalism. These Mercersburg theologians termed Methodism to be American religion at its worst. Charles Yrigoyen, Jr. charts **"Mercersburg's Quarrel with Methodism,"** and parades the epithets thrown—inauthentic, un-Protestant, anti-intellectual, un-Biblical, sectarian, unchristological, unchurchly, unsacramental. He also explores Methodism's response. Hyper-sensitivity on both sides derived, he argues, from evangelical/Methodist influenced divisions within the German community.

Roles played by women in the creation and maintenance of Victorian culture and particularly the relation of cultured women and ministers in those fabrications we now recognize as critically important. Phyllis Tholin in **"Samantha and her Sisters: Images of Women in the Writings of Marietta Holley,"** contributes some complicating and interesting Methodist wrinkles to those patterns. The literary career she examines rivaled that of Mark Twain. Holley's immensely popular Samantha stories stayed in print for 10-20 years, enjoyed serialization in *Petersen's* and *Ladies' Home Journal* and in one case sold over a million copies. Premised on the marriage of a literary woman and a minister and narrated by Josiah Allen's wife, these stories caricatured the social scripts of Victorian culture. In dialect humor, Samantha exposed male and clerical authority and pretensions and advocated woman suffrage, temperance, and various reforms. The rational, practical, effective partner in the marriage, Samantha and other women around her modeled powerful alternative images for American women. Thereby these stories encouraged political consciousness, as the encouragement of Susan B. Anthony and Frances Willard would indicate.

With documents released under the Freedom of Information Act, George D. McClain investigates **"Social Ministry and Surveillance: Harry F. Ward and the Federal Bureau of Investigation."** Cofounder and long-time executive of the Methodist Federation for Social Service and professor at Union Theological Seminary, Ward emerged as the premier Methodist activist in a panoply of causes and organizations. Criticism of intelligence policy earned him harassing surveillance for two periods, 1922-25 and 1941-65. His dossier, apparently shared with other governmental agencies, for a period fingered Ward for custodial detention in national emergency. Assembled in a fashion calculated to force conformity rather than gain accurate information, the file was biased by its virulent anti-communism and contemptuous hostility, by unsubstantiated allegations, by magnification of Ward's influence, and by the "hope that church authorities would censor or expel Ward." McClain's probe suggests new directions for the study of church and society, the church as specter in political hallucination.

After the white conference had defeated one plan for integration and the black conference a second, South Carolina United Methodists approved a third under pressure of a 1972 deadline. The background, details, and implementation of the merger of the largest black conference with a large white conference, Charles H. Lippy examines in **"Towards an Inclusive Church: South Carolina Methodism and Race, 1972-1982."** Lippy suggests that leadership mattered, that the media (*Advocate*) and joint activities broke resistance, that symbols of inclusion proved critical. Initial success at the conference level resulted. The next stage—real integration at the local level and open itineracy—has wanted "signs of inclusiveness," occasions for interaction, adequate coverage and leadership. In fact, new conference leadership—spared the exacting attention to racial sensitivity that the merger generation experienced—has been "less alert" to the "nuances and subtleties" of inclusiveness. That failure, Lippy notes, comes at a point when the agenda of inclusion demands the recognition of diversity in the two communities, resourcing of black ministry so as to make it an attractive career option and inclusion of blacks without sacrificing their rich heritage.

"Organizational Patterns of Korean-American Methodist Churches: Denominationalism and Personal Community," by Illsoo Kim, seeks explanation for the dramatic growth of Korean and Korean-American Christianity in the congruences of Christianity with Korean culture. While acknowledging the importance of ideological factors, Kim suggests that missions to Korea prospered in proportion to their accommodation to traditional communal patterns of self-governance and Confucian social codes. Presbyterians succeeded most completely in meshing their polity with this intense localism and hence predominate. Korean Methodists, in both Korea and the U.S., have compensated by yielding to very un-connectional and seemingly presbyterial patterns of local and lay authority.

Congregations built on this basis in the U.S. have multiple appeal. Nonterritorial, open, integrative, grass-roots communities, they function as a cultural-linguistic social service center. At the heart of this personal community is a strong, pioneering pastor who sustains its traditional culture, homeland polity, family atmosphere, ethnic ethos, social service. The Korean-Methodist patterns of community, polity, and leadership pose new questions for the United Methodist hierarchy as much as for scholars. What is the Methodist vision and from where does it derive? That, as these essays have shown, has been a recurrent issue for Methodism.

Conclusion

Whether during its bicentennial Methodism proclaimed grace and freedom, readied itself for its third century, and looked ahead, time will surely tell. There can be little doubt that Methodism looked back, steadied its grasp on the past two centuries, and proclaimed history. The writer attended six major conferences on Methodist history and without straining to research the matter was aware of serious local and regional scholarly endeavors across the continent. Those diverse facets of the Methodist teaching office—media, conference leadership, offices charged with interpretation in the various agencies of the churches, publishing houses, educational institutions—took the scholarly challenge of the bicentennial quite seriously. Publication of Methodist history took a quantum leap. Some of that will be ephemeral and unfortunately not soon enough. But the number of highly competent books, the reprinting of documents, the reissuing of out-of-print standards has made the bicentennial an important phase of Methodist self-examination.

When historians re-view the bicentennial, they will doubtless discover that this scholarship resulted less from the spontaneous outpouring of the Methodist spirit than from the endeavor on the part of historians and other interpreters of Methodism to gain a hearing for what they had already been thinking and perhaps saying. For good or ill, this book may well serve as evidence for such an argument. Its sponsorship shows the Division of Ordained Ministry of the General Board of Higher Education and Ministry of The United Methodist Church to have taken advantage of the bicentennial to labor for a better understanding of ministry and a ministry better informed.

Indeed, what this volume best attests is that the bicentennial both elicited and exhibited ongoing Methodist efforts at historical self-understanding. The essayists here included wrote for the occasion—the consultation and this volume—but in every case did so out of larger research projects in which they have been engaged. Hence this volume points beyond itself to the considerable rethinking of Methodist history which the bicentennial did not so much cause as air. Rightly used, this volume becomes an invitation to readers to the Methodist past, perhaps to their own research, certainly to engagement with what is here sampled. And fortunately, further sampling is also possible, most immediately in the companion theology volume whose strong historical note evidences just how much Methodists have to look back in order to look forward. *Methodist History* provides ongoing access to new Methodist scholarship. A 1984 issue of *The Drew Gateway* contained other essays delivered at the Drew consultation. The *Canadian Historical Society Papers* for 1984 consid-

ered U.S., Canadian, and British history. The *Newsletter* of the World Methodist Historical Society features papers delivered at its conference at Asbury Seminary. *Quarterly Review* offered a bicentennial issue. And finally, the two volumes of *Women in New Worlds*[3] dramatically display the directions and quality of contemporary Methodist scholarship.

Whatever else the bicentennial of 1984 accomplished, it revealed and encouraged the rethinking of Methodist history.

NOTES

1. Frank Baker, *From Wesley to Asbury* (Durham: Duke University Press, 1976).
2. Donald G. Mathews, *Religion in the Old South* (Chicago: University of Chicago Press, 1977).
3. Hilah F. Thomas, Rosemary Skinner Keller, and Louise L. Queen, eds., *Women in New Worlds*, 2 vols. (Nashville: Abingdon Press, 1981, 1982).

I. REAPPRAISALS

Counting the Converts:
Progress Reports as Church History

Kenneth E. Rowe
Drew University

American Methodism's confidence in God acting in and through history endows the past with momentous importance. It becomes a potent force for the historian. Each successive generation of Methodists, and each successive member of the Methodist family of churches, demanded a fresh telling of the story from its own perspective and for its own purposes. As a case study, I have selected for analysis five general histories of the Methodist Episcopal Church—(1) Jesse Lee's pioneering work of 1810; (2) the establishment-securing history of Nathan Bangs in the early 1840s; (3) Abel Stevens' mid-century celebration of Methodism's achievements; (4) James M. Buckley's Gilded Age chronicle of the 1890s; and (5) William Warren Sweet's upbeat history which gave the church a much-needed lift during the Depression of the 1930s. These were the histories which largely expressed and shaped the Methodist Episcopal Church's historical self-understanding. Widely read in their time by layfolk and clergy alike, several were also required reading for the church's candidates for the ordained ministry.

Although Methodism's histories and historians have been a matter of interest for the curious for more than a century, no comprehensive study of them has been attempted. Completion of the project would entail examination of the principal histories of the Methodist Protestant Church, the Methodist Episcopal Church, South, the Evangelical and United Brethren Churches, the independent black Methodist churches, and the independent evangelical Methodist churches. The focus of my paper, however, is solely on the principal histories of the northern branch of Methodism through unification in 1939.

In a letter which was written to Ezekiel Cooper a few weeks before his death in 1791, John Wesley called for his American preachers to give "a connected relation of what our Lord has been doing in America."[1] Following Wesley's advice and example, the founding Bishops Coke and Asbury kept extensive journals, published them from time to time, and encouraged the preachers they deployed to do the same. Brief historical prefaces appeared in the newly organized church's book of discipline from the beginning. In 1805 Asbury published extracts of letters written to him by preachers and members containing "state of the church" reports from various regions.[2] But thirty years after Wesley's movement spilled over to the American colonies, no "connected relation" of the Lord's doings among them had been published.

The project of writing a full-scale history of the Methodists in America got off to a bad start. The first manuscript, penned by a journal-keeping preacher, was formally rejected by the church's General Conference of 1808. Jesse Lee (1758-1816) must have been stung when a committee of his peers labeled his manuscript "more like a simple and crude narrative of the proceedings of the Methodists than a history," declined to publish it, and passed legislation which would prevent preachers from publishing any book or pamphlet without conference approval."[3]

I. Setting the Pace: Jesse Lee's *Short History of the Methodists* (1810)

Next to Asbury himself, Jesse Lee was one of the most able and influential preachers in the founding era. He joined the Methodists a scant three years after Asbury arrived, preached his first sermon in the middle of the Revolutionary War, declared himself to be a conscientious objector, and when drafted, served as a non-combatant. Afterward, he rode circuits from Canada to Florida, but especially in New England where he was Asbury's chief lieutenant. He took a prominent role in the conferences of preachers as the church's governance structures were being hammered out by trial and error. In his later years he served several terms as chaplain to Congress. This was the man whose manuscript was summarily rejected in 1808.[4]

Despite the rebuff by his colleagues and the ban on private publishing, Jesse Lee brought out his history two years later in the spring of 1810 through a Baltimore publisher. Publication was possible only because of the financial backing of more than seven hundred history-minded clergy and layfolk, more than half of them from his native Virginia. Lee had circulated a prospectus to his many friends throughout the church in June of 1809 soliciting their support. It was a highly successful referendum in effect overturning the decision of the general conference.[5]

It is not surprising that Lee's *Short History* was greeted with such hostility by those about whom it was written. Lee was chronicling a difficult period for the church. Wesley's renewal movement had become an established American church. Preachers chafed under Asbury's imperial episcopacy, regional conferences squabbled about supremacy, layfolk and clergy vied for leadership, tempers flared, schisms sizzled. Debates about the title and garb of bishops, the merits of Wesley's prayer book, the uses and abuses of episcopal power, slavery and black presence in the churches, and even debates over what later became hallmarks of evangelism Methodist-style—camp meetings and Sunday schools—all were set forth by Lee in a brutally honest and simple narrative, in undiplomatic language and often with uncomplimentary effect.

All this tended to give the manuscript the element of an exposé. There is no cover up here; neither are there halos. To some, Lee's frequent use of the first person smacked of egotism; to others the manuscript lacked literary polish. But the chief drawback was its portrait of Asbury. Many, including Asbury himself, felt that Lee had not given the founding bishop his due. Henry Boehm said that when Asbury first saw a copy of Lee's manuscript, it "made him nervous."[6] One of the sections that made him most nervous was Lee's "chicken in the attic" theory about Asbury's wartime hideaway at Judge White's farm. While lesser members of his flock were marching up to their colonial draft boards and either signing up and taking British fire or announcing themselves to be conscientious objectors and taking American ire, said Lee, Asbury was lying low in an attic in Delaware for the better part of two years.[7] What Asbury wanted was a history that furthered what God was doing by reporting what he had done.[8] "As a record of the early history of Methodism in America," Asbury wrote in 1815, "my journal will be of use; and accompanied by the minutes of the conference will tell all that will be necessary to know."[9]

Lee's preoccupation was not with Asbury but with church growth. An increase from fewer than a thousand members to more than two hundred thousand in forty years was impressive. In his narrative he moved from the conference to the revival and to the organization of new circuits, and then back to the conference, with the plodding rhythm of the itinerant preacher on horseback. By focusing on how the Methodists kept pace with the nation's march, Lee set the pace for all Methodist historians who were to follow. His analyses were simplistic, his sources scanty, and his subject matter frustratingly restricted. Yet in many ways Lee's *Short History* is the most delightful of them all to read and gives a fine feeling of contemporaneousness. He also included important statistics and large blocks of documentary materials not then available in printed form. His work thus became a textbook for future historians and happily has been recently reprinted in facsimile with illustrations, indexes, and a map.

II. Defending the Establishment: Nathan Bangs's *A History of the Methodist Episcopal Church* (1838-1841)

Within one year of the publication of Lee's unauthorized history, Ezekiel Cooper, the American preacher to whom Wesley had suggested the need for a history of his American flock twenty years before, presented to the Baltimore conference a plan for what he called a "complete history of the Methodist Episcopal Church in America."[10] Cooper envisioned an episcopally-led, church-wide drive for materials and documents, the establishment of a central archives to house them, and the enlisting of a competent historian to examine the sources and prepare a manuscript for publication. The general conference of 1812 adopted Cooper's plan and appointed a three-person committee to carry it out. Although the ambitious project was never implemented,[11] one young member of the committee was bitten by the church history bug. For the next thirty years Nathan Bangs (1778-1860) carried on his own church history project.

Contrary to the cooperative spirit of the "era of good feelings" symbolized among American churches by the "benevolent empire" or "the evangelical united front," Bangs urged stronger denominational loyalty. He first rose to prominence in the church as a result of his verbal and printed defense of Methodist theology against assaults of the Calvinists. He then championed Methodist polity by rejecting external charges of an invalid ministry and internal demands for democratic reforms. In order to protect and promote Methodist interests, he expanded the Book Concern, launched a church-wide weekly newspaper, upgraded the church's clergy journal, helped found Methodist benevolent societies, and wrote a four-volume history 1838-1841.[12]

As second-generation Methodists in America sought to explain and consolidate their spectacular success, Nathan Bangs provided the underlying interpretation. Standing in the shadow of the founding fathers and mothers and living in fear of attack from denominational rivals without and ambitious reformers within, Methodists in the early national period struggled with issues of purpose and method, continuity and change.

Bangs looked to the past for guidance. Choosing as the theme of his history how Methodism "won its way through every opposition maintaining the purity of its character, and exerting its hallowing influences on society,"[13] he related the story of its rise and progress. Working year by year Bangs chronicled the actions of general conferences, recounted geographical expansion, described extensive revivals, reported new missionary endeavors, included obituaries of recently-deceased itinerants, and counted the years' converts. The results of his research led him to conclude that Wesley's mandate—"to reform the nation and to spread Scriptural holiness over the land"—and Asbury's methods—a disciplined army of itinerant preachers deployed by roving field marshalls called bishops—were still valid.[14]

Bangs also looked to the past for ammunition to silence the church's critics. The completion of Methodism's formative period and its attainment of a self-conscious identity did not automatically bring recognition from sister churches. Its stunning growth alarmed denominational rivals. Joining forces to beat back the interloper, they assailed Methodist doctrine and polity. Bangs sought to secure for the Methodists their rightful place in American religious life. He told the story of a small, unprepossessing band of Christians who became America's largest church. Lacking all the normal attributes of success, Methodists could only trace their fortune to the active blessing of God. If God's approbation could be clearly demonstrated in his church's prosperity, the religious community would have to take note.

From within, second generation Methodism was racked by a reform movement fighting for a redistribution of power. Beginning with O'Kelly in the 1790s, the movement reached full force in the 1820s. Expulsion of the radicals by 1828 blunted its strength, but remnants of the reform caucus remained. In addition, abolitionists were pulling the church away from its commitment to colonization toward immediate emancipation of blacks. Thrown on the defensive, Bangs labeled the reformers "malcontents," "heedless and enthusiastic lecturers," and found their actions and ideas "inflammatory" and "unjust."[15] Since he felt Methodism's adversaries intentionally distorted the church's position, he sought to set the record straight by frequently including in the text large portions of primary material—for instance, the entire report of the 1828 General Conference against the reformers, which takes up sixteen full pages in his history.[16] Counting the converts was another handy weapon. To Bangs a shrinking church like O'Kelly's Republican Methodist Church or a slow-grower like the Methodist Protestant Church signaled God's disfavor. A rapidly expanding church like his own was obviously God's favorite American church.

Bangs' history remained standard for a quarter of a century until it was replaced by Abel Stevens' history in 1864. Despite its limitations, it provided Methodists of his day with information not readily available elsewhere. It was the most authoritative guide to the actions of the general conference whose journals remained unpublished. It documented the numerical and geographical growth of the church. It gave persuasive rationale for its beliefs and practices. Most of all, it gave Methodists in the early national period a sense of identity: They were part of a dynamic church whose labors God abundantly blessed.

III. Providential Progress: Abel Stevens' *History of the Methodist Episcopal Church* (1864-1867)

Two events in the middle of the nineteenth century provided occasion for a fresh telling of the Methodist story—the centenary celebration of American Methodism and the end of the Civil War. By the end of their first century the Methodists had become the vanguard of the Protestant establishment in the nation. Northern Methodists could also proudly point to their patriotic support of Lincoln and the Union cause.

The northern church's publishing house and its national centenary committee planned an ambitious and expensive program of historical publications. They secured as author a man whose whole career fitted him for the task and who ended up taking early retirement in 1860 to complete the job. Trained at Wesleyan University, Abel Stevens (1815-1897) for twenty years had been publishing a series of regional histories and biographical works as well as editing two of the church's chief weekly newspapers—first Boston's *Zion's Herald* and then New York's *Christian Advocate*.[17]

The first of Stevens' centenary publications to be issued was a history of world Methodism in three volumes (1858-1861), which exhaustively explored the British roots and the expansion of the movement to all parts of the globe. That series merely set the stage for a four-volume history of Methodism in America (1864-1867). For busy pastors and poor seminarians, Stevens published the next year (1868) a popularly-priced one volume abridged edition of the church's American story. For the masses he prepared a popularly written centenary commemorative volume (1865). For the ladies Stevens produced *The Women of Methodism* (1866), highlighting for the first time the significant role of women in the denomination. It was Stevens' four-volume *History of the Methodist Episcopal Church*, however, which replaced Bangs's history as the church's standard for many years to come.

In the midst of the agony of the Civil War, Stevens allowed himself the luxury of taking the long view of the progress of Methodism up to that time and of its interrelationships to its national setting. Out of the eighteenth century cauldron came a revolution in science, commerce and government, and a revival of religion. America was the locus of the new birth of civilization and Methodism was the chief molder of its moral sensibilities.

Stevens combined the idea of progress, which saw for America continuing moral and material advancement, with providence which saw history as the unfolding of divine perfection. The progress of American Methodism from its humble origins to the "chief religious embodiment of the common people," says Stevens, is the most remarkable religious movement of this country.[18]

> The influence of this vast ecclesiastical force on the progress of the New World [he confidently wrote] can neither be doubted nor measured. It is generally conceded that it has been the most energetic religious element in the social development of the continent. With its devoted and enterprising people dispersed through the whole population; its thousands of laborious itinerant preachers, and still larger hosts of local preachers and exhorters; its unequaled publishing agencies and powerful periodicals, from the *Quarterly Review* to the child's paper, its hundreds of colleges and academies; its hundreds of thousands of Sunday-school instructors; its devotion to the lower and most needy classes, and its animated modes of worship and religious labor, there can hardly be a question that it has been a mighty, if not the mightiest, agent in the maintenance and spread of Protestant Christianity over these lands.[19]

Stevens attributed Methodism's success unabashedly to God's special favor. Providence had called and equipped the Methodists not solely to convert sinners but also to shape history. For American Methodists celebrating their one-hundredth birthday, there was concrete evidence that God had a special plan in mind for them. The evidence was their remarkable growth in the first half of the nineteenth century and the increasing wealth and national prestige of the denomination in the middle years. These historical occurrences were clear manifestations of divine favor and as such implied social responsibility. Through its itinerant system and the piety of its preachers, the church could reach and attract the common people. Its success in both wilderness and urban landscape enabled Methodism to shape the national conscience and to foster patriotic loyalty.

Stevens' early writings on local history and biography brought into focus ordinary people and conditions of early Methodism at the grass roots level. In his histories for the first time laywomen and laymen share the spotlight with clergy. But his work contains serious flaws. Sentimental hagiography abounds. His narrative is generously laced with biographical bits extolling common folk as heroic bearers of the church's faith. More importantly, whereas his two predecessors tended to revel in controversy and conflict within the tradition—Lee relentlessly pressing the reformist side and Bangs pressing the establishment side—Stevens concocted a peaceful and serene century. By closing the story with the passing from the scene of the chief leaders (1820), Stevens avoided discussing the turbulent twenties with its laity rights crises, the terrible thirties with its colonization and abolition crises, and the explosive forties which led to bitter divisions.[20] An imaginary church thus arose in the mind of its creator which seriously distorted the church's self-understanding for decades, since Stevens' history was required reading for candidates for the ministry until 1936!

IV. Victorian Pitfalls: James M. Buckley's *History of the Methodists in the United States* (1896)

The impetus for the publication of American Methodism's turn-of-the-century history came from outside the fold. During the latter part of the nineteenth century, historical writing became professionalized and turned academic. The formation of the American Society of Church History in 1888 marked the impact of the new movement on religious history. The new society's first major project was the commissioning of a thirteen volume history of the principal denominations in America.[21] Volume five was assigned to the Methodists and an editorial board chaired by Philip Schaff chose the Methodist Episcopal Church's chief spokesman for the job—James Monroe Buckley (1836-1920).

Buckley was then in the middle of a thirty-year career as editor of Methodism's chief weekly newspaper, the New York-based *Christian Advocate*. For many years he had taken upon himself responsibility to defend unchanged every feature of the church's doctrine and polity. To sustain his cause he used generous doses of the church's history. Widely respected for his incisive mind and combative spirit, Buckley championed the conservative cause weekly in his editorials and quadrennially on the general conference floor. He dominated every general conference of the Methodist Episcopal Church from 1872 to 1912. He knew, when it suited him, how to stop change in its tracks. Almost single-handedly Buckley kept women out of the ministry and out of the legislative conferences of the church for a generation. Upon his retirement as editor in 1912, he joined the Drew Seminary faculty where he taught "ecclesiastical law" until his death in 1920.[22]

Buckley's *History of the Methodists in the United States* was first published in 1896 in the American Church History series. The next year it was re-issued in a two-volume deluxe edition with numerous illustrations, a slightly revised title, but without series identification.[23] Buckley took the opposite stance from Stevens in both content and style. Methodism was not improving but deteriorating. Secular values and worldly amusements were diverting Methodists from their historic mission. Numerical growth continued, but at a much slower pace. To halt the slide, Buckley proposed to clarify the church's historical distinctiveness, to describe the controversies which shaped her life, and to recall the church to its God-given, discipline-ordered mandate. The needs of church growth had to be kept foremost. Since forces of dissent and reform diverted the church from its fundamental mission, the church required authority and discipline, not individual rights and congregational polity. Romantic sketches of heroic preachers and pious layfolk are not to be found here. Bishops, bureaucrats, and clergy members of legislative committees are the key figures in Buckley's holy history.

A college drop-out during his freshman year at Wesleyan, Buckley was a self-taught student of historical method. He was more sensitive than most to the standards for acceptable research.

He prefaced his history with a brief discussion of his sources and sought to verify the most important facts. A full-scale bibliography plus footnotes showed up for the first time in a major Methodist history. Buckley apparently agreed with the late nineteenth-century assumption that accumulated data organized chronologically constituted history, for his history reads more like an endless string of news releases from legislative assemblies rather than the story of the unfolding of God's plan through a spirit-filled people.

Although seriously deficient, Buckley's history is nevertheless important because it reflects a new direction in historical thought. Methodism's past did not flow out of sacred history, but was played out in the decisions of human actors set upon an institutional stage. Further, the subject matter of Methodist history was broadened. Recognizing the church's pluralistic character, Buckley included for the first time the history of other American Methodist bodies—the three independent black Methodist churches, the several evangelical Methodist churches, along with the Methodist Episcopal Church South and the Methodist Protestant Church. Yet his glancing attention to them displayed a patronizing attitude.

In the Gilded Age, with its pursuit of money, respectability, and efficiency, professional revivalists gave way to professional managers as agencies proliferated and Methodism became more bureaucratic. Buckley's history fit nicely into that ethos. Although never fully displacing Stevens as standard, Buckley's history was many times reprinted and the two volumes of the deluxe edition with their gilt-trimmed red backs and marbled boards doubtless found their way onto coffee tables in countless Methodist parlors.

V. The Most American of Churches: William Warren Sweet's *Methodism in American History* (1933/1953)

In the previous century preachers like Lee and Bangs and journalists like Stevens and Buckley wrote Methodist history. In the twentieth century the professionally-trained scholar based in seminary or university undertook the task. While most professional historians were writing about politics, patriotism, or the emergence of industrial America, William Warren Sweet (1881-1959) schooled himself in the best ways to go about writing history in his time. He majored in history at Ohio Wesleyan (1902) and took the doctorate in history at the University of Pennsylvania (1912) where he debated the merits of Turner's frontier thesis and soaked up McMaster's scientific focus on the facts. Sweet also brought a lifelong interest in religion to his vocation. Firmly rooted in the Methodism of middle America (Baldwin, Kansas, to be exact), he had already taken the B.D. degree with honors at Drew Theological Seminary (1906). His fusing of the two elements—rigorous academic training in the historical disciplines and strong identification with one of the most American of churches—led to the development of a new discipline when, in 1927, the University of Chicago invited him to a chair in American church history. During the next two decades, Sweet busied himself getting out of the chair to gather documents, chiefly on religion on the frontier, and then getting back to it to edit and write volume upon volume.[24]

Sweet was interested primarily in chronicling the growth of successful churches, churches whose large size and national distribution determined for him their "typically American" status. None was more successful, more ubiquitous, and therefore more typically American than his own church. All Sweet's early research and writing focused on telling the story of the Methodists. His Penn dissertation dealt with the causes of the division betwen north and south in 1844. After he came to Chicago, he became a vigorous advocate of the use of Methodist history as a basis for uniting the separated branches of Methodism. In the early 1930s he was commissioned by Methodist Episcopal Church's Board of Ministerial Training to write a new history of Methodism in America, emphasizing the historic bonds which united the three main branches. Moonlighting to make ends meet during the Depression, Sweet spent two fall terms at his theological alma mater, where he taught church history and ransacked the stacks in Drew's old Cornell Library. In 1933, in between those two excursions to Drew as visiting professor, the Methodist Book Concern published his *Methodism in American History*. It became the standard for a generation. A revised edition bringing the story up to date was published in 1953 and Abingdon Press still keeps it in print.

Sweet's new text reflected the growing spirit of optimism and unity within Methodism. His career coincides roughly with what may be called the triumphalist phase of American Methodist history, the era when traditional Methodist condemnation of liquor became the law of the land, and when stately buildings, ordered worship, and educated ministers became typical in Methodist churches. When reunion was achieved in 1939, Methodism became the largest and richest Protestant denomination, the un-

questioned leader of the mainstream churches of America. Its future would be even brighter than its glorious past which he knew so well.

Sweet's training at Penn taught him that history emerges out of the environmental context and that historical analyses must rest upon a verifiable base. When he began to focus on church history, he therefore placed the churches firmly within the context of American history and found the explanations for its development in the cultural and historical forces of the time.

At the heart of Sweet's synthesis lay the conviction that the first wave of westward expansion, which took place in the Mississippi valley during the two generations after the Revolution, determined the shape of American religion. The territory into which the churches were expanding was an uncivilized frontier which rendered many elements of eastern church life counterproductive or obsolete. The frontier functioned as a kind of Darwinian testing-ground in which the churches with old world, vestigial encumbrances declined or died, whereas the younger vigorous churches, more fit for frontier life, survived and prospered. In Sweet's words, "the churches which devised the best methods for following the population westward were the ones destined to become the great American churches."[25] Methodism's successful methods, Sweet said, included a strong, centralized organization capable of planning, coordinating, and executing westward expansion, a theology in tune with the American spirit, and the use of revivalism as a technique to reach the mass of unchurched settlers.

In his desire to explain institutional growth, Sweet followed the tradition of other Methodist historians we have examined. All assumed that true religions spread fastest, that the basic task of the church was to maximize expansion, and that the strength and influence of a denomination were best measured in membership statistics. Sweet shared these assumptions with Buckley, Stevens, Bangs, and Lee.

Sweet shared some of their weaknesses as well. By focusing on the frontier, Sweet gave the impression that what was occurring in the cities or in the east was of secondary importance, an assumption which few historians today would accept. He paid little attention to those who were not quite a part of church history and who had done little on the frontier. Under the influence of the melting-pot notion, Sweet largely ignored Methodism's ethnic and racial diversity. Blacks were people for whom abolitionists had done something; native Americans were folk whom Methodist missionaries tried to civilize; both were hardly agents of their own history. And then there are women who will no longer permit the story to be told as Sweet told it—almost macho style, with a tinge of frontier swagger.

Despite these flaws, Sweet's history gave mid-twentieth-century Methodists a much clearer notion of their church's developmental process. And his balanced, irenic account of past conflicts within the church helped to forge a common and sympathetic view of their history, which carried Methodism closer to unification in 1939.

Wesley's own *Short History of Methodism* (1765) and a much fuller "short history" in volume four of his *Concise Ecclesiastical History* (1781) were produced partly in defense of his evangelical movement, partly as examples of his favorite Biblical theme: "What hath God wrought!" Asbury found history in the form of "religious intelligence" to be an important adjunct to the preached word in the evangelistic task. It is not surprising that succeeding generations of Methodist historians—until our own time—followed their lead and produced progress reports as church history.

From Jesse Lee's first to William Warren Sweet's last, histories of the Methodist Episcopal Church betray Wesley and Asbury's confidence in the converting power of "religious intelligence." In each history numerical growth and geographical expansion are primarily explained by an ingenious church polity and a democratic theology. Caught up on the tradition of the new beginning, Methodist historians credited divine providence with their spectacular accomplishments and boundless potential. There was no question about the grand design in God's mind to spread Scriptural holiness over the land by means of the Methodists. History was used to demonstrate this end. Protestant Christianity, typified in mainstream Methodism, was the defender of democracy, the guarantor of social stability, the foundation of morality, the provider of education—in short, the bearer of American culture.

NOTES

1. John Wesley to Ezekiel Cooper, February 1, 1791, in John Wesley, *Letters*, edited by John Telford (London: Epworth Press, 1931), VIII, 259-60.
2. *Extracts of Letters Containing Some Account of the Work of God Since the Year 1800* (New York: Published by Ezekiel Cooper and John Wilson for the Methodist Connection in the United States, 1805).
3. *Journals of the General Conference of the Methodist Episcopal Church* (New York: Carlton & Phillips, 1855), I, 87. See also Nathan Bangs, *A History of the Methodist Episcopal Church* (New York: Published by Thomas Mason and George Lane for the Methodist Episcopal Church. 1838-1841), II, 322.
4. The best overall study of Lee is William L. Duren, *The Top Sergeant of the Pioneers* (Atlanta: Emory University Press, 1930). Two nineteenth-century biographies are still useful since they contain extensive extracts from Lee's journals: Minton Thrift, *Memoir of the Rev. Jesse Lee* (New York: Published by Nathan Bangs and Thomas Mason for the Methodist Episcopal Church, 1823) and Leroy M. Lee, *Life and Times of the Rev. Jesse Lee* (Nashville: Southern Methodist Publishing House, 1860).
5. See list of subscribers in Jesse Lee, *Short History of the Methodists in the United States of America* (Baltimore: Magill and Clime, 1810), 367-76. See also Thrift, *Memoir*, 328. A facsimile reprint with illustrations, indexes, and a map was published in 1974 (Rutland, VT: Academy Books).
6. Henry Boehm, *Reminiscences, Historical and Biographical, of Sixty-Four Years in the Ministry,* edited by J.B. Wakeley (New York: Carlton & Porter, 1865), 291. See also *Journal and Letters of Francis Asbury*, edited by Elmer T. Clark (Nashville: Abingdon Press, 1958).
7. Lee, *A Short History*, 64.
8. For this felicitous phrase, I am indebted to my colleague, Russell Richey.
9. *Journal and Letters of Francis Asbury*, II, 783.
10. Frederick A. Norwood, *Sourcebook of American Methodism* (Nashville: Abingdon Press, 1982), 149-152.
11. Bangs, II, 322-23; Abel Stevens, *Life and Times of Nathan Bangs* (New York: Carlton & Porter, 1863), 325-26; *Journals of the General Conference of the Methodist Episcopal Church* (New York: Carlton & Phillips, 1855), I, 120.
12. The best critical study of Bangs is Richard E. Hermann, "Nathan Bangs: Apologist for American Methodism" (doctoral dissertation, Emory University, 1973). The standard nineteenth century biography is Abel Stevens, previously cited.
13. Bangs, II, 3.
14. Bangs, I, 366.
15. Bangs, III, 395-440; IV, 242-65.
16. Bangs, III, 413-29.
17. No biography of Stevens has been produced. For a helpful discussion of the theme of providence in his historical writings, see Donald G. Jones, *The Sectional Crisis and Northern Methodism: A Study in Piety, Political Ethics and Civil Religion* (Metuchen, N.J.: Scarecrow Press, 1979).
18. Abel Stevens, *Compendious History of American Methodism* (New York: Carlton and Porter, 1867), 527; see also his *Centenary of American Methodism* (New York: Carlton & Porter, 1865), 210.
19. Stevens, *Compendious History*, 576-77.
20. Stevens' one-volume abridged edition, *Compendious History of American Methodism* (1867), included four skimpy chapters at the end bringing the story down to 1866, but it was the four-volume work which remained on the church's "course of study" for preachers until 1936. Stevens also published a *Supplementary History of American Methodism* (New York: Eaton and Mains, 1899), bringing the story down to 1890.
21. See Henry Warner Bowden, *Church History in the Age of Science* (Chapel Hill, N.C.: University of North Carolina Press, 1971), 58-68.
22. The sole biography is George P. Mains, *James Monroe Buckley* (New York: Methodist Book Concern, 1917).
23. James M. Buckley, *A History of Methodists in the United States* (New York: The Christian Literature Co., 1896; American Church History series, vol. 5); *A History of Methodism in the United States* (New York: The Christian Literature Co., 1897, 2 vols). A seventh edition of the original printing was issued by Scribners in 1909.
24. The best critical study of Sweet is James L. Ash, *Protestantism and the American University* (Dallas: SMU Press, 1982).
25. William Warren Sweet, *Methodism in American History* (New York: Methodist Book Concern, 1933), 143.

The United Methodist System of Itinerant Ministry

E. Dale Dunlap
Saint Paul School of Theology

Methodism began as a missionary movement. The strategies and structures of the movement developed, largely pragmatically, as a means of fulfilling that missionary vocation.

Methodism has always been, and The United Methodist Church continues to be, connectional rather than congregational in polity. The essence of a connectional system is that every church is a part of every other church, and that no one church can live to itself alone. Within such a system common consideration is given to the needs of all the churches, the good of all the churches is promoted, and decisions take account of all the churches. Connectionalism is a corporate covenant as one means of fulfilling the church's reason for being—God's call to embody and carry forth Christ's ministry in and for the world.

The promise of connectionalism is best fulfilled by an itinerant system of ministerial supply. A writer in *The Methodist Magazine* in 1843 identified an itinerating ministry as the distinguishing feature of Methodism, "that feature which constitutes the main difference between ourselves and other evangelical denominations . . . ."[1] In one way and another Abel Stevens' judgment that "the grand peculiarity of the Methodist *ecclesiastical system* is the *itineracy of its ministry* . . . the cornerstone of the whole structure"[2] has been a recurring theme throughout the years. Even those who have been critical of some aspects, or even most of the system, form a consensus that it still is the best system: Distinctive of United Methodism, the itinerant system accounts in very large measure for the phenomenal effectiveness of the movement in the United States.

Itinerant ministry is a kind of team ministry created by and for the connection as a whole. It is designed to provide careful and strategic deployment of the totality of the ministers for the fulfilling of their corporate goal and reason for being—namely, the effectiveness of the church in mission. It aims to balance the needs of the connection (the totality of the churches) with the opportunity for the minister to make her or his best contribution toward that common goal.

The "bed-rock" essence of the system of itineracy is a disciplined and directed mobility of preachers. This involves three components:

1) The context of mission, and a necessary overall strategy for the deployment of ministerial resources.

2) A covenanted commitment on the part of congregations, clergy, and connection (personified by some kind of third-party appointing power, which historically has been the bishop), which involves the surrender of certain individual rights in order to benefit from the values of convenantal rights and principles, and in the interest of the common cause.

3) The principle of mobility of clergy who are committed to the mission of the Church and the United Methodist system, though requiring no particular length of tenure.

The covenant relationship that characterizes itineracy is double in nature: clergy members of an annual conference covenanting with each other to form an interdependent and complementary "group" ministry, and the clergy covenanting with the connection and the churches to provide their ministerial needs—all within the context of commitment to the mission of the church. The system promises that each church will be provided ministerial leadership, and that each clergyperson will be provided a charge. It requires that each charge must receive and support the minister appointed, and that each clergyperson must go to and serve faithfully the appointed charge. Being a covenant, it is voluntarily entered into and mutually binding. No one called to preach has a "natural," religious right to fulfill that calling as an itinerating United Methodist church. They become so by voluntarily entering a covenant relationship, the conditions of which are known in advance and accepted, and the fulfillment of which is characterized by obedience—joyful obedience, hopefully. Such a system can operate successfully only when there is a mutual concession on the part of churches and preachers, both giving up the right and power of absolute choice, and in the final analysis accepting the decision of a duly constituted third party—the appointing power, which in United Methodism is the bishop.

Loyalty to the system, albeit sometimes critical — and properly so—is necessary to the effective functioning of itineracy. Historically United

Methodism has taken the position that the preacher has voluntarily entered into the covenant relationship for evangelical religious purposes, and that if one becomes convinced that the system is wrong, or finds it unacceptable, or becomes unable to fulfill the covenant, after all constitutional efforts to improve or change the system have failed, the appropriate alternative is to withdraw from the traveling ministry of The United Methodist Church.

The origin of the itinerant ministry in Methodism was incidental and providential. It certainly was not a premeditated and carefully projected design in the mind of John Wesley. His passion was the saving of souls, and his sole aim, as he wrote to Samuel Walker, a clergyman of Truro, in 1756, was and still remained "to promote . . . vital, practical, religion; and order, then, is so far valuable as it answers these ends.[3] Itineracy was a strategy for meeting the spiritual and religious needs of those who responded to Wesley's evangelism—the people called Methodists. Of necessity Wesley was forced to use lay persons to assist him in the various bands, classes, and societies. The next step was the use of some of the more promising laity as "sub-pastors." Then came the use of "lay preachers," local and itinerant.

In his description in the *Minutes* of 1766 Wesley says that "after a time a young man, named Thomas Maxfield, came and desired to help me as a son in the gospel. Soon after came a second, Thomas Richards; and then a third, Thomas Westell. These severally desired to serve me as sons, and to labour when and where I should direct."[4]

As a matter of fact Wesley had no alternative but to use lay preachers if he was to accomplish anything at all. The clergy would not help. In his *Farther Appeal to Men of Reason and Religion* Wesley defends his use of lay preachers by showing that circumstances forced him to accept "this surprising apparatus of Providence," which certainly ran counter to his own prejudices.[5] As far as he was concerned the fruit of their labors was vindication of their use. The spread of Methodism would have been impossible without the itinerant lay preacher.

John Wesley laid down certain unalterable conditions for itinerant ministers who asked to join him in his work. "None needs to submit to it (his direction)," he says, "unless he will . . . Every Preacher and every member may leave me when he pleases. But while he chooses to stay, it is on the same terms that he joined me at first,"[6] —namely, that it was needful that they should do that part of the work which Wesley advised, at those times and places which he judged most for God's glory.[7]

The strategy of being able to send his helpers when, where, and how they were needed for the good of the connection and its mission was only a part of the value of a system of itinerant ministry for John Wesley. He found great value in itineration *per se*. Again replying to Samuel Walker, Wesley insisted that to restrict the preachers to individual societies would ruin the work as well as the preachers themselves— whether ordained or unordained . . . .

> I know, were I myself to preach one whole year in one place, I should preach both myself and most of my congregation asleep. Nor can I believe it was ever the will of our Lord that any congregation should have one teacher only. We have found by long and constant experience that a frequent change of teachers is best. This preacher has one talent, that another. No one whom I ever yet knew has all the talents which are needful for beginning, continuing, and perfecting the work of grace in an whole congregation.[8]

Wesley was convinced that the societies would become as dead as stones if preachers remained in the same place too long.[9]

Whatever gave promise of usefulness in the promotion of evangelism and meeting the needs of the societies was used by Wesley, and if fruits were forthcoming, that was sufficient validation of divine approval. Nearly everything Wesley did was basically pragmatic and prudential—or, as he would prefer, providential. This is not to say, however, that there was no theological rationale, but only that his mode and means of promotion and administration derived from practicality rather than theory.

It was this system of itinerant ministry that was instrumental in the mission of Methodism to America. And it was this system of itinerant ministry, adapted to a new and radically different environment, that was to be the distinguishing mark and instrumentality of the Methodist Episcopal Church.

There were similarities between the system of itineracy in England and in America. There was the same directed and disciplined mobility, with the same "double" itineracy—movement from circuit to circuit with limited tenure, and movement from charge to charge within the circuit. There were distinct and significant differences also. With the end of the Revolutionary War Methodism became a church, not a connection of societies—an *ecclesia* rather than *ecclesiolae in ecclesia*. It had to operate in a geographic expanse and contour unlike and more expansive than anything in England. It found itself in the context of an unsettled and dynamic cultural climate that was "in process" of becoming in a way unfamiliar to England, even on the eve of social revolution. American Methodism began its independent existence with a notion of ministry markedly different from that in English Methodism of the time. American traveling preachers, for the most part, were ordained, which involved them in a priestly function. In a way and to an extent not to be characteristic in England until sometime after Wesley's death, Methodist ministry in America combined the pastoral office with the prophetic. Dr. J. D. Lynn suggests that an additional factor added by the Americans to the Wesleyan notion of ministry is that of identifying willingness to travel with an authentic call to preach. A call to preach is a call to travel. Itineracy became the norm of ministry.[10]

The system of itinerant ministry was peculiarly suited to the Methodist missionary enterprise in frontier America. Whether positive or negative, the dairies, journals and letters of the preachers attest, as Professor Frederick Norwood observes, to the "universal domination" of the itinerant system in American Methodism[11] and it is apparent that "until about the end of the Civil War, frontier conditions favored the itinerant system, in spite of the natural difficulties."[12]

Reading the literature of Methodism in general and American Methodism in particular, one is struck by the paucity of direct spiritual and theological apology for the system of itinerant ministry. Claims of a scriptural mandate or warrant for the system are not made by the Methodists, but beginning with Coke and Asbury in their *Notes to the Discipline*, and continuing throughout most of the nineteenth century, Methodists extolled the system as "the primitive and apostolic plan"—" . . . *that plan* which God has so wonderfully owned, and which is so perfectly consistent with the apostolic and primitive practice."[13] The theological rationale for the system has to be discovered more by extrapolation from general descriptions and discussion of pragmatic values than from intentional theological analyses. Bishop McKendree's phrase, "the universal spread of the Gospel," provides the clue to the fundamental theological rationale of Methodism's system of itinerant ministry. Itineracy is tied intimately to the mission of the church, an outgrowth of the New Testament message. Pragmatic justifications are voluminous. Methodists have never supposed that there was any particular form of church polity of divine prescription. The mode of governing the church is left, as Abel Stevens wrote, "to its own discretion and the exigencies of time and place."[14]

It has been well observed that "if the itinerant ministry had its beginning under the leadership of Wesley, it had its greatest development under the direction of Francis Asbury."[15] Asbury believed in the plan of itineracy, heart and soul — and he modeled it with uncommon intensity. It was clear to him that it was absolutely essential to the fulfillment of the Methodist mission in the new nation. Very quickly after his arrival he saw that while the work was to be found chiefly in the towns, it could have much greater extension if taken into the villages and crossroads. Within weeks of his arrival in America in 1771 he wrote in his *Journal*:

> I remain in New York, though unsatisfied with our being both (himself and Boardman) in town together. I have not yet the thing I seek—a circulation of preachers, to avoid partiality and popularity. However, I am fixed to the Methodist plan, and do what I do faithfully, as to God. I expect trouble is at hand. This I expected when I left England.[16]

Two days later he wrote:

> I judge we are to be shut up in the cities this winter. My brethren seem unwilling to leave the cities, but I think I shall show them the way.[17]

And "show them the way" he did, traveling an estimated 270,000 miles, much of the time suffering illness that normally ought to have caused his death in short order. But he kept it up to the end.

Professor Frank Baker identifies Asbury as "an ecclesiastical Darwinist" (*i.e.*, a religious pragmatist) who honored the past, but for whom no practices were sacrosanct (except the system of itineracy?). "Even his doctrine of the ministry was functional: you were a minister because you were used of God, and only as long as you were used by God."[18] Asbury was certain that to have

an efficient itineracy it was essential that the preachers should be tightly ordered and firmly disciplined—though the specific rules and administrative practices to which they must respond and which they in turn would enforce should be flexible enough for variation in face of constantly changing circumstances. To ensure a disciplined people, an adequate ministry, and a smoothly running itinerant organization, it was essential in Asbury's view to have an acknowledged leader or leaders—an apost late, and episcopacy.[19]

In his "valedictory," his advice offered to Bishop William McKendree in 1813, Asbury was still reinforcing his conviction about an itinerant ministry. "I wish to warn you," he said, "against the growing evil of locality in bishops, elders, preachers, or Conferences."[20] And at the end of the address he commends the itinerancy as distributing talents more broadly and diversifying services more widely than any other system.

The system was a demanding one and the itinerants were subject to rigorous discipline. Once Asbury had been made General Superintendent in 1784 he had the power to send preachers to circuits "with the comprehensive view of a statesman whose eye is on the far horizon, and with the disciplined strategy of an army commander who deploys men as seems best to serve the cause."[21] And he used that power. The "cause" was everything with Asbury, and the preachers (including himself) were servants to that end. It must be remembered, however, that they had voluntarily entered into this covenant of service and sacrifice. While Methodist bishops theoretically had absolute power and discretion in appointing preachers, by 1844 most of them practically received the counsel of their presiding elders and communications from both preacher and people—in greater or lesser degree.

In Coke's and Asbury's view the episcopacy was as itinerant as the traveling preachers—an itinerant general superintendence. In their "Notes" in the *Discipline* of 1798 they wrote:

> It would be a disgrace to our episcopacy, to have bishops settled on their plantation here and there, evidencing to the world, that instead of breathing the spirit of their office, they could, without remorse, lay down their crown, and bury the most important talents God had given to men.[22]

In the system bishops are regulated by the same itinerant principle as the other preachers. They go on to say that if through improper conduct the episcopacy loses the confidence of the preachers and conference, the appointing power can be taken from it and invested in other hands.[23]

The cost of the system in human effort and sacrifice was fantastic. The preachers were constantly on the go, exposed to all kinds of weather, especially vulnerable to epidemics and disease, for which, in addition to the expectancy of an eternal reward, they received less than $100 cash per year. Most of the men were young when they died. "Promised nothing either as they entered the traveling ministry or as they retired from it, they were nevertheless expected

to give all of themselves to their calling. And they did, by the hundreds worn out before they were forty."[24]

Professor Norwood is right in identifying the early itinerant Methodist preachers as being "as close as one could come in Protestantism to the absolute vows imposed on members of monastic orders."[25]

Demanding as the system was, it was not inflexible. From the beginning it was able to respond to the ever-changing circumstances of the geographical frontier, and during the two centuries of its development it has adapted to the new conditions created by social, economic and cultural changes. There would have been, all along, general agreement with "Nathan Plainspeak" in his view that "the itinerancy is a human invention. As such it is from its very nature constantly in need of repair and renovation, as such is capable of unlimited improvement, as such must be adapted to new conditions as fast as they arise."[26]

Thomas Coke and Francis Asbury were unwilling to consider any change that might run the least chance of "wounding" the itinerant system. To an astonishing extent the dedicated preachers responded to the bishop with an "I'll go where you want me to go." They knew the system was a hard one, but they saw its superiority in the field and "dreaded experimentation" that might disturb the foundations. They viewed "the gospel *and the itinerancy* (as) a fine illustration of power geared to adequate machinery."[27] William Watters wrote in 1806, "I never moved from one Circuit to another, but what it reminded me that I was a Pilgrim—that here I had no continuing city—that I was a tenant at will, and ought to be always ready." Alfred Brunson shared this positive view, opposing the change to the two-year time limit—because it was too long.[28]

Everyone, however, did not view the system as an unmixed blessing or the pinnacle of perfection. Thomas Ware, certainly a committed itinerant, felt that the system was "too severe." Nicholas Snethen and Benjamin Lakin expressed similar reservations.[29] Professor Norwood makes the following cogent observation:

> That the system of itinerant ministry was not universally popular is indicated by the number of locations of men who for one reason or another simply couldn't take it any longer. A substantial report of the Committee on Ways and Means of the General Conference of 1816 dealt with the problem and recommended a series of improvements to render the plan more tolerable. Salaries (allow-

ances) should be higher (though still very low); parsonages should be provided, along with fuel and food; provision should be made for support of retired preachers; a plan for a course of study should be set up.[30]

In addition to the severity of the system itself, there was early resistance to the way in which the appointing power was being exercised. Men dropped out rather than continue under it. Others balked and were disciplined. There were frequent trials and expulsions. All of this surfaced under the leadership of Thomas O'Kelly, who enlisted Coke's aid in calling a conference on October 31, 1792, to consider abolishing arbitrary aristocracy (Asbury's), giving the conference of the district the right to nominate presiding elders, limiting of districts in the general conference, allowing each preacher to appeal his appointment to the conference, and establishing a conference of at least two-thirds of the preachers to check up on everything. The crux of the matter is found in the following motion offered by O'Kelly on the second day of the conference: "After the bishop appoints the preachers at conference to their several circuits, if any one thinks himself injured by the appointment, he shall have liberty to appeal to the conference and state his objections; and if the conference approve his objections, the bishop shall appoint him to another circuit."[31] After lengthy debate the motion was overwhelmingly defeated. O'Kelly and others, including young William McKendree, later to return and become Asbury's "successor," walked out and left the Methodists.

"The itineracy," President Horace G. Smith wrote some time ago, "proved to be a system tailor-made to reach the people and to create a church under conditions that prevailed for half a century after the organization of Methodism." Adapted to reach the multitudes moving westward, it was marked by discipline and flexibility. "Only the other system," he says, "—the lay ministry of the Baptist Church—was able to cope with this pioneering situation."[32] The success of the system needs no proof beyond the telling of the story itself. Professor Norwood quotes Abel Stevens to the effect that the operation of the Methodist itinerant system was analagous, not to American democracy, but to military discipline, and then observes:

The frontier produced a curious combination of rigid authoritarian discipline associated with a high degree of independent responsibility—authoritarianism tempered with individualism, obedience invested with freedom. Sent out under the sole authority of the bishop from the annual conference, his was not to reason why but only to accept obediently whatever appointment was his, always under the necessity of giving up that appointment in return for another at regular intervals—this same preacher enjoyed a degree of freedom in the accomplishment of his task almost unparalleled in the annals of the ministry . . . . This curious combination of discipline in the annual conference with freedom on the circuit has entered into the permanent fabric of the American Methodist ministry.[33]

Bishop F. Gerald Ensley observed that "while the Methodist system may have been Hamiltonian in its ideals of authority and efficiency, the personnel who made it go were Jeffersonian in their sympathies and willingness to sacrifice for the people."[34]

The values of the system were simple and clear. It was intensely motivated by the missionary objective to "go into all the world" that all might be saved. It was mobile, following people wherever they went on the frontier. It was strategic, putting preachers where and when they were needed for purposes that meshed into an overall pattern of missionary and evangelistic endeavor. It provided a freedom from congregational control that encouraged and made possible prophetic preaching and pragmatically creative pastoral functioning.

There were problems also. To begin with there was the difficulty of finding men who would submit to the rigors of the system. "I am shocked," wrote Asbury in 1801, "to see how lightly the preachers esteem, and how readily they leave, the traveling plan. O Lord, by whom shall Jacob arise?"[35] Apparently some of the itinerants could not discipline themselves in their freedom, and there were complaints that some developed the habit of appearing for the first time on their appointed circuits immediately prior to the first quarterly conference and departing immediately after the fourth, and while preaching and classes were promoted, pastoral duties and instruction of children were neglected.[36] For the total sacrifice required of the itinerants, there was no security for families, which had to be neglected during their almost continuous absence; no provision in the case of disability, which was almost the rule; and no support in old age. Even at the earliest stages there were pressures from the laity to obtain and retain "the most able and lively preachers for their respective circuits," thereby subverting the itinerant plan.[37]

The most serious and prevailing problem had to do with marriage. Anyone involved in the discipline of the itineracy could never expect to have a normal home and family life. It was almost impossible to stay with the traveling ministry for any length of time unless one remained celibate. Most of the men who continued in the itineracy did not marry. Asbury preferred it this way. When it was called to his attention that the low and precarious financial support resulted in an "involuntary celibacy," he responded, "All the better!"[38] That this was not widely accepted by the preachers is attested by Asbury's response to the news that a favored preacher was to be married: "I believe the devil and women will get all my preachers."[39] Not only did marriage make for problems of appointment, it also was resisted by the circuits who were in no mood to support a minister's wife. If a preacher did marry, it often meant that he would locate. The early *Disciplines* admonish: "Take no step toward marriage without first consulting with your Brethren."[40] The whole matter of marriage and location constituted a serious problem, summarized by Dr. W. W. Sweet:

The great loss of traveling ministers through their 'location' is showed by the fact that, of the 1,616 preachers received into the conferences from the beginning of American Methodism to 1814, 821 had located, most of them within a relatively few years after their admission; 131 had died in the service; 34 had been expelled; and 25 had withdrawn. As late as 1809, of the 84 preachers in the Virginia Conference, only 3 had wives.[41]

Bishop Coke did not agree with Asbury on the desirability of a celibate traveling ministry, believing that preachers could do better work and serve longer in effective ministry if consideration was given to basic needs, normal family life, and provision of old age.[42] But Coke did not stay around long enough to have any moderating influence. Actually, however, the celibate ministry of Asburian Methodism appears to have been on the way out by the time Asbury died in 1816.[43] With the change in the time limit set on tenure in a circuit, Methodist ministers began to marry and establish homes. Even so, the episcopal address to the 1844 General Conference addresses a continuing concern:

The admission of married men into the itinerancy (has) had a debilitating influence upon the energies of the itinerant system . . . . A large proportion of the young preachers marry before they graduate to the Eldership, and no small number while they are on trial. And this has almost ceased to be an objection to their trial. In general it is quite sufficient that they have 'married prudently.'

It is not easy to calculate the extent of the influence of this practice to enervate the operations of the itinerant ministry. . . . The circuits which would have received and sustained them with cordiality as single men, in consideration of their youth and want of experience, have very different views and feelings when they are sent to them with the encumbrance of a family . . .

It is to be feared that these men have either mistaken their calling in the beginning, or by early temptation lost the spirit and power of it.[44]

Given the very nature of the system of itinerant ministry, the length of time an itinerant is permitted to stay in the same place is a crucial issue. It appears to be the perennial concern that has engaged the traveling preachers more existentially than any other.

The first *Discipline* of the Methodist Episcopal Church, printed in 1785, but containing the actions of the organizing Conference of 1784, identifies the duty of the superintendent (bishop) among others, "to fix the Appointments of the Preachers for the several Circuits: and in the Intervals of the Conference, to change, receive, or suspend Preachers, as Necessity may require; . . ."[45] In the beginning, at Asbury's discretion, the appointments were changed every three months, with a tenure rarely exceeding six months. The first formalization of a time limit seems to be the following note in the *Minutes* of 1794: "The bishop and Conferences desire that the preachers would generally change every six months, by the order of the presiding elder, whenever it can be made convenient."[46] In fact, "between 1794 and 1804 the terms greatly lengthened. Many remained *two* years, and several stayed *three* years, and Francis Asbury *could not* prevent it."[47]

In 1800 a pastor named Stebbins was appointed to Albany, New York. He was very popular and the people wanted continued reappointments. Asbury thought it a mistake, but the pressure was so great that he did so against his better judgment. Some of the preachers proposed that to avoid this kind of thing, the conference set a maximum limit. Asbury had some reservations about this restricting of the appointive power, but made no real objection. As a result the conference of 1804 directed that no preacher was to remain in the same station more that two years successively (excepting the presiding elders, the editor and general book steward, the assistant editor and general book steward, the supernumerary, superannuated, and worn-out preachers).[48]

Bishop Asbury made the appointments without consultation. This changed with William

McKendree who was elected bishop in 1808 and took the leadership after Asbury. He introduced the practice of consulting with the cabinet on ministerial appointments, "getting around Asbury's objections to this innovation adroitly by explaining that, unlike his old father in the faith, he needed the help of the presiding elders."[49]

From 1836 onward efforts were made to lengthen the time limit, but without immediate success. The conference that year held that "it is inconsistent with the genius of Methodism to continue a preacher for many years in succession in the same part of the work, and, therefore, the bishops are advised not to continue any preacher for many years in succession in the same city, town, or district."[50] "The *Journal* of the General Conference of 1840 recorded the opinion of the Committee on Revisals that 'the time has not yet arrived for such alteration of the *Discipline.*' "[51]

The General Conference of 1844 provided "that, with the exceptions above mentioned, he (the bishop) shall not continue a preacher in the same appointment more than two years in six, nor in the same city more than four years in succession, nor return him to it after such term of service till he shall have been absent four years."[52] This was repealed in 1856. The Methodist Episcopal Church, South, carried the two-year limit into its structure in 1844. (Eventually an exception was made for New Orleans, where a man might serve longer because it was felt it took at least two years to build up immunity to yellow fever.)[53]

The pressures of changed circumstances, however, could not be resisted forever. As Bishop Harmon observes, "with the development of more and more station churches, and the establishment of parsonage homes in connection with these, and also with the growth in membership and the ongoing of time, there was increased pressure to obtain relief from the ironclad time limit of earlier years. In every Annual Conference there proved to be situations where it was clearly in the interest of the work for a man to be continued longer in a special situation than the law allowed."[54] Evidence suggests that the real breakthrough on the time limit began with the appointment of special editors, secretaries, missionary personnel, and other ministries, whose work could not be adequately consummated under the strict time limits applied to the regular traveling preachers.

The Methodist Episcopal Church was the first to respond to these pressures. In 1864 the limit was extended to allow an appointment of not more than "three years in six."[55] As an experiment, it was further extended to five years for regular preachers-in-charge in 1888.[56] By 1900 that experimental rule was dropped, and there was no further time limit established. In the Methodist Episcopal Church, South, there was growing feeling that a more settled pastorate would greatly enhance the interests of the church, and at the conference of 1866 a committee recommended the removal of all time limits. The recommendation was overwhelmingly accepted. Under the pressure of conservative "elders," led by Bishop Pierce, who threatened to resign, the action was reconsidered the following day and the conference settled for a maximum limit of four consecutive years.[57] Provision was made later for exceptions if the bishop had the approval of a majority of district superintendents given by ballot. This legislation continued until the time of union in 1939.

The Methodist Church, in its initial *Discipline* in 1939, placed no time limits upon the tenure of a traveling preaching in a given charge. At this point, however, changes begin to appear in the conditions under which appointments are to be made. In that first *Discipline* it is stated that the bishop "shall appoint Preachers to Pastoral Charges annually after consultation with the District Superintendents; *provided* that, before the official declaration of the assignments of the Preachers, he shall announce openly to the cabinet his appointments."[58] The 1940 *Discipline* stipulates that "*provided*, further, that before the final announcement of appointments is made the District Superintendents shall consult with the Pastors when such consultation is possible."[59] A move to force the Superintendent to consult also with the Pastoral Relations Committee involved was voted down.[60] This seemingly modest provision was a significant restriction upon the unlimited authority of a bishop to make appointments that was to lead to even further modifications. This restriction was made explicit in 1953 when an Annual Conference appealed to the Judicial Council for an interpretation of the meaning of "consult." The decision makes clear that while the final authority in appointing preachers to their charges rests upon the presiding bishop, "it does not relieve the District Superintendent of the responsibility of consulting with the preacher in order to ascertain whether there are any reasons why the appointment should not be made. Therefore, the final reading of the appointment of preachers to their charges must be preceded by consultation of the District Superintendent with the preacher."[61] Clearly, the District Superintendent is now mandated to participate in the appointing process which up to this point legally had been the exclusive prerogative of the Bishop. A minor revision in 1948 provided that the District Superintendent did not have to consult the pastor when that person had left the seat of the Annual Conference without permission.[62] In 1964 a further provision was made: "Bearing in mind the stated goals of an inclusive church, he shall seek the co-operation of the Cabinet and congregations in the appointment of pastors without regard to race or color."[63]

The Evangelical United Brethren Church and The Methodist Church came into the union of 1968 with no time limits upon the tenure of a traveling preacher in a given charge. The first *Book of Discipline* of The United Methodist Church contains Paragraph 432.1 (now 391.1) of the 1964 *Discipline* of The Methodist Church without a change of any kind.[64]

The movement to require consultation with the Pastoral Relations Committee in the appointment-making process that failed in The Methodist Church in 1940 came to fruition in The United Methodist Church in 1972. That legislation provided that "the bishop shall provide for consultation with the Pastor-Parish Relations committee or its representative," and that "before any announcement of appointments is made, the district superintendents shall consult with the pastors and the local Pastor-Parish Relations committees or their chairpersons concerning their specific appointments . . . ."[65]

Dramatic evidence of the movement to restrict the power, if not the authority, of both bishop and cabinet and to broaden the participation of both pastors and local churches in the decision-making process of appointment-making is provided in the 1976 *Book of Discipline*. In it there is an entire section on appointment-making that requires consultation with the parties affected by the process of appointment-making, and announcement of the appointment to these parties before public announcement is made. It spells out the consultative process in detail and identifies the criteria to be used in making appointments.[66]

Both the fact and the far-reaching implications of this action constitute the most revolutionary adjustment of the system of itineracy to the challenge of changing circumstances in the two centuries since it was laid down as the foundation of American Methodism. One can almost feel the vibrations of Bishop Asbury turning over in his grave. The extent to which it is responsive to the concerns the traveling preachers have with the system is astonishing. The test, of course, lies in the extent and spirit of its implementation.

The simplest description of what has hap-
pened to the system of itineracy in American Methodism is that it has undergone a slow but steady change from radical itineracy to localism. In different ways Dr. Lynn and Professor Norwood provide impressive illustration of this thesis.[67] Dr. Lynn holds that between 1784 and 1844 the role of minister in Methodism shifted from simple evangelical proclamation to denominational promoter and administrator, with the concomitant change that called for a more settled ministry.[68] Professor Norwood says that during the nineteenth century the traveling ministry became localized, both in the sense of the increase of stations as against circuits and the lengthening of pastorates. In this process he sees two sociological factors at work, the western movement of the frontier which tended to foster the itineracy, and the urbanization of society which tended to destroy it. He makes an interesting value judgment:

> The change was probably necessary, to fit the changing times, for, after all, the itineracy was a human invention. But something of the light of the Wesleyan tradition was extinguished, for out with the itineracy went the fundamental concept of a world parish, an unlimited ministry called to publish the glad tidings in the great unknown. Location could too easily mean stagnation. That is why I suggest that the missionary has inherited one of the central features of the Methodist ministry.[69]

As early as 1774 Asbury was having to deal with the pressures toward localization when friends of Thomas Rankin requested that he be left in New York for a longer time. His *Journal* recounts other similar requests.[70] While the system was being regularly extolled in the literature, the frequent expression of concerns about this aspect of the itineracy in the bishops' addresses to conference—as early as 1828—underscore the reality of the problem. By 1844 there were few circuits left in the north and east. That year in their Address to conference the bishops deplored the fact that "in some Conferences little or nothing remains of the itinerant system, but the removal of the preachers once in two years from one station to another." At the same time they were insisting that "the itinerant plan of preaching the Gospel is an essential element of this system. It was laid as the chief stone in the foundation of the whole building."

A major problem arose with the appearance of the large churches. Increasingly the prestigious city churches tended to disregard the obligations of the itinerant system and to subvert the appointive system by operating on what was practically a "call" system—initiating and making prearrangements with a pastor, and then "seeking" the consent of the bishop to make the appointment. Some even thought their decision should be final. The Methodist Episcopal Conference of 1884 took the position that "direct negotiations between pastor and churches in advance of the making of the appointments by the bishops are contrary to the spirit of our itinerant ministry and subversive of our ecclesiastical polity, and as such should be discouraged by our Bishops, Pastors, and people."[71] Apparently this did not have the desired effect, for in 1912 conference enacted the same resolution again. The episcopal address that year dealt with the problem at length. Bishop Thomas B. Neely felt strongly that if the practice was allowed to continue it would weaken or even destroy the appointing power, work injury to everyone, and work disaster in the church. He observed that the problem was not with the system, but with too many interfering with it—a few laymen of prominent churches, some preachers, and some presiding elders.[72] More than half a century later this problem is still not unknown.

Further pressure was put on the system and the goodwill of the regular traveling preachers by the steady increase of special appointments, which by 1880 involved over three hundred ministers in the Methodist Episcopal Church. While still remaining officially traveling preachers, they were virtually located. This phenomenon, too, has increased steadily to the present.

The very success of the itinerant system was a significant factor in its modification. As membership in local congregations grew and more churches developed on a circuit, it became necessary for the traveling preacher to travel less extensively and devote his time to fewer churches. The inevitable outcome was that the station (a one-point charge) became common. And, as Dr. Gerald F. Moede has observed, in this development the pastoral office assumed a new importance, occasioning a new relationship between Methodist preachers and their people.[73] When this relationship grew into mutual satisfaction and appreciation, the natural tendency was to resist change and to seek a continuation of it.

By the turn of the century it was clear that the Methodist system of itinerant ministry was experiencing an irresistible and irreversible metamorphosis. During the early period of American Methodism itineration meant that a preacher literally was constantly traveling—on the move from place to place within a circuit and from circuit to circuit, at the direction of an appointing power with absolute authority. For a long while now itineracy basically has meant that

the preacher is amenable to periodic (at increasingly lengthening intervals) change of appointment, with increasing participation in the decision-making related to it. There is almost no comparability between the present condition of relative stability of time, opportunity for settled family life, adequate to luxurious parsonages, minimum salaries, and health and retirement provisions, and the earlier one of constant mobility, no chance for a settled family life, few amenities for living, meager financial support, and no security in infirmity or old age. How the change has affected the traveling preachers' ministry, particularly its missionary thrust and sacrificial mode, is a moot matter.

The social and cultural context in which connectionalism and itineracy have to do mission and ministry today, if it is to be done at all, has changed—as it always has. The rigors of a radical itineracy were relatively subject to acceptance and fulfillment by a celibate itineracy to a degree not realistic by a largely married one. Legitimate family responsibilities mean that some kind of accommodation is required between the claims of itineracy and family. Spouses' right to self-identity and fulfillment in their own vocations has to be acknowledged. The insistence upon a greater measure of participation in self-determination, by both clergy and congregation, cannot be ignored.

The system of connectionalism and its strategy of itinerant ministry has worked well throughout Methodist history, and in the light of past crises calling for change and adaptive reponsiveness of the systems, there is hardly warrant for anticipating or predicting its demise at this time. It has always been a pragmatic and flexible system in its functioning—and still is. The working of the system obviously requires a very high level of commitment and willing cooperation of churches and preachers. In the last analysis, however, the effectiveness of the system is going to lie in great measure with bishops and cabinets—prepared to work the system with equity, sensitivity, and as much skilled consultative collegiality as possible, but ultimately clearly on the basis of missional strategy and thrust.

Without doubt United Methodism finds itself in this kind of a situation. It is a moot question whether the new social order is either in principle or in fact any more fluid than the frontier society of Methodism's first century in America. There is a remarkable similarity between them. Once again the flexibility and adaptability of the system is being put to the test. Historically the system has always been able to adapt, but always in such a way as to preserve the integrity and essence of connectionalism and itinerancy. The question is, Can and will we adapt the present-day version of United Methodism's system of connectionalism and itinerant ministry to meet the challenge?

NOTES

1. *The Methodist Magazine*, Vol. XXV, 1843, p. 278. Quoted by James David Lynn, *The Concept of Ministry in the Methodist Episcopal Church, 1784-1844* (Ann Arbor: University Microfilms, 1978), p. 223.
2. Stevens, Abel. *An Essay on Church Polity: Comprehending an Outline of the Controversy on Ecclesiastical Government, and a Vindication of the Ecclesiastical System of the Methodist Episcopal Church* (New York: Lane & Tippetts, 1847), p. 172f.
3. Wesley, John. *The Letters of the Rev. John Wesley, A.M.*, John Telford, editor. Volume 3 (London: The Epworth Press, 1931), p. 192.
4. Wesley, John. *The Works of the Rev. John Wesley, M.A.*, Thomas Jackson, editor. Vol. VIII (London: John Mason, 1829), p. 311.
5. *Ibid.* p. 227. (See all of Part III, pp. 201-247.)
6. *Ibid.*, p. 313.
7. *Ibid.*, p. 310.
8. Wesley, *Letters*, Vol. 3, p. 195.
9. Lawson, A.B. *John Wesley and the Christian Ministry* (London: S.P.C.K., 1963), pp. 103-104.
10. Lynn, James David. *The Concept of Ministry in the Methodist Episcopal Church 1784-1844* (Ann Arbor: University Microfilms, 1973), p. 81ff.
11. Norwood, Frederick A. "The Church Takes Shape, 1784-1824," *The History of American Methodism*, Vol. I, Emory Stevens Bucke, editor (New York: Abingdon Press, 1964), p. 469.
12. Norwood, Frederick A. "The Americanization of the Wesleyan Itinerant," *The Ministry in the Methodist Heritage*, Gerald O. McCulloh, editor (Nashville: The Board of Education of The Methodist Church, 1960), p. 44.
13. Quoted by Abel Stevens, *op. cit.*, pp. 140f, from *1798 Discipline.*
14. Stevens, *op. cit.*, p. 1.
15. Smith, Horace Greeley. "The Itinerant Ministry," *Methodism*, William K. Anderson, editor. (Cincinnati: The Methodist Publishing House, 1947), pp. 161-166.
16. Asbury, Francis. *The Journal and Letters of Francis Asbury*, Vol. I, Elmer T. Clark, J. Manning Potts, and Jacob L. Payton, editors (Nashville: Abingdon Press, 1958), p. 16.
17. *Ibid.*
18. Baker, Frank, *From Wesley to Asbury: Studies in Early American Methodism* (Durham: Duke University Press, 1976), p. 120.
19. *Ibid.* p. 122.
20. Norwood, "The Church Takes Shape," *op.cit.*, pp. 486-87.
21. Smith, *op.cit.*, p. 167.
22. Norwood, "The Shaping of the Methodist Ministry," *op.cit.*, p. 346f.
23. Robert W. Goodloe, *The Principles and Development of Church Government with Participation Application to Methodism* (Nashville: Cokesbury Press, 1932), p. 233. (Quoting Coke and Asbury's *Notes to the Discipline*.)
24. Norwood, "The Church Takes Shape," *op. cit.*, p. 469.
25. *Ibid.*
26. Quoted in Norwood, "The Americanization of the Wesleyan Itinerant," *op. cit.*, p. 50.
27. James A. Hensey, *The Layman in the Itinerancy* (New York: The Methodist Book Concern, 1919), p. 153f. Italics in the original.
28. Cited in Norwood, *The Story of American Methodism, op. cit.*, p. 137.
29. *Ibid.* p. 138.
30. Norwood, "The Shaping of Methodist Ministry," *op. cit.*, p. 342.
31. Norwood, "The Church Takes Shape, 1784-1824," *op. cit.*, p. 437.
32. Smith, *op. cit.*, p. 167.
33. Norwood, "The Americanization of the Wesleyan Itinerant," *op. cit.*, P. 36f.
34. F. Gerald Ensley, "American Methodism: An Experiment in Secular Christianity," in Bucke (ed.), *The History of American Methodism*, Vol. III, p. 622.
35. Asbury, *op. cit.*, Vol. II, p. 288.
36. Norwood, "The Americanization of the Wesleyan Itinerant," *op. cit.*, p. 42f.
37. Harmon, *op. cit.*, p. 51. (Quoting from Coke and Asbury's *Notes*, p. 34.)
38. Norwood, "The Church Takes Shape, 1784-1824," *op. cit.*, p. 469. (Quoting from Asbury's Journal for February 1, 1809.)
39. Don W. Holter, "Some Changes Related to the Ordained Ministry", *Methodist History*, Vol. XIII, No. 3, April, 1975, pp. 183f. (Quoting from W. W. Sweet, *Virginia Methodism, A History*, Richmond, 1955, p. 155.)
40. *Ibid.*, p. 132.
41. *Ibid.*, p. 183f. (Quoting from W. W. Sweet, *The Methodists, Religion on the American Frontier*, 1783-1840, Vol. IV, p. 50.)
42. Norwood, *The Story of American Methodism, op. cit.*, p. 139.
43. *Ibid.*
44. Lynn, *op. cit.*, p. 94. (quoting *The Address of the Bishops to the General Conference*, 1844, p. 11.)
45. Thomas B. Neely, *The Bishops and the Supervisional System of the Methodist Episcopal Church*. (Cincinnati, Jennings and Graham, 1912), pp. 93f. (Quoting the answer to Question 26. What is the office of a Superintendent? from the *Discipline* of 1785.)
46. Harmon, *op. cit.*, pp. 98f.
47. Buckley, *op. cit.*, pp. 153ff.
48. Harmon, *op. cit.* (Citing *Journals of the General Conferences*, 1796-1836, New York, Carlton and Phillips, 1855, p. 56).
49. Norwood, *The Story of American Methodism, op. cit.*, p. 144. See also Smith, *op. cit.*, p. 169.
50. Harmon, *op. cit.*, p. 9.
51. *Norwood, "The Americanization of the Wesleyan Itinerant," in McCulloh (ed.), op. cit., p. 38.*
52. Buckley, *op. cit.*, p. 134.
53. Charles T. Thrift, Jr. "Rebuilding the Southern Church," in Bucke (ed.), *The History of American Methodism*, Vol. II, p. 277.
54. Harmon, *op. cit.*, pp. 9f.
55. Buckley, *op. cit.*, p. 134.
56. Harmon, *op. cit.*, p. 16.
57. Thrift, *op. cit.*, p. 277.
58. *Doctrines and Discipline of The Methodist Church* (New York: The Methodist Publishing House, 1939), Par. 400.1, p. 118.
59. *Doctrines and Discipline of The Methodist Church* (New York: The Methodist Publishing House, 1940), Par. 332.1, p. 99.
60. Frederick E. Maser, "The Story of Unification, 1874-1939," in Bucke (ed.), *The History of American Methodism*, Vol. III, p. 477.
61. Judicial Council Decision No. 111, 1954 *General Minutes*, pp. 633-34, cited in Murray H. Leiffer, "United Methodism, 1940-60," in Bucke (ed.), *The History of American Methodism*, Vol. III, p. 514.
62. *Doctrines and Discipline of The Methodist Church* (Nashville: The Methodist Publishing House, 1948), Par. 432.1, p. 122.
63. *Doctrines and Discipline of The Methodist Church* (Nashville: The Methodist Publishing House, 1964), Par. 431.2, p. 176.

64. *The Book of Discipline of The United Methodist Church* (Nashville: The Methodist Publishing House, 1968), Par. 391.1, p. 143.

65. *The Book of Discipline of The United Methodist Church* (Nashville: The United Methodist Publishing House, 1972), Par. 391.1, p. 183.

66. *The Book of Discipline of The United Methodist Church* (Nashville: The United Methodist Publishing House, 1976), Pars. 527-531, pp. 228-230.

67. Lynn, James David, *Op. Cit.*, and Norwood, Frederick A., "The Americanization of the Wesleyan Itinerant," *Op. Cit.*

68. Lynn, *op. cit.*, pp. 25f.

69. Norwood, "The Americanization of the Wesleyan Itinerant," in McCulloh (ed.), *op. cit.*, p. 53. His theses are stated on p. 35.

70. Goodloe, *op. cit.*, p. 237.

71. Cited by Lynn, *op. cit.*, p. 226.

72. Thomas B. Neely, *The Minister in the Appointive System* (New York: Fleming H. Revell Company, 1914), p. 89.

73. Gerald F. Moede, *The Office of Bishop in Methodism. Its History and Development* (New York: Abingdon Press, 1964), p. 115f.

The Status of Methodist Preachers in America, 1769-1791

Frank Baker
Duke University

Wesley's Methodism was not planned in advance, but was a step by step response to situations, a slowly accumulating series of experiments at bringing new spiritual life to the Church of England, an institution seemingly being strangled by forms and traditions. Wesley introduced new methods derived from new concepts of God's work, and these new methods were frequently embodied in new terminology—or rather in old terminology given a new ecclesiastical meaning. As Methodists in America, we have inherited many of these new terms, whose existence from antiquity we have sometimes taken for granted. From time to time, however, we discover those who interpret these terms differently, or who—"How can it be!"—have never heard of them in a religious context. We have our own Methodist gobbledegook, or babblegab, or perhaps we should call it "Methodese." This essay, therefore, attempts an exploration of the early Methodist preachers against the background of some unfamiliar history and some peculiar terms in order that we may feel our way into a fuller understanding of the essential ethos of Methodism and its ministry.

In 1738, as a clergyman of fourteen years' standing, John Wesley became convinced that salvation by faith alone was neglected by his mother Church, both as an ancient theological belief and as an authentic personal experience. In proclaiming his own personal assurance of this experience in Bristol in 1739, he both preached in the open air and by his testimonies revitalized two old religious societies of the Church of England. Later that year he accepted the invitation of a group of people in London who wished him to become their spiritual director—the first truly *Methodist* society, in the sense of owing complete allegiance (under God) to him alone.[1] Either late in 1740 or early in 1741 he deliberately enrolled his first full-time itinerant lay preacher, Thomas Maxfield.[2] Apparently it was this growing volunteer army of lay itinerants which became increasingly responsible for the spread and administration of Methodist societies throughout the British Isles. In 1743 Wesley prepared a set of *General Rules* for his followers, in order to distinguish them both from worldly people and from nominal Christians; this gave them visible identity through higher standards both of personal and corporate discipline. In 1744 he invited both his handful of clerical colleagues and some of his lay helpers to confer with him about the doctrinal content of their message and the organization of their societies—the first annual *Conference*. At the 1746 Conference he discussed for the first time the division of England into *circuits*, and his periodical *stationing* of the preachers in them. Late in 1746 he began to publish a series of *sermons* expounding his confirmed beliefs about the way of salvation. At the Conference of 1747 he maintained that although bishops, priests, and deacons were scriptural orders, yet it was the will of God that in church government there should be a "necessary variety."[3] In 1749 he instituted the *quarterly meeting* for the preachers and leaders in every circuit.[4] He also appointed one of the lay *helpers* to be his chief *assistant* in each circuit. Thus during Methodism's first decade Wesley had established a new ecclesiastical entity. This was set forth in two pamphlets, published in 1749, which codified the discussions on *doctrine* and on *discipline*, and established Methodism's position as a *society* within the Church of England, yet with its own integrated unity because both preachers and people were *in connection* with John Wesley. Although much more development was to take place on both sides of the Atlantic, in effect Methodism had come of age.

Wesley's beginnings in England were in a measure re-enacted during the first twenty years of Methodism in America. The enthusiastic lay pioneers in New York had appealed in 1768 for one of Wesley's itinerant preachers to direct them: "We want [i.e. need] an able, experienced preacher, one who has both gifts and graces necessary for the work . . . The progress of the gospel here depends much on the qualifications of the preachers."[5] Wesley sought to engender comradeship in America rather than undue individualism, and consistently sent out his preachers in pairs, beginning with Boardman and Pilmore in 1769, continuing with Asbury and Wright in 1771, Rankin and Shadford in

29

1773, and in 1774 Dempster and Rodda to replace Boardman and Pilmore.[6] The ranks of these "official" itinerants were supplemented by British local preachers, who came out as free lances at their own charge, or in the course of some secular undertaking, men like Strawbridge, Williams, Dromgoole, King, Glendenning, and others, some of whom became almost indistinguishable to later eyes from the native preachers, whom they greatly helped to stabilize. Two immigrant volunteers in effect founded the Methodist Publishing House, Robert Williams and John Dickins, and another, Robert Strawbridge, was the pioneer and driving force behind the explosion of Methodist preaching in the south, especially through the agency of the steadily growing band of young American preachers whom he enrolled.[7] Even by 1774 these American-born preachers outnumbered the British.

The British travelling preachers found it somewhat difficult to assimilate these disparate individuals into their own more ordered ways, especially as they themselves mostly shuttled between New York and Philadelphia. This was true even after the arrival of Asbury, who was eager to dislodge the English from their rootage in the cities. Indeed they were slow to learn of what was happening in the south quite independently of their own oversight, and not until 1772 did Pilmore set out on a lengthy missionary tour down as far as Georgia, nor did Asbury himself visit that state until 1788. Nevertheless, by 1773, when the newly-arrived "General Assistant," Thomas Rankin—aged 35 to Asbury's 27—summoned the first American Methodist Conference, understanding and integration were at least beginning. Along with three of the latest four of Wesley's itinerants were present four of the volunteer British preachers, and even one of the native preachers, William Watters, who could not disguise his awe on the occasion, as one "unworthy of a name and place amongst the servants of God."[8]

The Minutes of the 1773 Conference made it clear from the outset that the preachers were all very much under discipline, and that that discipline was exercised by Wesley himself. Each solemnly responded "Yes" to a series of written questions posed by Wesley's "General Assistant":

Ought not the authority of Mr. Wesley and that conference to extend to the preachers and people in America, as well as in Great Britain and Ireland?
Ought not the doctrine and discipline of the Methodists, as contained in the Minutes, to be the sole rule of our conduct who labour in the connection with Mr. Wesley in America?[9]

With the acceptance of this general approach they came down to six specific rules, of which the first two were:
"Every preacher who acts in connection with Mr. Wesley and the brethren who labour in America is strictly to avoid administering the ordinances of baptism and the Lord's Supper.
"All the people among whom we labour to be earnestly exhorted to attend the church, and to receive the ordinances there; but in a particular manner to press the people in Maryland and Virginia to the observance of this minute." (This was directed, of course, at misguided southern enthusiasm.)

It was, of course, perfectly natural for the two preachers whom Wesley had sent out to America in 1769, and for their successors, to build other societies and to shape other preachers, after the patterns made normal by Wesley—indeed this was the very task for which they had been invited. This implied that their own status, and that of their colleagues, remained that of "extraordinary messengers" of God, who might help the regular evangelical clergy to revive the Church of England,[10] whose public worship would offer the normal ministry of word and sacrament. They were to challenge the sluggish and the sinful in public, and to witness to their personal experience of God in class-meeting and society-meeting. The full range of Methodist activities was speedily embraced in America, including the regular itinerancy of those who were authorized as preachers at one level or another.

The stories of these "extraordinary messengers" in America are reminiscent of the autobiographies which Wesley commissioned from his own preachers, which from 1791 became bestsellers on the American Methodist scene as The Experience of the Most Eminent Methodist Preachers.[11] William Watters describes his earlier activities with other young converts in Maryland: "On the Lord's day we commonly divided into little bands, and went out into different neighbourhoods, wherever there was a door open to receive us, two, three, or four in company; and would sing our hymns, pray, read, talk to the people, and some soon began to add a word of exhortation."[12] After such exhorting for five or six months, Watters accompanied Robert Williams into Virginia, was asked by Pilmore to fill in for him at Norfolk while he travelled farther south, and thus became the only native preacher to attend the 1773 Conference, when he came "on trial" for a year. At the 1774 Conference he was not only "admitted" (i.e. into "full connection"), but also appointed an "Assistant." Watters exhibited that essential ingredient in an early

Methodist preacher, whether in England or America, a readiness to sit light to all earthly cares and ambitions as he accepted an arduous and unsettled itinerancy: "Mr. Rankin thought that D. Ruf[f] and I had better change for a quarter, but with the promise that I should then return and stay till the following Conference. I never moved from one Circuit to another but what it reminded me that I was a pilgrim, that here I had no continuing city, that I was a tenant at will, and ought to be always ready."[13]

Freeborn Garrettson's autobiography first appeared in the U.S.A. in 1791, but also delighted English readers by its serialization in the pages of Wesley's *Arminian Magazine*. He came from British emigrants who had settled in Maryland and were loyal members of the Church of England. His conscience was awakened by a Methodist exhorter about 1774; he was converted, and speedily sought to share his experience with others. He described his visits to his weekly class-meeting, from which as an exhorter he "began to hold evening meetings in different places several times a week, and united those who were awakened into a kind of society." Two of the British preachers, Rankin and Rodda, encouraged him. Martin Rodda, he says, "forced me into the pulpit . . . I travelled a few days with him, after which he sent me on a circuit alone. This was the Fall after my conversion . . . I was now quite willing to be an exhorter, but thought I would not take a text." (This was the narrow line dividing exhorting from preaching which Thomas Maxfield had crossed to become Wesley's first lay preacher, for expounding Scripture was supposedly the prerogative of the ordained deacon only.) Yet his conscience and what seemed a divine revelation so exercised him that soon he took even that decisive step, and attended the 1776 Conference in Baltimore. Here, he says: "I . . . passed through an examination, and was admitted on trial, and my name was, for the first time, classed among the Methodists; and I received of Mr. T[homas] R[ankin] a written licence."[14] He spent six months in his first circuit, and three months each in two others, at the Deer Creek Conference in May 1777 was "admitted into full connection," and at the Leesburg Conference in 1778 made an Assistant, as a young man of twenty-six supervising the three men stationed in the Kent Circuit. All this, of course, and much more, might perfectly well have been happening on the British Methodist scene, except that the average age of the preachers there was now greater.

The rapidity of the rise to responsibility of the American preachers demonstrates not only their innate ability but the unsettled state of the nation during the Revolutionary War, even in its opening stages. Their multifarious activities and wide travels, however, had matured them far beyond their years. Those who had been followers had now become leaders, and were preparing themselves for whatever American independence might bring for them and expect of them both in State and Church. It was not unnatural that those who had followed the call in 1773 to dedicate themselves to the unquestioning service of Wesley's brand of Methodism might now be entertaining second thoughts. In the seventies, indeed, there was being re-enacted in America the unrest of the preachers in England during the fifties and sixties, an unrest focussing on their lowly status as preaching "helpers," or even as the somewhat less lowly "Assistants" (i.e. to Wesley), responsible for the oversight of other preachers, rather than the conventionally recognized standing of priest or presbyter, or even of a humble deacon, who could display at least an ordination parchment to confirm his call to proclaim the gospel in the Church of God. If indeed they were expected to urge attendance at the public worship and the sacraments of the Church of England, surely Mr. Wesley could do more for them than furnish a mere preaching-licence! Perhaps in a new country, soon to be under a new rule, they should take matters into their own demonstrably capable hands.

Wesley had faced similar rumblings in the British Conference of 1766, challenged by the question: "But what *power* is this which *you* exercise over the Methodists in Great Britain and Ireland?" The essence of his reply was that this was the burden which God himself had laid upon him through the request of those who originally sought his spiritual direction, nor dare he yet lay it down. He went on to call for "arbitrary power," in that he exercised it alone, but continued: "If you mean *unjust*, *unreasonable*, or *tyrannical*, then it is not true." Wesley then called for renewed personal and family religion, more courage in proclaiming God's word, more faithfulness in pastoral practice, closer discipline in study. The 1766 *Minutes* was doubled in size to include this document, which was then incorporated in three blocks of the "Large" *Minutes* of 1770—significantly the manual which formed the background of early Methodist administration in America.[15]

Public antagonism against the British Methodist preachers was making it ever more likely that they must soon leave the conduct of American Methodism, if it were to survive, to native Americans. The anxiety of the British preachers about the future came to a head at the 1777 Conference, assembled in the Deer Creek preaching-house, Maryland. In the intervening years since 1773 the body of preachers had quadrupled, but Methodism's standing still remained precarious because of their comparative youth and inexperience. Added to that was the natural erosion in their ranks, similar to that earlier faced by Wesley. Dozens of preachers entered the itinerancy briefly, and disappeared without trace. Of the eight itinerants sent by Wesley only two remained in America after 1777, and one of these (James Dempster) had left the connection, and later became a Presbyterian minister. Of over fifty native and immigrant preachers given appointments during the years 1773-78, only 28 were listed in the 1778 stations. In 1778 both preachers and membership were down from 1777. Some preachers, like William Duke, were admitted on trial in their teens, and all but three seem to have been in their early twenties.[16]

As William Watters and his companions assembled in 1777 with their British leaders, who had so successfully laboured to weld them into a strong preaching brotherhood, he wrote: "Our hearts were knit together as the hearts of David and Jonathan, and we were obliged to use great violence to our feelings in tearing ourselves asunder."[17] The group "warmly debated" whether they should continue to take communion with other churches wherever possible, especially in the parish churches of the Church of England, and eventually agreed that it was "highly expedient that the preachers and people pursue the old plan as from the beginning."[18] Then they turned again to the "Large" Minutes of 1770, in which Wesley had printed—in addition to his reply to the 1766 challenge against his "power"—a lengthy document prepared in 1769, which sought to secure peace and unity among the Methodist preachers after Wesley's death. And as their British colleagues had done and were to do periodically, they re-affirmed their loyalty to Wesley and the goals and methods of his Methodism:

We whose names are underwritten, being thoroughly convinced of the necessity of a close union between those whom God hath used as instruments in his glorious work, in order to preserve this union, are resolved, God being our helper,

1. To devote ourselves to God, taking up our cross daily, steadily aiming at this one thing, to save our souls and them that hear us.

2. To preach the old Methodist doctrine, and no other, as contained in the Minutes [i.e. the "Large" Minutes of 1770].

3. To observe and enforce the whole Methodist Discipline, as laid down in the said Minutes.

4. To choose a committee of Assistants to transact the business that is now done by the General Assistant and the old preachers who came from Britain.

Twenty-five signatures were appended, and the committee was named as Daniel Ruff, William Watters, Philip Gatch, Edward Dromgoole, and William Glendenning.[19]

When the preachers re-assembled in Conference in Leesburg a year later they found that not even Asbury was able to be with them. Watters exclaimed: "Having no old preachers with us, we were as orphans bereft of our spiritual parents"; but "though young and unexperienced" they set themselves "to transact the business of Conference."[20] As to the administration of the ordinances, once more they stayed with Wesley's plan, deferring any other decision until the following Conference. In 1779, however, the preachers met in two separate conferences, the northern circuits continuing to maintain the status quo, while those in Virginia decided to elect a presbytery, who should both administer the sacraments and ordain other preachers by the laying on of hands.[21] In order to avoid a permanent division, however, in 1780 a deputation consisting of Asbury, Watters, and Garrettson persuaded the Virginians to rescind their previous decision, and once more to wait until Wesley might be able to offer some more orthodox solution to their problem.[22] Ordination could be purchased at too expensive a price, it seemed, though Philip Gatch made a note on Asbury's expurgated edition of the Fluvanna Minutes: "May 1779, some of the Preachers undertook to administer the ordinances through necessity. It was to keep our societies together. I believe it was of the Lord, for he greatly blessed us."[23]

This deferment of ordination for a further year was agreed to on condition that the participants consult Wesley during the interval, and this they did, in spite of the logistical problems of wartime. Asbury wrote on May 12, and several times more during the following months, though all that survives is a transcript of his letter to Wesley of September 3, 1780.[24] John Dickins also wrote.[25] Wesley's reply came through in time for the Conference beginning

April 16, 1781, which Garrettson thus described: "We met and received Mr. Wesley's answer, which was that we should continue on the old plan until further direction. We unanimously agreed to follow his counsel, and went on harmoniously."[26] On October 19 that year Lord Cornwallis surrendered at Yorktown, the beginning of the end of the war. In March 1782 a new government came into power in England, preliminary peace plans were signed in November 1782, and after lengthy negotiations between all the nations concerned, the Treaty of Paris was signed September 3, 1783, to be ratified January 14, 1784. Thus three years passed between the virtual cessation of military activities in America and the accomplishment of Wesley's mission to export an ordained Methodist ministry to America.

Wesley seems to have done little during 1782, lulled by Watters' reassurance that the ordination controversy had died down.[27] This was later confirmed by Asbury. Not until April 5, 1783, when Asbury heard (incorrectly) "that peace was confirmed between England and America" did he himself undergo "various exercises of mind" about what the new circumstances might imply for their ecclesiastical situation.[28] He believed that so far Methodist sacramental needs had been adequately satisfied by such clergy as "Mr. Jarratt, in Virginia, . . . Mr. Pettigrew, North Carolina, Dr. Magaw, Philadelphia, and Mr. Ogden in East Jersey."[29] Wesley's own mind had also been genuinely exercised as he realized that loyal and patient preachers were waiting for him to take the initiative that should transform them into a sacramental society, an independent church having its roots in a Church of England reformed by Methodism. He was not yet sure how to approach the task, however, nor was he convinced that the time was yet ripe. It seemed clear that it would be fruitless once more to approach the Bishop of London to ordain Methodist preachers, as he had done in nominating John Hoskins for Canada in 1780.[30] He tried to keep abreast of trans-Atlantic conditions, however,[31] and in February 1783 informed William Black in Nova Scotia: "Our next Conference is to begin in July, and I have great hopes, we shall be then able to send you assistance."[32] (Wesley, of course, was thinking in global terms, the United States forming one field, their northern neighbours another.) On May 23, 1783, Edward Dromgoole wrote from Virginia about the great and effectual door now opened in America, and assured Wesley that the Methodist preachers were so united to Asbury that they wished to keep him there, to which Wesley replied on Sept. 17: "When the Government in America is settled, I believe some of our brethren will be ready to come over. I cannot advise them to do it yet. First let us see how Providence opens itself. And I am the less in haste because I am persuaded Bro. Asbury is raised up to preserve order among you, and to do just what I should do myself, if it pleased God to bring me to America."

Asbury was becoming somewhat anxious, however, and warned Wesley on Sept. 20, 1783, that after all "the friendly clergy are located, and do but little for us." He urged that the young hotheads "of our connection" must be forestalled from seeking ordination on their own, so that Wesley ought to move swiftly and decisively if he would prevent disruption. With little disguise he offered his own services to maintain order. Wesley had already acted decisively, on October 3 sending a letter to the American preachers underlining the dangers which might well arise from an influx of unauthorized British preachers, and pleading that they should not receive any "who will not be subject to the American Conference, and cheerfully conform to the Minutes both of the American and English Conferences", or any who would be reluctant to place themselves under the supervision of Francis Asbury as the General Assistant.[33]

Further correspondence, interviews with Coke and others in England, inquiries into ecclesiastical law, literary preparations for the new church, the screening of suitable preachers, took up almost another year before Wesley was able to send his long-awaited solution of the ordinance problem in America. It comprised a "little sketch" of a new church, a thoroughly revised Book of Common Prayer, Ordinal, and Articles of Religion, a new *Collection of Psalms and Hymns*, and a commendatory letter addressed "To Dr. Coke, Mr. Asbury, and our Brethren in North America." He also sent two of his trusted preachers, newly ordained as deacons and elders, together with his clerical colleague Dr. Thomas Coke, whom Wesley had commissioned by the laying of hands as his first Superintendent of the whole work in America, with instructions that he should set apart Asbury for the same office. "Superintendent" was the term which replaced "bishop" in his revised Ordinal—a simple translation of that Greek word into ecclesiastical Latin, a title used in the early church and by the Reformed Churches both in Europe and Scotland, which avoided any overtones of pomp and power while underlining the pastoral function of oversight.

The actual content of his "little sketch" had been simmering in Wesley's mind for months, and had been carefully discussed with Coke. As soon as Coke landed in New York on November 3 he described to John Dickins, stationed there, "our new plan of Church government," and delivered a similar talk to the whole society in Philadelphia. On November 14 he met Asbury at the Quarterly Meeting in Barrett's Chapel, whose reaction was, "It may be of God," but insisted that his own appointment should be left to the preachers.[34] He had discussed it with a few of them, and all agreed that the whole plan should be placed before a conference. Freeborn Garrettson was therefore sent off to invite the preachers to Baltimore for Christmas Eve, while Asbury took Coke for a little exercise to work off his fat—a thousand-mile tour of the southern societies. Most of the preachers who assembled in Lovely Lane on Christmas Eve had already had plenty of time to talk over at least some details of the plan with others. Most welcomed it, but not all. Thomas Haskins and his companions felt that Wesley was rushing things too much, and that other clergy should first be consulted.[35]

The crucial early events of the Conference were the ordination of deacons, elders, and superintendents. These three orders—and no others—are mentioned by Richard Whatcoat (already ordained by Wesley), Thomas Haskins, Jesse Lee, and Asbury himself.[36] Yet when the official record of the sessions eventually appeared it was worded somewhat strangely. In reply to Question 3, "What Plan of Church-Government shall we hereafter pursue?" came the sentence: "We will form ourselves into an Episcopal Church under the Direction of Superintendents, Elders, Deacons, and Helpers, according to the Forms of Ordination annexed to our Liturgy, and the Form of Discipline set forth in these Minutes."[37]

Familiarity with the phraseology disguises the strange mixture in this Brunswick stew. Each ingredient calls for careful scrutiny: neither fish, flesh, nor fowl predominates, but together they form an exotic conglutination of Scripture, episcopalianism, and presbyterianism, strongly seasoned with Wesley's Methodism. Perhaps strangest of all is the intrusion of the word "Helpers," for though such persons appear in the *Discipline*, they are there as unordained pastor-preachers.[38] Clearly they held a lower status than the new deacons. It seems, however, that this category was not intended as a kind of glorified Local Preacher, but as a continuation of the regular itinerant preachers of 1769-84—in the 1789 *Discipline*, indeed, "Helpers" is altered to "Preachers." Apparently, in the urgent and overriding need to ordain sufficient Methodist preachers, all the ramifications of such a decision

had not sufficiently been thought through—as Thomas Haskins had complained so that the members of the Conference were faced with the danger of having disenfranchised those preachers not present, those who might prefer not to be ordained, or whose who were not sufficiently proven in the work to be considered ready for ordination. What was their status, those untidy remnants of the previous all-embracing brotherhood of preachers termed Wesley's "Helpers"? Here was fertile soil for ecclesiastical envy! There was another anomaly, of course. Was being a deacon, ordained to preach only, really more important, more definitive, than being received into Full Connection by the Conference as a Helper? In embracing ordination as the solution for their problems, were the preachers forfeiting a rich element in their heritage, the brotherhood of the preaching itinerancy? Had their repeated vows of loyalty to Wesley's "old plan" been sabotaged by the "new plan," even though it apparently originated with him?

In spite of complaints about Wesley's autocracy and lack of understanding of their unique circumstances, they owed to him, under God, much of their spiritual heritage, and many of them—probably most—still wished to retain the familiar setting of the methods of Methodism, always provided that their ecclesiastical status was improved. They were content to remain under orders, so long as they were in undisputable Holy Orders. But *how* were these to be secured? It seemed that the essence of the new form of imported episcopalian government remained similar to Wesley's Methodism, except that a benevolent ecclesiastical monarchy was being replaced by an ecclesiastical oligarchy, a rule by superintendents. The actions of Wesley, Coke, and Asbury in this are fairly clear, but their ultimate intentions remain a matter of speculation. As Bishop Tigert suggested, the superintendents alone were probably intended to retain all appointive powers, but by Asbury's appeal to the Conference this power was partially stripped from them, and the preachers themselves in general gained at least *elective* powers over all appointments.[39] Wesley himself had readily separated the functions of ruling priest and serving prophet, but now the prophets—the preachers—came to have a voice in their own standing. Wesley's expedient vicarious ordination of only a few of them—surely to have been appointed by the superintendents—had become a few ordinands elected by the preachers themselves, with the implication that others similarly would eventually be elected and ordained, including most of those now omitted.

In the meantime, what? Surely the time-tested fellowship of Wesley's lay "Helpers" should be preserved! And so, apparently after the close of their founding Conference, its decisions were patched up by the addition of their old title, in a context which made it quite clear that this was not an unimportant vestigial appendix, but that the whole new church was to be "under the direction" of "Superintendents, Elders, Deacons, *and Helpers*"! By this action, probably initiated by Asbury—witness his initial response to Coke's outline of Wesley's plan, "It may be of God"[40]— they moved a step nearer to democracy in American Methodism. The Christmas Conference had sown the seeds of a general ordained status for Wesley's lay "Helpers" in America, which after many days and much uprooting of troublesome tares, eventually bore a bountiful harvest.

After 1784, and far beyond Wesley's death in 1791, apart from the enhanced status of the preachers, and the fulfilling of their sacramental ministry, things continued much as they had been, church or no church. The term *Circuit* continued in use, though steadily reduced in importance with the diminishing number of societies encompassed. The societies themselves were increasingly called charges, or stations, while the Circuit Quarterly Meeting, from covering a huge area, gradually dwindled to a Quarterly Conference for a restricted charge or charges, and was renamed in recent years the Quarterly Charge Conference. The quarterage, or quarterly allowances paid to the travelling preachers at the Quarterly Meeting, became simply allowances, though for a time they were referred to as his "salary," almost as if profession-alism were creeping in—even though the sums allowed were small enough to offer little induce-ment to transform a vocation into a profession. The term *Assistant* gradually became quite redundant in Wesley's technical sense of the preacher in charge of a circuit, as did the practice of preachers itinerating around a circuit, though itinerating from circuit to circuit remained an issue constantly refuelled by official pronounce-ments. The importance of Methodism as an integrated system, a connectional organization, remained paramount, however, and being re-ceived into Full Connection by the Conference was by some regarded as of equal importance with being ordained. The Annual Conference, of course, remained the major structural feature linking Methodists throughout the world, though the new idea of a quadrennial General Conference was introduced in America in the year after Wesley's death. The annual "Stations" of the preachers eventually became their "ap-pointments," and the double choice of *Minutes* and *Discipline* for Methodism's administrative handbook was resolved in favour of the latter title. Strangely enough the preachers themselves were called preachers still, even after ordination, not "ministers"—a title which Wesley himself had reserved for the ordained clergy of the Church of England. "Priest" and "presbyter" were never used, and even the term "elder" (except in certain contexts, as in "presiding elder") was of limited currency. The fullest justification for having deacons seemed to be that Wesley had clearly recommended a three-fold order of ministry, but the office has caused problems to this day. Even before Wesley's death "superintendent" was replaced by "bishop," to Wesley's disgust, but the discarded title refused to die: not only did it remain in later years as an integral part in the title of the presiding elder's successor, the district superintendent; even in the present United Methodist Church the third restrictive rule prohibits "doing away with our plan of itinerant general superintendency"—i.e., of course, the episcopacy, in Wesley's own interpretation of that office. Indeed Wesley's deliberate delay, combined with Asbury's patient persistence, had secured as much as could have been hoped for in adapting an old ecclesiastical model to a new environment, while at the same time greatly enhancing the status of its hitherto lay preachers.

Perhaps of equal importance to the ecclesiasti-cal status gained in 1784 through Wesley's initiative was the greatly improved democratic status gained for the preachers by Asbury's unexpected stubbornness. As noted above, it seems almost certain that both Wesley and Coke envisaged, and expected Asbury to embrace, government by the two bishops in America, who would ordain and station the preachers largely in 'accordance with their own judgment, though subject during his lifetime to Wesley's approval. What Asbury did by his appeal to the conference was to secure for the preachers what would otherwise have been regarded as an episcopal prerogative, the election of subsequent bishops, and their answerability to the preachers in conference. For this kind of government in England *after his death*, Wesley had of course made provision in his Deed of Declaration in 1784, but here also, as in declaring themselves an autonomous Church, the American preachers were ahead of their greatly respected British mentors.

NOTES

1. Davies, Rupert, and Gordon Rupp, eds. *A History of the Methodist Church in Great Britain*, Vol. I, London, Epworth Press, 1965, pp. 220-1.
2. Wesley Historical Society, *Proceedings*, Vol. XXVII (1950), pp. 7-15.
3. Wesley Historical Society, *Publication* No. I, The Manuscript Minutes, 1747, p. 48.
4. Ibid., Supplement (1904), pp. 61-6.
5. Baker, Frank, *From Wesley to Asbury*, Durham, NC, Duke University Press, 1976, p. 80.
6. Ibid., pp. 84-98.
7. Ibid., pp. 33-4.
8. Watters, William, *A Short Account of the Christian Experience and Ministereal* (sic) *Labours of William Watters*, Alexandria, Snowden, nd, p. 30.
9. Methodist Episcopal Church, *Minutes of the Methodist Conferences, annually held in America, from 1773 to 1794 inclusive*, Philadelphia, Tuckniss, 1795, pp. 5-6.
10. Wesley Historical Society, The Manuscript Minutes, 1746, p. 34.
11. Baker, Frank, *A Union Catalogue of the Publications of John and Charles Wesley*, The Divinity School, Duke University, Durham, NC, 1966, No. 368B.
12. Watters, op.cit., p. 19.
13. Ibid., p. 43.
14. Garrettson, Freeborn, *Experience and Travels*, Philadelphia, Hall, 1791, pp. 26, 37-41, 44, 47, 52, 55.
15. Methodist Church (United Kingdom), *Minutes of the Methodist Conferences*, Vol. I (1744-98), London, Mason, 1862, pp. 60-70, 638-48, 472-8, 516-22, 523-4: in the 1766 original, pp. 9-23, and in the 1770 original, pp. 49-53, 7-15, 33-5, 22-5.
16. According to his MS Journal he was born in Baltimore Sept. 15, 1757, and his MS Minutes of the Philadelphia Conference beginning May 25, 1774, note his admission on trial. (For both these documents I am indebted to Edwin Schell.)
17. Watters, op.cit., p. 57. Cf. Asbury, Francis, *Journal and Letters*, ed. Elmer T. Clark *et al.*, 3 vols, Nashville, Abingdon, 1958, I, 238, and Rankin, Thomas, MS Journal (at Garrett-Evangelical Seminary, Evanston, Ill.), May 20, 25.
18. Duke, William, MS Minutes of the 1774-7 Conferences, transcribed by Edwin Schell, 1964.
19. This document is not present in the printed *Minutes*, but see the MS Minutes prepared by Philip Gatch, Question 11. These are preserved in the Methodist Theological School in Ohio, Delaware, Ohio, and were published in *The Western Christian Advocate*, May 19, 26, 1837, and reproduced by Edwin Schell for the Baltimore Conference Historical Society; cf. Elizabeth Connor, *Methodist Trail Blazer*, Creative Publishers, Cincinnati, Ohio, 1970, pp. 75-7. The document was based on one appearing in the British annual *Minutes* for 1769, 1773, 1774 (and signed on other occasions), which was also reproduced in the "Large" *Minutes* of 1770.
20. Watters, op.cit., p. 68.
21. Gatch, MS Minutes; cf. Garrettson, op.cit., p. 176, etc.
22. Watters, op.cit., pp. 71-3, 79-81; Garrettson, op.cit., pp. 176-8; Connor, *Methodist Trail Blazer*, pp. 97-112, 118-25; William Warren Sweet, *Virginia Methodism*, Richmond, Whittet and Shepperson, 1955, pp. 79-86.
23. Connor, op.cit., p. 109.
24. Asbury, *Journal*, I, 350; III, 24-6.
25. Watters, op.cit., p. 102; Garrettson, op.cit., p. 177.
26. Garrettson, op.cit., p. 207.
27. Cf. John Wesley, Feb.22, 1782, to Watters: "It is a great blessing that there is an end of that unhappy dispute, which otherwise would have torn you all in pieces. Again and again it has been set on foot in England and Ireland, but it never came to any height. We always took care to suppress it at the very beginning, so that it could not do much mischief."
28. Asbury, *Journal*, I, 440.
29. Cf. Asbury's letter of August 1783 to George Shadford in England, *Journal*, III, 28. "Mogden" in the (misread ?) original clearly refers to the Rev. Uzel Ogden: cf. Wesley's letter to Asbury of Oct. 31, 1784, and Asbury, *Journal*, I, 442.
30. Baker, Frank, *John Wesley and the Church of England*, London, Epworth Press, 1970, pp. 259-70.
31. Cf. his letter from Dublin, written May 2, 1785 to his brother Charles in London: "Tell me all you know of the good Congress, the loyalists, and the colonies."
32. From the original in Victoria University, Toronto, Feb. 26, 1783.
33. Lee, Jesse, *A Short History of the Methodists*, Baltimore, Magill and Clime, 1810, pp. 85-6.
34. Asbury, *Journal*, I, 471.
35. Sweet, William Warren, *Men of Zeal*, New York, Abingdon, 1935, pp. 170-2.
36. Sweet, *Men of Zeal*, pp. 166-7, 173; Lee, op.cit., pp. 94-5; Asbury, *Journal*, I, 474.
37. Tigert, John J. *A Constitutional History of American Episcopal Methodism*, 6th ed., Nashville, Smith and Lamar, 1916, pp. 534-5.
38. Ibid., pp. 550-2 (Questions 32-4).
39. Tigert, op.cit., pp. 192-4.
40. Whoever pointed out the oversight, it was probably Coke who was responsible finally for setting it right: see Baker, *From Wesley to Asbury*, p. 155n.

Thomas Coke's Contribution to the Christmas Conference: A Study in Ecclesiology

Warren Thomas Smith
Interdenominational Theological Center

American Methodism moved from a somewhat vague, albeit dynamic, group of societies to become a church during the ten days known as the Christmas Conference, December 24, 1784- January 2, 1785. It was an epoch-making event. The Methodist Episcopal church in America came into being, and Church it was, wherein "the pure Word of God is preached, and the Sacraments duly administered." It was not a sect nor a faction of religious malcontents. The Christmas Conference is a milestone in the history of America, and the story of the Church of Jesus Christ, an event worthy of study.

The Problem of Sources

The paucity of primary data on the Christmas Conference is a major concern. No official *minutes* have survived. We do not even have a full roster of those in attendance: some sixty—or more—preachers, with lay people in the congregation at worship services. (Thomas Coke Ruckle's painting "The Ordination of Francis Asbury"—a composite of those the artist thought were present— was not completed until 1882. Obvious errors were made.) We are forced to rely on a handful of journal entries, diaries, letters, and an occasional pamphlet. Thomas Ware's significant "The Christmas Conference of 1784" was not published until 1832. The indication is clear: it was written largely in retrospect by a man advanced in years. The same holds true of other brief reminiscences. Regrettably, Jesse Lee's history is not an eyewitness account of the Conference.

A great deal is obviously missing, especially those intriguing documents which reveal behind-the-scenes planning. What of give and take on the floor of conference? In short, who is responsible for the structure, the wide and many spheres of interest of both the conference and the church which was born of it? Wesley's *Large Minutes* served as guide for the conference and the 1785 *Discipline*, but who possessed sufficient personality and sagacity to work, cajole, bargain, reason through an overarching plan acceptable to that founding body? One who may provide a number of answers is that clergyman who came to America as John Wesley's representative: Dr. Thomas Coke.

The Welshman

Thomas Coke[1] (1747-1814) is the forgotten figure not only of the Christmas Conference but of American Methodism. Asbury remains the dominant personality who can never be ruled out. He had known frontier America for some thirteen difficult—and heady—years. Coke had not. Nonetheless, our thesis maintains: the "little doctor" played a major role, and his influence—imperceptibly—manifested itself in the Baltimore deliberations, and in the subsequent formation of the Methodist Episcopal Church. It becomes an exploration—an analysis really—in ecclesiology. Unfortunately, primary sources from Coke himself are hard to come by. His *Journals* are inordinately brief. He devoted a few, possibly hastily written, paragraphs to the conference, yet he meticulously notes certain incidents and individuals he regarded as essential. His surviving letters—possibly not more than five hundred—have yet to be published in a single volume. These give only a few allusions to that pivotal assembly. His conference sermons do provide a number of substantial clues as to the direction in which the new church would move. What, then, did he actually bring to the Christmas Conference?

Collegiate Background

Coke sprang from a middle class Welsh family of Brecon. His father Bartholomew, an apothecary, served as common councilman, as alderman, and was twice elected baliff (mayor). Thomas followed in father's footsteps, serving on the Brecon council for years. He paid the "usual fees at dinners, &c. in the Corporation" as late as 1801.[2] He was no stranger to the ups and downs of political life—and the ways of prudent statecraft.

AUTHOR'S NOTE: A word of profound gratitude is expressed to Bishop Nolan B. Harmon, Mr. John Vickers, and Professor Arthur W. Wainwright for insights, comments, and advice.

Thomas received his elementary education at the local Christ Church College and then matriculated as a "gentleman commoner" at Jesus College, Oxford "6 Apr. 1764"—according to the Battle Book. The University Register mentions 11th of April of that year. It was the Paschal Term. He received the B.A. "4 Feb. 1768" and on the 5th was advanced to "fellow commoner."[3] He was ordained deacon at Oxford on June 10, 1770 and his M.A. was conferred three days later, June 13th, "1768 Bre. Thos. Coke B.A. 1768 (M.A. 1770)." His ordination as priest was held in Wales on Sunday, August 23, 1772 at Abergwili.

Legal Training

During these years, beginning no later than July 14, 1771, Coke served as assistant curate at South Petherton in Somerset, during which time he was introduced to the Wesleyan Revival. In June of 1775 Coke was back at Oxford petitioning for two degrees—Bachelor and Doctor—in Civil Law. These degrees, and the academic work required for them, play no small role in Coke's contribution to Methodism in Britain and America. Lord North, the Chancellor (and Prime Minister), wrote from Downing Street "8th June 1775"

Reg. Conv. Term. Trin. Conv.
14 June 1775

Mr. Vice-Chancellor & Gentlemen,
I have been moved in behalf of Thomas Coke M.A. of Jesus College who is from his matriculation of full standing for the Degree of Doctor in Civil Law, but was prevented by circumstances from proceeding regularly to the Degree of Batchelor in that Faculty. He therefore humbly prays that by Favour of Convocation he may be allowed to accumulate the Degrees of Batchelor and Doctor in Civil Law, paying Fees for both Degrees but doing exercise for that of Doctor only, in order to his being a Candidate for the Degree of Doctor in Civil Law next Term. To this [request I give my Consent, and am
Yr. Affectionate Friend and Servant]
North[4]

An engrossing Latin phrase was penned at the close of North's letter: "Sex hasce Literas Venerabilis Domus ratas habuit." What does it mean?

The phrase *aliquid ratum habere*, used in Classical Latin, means "confirm or approve". *Venerabilis Domus* is, of course, a reference to the Ancient House of Congregation which is the degree

granting body. The entire line can thus be translated: "The Ancient House of Congregation has approved the request in these six letters."[5]

Lord North's was but one of six letters written in Coke's behalf. Obviously young Coke had been busy securing letters from influential friends and associates. (John Morgan, M.P. from Brecon may have been one. Another might have been Joseph Hoare, B.D., who became Principal of Jesus College on April 27, 1768 and held the post until 1802. These are but assumptions. A further question regarding the five other letters: are they extant?)[6]

If Coke acquired the degrees of B.C.L. and D.C.L. "by accumulation," he would have taken both at the same time—the requirements for the doctorate satisfying those for the baccalaureate. The two degrees in civil law can be substantiated by Coke's letter of May 14, 1791, to Connecticut's Bishop Samuel Seabury of the Episcopal Church:

Being educated a member of the Church of England from my earliest Infancy, being ordained of that Church, and having taken two degrees in Civil Law in the University of Oxford which is entirely under the Patronage of the Church of England.[7]

Coke's doctorate was conferred on June 17, 1775, and the formal record in the Register of Congregation of the University is, of course, in Latin. The translation:

1775 Thomas Coke, Master of Arts, a student of Civil Law from Jesus College begs etc. In-so-far-as it has been dispensed to him by the venerable House of Convocation in regard to the grades to be required in Civil Law; [and since] he has diligently heard a public lecturer; [and since] he has had according to requirement three lecture courses in the School of Jurisprudence; [and since] he has performed all other things which required by the Statutes (unless in-so-far-as he has been dispensed therefrom etc). It is granted as above petitioned. 17 June[8]

Coke's degree, D.C.L., represents an English phrase. Those who wrote in Latin frequently Latinised it as LL.D. (Legum Doctor), and Coke himself frequently employed these letters following his name. Oxford, unlike Cambridge, was forbidden by parliamentary statute to grant a degree in Canon Law.[9]

Coke's doctorate has usually been dismissed as *honoris causa*, as in Lord North's D.C.L. conferred on October 10, 1772 at the time he became

Chancellor, or Samuel Johnson's, "by diploma" on April 1, 1775. Coke had far more expertise in jurisprudence than has been recognized, and this legal know-how was to stand him in good stead. He was not naive. All one has to do is read Coke's correspondence with his relative and lawyer, Thomas Williams, at Brecon. Coke the clergyman-lawyer could be a shrewd business-man, demanding an accounting from his renters and debtors. He displayed a bulldog tenacity, demanding payment.

Methodist Activities: 1783-84

By 1783, Coke was heart and soul in the Methodist societies (having been callously driven from his Anglican curateship by disgruntled parishioners in 1777). The years 1783-84 saw a number of noteworthy events. Among them, publication of Coke's *A Plan of the Society for the Establishment of Missions among the Heathens*, a bold—but abortive and premature—call to missions. This was the initial in a series of publications to come from his facile pen during the course of his lifetime as "Father of Methodist Missions."

Of greater importance in the American story is Coke's relationship as John Wesley's secretary/confidant during 1777-84. There were odd jobs aplenty throughout the societies. Among them, the selling of books. In 1782 Wesley established his Society to Distribute Religious Tracts to the Poor, and Coke became something of a colporteur. Wesley once remarked to Henry Moore that Coke was so "sound in the faith" and "zealous of good works" that he could be left in charge while Wesley was away.[10] Obviously, Wesley and Coke had rapport. On August 6, 1781 Wesley noted, "I desired Mr. Fletcher, Dr. Coke, and four more of our brethren to meet every evening, that we might consult together on any difficulty that occurred."[11] It was spine-tingling. "He admitted me to his most secret councils," recalled Coke, "and in some things placed a confidence in me, the recollection of which even fills me with surprise."[12]

In 1782, at Wesley's request, Coke presided at the Irish Conference. He was indeed Wesley's representative to the Emerald Isle, and Coke continued to preside at that Conference—with one or two exceptions—for some thirty years (until 1813, when he left Britain for the last time). The role of presiding officer at a Methodist conference was not new to Coke when he arrived in America in 1784.

Alas, it was contention among the societies that consumed a substantial amount of time. There were disputes, as at Bath. "I am endeavouring to bring matters, respecting the Bath Chapel, a conclusion," Coke wrote Wesley on December 15, 1779. He went on:

> I find it very difficult to get money: yet, I hope, through the Divine blessing, it will be raised, and settled upon the plan prescribed in the Minutes. Brother B. shall be appointed steward, if you do not object to him. He is a man of peace, loves you, loves the Church of England, and is beloved by all the people.[13]

Coke accepted this sort of unpleasant responsibility with alacrity.

It was the Birstal Chapel, constructed in 1751 and rebuilt in 1782, that opened a Pandora's box and became a *cause célèbre*. A new deed provided that on the death of the Wesleys "the major part of the trustees and class leaders to deprive, remove or suspend the preacher or pastor, for the time being, at their free will or pleasure." Conference was immediately—and rightly—concerned: who owned the chapels? who stationed the preachers? Wesley's entire *modus operandi* was at stake. Would the societies become presbyterian in polity?

The *Minutes* of the London conference of August 1782 asked: "What can be done with regard to the preaching house at Birstal?" The answer:

> If the trustees still refuse to settle it on the Methodist plan (1). Let a plain state of the case be drawn up; (2). Let a collection be made throughout all England in order to purchase ground and to build another preaching house as near to the present one as may be.[14]

Coke was chosen to put into execution this important minute, and he seems to have relished the opportunity. His *Address to the Inhabitants of Birstal and the adjacent Villages*, published in November, 1782, spelled out the Methodist plan, which insisted on conference ownership of property and appointment of preachers. Coke concluded his case with a collect, "O thou Lover of Concord and Prince of Peace, keep these Little Ones under thy fostering wing," requesting of God, "Keep them close to the Bleeding Side of Jesus, and close to the affectionate hearts of their faithful Pastors, forever."[15]

In 1783 Coke was responsible for visiting all societies to "get all our preaching-houses settled on the Conference Plan." Later, September 5, 1788, Coke issued his *The State of the Dewsbury-House, in Yorkshire: being a Vindication of the Conference respecting it*. The identical issue was once more raised: ownership and control of property and stationing of preachers. "The grand point in contest between the Conference and the Trustees of Dewsbury, is, and has been from the beginning," said Coke, " 'whether the Trustees ought to have power, *by themselves,* and *of their own authority alone,* to reject any preacher sent to them by the Conference, or not?' "[16] Coke was still battling this problem in Britain after Wesley's death.*

While the polemics may appear extremely tedious, throughout this controversy a philosophy of church government was in process of being hammered out. At the heart of the matter was the question of authority: who would station the preachers? Where did ownership of property finally reside? Were Methodists to evolve as a loosely organized fellowship, with central magisterial power at a minimum, and scant cohesiveness among the membership? Was real power to be vested in local trustees, or possibly the congregation? In Coke's thinking, the conference ought to be the arbitrator in all matters, holding a tight reign—in military fashion. Methodists were here coming to terms with the *bene esse* of the fellowship. It was more than a matter of control, it was liberation of the pulpit. If the pastor was to be free from the tyranny of autocratic lay people—as Coke had sadly learned at South Petherton—measures must be taken. All Methodists were part of a total fellowship, not separate societies.

We cannot gainsay that when he came to America, Coke pondered these British experiences. After all, the clergyman with legal training was encountering the stuff of which religious institutions seem to be made: there is always the human element. No matter how godly, no matter how righteous, there is always the question of people relating to people.

Securing Legal Status of the Conference

In 1763 a *Model Deed* had provided that after the demise of the Wesleys and William Grimshaw, preachers were to be appointed by "the yearly Conference of the people called Methodists." It was not so much a question of who were "the people called Methodists" as what was the conference in legal eyes. Coke was assuredly part of the answer. At the close of the 1782 conference, he and William Clulow—Wesley's solicitor—began work on a suitable "Declara-

*EDITOR'S NOTE: See the chapter in this book, "The United Methodist System of Itinerant Ministry," by E. Dale Dunlap.

tion . . . to be enrolled in the Court of Chancery for safe custody, naming the present members and prescribing the mode of election to fill vacancies."[17] The outcome was the *Deed of Declaration*, enrolled on March 9, 1784. It was Methodism's *magna carta*, whereby the term "conference" was given legal status, and declared owner of all property and holding power of appointment of preachers. By becoming a legal entity, the Methodist Conference possessed enormous power. One hundred preachers were listed as constituting the body—named by Wesley himself, who defended Coke against vociferous attack by those not listed, *Non vult, non potuit* (he would not, he could not). An assumption has been that Coke had little to do with the actual preparation of the *Deed*—certainly a false premise in light of Coke's Oxford degrees, and his consociation with Clulow. "All things necessary being completed in the Court of Chancery according to law," said Coke, "I thought it my duty to send copies of the Deed to all Assistants of circuits throughout Great Britain; and I afterward carried copies of it to Ireland."[18]

America

As early as Monday, January 20, 1746, John Wesley recorded, "I set out for Bristol. On the road I read over Lord [Peter] King's *Account of the Primitive Church*." He continued, "In spite of the vehement prejudice of my education, I was ready to believe that this was a fair and impartial draught; but, if so, it would follow that bishops and presbyters are (essentially) of one order, and that originally every Christian congregation was a Church independent on all others!"[19]

High churchman that he was, John Wesley was likewise a sensitive, practical man who in all things sought to reach the heart of an issue. For him, governance was of the *bene esse*, not the *esse* of the church.[20] A reading in 1756 of Bishop Edward Stillingfleet's *Irenicon* had furthered Wesley's understanding of church government. "I think he has unanswerably proved," noted Wesley, "that neither Christ nor His apostles prescribed any particular form of church government; and that the plea of Divine right, for diocesan episcopacy, was never heard of in the primitive church."[21]

Wesley's contemplation of church structure and orders can be seen in clear juxtaposition to the American societies. He had long pondered the situation in the colonies. The Treaty signed in Paris, September 3, 1783, officially terminated the Revolutionary War. What were the American Methodists to do? Letters with Wesley had been exchanged for years. The surging cry from

America was for the administration of Baptism and the Lord's Supper. Clearly, it was a matter of the sacraments, and only an ordained clergy could administer them. Wesley's repeated requests for aid from the Bishop of London had been rejected. Pragmatist that he was, John Wesley saw that action had to be taken.

The possibility of Coke's being sent to America had been the topic of conversations between Wesley and Coke. The precise purpose for such a trip, and in what role Coke should go, remain somewhat mysterious. The conference at Leeds, July 27-August 3, 1784 heard the announcement that Coke would make a voyage to America. "Mr. *Richard Whatcoat* and Mr. *Thomas Vasey* offered themselves as Missionaries for that purpose, and were accepted."[22]

Immediately after conference, Wesley journeyed to Bristol and Coke to London where he was to make ready for his journey to America. On August 9th Coke wrote a lengthy—and fascination—epistle to Wesley:

> The more maturely I consider the subject, the more expedient it seems, to me that the power of ordaining others, should be received by me from you, by the imposition of your hands, and that you should lay hands on Brother Whatcoat and Brother Vasey.[23]

Coke proceeded to outline a plan, including using the Reverend James Creighton—an Anglican priest—and meeting at John Castleman's house in Bristol. It is no surprise that Coke's critics insisted that what followed was all Coke's doing. In truth, Wesley followed the outline. Was it Coke's idea? Or was Coke merely repeating plans previously worked out by Wesley? Coke did receive word from Wesley, directing him to come to Bristol and bring Creighton.

On Wednesday, September 1, 1784, Wesley recorded, "Being now clear in my own mind, I took a step which I had long weighed in my mind, and appointed Mr. Whatcoat and Mr. Vasey to go and serve the desolate sheep in America." The service took place at Castleman's home at 6 Dighton Street. For Thursday, September 2nd, Wesley noted in his *Journal*, "I added to them three more; which, I verily believe, will be much to the glory of God." The diary entry begins at 4 a.m. "Prayed, ordained Dr. Coke."[24]

Coke was the logical instrument—executor—of Wesley's design for American Methodists: he was in full orders, held Oxford degrees, independently wealthy (he usually paid his own expenses in traveling on business for the societies), still comparatively youthful, and of enormous evangelical vitality. He had all neces-

sary trappings and qualifications. His background groomed him for a particular task and responsibility, not the least of which was juristic experience. Coke was going to bring more than just courtly manners and a 5'1" stature to America. His parchment, in Wesley's hand, read, "I have this day set apart as a Superintendent, by the imposition of my hands and prayer . . . Thomas *Coke*, Doctor of Civil Law, a Presbyter of the Church of *England*, & a man whom I judge to be well qualified for that great work."[25]

The Bristol ordinations by Wesley on September 1 and 2, 1784, provided credentials for a venture frought with uncertainty. Action had been taken: two lay preachers, Whatcoat and Vasey, were first ordained deacons, then elders, Coke was set apart as superintendent. Clutching their parchments to which Wesley's name and seal were affixed, and bearing a cluster of important documents from the founder of Methodism, the three clergymen sailed for America.

A myth has developed that Thomas Coke was a delightful nonentity, exuding amiability, ingratiating himself to one and all. Indeed, as William Wilberforce noticed, Coke had a cherubic face with a complexion as smooth as an apple. These cheery features belie the character and personality of the man. He was, among other things, one who had encountered tough opposition in matters personal, legal, and ecclesiastical.

Arrival

Coke used the voyage to engage in additional homework in church history, reading—among others—Augustine's *Confessions*. Coke, Whatcoat, and Vasey disembarked from the *Four Friends* at New York on Wednesday, November 3, 1784. Coke preached at the John Street meeting house, Wesley Chapel, and had long and interesting conversations with John Dickins, but no public announcement was made of Wesley's plans. In Philadelphia, Coke preached at St. George's and there told the Methodists of "our new plan of Church Government," but avoided any hint of the plans to the Anglican clergymen Samuel Magaw and William White.

Coke and his associates had as a target meeting Asbury further south. The dramatic encounter of Coke and Asbury took place at Barratt's Chapel—a few miles from Dover, Delaware—on Sunday, November 14th. Noted Coke:

> . . . .About ten o'clock we arrived at *Barret's Chapel*, so called from the name of our friend that built it, and who went to heaven a few days ago. In this

Chapel, in the midst of a forest, I had a noble congregation to which I endeavoured to set forth our blessed Redeemer, as our Wisdom, Righteousness, Sanctification, and Redemption.

He concluded, "After the sermon, a plain, robust man came up to me in the pulpit, and kissed me: I thought it could be no other than Mr. *Asbury*, and I was not deceived."[26] It was a moment of high emotion, especially for Coke and the congregation.

"After dining in company with eleven of our Preachers at our Sister *Barret's*, about a mile from the Chapel," observed Coke, "Mr. *Asbury* and I had a private conversation concerning the future management of our affairs in *America*."[27] For the first time, Asbury heard the full plan. He was to be named superintendent. "I privately opened our plan to Mr. *Asbury*. He expressed considerable doubts concerning it," admitted Coke, "which I rather applaud than otherwise."[28] Asbury was cautious, and well he might be. Was he to assume power by fiat of John Wesley?

Asbury opened his mind and heart to Coke. Said Coke:

He informed me that he had received some intimations of my arrival on the Continent; and as he thought it probably I might meet him that day, and might have something of importance to communicate to him from Mr. *Wesley*, he had therefore collected a considerable number of the Preachers to form a council; and if they were of opinion that it would be expedient immediately to call a Conference, it should be done.[29]

Asbury sought the opinion of his fellow preachers. "They were accordingly sent for, and after debate, were unanimously of that opinion," noted a thoughtful Thomas Coke. He also tended to gloss over events: the debate among the preachers may have been rather heated.

At Asbury's insistence, a conference was called, and the institutional wheels started to turn. "We therefore sent off *Freeborn Garretson*," said Coke, "like an arrow, from North to South, directing him to send messengers to the right and left, and to gather all the Preachers together at *Baltimore* on Christmas-Eve."[30] (It is doubtful that John Wesley would have agreed to submit the scheme to the preachers, as Coke did.)

Planning the Conference

After a preaching tour with Harry Hosier,[31] Coke met Asbury and they journeyed to Perry Hall, elegant home of the Henry Dorsey Goughs. From December 17th until the 24th they talked with Whatcoat, Vasey, and William Black (who had just arrived from Nova Scotia). "Here I have a noble room to myself," said Coke, "where Mr. *Asbury* and I may, in the course of a week, mature every thing for the Conference."[32] Was it here that, as Edward Drinkhouse insists, "the business was 'cut and dried' before the Conference assembled"?[33] Was Perry Hall the scene of Coke's unfolding of ideas, warnings, admonitions, regarding structure of the nascent Church? Here, in confidence, he would have been at liberty to spell out dangers in congregational polity—hazards personally experienced as an Anglican curate and seen firsthand in the Methodist connection in Britain. It may well be that at Perry Hall the destiny of American Methodism was decided.

Coke could have relied on personal encounters. Would the "free church" system work? Had not the fracas at Birstal been the result of lay people aspiring for too much authority? Did not the *Deed of Declaration* spell it out? If Methodism was to move into frontier America, would not a firm hand be required at the helm? Credit for the gestalt whereby Methodists conquered a wilderness for Christ has usually been given to Francis Asbury. Was it exclusively his idea? The preacher/attorney from Brecon may well be responsible.

Conference in Session

Thomas Coke called the Christmas Conference to order at 10:00 a.m. on Friday, December 24, 1784. "Our friends in *Baltimore* were so kind as to put up a large stove, and to back several of the seats," said an appreciative Thomas Coke, "that we might hold our conference comfortably."[34]

Coke presided at all sessions. "On Christmas-Eve we opened our Conference: which has continued ten days." The doctor continued, "I admire the American preachers. We had near sixty of them present. The whole number is eighty-one. They are indeed a body of devoted, disinterested men, but most of them young."[35]

The reading of Wesley's letter *To Our Brethren in America*, by Coke, would have been dramatic—the Welsh voice resounding in Lovely Lane. Thomas Ware tells us that it was John Dickins who proposed the name the Methodist Episcopal Church in America, and it passed without a negative voice. Would it be too much to hazard a speculation that Coke may have been party to the suggested name? He and Dickins had spent hours in conversation in New York, and Dickins heard of Wesley's plans with delight. The idea that it would be an *Episcopal* denomination would have pleased Coke mightily.

After having been elected by the conference, Asbury was ordained a deacon by Coke on December 25th. On the 26th Asbury was ordained elder, at which time Coke preached *A Sermon on the Godhead of Christ* (a favorite theme). On the 27th, assisted by Whatcoat, Vasey, and Philip William Otterbein of the German Reformed Church, Coke placed his hands on Asbury's head, setting him apart for the office of superintendent—precisely the same title bestowed on Coke by Wesley." (Brother *Asbury* has so high an opinion of Mr. *Otterbine*," noted Coke, "that we admitted him, at brother *Asbury's* desire, to lay hands on brother *Asbury* with us, on his being ordained bishop.)"[36]

The ordination sermon—Coke's terms—was on the "character of a Christian Bishop." There was no mistaking Coke's semantics. It was *ordain* not *set apart*, and the office was *Bishop* not *Superintendent*. Coke's lengthy message was replete with references to Sts. Jerome, Clement, Polycarp as well as the celebrated Bishop Hoadley and Dr. Calamy—all of whom Coke had been studying during the voyage to America. "But what right have you to Ordain?" was Coke's rhetorical question. The answer: "The same right as most of the Reformed Churches in Christendom." It was unmistakably clear as to title and function within the historic catholic tradition (Anglican, Roman, and with the Reformed added). "But of all the forms of Church-Government, we think a moderate Episcopacy the best. The executive power being lodged in the hands of one, or at least a few," Coke explained, "vigour and activity are given to the resolves of the body, and those two essential requisites for any grand undertaking are sweetly united—calmness and wisdom in deliberating; and in the executive department, expedition and force."[37]

The Episcopacy

Was it Coke who set the tone—despite Wesley's later protestations—which resulted in title change? Was Coke thus responsible for the episcopal tradition, vis-a-vis a milder, more democratic superintendency? This assumption may be corroborated by the meeting which occurred sometime during the first days of the conference between Coke, Asbury, Henry Gough and John Andrews and William West, Anglican rectors in Baltimore. They drank tea and talked of a rapprochement between Methodists and Episcopalians, with the suggestion that Coke be consecrated a bishop in the new church. Alas, no mention was made of Asbury's being given the same office. Considering Asbury's lack of suitable social and academic background, such may not have been even a possibility.

Undoubtedly Asbury's autocracy enforced the concept of episcopal power in America, and he was but following the pattern set by the autocratic Wesley—a pattern exercised before either Asbury or Coke were born. Coke, however, may be the progenitor of the idea and ideal of Methodist bishop. This was, after all, explicitly the point of Charles Wesley's acrimonious charge that Coke was returning from the conference with episcopal power, to ordain Methodist preachers in Britain. "Do you not know and approve of his avowed design and resolution to get all the Methodists of the three kingdoms into a distinct, compact body?" Charles wrote to John, "a new episcopal Church of his own?"[38]

Charles' was the same accusation voiced by Coke's enemies—and they were multitudinous—of inordinate ambition, that of seeking to become a bishop, not as American Methodists subsequently interpreted the office (not a third order) but in the high Anglican tradition. Indeed, Coke's attempts in 1791 at a conjoining with the Episcopal Church were so construed by many.

Ministry

Coke spoke of the preachers in glowing terms, "The spirit in which they conducted themselves in choosing the Elders, was most pleasing." He went on, "I believe they acted without being at all influenced either by friendship, resentment, or prejudice, both in choosing and rejecting."[39]

With almost a parent's concern, Coke painstakingly listed the ordinands. Thirteen preachers were elected Elder:

One elder was elected for *Antigua, Jeremiah Lambert*: two for *Nova Scotia, Freeborn Garretson*, and *James Cromwell*: and ten for the states; *John Tunnell, John Haggerty, James O'Kelly, LeRoy Cole, William Gill, Nelson Reed, Henry Willis, Rueben Ellis, Richard Ivey*, and *Beverly Allen* . . . He continued the list of elections to Deacon's Orders:
They also elected three deacons, *John Dickins, Caleb Boyer*, and *Ignatius Pigman* . . . Four of those elected were unable to attend Conference:
Brothers *Tunnell, Willis,* and *Allen*, of the elected elders, were not present at the conference; nor brother *Boyer* of the deacons.[40]

Coke, who did not suffer from false modesty, was exultant, "The Lord, I think, was peculiarly present whilst I was preaching my two pastoral sermons; the first when I ordained brother

Asbury a bishop, the second when we ordained the elders. GOD was indeed pleased to honour me before the people."[41]

American Methodist preachers were at first chary about the "little doctor"—his voice, manners, academic background. His moving prayers soon melted the brothers' hearts, and they took him to their hearts. They did not stand in reverence before him, however, and they did not hesitate to disagree with him.

Ritual

Gleaning the activities of the Christmas Conference, one is made aware that contributions—great and small—came from Coke. Not the least is the omission (probably deliberate) of the "descended into hell" clause in the Apostles' Creed. "Dr. Coke made two or three little alterations in the Prayer-Book without my knowledge,"[42] admitted Wesley. What the "little alterations" were and in what sense Coke made them remains problematical. Wesley had certainly made some very substantial ones already. If Coke did remove the "descended into hell" clause, did Wesley find theological objections? If, on the other hand, the American Methodists found they wanted the clause restored, was any attempt made to do so? It would appear that Coke's action—if he indeed is responsible—was quite acceptable to Methodists in America.

The loss of the "Little Sketch" which may have contained instructions for *The Sunday Service* has been blamed on Coke. Drinkhouse—writing in late nineteenth century—insists Coke did so intentionally; but is Drinkhouse to be trusted at this point? There is wide disagreement as to the nature of the "Little Sketch." What did Wesley mean? Is it a sheaf of documents, all relating to American Methodists, and to *The Sunday Service*? Whatever the case, it was Thomas Coke who conveyed the liturgy from Britain to America, and had *The Sunday Service* bound as separate volumes to be distributed among the members of the new church.

A College

Cokesbury College is Coke's gift—along with John Dickins—to American Methodism. At the initial meeting with Asbury at Barratt's Chapel, Coke raised the issue of need for a college. The "little doctor" gave himself unstintingly to fund-raising for Cokesbury as well as securing a faculty. Asbury's summation of the noble but ill-fated project says it best, "I wished only for schools—Doctor Coke wanted a college."[43]

Cokesbury as an institution did not survive, but the idea and ideal did. Higher education in America owes a debt to Thomas Coke. In the years following the conference, the people called Methodists made an admirable contribution, attempting to unite knowledge and vital piety.

The Slavery Issue

The trenchant attack on slavery, clearly spelled out in the *Discipline*, very likely came from Coke. If it did not originate with him, it certainly had his approval. During 1785, in the six months following the Conference, Coke conducted a private war on slavery in Virginia and the neighboring territory, much to the consternation of slaveholding Methodists and Anglicans—the Reverend Devereux Jarratt, among others.

Coke faced mob action:

The testimony I bore in this place against slave-holding, provoked many of the unawakened to retire out of the barn, and to combine together to flog me . . . as soon as I came out. A high-headed Lady also went out, and told the rioters . . . that she would give fifty pounds, if they would give that little doctor one hundred lashes. When I came out, they surrounded me, but had only the power to talk . . . But God restrained the rage of the multitude.[44]

The tragedy of slavery became increasingly real to Coke: "I rode to Brother *Kennon's*, preaching a funeral sermon in the way at a Planter's house for a little child, and reading our burial service in the woods over the grave." He continued, "They have a funeral sermon in these parts for every human creature that dies, except the Blacks."[45]

There were genuine conversions, as in the case of Brother Kennon who "has emancipated twenty-two Slaves. These are great sacrifices: for the Slaves are worth, I suppose, upon an average, thirty or forty pounds sterling each, and perhaps more."[46]

This campaign was a magnificent witness by Coke. The crusade concluded with a visit to Mt. Vernon, "Mr. *Asbury* and I set off for General *Washington's*," observed Coke. He told of the reception. "After dinner we desired a private interview, and opened to him the grand business on which we came, presenting to him our petition for the emancipation of the Negroes, and intreating his signature." The General did not sign, "but if the Assembly took it into consideration, [he] would signify his sentiments to the Assembly by a letter."[47]

With the passing of time American Methodists had second thoughts about the expediency of the abolition of slavery—a victory for the conservative wing. Coke's bold antislavery proviso was weakened. Why did he not resume his fight? Was he weary? Was he away too long? One cannot champion a cause *in absentia*. The evangelistic outreach and stability of the young church became primary concerns. Liberation of blacks was never a forgotten issue, however, neither in Coke's mind nor that of many Methodists. The war did not end!

Missions

It was said of Coke that if he were dead, the word *missions* would bring him back to life. As he planned the trip to America, he had originally planned to make a pastoral visit to both Nova Scotia and the Caribbean. Time would not permit such a tour, but he was able to raise funds—at the Christmas Conference. "One of the week-days at noon," said Coke, "I made a collection towards assisting our Brethren who are going to *Nova-Scotia*: . . . fifty pounds currency, (thirty pounds sterling)."[48] He did send Garrettson and Cromwell to Nova Scotia. Lamentably, poor Lambert died before sailing for Antigua. Fortunately, John Baxter—who had been preaching in Antigua since 1778—was in the United States. One of Coke's last acts before returning to Britain in the spring of 1785, was to ordain Baxter for continued ministry in the West Indies.[49] (Baxter is not listed among those chosen, or ordained, at the Christmas Conference.)

The beautiful Caribbean indeed became the scene of Coke's four eventful tours. These visits hold tremendous importance. Methodist missions, under British supervision, made remarkable advance. From that experience Coke made a notation, "Who knows but the Lord is preparing me for a visit in some future time to the coast of *Africa*."[50] A permanent mission in Sierra Leone became a reality.[51] Missions reflect the heartbeat of the man who gave his personal fortune to finance an impressive mission to Ceylon. He died on this missionary voyage, enroute to Asia.

Discipline

Along with Asbury, the *Discipline*[52] of 1785 was the product of Coke's mind and heart. Following Wesley's *Large Minutes* scrupulously, a guide was made available for the new church. The circuit riders carried in their saddlebags: a Bible, a hymnal, and the *Discipline*. Along with the Bible, the *Discipline* became part of the life of the Methodist, be that person ordained, licensed, or active layman or laywoman. It was a rule, and it was to be followed. It set a pattern for living, reforming the continent and spreading scriptural holiness over the land.

Adjourn

The Christmas Conference adjourned on January 2, 1785. What had Thomas Coke given to it? Perhaps his outstanding contribution was himself: his ebullient personality, his charm, his optimism.[53] He loved people; he was concerned about the plight of the downtrodden of the earth. He was devoted to the church he helped establish—its first bishop. He sought, above all, to be faithful to the Christ whose gospel he gladly preached and lived.

The question remains: did Coke, along with the American Methodists, create an altogether different, independent church, unlike that which John Wesley intended? Of this we are certain: the Americans declared their independence at the time of the signing of the *Declaration*. They were no longer subservient to the British king. At the Christmas Conference, American Methodists let it be known they would not be ruled by him. Thomas Coke, a Britisher, seems to have caught that spirit in a glorious fashion, and understood his American brothers and sisters.

Leave Taking

"On *Thursday* the doctor took his leave of America for this visit," recorded Asbury. "We parted with heavy hearts."[54] It was June, 1785. Coke was preparing to return to Britain, concluding his initial visit to America. As the "little doctor" boarded the *Olive Branch* for his return voyage, he paused for a moment of reflection, "In my younger days, one of the greatest afflictions in life to me during the time it lasted, was to be torn away from my friends whom I dearly loved." He then concluded, "But I think for many years I have not felt myself so effeminate (shall I call it?) as I did on parting with my *American* Brethren, the Preachers: and the sensation continued very painful for a considerable time after I left them."[55]

Coke would, in the course of the coming years, make eight additional visits to the United States, presiding at conferences, conferring with Asbury and others, preaching, raising funds for Cokesbury College and missions, expressing concern for black people.

Tribute

Thomas Coke died May 3, 1814, and was buried in the Indian Ocean. The following year, on Sunday, May 21, 1815, Francis Asbury recorded:

By vote of conference, I preached the funeral sermon for Doctor Coke—of blessed mind and soul—of the third branch of Oxonian Methodists—a gentleman, a scholar, and a bishop, to us—and as a minister of Christ, in zeal, in labours, and in services, the greatest man in the last century.[56]

It was *Sabbath*, September 24, 1815 that Asbury noted:

I preached at Lebanon, by request of conference, a memorial sermon for Doctor Coke: my subject was Matt. v. 16: "Let your light so shine before men." The Gospel light, in all its fulness of grace and power, the reflected light of that Light of the world, manifested in faith and in obedience in every grade and class of believers. Ministers should be resplendent like a city illuminated in the night; a great light amidst Churches in darkness and slumber; like Doctor Coke, whose effulgence beamed forth in missions, in labours, in Europe, in America, in the isles of the sea, and in Asia. I took occasion to particularize the abundant labours of this distinguished man of God.[57]

NOTES

1. Coke's name should be pronounced "Cook," as it was in the eighteenth century and earlier by upper classes, and often spelled Cooke. See Robert Charles Hope, *A Glossary of Dialectal Place-Nomenclature* (London: Simpkin, Marshall & Co., 1883), p. x. Charles Wesley rhymed Coke with *took* and *forsook*. See Frank Baker, *Representative Verse of Charles Wesley* (London: The Epworth Press, 1962), pp. 367-368. But habit is hard to break, and coming from Atlanta, we are constantly reminded "Coke is it." In all matters pertaining to Coke, required reading is John Vickers, *Thomas Coke: Apostle of Methodism* (Nashville: Abingdon Press, 1969), a superb biography.
2. See Vickers, p. 19.
3. Battle Book, Jesus College, Oxford. The author is indebted to the College Bursar who sent extensive data, September 9, 1961, and to Principal John T. Christie who furnished auxiliary material in 1964.
4. Copy owned by the Methodist Missionary Society, London.
5. Thanks to Mr. E.E. Sabben-Clare, Oxford University Information Officer, in a letter to the author, September 17, 1976.
6. See Warren Thomas Smith, "Thomas Coke's Doctorate" in *Proceedings of the Wesley Historical Society*, Vol. XLI, Part 6 (October 1978), pp. 169-173. Also see Warren Thomas Smith, "The University of Oxford as Thomas Coke Knew It" in *The Journal Of The Interdenominational Theological Center*, Vol. V, No. 1 (Fall 1977) pp. 33-46.
7. Copy at Bodleian Library, Oxford. See Vickers, p. 177.
8. The Latin original was supplied by the Secretary of Faculties, University Registry, in 1951.
9. See *Proceedings*, XI, pp. 94, 144. Also see Vickers, pp. 29-30.
10. See Henry Moore, *The Life of the Rev. John Wesley, A.M.* (New York: N. Bangs and J. Emory, 1825), II:315. Also see George Smith, *History of Wesleyan Methodism* (London: Longmans, Green, etc., 1872), I:417. Also see Vickers, p. 40.
11. Nehemiah Curnock, ed., *The Journal of the Rev. John Wesley, A.M.* (London: The Epworth Press, 1938), VI:329.
12. See *The Substance of a sermon preached in Baltimore and Philadelphia, on the Death of the Rev. John Wesley* (London: 1791), p. 5.
13. See Coke's letter to Wesley, December 15, 1779, in *The Arminian Magazine* (London: 1790), pp. 50-51.
14. *Minutes*, 1782.
15. Thomas Coke, *An Address to the Inhabitants of Birstal and the adjacent Villages* (Leeds: J. Bowling, 1782), p. 10.
16. Thomas Coke, *The State of the Dewsbury-House, in Yorkshire; Being a Vindication of the Conduct of the Conference respecting it* [London: 1788], p. 3.
17. See John S. Simon, *John Wesley: The Last Phase* (London: The Epworth Press, 1934), p. 210.
18. *An Address to the Methodist Societies in Great Britain and Ireland on the Settlement of the Preaching Houses* (Edinburgh: 1790).
19. Wesley, *Journal*, III:232.
20. See Emory Stevens Bucke, ed., *The History of American Methodism* (Nashville: Abingdon Press, 1964), I:198.
21. Quoted in L. Tyerman, *The Life and Times of the Rev. John Wesley, M.A.* (London: Hodder and Stoughton, 1871), III:430.
22. Dr. Coke and Mr. Moore, *The Life of the Rev. John Wesley, A.M.* (London: 1792), p. 458.
23. See John Whitehead, *The Life of the Rev. John Wesley, M.A.* (Boston: Hill and Broadhead, 1846), II:255-256.
24. Wesley, *Journal*, VII:15.
25. Ibid., VII:16.
26. *Extracts of the Journals of the Rev. Dr. Coke's Five Visits to America* (London: G. Paramore, 1793), pp. 15-16. Coke's original spellings have been retained.
27. Ibid., p. 16.
28. See *The Arminian Magazine* (Philadelphia: 1789), I:243. This is the American edition of Coke's *Journal*.
29. Coke, *Journal*, p. 16.
30. Ibid.
31. See Warren Thomas Smith, *Harry Hosier: Circuit Rider* (Nashville: The Upper Room, 1981). Also see Warren Thomas Smith, "Harry Hosier: Black Preacher Extraordinary" in *The Journal of The Interdenominational Theological Center*, Vol. VII, No. 2 (Spring 1980), pp. 111-128. Also Warren Thomas Smith, "The Incomparable 'Black Harry'" in *Together*, October 1970, pp. 40-41. Related information is to be found in Warren Thomas Smith, "Sketches of Early Black Methodists" in *The Journal Of The Interdenominational Theological Center*, Vol. IX, No. 1 (Fall 1981), pp. 1-18.
32. Coke, *Journal*, p. 22.
33. Edward J. Drinkhouse, *History of Methodist Reform* (Baltimore and Pittsburg: Board of Publications of the Methodist Protestant Church, 1899), I:287.
34. *The Arminian Magazine* (Philadelphia: 1789), I:291-292.
35. Coke, *Journal*, p. 23.
36. *The Arminian Magazine* (Philadelphia: 1789), I:291.
37. *The Substance of a Sermon Preached at Baltimore in the State of Maryland before the General Conference of the Methodist Episcopal Church, On the 27th of December 1784 at the Ordination of the Rev. Francis Asbury* (London: J. Paramore, 1785).
38. See Thomas Jackson, *Life of The Rev. Charles Wesley* (London: Mason, 1841), II:397.
39. Coke, *Journal*, p. 23.
40. *The Arminian Magazine* (Philadelphia: 1789), I:291.
41. Ibid.
42. John Telford, ed., *The Letters of the Rev. John Wesley, A.M.* (London: The Epworth Press, 1931), VIII:144-145, to Walter Churchy, June 20, 1789.
43. Elmer T. Clark, ed., *The Journal and Letters of Francis Asbury* (Nashville: Abingdon Press, 1958), II:75 *Journal* entry for Tuesday, January 5, 1796.

44. Coke, *Journal*, p. 35.
45. Ibid., p. 36.
46. Ibid. By present currency standards, the twenty-two slaves would represent an investment in excess of $22,000.
47. Ibid., p. 45. Also see Warren Thomas Smith, "Thomas Coke's War on American Slavery" in *The Journal Of The Interdenominational Theological Center*, Vol. II, No. 1, (Fall 1974), pp. 44-54.
48. *The Arminian Magazine* (Philadelphia: 1789), I:291.
49. Ibid., I:398. Also see Vickers, p. 99. Also see Warren Thomas Smith, "Thomas Coke and the West Indies" in *Methodist History*, Vol. III, No. 1 (October 1964), pp. 1-11.
50. Coke, *Journal*, p. 67.
51. See Warren Thomas Smith, "An Appraisal of Thomas Coke's Africa Mission: 1791-1811" in *Church History*, Vol.

40, No. 3 (September, 1971), pp. 306-316.
52. *Minutes of Several Conversations between The Rev. Thomas Coke LL.D. and The Rev. Francis Asbury and others, at a Conference, begun in Baltimore, in the State of Maryland, on Monday, the 27th of December, in the Year 1784. Composing a Form of Discipline for the Ministers, Preachers and other Members of the Methodist Episcopal Church in America* (Philadelphia: Charles Cist, 1785).
53. See Warren Thomas Smith, *I Remember the Christmas Conference*, adapted for drama by William S. Vance (Nashville: Abingdon Press, 1983).
54. Asbury, *Journal*, I:490, entry for Thursday, June 2, 1785.
55. Coke, *Journal*, p. 47.
56. Asbury, *Journal*, II:780.
57. Ibid., II:792.

Methodist Mission Among the Dakotas:
A Case Study of Difficulties

Bruce David Forbes
Morningside College

Prior to the Dakota War of 1862, five Christian groups attempted missions among the Dakota or Sioux people of southern Minnesota. Among them, the Methodist mission seemed a negative example, yielding few results in conversion or cultural impact after five years of effort.[1] Church historians frequently select notable, "successful" persons and efforts as the foci for historical narratives, but attention only to such examples tells an incomplete story and hinders full evaluation. In the study of Methodist missions to Native Americans, it is instructive to examine troubled efforts as well, especially in situations such as Minnesota which permit comparison with other missionary approaches among the same people. The resulting analysis highlights mission difficulties involving itinerant church polity, patterns of training and financial support, an educational approach that slighted native languages, and other evidences of cultural misunderstanding.

The missions discussed here focused upon the Dakota or Sioux people.[2] "Sioux" is the term officially recognized by United States and Canadian governments, but the word is derived from a derogatory name which means snakes, adders, or enemies, given them by the Chippewa or Ojibwe, their northern rivals. The people called themselves "Dakota," meaning friends or allies. ("Lakota" and "Nakota" are essentially dialect differences used by related people who had moved further west into what is now South Dakota.) Dakota was the term employed most frequently by the missionaries considered here.

Unlike their western plains relatives who would eventually become the stereotypical warrior Indians of Western movies and novels, the Dakotas of southern Minnesota in the early 1800s were largely a woodland people, with many features resembling Central Algonquian tribes. They clustered in wooded areas along rivers and lakes, venturing onto neighboring prairies or into more wooded territory to the north for hunting and foodgathering. Their combination of a settled and a wandering lifestyle might be termed semi-nomadic. Most Dakotas lived in relatively permanent villages of gable-roofed bark houses during the spring and summer. They planted and harvested corn but gave limited attention to such domestic agriculture, augmenting their subsistence with frequent excursions for fishing, hunting, and the gathering of wild crops. Throughout the winter they lived in tipis or similar conical structures made of hide, which afforded protection against the weather that the bark houses could not provide. They traveled in the early winter, seeking game, and eventually settled in their tipis somewhere near their summer village locations.

The Dakotas in southern Minnesota were organized into four major "bands" (Mdewakanton, Wahpekute, Sisseton, and Wahpeton), subdivided further into villages. Bands were led by a hereditary chief and a band council, but in the eighteenth and nineteenth centuries internal developments and the encouragement of whites who insisted on dealing only with formal leaders prompted each village to establish its own chief and council. The authority of the hereditary chief was subject to the advice and consent of councils; a chief was influential only to the extent that his oratorical skill and personal character were persuasive.

Like that of many other tribes, Dakota spirituality emphasized relatedness. Specific beliefs about spirits and gods, afterlife, etc. were flexible and diverse, frustrating many inquiring missionaries who sought a clear, single answer to their questions. Yet underlying the various specifics was a basic unitary worldview, in regard to the natural order and to the human community. What appeared to the missionaries as pantheism was a conviction of spiritual kinship with the entire natural order. The controlling power of the universe was pervasive; all of creation had a sacred status. "As visible and invisible, as material and immaterial, as human and as animal, the gods embodied all manifestations of nature . . . For the Sioux, any concept which denied or minimized the cohesiveness of this system would have been as naive as it was unreal."[3] This spiritual sense of kinship was expressed through legends in which animals with human characteristics predominated and through rituals related to natural cycles.

The unitary worldview also was expressed socially in the Dakota sense of community. Whatever the individualism involved in vision quests or personal status, it was submerged by basic communal identification and activity. Community rituals, economic communalism, ethics of generosity and hospitality, and the strong bonds of extended family units all pointed to the centrality of human relatedness in Dakota life.

Further, this unitary approach rejected any cultural dichotomy between sacred and secular. It was impossible to completely separate Dakota spirituality from their economy, their health and well being, and even their recreation. As one missionary wrote, "The Dakotas carried their religion into almost everything, for, unlike the Christian religion, it was of such a nature that it was never out of place. There was no incongruity between it and the most thoughtless levity or reckless dissipation."[4] Even with the missionary's negative evaluation, the unitary nature of Dakota spirituality was acknowledged.

In brief, these were the Dakota people missionaries met and worked with between 1834 and 1862. One must be cautious about the oversimplifications inevitable in such a thumbnail sketch of ethnology, but at least a token introduction is vital in reminding us that the following story is of two peoples and cultures meeting, not of visitors making offerings into a cultural void.

The year 1834 marked the beginning of sustained missionary efforts among natives in what would become southern Minnesota. Dakotas had experienced earlier contact with French explorers and priests in the late seventeenth and early eighteenth centuries, but most had the character of visits rather than settlements. The only substantial French Jesuit attempt to establish a mission occurred in 1727 when a party arrived to establish a trading post and mission on Lake Pepin; Fort Beauharnois was abandoned after a year. A second attempt at the same location several years later was similarly short-lived.[5] British exploration followed; U.S. involvement in the area began with the 1805-06 expedition of Zebulon Pike. In 1819 the United States established a fort (renamed Fort Snelling in 1825), which provided the first sustained institutional white presence in Dakota lands, but missionaries were not yet involved. Finally, in 1834 and 1835, missionaries arrived to stay, and various efforts continued until the Dakota War of 1862, often called the Great Sioux Uprising. In the aftermath of the war, Dakotas fled to the west and into Canada or were imprisoned and removed from the state. Missions that continued were transplanted to the new lands, with only a trickle of the Dakotas and their Christian institutions returning to Minnesota after 1869.

Between 1834 and 1862, then, five groups attempted to evangelize the Dakota people. The dominant mission was that sponsored by the American Board of Commissioners for Foreign Missions (ABCFM), a cooperative Congregationalist-Presbyterian agency. It was first in the field and the only mission to span the entire period under consideration; it also surpassed the others in number of stations and personnel, duration, and impact. Founded in 1810, the ABCFM became a major factor in the story of American missions both overseas and among American Indians, because of the magnitude of its own work and the stimulus it provided for the creation of other denominational missionary societies. The Board was not only a funding organization but exerted significant oversight through the articulation of missionary theology and strategies, recruiting and sometimes training of missionaries, regular correspondence, and visits by Board officers in the field.[6]

Following preliminary reconnaissance visits sponsored by the Board in 1829 and 1834, Thomas S. Williamson arrived with other mission workers in the spring of 1835. Two brothers, Samuel and Gideon Pond, had arrived a year earlier, inspired by a Connecticut revival to evangelize but with no official connections. The Indian Agent had put them to work with "civilizing" activity among the Dakotas, but upon Williamson's arrival he included them in the mission. In addition to Williamson and the Ponds, the other well-known name associated with the mission was Stephen Return Riggs, who arrived in 1837. These four, and numerous less publicized workers, encouraged farming (i.e. greater reliance on domestic agriculture), opened schools, and plunged into the task of learning the Dakota language. The linguistic work was their most significant accomplishment in the first decade and a half, reducing the Dakota language to writing, compiling dictionaries, producing a spelling book, and translating the Bible and other "spiritual literature" (including Bunyan's *Pilgrim's Progress*, Watt's Second Catechism, hymnbooks, and more).[7]

Conversions were few; of those who accepted Christianity, several were from the family of Joseph Renville, a mixed-blood trader. Yet even as the mission met active resistance and seemed to be a "difficult and almost unproductive field," the ABCFM continued to reinforce the mission with additional workers.[8] After 1851, when traditional ways were disturbed by treaties restricting the Dakotas to reservation lands in southern Minnesota, a few more conversions came. Yet on the eve of the Dakota War, Williamson could report only 52 full-blood and 15 mixed-blood Dakota members of ABCFM mission churches.[9] Wholesale conversions followed the Dakota War of 1862, as the imprisonment and relocation which took place in the conflict's aftermath disrupted traditional ways even further.

Protestants from Lausanne, Switzerland, sponsored a second mission effort. The "Societé des missions évangeliques de Lausanne" was a modest, local effort which attempted to send missionaries among Canadian Indians. The first full-time missionary returned with health problems after three years. In 1835 the society appointed two other missionaries, Daniel Gavin and Samuel Dentan. The intention was to send them to Canada as well, but upon arrival in North America Dentan and Gavin wrote that their survey of the situation led them to work among the "Sioux." The Swiss society was Reformed (Calvinist), theologically akin to Presbyterians and Congregationalists. With no training or guidance except for financial support from Lausanne, the two missionaries relied upon ABCFM assistance, visiting their missions, using their primers, and generally adopting their mission approach. Gavin married Lucy Stevens, an ABCFM mission teacher, and the marriage appropriately symbolized the close relationship between the Swiss and American Board missions. The Lausanne society even corresponded with the ABCFM. When the Gavins left the mission in 1845, and the Dentans in 1847, the ABCFM took responsibility for continuing work at the site, at Lausanne's request.[10]

A Catholic mission was the most short-lived of the five. In 1841 Augustin Ravoux, a French priest who had been recruited to come to America as a missionary three years earlier, toured various trading posts to investigate possible mission sites and to begin learning the Dakota language. In 1842 he established himself at Little Prairie, near the trader J. B. Faribault. Thereafter he translated a question and answer catechism, prayers, and hymns, published a little book in the Dakota language, built a rough chapel, and opened a school. The mission was abandoned in the spring of 1844, because of financial difficulties, native resistance, and a need to serve a growing community of white and mixed-blood Catholics at Mendota. Ravoux hoped that his reassignment would be temporary, permitting him to return to Indian work, but it was not to be. From 1844 until the coming

of Joseph Cretin as St. Paul's first Catholic bishop in 1851, Ravoux was the only resident Catholic priest within what is now Minnesota. His Indian efforts were too brief to provide a full contrast with the other missions, but even his short tenure seems notable for its disinterest in any agricultural program similar to that promoted by government agents and the other missions; Ravoux concentrated on acquisition of the native language, education, and baptisms.[11]

The final entry into the Dakota mission field was Episcopalian. Henry B. Whipple, Minnesota's first Episcopal bishop, arrived in 1859. Within two weeks he toured Episcopal missions among the Ojibwe to the north, and in June 1860 he visited part of the Minnesota "Sioux" reservation which appeared devoid of missions. By October he had appointed Samuel Hinman to establish St. John Baptist's Mission, at the Lower Sioux Agency. Little time remained before the Dakota War, but in that interim Hinman worked at learning the Dakota language, opened a fairly successful day-school, and baptized at least eighteen Dakotas into the church, a majority being full-bloods. Although relatively fresh on the scene, Hinman and Whipple continued to give attention to the Dakotas following the war, sharing in the massive conversions that resulted.[12]

In the context of these four other efforts, Methodists also attempted to evangelize and "civilize" the Dakotas. They arrived in 1837, only two years after the American Board and the Swiss Reformed, but both predecessors outlived the Methodist mission. The brief Catholic foray overlapped the Methodists. Episcopalians arrived much later, after the Methodist, Catholic, and Swiss Reformed efforts all had left the field.

On the national level as well, Methodists were later than the American Board in seriously beginning missions among Native Americans. As Wade Barclay, the major historian of Methodist missions, has observed,

> It cannot be said that the missionary zeal of the earliest Methodist pioneers expressed itself in extensive efforts for the conversion of the Indians. Wherever their labors extended they must have come in contact with them but evidence is lacking that, at any time during the closing years of the eighteenth century and the beginnings of the nineteenth organized effort was made by Methodists for their evangelization.[13]

The "first appointment by the Methodists of a missionary, officially designated as such, to the American Indians" was made by the Ohio

Annual Conference in 1819.[14] James Montgomery was appointed to work with the Wyandot Indians, building upon some previous, unofficial missionary activity by other Methodists. From that beginning, work extended into the Great Lakes region in the 1830s, while southern portions of the church also initiated efforts among the "five civilized tribes" and followed them after removal into Indian Territory (Oklahoma).

A related development during the period of birth of Methodist Indian missions was the organization of the Missionary Society of the Methodist Episcopal Church by the General Conference of 1820. The Society gave the bulk of its support to domestic missions on the white frontier, but Indian missions were included within its scope. In contrast to the initiative and supervision exerted by the ABCFM, the Methodist Society was largely restricted to being a mechanism for financial support. A constitutional provision at the time of the Society's founding lodged the responsibility for establishing and maintaining missions with the annual conferences and the bishops; missions under such localized conference supervision could draw from financial resources of the Society. This situation obviously left the Society with limited authority, and any that was exercised was done so guardedly. Even though missionaries appointed by bishops were considered "missionaries of the Society" and were listed as such in annual reports, they actually were related more closely to their annual conferences than to the Society. An indication of the loose relationship was the trouble the Society had in persuading missionaries to submit regular reports. As years passed, the Methodist Missionary Society attempted to exert increased initiative and authority, but developments were very gradual. For our period, in Barclay's words, "the relation between the Missionary Society and the missionaries . . . was not a close and intimate one."[15]

The Society's weak role is better understood when one recognizes that the Methodists saw their *whole system* as missionary in character. To some, a special missionary society seemed unnecessary. Yet the Methodists were aware of the founding of the American Board and other denominational mission societies, and they shared the missionary impulse of the time. A missionary society was deemed an appropriate structure to undergird special efforts on the moving frontier with needed finances, but initiatives remained decentralized, resting with the annual conferences.

Methodists were also relatively late in gaining cross-cultural experience. From its beginning the ABCFM, with its focus upon foreign missions, gained experience in cross-cultural contexts overseas that was potentially applicable to cross-cultural missions with Native Americans. However, the Methodists' first, limited "foreign" experiences did not come until the late 1830s, and even those experiences could have helped little in learning about evangelization between markedly different cultures. The beginnings of "foreign" Methodist missions were in the independent nation of Texas, among black American colonists in Liberia (neither of which were radically cross-cultural situations), and in short-lived forays into South America.[16] Even if more cross-cultural experience had been gained, the loose, decentralized Methodist missionary strategy might have hindered the sharing of lessons. As it was, Methodist missionaries to Native Americans were in their denomination's vanguard of cross-cultural evangelization; any learning would have to take place in the midst of their labors.

The Methodist mission among the Dakotas began in this context of annual conference independence and limited prior experience. The initiator of the Dakota mission was Alfred Brunson, a minister from the Pittsburgh Conference. He was inspired to take the gospel to Indians of the Old Northwest after reading a report about the 1832 Henry Schoolcraft expedition to find the source of the Mississippi River. With no special background or preparation, Brunson was transferred to the Illinois Conference in 1835 and was assigned a missionary circuit hundreds of miles long, extending into Minnesota.[17]

In 1836 Brunson led a party including David King, John Holton, and Holton's family, to Prairie du Chien.[18] The group wintered there, making further preparations and attempting to learn about the region. Brunson there encountered James Thompson, a black slave owned by Captain Day of Fort Crawford at Prairie du Chien. Thompson's previous owner had spent time at Fort Snelling, where Thompson had married a Dakota woman and become acquainted with some of the language. Thompson is said to have represented himself as a "good Methodist," eager to act as an interpreter and, not incidentally, to return to Fort Snelling where his wife and children remained.[19] Brunson, convinced of the need for an interpreter, wrote to J.F. Wright of the Cincinnati "Book Room" and solicited funds through the *Western Christian*

Advocate. In the spring of 1837 Wright sent Brunson a draft for $1,200, which was used to purchase Thompson's freedom. Thompson stayed with the mission only a year, prompting Brunson to write that he had "proved unfaithful."[20] The negative evaluation was echoed by later church historians; Chauncey Hobart wrote that Thompson was selected "not because he possessed the character and requirements desired, but because he was the best and most promising help that could then be obtained."[21]

Brunson's later work led him to the Ojibwe people of northern Minnesota and to the whites and Indians in what is now Wisconsin, but he began by establishing a mission among the Dakotas. In May, 1837, Brunson and his party arrived at Fort Snelling and presented their credentials from the Secretary of War to the officials there. The region was still Dakota land, with only a small triangle negotiated to the United States government as the site for Fort Snelling. Brunson reported that "we found the officers, and Major Taliaferro, the Indian agent, very favorably disposed toward our objects."[22]

Lawrence Taliaferro has been called "the most important and influential civil official on the upper Mississippi" during his tenure at Fort Snelling (1820-1839).[23] Among his intentions was a desire "to conduct his charges along the road toward civilization," especially by encouraging Indians to adopt white methods of farming, including the plow and harness.[24] Taliaferro thus welcomed missionaries such as the Ponds, Williamson, and Brunson because he saw them as potential assistants in his agricultural program. On Taliaferro's recommendation, and apparently with Chief Big Thunder's invitation, the Methodists established a mission at Kaposia, "Little Crow's Village," several miles below Fort Snelling on the west side of the Mississippi River.[25] There they intended to establish a farm and a school, as a base from which they might preach the gospel in the region.

After several weeks Brunson left the party at Kaposia to return to Prairie du Chien for supplies.[26] There he encountered three Ojibwe converts associated with the Lake Superior mission of John Clark: John Johnson, George Copway, and Peter Marksman. They returned to Kaposia with Brunson and helped construct a two-story log house. Brunson's autobiography, written much later, remembers that the Dakota people of Kaposia were amazed by the building skill of the three visitors and could not believe that they were actually Ojibwes, their despised rivals. Thompson, Brunson's interpreter, told the Dakotas that they could become just as skillful if they would listen to the teachings of the missionaries.[27]

The three Ojibwe assistants represented native leadership and training that had no counterpart at the Dakota mission. In the fall of 1837 the Illinois Conference voted $1,400 for the education of the three at Ebenezer Manual Labor School, near Jacksonville, Illinois. They were to be students alongside three white youth who had committed themselves to missionary service: Samuel Spates, Allen Huddleston, and "One Weatherford" (first name unknown). The Ojibwe youths were to gain knowledge of Christianity and "civilization," while the whites were to gain knowledge of native language and culture through acquaintance with their Ojibwe fellow students. Weatherford did not fulfill his missionary commitment, but the other five provided substantial leadership for the Methodist Ojibwe mission stations of northern Minnesota from 1839. Copway and Johnson became quite renowned. Copway, although criticized by some fellow workers and historians, published a widely distributed autobiography.[28] Johnson was an active Methodist missionary until 1848; thereafter he achieved greater prominence as an Episcopal priest (Enmegahbowh) and an associate of Bishop Whipple. Huddleston died of illness in December, 1839; Spates worked among the Ojibwe until the general unrest surrounding the Dakota War of 1862, when he began serving non-Indian parishes in the Minnesota Conference.[29]

In contrast, the Methodist Dakota mission managed few if any native converts and no native leadership. The most substantial indication of Dakota conversions in five years of work is the unelaborated classbook record of the baptism and reception into the church in 1841 of three full-blood Dakotas: Mary Thompson, Hannah Martin, and John F. Cooks.[30] The lack of any celebration of this event in the retrospective writings of the missionaries or early historians might be explained in three ways: the Dakotas may have lapsed quickly from their Christian professions; the credit for the conversions might belong to other missionaries; and the women may have been married to non-Indians, making their conversions somewhat expected. (Was Mary Thompson the wife of the mission's first interpreter?) The only other report of any Dakota conversion to Methodism is a passing reference by Thomas Williamson, who established an ABCFM mission at Kaposia after Methodists abandoned the work; an 1850 letter from Williamson mentioned that a Dakota woman in his congregation had been admitted to the Methodist church's membership sometime in the late 1830s.[31] Whatever the explanation of these brief indications, it is clear that the Methodists' accomplishments in terms of the conversion of Dakotas was negligible. Alfred Brunson claimed that the one event that made the mission worthwhile was the conversion, not of an Indian, but of a Swede (Jacob Falstrom) who became an active, lifelong Methodist.[32]

In addition to preaching throughout the area, with the general concern for evangelization, the mission's first priority was the establishment of a school. "As soon as the school house was ready," Brunson wrote in a retrospective letter, "Bro King opened a school for the children, which he taught & at the same time studied the language, with a view to preaching in it."[33] Although the Methodists recognized that some acquisition of the Dakota language was necessary for communication, their interest in the language was limited. The Methodist mission school taught reading and writing in English alone. Brunson, the superintendent and policy maker, was aware that the American Board missionaries had set a precedent of teaching Dakota reading and writing first and English second, but Brunson believed that energy spent on the Dakota language was wasted. In his autobiography he wrote,

with me the chief thing was the use of education to them. Their business transactions must be mainly with the whites. There were no books or literature in their mother tongue, and but little, if any could ever be expected; while, if they learned to speak, read, and write the English language, they would be prepared for intercourse with the whites, and the whole literature of the whites would be open and accessible to them.[34]

Brunson and King believed that "English would finally become the universal speech of the savages."[35]

Whatever the practical arguments for the use of English, insistence on this approach also had potentially far-reaching cultural implications. Language can be a subtle vehicle for cultural identity, assumptions, and thought patterns. The missionary society of the Methodist Episcopal Church emphasized these implications in an 1856 report (more than a decade after the Methodist mission in Minnesota had been abandoned):

With the English language, the Indian will acquire the elements of English literature, and the forms of thought, and the feelings which it represents, both social and religious. We doubt whether the Indians

will ever be raised to a good state of civilization and religion, without the use of the English language. The influence of a language upon the principles, feelings, and habits of a people, is not appreciated as it ought to be.[36]

Evaluated from one perspective, English language education assisted the introduction of a superior way of life. From another perspective, it was yet another facet of cultural imperialism.

However, as earlier American Board experience in other settings could have told them, the English approach yielded scant results in education. First of all, because these Methodists had little commitment to the Dakota language, they had difficulty giving much effort to learning it. In spite of the recognition that some acquaintance with the language was necessary for basic, introductory communication, they made little progress. In 1842, after five years in the field, David King wrote to Samuel Pond: "I am still trying to learn a little Sioux and you know I dont[sic] learn much. I am a lazy student."[37] King was undoubtedly being deferential to a man who was an acknowledged superior in the Dakota language, but the humble stance was justified. The Methodists in the short-lived Dakota mission never gained noted facility in Dakota.

Secondly, the English-only approach failed to take account of the interest of the Dakotas. The American Board discovered that American Indian students were usually more interested in learning to write their own language than some strange, unknown words; if Dakota literacy came first, English instruction might then be added as a second step. In bypassing the Dakota language, the Methodist missionaries lost the interest of many students. They also proved insensitive to Dakota culture by ignoring a natural Dakota attachment to their own language. Chief Big Thunder reportedly tried to induce the Methodist missionaries "to teach his people to read and write their own language, as the Pond brothers were doing, but the 'sacred white men' refused."[38]

Another thrust of the mission was agricultural, consistent with Indian Agent Taliaferro's interest. In the fall of 1837 three more persons, with families, "were added to the mission, with a view to open a farm from which the Mission family could derive its main support in provisions, & to extend operations into other lands."[39] Once established, the farm was also to be an instructional model for the Dakotas. Indeed, agricultural achievements constituted the Methodist mission's greatest "success." "We have done far more than they [American Board missionaries] in the way of *farming*," Brunson wrote. "Our Indians have been able to plant and raise more corn than theirs."[40] By the end of the summer, 1838, eighty acres of ground were reported under cultivation.[41]

This attention to farming was prompted in part by humanitarian concern. In the view of Euroamericans, native hunting and foodgathering left too much to chance, resulting in unfortunate cycles of feast and famine. In addition, there was evidence that hunting encouraged by traders had caused a declining population of game, forcing Dakotas to travel further in their hunts. Subsistence was becoming more difficult, and the far-flung expeditions sometimes increased conflicts with other bands and tribes. To Taliaferro and the missionaries, the Dakotas had an inadequate system of subsistence, and a diminishing supply of game would only increase problems in the future. It seemed that a greater reliance on domestic agriculture, with crop surpluses that might be stored, would better supply the Dakotas with food. Thus, wrote Brunson, the Indians "are in a state of starvation themselves, and one object of our mission is to teach them to cultivate the soil, and thus save themselves and families from starvation."[42]

It was true that use of the plow and certain Euroamerican agricultural techniques might enable increased crop production for the Dakotas, but near-total reliance on domestic agriculture did not prove as superior as it seemed. The native subsistence pattern had the advantage of diversification, combining various hunts with fishing, food gathering, and limited agriculture. Farming was a gamble against weather, diseases, and insects; in later reservation years, crop losses were especially devastating to "farmer Indians" who had dedicated all their efforts to tilling the soil.

Besides humanitarian intentions, other motives influenced the agricultural program. More reliance on domestic agriculture might produce a more settled lifestyle for the Dakotas, breaking the semi-nomadic pattern that made mission activities difficult. Brunson wrote that the "migratory habits" of the Dakotas were a hindrance to the mission school; "the children were so often away from the village on hunting and fishing expeditions with their parents."[43]

Also involved was the inculcation of the value of "industriousness," a cultural ideal related to the Protestant work ethic, especially highly esteemed in nineteenth century America. An article in an ABCFM Dakota newspaper sermonized: "we say, either determine to be nothing at all, or else determine to *be industrious*."[44] Missionaries tended to view hunting as sport, while farming was properly industrious labor. The disinclination of Dakotas to farm after the style of white men was thus interpreted as a sign of laziness. Brunson complained that "the Indians do not know how to work, and if they did, they have a foolish prejudice, of which they must be cured to be civilized, that it is derogatory to the dignity of a *man* to work."[45]

The last phrase in Brunson's statement raises an additional issue, of sex role definitions. In traditional Dakota society men hunted and assumed other responsibilities away from the village, while women took charge of domestic tasks including limited crops. Asking Dakota men to farm was, in effect, asking them to become women, from a traditional perspective. The missionary agricultural program, then, involved much more than the simple introduction of techniques. It carried with it a number of missionary assumptions and intentions, and it confronted obstacles in native culture.

Accomplishing these tasks of evangelism, education, and farming was made difficult by frequent shifts in personnel. Alfred Brunson, whose autobiography serves as a major source of information about this mission, functioned as superintendent only from 1837 through 1839. Brunson spent relatively little time at Kaposia. He attended the Illinois annual conference in the fall of 1837, not retuning until the next spring. He spent most of the summer of 1838 travelling through northern Minnesota, surveying mission possibilities among the Ojibwe.[46] Additional time was spent at Fort Snelling and Prairie du Chien. When Brunson requested superannuation for health reasons in the fall of 1839, also chafing at some apparently unjustified charges that he exploited mission work for personal gain, the Rock River Conference (Illinois) appointed Benjamin T. Kavanaugh as his successor.[47] Kavanaugh promptly visited Kaposia and then, continuing the pattern of the superintendent's absence, returned to Kentucky, his native state, to lecture and raise money for the work. He returned in the spring and built a residence within two miles of the mission, but his responsibility for Ojibwe missions as well as Kaposia necessitated other absences.[48] The superintendent's role was administrative, for the region; day to day work with the Dakotas fell to others.

Those other persons tended not to remain for long terms. David King was the mission's most stable resident, arriving with the original party and remaining after the mission's closing; he was not ordained and was usually designated as the mission teacher, although he also participated in preaching and farming. Mission personnel officially appointed by the government as farmers changed almost annually: Hiram Delap arrived in the fall, 1837, and departed in May 1838; Thomas W. Pope succeeded him but left in 1839; John Holton, a member of the original party but whose role with the mission in the next two years in unclear, became the next government appointed farmer; David King succeeded him in 1840. Other preaching and teaching missionaries passed through briefly: J.G. Whitford served for about two years, among both the Dakota and Ojibwe people; Allen Huddleston, after his graduation from Ebenezer, spent a month or two with King; Rollin Brown was appointed to Kaposia after serving an Ojibwe mission, but it is unclear if he ever arrived.[49] Benjamin Kavanaugh brought his brother William with him in 1840; at the 1841 conference William Kavanaugh was appointed missionary in charge of the Dakota mission, to be assisted by David King. Several of the departures were for reasons of health, but the shifts were also consistent with the mobility of the Methodist itinerant system.

Mission difficulties climaxed in the years 1841 and 1842. It was apparently in 1841 that Big Thunder ordered the mission school closed. In the same year Methodists opened a new boarding school across the river at Red Rock, primarily serving mixed-blood children. Red Rock is claimed to be the starting point of (white) Minnesota Methodism. King and Kavanaugh remained, but the focus of attention had changed. Benjamin Kavanaugh's relationship with the Indian Agent deteriorated so severely that the Secretary of War ordered Kavanaugh from the region in January 1843. David King remained nearby as a government appointed farmer, but the Methodist Dakota mission was abandoned.

Clear understanding of the circumstances and reasons behind the final events are difficult to sift from the evidence, but opinions have been offered. Stephen Riggs, an ABCFM missionary in the same period, wrote that the Indians near the Methodist mission "became insolent and exacting." He speculated that the Dakotas "had been spoiled from the beginning by having too much done for them by the [Methodist] missionaries."[50]

A more demonstrable partial explanation is that, in the context of increasing Dakota-Ojibwe rivalry, various leaders believed that the missionaries were undermining the Dakotas' ability to wage war. In 1842 David King wrote to Samuel

Pond: "The Indians or Big Thunder or somebody else dont [sic] like me. He blames me with all the misery in the band[.] He says that I am on the side of the enemy and pray to God to help them."[51] King's statement suggests continuing themes of white-Indian relations: missions sometimes served as a scapegoat for tribal problems; missionaries' efforts to prevent warfare were frequently interpreted as efforts to aid the enemy; and white "civilized" education did not help an Indian child become a successful warrior. The last of these themes was said to be the immediate reason for the closing of the mission school. Minnesota historian William Watts Folwell claimed, on evidence not ascertained by this writer, that Big Thunder ordered the school closed "because he did not want the boys spoiled as soldiers."[52]

The attitude of Big Thunder was crucial to the mission's existence. In the beginning the chief welcomed the missionaries to his village, enrolled his own children in the mission school, and encouraged his tribe to listen to the missionaries.[53] On one occasion in 1838, when threats of an Ojibwe attack frightened the mission personnel enough to leave, Big Thunder told them to stay and provided armed protection for them.[54] Big Thunder eventually turned against the Methodists, but he not seek to eliminate all whites. He asked the Indian Agent for another farmer, other than David King.[55] Later, in 1846, Big Thunder's son, the Little Crow of the Dakota War, invited Thomas Williamson to reestablish a mission at Kaposia.[56] Thus, there is reason to believe that some of the hostility was directed at these particular Methodist missionaries. Considering the missionaries' lack of training in cross-cultural relationships, symbolized by their disinterest in native langauges, personal clashes are quite conceivable.

A major feud also developed between Benjamin Kavanaugh and Major Amos Bruce, Lawrence Taliaferro's successor as Indian Agent. Kavanaugh wrote to the United States Indian Office, accusing Bruce of "drunkenness, favoritism to the Catholic missionaries, and general disqualification for so important an office."[57] Bruce defended himself, and trader Henry Hastings Sibley and other men countercharged that Kavanaugh was guilty of voyeurism. They claimed that he had drilled holes through the partition separating his stateroom from that occupied by a newly married couple on the steamboat Amaranth. Kavanaugh not only left the mission but later underwent an investigation by church officials.[58]

In October, 1842, David King wrote, "Our missions and school have all been abandoned. The property is all for sale."[59] When Thomas Williamson began American Board mission work at Kaposia four years later, he used the buildings that had been left by the Methodists. Stephen Riggs attributed the Methodist abandonment of the mission to impatience. "This was unreasonable," he wrote, "but Methodism then had not learned to work and wait for fruit in such unpromising fields. . . . To us it seems as if they did not hold on until the harvest came, and the reaping has fallen mainly into other hands."[60]

Some problems encountered by the Methodists were common to all the missions among the Dakotas. Many traditional Dakotas resented the intrusion of the "white man's" religion and culture, whatever the denominational label. No mission obtained really massive conversions until the war, no matter what the mission strategy. The war's radical cultural disruption and seeming defeat of traditional ways prompted many Dakotas to embrace a new religion and lifestyle, as much because of the changed external context as because of the missionaries. Methodists were not "fortunate" enough to be in place when the changes occurred.

Yet it was more than simply happenstance that the Methodist mission did not continue until 1862. In essence, the Methodists took an itinerant style of ministry that had served them well on the white frontier and attempted to apply it to Indian missions, where it was less appropriate. The difference was a cross-cultural situation, which required preparation for cultural understanding, more patience and sensitivity in communication, and more stable, long-term support. On the white frontier, rough-hewn preachers might communicate with the "common people" more effectively than would seminary educated clergy, but in Indian missions unprepared white preachers had no such automatic advantage. The mobility of wide circuits and frequent shifts in personnel might be efficient in extending ministry among people of somewhat similar Euroamerican backgrounds, but it was a mistake to view circuit riders as interchangeable chess pieces when they were assigned to tribal cultures so dissimilar that they spoke mutually unintelligible languages and held entirely contrasting cultural assumptions. As an Oklahoma Methodist missionary complained some years later: "Imagine a missionary being changed from China to Japan and from Japan to Africa every four years. What could the church expect of him?"[61]

In such matters, the Methodists provided a striking contrast with the more successful ABCFM Dakota mission. The American Board did not have extensive training programs prior to sending missionaries into the field, but the Board did provide substantial direction and oversight through letters, reports, and visitations, based upon an articulated mission theology and strategy and upon foreign experience. Brunson, Kavanaugh, and other Methodists entered Minnesota from white circuits, with little or no previous contact with Indians and little or no contact with other Methodist missionaries among Native Americans. Williamson, Riggs, and the Ponds worked with the Dakotas for more than twenty-five years; only David King was a part of the Methodist mission for the entirety of its five year life. The ABCFM Dakota missionaries focused on that tribe, while the Board sent others among the Ojibwe; several Methodist missionaries were shifted between the Dakota and Ojibwe peoples. All of the other mission efforts gave substantial early effort to learning the Dakota language; Methodists showed the least interest, and supported English-only education. The American Board provided comparatively solid and enduring financial support, underwriting many years which showed missionary acquisition of the language as almost the only result; before Brunson departed he complained that eastern supporters provided inadequate financial assistance and yet complained that it was too expensive.[62]

Some of these contrasts may be a bit overdrawn, but they highlight real differences in mission strategy and support. Such difficulties can be overlooked when particularly effective missionaries surmounted them. The situation of the struggling Dakota mission, however, raises questions about the general Methodist mission strategy among Native Americans that should be tested through examination of other settings and other eras.

NOTES

1. This essay is a revision and expansion of the section of the author's dissertation pertaining to Methodist missions. Bruce David Forbes, "Evangelization and Acculturation Among the Santee Dakota Indians, 1834-1864" (Ph.D. dissertation: Princeton Theological Seminary, 1977), chapter 3.
2. The following ethnological summary is derived from the Forbes dissertation, chapter 1, and from the following sources:
   Royal B. Hassrick, *The Sioux: Life and Customs of a Warrior Society* (Norman: University of Oklahoma Press, 1964).

James H. Howard, "The Cultural Position of the Dakota: A Reassessment," in *Essays in the Science of Culture in Honor of Leslie A. White*, edited by G. Dole and R. Carneiro (New York: Thomas Y. Crowell Co., 1960), pp. 249-268.

Roy W. Meyer, *History of the Santee Sioux: United States Indian Policy on Trial* (Lincoln: University of Nebraska Press, 1967).

Samuel Pond, "The Dakotas or Sioux in Minnesota as They Were in 1834," *Collections of the Minnesota Historical Society* XII (1908), pp. 319-501.

Claude Edwin Stipe, "Eastern Dakota Acculturation; the Role of Agents of Culture Change" (Ph.D. dissertation: University of Minnesota, 1968).

3. Hassrick, p. 246.

4. Pond, "Dakotas . . . 1834," p. 429.

5. Mary Aquinas Norton, *Catholic Missionary Activities in the Northwest, 1818-1864* (Washington, D.C.: Catholic University of America, 1930), pp. 10-14.

6. For general histories of the ABCFM, see Clifton Jackson Phillips, *Protestant America and the Pagan World: The First Half Century of the American Board of Commissioners for Foreign Missions, 1810-1860* (Cambridge, Massachusetts: East Asian Research Center, Harvard University, 1969) and William E. Strong, *The Story of the American Board: An Account of the First Hundred Years of the American Board of Commissioners for Foreign Missions* (Boston: Pilgrim Press, 1910).

7. For further information about the ABCFM Dakota mission, consult chapter 2, Forbes dissertation, and the following beginning bibliography:

Samuel W. Pond, Jr., *Two Volunteer Missionaries among the Dakotas, or the Story of the Labors of Samuel W. and Gideon H. Pond* (Boston: Congregational Sunday School and Publishing Society, 1893).

Stephen R. Riggs, *Mary and I: Forty Years With the Sioux* (Chicago: W.G. Holmes, 1880; Minneapolis: Ross & Haines, Inc., 1969 reprint edition).

Stephen R. Riggs, *Tah-koo Wah-kan: or, The Gospel among the Dakotas* (Boston: Congregational Sabbath-school and Publishing Society, 1869).

Jon Willand, *Lac Qui Parle and the Dakota Mission* (Madison, Minnesota: Lac Qui Parle County Historical Society, 1964).

8. ABCFM *Annual Report* (1848), pp. 261-262.

9. Thomas S. Williamson, "List of the Members of the churches among the Dakotas, August 18, 1862," manuscript list in Williamson Papers, Archives and Manuscripts Division, Minnesota Historical Society, St. Paul.

10. For further information regarding the Swiss Dakota mission, see pp. 91-96, Forbes dissertation, and the following:

J. Cart, *Histoire du Mouvement Religieux et Ecclésiastique dans le Canton de Vaud*, six volumes in four (Lausanne: Georges Bridel, 1870-1880), especially II, pp. 171-180.

"Reports of the Evangelical Society of Missions of Lausanne," 1835-1850, English translations in Box 4, Manuscripts Relating to Northwest Missions, compiled by Grace Lee Nute; Archives and Manuscripts Division, Minnesota Historical Society.

Stephen R. Riggs, "Protestant Missions in the Northwest," *Collections of the Minnesota Historical Society* VI (1894), pp. 134-135.

11. For further information regarding the Catholic Dakota mission, see pp. 96-111, Forbes dissertation, and:

Mary Aquinas Norton, *Catholic Missionary Activities in the Northwest, 1818-1864* (Washington, D.C.: Catholic University of America, 1930), pp. 46-73.

Augustin Ravoux, "The Labors of Mgr. A. Ravoux Among the Sioux or Dakota Indians from the Fall of the Year 1841 to the Spring of 1844," *St. Paul Pioneer Press* (March 7, 1897); also reprinted in pamphlet form.

Augustin Ravoux, *Reminiscences, Memoirs and Lectures of Monsignor A. Ravoux* (St. Paul: Brown, Treacy & Co., 1890).

Eugene J. Roden, "Augustin Ravoux, Pioneer Priest" (Master's thesis: St. Paul Seminary, 1955).

12. For further information regarding the Episcopal Dakota mission, see pp. 111-124, Forbes dissertation, and:

William Joseph Barnds, "The Ministry of the Reverend Samuel Dutton Hinman Among the Sioux," *Historical Magazine of the Protestant Episcopal Church* XXXVIII (1969), pp. 393-401.

George C. Tanner, "Early Episcopal Churches and Missions in Minnesota," *Collections of the Minnesota Historical Society* X, Part I (1905), pp. 203-231.

George C. Tanner, *Fifty Years of Church Work in the Diocese of Minnesota 1857-1907* (St. Paul: Published by the Committee of Publication and Sold by the Rev. W. C. Pope, 1909).

William Welsh, *Taopi and his Friends, or the Indians' Wrongs and Rights* (Philadelphia: Claxton, Rensen & Haffelfinger, 1869).

Henry Benjamin Whipple, *Lights and Shadows of a Long Episcopate* (New York: The Macmillan Company, 1900).

K. Brent Woodruff, "The Episcopal Mission to the Dakotas, 1860-1898," *South Dakota Historical Collections* XVII (1834), pp. 553-603.

13. Wade Crawford Barclay, *The History of Methodist Missions*, three volumes (New York: The Board of Missions and Church Extension of the Methodist Church, 1949-1957), I, p. 200.

This early American Methodist inattention to Indian missions was in spite of founder John Wesley's clearly exhibited concern for evangelization of Native Americans. A major motivation for Wesley's ill-fated expedition to Georgia was evangelization of Indians, although the intention was not fulfilled; Wesley greatly admired David Brainerd and published an abridged version of Jonathan Edwards' *Life of Brainerd*; one of Wesley's letters to Francis Asbury contains a significant passage about American Indians (November 25, 1787).

14. arclay, *Methodist Missions*, I, p. 203.

15. *Ibid.*, p. 285. Material in this paragraph is summarized from pp. 205-208, 282-285.

16. For a brief summary of these beginninngs, see William R. Cannon, "Education, Publication, Benevolent Work, and Missions," in *The History of American Methodism*, edited by E.S. Bucke, three volumes (New York, Nashville: Abingdon Press, 1964), I, pp. 586-599.

17. The major source for information on the life and work of Alfred Brunson is his own book: Alfred Brunson, *A Western Pioneer: or, Incidents of the Life and Times of Rev. Alfred Brunson . . .* , two volumes (Cincinnati: Hitchcock and Walden, and New York: Phillips and Hunt, 1879); II, chapters 3-5 are most pertinent to our subject. J. Christian Bay's *Going West: The Pioneer Work of Alfred Brunson* (Cedar Rapids, Iowa: The Torch Press, 1951) is simply a precis of Brunson's life based on *A Western Pioneer*, sprinkled with quotations from it: Brunson's own work is preferable for the historian. Ella C. Brunson, Alfred's daughter, wrote "Alfred Brunson, Pioneer of Wisconsin Methodism," *Wisconsin Magazine of History* II, 2 (December 1918), 129-148: it ignores unpleasantries and is highly unreliable. For secondary treatments of Brunson and the Methodist Dakota mission, in addition to general histories of Minnesota, see: Chauncey Hobart, *History of Methodism in Minnesota* (Red Wing: Red Wing Printing Co., 1887), pp. 13-33; Return I. Holcombe, *Minnesota in Three Centuries, Volume Two* (Mankato: The Publishing Society of Minnesota, 1908), pp. 261-270; Margaret Lowe, "Methodist Missions in Minnesota from 1837 to 1845," 32 pages typescript in library of Minnesota Historical Society, St. Paul; Stephen R. Riggs, "Protestant Missions in the Northwest," *Collections of the Minnesota Historical Society* VI (1894), pp. 135-143.

18. *Christian Advocate and Journal* XI: 48 (June 30, 1837), p. 198.

19. Chauncey Hobart, *History of Methodism in Minnesota* (Red Wing: Red Wing Printing Co., 1887), p. 15.

20. *Christian Advocate and Journal* (September 28, 1838).
21. Hobart, p. 14.
22. Brunson, *Western Pioneer*, II, p. 75.
23. William Watts Folwell, *A History of the Santee Sioux: United States Indian Policy on Trial* (Lincoln: University of Nebraska Press, 1967), p. 36.
24. Roy W. Meyer, *History of the Santee Sioux: United States Indian Policy on Trial* (Lincoln: University of Nebraska Press, 1967), p. 36.
25. References to "Little Crow" can be confusing because the name was passed along a line of hereditary chiefs and could refer to at least four different persons. The Little Crow who invited Brunson to Kaposia was also called Wakoyantanke, or Big Thunder. Big Thunder's son became the best known Little Crow, who participated in the Dakota War of 1862. The son's alternate name was Tayoyateduta, or His Scarlet People.

The clearest indication of an invitation from Big Thunder to the Methodists is found in Brunson's *Western Pioneer*, II, p. 78: "the chief having expressed a desire for us to establish a mission in his village . . . " The historian would be wise to exhibit some skepticism about the claim of invitations to this and other missions; the mythic image of an Indian reaching out to the missionary for help appears to be almost a formal requirement in missionary narratives. One should be especially cautious about interpreting invitations as implying spontaneous initiatives on the part of Dakota leaders; invitations are often better described as Native American willingness to accede to certain missionary suggestions. Whatever the spontaneity in this case, sources generally agree that the missionaries were amicably received.
26. Margaret Lowe, "Methodist Missions in Minnesota from 1837 to 1845," typescript essay held by the Minnesota Historical Society library, St. Paul, p. 3.
27. Brunson, *Western Pioneer*, II, p. 81. George Copway, *The Life, History, and Travels of Kah-ge-ha-gah-bowh . . .* (Albany: Weed and Parson, 1847), p. 122.
28. "George Copway, after a few years of most unsatisfactory connection with the missions, made himself notorious by various exploits throughout the country and finally drank himself to death." Hobart, p. 28.
29. Lowe, pp. 5-6, 12-22. Hobart, pp. 16, 25-33.
30. Classbook of St. Peter's Missionary Station and Sioux Mission; Methodist Papers, Archives and Manuscripts Division, Minnesota Historical Society.
31. *Missionary Herald* XLVI (1850), p. 169.
32. "The conversion of this family and their subsequent respectability and usefulness, as the fruit of our missionary operations in that country, was worth all its cost." Brunson, *Western Pioneer*, II, p. 120.
33. Alfred Brunson to B.F. Hoyt, March 28, 1859; Methodist Episcopal Church, Minnesota Annual Conference Historical Society Papers, Minnesota Historical Society.
34. Brunson, *Western Pioneer*, II, p. 96.

35. Holcombe, p. 264.
36. *Annual Report of the Missionary Society of the Methodist Episcopal Church*, 1856, p. 71. Quoted by Robert Berkhofer, Jr., *Salvation and the Savage: An Analysis of Protestant Missions and American Indian Response, 1787-1862* (Lexington: University of Kentucky Press, 1965), p. 33.
37. David King to Samuel W. Pond, October 25, 1842; Pond Family Papers, Archives and Manuscripts Division, Minnesota Historical Society.
38. Holcombe, p. 264.
39. Alfred Brunson to B.F. Hoyt, March 28, 1859; Methodist Papers. The additions to the mission mentioned here were "Rev. J.G. Whitford, T.W. Pope & family, & Hiram Delap & family."
40. Brunson, *Western Pioneer*, II, p. 135. However, Brunson acknowledged that the greater attention given by ABCFM missionaries to the Dakota language had resulted in more conversions.
41. Thomas W. Pope to Lawrence Taliaferro, August 24, 1838; Taliaferro manuscript Letter Book, Minnesota Historical Society.
42. Brunson, *Western Pioneer*, II, p. 131.
43. *Ibid.*, p. 95.
44. *Dakota Friend*, January 1851. Emphasis is original.
45. Brunson, *Western Pioneer*, II, p. 131.
46. Lowe, pp. 4-7.
47. "Misrepresentation of Missionaries," *Christian Advocate and Journal*, March 22, 1839. Brunson, *Western Pioneer*, II, pp. 126-135.
48. *Christian Advocate and Journal*, May 1, 1840.
49. Lowe, pp. 6-10.
50. Riggs, "Protestant Missions," p. 142.
51. King to Pond, October 25, 1842; Pond Family Papers, MHS.
52. William Watts Folwell, *A History of Minnesota*, four volumes (St. Paul Minnesota Historical Society, 1956 reprint edition) I, p. 206.
53. Holcombe, p. 263.
54. Brunson, *Western Pioneer*, II, pp. 115-116.
55. King to Pond, October 25, 1842; Pond Family Papers, MHS.
56. For speculation about Little Crow's reasons for inviting Williamson, see Folwell, *History of Minnesota*, I, pp. 201-202.
57. Lowe, p. 11. Meyer, p. 70.
58. Meyer, p. 70.
59. King to Pond, October 25, 1842; Pond Family Papers, MHS.
60. Riggs, "Protestant Missions," pp. 140 and 143.
61. Milton A. Clark, "Work Among the Kiowa and Comanche Indians," *Western Methodist* (August 15, 1907), p. 4.
62. Brunson, *Western Pioneer*, II, pp. 131-135.

The Holiness Complaint with Late-Victorian Methodism

Charles Edwin Jones

Without doubt the times are ripe in all of our large cities for just such churches as the Nazarene in Los Angeles. There is a stiffness and coldness in our city churches that freezes out the common people, and, worst of all shuts out the Christ of the common people. The pastors of our city churches are not soul winners. There may be exceptions, but they are very rare. So far as the Holy Ghost is concerned, in most all of the great city churches, it is well understood that if He cannot come in without sanctifying the people from all sin, and putting in their mouths a testimony to the fact, He can, and shall stay out. —H. C. Morrison, *Pentecostal Herald*, January 25, 1899

In January 1899, Evangelist Henry Clay Morrison[2] of Kentucky, a local elder in the Methodist Episcopal Church, South, conducted an eleven-day meeting in the tabernacle church of P.F. Bresee[3], former Methodist Episcopal pastor and presiding elder, in Los Angeles. The evangelist, who himself had narrowly escaped expulsion from Methodist ministry and membership for independent revivalism in Texas three years earlier, was vastly impressed with what he saw. The pastor, Morrison felt, enjoyed freedom to work "for the salvation of souls" utterly untrammeled with ecclesiastical complications."[4] The unspoken message in his January 25th editorial in the *Pentecostal Herald* was clear. Given the current state of Methodism, was not the revolutionary course taken by the Los Angeles pastor thoroughly justified?

Morrison reported, "For about fifteen years, Rev. P. F. Bresee, D.D., had preached in and around Los Angeles, serving two of the largest churches in the city. A few years ago, a combination of circumstances led to the doctor's withdrawal from the membership of the M. E. Church, and his entering upon an independent work in the city for the salvation of souls. About a year later he organized 'the Church of the Nazarene' with sixty members" and began "a marvelous career of soul winning for Christ." It was, Morrison thought, a vindication of Bresee's belief "that a church ought to be able to have a revival the year" around, a church "at whose altars sinners were being constantly [sic] converted, and believers sanctified." For the evangelist, preaching in the Los Angeles tabernacle was a refreshing experience. "It was wonderful to look on the great throng of uplifted, shining faces." "This meeting," he exclaimed, "will ever be remembered as one of the green spots in my life."[5]

The careers of Bresee, a Northern partisan who had draped his pulpit in Iowa with an American flag during the Civil War, and Morrison, the son of a Kentucky slaveholder, illustrate the dilemmas faced by holiness advocates in established Methodism. Both men were lifelong Methodists. Both had begun their ministries on the circuit, Bresee, the senior by nineteen years, at a time when much of Iowa was at the pioneer stage. Each had experienced entire sanctification (what Wesley called "the second blessing, properly so-called") after becoming well established in the ministry, and each felt that such an experience was an essential step for every believer. Each had developed close ties with the National Association for the Promotion of Holiness and had served as an evangelist under its auspices. And each had suffered what seemed to him unfair treatment by church officials for commitment to what he himself believed to be foundational truths of early Methodism.

Phineas F. Bresee was born December 31, 1838, in Delaware County, New York. (In adulthood he replaced his middle initial with Franklin, the name of the township in which he was born.) At age seventeen he was converted during a protracted meeting in the church of which his parents were members. Phineas launched into Christian activity immediately, leading prayer meetings, exhorting, and doing all he "could to push along the work." A few months later, the pastor issued him an exhorter's license which, he recalled: "I proceeded not to use." He recognized his call only after a leading citizen queried, "You will be a minister, won't you?"[6] Soon thereafter Bresee's father decided to move to Iowa. On the eve of his departure the youth made his first attempt at preaching. "I" went "to Iowa with one sermon."[7]

In the fall of 1857 (the year Morrison was born), young Bresee was appointed to the Marengo circuit as junior preacher to A. C. Barnhart. William Simpson, his presiding elder, was a distant relative of Bishop Matthew Simpson, by whom Bresee was ordained as a deacon and admitted to full connection two years later.[8] (Bresee held the bishop in high regard, sought his advice in the crisis which precipitated the move to California, and, in all likelihood, supported moves to name the college in Indianaola, Iowa, and a church he later served in Los Angeles after Simpson.) As pastor or presiding elder, Bresee was to continue the ministry he began the year he arrived in Iowa until 1911, when he resigned to devote full time to the general superintendency.

In Iowa, Bresee experienced the full range of challenges presented by pioneer Methodism. In later summer of 1860, he returned to his old home in New York state to take Maria G. Hibbard, distant relative of Freeborn Garrettson Hibbard,[9] as his bride. The first appointment following his marriage was Grinnell, a circuit of five or six churches which included one particularly difficult congregation made up largely of Southern sympathizers who resented the "Abolition doctrine" of their young pastor. "We lived largely on faith. You would hardly believe that one sack of flour" and "a few pounds of buckwheat to make pancakes, did us that year." At the 1861 conference, during which he was ordained an elder by Bishop Scott, Bresee asked to be moved. "I told the presiding Elder that I did not want to go back. He intimated to me that I might get a poorer appointment." And he did indeed: the Galesburg circuit, a half-dozen preaching points, mostly schoolhouses, and no parsonage. Quarters for the preacher's family (Maria had given birth to their first son while the conference was in session) consisted of "one room with a very small bedroom connected with it, access to which was gained solely by going through" the landlord's "living room."[10]

A number of convictions about the essentials of the Methodist ministry took shape in Bresee's thinking during these years, principles which would make later developments in the church intolerable to him. Grieved that he should be appointed to such a place, he was seized with "an awful determination to win and succeed in accomplishing something." Later, he remembered, "I had a very good horse, which I immediately traded off to get a poorer horse, and money enough to pay my debts on the circuit where I had lived, so that there need be no feeling of lack of confidence in a Methodist

preacher." Convinced that his chief responsibility was to see revival on his charge, he determined to conduct a two-week protracted meeting in each of the six churches on the circuit. He began in October. By spring he had conducted meetings in all the churches. "That charge did me more good than any I ever had." He recalled, "It broke me up" and "taught me . . . that desperation, earnestness, intensity, would win, God helping, in doing God's work."[11]

This beginning, so similar to others in pioneer Methodism, was certainly not limited to those destined to be drawn into the holiness movement but it was typical of many future holiness adherents. About twenty years later in Kentucky, Henry Clay Morrison's second appointment, the Jacksonville circuit, consisted of five points located in three counties.[12] The third year his three-point circuit centering on Buckner's Station, a hamlet on the Ohio River twenty-five miles above Louisville, paid $11.08 per month. Morrison, then a bachelor, purchased a meal ticket at a boarding house, abstaining from meals when the dots on the ticket gave out before he had the wherewithal to buy another. He, nevertheless, counted the year a success because of revivals which broke out at all points on the charge.[13]

The aggressive revivalism which characterized the early ministry of Bresee and Morrison made plain in broad outline their vision of some Methodist essentials. At this time, neither man claimed to have been entirely sanctified. Nor had either yet adopted the puritanical stances which later became the hallmarks of holiness advocates, such as plain dress and abstinence from tobacco. Pictures of women in the Bresee family taken in the 1870s indicate, for instance, that they wore necklaces and earrings.[14] Morrison himself stated that he continued to use coffee and tobacco after he entered the Methodist ministry and that for reasons of health he gave up coffee before he quit smoking cigars.[15]

In conformity to what they regarded as Wesleyan fundamentals, the future holiness leaders carried the charismatic style developed in their early ministry into later pastorates. Bresee's rapid ascent in Iowa carried him to leading pastorates in Des Moines (the capital city), Red Oak, and Council Bluffs. Upon removal to California in 1883, he was assigned to the First M.E. Church of Los Angeles. This appointment was followed by the First Church of Pasadena (here in 1888 he commanded an annual salary of $4,350, more than five and a half times the national average for ministers)[16] and service as presiding elder of the Los Angeles District. In all these places, especially after 1884 when he entered the holiness ranks in earnest (he had claimed entire sanctification sixteen years earlier at Chariton, Iowa), Bresee pursued an aggressive evangelistic ministry.[17]

A number of changes both within the church and outside it contributed to revivalistic fervor. The time limit on pastoral appointments in the Methodist Episcopal Church was raised twice in the last half of the nineteenth century. The two-year limit in effect when Bresee launched his ministry encouraged vigorous action. The brevity of appointments coupled with the distance between preaching points on circuits in rural areas made each pastor into an itinerant evangelist. Committed as he was to this way of ministering, Bresee opposed relaxing the time limit in 1864 when the General Conference raised it to three years. Bresee's reaction in 1888 when that body set the limit at five years is not known.[18] The time limit for the Southern church was set at four years in 1866, when Morrison was still a child.

Longer tenure for pastors was not an insignificant matter inasmuch as it indicated a change in their primary role. The growing settledness and respectability of Methodist members indicated the need for a different kind of minister, less the evangelist and more the administrator. Church architecture registered the change. Following the lead of Christ Church, Pittsburgh, which had built the first gothic edifice in American Methodism in 1855, hundreds of congregations abandoned the simple buildings of an earlier day for substantial and costly ones reflecting the new prosperity. It was into such a gothic structure that in 1874 the Methodist congregation at Red Oak, Iowa,[19] moved following an outstanding revival, the first so-called Home Camp Meeting, conducted by P. F. Bresee, its pastor.

The Home Camp Meeting was to become an annual event in churches served by Bresee. The new gospel music of the type used by Moody and Sankey (and the National Holiness evangelists, which he introduced at this time, also became a standard feature in Bresee's pastorates.[20] Skillful ministers such as Bresee were able, for a time at least, to pursue revivalism and to support the desire of their people for secular respectability. Conflict between the two, such as that touched off by his appointment to the debt-ridden, elegantly-housed Simpson Church in Los Angeles, lay two decades in the future.[21]

For Henry Clay Morrison the decade of the 1880s was one of great professional advancement and of wholehearted acceptance of the holiness message. These years, which included training at Vanderbilt University, ordination as deacon and elder, and admission to full connection in the Kentucky conference of the Methodist Episcopal Church, South, witnessed a steady progression in the prestige of appointments held: Eleventh Street in Covington, Highlands, Stanford, Danville, and Frankfort, the state capital.[22] In 1887 upon the urging of friends he read Wesley's *Plain Account of Christian Perfection*. Morrison reported that a short time later while reading a letter from Horace Cockrill, one of very few holiness men in the conference,

The Truth broke in upon me like an inspiration. I saw the doctrine and experience of full salvation as clearly as the sun in a cloudless noonday sky. My whole heart said, "It is the truth," and I laughed and wept for joy. It seemed as if the following conversation went on within my breast: "I am the Lord's child. Yes, but not his holy child. He wants me to be holy, but I cannot make myself holy. That is so, but he can make me holy." "Yes, he can," was the response of my whole heart. I saw clearly the reasonableness of it all, and the will and power of God in the matter. I felt assured that I should return to my boarding house after dinner, go to my room, and receive the blessing as a free gift of God.[23]

The reception of this experience, which in Morrison's case was accompanied by swallowing a mystical ball of fire, accentuated his confidence as a God-appointed leader and his fear of worldliness. (Bresee had a similar experience with fire. Neither man, however, regarded this phenomenon as normative.) Although he himself had quit smoking only a year previously (after realizing that his habit was being supported by the sacrificial giving of working girls),[24] Morrison preached straight-out against dancing, card playing, theater going, and horse racing. The revivalistic emphasis, always a prominent feature in Morrison's ministry, became even more pronounced. During the two years at Frankfort, his last pastorate before plunging into evangelism full time, four protracted meetings (one lasting six weeks) were held there. In addition to these meetings in his own church, Morrison conducted revival series at Maysville, Carrolton, Cedar Chapel, Louisville, Mount Sterling, and Henderson, Kentucky, and launched the *Old Methodist* during these years. In the fall of 1890 he requested location to devote fulltime to itinerant evangelism and editorial work.[25]

The reformist impulse behind Henry Clay Morrison's career change was indicated by the succession of names under which his paper appeared in its first decade. The *Old Methodist,* first issued in December 1888, became the *Kentucky Methodist* at the time of Morrison's location, the *Methodist* four years later, and the *Methodist and Way of Life* with the absorption of W. A. Dodge's Atlanta-based paper in 1895. The *Pentecostal Herald,* a title destined to continue for the remainder of the founder's life, was chosen two years later.[26] Morrison's great popularity as a revival preacher in central Kentucky during his pastorate at Frankfort led him to assume that his attractiveness to Kentucky Methodist pastors seeking a revivalist would increase with location. Although calls to other areas, notably Texas and California, came with increasing frequency, invitations to central Kentucky engagements plummeted. During his last year at Frankfort, he received at least thirty invitations to hold protracted meetings in Kentucky Conference churches. The next year he received only one.[27]

The names borne by his paper during its first decade reflected Morrison's vision for the church and his strategy for realizing that vision. Itinerant evangelism was to be the method whereby the dynamism of the pioneer Methodist circuit was to be transmitted in the Gilded Age. The evangelist's first goal was renewal of "old" Methodism in his native state. Frustrated by the coolness of his former connectional brethren at home, he ranged much farther afield, achieving a national circuit within a very few years. At this time Morrison underlined the grandeur of his crusade to save the church by the prominence he gave to "Methodist" in the paper's name.

Although location provided Evangelist Morrison with freedom from restraints imposed by conference membership, he was to find as a local elder little to shield him from the darts of ecclesiastical foes. Morrison's popularity as an evangelist grew steadily and he continued as a much-desired revival and camp meeting speaker with a national, even international, clientele, to the end of his life more than a half-century later. He, like Bresee, joined the National Association for the Promotion of Holiness, a largely Methodist committee of evangelists which had organized in 1867 to revive Wesleyan perfectionism by means of camp meetings. (Permanent encampments such as the one sponsored by the Ocean Grove Camp Meeting Association of the Methodist Episcopal Church had been founded and sustained in their early years by National Holiness backers.) The National Association, together with state and local affiliates, created a gigantic evangelistic circuit which, in its supporters' eyes resembled in a greatly magnified way, the pioneer Methodist circuit of their youth.

It was on to this platform (revival of "old" Methodist teachings and practices outside the control of Methodist officialdom) that the young evangelist had stepped.[28]

Six years later Henry Clay Morrison was brought to trial *in absentia* (he was evangelizing at the time in California) by the Hill Street Church in Lexington, Kentucky, on charges referred to it by the presiding elder and preacher-in-charge of the Dublin, Texas, circuit. The case, which alleged that the evangelist had broken the law of the church by conducting a meeting within the bounds of the circuit without permission of the pastor, was eventually set aside by the Kentucky annual conference.[29] Victory was short lived, for the 1898 General Conference of the Methodist Episcopal Church, South, enacted legislation giving the pastor power to regulate preaching by "any traveling or local preacher or layman" in the environs of his appointment.[30] At Terrell, Texas, later that year and at Denton, Texas, six years later, Morrison evaded prosecution by hostile clergy by use of extralegal devices: in the first instance by withdrawing from membership in the church temporarily, and in the other by placing himself at the mercy of his enemy.[31]

Ultimately, Morrison found a way to survive in the church. He was destined to serve for more than a quarter century as president of Asbury College, an independent institution supported by holiness loyalists in the church. In 1923 he would found the Asbury Theological Seminary to supply holiness clergy for the church. From the church, in turn, he was to receive numerous tokens of affirmation, serving in 1921 as delegate to the Ecumenical Methodist Conference in London, and between 1918 and 1938 as delegate to five general conferences of the Methodist Episcopal Church, South. Although he himself would reach a *modus vivendi* in the church, Morrison often stood on the edge of despair. His followers could expect little affirmation in a church whose bishops in 1894 had decried the very existence of "holiness evangelists, and holiness property." There was, he thought, little hope. "The ecclesiastics of the times are against the holiness movement. They are against the humility, zeal, and holy excitement that must characterize a genuine Holy Ghost revival of religion. They are," he concluded, "against the Holy Ghost in His manifestations among the people." Church officials, he declared, "are against the great masses of common people. They are blind to the marvelous opportunity that surrounds us to sweep the multitudes into the kingdom of heaven."[32]

Perhaps Methodism in some reincarnation such as Bresee's Church of the Nazarene was the answer. At least so it seemed for one brief moment following the meeting in Los Angeles.

Holiness tradition on separation from the mother church lays blame on the neglect of the Wesleyan doctrine of perfect love. Bresee and Morrison would agree. Yet, however steadfastly they and their colleagues promoted holiness doctrine, their actions and rhetoric point to an even more central Wesleyan issue: the decline of zeal which each man regarded as characteristic of the church of his youth. The diversion of enthusiasm from the salvation of souls to the building of institutions had sidetracked the church from its true purpose. Keeping the "glory down," Bresee's formula for churchly success, required charismatic leaders like those remembered from pioneer days. As true Methodists, the holiness leaders never doubted the necessity of church order. When, however, that orderliness crowded out the fervor which lay near the heart of Wesleyan piety, they felt impelled to rally that part of the Methodist constituency most anxious for the recovery of primitive zeal. A key element in this nostalgic band were country people then flocking into Louisville and Los Angeles. How to present essential Methodism (which for Bresee and Morrison was the gospel indeed) to these chosen ones among God's "poor" was the obvious task. In their view, the church blocked the way. The remedy lay in establishing "centers of holy fire" outside or on the border of official Methodism. For Bresee, the solution was a new Methodist church, the Church of the Nazarene. For Morrison, it was the zealous young workers who would be formed by the Asbury institutions for the benefit of official Methodism, but free from its cold heavy-handedness.

NOTES

1. H.C. Morrison, "The Church of the Nazarene," *Pentecostal Herald* (Editorial), 11 (Jan. 25, 1899), 8.
2. For biography see his *Some Chapters from My Life Story* (Louisville, Pentecostal Publishing Co., 1941); his *Life Sketches and Sermons* (Louisville, Pentecostal Publishing Co., 1903); and his *Remarkable Conversions, Interesting Incidents and Striking Illustrations* (Louisville, Pentecostal Publishing Co., 1925); also Percival A. Wesche, "The Life, Theology, and Influence of Henry Clay Morrison" (Unpublished Ph.D. thesis, University of Oklahoma, 1954); Percival A. Wesche, *Henry Clay Morrison, Crusader Saint* (Berne, In., Herald Press, c1963); and C. F. Wimberly, *A Biographical Sketch of Henry Clay Morrison, D. D., Editor of "The Pentecostal Herald": the Man and His Ministry* (New York, Fleming H. Revell Co., 1922).
3. For biography see E. A. Girvin, *Phineas F. Bresee: a Prince in Israel* (Kansas City, Mo., Pentecostal Nazarene Publishing House, 1916; reprinted: Kansas City, Mo., Nazarene Publishing House, 1981); Donald Paul Brickley, "The Life and Work of Phineas F. Bresee" (Unpublished Ph.D. thesis, University of Pittsburgh, 1958); Donald P. Brickley, *Man of the Morning: the Life and Work of Phineas F. Bresee* (Kansas City, Mo., Nazarene Publishing House, 1960); H. D. Brown, *Personal Memories of the Early Ministry of Dr. Phineas F. Bresee: Character Study* (Seattle, 1930); A. M. Hills, *P. F. Bresee: D. D., a Life Sketch* (Kansas City, Mo., Nazarene Publishing House, 1930); and I. G. Martin, *Dr. P. F. Bresee and the Church He Founded* (Mansfield, Il., Printed by Nazarene Publishing House, Kansas City, Mo., 1937); also Ward B. Chandler (comp.), *Sayings of Our Founder* (Houston, Chandler and Roach Religious Publications, 1948); Timothy L. Smith (comp.), *The Certainties of Faith: Ten Sermons by the Founder of the Church of the Nazarene* (Kansas City, Mo., Nazarene Publishing House, 1958); and Carl Bangs, "The Making of a Founder: Phineas F. Bresee," in his *Our Roots of Belief: Biblical Faith and Faithful Theology* (Kansas City, Mo., Beacon Hill Press of Kansas City, 1981), 9-25.
4. Morrison, "The Church of the Nazarene," *Pentecostal Herald*, 11 (Jan. 25, 1899), 8.
5. *Ibid.*
6. Girvin, *Phineas F. Bresee: a Prince in Israel*, p. 28.
7. *Ibid.*, p. 29.
8. *Ibid.*, p. 32-36; Brickley, *Man of the Morning*, p. 59-62.
9. The testimony of Hibbard, the biographer of Bishop L. L. Hamline, is included in Phoebe Palmer, *Pioneer Experiences; or, The Gift of Power Received by Faith, Illustrated and Confirmed by the Testimony of Eighty Living Ministers, of Various Denominations*, by the author of "Way of Holiness" (New York, W. C. Palmer, Jr., 1868), 34-45.
10. Girvin, *Phineas F. Bresee: a Prince in Israel*, 38-41.
11. *Ibid.*, 40, 43.
12. Wesche, "The Life, Theology, and Influence of Henry Clay Morrison," 34; Wesche, *Henry Clay Morrison: Crusader Saint*, 30.
13. Wesche, "The Life, Theology, and Influence of Henry Clay Morrison," 38-39; Wesche, *Henry Clay Morrison: Crusader Saint*, 32-33.
14. Pictures in the possession of Carl Bangs, Prairie Village, Kansas.
15. For circumstances surrounding Morrison's giving up coffee, see Wesche, "The Life, Theology, and Influence of Henry Clay Morrison," 36-37.
16. Bresee's salary at Pasadena is given in Brickley, *Man of the Morning*, 103. In 1890 the average compensation for ministers in the United States was $794. See U.S. Bureau of the Census. *Historical Statistics of the United States, Colonial Times to 1957* (Washington, Government Printing Office, 1960), 92.
17. Girvin, *Phineas F. Bresee: a Prince in Israel*, 51, 54-96.
18. *Ibid.*, 46-47, 88-89.
19. See Bangs, "The Making of a Founder: Phineas F. Bresee" in his *Our Roots of Belief*, 16. A photograph of the M. E. Church, Red Oak, Iowa, 1874 is included in Girvin, *Phineas F. Bresee: a Prince in Israel*, between 226 and 227; for an account of the Red Oak pastorate as a whole see 59-65.
20. For an account of the introduction of the gospel songs of P. P. Bliss at Red Oak see Bangs, "The Making of a Founder: Phineas F. Bresee" in his *Our Roots of Belief*, 15-16.
21. Girvin, *Phineas F. Bresee: a Prince in Israel*, 98; Brickley, *Man of the Morning*, 114-115.
22. Wesche, "The Life, Theology, and Influence of Henry Clay Morrison," 44-68; Wesche, *Henry Clay Morrison: Crusader Saint*, 35-50.
23. Quoted in Wesche, "The Life, Theology, and Influence of Henry Clay Morrison," 57.
24. *Ibid.*, 52. Morrison's later statements comments on tobacco are strongly condemnatory. See, for instance, his *Open Letters to the Bishops, Ministers and Members of the Methodist Episcopal Church, South* (Louisville, Pentecostal Publishing Co., 190-), 3, 12, 14-18.
25. Wesche, "The Life, Theology, and Influence of Henry Clay Morrison," 61-68, 70-71.
26. *Ibid.*, 72, 74, 79, 85-86.

27. *Ibid.*, 97-98.
28. Jones, "The Camp Meeting" in his *Perfectionist Persuasion: the Holiness Movement and American Methodism, 1867-1936* (Metuchen, N.J.: Scarecrow Press, 1974), 16-46.
29. *Ibid.*, 93; Wesche, "The Life, Theology, and Influence of Henry Clay Morrison," 125-144; Wesche, *Henry Clay Morrison: Crusader Saint*, 82-92; and W. E. Arnold, *The H. C. Morrison Case: a Statement of Facts, an Investigation of the Law* (Louisville, Kentucky Methodist Publishing Co., 1897).
30. Wesche, "The Life, Theology, and Influence of Henry Clay Morrison," 139.
31. *Ibid.*, 140-144; Wesche, *Henry Clay Morrison: Crusader Saint*, 89-92.
32. Morrison, "The Church of the Nazarene," *Pentecostal Herald*, 11 (Jan. 25, 1899), 8.

The Well-Furnished Minister:
The Conference Course of Study in the M. E. Church, South, 1900-1939

Robert W. Sledge
McMurry College

With a Fellow of Oxford as its founder, the Methodist Church in America could hardly be expected to ignore the education of its ministers, no matter how uncouth might be the frontier constituency they served. The first phase of that educational process paralleled the educational process in other professions—apprenticeship. Thus a fledgling preacher was attached to an experienced man as they travelled their appointed circuit together, the junior preacher learning by direct observation and conversation from his senior partner.[1]

In 1816, the Methodist Episcopal Church (the name under which American Wesleyans first organized themselves) adopted a new system which would first supplement and then supplant the apprenticeship process. It centered on a two-year regimen called "the course of study." At the same General Conference that divided American episcopal Methodism into northern and southern wings in 1844, the body first provided for expansion of the course of study to four years, and each branch carried that legislation into their separate existences. In the new Methodist Episcopal Church, South, after some difficulty getting started, the course of study served as the mainstay of theological education until the reunification of 1939. To be sure, the Church South established theological seminaries at Vanderbilt in 1875 and at Emory and Southern Methodist universities after the church divested itself of its relations with Vanderbilt in 1914. But seminary education was still in the process of being phased in as the next form of theological education in 1939. A survey made in 1926 showed only 12% of Southern Methodist ministers with seminary training.[2] A dozen years later, in the period just preceding unification, only about one-third of the newly ordained elders each year were seminary graduates. The remainder came through the course of study.[3]

Preparation of the Course of Study

Take thousands of committed young men, drill them thoroughly in a certain set of ideas, scatter them systematically in positions of leadership in every village and town in the South, and set them to work disseminating those ideas daily and weekly to large numbers of receptive people in that area. It is an extremely important position to determine the content of such a set of ideas. The very life of the church could depend on it. So the M. E. Church, South, did not take lightly the decisions of selection of books for the course. The church entrusted the choice of materials to the most respected, mature, reliable and influential men it knew—the college of bishops. That the bishops took their task seriously can be seen from Bishop Collins Denny's comment in 1926: "No more important work lies before us than the selection of the Courses to be pursued by our coming preachers. We may make them or mar them by our choice of books."[4]

Unfortunately, we know little of what went on in the college when the course of study was being discussed. The Bishops kept their deliberations completely to themselves, so much so, in fact, that they issued all statements as if they were unanimous under the policy they called the "unit rule."[5] This self-imposed vow remained intact until the special session of the General Conference in 1924, called to discuss unification. We can see, however, that the basic work of outlining the courses (including courses for seminary graduates, Spanish-speaking ministers and others along with the principal course) fell to subcommittees of from two to four bishops, though one especially interested bishop might do most of the work. The subcommittees then reported back to the college of bishops for discussion, amendment and final ratification of their labors.

The bishops were not all alike. Some were staunch conservatives while others were much more progressive, so any course of study they worked out was likely to be some sort of compromise. The behind-the-scenes maneuverings of the group were an internal manifestation of their public differences. During the two decades following 1914 especially, Southern Methodist bishops took public issue with one another on a broad range of subjects, following the lines of cleavage that threatened to rend the denomination at large. The issues of Vanderbilt, democratization, unification, the role of the general boards, clergy in politics and several other problems drew written "deliverances" from the episcopal leaders, often in the form of direct personal clashes in print.[6]

In particular, Bishops Collins Denny and Edwin Mouzon took leadership in planning the course of study. Both had served at least briefly as college professors and both were well educated and confident men. But Denny was the more conservative of the two by far and was often disturbed by the direction the course of study took. In a letter to Bishop Candler in 1926 he stated succinctly the conservative viewpoint:

> We may not be able to get the votes to use Ralston, but I am in favor of returning to that book. The objection will likely be made that the book is old, out of date. I am not much influenced by that cry. Changed conditions may and indeed do often call for a changed presentation of truth, but truth does not change. Many of us profited greatly by Ralston, and our coming preachers need to know exactly what Ralston stresses.[7]

Later in the same note, he called for inclusion of a book on the founding of the M. E. Church, South, as a device to discomfit the advocates of unification. On another occasion he opposed the inclusion (successfully, as it turned out) of "Buckham's Personality and Psychology" on the grounds, among other things, that it "seems to accept the fact of evolution."[8]

Bishop Mouzon also exerted great influence on the course. In 1922, he claimed almost full responsibility for the revision of 1918. Though it was criticized as being too liberal, he affirmed his orthodoxy by saying:

> Indeed the course of study as it now is—with the exception of those books by Prof. Davis which Bishop Denny put in, and two biographies—is the course as I prepared it, and no book that I suggested was objected to by the Bishops. *Per contra*, such men as Bishops Hoss, Hendrix, and Candler congratulated me and said that we now had the best course we had ever had.[9]

To Denny's distress, the Davis books (one on deductive logic, one on psychology, each with commentary by Denny, plus another on ethics) were omitted from the 1922 revision though Denny lamented the exclusion of the Ethics book, "the sanest, safest and most satisfactory work I have ever read."[10] He was happier after the 1926 revision made the course more conservative. "Our Lord helped us," he said, "on the Courses of Study, and we are better off than we have been for four years."[11]

Other criteria affected the bishops' choices. Sometimes an adequate book could not be found for various reasons. George P. Fisher's *History of the Christian Church* wound up on the course in 1926 because one acceptable alternative was too expensive and another, Williston Walker's work of the same name as Fisher's, was considered by Denny to be "a dangerous and a bad book" because of its anti-Methodist tone.[13] Other works such as John Laidlaw's *Bible Doctrine of Man* and J. Agar Beet's *The New Life in Christ*, had to be removed because they went out of print and the same thing nearly happened to R. W. Dale's *Christian Doctrine*.[14] One book, by Professor Andrew Sledd of Emory University, was approved for the course in 1918 but never included because Sledd did not complete it.[15] Southern Methodist Publishing Agent A. J. Lamar, making recommendations to Bishop Warren Candler on the subject of fit items for the course of study, felt that in the field of psychology there was really nothing acceptable in print.[16] So the bishops had to work with what was available as well as what was finally mutually agreeable.

Although the courses of study devised by the bishops were generally not too controversial in the church at large, sentiment began to develop aimed at taking that responsibility off their hands. Partly, this was an element of a general feeling that the episcopacy was too powerful. Partly, it was in emulation of the M. E. Church, where a special commission of educational professionals prepared the course. The Southern bishops were not very much in sympathy with such a structure. An exchange between W. C. Everett, manager of the Dallas branch of the Publishing House of the M. E. Church, South, and Bishop Edwin Mouzon served to illustrate the attitude. In 1922, Everett proposed to Mouzon the creation of a commission on courses of study after the northern model. Mouzon understood Everett's concern, but responded:

> Don't have a Commission on Course of Study appointed. The Northern brethren did that, and have been in a fight over it ever since. Their course of study has not been properly guarded. I fear that a Commission would do one of two things—either put in reactionary books or put in heretical books. Better leave it in the hands of the Bishops who are supposed to be up-to-date men, and who are also under a solemn obligation to guard the Church from erroneous and false doctrine.[17]

A sweeping change in the educational administration of Southern Methodism in the 1930 General Conference wrought precisely that change, however. A new "superboard" called the General Board of Christian Education contained a "Department of Leadership Training" which included supervision of a "Commission on Courses of Study." The commission, which would replace the college of bishops in this function, would be made up of five bishops selected by the college, and four other traveling elders, two of whom would be educators. In the modifications made by the General Conference of 1934, one of the bishops was replaced by the secretary of the Department of Schools and Colleges of the General Board of Education. Thus, while episcopal leadership was still present in the process of selecting the course of study books, they no longer had the majority voice in the process.

Minutes of the commission have survived in the files of two of the bishops who participated in the first commission, Bishops Warren Candler and Edwin Mouzon.[18] Mouzon, in fact, was the chairman of the commission for the quadrennium. Also serving were Bishops John M. Moore, Hoyt M. Dobbs and Paul B. Kern. In addition, Professor Franklin Parker of Emory University's Candler School of Theology, Dr. C. M. Bishop, sometime college president and seminary professor, Dr. Nolan B. Harmon, Jr. and Dr. W. W. Peele, both pastors, completed the group. Interestingly enough, all of these men except Dr. Bishop were elevated to the episcopacy, though Parker declined to serve in the office.

While the minutes do not reveal the kinds of participation in any debates that may have been held in the commission meetings, the tone of the meetings suggests that partisan feeling was far from their minds. The existing course was modified book by book as seemed necessary, and no one seemed to have a prepared agenda of books to promote. Often, decisions were reached "by common consent." Even more often, final decisions were entrusted to one or more members of the commission, with the understanding that whatever they came up with would be satisfactory to the rest of the members. This spirit of cooperation is predictable, given the general spirit that prevailed in the church at that time (in sharp contrast to the loud confrontations of the preceding decades), and also given the makeup of the committee, which was filled with men of progressive temperament. The exception was the conservative Bishop Candler, but he was absent from the 1933 and 1934 meetings anyway.

Even the modest change of 1934 in placing the secretary of the Department of Schools and Colleges on the Commission did not create much ripple, since the man in question, Dr. W. M. Alexander, was already serving as the secretary of the body though not holding voting membership prior to 1934. While the commission made many modifications from the course it had inherited from the bishops, the essential thrust of the course was not changed appreciably for the remaining few years of the denomination's separate existence.

Administration of the Course of Study

Through the 19th century, committees of the annual conferences administered the course of study drawn up by the bishops. Each class met with a designated group of specially trained interrogators picked from the travelling elders of the conference. These men were veterans of the circuits who had carefully prepared themselves to examine the candidates of each level when all the preachers gathered for the meeting of the annual conference, usually in the fall.

But the lack of uniformity from conference to conference inevitably raised questions about the need for a more centralized system of guidance for examining committee and candidate classes alike. This concern surfaced in the General Conference of 1898 when the Arkansas Conference petitioned the governing body of the M. E. Church, South, to create a correspondence school to oversee the course of study.

The committee on memorials referred it to the committee on education. Subsequently, in the committee's report No. 2, which was adopted by the General Conference, section 1, read:

1. The Committee on Education had had under consideration a memorial from the Arkansas Conference, asking that a plan of correspondence-instruction be provided by the General Board of Education to assist undergraduate preachers in the prosecution of their studies in the Conference course, and recommends nonconcurrence.[19]

Section 3 of the same report dealt with another proposed reform in the use of the Course of Study in a similar fashion:

3. The Committee has also carefully considered a memorial from the Theological Faculty of Vanderbilt University, requesting that applicants for admission to any Annual Conference shall be excused from examination on that part of the Course of Study which they may be certified to have completed in that department of the University to the satisfaction of its faculty. We recommend nonconcurrence.[20]

However, the committee did approve one

proposed reform having to do with the administration of the course of study, and commended it to the General Conference for consideration in report No. 5:

Your committee has had under consideration the following resolution referred to them by the Conference, and recommend its adoption:

Resolved, That the presentation of the Bachelor of Divinity diploma from Vanderbilt University by an applicant for admission on trial in any of our Annual Conferences shall be considered the equivalent of the required examinations in the books that are covered by this degree, and that in these studies the examination may be omitted.[21]

This motion by the committee was tabled by a vote of 60-45. A last minute motion to reconsider was also tabled just before final adjournment. The mood of the General Conference of 1898 did not allow any improvement in the matter of ministerial education. However, 1902 was a different story. A new awareness permeated the meetings of the committee on education and indeed, the whole conference. A new chairman, W. B. Murrah, presided over the committee. Its first report dealt in eight points with ministerial education. The first point set the tone of the report when it recommended:

1. That our Conference generally be urged to advance the standards for admission on trial in accordance with the advanced standards in all callings. Our preachers should be leaders of men, and in an age of general education, they need to be educated men.[22]

In line with this new thrust in education, the correspondence school which had been defeated in 1898 was proposed again, and this time it passed through committee and gained the approval of the General Conference. It was resolved:

4. (1) That for the guidance of all candidates for admission and undergraduates in the Conferences, and also of those who, having completed the Conference course, desire to prosecute a post-graduate course of study, the Board of Education is instructed to establish at Nashville, in connection with the Biblical Department of Vanderbilt University, and under the direction of its Faculty, Correspondence Courses, which shall be offered to all ministers or candidates for our ministry under such regulations as may be approved by the Board and Faculty.

(2) The Secretary of this Correspondence School shall issue a certificate to every one who prosecutes, under the direction of the school, the

study of any book embraced in the Course of Study, and passes a satisfactory written examination on the same. He shall send this certificate along with the questions and examination papers to the chairman of the Annual Conference committee having charge of the candidate or undergraduate concerned. The Conference committee may then, if the Conference sees fit, accept this certificate in lieu of examinations held by themselves.[23]

Also proposed at this time as an additional aid to ministerial training was the establishment of "Preachers' Institutes." They were to be held in various areas of the church under the direction of the correspondence school and with the cooperation and support of the adjacent annual conferences' examining committees. The conference appropriated the sum of $5000 for the correspondence school and the preachers' institutes.

In additional contrast to 1898, the same report urged that the annual conferences grant credit in the course of study for related work done in approved colleges. Both the Board of Education and the college of bishops had earlier suggested this to the General Conference. The entire report was debated part by part and adopted by the General Conference.[24]

The correspondence school was organized the same year by the Board of Education working in consultation with the theological faculty of Vanderbilt. The Rev. J. L. Cuninggim was elected director in June 1902 and operations began the following month. By April 1903, 236 students had enrolled in the School. The school was organized into two major divisions, one administrative and the other educational, closely parelleling the work of the annual conference examining committees and the presiding elders respectively. The administrative section consisted of six departments: information, supplies, correspondence, records, mailing, and filing. The educational section also had six departments: correspondence instruction, preachers' institutes, extension lectures, extension library, the prayer league and the *Correspondent*. The most important of all these departments was the one dealing with correspondence instruction. The *Correspondent* was a monthly newsletter sent to all enrollees. The faculty felt that it enabled them to keep in better touch with the students. Extension lectures, dealing with the books in the conference course, were given by the faculty of the correspondence school through the annual conferences. Twelve of these were conducted during 1905. The school established an extension library to help those preachers who were unable to afford the books they might be needing in the course of their studies. Books were lent to the students "for a nominal fee."[25] The theological faculty of Vanderbilt University served as the faculty of the correspondence school, for which they also received a nominal remuneration.

The General Conference expressed satisfaction at the work of Dr. Cuninggim and his associates at the end of their first four years of work. In the Journal of the 1906 General Conference, the committee on education reported thus about the correspondence school:

The Correspondence School. The history of this work in the past quadrennium has more than justified the action of the last General Conference in establishing it. A splendid beginning has been made, but it is only a beginning. In addition to correspondence courses covering the Conference Course of Study, the Director of the School is planning correspondence courses for candidates for admission on trial, for graduate students, for lay workers in the Sunday school and Church; also a circulating library for young preachers, and larger work in preachers' institutes and extension lectures.[26]

The correspondence school had indeed served its purpose thus far. At the end of the first year of operation, April 1903, there were 236 students enrolled. By April, 1904, there were 424 taking courses. This increased to 512 in 1905 and to 660 by the time General Conference met in 1906.[27]

Another step in the examination procedure took place in 1910. Up until this time the annual conference examining committees had had to examine the candidates themselves, even though they had received from the candidates both certificates and full data on the examination as conducted by the correspondence school. Now the General Conference decided that they could accept correspondence school certificates without any further examination. The same provision applied to certificates from accredited colleges.[28]

Meanwhile, the school continued to grow. April, 1909, saw 1165 students on roll. The financial statement of that year showed that their tuition fees netted $5,796.32 while annual conferences contributed $3,596.22. From this, the director received a salary of $2,000 and the cost of instruction totalled $3,847.12.[29]

The next few years saw a traumatic upheaval in the life of the M. E. Church, South, which vitally affected the correspondence school. Events concerning the relationship of the General Conference to Vanderbilt University came to a head when the Vanderbilt trustees refused to accept certain nominees to their Board from the

General Conference of 1910, stating that they had the right to fill vacancies themselves. The college of bishops brought suit on behalf of the Church. However, the suit was decided March 21, 1914, in favor of the trustees. The General Conference moved immediately to withdraw all support from Vanderbilt. This left the correspondence school temporarily high and dry, for it had depended on the Vanderbilt theological faculty. In October, the correspondence school was removed from Vanderbilt and set up at Emory University in Atlanta.[30]

The same year, the Rev. Richard Heber Bennett succeeded Dr. Cuninggim as head of the Department of Ministerial Supply and Training. Bennett had been professor of moral philosophy at Randolph-Macon College and held the post of missionary secretary for the Virginia conference at the time of his appointment to the ministerial training post.[31]

When the Board of Education met again in April, 1915, they took up a request by the new Southern Methodist University in Dallas, Texas, to convey the work of the Correspondence school west of the Mississippi River to their theological school. The board agreed to try, and directed the secretary of the correspondence school to look into the possibilities. He felt that financial difficulties would be the only obstacle, and said that if the Board could give him more money, he could do it, but that the current budget would not allow such a move. This was brought before the General Conference of 1918. The committee of education of that conference recommended that

. . . the work of the Correspondence School be carried on in the future in connection with the two schools of theology, so that the territory east of the Mississippi River shall be served by the Candler School of Theology (at Emory University), and that west of the Mississippi River by the School of Theology of Southern Methodist University, provided the details of the plan can be satisfactorily worked out by the Board of Education in connection with the universities.[32]

To administer this new phase of the work, they proposed

That a Secretary of Ministerial Supply and Training and of Religious Education be elected by the Board of Education, who shall give practically all his time to ministerial supply and religious education, and only general superintendence to ministerial training. This work shall be done under the immediate care of the Board of Education who shall have authority to elect two directors of the

Correspondence School, one of whom shall be located at Emory University and one at Southern Methodist University.[33]

These recommendations were approved and put into effect. By the time of this shift the correspondence school had grown to well over 1,500 students, despite a temporary decline in enrollment in the wake of the Vanderbilt dispute.[34]

J. L. Cuninggim had in the meantime become professor of religious education at the theology school at Southern Methodist and he accepted leadership of the correspondence school work to be conducted from Dallas along with his teaching duties. He held the post until 1921 when he moved on to another school. Charles C. Jarrell, professor of English Bible at Emory University, took the other half of the correspondence school work from his office in Atlanta. He was succeeded by Dr. W. J. Young on December 1, 1919. R. H. Bennett continued at his work as secretary of ministerial supply and training with the additional words "and of Religious Education" tacked on as the General Conference had suggested.[35]

The work of the correspondence school was to be intensified even more by another provision of that report. This made it *mandatory* for the candidates for admission and the undergraduates to pass their examinations through the correspondence school before they could be passed by the annual conference examining committees. Students could take courses either by mail with the headquarters of the correspondence school or in mid-year meetings of the preachers' institutes. The examining committees were to receive the certificates from the correspondence school and give their own examination to the candidate, usually an oral one. In lieu of the correspondence course, however, certificates from standard colleges could be accepted and applied to the "collegiate subjects prescribed for Conference undergraduates." Certificates from theological seminaries and Biblical departments of standard colleges might be accepted in place of Biblical and theological subjects in the course of study. The General Conference authorized the examining committees to conduct their examinations at any convenient times other than the session of the annual conference, such as preachers' institutes or other mid-year meetings.[36]

This set the form which the correspondence school would keep, with minor changes, throughout the rest of the life of the Southern church. The seminaries began to remove some of the load as more and more men began to enroll in them. Yet even then their work did not lighten much, for the 1930 General Conference provided that the bishops should draw up a course of study for the seminary graduates. This course appeared in the *Discipline* in 1934, divided into four areas with about four books in each. The seminary graduates were to read these and write a thesis in each of the areas. These were to be approved by "the Committee on Correspondence Schools," made up of the deans of the two seminaries, the directors of the two branches of the correspondence school, and the secretary of schools and colleges of the General Board of Christian Education. These provisions were in effect up to the time of unification in 1939.[37]

Structure and Content of the Course

The course of study had several branches. The most important one was the course for travelling preachers, the normal route to full ordination and full annual conference membership. Throughout the period under consideration, this was one year of studies for admission on trial followed by four years of studies leading to full connection. Adjunct courses were appointed for "postgraduates" from 1915 on, but, being optional were never too popular. They were administered by the correspondence school. In 1934 the General Conference added another adjunct in the form of a brief selection for "graduates of schools of theology."

A second branch of the course of study applied to local preachers. The General Conference first authorized a two-year course for them in 1886 and continued it intact until 1918, when it was modified somewhat. A third year was added in effect in 1930 with the creation of a preliminary course for license to preach.

As missionary activity began to garner non-English-speaking ministerial candidates, the church had to make provision for their special needs. The first such courses made their appearance in 1898 with a course for Mexican local preachers and one for Japanese-speaking itinerants. The Spanish course grew in 1902 to a full five-year sequence, accommodating Mexican and Cuban ministers. Eventually there were courses for German, Korean, Brazilian (Portuguese), Czech, Belgian, French, and American Indian preachers.

A major overhaul of the type and number of books in the main course of study in 1886 lasted into the twentieth century. It included a much decreased emphasis on old Wesleyan standards, retaining as its mainstays Richard Watson's

Institutes of the Christian Religion in each of the four years, along with Wesley's *Sermons* and the *Discipline* for two years each. Wesley's *Notes on the New Testament* were also added. Study of the text of the Bible was dropped and topical Bible studies relegated to the reference category. The study of theology in systematics texts and monographs increased in this installment of the course.[38]

For the next twenty years, there were virtually no changes in the course of study. However, 1906 saw the most drastic revision of the course in the history of the Church, South. The omission of Watson's *Institutes* for the first time in over 75 years epitomized a new theological stance. *Institutes* had been one of the mainstays of the course since it first came out. In its place, Sheldon's *System of Christian Doctrine* became the systematics textbook, but only in the second and third year classes. Biblical studies were shifted from Wesley's *Notes on the New Testament* to Samuel Green's revision of Joseph Angus's *Handbook of the Bible*, which had previously served as a reference work in the 1870's and 80's. It was used in each of the first three years, while Wesley's *Notes* had only covered the initial two years. Great emphasis was placed on Christian education, with such works as *The Kingdom in the Cradle* and Lawrence's *How to Conduct a Sunday School*. A new emphasis in missions came with John R. Mott's *The Pastor and Modern Missions* and Freemantle's *The World as a Subject to Redemption*. Social concern was exemplified in Peabody's *Christ and the Social Question*. The course of study for admission on trial was revised in this year by the elimination of Bible study. "The ordinary branches of an English education" was clarified to mean studies in English grammar, rhetoric, geography, history, and arithmetic. John S. Banks's *Manual of Christian Doctrine* became the first systematic theology text for the neophytes.[39]

A sort of "Back to the Bible" movement appeared in 1918's revision of the course. Study of the text of Scripture, along with appropriate commentaries was restored for each class. Another mark of the 1918 course of study was a heavy dose of church history. The concentration in the first two years was on Methodist history, and in the latter two years on general church history. All told, the historical studies accounted for over one-third the entire Course that year. Each class had at least one text on practical theology, using such books as Kern's *Ministry to the Congregation*, Brook's *Lectures on Preaching*, Chappell's *Building the Kingdom*, and Jefferson's *The Building of the Church*, along with studies in the *Discipline*. The studies for admission on trial received similar attention, with the requirement on general education being omitted entirely. Church legislation regarding the educational level of applicants for this course had rendered continuation of basic educational requirements in the course itself unnecessary.[40]

The year 1918 marked the beginning of a period of "tinkering" with the course of study. Where there had been only a handful of changes between 1886 and 1906, and no changes at all from 1906 to 1918, now serious alterations in structure and content were made in 1922, 1930, and 1934. This was true of the course of study at all levels. In 1922, practical theology received an even greater emphasis with the addition of books on evangelism, the Sunday school, sociology of religion, and more on preaching.[41] The revision of 1930 was largely a reshuffling of books already on the course, with a few additions in church history, theology, and ethics.[42]

By 1934, the course of study showed a great diversity. It dealt with a variety of subjects aimed at making the fledgling ministers well-rounded men. The tendency was for the works to be more difficult than in previous years. The writing of sermons was omitted for the first time since 1870. Interest in Methodist beginnings was exhibited in the course for admission on trial and in the four years course. Perhaps this was stimulated by the new "studies for Graduates of Schools of Theology" which placed heavy stress on Methodism and the genesis of the Methodist movement. The course had had books on Methodist history before, but not with such an interest in Wesley and his age, and often as primary sources, not secondary as in 1934. The business of running a local church received considerable attention with new books on Christian education, preaching, ministerial ethics, administration and worship. This was the first time that any concern for worship had been expressed in the course of study, except for incidental mention of texts on preaching and theology.[43]

Model for Ministers

What, then was the model for ministry that the M. E. Church, South, adopted in training preachers for their high calling?

For one thing, though there was some divergence of opinion on the point, they expected preachers to be better educated than the bulk of the people they served. This meant not only a higher spiritual development but also a better quality of general education. The committee on education of the 1902 General Conference said, in calling for a stronger educational level among clergy, "Our preachers should be leaders of men, and in an age of general education, they need to be educated men."[44]

As the century began, for example, a phrase in the requirements for admission on trial called for "the ordinary branches of an English education."[45] Since no other educational standard applied at the time, this was a minimum that they dared not overlook. The 1906 revision spelled this out in more detail: "English grammar; Rhetoric; Geography; Arithmetic with special reference to bookkeeping; 'Outlines of World's History' (Swinton) . . . "[46] Several theological works and a written sermon completed the requirements, and it may be noted that the sermon was to be judged on literary and grammatical quality as well as on logical and theological merit.

After 1918, these requirements were no longer mentioned, although the written sermons continued to undergo scrutiny for literary standards. A safeguard here was the notice beginning in 1914 that "the requirements for admission on trial shall be equivalent, so far as English branches are concerned, to the requirements set by the Educational Commission for admission into a standard college."[47] However, even this minimal standard could be set aside in exceptional cases. In 1926, an otherwise cautiously conservative General Conference increased the level to "at least two years of work in a standard college, or its equivalent," again allowing exceptions in cases clearly recognized unusual.[48] In 1934 the standard went up again, calling for a college education in all but the most unusual cases, in which case two years of college became the absolute minimum. Conservatives at this General Conference argued in vain that the exception should still allow admission of highly motivated and otherwise well-equipped individuals who might not be able to meet the two-years-of-college minimum.[49]

The image of the ideal minister included not only his general breadth of mind but also his professional competence. The course of study concerned itself principally with this aspect of ministerial quality.

It is not surprising, given the fact the Southern Methodist clergyman was usually known as "the preacher" rather than as "the minister," "the pastor," or "the priest," that a heavy stress of the course of study was on preaching. Up until 1934, the requirements for each year of the course included a written sermon. A study of Wesley's sermons, included throughout the period, was mainly for theological enhancement, but was also

a source of wisdom on preaching. A staple of the course was the inclusion of books on the practical aspects of preaching.

The minister's role included the leading of worship. John A. Kern's *Ministry to the Congregation* became a basic staple of the second year course in 1898. Though it is really a series of lectures on homiletics, a very good short section dealt with general principles or worship, scripture reading, hymns, prayers and prayer-meetings. [50] It endured in the course throughout the period. Not until 1934 was a book strictly related to worship added. This was G. W. Fisk's *The Recovery of Worship*, which was mainly a plea for more dignified services.[51] It reflected also a change in Southern Methodist thinking about spiritual matters, for the old notion of worship as an evangelistic event had been eroding, though not without its conservative defenders, throughout the century. Conservatives felt that the progressives' lack of interest in revivalism reflected a loss of spirituality. In the new stress on worship that swept the denomination in the 1930's, both groups could find a congenial interest and a point of agreement. Indeed, "worship" became a shibboleth of the 30's as "democracy" had been in the two preceding decades.[52] With the exception of a couple of books on the sacraments, the course of study contained little else of guidance for the minister. In other words, the inclusion of Kern is the only real indication that the leading of worship was a high priority before the 1930's.

Much greater stress went into congregational administration. A baseball umpire once said that he did not have to worry about arguments from the players. As long as he knew the rule book better than they did, he had the upper hand. Something of the same psychology went into the course of study. The rule book in this case was the *Discipline*. Such study was always required, with the companion *Manual of the Discipline* also required between 1870 and 1934. If the Wesleyan minister was to be "a man of one book," as the movement's founder desired, that one book would be the Bible. But a near (some said blasphemously near) second was the *Discipline*.

Educational supervision, particularly of the Sunday school, also fell to the minister. One of the landmark changes in the course of study came in 1906, and a major feature there was the new stress on Christian education. It had hardly been mentioned prior to that time. The 1906 revision contained several books in the studies of the second year aimed at making up that deficit. They were titled *How to Conduct a Sunday School*, *The Kingdom in the Cradle*, and *The Training of the*

Twelve. Though they were removed in the revision of 1918, similar works replaced them in large part.[53] *The Organization and Administration of the Sunday School* entered the course in 1922 as a specially commissioned work for both the M. E. and M. E. South courses of study. The authors, Jesse L. Cuninggim and Eric North, represented educational leadership in the two branches of episcopal Methodism.[54]

The course of study included other items that need not be detailed here, works that introduced the fledgling minister to theology in the general Christian sense and in the special Methodist arena; evangelism; Biblical scholarship; ethics; church history and other concerns. It might be instructive to note some of the things it did *not* contain as well. For example, the nineteenth century course of study was heavy on polemics directed against the doctrines of rival Christian denominations. The twentieth century course was largely purged of such works, reflecting the dawn of a new era of ecumenism. No anti-semitic materials of any significance can be found in the course in either century. Discussions of such social issues as race relations in the South were virtually non-existent, and when they did occur, they supported the prevailing Southern paternalistic view, though the church's slant on that issue was more humane, perhaps, than that of the secular South. Neither did the holiness issue which troubled the American Methodists around the turn of the century have any consideration in the course. Whether because no adequate works on the subject could be found, or because the bishops did not wish to open that very controversial question, no mention, even oblique, is contained in the twentieth century course of study. Another issue appeared only briefly. Two books on Christian social concerns made an appearance in the revision of 1906, only to be removed in 1918. They were Francis Peabody's *Christ and the Social Question* and W. H. Fremantle's *The World as a Subject for Redemption.* They came into the course at the height of the social gospel movement, and disappeared from it in the wake of the general disappointment in liberalism which accompanied World War I. But a later book by David Adam spoke of social ethics in such a way as to show that the work of the social-gospellers had not been in vain. By 1934, social ethics were considered a proper branch of moral investigation.[55]

The Methodist Episcopal Church, South changed appreciably during the last four decades of its existence. Its attitudes about its own inner nature changed and so did its understanding of the ministry. These new attitudes showed clearly in the course of study. The administration of the course was modified in ways similar to the reordering that took place in the church at large. The episcopacy was supplanted by a committee of experts in planning the course of study. This was just one aspect of the general weakening of the episcopacy, of which another example was the creation of the Judicial Council. The administration of the course fell increasingly into the hands of an educational bureaucracy in Nashville as part of the wider development of influential general boards in all areas of the church's life.

By 1939, the image and role of the minister in the M.E. Church, South was different too, and the course of study showed this quite clearly. The educational level expected for entry into the course was raised substantially. Indeed, there had been practically no minimum requirement for formal education in 1900. The mid-century preacher, if the course of study is an indication, was expected to become an more efficient administrator, a better trained educator, a more sophisticated theologian, a less sectarian churchman than his predecessors. These new skills came, perhaps, at the expense of his preaching ability. There were some who sorrowed over these developments, but the changes were present in the denomination first and it then fixed them in its ministerial training program.

In short, the course of study very predictably reflected the prevailing Southern Methodist views on most subjects, though it was probably skewed a bit toward the progressive end of the spectrum. It showed what aspirations the M.E. Church, South had for its future leaders.

NOTES

1. This paper is based on the author's M. A . thesis at the University of Texas, entitled "The Conference Course of Study in the Methodist Episcopal Church, South." The degree was granted in 1964.
2. Mark May, *The Profession of the Ministry, Vol. II: The Education of American Ministers* (New York: Institute of Social and Religious Research, 1934), p. 17.
3. Curtis B. Haley, ed. *General Minutes and Yearbook of the Conferences of the Methodist Episcopal Church, South, 1935-1938* (Nashville: Publishing House of the Methodist Episcopal Church, South, 1935-1938), *passim.*
4. Denny to Bishop Warren A. Candler, July 15, 1926, Candler Collection, Emory University.
5. Robert W. Sledge, *Hands on the Ark: The Struggle for Change in the Methodist Episcopal Church, South, 1914-1939* (Lake Junaluska, N. C.: Commission on Archives and History of the United Methodist Church, 1975), p. 131.
6. Ibid., pp. 29-49, 90-188.
7. Denny to Candler, July 15, 1926, Candler Collection. Thomas N. Ralston's *Elements of Divinity* was in the course from 1870 to 1886, but never included after that.
8. Denny to Candler, December 27, 1926, Candler Collection.
9. Mouzon to John W. Holt, Blanket, Texas, January 23, 1922, Item #322 in Mouzon Collection, Bridwell Library, Southern Methodist University.

10. Denny to Candler, June 24, 1922, Candler Collection.
11. Denny to Candler, December 27, 1926, Candler Collection.
12. (New York: Charles Scribner's Sons, 1893.)
13. Denny to Candler, December 27, 1926, Candler Collection.
14. Correspondence School to Denny, February 19, 1926, Candler Collection.
15. Mouzon to Candler, October 25, 1918, Candler Collection.
16. A. J. Lamar to Candler, May 26, 1926, Candler Collection.
17. Everett to Mouzon, January 25, 1922; Mouzon to Everett, January 28, 1922; both part of item 256, Mouzon Collection.
18. One dated February 22-23, 1933 in Candler Collection; the other dated February 20, 1934, item 4815 in Mouzon Collection.
19. General Conference of the Methodist Episcopal Church, South, *Journal* (Baltimore, 1898), p. 121.
20. Ibid.
21. Ibid., pp. 225-26.
22. Ibid. (Dallas, 1902), p. 226.
23. Ibid.
24. Ibid., pp. 227, 114, 115.
25. Thomas N. Ivey, ed., *Southern Methodist Handbook* (Raleigh, N. C.: Commercial Printing Co., 1907), p. 93.
26. General Conference of the Methodist Episcopal Church, South, *Journal* (Birmingham, Ala., 1906), pp. 181-82.
27. Ivey, *Handbook*, p. 93.
28. General Conference of the Methodist Episcopal Church, South, *Journal* (Asheville, N.C., 1910), p. 325.
29. Thomas N. Ivey, ed., *Southern Methodist Handbook* (Nashville: Publishing House of the Methodist Episcopal Church, South, 1910), pp. 88-90.
30. I. Frank Dent, "Efforts of Methodism to Educate Her Ministry." (B. D. thesis, Perkins School of Theology, Southern Methodist University, 1930), pp. 51-57. See also Ivey, *Handbook* (1917), pp. 72-73.
31. "Jesse Lee Cuninggim" and "Richard Heber Bennett," *Who's Who, 1922-23* (Chicago: A. N. Marquis Co., 1922).
32. Ivey, *Handbook* (1917), pp. 72-73. See also General Conference of the Methodist Episcopal Church, South, *Journal* (Atlanta, 1918), pp. 243-45.
33. Ibid.
34. Ivey, *Handbook* (1917), p. 73.
35. "Jesse Lee Cuninggim," "Richard Heber Bennett," and "Charles C. Jarrell," *Who's Who, 1922-23*. See also Methodist Episcopal Church, South, *Bulletin of the Board of Education*, May, 1919, pp. 34-35 and February, 1920, p. 171.
36. General Conference of the Methodist Episcopal Church, South, *Journal* (Atlanta, 1918), pp. 243-45.
37. Ibid. (Dallas, 1930), pp. 452, 225. See also *The Doctrines and Discipline of the Methodist Episcopal Church, South* (Nashville: Publishing House of the Methodist Episcopal Church, South, 1934), p. 230n. (Hereafter cited as *Discipline*.)
38. *Discipline* (1886), paras. 252-255.
39. *Discipline* (1906), paras. 543-547.
40. *Discipline* (1918), paras. 779-783.
41. *Discipline* (1922), paras. 791-794.
42. *Discipline* (1930), paras. 887-890.
43. *Discipline* (1934), paras. 463-471.
44. General Conference of the Methodist Episcopal Church, South, *Journal* (Dallas, 1902), p. 227.
45. *Discipline* (1898), para. 525.
46. *Discipline* (1906), para. 543.
47. *Discipline* (1914), para. 730.
48. *Discipline* (1926), para. 624.
49. Sledge, *Hands on the Ark*, p. 219.
50. (Nashville: Publishing House of the Methodist Episcopal Church, South, 1897).
51. (New York: The Macmillan Co., 1931.)
52. Sledge, *Hands of the Ark*, p. 213.
53. Marion Lawrance, *How to Conduct a Sunday School, or Twenty-Eight Years a Superintendent* (New York and Chicago: Fleming H. Revell Co., 1905); James A. Atkins, *The Kingdom in the Cradle* (Nashville: Publishing House of the Methodist Episcopal Church, South, 1907); Alexander Balmain Bruce, *The Training of the Twelve* (Edinburgh: T. and T. Clark, 1871).
54. (New York and Nashville: Methodist Book Concern, 1919.)
55. David S. Adam, *A Handbook of Christian Ethics* (Edinburgh: T. and T. Clark, 1925), Section III.

Reexamining the Public/Private Split: Reforming the Continent and Spreading Scriptural Holiness

Jean Miller Schmidt
Iliff School of Theology

When the Methodist Episcopal Church was formally organized in 1784, the preachers assembled there in Baltimore followed John Wesley's example forty years earlier in asking: "What may we reasonably believe to be God's Design in raising up the Preachers called *Methodists?*" The answer of course was a reaffirmation of Wesley's earlier one: "To reform the Continent, and to spread scriptural Holiness over these Lands."[1] In this address I want to explore what these terms, "reforming the Continent" and "spreading scriptural holiness" (roughly equivalent to "public" and "private") have meant in American Methodist history, especially during the period from 1840 to 1939. Before turning to this history, however, I want to explain briefly what I mean by "the public/private split" and why I think it merits our attention as we look at our own Methodist past for the sake of the future.

During the turbulent decade of the 1960s, when many graduate students tried to assuage consciences burdened with the luxury of the academic enterprise in such troubled times by writing a "relevant" dissertation, I completed my graduate work at the University of Chicago Divinity School with a thesis entitled, "Souls or the Social Order: Polemic in American Protestantism." Concerned by the painful and sometimes bitter division between social activist and conservative evangelical Christians in the 1960s, I tried to discover how two parties which obviously laid claim to the same tradition of evangelical Protestantism in mid-nineteenth century America could have arrived at such different convictions about the appropriate role of the church in relation to society. Because my research indicated that the same evangelical Protestants were likely to be involved in saving souls *and* social reform in the 1830s to 1850s, I surveyed the period from 1857 to the 1920s in an effort to discover how and why a split of such consequence had occurred.

If this sounds familiar, it is probably because you are acquainted with Martin E. Marty's prize-winning historical essay entitled *Righteous Empire: The Protestant Experience in America*, in which (as Marty himself indicated clearly in the footnotes) my dissertation formed the basis for chapter 17.[2] In that book, Marty described the fateful "public/private split" which developed in American Protestantism, claiming that without an understanding of that "two-party system" twentieth century Protestantism was incomprehensible.

Marty's book was published in 1970. Since then the two-party thesis has been subjected to sociological research, and some writing has explored possible approaches toward overcoming the split. Evangelical scholars like George Marsden and Donald Dayton have questioned the adequacy of the label "private" as a description of their own tradition, reminding us of the social concern of evangelicals and holiness groups prior to the "Great Reversal" which began about 1900.[3] There has also been much more sophisticated reflection upon the meaning of the term "public."[4] Perhaps most surprising of all has been the way in which the so-called "private party" of the 1960s has gone public in the 1980s as the Moral Majority or new religious right, seeking to impose its private vision on the public realm.

If I had been asked to write an article for the recent *Christian Century* series on "How My Mind Has Changed" (covering the decade 1969-1979),[5] there is much I would have had to confess or take into account as well as bring up to date. There was the strong trend toward private religion in the 1970s, but at the same time, the rediscovery by "young evangelicals" of a prophetic social witness (Sojourners, for example). My 1969 dissertation had almost no mention of black religious history during this period, nor of women's history, nor the relationship between denominational religion and "civil religion" in America. Clearly the contribution of social historical studies in the past twenty years has had a tremendous impact on the way historians now interpret the American religious past. Finally, perhaps in an effort to avoid doing denominational history (with its attendant dangers of parochialism and triumphalism), I paid little attention in my dissertation to the Methodists, concentrating on those who were first to develop a social gospel (Congregationalists and Episcopalians) and those who were most involved in the Fundamentalist-Modernist struggle of the 1920s (Presbyterians and Baptists).

For a number of reasons, I decided that this issue needed to be addressed in our Bicentennial Consultation. First, because the phenomenon which the two-party system attempted to explain is far from being resolved in contemporary American religion. Many Americans have yet to be convinced that religion should be anything but private. Second, because the split, however it be described, has had destructive and damaging consequences to the churches as well as to the quality and health of American public life. Most important of all, I believe that the Wesleyan denominations in America (including all those groups which regard the Christmas Conference of 1784 as in some way a part of their founding history) have within our traditions resources for nurturing a vision that moves beyond the public/private split.[6] It is especially for this last reason that I think the issue demands our attention here.

In quest of such a vision, which moves beyond the split to embrace both personal and social transformation, I want to lift up examples of Methodists who combined conspicuously well the spiritual and social dimensions of their faith. As a group they represent *a* Methodist tradition, true (I believe) to the thought and example of their mentor John Wesley, and worthy of our exploration. Because of time limitations, I intend to use aspects of their stories to illuminate public/private issues at certain revelatory moments in our common past as Methodists. Here symbolic dates will serve as windows on a larger period: the dates I have selected are 1840, 1866, 1884, and 1919.

I am suggesting here one possible approach to a new history for our times. While by no means claiming to have done prophetic history, I have intentionally concentrated on stories of women and black Methodists that were missing from the histories to which Kenneth Rowe referred.[7] I am convinced that the figures I have chosen are important for us precisely because they were able to relate private faith to public order in a way not typical for their historical moment.

1840

The account of the American Methodist struggle to establish an antislavery norm is important background for an exploration of this first period.[8] By the General Conference of 1804, the mood was clearly one of retreat in the face of public outcry, especially with the approval of an expurgated edition of the *Discipline* for use in conferences south of Virginia.

Francis Asbury's moral anguish over this defeat was reflected in a journal entry of 1809. In it, he conceded that if Methodist preachers were to have access to the *souls* of slaves, they might have to settle for amelioration of their condition within the system, rather than continuing to work for their emancipation.[9] By 1816, Methodist accommodation to the system of slavery was marked by a sense of futility that "little can be done to abolish a practice so contrary to the principles of moral justice." This disillusionment over the failure to enforce an antislavery norm, and the shift in early Methodism from attacking the institution of slavery to a religious concern for slaves *within* the system, helped establish the pattern of overcoming social evils by changing individuals. Bishop McKendree seemed to articulate this orientation when he told the preachers at the General Conference of 1816 that God's design in raising up the preachers called Methodists was "to reform the continent *by* spreading scriptural holiness over these lands."[10]

While Southern preachers engaged in a vigorous evangelizing mission to the slaves, most Northerners managed to avoid endorsing either slavery or abolition by supporting the new scheme of African colonization. The recovery of the earlier emphasis on social reform with regard to slavery would have to await the Christian abolitionism of the 1830s.[11]

In 1837-38, preachers in the South Carolina and Georgia Conferences declared that slavery was not a "moral evil" but merely "a social and domestic institution . . . with which, as Ministers of Christ, we have nothing to do."[12] By the time the General Conference met in 1840, Southerners and Northern anti-abolitionists alike were determined to defeat the troublesome abolitionist minority in the church. That conference commended the work of the American Colonization Society, and in the infamous Silas Comfort case resolved to prohibit the testimony of black church members in church trials in any state where blacks were denied that privilege by law. Declaring that "the simple holding of slaves constitutes no legal barrier to the election or ordination of ministers," the conference asserted that it would be "a sore evil to divert Methodism from her proper work of 'spreading Scripture holiness over these lands.'"[13]

By the early 1840s, the Methodists had become the largest Protestant denomination in America.

Thus at the very time when American Methodists were rejoicing at God's approbation, evidenced in their remarkable success in evangelizing the nation, they also succeeded in silencing the radical antislavery minority in their midst. These Christian abolitionists took the uncompromising position that slavery was a sin regardless of circumstances and that good people could be the bulwarks of an evil system. Orange Scott had been a key figure in the debates on slavery in the 1836 and 1840 General Conferences. Although he was deeply troubled by the possibility of secession, by 1842 he was convinced that the Methodist Episcopal Church would never take action against slavery, and he did withdraw. In 1843 Scott and La Roy Sunderland led in forming the Wesleyan Methodist Connection on the basis of abolitionism and John Wesley's doctrine of Christian perfection. As the pastoral address at the organizing conference explained: "It is holiness of heart and life that will give you moral power to oppose the evils and corruption in the world, against which we have lifted up a standard."[14]

For 1840 then, we would point to the examples of Orange Scott and Scott's successor in leadership of the Wesleyan Methodists after his early death in 1847, Luther Lee. Both men were born in 1800, they grew up in impoverished homes in Vermont and upstate New York, received little education, and gave themselves to the Methodist ministry after conversion experiences in their young adult years. Both rose to prominence among the Methodists because of their powerful preaching and leadership abilities. Both became converted to abolitionism in the 1830s. As Orange Scott later described it, "being wholly devoted to the one idea of saving souls, I omitted to examine, faithfully and critically as I should, the condition of the country in respect to great moral evils. My eyes, however, were at length opened." For the rest of his life, Scott would insist on the conjunction of "piety and radicalism."[15]

After Scott's death, the mantle of leadership passed to his cohort Luther Lee, who presided over three of the first six general conferences of the new denomination and became editor of its paper, The True Wesleyan. While serving pastorates in upstate New York and Ohio, he was active in the Underground Railroad, and in 1864 became professor of theology at Wesleyan Adrian College before returning to the M.E. Church after the Civil War. In a sermon entitled "The Radicalism of the Gospel," Lee argued that "the Gospel is so radically reformatory, that to preach it fully and clearly, is to attack and condemn all wrong, and to assert and defend all righteousness."[16] He understood that religion must not be divorced from political responsibility and in 1840 had helped to organize the antislavery Liberty party. In 1853, Luther Lee preached the ordination sermon for Antoinette Brown, the first woman to be fully ordained to the Christian ministry in an American denomination. As one historian said of leaders like Scott and Lee: "The implication of the abolitionist preaching was a new kind of society much different from the old—an implication only gradually being realized in the 20th century."[17]

1866

By 1861, each of the two Methodist bodies that had separated in 1844 had become the largest Protestant church in its geographical area. The two churches were separated not only by sectional interests, but by different understandings of the appropriate role of the church in society. The Southern church in its defense of slaveholding claimed to be faithful to the only Scriptural mission for the church, namely preaching repentance, faith, and holiness, and leaving the affairs of state to those competent to deal with them. It accused Northern Methodism of being a "political" church, intent on subjugating the South. To the end of the struggle, Southern Methodists insisted that their church had appropriately avoided political involvement.[18]

The view of many Methodists in the North that the church must influence political action on the slavery issue (particularly after the passage of the Fugitive Slave Law in 1850), reflected the growing sense of responsibility for shaping the national conscience associated with the denomination's new institutional prominence. The antislavery stance of the Methodist Episcopal Church, however, was considerably qualified by its concern over the possible loss of the border conferences. It was not, therefore, until 1864 (more than a year after the Emancipation Proclamation) that the General Conference acted to alter the General Rule and exclude all slaveholders from church fellowship.

The preeminent symbol of Northern Methodism's new status in the 1860s was Bishop Matthew Simpson, whose popular War Speech concluded with the affirmation (made, he said, with all due reverence) that God "cannot afford to do without America."[19] The Methodist bishop believed about equally in the triumph of Christianity, the peculiar destiny of the American nation, and the greatness of the Methodist Episcopal Church.

That church had "come of age" when *Harper's Weekly* could comment, during the centennial observance of 1866, that Methodism had become "for good or ill . . . the predominant ecclesiastical fact of the nation."[20] Methodist celebration of that centennial was marked by Abel Stevens' historical volumes, by the raising of over $8.5 million for the Centenary Educational Fund and the opening of Drew Theological Seminary in 1867, and by the American Methodist Ladies' Centenary Association's raising money to erect Heck Hall on the campus of Garrett Biblical Institute in honor of founding mother Barbara Heck.[21]

Northern Methodists made the centennial of American Methodism a time for a great push forward, particularly in the areas of church extension into the West, and missionary, educational, and social work among the freed people in the South.[22] Some Methodist Protestants participated in this centennial observance. The Methodist Episcopal Church, South, preoccupied with its own struggle to survive as a separate church, noted that it would hold no formal centennial celebration until 1884.[23] As northern black Methodists engaged in their own mission to the southern freed people, the A.M.E. Church celebrated its own semi-centennial in 1866, commemorating its first general conference.

At least one important voice was missing from the Methodist scene for most of 1866. Gilbert Haven, the New England Methodist preacher, noted abolitionist, and outspoken defender of racial equality in church and society was in semi-retirement most of that year recovering from what was then called "nervous prostration."[24] Raised in a religious home in which Puritan and Methodist influences were equally strong, Haven's abolitionism and the New England insistence on the church's role as the conscience of the social order were already evident in his sermon of 1850 entitled "The Higher Law." During the decade from 1851-61, Haven held five pastorates in the New England Conference and identified with the radical antislavery contingent in the church. Like the evangelical abolitionists of the 1830s, Haven was openly critical of reformers like William Lloyd Garrison who had abandoned evangelical faith and declared the fundamental immorality of American society. Haven retained his basic confidence in both American politics and evangelical religion. He also declared himself to be a *loyal* abolitionist; that is, he would stay in the Methodist Episcopal Church, to which he was devoted. His ministry, however, must be one of social reform. In Haven's view, it was the task of

preachers to preach "salvation from all sin, personal, social, and national."[25]

In the 1860s, Gilbert Haven shared the views of many northern Methodists that the Divine purpose was being worked out in the Civil War, that God's millennium was coming, and that American evangelical Protestants in general, and the Methodists in particular, had a special mission. There were, however, crucial differences in the way he interpreted these matters.[26] Even before the outbreak of the war, he emphasized the complicity of both North and South in the sins of slavery and racism, and urged the necessity for national repentance. As he reflected on the Civil War in 1862, he was more than ever convinced that through it God was working out his sovereign purpose of purging the "model republic" from the evil of slavery and inaugurating an era of interracial harmony. After the Emancipation Proclamation, Haven was optimistic about the coming of God's kingdom, seeing it as "God's bringing all into subjection to him."[27]

The new order would be characterized by liberty, equality, and unity. While confident of America's destiny in relation to the millennium, Haven was aware of the contradiction of racism. His view of America's chosenness was conditional: "If we cooperate with Him [by inaugurating this interracial brotherhood], He will make us his vanguard. If we refuse, He will . . . cast us off, and raise up another people who shall follow his guadance."[28] It was the church's role to become a racially inclusive community in order to prod the nation toward "a racially integrated and just society."[29] This insistence that the church take "the more excellent way" and "entirely ignore the idea of color in the organization of our Churches and conferences throughout the whole land"[30] earned Haven little support. He was widely criticized in the church when he refused to accept an appointment as missionary to black people in Vicksburg, Mississippi, because he objected to the segregationist policy of the missions. The basic cause of Haven's breakdown in 1866 was his agonizing realization that so few of his contemporaries shared his vision of the transracial character of America's national mission.[31]

He described this vision in a sermon explaining why colonization could never solve America's race problem:

"They [American blacks] will never leave us or forsake us . . . They must abide with us till we acknowledge by word and act that they are one with us . . . God will keep them with us till He has cured us of our sins. Then shall we rejoice to abide with them always, and to build up a grand nationality of one humanity, of one language, having one Redeemer, and one future on earth, and, if in Christ, forever."[32]

In March 1867, Haven (having recuperated from his illness) was elected editor of *Zion's Herald*. From this post, he resumed the crusade for racial equality in church and state, advocating civil rights, social equality, and racial assimilation. In addition, he was a zealous advocate of prohibition and women's rights, including both suffrage and ordination.[33] Haven campaigned unsuccessfully for the merger of the A.M.E. and A.M.E. Zion Churches with the M.E. Church. In spite of some opposition, he was elected bishop in 1872, and assigned to Atlanta. His outspoken protests notwithstanding, in 1876 the General Conference of the M.E. Church approved the segregationist policy of separating all the annual conferences according to race. Most northern Methodists accepted this new segregationist policy and the accompanying spirit of cooperation with the Southern church called "Methodist fraternity." Haven could not welcome it because of the price that had been paid in terms of racial attitudes and commitments.

When he died in January of 1880, a somewhat lonely man, it was the black Methodists who understood best the convictions that had motivated his entire career. As Benjamin Tanner put it in the *Christian Recorder*:

"He was one of the few that *made* public opinion instead of following it; and happily for mankind, like the great Master he loved, he made it on the side of the poor, the bond, and the ostracized. We have spoken of him as the finest type of our American religion—a religion that, to a large extent, sanctioned slavery in the past and both sanctions and practices caste in the present. But the great soul of Gilbert Haven was against both."[34]

1884

Classic accounts of the rise of the social gospel in American Protestantism (like those of Henry May and C.H. Hopkins)[35] tended to focus on the formation of the Methodist Federation for Social Service in 1907, and the adoption of the Social Creed by the General Conference of 1908, and therefore to stress the "lateness" of a Methodist social gospel. Scholars who looked elsewhere than to episcopal pronouncements and General Conference decisions could discern signs of a social awakening in the 1890s in the Methodist press, in the city missionary work of people like Frank Mason North, and in memorials to General Conference from the New York East and Rock River annual conferences.[36] For the most part, the story prior to the 1890s, however, was one of neglect, inattention, and complacency with regard to urban and industrial problems.[37] Yet during the 1880s, Methodist women initiated a whole range of activities that not only would constitute a pragmatic social gospel in its own right, but would result in a greatly enlarged sphere of influence for the women themselves, in both church and society. As Beverly Harrison pointed out nearly ten years ago, these women were responding to the subtly encroaching split between the interpersonal and the public sphere that industrialism was effecting.[38] They wanted to "feminize" the ever more remote public world. I want to use the stories of three women here, to lift up both their personal example and the cumulative impact of their efforts. As a window into the decade, I've chosen the symbolic date of the Methodist centennial in 1884.

The 1884 celebration appears to have differed in two important respects from the one in 1866: it involved both major branches of episcopal Methodism, as well as smaller Methodist bodies, and it seemed to strike a more sober note, warning of the dangers of neglecting the poor, and of becoming assimilated to the world.[39]

In 1866, Frances Willard was corresponding secretary of the American Methodist Ladies' Centenary Association. By 1884, she had been national president of the W.C.T.U. for five years; in 1888 she would actually be elected a lay delegate to the M.E. Church General Conference.[40] Although that 1888 General Conference ruled the five women delegates ineligible, the struggle for full laity rights for women in the church had begun. That same General Conference officially recognized the new Methodist deaconess movement, begun the preceding year by Lucy Rider Meyer. In 1886, women of the Southern Methodist Church had gained approval of their General Conference for a Woman's Department of Church Extension which would become the Woman's Home Mission Society. Its outstanding leader was Belle Harris Bennett, who would lead the fight in her church for full lay rights for women. As women moved into these expanded roles, it is no wonder that James M. Buckley as historian and guarantor of the old order saw Methodism deteriorating![41]

The movement of middle-class Protestant women in America beyond the world of home and church into larger spheres of influence and "usefulness" came primarily through their creation of organizations "for women only."[42] The New York Ladies' Home Missionary Society was organized as early as the 1840s, and in 1850, at the instigation of holiness evangelist Phoebe Palmer, women undertook support of the Five Points Mission in one of New York City's bleakest neighborhoods. The greatest impetus to women's activities came, however, with the Civil War and the important role women played in nursing and relief efforts. After the war, American Protestant women perceived other needs calling them from their homes into the world.

Frances E. Willard (1839-1898) was the means by which countless Victorian "ladies" left the sanctuary of their homes to support the causes of temperance and woman suffrage for the sake of "home protection."[43] Intrepid leader of the W.C.T.U. for nearly two decades, her story is almost too familiar to be fully appreciated by an age less enthusiastic about teetotalism than was her own. Recent research on her life and thought has made clear both the extent of her involvement in a wide range of social reform issues, and the early social gospel character of her mature religious convictions.[44] On the Wisconsin frontier where she spent much of her childhood, Frances was able to escape many of the limitations of prescribed roles for young women, but she early envied her brother's rights to an education, the vote, and a ministerial career. After a decade of teaching and administration, Willard was converted in the 1870s to the two causes to which she would give the rest of her life—women and temperance.[45]

Proclaiming itself "organized mother-love," the W.C.T.U. began with a commitment to prohibition, and under Willard's "Do-Everything Policy" moved into active participation in a wide range of issues, including woman suffrage, social purity, concerns of labor, peace and arbitration, welfare work among blacks and immigrants, temperance education, health and hygiene.[46] Frances Willard challenged women to redefine the ideal of womanhood, rejecting the notion that women's nature and virtues were inherently different from men's, requiring different spheres of existence and influence.[47] Under her leadership, women gained an increased sense of their own power and a new self-assurance. She raised women's consciousness on important public issues, and instructed them in the rudiments of what she called "Gospel politics," which included petitioning legislative bodies and participating in political parties such as the National Prohibition Party. As the motto "for God and home and native land" suggests, W.C.T.U. women were urged to develop their gifts for the sake of the christianization of their nation. "To help forward the coming of Christ into all departments of life," Willard said, "is, in the last analysis, the purpose and aim of the WCTU."[48]

Compared with the progress of the social gospel, Willard's own commitments in the 1880s and 1890s were remarkable. She became a member of the Knights of Labor in 1887, wrote articles for the Christian Socialist journal the *Dawn*, and joined the Fabian Socialists in England in 1893. During these years, there is no question that she increasingly perceived the relationship between poverty and alcoholism in such a way as to understand the latter as a social evil, and not simply a personal vice.[49]

Like Orange Scott, Luther Lee, and Gilbert Haven, Frances Willard's social reform was motivated by a deep Methodist piety. Had she been a man, she would very likely have become a Methodist minister.[50] Having become a full member of the Methodist Episcopal Church in Evanston at age twenty-two, she later consecrated herself completely to God during holiness meetings led by Phoebe Palmer and her husband. For a time during the 1870s, she led inquiry meetings and Bible studies in Moody's revivals. After the unsuccessful attempt of Anna Oliver and Anna Howard Shaw to be ordained in the M.E. Church in 1880, she wrote *Woman In the Pulpit* to urge the cause of women's ordination and to claim its biblical basis. Her concern for health was reminiscent of Wesley's, and she urged women to care about diet and exercise (especially recommending riding a bicycle as excellent exercise for women!). She saw Christian commitment and social reform as fundamentally connected. As she put it, "When the spirit of God has been generated in a human being, it must not be shut up in the prayer-meeting or the church building, but turned on the saloons, the gambling houses, the haunts of shame."[51]

This same phenomenon of women's beginning with the simple intention of extending the influences of the home and gradually increasing their involvement in the public sphere occurred in both the deaconess movement and the women's missionary movements.[52] The woman chiefly responsible for founding the deaconess order in the Methodist Episcopal Church was Lucy Rider Meyer (1849-1922).[53] Born in Vermont to parents of Puritan stock, she was raised in a strongly religious home where she "came to Jesus" at age thirteen in a Methodist revival and subsequently joined the church. She graduated from Oberlin College and Cook County Normal School, was Professor of Chemistry at McKendree College for a time, and later completed a medical degree. While serving as field secretary of the Illinois State Sunday School Association, she met many young women whose lack of preparation kept them from lives of usefulness.

After her marriage in 1885 to Josiah Meyer, the couple opened the Chicago Training School for City, Home, and Foreign Missions. The course of study was comprehensive, including Bible classes, but also studies in "hygiene, in citizenship, in social and family relationships, in everything that could help or hinder in the establishment of the Kingdom of Heaven on earth."[54] An important aspect of the program was the provision for field work in the city, since most of the students came from rural or small town homes. In the summer of 1887, Lucy Meyer enlisted several of her trainees in a program of visiting and assisting the immigrant poor and needy in Chicago. It was the beginning of the Methodist deaconess movement, which spread rapidly to other cities like Cincinnati.

Methodist deaconesses were determined to transform the city. They began by "visiting," canvassing tenement neighborhoods to discover those in need of help. While ministering to people's basic needs and demonstrating neighborly concern, they also gathered important information on prevailing social conditions. As literature like the *Deaconess Advocate* reveals, they came increasingly to look for the underlying causes of the misery they found, and then to attack the evil social structures responsible. (The same might also be said about holiness social work among the poor in the 1880s and 1890s.)[55]

These women were activists rather than theorists. They saw what they were doing as "pure practical Christianity." They responded to Christ's call with the resolve to become *useful*, to further God's purpose for the world. Methodist deaconesses formed a new breed of church women. Trained for and consecrated to the order, they became experts in the field of Christian social service.[56]

Women in the Methodist Episcopal Church, South, were like their northern sisters in developing a sense of responsibility for Christian work that reached beyond the local congregation.[57] The Woman's Department of Church Extension was originally established to raise funds for building and repairing parsonages in the West. In spite of considerable opposition, the women continued to expand their home mission work. By the early 1890s, they had become convinced of the need for organized city mission work among the poor in cities like St. Louis, Nashville, Atlanta, and New Orleans. The Womans' Home

Mission journal, begun in 1892, was significantly entitled *Our Homes*.

In 1884, a young woman named Belle Harris Bennett (1852-1922), from a prominent Kentucky family, gave her life wholly to God at a summer conference at Lake Chautauqua, New York.[58] A few years later whole attending a missionary meeting, she became concerned about the evident lack of preparation of missionaries and wrote to Lucy Rider Meyer for information about her training school. Feeling called by God to establish a training school for missionaries, she presented her idea to the Woman's Board of Foreign Missions in 1889, and was promptly appointed "agent" of the Board to raise funds and promote the idea. As a result of her efforts, the Scarritt Bible and Training School was opened in Kansas City in 1892.

In 1897, she established the Sue Bennett School for poor children in the mountains of Kentucky in honor of her sister who had died several years earlier. As president of the Woman's Home Mission Society from 1896, and of its governing board from 1898, she urged the establishment of church settlement houses (judiciously calling them "Wesley Community Houses"). The first was begun in Nashville in 1901. In 1902 she persuaded the General Conference of the Southern Methodist Church to authorize deaconesses. She led the home missions women in educational work among blacks, supported woman suffrage, and worked for more restrictive child labor laws.

When in 1910 the Southern Methodist women's home and foreign mission boards were merged into a single Woman's Missionary Council under a largely male Board of Missions, Bennett had the difficult job of serving as president. Although the change resulted in a significant loss of autonomy for the women's work, they had not been consulted, nor were their protests heeded. Belle Bennett immediately launched the struggle for full laity rights for women in her church. With the vote of the General Conference in 1918 and ratification by the annual conferences in 1919, women were finally seated as delegates in the General Conference of 1922. Although elected by the Kentucky Annual Conference as its first woman delegate, Belle Bennett was too ill to attend; she died of cancer that July.[59]

The standard biographies of Lucy Rider Meyer and Belle Harris Bennett, written by women who were also deeply involved in deaconess and home mission work, make clear how deeply spiritual these women were, and how untroubled by any distinction between spiritual and social spheres. As Belle Bennett's biographer Tochie MacDonell explained: "The motive of Miss Bennett's missionary zeal was the building of God's victorious kingdom on earth. She sought to show the way of regeneration through Christ to the individual and fought to conquer the evil that clogs the salvation of society. 'Eternal life for the individual, the kingdom of God for humanity,' was the slogan of her life. For this reason she led the women of the Church in much endeavor for human betterment, not then classed as religious work."[60]

As Southern Methodist missions women came face to face with "the ugly realities of industrializing society," they gradually came to embrace a more public role and to engage in a more active political program to achieve social change. They were willing to say of themselves, "Grow we must, even if we outgrow all that we love."[61]

1919

Black Methodists in the 1880s and 1890s had to deal with two sets of challenges: those facing Christian America, and those confronting black America.[62] A central theme in Afro-American religious thought had always been the interpretation of black suffering, the conviction that God would soon bring a slaveholding society to judgment. A primary issue for black Christians after the failure of Reconstruction, therefore, was the death of hope, the question of meaning.[63] In 1883, the Civil Rights Act of 1875 was struck down by the Supreme Court. With the approval of the legality of racial segregation in the 1890s, private discrimination became public policy. There were 2500 lynchings of black Americans in the years from 1884 to 1900. Thus black Christians had to cope with both a racial and a religious crisis.

In addition, black Methodists were experiencing a lack of leadership in the 1890s.[64] Between 1890 and 1895, for example, all five of the bishops of the A.M.E. Church who had been elected before 1880 died. Chief of these was Bishop Daniel Alexander Payne, who died in 1893. From the time he joined the A.M.E. Church in 1841, his vision of a black Christian culture and of what the A.M.E. Church should be had become increasingly dominant. He had a central role in launching the A.M.E. effort to reach the freed people in the South as early as 1863. His belief in the traditional Wesleyan values of education, disciplined living, and service was formative for his church. Wilberforce University, of which he was president, was the

"black Athens," the *A.M.E. Church Review* was the leading black journal. After Bishop Payne's death, it was Bishop Henry McNeal Turner who was the next great leader of the A.M.E. Church. Bishop Turner's disillusionment with America after the reverses of the 1880s was so strong that he became an outspoken advocate of African colonization. In late nineteenth and early twentieth century America there was also the beginning of an autonomous black culture no longer under the tutelage of the A.M.E. or any other Protestant church, and the massive movement of blacks into the cities. The A.M.E. Church, in short, was overwhelmed by the combined forces of industrialism, urbanization, and racism.[65]

In 1919, Methodists were celebrating yet another centenary, this a $100 million drive commemorating the beginning of the Methodist missionary enterprise and closely associated with the interdenominational Protestant missionary effort called the Interchurch World Movement. That year was also important for Methodists since the Joint Committee of Reference was appointed in 1919 to draw up a proposed constitution for a unified Methodist Church.[66] In the country as a whole, 1919 saw the passage of both the Volstead Act to enforce Prohibition and the amendment for woman suffrage; these went into effect in 1920 as the Eighteenth and Nineteenth Amendments. Later that summer of 1919, the first widespread radical urban black resistance broke out in cities like Chicago and Washington, D.C. Black Americans, "in sackcloth and ashes" commemorated the offical anniversary of the coming of the first Africans to Virginia as slaves three hundred years earlier.[67]

For 1919, it seemed appropriate to look at two figures, one the man most responsible for providing the A.M.E. Church with a new vision of what its place might be in the modern city, Reverdy Ransom, editor of the *A.M.E. Church Review* and pastor of the mission Church of Simon of Cyrene in New York City.[68] The other is Francis McConnell, bishop of the Methodist Episcopal Church since 1912, and also president of the Methodist Federation for Social Service since that same year. In 1919, he was forty-eight years old and had already earned an outstanding reputation both as a presiding officer and as a prominent churchman vitally concerned about the industrial order in America.[69]

Unlike his predecessors in leadership of the A.M.E. Church, Reverdy Ransom was a man of the city. Born in 1861 in Ohio, educated at Oberlin and Wilberforce, Ransom had entered the A.M.E. ministry in 1886. After serving in small mission churches in Pennsylvania for four years, he was moved by Bishop Payne in 1890 to the prestigious North Church in Springfield, Ohio. From there he was moved to Cleveland, and in 1896 to Bethel Church in Chicago. In 1900, he left Bethel to launch the Institutional Church and Settlement House, "the only colored Social Settlement in the world."[70] In 1905, he began a two-year pastorate in Boston and was actively engaged in the Niagara Movement. From 1907 until his election as editor in 1912, he was pastor of Bethel Church in Harlem. He was elected bishop in 1924 at age 63, and lived to be 98, serving as bishop until 1952!

After the death of Bishop Turner in 1915, it was Reverdy Ransom who was most responsible for carrying forward under changed circumstances the A.M.E. Church's traditional concern with forming a black Christian culture. Ransom's vision differed significantly from that of Payne in terms of theology, worship, and his view of the Christian life. Although he wrote no extended theological works, his was clearly a "liberal, social gospel theology." While sharing some of Payne's sense of propriety in worship, he believed black churches should know and own their own tradition of "spontaneous enthusiasm." For him, the heart of the Christian life lay in "active concern and forgiving love for the downtrodden and outcast." He was thus a good deal less stringent than Payne about the "weaknesses of the flesh," and "greatly softened" the authoritarian cast of Payne's "strictly ordered" vision of what African Methodism should be.[71]

Ransom encouraged an expanded role for women in the A.M.E. Church, supporting deaconesses and woman suffrage. From the time of his 1896 article on "The Negro and Socialism," he worked for the amelioration of the working class in contemporary society. In that article he said, "The present social order with its poverty and vast reserve army of the unemployed cannot be accepted as final, as the ultimate goal for which the ages have been in travail. If man is the child of God, the present social order is not divine. God has never sanctioned, as by divine right, a social order into which the vast majority must be born only to find, 'no trespass' posted upon every portion of the domain of nature, which is their heritage, and to lead a life of privation and suffering in a struggle to maintain an existence."[72]

He looked to democratic socialism as the movement which could transform this situation, and he dreamed of the day when black and white workers would join in a common movement, and when a new civilization would arise, recognizing the solidarity of the human race, and allowing all to share the blessings of their common heritage.

Ransom's chief service to the A.M.E. Church was offering it a way into the future. In his sermon before the General Conference of 1936, he described the "church that shall survive" as a church that knows "neither race, color, nor nationality." Yet he was concerned for the totality of black Christians in America. He believed that the A.M.E. Church must be enlisted in the struggle for social justice and unafraid to bring prophetic judgment to bear on the evils of American society. "I see little hope for the survival of the A.M.E. Church," he warned, "if we do not so apply the Gospel of Christ as to make it a vital force in the life of society."[73] Ransom's vision "rested upon a deep personal commitment to the Christian faith, a preoccupation with remoulding the surrounding world under the impetus of that faith, and a conviction that the A.M.E. Church could be a place where that commitment and that preoccupation significantly affected the life of black America."[74] The church from whose service he retired in 1952 was not the activist community he wished it to be, but it was far better prepared for the civil rights struggles of the 1960s than it would have been without him.[75]

In 1919, Bishop McConnell was chosen to chair the commission of inquiry investigating the strike against U.S. Steel (under the auspices of the newly-organized Department of Industrial Relations within the Interchurch World Movement). Before 1912 it would have been difficult to predict such a role for McConnell. Born in rural Ohio, the son of a Methodist preacher and an intensely devout mother, he graduated from Ohio Wesleyan, studied for the ministry at Boston University, and went on to complete a Ph.D. under Borden Parker Bowne. He served four appointments in Massachusetts and one in Brooklyn, New York, before becoming president of DePauw University. At heart a philosopher and theologian, he apparently became interested in the social movement only in 1912. He was, in fact, the first of Bowne's students to demonstrate the theoretical significance of Boston personalism for social reform.[76]

The special commission of inquiry for the steel strike included both prominent church people and experts in industrial research who were competent to handle the technical investigations. The strike itself, which involved half of the nation's steel workers in a fight for union recognition, has been regarded in labor history as a pivotal struggle. (It was made even more interesting to Methodists by the fact that the chairman of U.S. Steel was Judge Elbert Gary, a devout Methodist!)[77]

In spite of the collapse of the strike, the commission completed and published its report in January 1920. The report corroborated the grievances of labor and helped to end the twelve-hour day and seven-day work week in the steel industry. It also revealed an extensive "spy network" operated by the steel management and the systematic denial of the workers' civil liberties. The report therefore explicitly requested the intervention of the federal government in the regulation of industry and the protection of the civil liberties of the workers. That the report was finally adopted by the Interchurch World Movement in spite of attempts to suppress it was largely due to Bishop McConnell's determination and courage. He himself admitted that the report might have caused the demise of the movement's financial campaign "if the movement had not already been dead when the report was published."[78]

As chair of the commission of inquiry, McConnell came under intense pressure, including sometimes vicious personal attacks. Associates who knew him well credited his profound faith in God as the foundation for his courage and social hope. As one of them put it, "the quiet courage of Bishop McConnell, the relative indifference to immediate results, a certain half-humorous detachment which often marks him, roots here."[79] In his autobiography *By the Way* (1952), McConnell warned oversensitive souls to find something else to do for the kingdom than to attempt to be socially radical preachers.[80] For his work in the steel strike investigation, the University of Colorado awarded Bishop McConnell the LL.D. degree. A New York rabbi, probably Stephen S. Wise, wrote to him, "I feel you are my bishop. You are bishop of my people."[81] Recent scholarship on this period suggests that the steel strike investigation was a decisive factor in causing the dissolution of the older social gospel coalition and the emergence of social gospel radicalism.[82] During the 1920s, McConnell's example served as a "prophetic symbol" for many younger radicals, to whom he gave new faith in the church. Reinhold Niebuhr said of him even after his own disillusionment with social gospel liberalism, he is "one of the most honest, courageous, and prophetic voices of American church history."[83]

Bishop McConnell's commitments were deeply theological and pastoral as well as social. He warned against an activism that was not thoroughly grounded in the intellectual pursuit of truth. In a little book he wrote in 1916 entitled *The Essentials of Methodism*, McConnell listed the new birth, entire sanctification, and the witness of the Spirit as essentials of the theological tradition to which he believed himself faithful.[84] He described conversion as a gift of God, as passage into new life through surrender to the Divine Will, as transformation so radical that it must manifest itself in one's life. Sanctification meant bringing all of life under subjection to God's Kingdom. Clearly personal salvation was fundamental for him, and engaging in a penetrating critique of American culture was not to be divorced from one's deep religious faith.

There are striking similarities between Ransom and McConnell in terms of personal faith. "Though reared in an atmosphere of prayer by a devout Christian mother" and nurtured in the piety of the A.M.E. Church, Ransom had neither been converted nor joined the church before he went off to Wilberforce. Part of the problem, as he himself recognized, was his unwillingness to submit to the "spectacle" of the mourner's bench. At Wilberforce, he experienced "one of those rapturing moments . . . when earth and heaven meet and blend in the happy consciousness that God has entered into our life making Himself known." He never ceased to testify to the importance of this life-changing experience. Similarly, Francis McConnell's mother was known for her profound Wesleyan piety (which he always honored). Yet when he became a member of the church of which his father was pastor, he simply "went forward and shook hands at the altar rail" with his father; "that was all there was to it."[85]

Both Ransom and McConnell were theological liberals and social gospel figures. It would be a serious mistake, however, to underestimate the depth of their personal faith, which was basic to all of their efforts for social transformation. Their inclusion in this address is in part to urge that the power to transform the world must be rooted in profound spirituality, biblical faith, and theological reflection (and not simply human effort), while insisting equally that this must *not* mean conforming to a particular type of piety.

I claimed at the outset that the individuals at whom we would look were faithful to the thought and example of John Wesley. During the formative years of the Methodist social gospel, there was a spate of research and publication on the "social implications of Methodism."[86] I believe that contemporary Wesleyans seeking a vision which embraces both personal and social transformation can claim to be in the Wesleyan tradition. Although after Aldersgate, John Wesley understood justification to be the indispensable foundation for salvation (never to be superseded), he clearly believed that the divine intention was the actual transformation of both persons and society, bringing them into active conformity to the will of God.[87] The General Rules outlined and the entire Methodist organization served this conception of the Christian life as social holiness, as character organized around a habitual disposition which embraced both spiritual and social concerns. The early Methodist people were taught to feel a personal responsibility for relieving social need.[88]

To sum up and conclude then, what have we said about reforming the nation and spreading scriptural holiness and what they have meant in our two hundred years as a denomination? In this address, we looked at the period from 1840 to 1939 and took "depth soundings" at revelatory moments for Methodists. Such, I have suggested, were 1840, 1866, 1884, and 1919. We wanted to explore the way public and private were related typically for Methodists in each of those moments. Then we looked at individuals who were visionaries, prophets, examples of holiness in the sense of relating their profound personal faith to a way of life that was morally courageous and socially transforming. They were usually also pioneers and innovators, relating private faith to public order in a way not typical for their historical moment.

In the 1960s when I wrote my dissertation, the dominant framework for interpreting the rise of the social gospel was the stimulus-response thesis formulated by Arthur Schlesinger.[89] A major weakness of that framework (as Robert Handy made clear in *A Christian America*)[90] was its inability to account for the dynamic, purposive, and culture-shaping power of the religious traditions which responded to those challenges. For all its diffuseness and apparent imprecision, the concept of modernization has seemed to me since to be a fruitful interpretive framework for looking at the relationship between public and private in American religion. It attempts to describe a process which includes different rates of change within various sectors of society and also counter-modern or re-traditioning trends. It is a concept which embraces the whole range of great cultural changes (social, political, economic, technological, and religious) which have marked modernity in western European and American life over the last four centuries.[91] I want to mention here only three aspects of religion in modernization.

First, all religious traditions in contemporary America are descriptively modern, in the sense that no tradition is immune to modernity. Traditions have to be reaffirmed, consciously kept alive by believers. Thus in this respect, the major difference between conservatives and liberals is one of response. Second, it has generally been assumed that the social gospel was a modern response to social change, while so-called private Protestantism was traditional. Yet I would submit to you that much of the thrust of the social gospel was an attempt to bring traditional values such as the importance of community into a modernizing public world. On the other hand, as many conservative Christian churches reveal, some of the most characteristic features of modern life—such as sophisticated use of media—are to be found there.

Finally, there is in modernization a wedge that compartmentalizes individual and social spheres of existence. One aspect of that split is the higher valuation of the individual than existed in traditional cultures. The ironic consequence, however, of the religious freedom of the individual is the inevitable tendency toward the privatization of religion. All religious traditions in the modern world have to struggle with this problem of how to articulate a credible public theology and ethics. The point of Martin E. Marty's *The Public Church* is that a "convergence of constituencies" of mainline Protestants, evangelicals, and Roman Catholics is needed so that those who share a concern for relating private faith to public order can contribute together to social and public morale.[92]

Perhaps we need a new conception of social ministry. This is the suggestion both of Presbyterian Dieter Hessel in a recent book and of Jane Cary Peck in a *Christian Century* article on ministry.[93] Both assert the need for a whole ministry which will express simultaneous concern for personhood, community, and global society. The relationship between the church and social transformation has usually not been deeply rooted in the local congregation. Hessel urges that we resocialize the private modes of ministry, such as preaching and pastoral care, and personalize the public modes so that they are meaningful to people at the local level.[94] Where the church ought to serve as a bridge between the public and the private, it has all too often been seen primarily as an extension of the private.[95] John Wesley understood well the relationship that Jane Cary Peck is reaffirming between transformed individuals, the nurturing and challenging of people in small groups (not only for personal growth but to enable social ministry), and the vision and power to change the world.

I am convinced that there is no greater need for the church of the 1980s and 1990s than to move beyond the public/private split to a vision which embraces both personal and social transformation. As United Methodists and others in our family of denominations look back on two hundred years of our history for the sake of moving forward, we have magnificent resources in our traditions for just such a vision. We need to encourage people who do not believe that their efforts make a difference by helping to acquaint them with heroes and heroines of their own tradition (as well as other traditions) who combined personal faith and social vision and action in their time. Methodist historians in particular might bring their awareness of history to the task of helping the church spell out the values inherent in the Methodist way of life. I think Earl Brewer was pointing to this when he urged that we develop and practice "new holistic disciplines of holiness, joining personal and social dimensions."[96]

At the 1884 General Conference of the Methodist Episcopal Church, one of the resolutions of the Committee on the Centennial affirmed: "For a church polity so effective, for doctrines so scriptural, for a ritual so precious, for leaders so heroic, for experience so vital, for a success so unexampled, we give God thanks."[97] What comparable affirmation would we make in 1984? Although surely they can no longer signify for us what they meant for Wesley or even for the Methodists in 1784, perhaps an appropriate way for us to move into our third century is by reflecting on what scriptural holiness and reforming the nation might mean!

NOTES

1. Several historians have referred to this. See, e.g. Wade Crawford Barclay, *To Reform the Nation*, vol. 2 of *Early American Methodism, 1769-1844* (New York: Board of Missions of The Methodist Church, 1950), 1-2.
2. Martin E. Marty, *Righteous Empire: The Protestant Experience in America* (New York: Dial Press, 1970). See chap. 17: "The Two-Party System: A Division Within Protestantism," and reference to my dissertation in Acknowledgments, 268, and Chapter Notes, 270.
3. Dean R. Hoge, *Division in the Protestant House* (Philadelphia: Westminster Press, 1976); Neill Q. Hamilton, *Recovery of the Protestant Adventure* (New York: Seabury Press, 1981); George M. Marsden, *Fundamentalism and American Culture* (New York: Oxford University Press, 1980); Donald W. Dayton, *Discovering An Evangelical Heritage* (New York: Harper & Row, 1976). Marsden discusses evangelical social concern in chap. 10, "The Great Reversal," 85-93. The term was also the title of a book by David O. Moberg. See *The Great Reversal: Evangelism and Social Concern*, rev. ed. (Philadelphia: J.B. Lippincott, 1977).
4. Hannah Arendt discusses the meaning of "public" in her book *The Human Condition* (Chicago: University of Chicago Press, 1958), especially chap. 2, 22-78. She emphasizes the public realm as common meeting ground and suggests that healthy public life depends upon discourse about the common good that transcends private interest. Also helpful are Parker J. Palmer, *The Company of Strangers: Christians and the Renewal of America's Public Life* (New York: Crossroad, 1981), and the older, but still useful work by John Dewey, *The Public and Its Problems* (New York: Henry Holt & Co., 1927). A good recent illustration of interdisciplinary inquiry into the meaning of "public" is the "Project on Religion and American Public Life" coordinated through the University of Chicago Divinity School.
5. James M. Wall, ed., *Theologians in Transition: The Christian Century "How My Mind Has Changed" Series* (New York: Crossroad, 1981). Interestingly, the basic change noted in most of the essays was the shift during the decade of the 1970s from the secular to the religious.
6. This includes the three denominations which became The Methodist Church in 1939 (M.E.; M.E., South; and M.P.), as well as black Methodist denominations (A.M.E.; A.M.E.Z.; C.M.E.) and holiness groups which broke away from Methodism (such as Wesleyan Methodists). I am not, of course, claiming that the Wesleyan traditions *alone* have such resources.
7. See Kenneth E. Rowe, chapter 1 of this book, "Counting the Converts: Progress Reports as Church History."
8. Two basic sources are: Donald G. Mathews, *Slavery and Methodism: A Chapter in American Morality 1780-1845* (Princeton: Princeton University Press, 1965) and William B. Gravely, "Methodist Preachers, Slavery and Caste: Types of Social Concern in Antebellum America," *Duke Divinity School Review* 34 (Autumn 1969), 209-229. See also Donald G. Mathews, *Religion in the Old South* (Chicago: University of Chicago Press, 1977).
9. From Asbury's *Journal*, II, 591. Quoted in Gravely, "Methodist Preachers," 214.
10. William B. Gravely makes this point in his article "Methodist Preachers," 214-15. See also Donald G. Mathews, *Slavery and Methodism*, 25-6, 28.
11. Mathews, *Slavery and Methodism*, chaps. 3 and 4, 62-110.
12. Gravely, "Methodist Preachers," 217-18.
13. Ibid., 219; Mathews, *Slavery and Methodism*, 196-211.
14. Mathews, *Slavery and Methodism*, 221-25, 229-31; quote on 231.
15. For the Wesleyan Methodists see Donald W. Dayton, *Discovering An Evangelical Heritage*, chap. 7, 73-84; also Luther Lee, *Five Sermons and a Tract*, ed. Donald W. Dayton (Chicago: Holrad House, 1975). Quotes in Dayton, *Discovering*, 74-5, 77.
16. Ibid., 81.
17. Donald G. Mathews, quoted in Dayton, *Discovering*, 84.
18. James W. May, "The War Years," in Emory Stevens Bucke, ed., *The History of American Methodism*, vol. 2 (New York: Abingdon Press, 1964), 207-8.
19. James E. Kirby, "Matthew Simpson and the Mission of America," *Church History* 36 (1967), 301.
20. Quoted in Donald G. Jones, *The Sectional Crisis and Northern Methodism: A Study in Piety, Political Ethics and Civil Religion* (Metuchen, N.J.: Scarecrow Press, 1979), 37.
21. Louise Queen, "The Centennial of American Methodism," *Methodist History* 4 (January 1966), 42-6.
22. John O. Gross, "The Romance of American Methodism," *Methodist History* 6 (October 1967), 19.
23. Queen, "Centennial," 48.
24. The major study of Haven is William Gravely, *Gilbert Haven Methodist Abolitionist: A Study in Race, Religion, and Reform, 1850-1880* (New York: Abingdon Press, 1973).
25. Gilbert Haven, *National Sermons. Sermons, Speeches and Letters on Slavery and Its War: From the Passage of the Fugitive Slave Bill to the Election of President Grant* (Boston: Lee and Shephard, 1869), 88-9.
26. See Gravely, *Gilbert Haven*, 117 (especially footnote 29).
27. Haven, *National Sermons*, 375.
28. Ibid., 405.
29. Gravely, *Gilbert Haven*, 127.

30. Ibid., 150, 140.
31. Ibid., 152.
32. Haven, *National Sermons*, 151.
33. Ibid., 626-30; Gravely, *Gilbert Haven*, 159-60. See also Nancy N. Bahmueller, "My Ordination: Anna Howard Shaw," *Methodist History* 14 (January 1976), 127.
34. Quoted in Gravely, *Gilbert Haven*, 256.
35. Henry F. May, *Protestant Churches and Industrial America* (New York: Harper & Brothers, 1949); Charles Howard Hopkins, *The Rise of the Social Gospel in American Protestantism 1865-1915* (New Haven: Yale University Press, 1940).
36. Philip D. Jordan, "Immigrants, Methodists and a 'Conservative' Social Gospel, 1865-1908," *Methodist History* 17 (October 1978), 19-25.
37. The Episcopal Address of 1888 (M.E. Church) referred to the labor problem as "comparatively new with us" and "not of easy solution." (*Journal of the General Conference*, 1888, 57.) It also raised the issue of the alienation of the workers for the first time. As late as 1891, J.W. Mendenhall, ed. *Methodist Review*, responded to criticism of the church for this inattention by claiming that "such questions are new, and it is a problem to know what more to do than discuss them." Wade Crawford Barclay, *Widening Horizons*, vol. 1 of *The Methodist Episcopal Church, 1845-1939* (New York: Board of Missions of The Methodist Church, 1957), 51.
38. Beverly Wildung Harrison, "Sexism and the Contemporary Church: When Evasion Becomes Complicity," in Alice L. Hageman, ed., *Sexist Religion and Women in the Church* (New York: Association Press, 1974), 202.
39. *Journal of the General Conference*, 1884, 380-381; Randolph S. Foster, *Centenary Thoughts for the Pew and Pulpit of Methodism in 1884* (New York: Phillips & Hunt, 1884), 166-69.
40. See her own account of the 1888 General Conference: Frances E. Willard, *Glimpses of Fifty Years: The Autobiography of An American Woman* (Chicago: Woman's Temperance Publication Association, 1889), 617-21.
41. Kenneth E. Rowe, "Counting the Converts," on Buckley.
42. Rosemary Skinner Keller, "Lay Women in the Protestant Tradition," in Rosemary Radford Ruether and Rosemary Skinner Keller, eds., *Women and Religion in America*, vol. 1, *The Nineteenth Century* (New York: Harper & Row, 1981), 242-43.
43. Carolyn D. Gifford, "Home Protection: The WCTU's Conversion to Woman Suffrage" (Unpublished paper, December 1980). Gifford describes the women's temperance crusade against the saloons in the 1870s, and the conversion of evangelical Protestant women to the cause of woman suffrage on realizing that laws were necessary to deal adequately with the liquor traffic rather than the persuasive tactics of "praying and pleading."
44. See, e.g. Carolyn DeSwarte Gifford, "For God and Home and Native Land: The W.C.T.U.'s Image of Woman in the Late Nineteenth Century," in Hilah F. Thomas and Rosemary Skinner Keller, eds., *Women in New Worlds: Historical Perspectives on the Wesleyan Tradition* (Nashville: Abingdon, 1981), 310-37. Also Gifford, "Women in Social Reform Movements," in Ruether and Keller, eds., *Women and Religion*, 294-303; and Ida Tetreault Miller, "Frances Elizabeth Willard: Religious Leader and Social Reformer" (Ph.D. diss., Boston University, 1978).
45. Willard, *Glimpses*, 334-41, 576-89.
46. Mary Earhart [Dillon], *Frances Willard: From Prayers to Politics* (Chicago: University of Chicago Press, 1944), especially chap. 9, "National President of the Union." On the subsequent narrowing of W.C.T.U. concerns after Willard's death, see Miller, "Frances Elizabeth Willard," 163.
47. Gifford, "For God and Home," 317.
48. Ibid., 327.
49. On Willard's developing commitment to labor, see Miller, "Frances Elizabeth Willard," 146-52. Also Earhart, *Frances Willard*, chap. 13, "Temperance and Labor," and 16, "Views on Many Subjects," and Mary Earhart

Dillon, "Willard, Frances Elizabeth," in *Notable American Women*, vol. 3, 618.

The question has often been raised as to how the issue of temperance/prohibition fits into the publicrivate scheme. Like prostitution, drugs, and gambling, this is an issue of personal behavior that has clear public consequences. On the one hand, the temperance crusade was part of the evangelical Protestant effort to create (and maintain) a "Christian America." On the other hand, it had deep kinship with the social gospel in its concern for the urban poor and its attack on big business, including the powerful liquor interest. It was primarily *after* the passage of Prohibition that this issue became a surrogate for the social gospel. On temperance/prohibition, see Richard M. Cameron, *Methodism and Society in Historical Perspective*, and Walter G. Muelder, *Methodism and Society in the Twentieth Century*, vols. 1 and 2 of *Methodism and Society* (New York: Abingdon Press, 1961); also Robert Moats Miller, "Methodism and American Society, 1900-1939," in Bucke, ed., *History of American Methodism*, vol. 3, 329-43.

50. Miller, "Frances Elizabeth Willard," 124. On Willard's religious development, see Willard, *Glimpses*, 622-28.
51. From Willard's Presidential Address to the W.C.T.U., 1897, quoted in Miller, "Frances Elizabeth Willard," 185.
52. Mary Agnes Dougherty, "The Social Gospel According to Phoebe," in Thomas and Keller, eds., *Women in New Worlds*, 1981, 200-216; Keller, "Lay Women," 242-53; Catherine M. Prelinger and Rosemary S. Keller, "The Function of Female Bonding: The Restored Diaconessate of the Nineteenth Century," in Rosemary Skinner Keller, Louise L. Queen, and Hilah G. Thomas, eds., *Women in New Worlds*, vol. 2 (Nashville: Abingdon, 1982), 318-37.
53. Isabelle Horton, *High Adventure: Life of Lucy Rider Meyer* (New York: Methodist Book Concern, 1928); Lucy Jane Rider Meyer, *Deaconesses, Biblical, Early Church, European, American, with the Story of the Chicago Training School for City, Home and Foreign Missions and the Chicago Deaconess Home*, 3rd ed., rev. and enlarged (Chicago: Cranston & Stowe, 1892).
54. Horton, *High Adventure*, 117.
55. Dougherty, "The Social Gospel," 206-10. On holiness social work, see Norris Magnuson, *Salvation in the Slums: Evangelical Social Work, 1865-1920* (Metuchen, N.J.: Scarecrow Press, 1977); also Timothy L. Smith, *Revivalism and Social Reform* (New York: Abingdon Press, 1957), 163-77, and Smith, *Called Unto Holiness: The Story of the Nazarenes* (Kansas City: Nazarene Publishing House, 1962).
56. Dougherty, "Social Gospel," 215-16.
57. John Patrick McDowell, *The Social Gospel in the South: The Woman's Home Mission Movement in the Methodist Episcopal Church, South, 1886-1939* (Baton Rouge: Louisiana State University Press, 1982).
58. Mrs. R.W. [Tochie] MacDonell, *Belle Harris Bennett: Her Life Work* (Nashville: Board of Missions, MECS, 1928). See also Carolyn L. Stapleton, "Belle Harris Bennett: Model of Holistic Christianity," *Methodist History* 21 (April 1983), 131-42. Stapleton stresses Bennett's integration of "traditional Christian piety with a deep commitment to social action." (131)
59. McDowell, *Social Gospel in the South*, chap. 5, 116-43; also Virginia Shadron, "The Laity Rights Movement, 1906-1918: Woman's Suffrage in the Methodist Episcopal Church, South," in Thomas and Keller, eds., *Women in New Worlds*, 1981, 261-75.
60. MacDonell, *Belle Harris Bennett*, 90.
61. Noreen Dunn Tatum, *A Crown of Service: A Story of Woman's Work in the Methodist Episcopal Church, South, from 1878-1940* (Nashville: Parthenon Press, 1960), 36.
62. David W. Wills, "Introduction," in David W. Wills and Richard Newman, eds., *Black Apostles At Home and Abroad: Afro-Americans and the Christian Mission from the Revolution to Reconstruction* (Boston: G.K. Hall, 1982).
63. Ibid. See also Vincent Harding, *The Other American*

Revolution (Los Angeles: Center for Afro-American Studies, UCLA, and Atlanta: Institute of the Black World, 1980), 79: "For a brief time, Reconstruction had provided the nineteenth century's most complete opportunity for the nation to forge a binding chain between the best possibilities of the white American revolution and the deep and pulsing movement of the black struggle for freedom. It was a magnificent chance for the two revolutions to become one in the creation of a new society . . . . Instead, America chose a 'New South.'"

64. David Wood Wills, "Aspects of Social Thought in the African Methodist Episcopal Church 1884-1910" (Ph.D. diss., Harvard University, 1975).

65. Ibid.

66. Robert Moats Miller, "Methodism and American Society," in Bucke, ed., *History of American Methodism*, vol. 3, 400-01.

67. Harding, *Other American Revolution*, 101 (the quote is from W.E.B. DuBois).

68. David Wills, "Reverdy C. Ransom: The Making of an A.M.E. Bishop," in *Black Apostles: Afro-American Clergy Confront the Twentieth Century*, eds. Randall K. Burkett and Richard Newman (Boston: G.K. Hall, 1978), 181-212.

69. William McGuire King, "The Emergence of Social Gospel Radicalism in American Methodism" (Ph.D. diss., Harvard University, 1977).

70. Wills, "Aspects of Social Thought," chap. 6, "The Vision of Reverdy C. Ransom," 243-4; Wills, "Reverdy C. Ransom," 197.

71. Wills, "Aspects of Social Thought," 247-52; Wills, "Reverdy C. Ransom," 195.

72. Reverdy C. Ransom, "The Negro and Socialism," *A.M.E. Church Review* 13 (October 1896), 196-7.

73. Quoted in Wills, "Aspects of Social Thought," 261.

74. Ibid.

75. Wills, "Reverdy C. Ransom," 205.

76. King, "Emergence of Social Gospel Radicalism," 118-21.

77. On the steel strike investigation, see Ibid., 292-326; also Muelder, *Methodism and Society*, 96-103.

78. Francis J. McConnell, *By the Way: An Autobiography* (New York: Abingdon-Cokesbury Press, 1952), 219.

79. Harris Franklin Rall, "Francis John McConnell," in Harris Franklin Rall, ed., *Religion and Public Affairs: In Honor of Bishop Francis John McConnell* (New York: Macmillan Company, 1937), 9-10.

80. McConnell, *By the Way*, 223.

81. King, "Emergence of Social Gospel Radicalism," 333.

82. King dissertation; also William McGuire King, "The Emergence of Social Gospel Radicalism: The Methodist Case," *Church History* 50 (December 1981), 436-49.

83. Reinhold Niebuhr, *Radical Religion*, quoted in King, "Emergence of Social Gospel Radicalism," 126.

84. Francis John McConnell, *The Essentials of Methodism* (New York: The Methodist Book Concern, 1916).

85. Reverdy C. Ransom, *The Pilgrimage of Harriet Ransom's Son* (Nashville: Sunday School Union, n.d.), 31-3; McConnell, *By the Way*, 36. See the group profile of the charter membership of the M.F.S.S. in King, "Emergence of Social Gospel Radicalism," 126.

86. For example, one of the chapters in the 1910 volume entitled *Social Ministry*, edited for the M.F.S.S. by Harry F. Ward, was on the "social activities" of John Wesley. Close to one-fourth of Bishop McConnell's 1939 biography of John Wesley was devoted to the social consequences of Wesley's evangelical revival. The literature here is considerable and generally well known. For a good recent essay on Wesley's theology in this connection, see Theodore Runyon, "Introduction: Wesley and the Theologies of Liberation," in Theodore Runyon, ed., *Sanctification and Liberation* (Nashville: Abingdon, 1981), 9-48.

87. See Runyon, "Introduction," 30-39.

88. Wellman J. Warner, *The Wesleyan Movement in the Industrial Revolution* (New York: Longmans, Green & Co., 1930), especially chap. 3, "The Basis of Wesleyan Social Ethics," 55-72.

89. Arthur Meier Schlesinger, "A Critical Period in American Religion, 1875-1900," Massachusetts Historical Society, *Proceedings* 64 (1932), 523-47.

90. Robert T. Handy, *A Christian America: Protestant Hopes and Historical Realities* (New York: Oxford University Press, 1971). Handy made the same point in *The Social Gospel in America* (New York: Oxford University Press, 1966), 4.

91. Among the works on modernization that I have found most helpful have been Richard D. Brown, *Modernization: The Transformation of American Life, 1600-1865* (New York: Hill & Wang, 1976) and Brown, "Modernization: A Victorian Climax," in Daniel Walker Howe, ed., *Victorian America* (University of Pennsylvania Press, 1976), 29-44. Robert Bellah, Peter Berger, and Joseph Kitagawa have also written extensively about modernization and religion in modernization.

92. Martin E. Marty, *The Public Church: Mainline-Evangelical-Catholic* (New York: Crossroad, 1981).

93. Dieter T. Hessel, *Social Ministry* (Philadelphia: Westminster Press, 1982); Jane Cary Peck, "A Model for Ministry," *The Christian Century* 100 (February 2-9, 1983), 94-7.

94. Hessel, *Social Ministry*, chap. 1, "To Reconstruct a Whole Ministry," 13-33.

95. Parker J. Palmer, *The Company of Strangers: Christians and the Renewal of America's Public Life* (New York: Crossroad, 1981), chap. 1, "Life Among Strangers," 17-33.

96. Earl D.C. Brewer, *Continuation or Transformation? The Involvement of United Methodism in Social Movements and Issues* (Nashville: Abingdon, 1982), 118.

97. *Journal of the General Conference*, 1884, 384.

II. NEW APPROACHES

Evangelical America—The Methodist Ideology

Donald G. Mathews
University of North Carolina

The Methodist Bicentennial celebrates an institution; but Methodism was first of all a movement. And movements begin beyond public action in the inner life of people who are ill at ease with the way in which institutions and elites have affected their lives. Movements begin when uneasiness becomes a subjective revolution that cuts ties to the past and sets people free to create selves and institutions anew. This is what Methodism did for the Revolutionary generation of Americans. Relying on preachers whose credentials were an ability to elicit intense emotion and to inspire religious commitment, Methodists became so effective at recruitment and mobilization that the post-Revolutionary generation would be called by religious historians "the Methodist Age." It was not that all Protestants had become Methodists, but that most Protestants had become so very much like Methodists in certain significant ways. This transformation was not so much the direct result of Methodism as it was of a larger process at work also with the Calvinist churches, a process that came to be called Evangelicalism.

Calvinist Evangelicals of the nineteenth century were to look back at revivals of religion in eighteenth century New England for their antecedents. There in Jonathan Edwards' Northampton, in Connecticut, Long Island, and areas scattered broadly enough to suggest a widespread phenomenon, there seemed to have been a Great (religious) Awakening. George Whitefield's tour of New England in 1739-40 was remembered as more than a metaphor for a blazing nova of New Light; it became in the memories of Evangelical historians a widespread, swift revolution in religious life throughout the colonies. But the memory had been inflated by romanticism, sentimentality, and time. Recent scholarship—the enemy of all illusions—has suggested that the awakening was not quite the tidal wave of emotion and transformation that Evangelicals remember. Scholarly skeptics could then conclude that the limited, sporadic, and scattered awakenings still conceded as actual events, could not have had any significant impact on the way in which men and women were prepared for the American Revolution and the Republicanism that pervaded political life thereafter. But here skepticism denied too

much. If there was no one event, there had nonetheless been a process of many events' changing the moods and forms of American religion. The result was an audience that repudiated deferential assumptions and habits, aristocratic display and waste, and rationalist skepticism repudiating these things not as a matter of principle (from outside the self) but as a matter of self-definition, a projection of the self into public discourse. If Evangelicalism did not cause the Revolution or create Republicanism, it was nevertheless a pervasive language for scrutinizing "authority," establishing "legitimacy," assuming "personal responsibility" and expressing "liberty."

The words were political words as well as religious words, words expressing a continuum of experience in which distinctions between politics and religion could be sustained perhaps during elections and revivals, but not necessarily all the time. When Methodist preachers rode into the American countryside to preach "liberty to the captives" "empowered" by the Holy Spirit, they were in a sense declaring the "politics of God" to people who were bound by race, sex, or social condition as well as personal predicament. Already ahead of them were New Light Baptists and New School Presbyterians. Divided by theologies of church and ministry, these Evangelicals shared emphasis upon the experience of the New Birth, a transformation worked by the Holy Spirit within the believer who had been convicted of sin, but graciously justified through God's intercession in Christ Jesus. One did not need to know how to read scripture or prayer book or to recite the creed. One did not need to explain the experience of grace in careful theological language. One needed only testify as to what was felt when receiving the Spirit within an "amazing grace" (once blind, now seeing; once dumb, now testifying; once fragmented, now whole).

Evangelicalism grew through its various manifestations to become the dominant mood of American Protestantism. Over the course of two centuries the processual transformation of volatile movement into orderly institution contained a logic at odds with the genius of early Evangelicalism. Any formalism that set ministers (authority) apart from most believers and regularized reception of the New Birth would be targeted as increasing the distance between the faithful and God. In response to such apostasy there were recurrent surges of radical supernaturalism. In the 1830s and 40s there were the Millerites; in the post-Civil War generation there was the elaboration of Evangelical motivation and vision in Bible conferences and holiness movements. In the twentieth century came fundamentalists and the current resurgence of "neo"-evangelicalism. Evangelical America, then, has been a movement, a series of movements, institutions, moods, and motivations that have affected our culture in a variety of ways that have yet to be fully understood. Within this persistent cultural form, Methodist ideology has been a significant force.

Ideology has been understood as a belief system serving the interests of those who propagate it as a mask or weapon in the universal struggle for advantage. For others, ideology has been explained as a symptom of and remedy for an imbalance in the social system. The problem with these conceptions of ideology, argues anthropologist Clifford Geertz, is that they do not deal analytically with symbolic forms and the search for meaning in ideologies which are essentially the creative attempts by people to understand social situations that have become incomprehensible to them. Ideology is an achievement of mind, making it possible for people to act purposefully—it is not only a map *of* a problematic social reality, but also a model *for* a more meaningful and new reality.[1] The attitude evoked is not that of scientific detachment, but of commitment; it is an investment of self in a transformation that is promised in vivid and evocative language, stretching the imagination beyond the known present and propelling it into an unknown and only partially charted future.

Methodist ideology was certainly that, and more. It was also a collage of sound, symbol, and act. It was style and mood evinced in oral communication. Some people called it noise. On February 11, 1807 a man in New Bern, North Carolina, reported such noise to a friend:

About a week past there was a methodist conference in this place which lasted 7 or 8 days & nights with very little intermission, during which there was a large concourse of people of various colors, classes & such, assembled for various purposes. Confusion, shouting, praying, singing, laughing, talking, amorous engagements, falling down, kicking, squealing and a thousand other ludicrous things prevailed most of the time and frequently of nights, all at once—In short, it was the most detestable farcical scene that ever I beheld.[2]

This report—so similar to other reports of Methodist conferences by non-Methodists—reminds us that American Wesleyans relied much less on the written word than that which was spoken. For all the tracts and treatises and sermons that Methodist preachers published and read, they were remembered first of all for their preaching and for the spontaneous verbal responses of their congregations—the shouts, the groans, the sobs of persons brought together to express their most interior and private thoughts. These acts and this noise were at the core of the movement. It is a fact often overlooked by historians who have read journals of circuit riders and come away disappointed because they were all too often merely reports of places visited, texts preached, and appointments kept. In such stark accounts there seems to be no substance because substance is assumed by scholars of the written word to be the written word. Substance for early Methodists, however, was the spoken word, the event and act of preaching and responding, the fusing together of individuals who poured their interior life out into a sharing community through testimony, song, shout, and laughter. The preachers could recall a "melting time" as the result of feeling such "liberty."

The psychodynamics of orality, as described by one of its most distinguished scholars, suggests the significance of early Methodist preaching. The "sounded word," he writes, is power and action in itself characterized by constructing through sound an event in which an audience becomes a community.[3] The often obsessive wrestling of self with self was to be prevented from turning into self-absorption in early Methodism through preaching that actually brought the interior life of each person out into a communal sharing of the drama of salvation and commitment. The religious experience of the one was to be more than the metaphor for the religious experience of the many; it was to be a common *bond* through which public discourse became a communally creative event. The preaching of early Methodism, therefore—the sound of the Holy Spirit—was at the heart of Methodist ideology precisely because it made the gospel an event.

If Methodist orality expressed the interior life of individuals becoming community, it also established, for awhile at least, the authority of the preachers. That authority was not resident in the office of itinerant but in the action that he made possible. If the words he spoke or chanted did not elicit communal response and regeneration, his authority was diminished for the moment, although expectation of the return of "power" through "liberty" in preaching could sustain the relationship between him and the people. The itinerants were, like the words they spoke, transitory, restlessly moving through the lives of their people, personifying a church beyond the isolated houses and little rooms within which they preached at pulpits made from kitchen chairs. Like the words they spoke, they were authoritative so long as they brought the interior life of their people into contact with the Spirit and through the Spirit, with their fellow believers in Christ. Thus the ordained preachers were not so much creatures of the local sacred community as were the ministers of the reformed tradition who were set aside to serve a single, gathered church for a long period of time. To be sure, itinerants achieved their position through recommendations from class meetings and quarterly conferences, but these existed within a larger conception of the church as a network of believers beyond any one place. The circuit rider did not belong to the locality after he had once left it, for he then belonged to the church above the stations, appointments, quarterly conferences and class meetings—the Church Militant, the annual conference. The Methodist movement was thus a dialectic between locality and universality. Cut as free of place as the early Apostles, the preachers came into the lives of the faithful from the outside, underscoring the societal, universal character of their ministry. Their universal relevance and the urgency of their message was also evident in the place and size of their audiences. They preached to persons of all faiths or none, to a congregation of "5 adults and 2 children" or to hundreds, in chapels, meeting houses, brush arbors, barns, cabins, taverns, jails, or court houses, in the homes of masters and in the quarters of slaves. If one had the stamina for such a life, a sense of the dramatic, a vivid experience of grace and the gift for making people feel God's presence and forgiveness, he could become the personification of the universal mission of Christianity and therefore a romantic figure in the eyes of the faithful.

Consistent with their orality and itineracy, Methodists made the entry-way into sacred community the compelling, inner sense of transformation—the New Birth. The immediate result of this conversion was commitment to the continuous struggle to live a holy life. There were two things happening in this in which *act* and *process* are both involved. The *act* is realization, through the oral dialectic of interior privacy and external community, of one's im-

portance. The result was commitment to a process of Christian maturation; the convert was not yet whole in perfect love, but he or she would know from experience itself that he or she could be: that God was making it possible for each person to win in the persistent struggle for life. All Evangelicals shared emphasis on such an experience, but unlike consistently Calvinist Evangelicals, the event in Methodism was no guarantee of final perseverence. The Methodist could not say "I have been saved!" and leave the sacred event at that. The Methodist had to say: "I have been saved, I am saved, I may be saved, I shall one day be saved." Both act and anticipation sustained the believer; but experience was a promise and not a final contract.

A basic characteristic of this New Birth was its openness, an openness to all those who professed to have experienced the presence of Spirit flowing from the Word. The radical nature of this openness in a racist and slaveholding society was revealed in the response by itinerants to the religious experience and exercises of the "poor Africans." The latter seemed to express more vividly than anyone else the power of the Spirit and the love of God who could thus exalt those who had been cast so low. Presbyterians responded warily and timorously to the expressiveness of Africans; but white Methodists—at least in the Revolutionary generation—approached stricken blacks prepared to acknowledge the experience of this exotic people as a manifestation of God's universal love, and evidence of a universal "spiritual sense." The blacks' response to the Methodists' orality was a concrete event, just as preaching had been an event; just as Christ and Moses had been events—not principles and not abstractions, but events. When frustrated and disappointed preachers felt no liberty in preaching to whites, their sense of failure was alleviated by the religious exercises of blacks because, as Frederick Dreyer points out in a recent article on John Wesley, what was important was "not what but *how* the Christian ought to believe." This emphasis meant, as Dreyer writes, "the believer's powers of self-consciousness" were the means through which the believer knew justification. He or she did not have to prove spiritual authenticity to skeptical ritual elders through affirmation of correct doctrine or citation of Biblical verses. But one could express the interior self's sensation of the spirit. As Dreyer points out, for Wesley—and one could add: for his preachers—faith was a "sensible experience."[4]

Orality . . . Itineracy . . . Sensible faith. These were the means of recruitment, each reinforcing the others, each flowing from the others, *all* creating an appeal to individuals that created a movement . . . Why? The answers to the question are familiar. The surge of Evangelicalism came from a counterattack by the clergy against infidelity. It came from a theological transformation soon expressed in popular terms. It came from a sense of guilt induced by a transformation of social relationships. It came from the translation into religious language of a sense of loss resulting from migrations, and changes within the vertical structure of society. It came as an organizing process parallel to that in government, politics, and commerce. These explanations all emphasize Evangelicalism as order without taking account of the very obvious but often ignored fact that Evangelicalism was first of all DIS-order. Orality, itineracy, and sensible faith were subversive of order. Orality repudiated the rationalist order of the written word that kept the illiterate out of political consideration save as the dangerous class. Methodist preachers could be understood as transforming into virtues what some considered to be disabling impediments to the exercise of power: illiteracy and passion. The itineracy also threatened order—or at least subverted it—by providing an alternative model for what constituted the legitimate relationship between clergy and laity, a relationship that was a metaphor for all power relationships. And the conversion experience or New Birth—a sensible faith—was especially disorderly in Methodism because it rejected or ignored those elements so crucial to good order in religion: the Creed, the Covenant, the Confession. Authenticity of the conversion experience, and therefore the legitimacy of the Christian's faith, was essentially established by the individual who had been drawn into a serious consideration of his or her personal destiny by first hearing that race, sex, and wealth did not dictate the worth of a person.

The full significance of this changed perception of self is clear when we understand the order that Evangelical Methodism rejected. It was an order in which wealth, prestige, race, and sex dictated who were powerful: relatively wealthy white men. The next stage in the argument, however, is not to conclude that the spread of Methodism had political implications that could make Evangelicalism into the Jeffersonian Republicans at camp meeting. The issue is not quite so simple because what is political is not limited to elections or parties. Power is exercised in many subtle ways, forming matrices of relationships, habits, values, and rules that can become so indelibly impressed in the consciousness of people who held little or no power as to be virtually legitimized by tacit acknowledgement that the way things are is the way things probably have to be . . . Any change in the way in which people think about themselves, what they should value, and how they should act can be a political change to the extent that the values of the ruling elites are challenged or repudiated and the sinews of social deference frayed. In some societies it has been a political act to drink water from a certain water fountain or sit down in a certain seat or pray in a certain pew. In the Evangelical movements of the early Republic, it could be a political act to meet at night to pray: blacks could be beaten for doing so, as many of them discovered. "This—" cried one black Methodist with blood rolling down his face from a club wielded by a sheriff, "This is what I have got for praising of my dear Jesus."[5]

To be clear in this, reconsider for a moment the slave's words. He had been physically attacked for "praising of my dear Jesus." The important word is "praising," because "praising" is an act and an event as befitted the response of an illiterate slave to the chanting orality of a Methodist preacher—James Meacham—himself obsessed by the demonic and pervasive power of the masters. "Blood!" he shouted at the whites: the *blood* of Calvary, the *blood* of oppression, the *blood* on the black man's face. All could be fused together in a free association of words in the homiletic chant of an itinerant feeling "liberty." In the meeting, demeanor and self-concept had been transformed in the slave—he was a new self that could not be contained in the ascribed status: black-and-slave. He had to shout to praise Him who had broken the shackles of slavery. If the skeptical insist that this was simply the self-delusion of religious fanaticism, they should consider the act of the sheriff who knew—if historians sometimes forget—that power suffuses all human life. Its expression occurs in all its aspects of dominance and subordination, in what Raymond Williams calls "the *whole* body of practices and expectations, the *whole* of living: our senses and assignments of energy, our shaping perceptions of ourselves and our world. It is a lived system of meanings and values . . . which, as they are experienced as practices appear as reciprocally confirming."[6] The New Birth broke into the system of traditional power relationships—sexual as well as racial and electoral—and announced that the traditional rules of the world no longer applied to the new person in Christ.

The New Birth was a *liminal* event. The

concept of the liminal comes from the work of Victor Turner and underscores the significance of the disorderliness of Methodist revival. The liminal is that aspect of life in which the ordinary rules of the world do not apply. They have been suspended, ignored, or declared void. Liminality characterizes *rituals through which persons move from one status to another* as in rites of passage. In them, the subjects are neither children nor adults; they are literally without social rank of any kind, neither dominant nor subordinate. In this situation one feels the essential equality of all human beings (distinctions are personal or individual and not social). As Turner points out, this egalitarian perception or experience can—if allowed to dictate life outside the liminal passage or situation—be dangerous to social order because it suspends all social distinctions. The New Birth as liminal event conveyed something quite significant, therefore, to those whose lives were most rigidly confined by the ordinary rules of the world.[7]

The liminal event was supposed to create a liminal people. The word that Methodist used to name this process was "holiness." The Methodists' goal was to preach "holiness throughout the land," and holiness was an order of life either in opposition to or alternative to worldly values. The difference between oppositional and alternative values was the difference between trying to replace values that sustained traditional patterns of dominance and subordination and trying merely to establish as binding for only a segment of the population values and behaviors different from those that dominated the larger society. Methodism in neither Great Britain nor the New World ever successfully developed an oppositional ethic even though the language of moral struggle was often expressed as opposition to the world. It was a language that Methodists shared with other Evangelicals, all of whom sought to fight or fend off the world. But they each did it within different intellectual contexts.

The context of Calvinist evangelicals embraced and explained the New Birth through ideologies grounded in theological understanding of the social dimensions of human life. Congregationalists, Presbyterians, and Baptists came from traditions tempered in the 17th century English revolution in which the structure of social life—not merely authenticity of the religious experience—was a major concern. Debate in that traumatized generation had ranged from establishing the only significant community as the gathered church to revolutionizing English society and establishing the Kingdom of God on earth—the Millennium. To

say that the social structure of Christian life was of intense interest in the tradition of non-Methodist evangelicals would be an understatement. In that tradition, there was a demand for a holistic system, one that was as logical and internally consistent as human thought could develop. The New England way was merely one of the earliest American elaborations of a holistic view of what social life should be like. Later, heirs of that fusion of faith and social context would spin their own holistic systems in Oneida, Brook Farm, the local Baptist church, or the social gospel. Although Methodists might later appropriate a practical system of thought such as social science to analyze a system (a social system), Methodism itself would not inspire the kind of total, systemic speculation that explained what the good society would be like. Methodism was more comfortable with the interior knowledge of the Holy Spirit, which the individual could know, than with trying to understand what only God could know.

Methodists, whose style and mood was often thought to betray fanaticism, sometimes found brother and sister Evangelicals too precise and insistent about matters that were really not very important from the Methodists' point of view (save as matters perhaps of taste). Methodists, for example, would baptize anyone anyway preferred, ranging from the application of a moist hand to total submersion in a creek; their latitudinarianism scandalized Baptists. Baptist particularism in insisting on closed communion was just as offensive to Methodists who opened their table to all those professing faith in Christ. Closed communion and insistence on immersion as the only form of baptism represented bigotry to Methodists who were also offended by the hyper-Calvinist insistence that once a person was converted he or she could not fall from grace. The rationale seemed to be imbedded in a theology more interested in maintaining the consistency of a highly speculative system of thought than in the healing and salvation of souls. Moreover, an assumption of the perseverance of saints seemed to encourage a rigidity and a sense of absolute righteousness that far surpassed what Methodists believed was supported by empirical experience. That is, the moral and religious failures of persons who had once had an experience of grace seemed to be obvious to Methodists. That such persons had lapsed after exemplifying the fruits of the Spirit demonstrated that they needed once more to throw themselves on the mercy of Christ. The Christian life was a struggle, a going on to perfection, the goal was ever ahead.

The point of setting up this contrast—inadequate though it may be in some respects—is to understand the openness of Methodist ideology. The conventional way of making the same point is to mention Arminianism, John Locke, and free will. But this litany does not quite convey the full meaning. Methodism struck at all forms and restrictions that prevented individuals from realizing a full life in Christ, whether conceived in formal theological systems or expressed in the one-and-only-church or limited to the orderliness of certain rituals. The Methodist goal was to make such forms irrelevant on matters that really counted in allowing each individual full access to the Spirit. "Liberty" was the word that Methodist itinerants used to express what they felt in a particularly effective preaching experience; and liberty was to be released from whatever bound the self to reach above the self. Liberty, John Wesley had written, was the "power of self-determination"; it was an experience open to "all human kind," he added, but it seemed to be understood most readily in its celebration by his preachers in the oral rituals of Methodist revival.[8]

But the question still remains as to how Methodist "liberty" or liminality could create Evangelical order out of Evangelical disorder. Personal holiness meant to show forth the fruits of faith. The faith that was sensed empirically (in one's feelings) was to be expressed in demeanor, mood, and self-discipline. The word was repudiated; friends who remained within it were to be left behind; the fiddles that invited dancing were put away; the ruffles on one's shirt were cut off; the strength of spirituous liquors resisted; the advances of worldly men rejected; and the winsome wiles of careless, frivolous young women withstood. The sexual repression demanded is suggested in this statement by a Methodist bishop:

> Therefore avoid the allurements of Voluptuousness, and fly every temptation that leads to her banquet as you would the devil himself. Oh how she spreads her board with delicacies. Her wine sparkles, her dainties invite, her Mirth charms. . . . Lascivious love stands in her bower. She spreads her temptations & begins to court their regard. Her limbs are soft and delicate; her attire loose & inviting, wantonness sparkles in her eyes. She woos with her looks and by the smoothness of her tongue endeavors to deceive.[9]

This description of voluptuousness when contrasted to the world one left behind in accepting Methodist discipline presents us with a problem. Why would anyone want to resist such allurement?

The question is that of the "world" that sees in sexual repression a misdirection of personal responsibility. Or it could be that of the skeptic who surrenders seriousness to a thoughtless wit. But it is also one that fails to see self-discipline within the personal and social context in which it occurred. Methodist holiness provided a way for individuals to feel the self-determination that Wesley called liberty—which may appear to be self-contradictory. It should seem ludicrous for the repressed, sober, serious, humorless caricature of Methodist holiness to feel liberty—unless of course the pejorative words are translated into "responsible," "sensible," "gracious." More important—even with the pejorative connotations—the power to establish a new order for oneself is a way of taking that power from someone else—masters, husbands, parents, or the worldly elites whose extravagant display and skeptical levity the Methodists joined other Evangelicals in repudiating. Persons who felt that the predominant values of the world did not assign them much honor, prestige, or importance—persons who felt unloved and rootless—could find haven and meaning through joining Methodist classes and societies. Not a few young women could be attracted to religion that specifically denounced the flirtatious silliness of giggly girls and elevated personal integrity, gentleness, reliability, and piety above good looks and fantasy. In Methodism was a pattern of relating to people that received public approval without deferring to the established customs and behavior of the aristocracy which only the wealthy could afford. In all of these situations and motives there is the persistent strain of self-discipline that enhances the self-esteem of persons who have the power of making themselves new, and it was this that was so attractive in Methodist order.

The aspect of practical Christianity that was MOST radical, that was most CLEARLY in opposition to the hegemonic values of early American society was the early Methodist assault upon slavery. It was an attempt to transform the liminal experience of basic human equality, *communitas*, into permanent form. From the very first, however, there was a schizophrenic quality to the move. After a few desultory discussions about slaveholding, the Christmas conference in a burst of liminal enthusiasm ordered all Methodists holding slaves to free them within two years. Francis Asbury had been uncomfortable with slaveholding since he had arrived in the New World over ten years earlier. But if the language adopted by the Methodists in justifying their excommunication of slaveholders is an appropriate guide, Methodist ideology had received a jolt from the politics of the American Revolution. Republican ideology apparently made the new rule possible.[10]

From the first attack on slaveholding, it was obvious that a radical, liminal demand of emancipation would not be effective. The itinerants had to rescind their edict within a few months because of intractable refusal by the slaveholding laity and a general "public outcry." The Methodist itinerants had assumed that the vision of *communitas* that has been elicited through the liminal sounds of the preaching event had the power to call forth the transformation of religious experience into the rules of everyday life. The preachers had themselves felt "liberty" to proclaim "liberty" to slaves as well as masters; but they had been betrayed by their own eloquence to believe it possible for slave and master both to return to the world of structure and rank with the same vision of *communitas*. For a few thousand slaves thus liberated, the hope was fulfilled. For the vast majority of course it failed. In response, antislavery Methodists turned to tactics which they hoped would re-capture the sense of spontaneous *communitas*: preaching and persuasion. In sermons, pamphlets, and animated discussions they tried to formulate an Evangelical-Republican ideology that could link the emotional transformation of conversion with a commitment to Republican equality. The tone of discourse varied with personal style and public place, but those defending slavery or holding slaves could find themselves condemned as "rogues," "oppressors," and "devils incarnate" with such vivid descriptions of their fate as to make one woman shout, "They will be slaves to the devil in Hell" just before she fainted.[11] That woman's personal vision of judgment and her immediate loss of consciousness are nice metaphors for the fate of the Methodist antislavery impulse. That impulse was more a moral judgment than a plan of action, a spontaneous exclamation rather than a reordering of structure. Denunciations of slaveholding and slavery became increasingly erratic and volatile, characterizing the idiosyncratic and eccentric; gradually the westward movement and death claimed antislavery Methodists and resistance to slavery remained in only a few pockets of the southern mountains or a few communities such as those of the Quakers.

Reasons for Methodist surrender to structure are so familiar as to constitute a Pavlovian response: economics and racism. But these were not *new* factors which eventually became strong enough to overpower revolutionary ideology; rather: they were the *context* within which the Methodist debate about slaveholding had taken place. And during that debate (between 1770 and 1810—more than a generation) both society and Methodism were changing. The exodus of non-slaveholding whites to the west—Kentucky, Tennessee, the Old Northwest—meant fewer dissenters in the Atlantic seaboard states. The movement of slaveholding whites into the southwest meant the further development of slavery. The volatility and movement of population required local religious and civic organizations to provide stability through regulation of social relations and the distribution of property. It is not surprising therefore that Methodist membership in the south should have jumped in geometric progression between 1770 and 1820. In the newer areas of the south and west this meant relatively large numbers of strangers present in each Methodist church that popped up as the result of sufficient population density. Thus, each new church, conference, or class had to decide, without reliance on ties of kinship, upon the rules governing decorum, public order, and social relations. This social role thrust upon Methodists responsibility for structure—defining "distinctive arrangements" of social position and authority, emphasizing differences, constraining action, creating boundaries, establishing social distance.

The inability of whites to create a consistently liminal place for black-white interaction has traditionally been the measure of early American Methodism. Focus, however, has been on Methodists of the wrong race. The full social meaning of Methodist ideology, the full implications of the liminal experience of the New Birth, are to be found in the process through which blacks in both sections of the new America developed in their own social lives the liminal experience of *communitas*.[12] Liminality of whites—those of high estate—has meant participation with those of low estate (blacks) in a ritual process expressing the essential humanity of those bonded by act, perception, and emotion. Suspension of the rules of slavery took place when white and black together heard preachers of both races, experienced conversion together, and came to camp meeting together. The camp became liminal space as both sexes and races mixed. The character of the experience there was recalled by one Methodist in this way:[13]

To see a bold and courageous Kentuckian (undaunted by the horrors of war) turn pale and tremble at the reproof of a weak woman, a little boy, or a poor African; to see him sink down in deep remorse, roll, and toss, and gnash his teeth . . . and return in the possession of a meek and gentle spirit, which he set out to oppose—who could say the change was not supernatural?

The "poor African," like those who had preached and prayed in Methodist churches for a generation, was not a liminal person simply because of his prayer in that Kentucky camp. He represented the fact of an Afro-Methodist faith which was itself a persistent statement of the liminal and *communitas*. The collective achievement of the blacks' religious experience, because of their social interaction with whites and their own cultural creativity, was to develop between the tensions of white structure and black liminality a community in which the logic of slavery and racism did not apply—that of black Methodists.

In that Kentucky camp meeting lay the metaphor for the Methodist ideology. There and in the conversion of blacks who first formulated Methodism in Charleston, and Wilmington, and Fayetteville, and Old St. George is the liminal insight, the fusion of orality, new birth (and liminal self), practical holiness and *communitas*. The innovation of the first itinerants' coming out of a universal mission into specific locality brought a psychological revolution—the source of all revolutions. The general illiteracy of blacks and the semi-literacy of many whites meant that the orality of Methodism was a revolution in perceptions of authority. Authority was to be thought not aloof from humankind but inherent within it. The metaphor is in the interaction of preacher and people and does not mean that the people are authority in themselves. Only the response *from* the congregation reveals the presence of authority: authority is the prevenient presence of the Spirit called forth from within the people, released in the ritual interaction of preaching.

A message sent to the audience—*to* them—from the aloofness of literacy, form, and reason, creates distance; a message developed from an outpouring of the Spirit within the holy community in a call and response cadence of a people expressing themselves in the preacher creates solidarity. That sense of human solidarity, of human equality—of essential humanness was what the Kentucky frontiersman found in campmeeting from an African. Thus, out of the liminal process of preaching is the liminal self revealed—a new birth.

The sense of the liminal self removed blacks from their slavery and the subordination of race. That this was a function not simply of their social condition is suggested by the fact that some slaveholders also understood the radical impli-

cations of the new birth. But the full implications of the Methodist ideology are in the blacks' experience. From their conversion they were cast free of all ties that bound them, and through the practice of holiness brought into being a community in which the ordinary rules of the world did not apply. In concrete terms, black Methodists received at least four things: (1) a language, (2) acknowledged legitimacy in a world where they had not been previously legitimate, (3) a personal discipline that authenticated the psychological revolution and broke the power of slavery, (4) a concrete institution in which *communitas* was acknowledged.

The language was a new means of communication between blacks and whites. Without a common language that acknowledged a common experience and a common obligation, the means of communication between white and black were that of power—work, sex, violence. A language of common religious experience—or failing that, of a common acknowledgement of obligation to the same moral authority—provided a way for blacks to celebrate their humanity in a public way. Whites—especially those professing Christianity—were now placed in a position of dealing with Christian blacks, knowing that the blacks understood the meaning of Christian obligation. The knowledge within black Methodists of that mutual obligation meant that their willingness to share the vision of *communitas* was the measure of the whites' Christian commitment professed in the new birth. To the extent that whites were themselves unable to embrace the full meaning of that vision they had failed to be truly Christian. The measure of Christianity, then, was reversed—it changed from white to black.

The legitimacy was that of the white world, not the black. Black conversion meant that within the world of structure—society—even the whites had to acknowledge that the blacks now, too, had a public institution—the church. The acknowledgement meant conceding—morally at least—a public claim of blacks to legitimacy outside their own culture and their own souls.

The personal discipline of holiness—the daily struggle to achieve the perfection of humanity in Christ—removed blacks from the power of whites to the extent that blacks now could wrest from whites the power to name themselves, to define themselves not with respect to white power but to the divine—the source of power. The new birth revealed to each black convert the incredible worth of self. The meaningful discipline was not white; the meaningful discipline was to answer to God for self, to act according to an inwardly developed sense of one's obligation and integrity. The achievement and limitations of this discipline are understood in a statement made by Uncle Tom to Simon Legree. He could not have Tom's soul; all he could do was to kill him.[14]

The concrete place in which *communitas* was acknowledged was of course the black Methodist class or society. It was the achievement and nurturer of the Methodist ideology—the model for all Methodists of any race and both sexes that conveyed the liminal insights of *communitas* in which the ordinary rules of the world did not apply. *Communitas* and holiness both underscored the transcendent legitimacy that was repeated over and over again in the religious sensibility of early Methodist ideology. The orality and itineracy that began the Methodist movement brought a dramatic disorderliness to the worldly order of the early Republic even as the liminal vision of community suggested an ideal orderliness. That a few emancipating white Methodists and the community of black Methodists could achieve "perfection" of the Methodist ideology was of course a function of social position and the individual moral heroism that transcends class. It was an ideology that denied the rules of class and exploitation; it was an abrupt, oral, radical intrusion into a world of rank, invidious distinctions, and careless convention. And it is this historic fusion of concrete reality and spiritual sensibility that we honor in celebrating the Methodist Bicentennial.

NOTES

1. Clifford Geertz, "Ideology as a Cultural System," in David Apter, *Ideology and Discontent* (London: Free Press of Glencoe, 1964), 47-76.
2. Thomas B. Houghton to James Iredell, Jr., 2 February 1807, James Iredell Papers, Duke University.
3. Walter J. Ong, *The Presence of the Word: Some Prolegomena for Cultural and Religious History* (New Haven: Yale University Press, 1967), especially Chapter 3.
4. Frederick Dreyer, "Faith and Experience in the Thought of John Wesley," *American Historical Review*, 88 (February, 1983), 12-30.
5. Donald G. Mathews, *Religion in the Old South* (Chicago: University of Chicago Press, 1977), 194.
6. Raymond Williams, *Marxism and Literature* (Oxford: Oxford University Press, 1977), 110.
7. Victor Turner, *The Ritual Process: Structure and Anti-Structure* (Chicago: Aldine Publishing Company) 94-120; Turner, *Dramas, Fields, and Metaphors: Symbolic Action in Human Society* (Ithaca: Cornell University Press, 1974) 272-99. See also Sally Falk Moore, "Epilogue" in Moore and Barnara G. Myerhoff, eds., *Symbol and Politics in Communal Ideology* (Ithaca: Cornell University Press, 1975), 210-239.
8. Dreyer, "Faith and Experience in the Thought of John Wesley," 27.
9. Diary of William McKendree, September 18, 1790, Vanderbilt University Library.
10. Mathews, *Religion in the Old South*, 66-73.
11. *Ibid.*, 66-80.
12. See Turner, *Ritual Process*, 94-165; Turner, *Dramas, Fields, and Metaphors*, 23-59, 271-99; Donald G. Mathews, "Evangelicalism in the Old South—*Communitas* and *Apocalypse*," unpublished essay.
13. Quoted in Dickson D. Bruce, Jr., *And They All Sang Hallelujah: Plain-folk Camp Meeting Religion, 1800-1845* (Knoxville: University of Tennessee Press, 1974), 87.
14. Harriet Beecher Stowe, *Uncle Tom's Cabin or Life Among the Lowly*, edited and with an introduction by Ann Douglas (Penguin American Library, 1981) 582-3.

The Attraction of Methodism: The Delmarva Peninsula as a Case Study, 1769-1802

William H. Williams
University of Delaware, Georgetown

In 1800, apprentice cabinetmaker William Morgan of Lewes, Delaware, was about to make a momentous decision. Only nineteen, Morgan was very concerned about his future and was convinced that a religious affiliation would give needed direction to his life. Shopping around for a suitable faith, he finally narrowed his choice to Episcopalianism or Methodism.

Cornelius Wiltbank, an elderly Episcopalian, advised young Morgan to join with the Episcopalians so that he could have religion and still enjoy himself. Wiltbank assured Morgan that "God did not require so much strictness as the Methodists said he did." Moreover, Christ's yoke, ". . . is easy and his burden is light. I am sure there is no harm in civil mirth, in going to balls and taking a civil dance; enjoying one's self among young people, hearing the fiddle; it revives one's spirits."[1]

Wiltbank's entreaties were appealing and his logic convincing. How could anyone choose the dour, strict world of Methodism over the enjoyments of Episcopalianism? And yet Morgan and thousands of other Delmarvans chose "strictness" over "enjoyment," causing Methodism to become the dominant faith on the Delmarva Peninsula.

The Peninsula

The Delmarva Peninsula begins about fifteen miles south of Philadelphia and pushes southward for more than two hundred miles. Bounded on the west by the mouth of the Susquehanna River and the Chesapeake Bay, and on the east by the Delaware River, Bay and the Atlantic Ocean, it includes all of Delaware and the Eastern Shore of Maryland and Virginia. Taking its name from these three states, the Delmarva Peninsula gradually widens as it proceeds south, reaching a width of almost seventy miles before receding to a long, narrow neck that finally ends at the confluence of bay and ocean. In the extreme north, Piedmont meets coastal plain. South of the fall line, only an occasional hill or swale interrupts the flatness of the land. The

The Delmarva Peninsula

western edge of the peninsula is serrated by hundreds of marshes, creeks, and rivers, producing a waterman's paradise. In 1790, except for the extreme north where the Scotch-Irish predominated, the white population was overwhelmingly of English ancestry. Blacks made up about 35 percent of the peninsula's population, and slightly more than 80 percent of the blacks were slaves.[2]

A few years prior to the American Revolution, the first Methodist itinerants visited Delmarva and planted spiritual seeds on extraordinarily fertile soil. By the end of the American Revolution almost one in three American Methodists lived on the Delmarva Peninsula. By 1820, approximately one in five adults—sixteen and over—Delmarvans was a Methodist, which is an astonishing figure considering the low percentage of Americans of that era belonging to any church. This unusually high concentration of Methodists makes the Delmarva Peninsula an ideal region for the study of why people became Methodists.[3]

The Ethnic Factor

During the colonial period, white Delmarvans were drawn to Anglicanism because it was their ancestral faith. Although the American Revolution brought an end to the colonial Anglican Church, the rise of the Protestant Episcopal Church from Anglican ashes continued to provide Peninsula Anglo-Saxons with an "English" church. After all, Episcopalianism was really colonial Anglicanism minus direct ties with England and the troublesome Anglican evangelists called Methodists. Although fresh from declaring their independence from the Church of England in 1784, Methodists also pointed to Anglican roots and, by doing so, offered Delmarvans a second "English" church.

The contest between Episcopalians and Methodists for the hearts and minds of the Peninsula's predominantly Anglo-Saxon population was decisively won by the Methodists for a number of reasons. But of considerable importance was the fact that the Methodists could claim a faith every bit as "English" as Episcopalianism and, therefore, a faith that descendents of Englishmen could feel comfortable with. William Morgan's mother had been of English stock and Anglican. When her son finally narrowed his choice to two churches, predictably they were both "English." It was no accident that Methodism on the Peninsula, as elsewhere, had its greatest success in areas previously dominated by the Church of England and the descendents of Englishmen.[4]

The movement of Delmarvans from Anglicanism to Methodism is amply chronicled in a number of biographies and autobiographies. At times, the sequential pattern included an Episcopalian interlude prior to Methodist conversion. The latter pattern was particularly true on Virginia's Eastern Shore, some scattered regions of Maryland's lower Eastern Shore, and some of the islands in the Chesapeake, because those areas were the last to be visited by Methodist itinerants.

Predictably, Methodism's opponents tried to discredit the "English" nature of Methodism. They would call attention to circuit riders of non-English extraction to make their point. When Joshua Thomas of Somerset County, announced in 1807 that he was going to a camp meeting, his uncle tried to dissuade him by declaring that Methodist preachers were "nothing but a parcel of Irishmen who ran away from their country to keep from being hanged." Asbury was sensitive to this issue and hesitated to assign to the Peninsula preachers of non-English background, particularly if they had heavy accents.[5]

The Demographic Factor

Peninsula Methodism received its greatest support in the countryside. Wesley's itinerancy system seemed ideally suited for reaching the isolated farmers and watermen who worked the flat land, and the creeks and sounds of the Chesapeake and Delaware bays. Riding his horse over fields, through forests, around marshes, and across rivers, the circuit rider made himself available to most of the rural folk of Delmarva. Where his horse wouldn't carry him, a waterman's log canoe would.

The location of Methodist chapels reflected Methodism's rural strength. By 1784, Methodists had built twenty chapels on the peninsula, and eighteen were in the countryside. Chestertown, Maryland, and Dover, Delaware, had the only in-town chapels, and even in Dover, the Methodist house of worship was "somewhat out of town." Many well-established communities didn't construct Methodist meetinghouses until well into the nineteenth century. Indeed, future Methodist Bishop, Levi Scott, noted the lack of an in-town Methodist church during his entire childhood in Odessa, Delaware, in the early nineteenth century.

Like most rural based movements, Peninsula Methodism was suspicious of towns and town dwellers. Wilmington, New Castle, and Dover, Delaware, and Elkton, Maryland, were subjected to Methodist criticism, but some of the strongest negative comments were reserved for Chestertown, Maryland. In 1776, one Methodist found the grain port on the Chester River "famous for wickedness," and nine years later Francis Asbury called it a "very wicked place."[6]

The cultural antipathy between the Methodist countryside and Delmarva's profligate towns came to a head in a bizarre controversy, sometimes called the "Great Pig Issue," in Georgetown, Delaware. In 1791, Georgetown was created by legislative fiat to be the new county seat for Sussex. From the beginning, the new county seat was governed by the Delaware General Assembly causing most serious town problems to be settled by legislative enactment in Dover.

As the newly founded community began to rise on former swamp and farm lands, two distinct visions emerged concerning Georgetown's future. On the one hand, in-town Episcopalians, drawn in part from judges, lawyers, and county officials, wanted Georgetown to become an aesthetically attractive and sophisticated county seat. By contrast, Georgetown's Methodists, drawn from residents with rural roots and including some farmers from the edge of town, wanted a community amenable to the less restrictive rural life-style.

The Wesleyans were less concerned with Georgetown's cosmetic appearance than they were with the right to turn loose their livestock to roam through its streets. Consequently, Methodist-owned pigs destroyed Episcopalian flower gardens, and irate Episcopalians demanded legislative action. Reflecting political pressures brought to bear by Methodists as well as Episcopalians, Delaware's General Assembly banned "swine running at large in Georgetown" in 1795, and subsequently stiffened, repealed, and finally in 1821, reenacted restrictions against free-roaming swine. The "Great Pig Issue" is just one example of the identification of Peninsula Methodism with the rural perspective.[7]

Inactivity of Other Faiths

Methodism's domination of all but the extreme north of the Peninsula was assured by the failure of other denominations to mount effective counteroffensives.

Lacking a clergy that was either numerous or energetic, Episcopalianism seemed capable of only verbal invective to stem the Methodist tide. Rectors focused their verbal attacks on John Wesley, calling him "a fallen Judas," and incorrectly insisting that Methodism's founder had been "disrobed by his [Anglican] Bishop and deprived of all ecclesiastical powers."

But beyond invective, Episcopalianism offered little resistance. Up and down the Peninsula, parishes lacking rectors waited to "be entirely eaten up by the Methodists." Typical was the scene in 1816 at St. Stephen's Parish, Cecil County, where parishioners were joining the Methodists because there was no Episcopal rector.[8] That year, on the entire peninsula, there were no more than twelve Episcopal clergy to compete with approximately thirty Methodist itinerants and more than two hundred local preachers. By 1820, Episcopalians were lamenting that there wasn't an Episcopal Church remaining in all of Caroline County, Maryland.

Lacking the energy of their Methodist counterparts, the few remaining Episcopal clergy demonstrated a general lassitude, particularly in inclement weather. In Accomack County, right after the American Revolution, English Methodist Thomas Coke was told that the Episcopal clergy "never stir out to church, even on Sunday's if it rains." A weakness for alcohol also seemed to hinder the performance of Episcopal clerics. In Lewes, Delaware, in 1799, the local rector often got so drunk at a local tavern that he had to be helped home by parishioners.[9]

In the early nineteenth century, Presbyterians were most numerous in New Castle and Cecil, the northernmost of Delmarva's counties, because it was here that the Scotch-Irish and their decendents were most heavily concentrated. There were some pockets of Presbyterians all the way south to the Virginia border, but insistence on an educated ministry limited the number of available Presbyterian clergy. The shortage of ministers was reflected in an urgent request in 1803 from the New Castle Presbytery that missionaries be sent into all of Delaware south of northern New Castle County, and into every county of Maryland's Eastern Shore. No effective response was made and signs of Presbyterian decline were evident throughout most of the peninsula. By 1813, four Presbyterian congregations in lower Delaware and one in Dorchester County, Maryland, had disappeared.[10]

Unlike other regions south of Pennsylvania, the Baptists never mounted a serious challenge in most areas of the peninsula. By 1812, for example, there were eleven times as many Methodists as Baptists in Delaware. On Maryland's Eastern Shore, Baptists were even less evident.

The only serious Baptist challenge came from Virginia's Eastern Shore. In 1776, Baptist preacher Elijah Baker left Virginia's Western

Shore and crossed the Chesapeake to Northampton County, on the southern tip of the peninsula. Two years later, the Lower Northampton Baptist Church was formed, probably the first non-Anglican church on Virginia's Eastern Shore. Despite wartime persecution, similar to what Methodist preachers were facing further north, Baker and fellow preacher George Layfield organized fifteen Baptist churches on the peninsula. Six were in Virginia, five in Maryland, and four in Delaware. By 1785, Virginia's Eastern Shore seemed ripe for a Baptist takeover. At the end of the eighteenth century, however, Baptist leader Elijah Baker died and the Baptist offensive came to a halt. By 1809, Methodists on Virginia's Eastern Shore outnumbered Baptists by 1,515 to 890.[11]

By the end of the eighteenth century other rivals to Methodism on the peninsula, such as the Quakers and their cousins the Nicholites, had long since lost their proselytizing zeal. The few Roman Catholics and Deists raised some concern, but it was more on account of their alien ideas than from the threat of their numbers.[12]

An Alternative Value System

During the late eighteenth century, a worship service at an Episcopal church in Dorchester County, was disturbed by a loud voice crying out, "choose ye this day whom ye will serve." The challenge came from the lips of a Methodist itinerant as he stood outside the sanctuary. After complaints from the parson, the Methodist remained silent until the congregation filed out. Then he repeated his stirring challenge with considerable effect, and one old lady responded, "I will serve the living God." Subsequently, the Methodist preacher converted so many of those present that the Episcopal church ceased to have a congregation.[13]

On the surface, this seems a straightforward account of Methodist success in converting Episcopalians. But on a deeper level it draws our attention to a compelling aspect of Methodism. The Methodist itinerant was making plain to that Episcopal congregation that one could not serve two masters. Simply put, Methodism maintained that to serve God and His ways required a rejection of the ways of men.

In the Chesapeake world of the eighteenth century, the ways of men were forged and shaped by the gentry and then emulated by the "middling and lower sorts." The same dancing, drinking, card playing, gambling, horse racing, cock fighting, and general revelling that marked the gentry's leisure moments also occupied the free time of those lower on the social scale. The "middling and lower sorts" showed their approval of another aspect of the gentry's value system by dreaming of the day when they too would be masters of black slaves.

But there were many who were increasingly uncomfortable with the dominant culture and its underlying value system. They found little that was attractive in a life-style that emphasized frivolity, competition, brutality, and deference to those of a higher social rank. Moreover, to the ambitious, it was self-evident that many of the ways of men were self-destructive and that adopting those ways, on a personal level, spelled nothing but disaster.

A few evangelists such as George Whitefield and Joseph Nichols, the founder of the Nicholites, had spoken earlier to some of this discomfort with the region's dominant mores. But it wasn't until the arrival of the circuit rider that the entire peninsula was offered a way to deal with this discomfort. The Methodist prescription called for a revolution in values. In order to move from the ways of men to the ways of God, the Methodist message demanded the substitution of seriousness for frivolity, cooperation for competition, compassion for brutality, and egalitarianism for deference.

To those seeking deeper human relationships than found in the surface comaraderie and the boozy haze surrounding the card game, horse race, or gala party, Methodist societies offered a supportive community. To a people facing a life time of long, harsh days that drained youth and high spirits from its young and prematurely aged its adults, Wesleyan societies offered far more than just a way to fight the boredom and loneliness of farm life. They provided a real sense of psychological security as Methodist brothers and sisters offered physical and financial help, or lent a sympathetic ear in time of tribulation. Moreover, while the Methodist class meeting kept its members on the road to perfection, it also encouraged each member to bare the innermost depths of his or her soul. What a wonderful catharsis! This type of activity could not go on in the outside world, dominated as it was by the competitive, self-assertive values of the gentry, which regarded self-revelation, particularly among males, as a sign of weakness.[14]

The Better Sort

That the Methodist challenge to the mores established by the peninsula's gentry excited and attracted members of the "lower orders" is understandable. More surprising was the willingness of some of the "better sort" to become

Methodist, to adopt a serious, pious air and to abandon revelry, gambling, sports, frivolity, and slavery. Evidently, many of the region's planters and their social peers were also searching for a new set of values to live by.[15]

On the peninsula, probably a higher percentage of the gentry and their peers became Methodists than anywhere else in the United States.[16] In part, the unusual number of Methodists among the "better sort" of the peninsula can be credited to the strength of "old Methodism."

During the American Revolution, American Methodists south of the Potomac moved to cut their ties with Anglicanism and set up an independent church. This schismatic movement came to a head in the Fluvanna Conference held in Virginia in 1779. Asbury was able to head off this schism by insisting that American Wesleyans adhere to "old Methodism," which maintained that Methodism was no more than a supportive, evangelistic movement within the Church of England and must remain so. Asbury won his battle against the Fluvanna schismatics because of his own strong leadership and because he fashioned for "old Methodism" a strong support base on the Peninsula while living there from December, 1777 to April, 1780.[17]

Because of their commitment to "old Methodism," Peninsula Wesleyans regarded themselves as Anglicans and worked in relative harmony with the Church of England. For this reason local Anglican gentry found Peninsula Methodism quite congenial and could comfortably support and even join Wesleyan societies while simultaneously remaining loyal to the Church of England. With the collapse of the Anglican Church during the American Revolution, some gentry simply continued their Methodist connection while others joined Methodist societies because, in many areas, that was all that remained of Peninsula Anglicanism.

By the end of the American Revolution, the Methodist seed had taken root among the gentry and even the Methodist declaration of independence from the Church of England in 1784 couldn't halt further germination and growth. The enthusiasm with which many of the wealthy and influential embraced Peninsula Methodism wasn't lost on "the middling and lower sorts." Accustomed as the latter two groups were to trying to mimic the activities of their betters, many followed the gentry into the Methodist camp. By contrast, the schismatic nature of Methodism elsewhere during the American Revolution probably so alienated Anglican gentry that they couldn't, in good conscience, become Methodists.[18]

The Middling Sort

Primarily made up of landed farmers but also including successful craftsmen, most merchants, attorneys, and physicians, was the peninsula's "middling sort." Although they might even have a few slaves, the "middling sort" fell far short of the gentry in number of slaves owned, acres possessed, and deference commanded. But falling short was hardly part of the ambitions of many of the "middling sort." They dreamed of upward mobility, worked at upward mobility, and a few were even confident that some day they, too, might be called "squire" or be deferred to in other ways. To reach those heights, the "middling sort" found Methodism very congenial because the Methodist faith reinforced the very assumptions that ambitious young men recognized as crucial to improving their own socio-economic status.

Isaac Davis is a case in point. Born in 1765 to a landed southern Delaware family in "the middle circumstances of life," at an early age he adopted the "habit of Labor, and [the] constant pursuit of activity and temperance . . ." By joining the Methodists as a young adult and by taking seriously the Methodist approach to work and temperance, Davis reinforced previously adopted living and working attitudes which, ultimately, led to the presidency of the Bank of Smyrna, appointment to the Delaware Supreme Court, and considerable wealth.

Moreover, ambitious young men like Isaac Davis found that the Methodist God provided "all things needful" for this world as well as "for eternity." Looking back from old age, Davis credited much of his worldly success to God's intercessions on his behalf. Not only did Methodism attract the "middling sort" because it reinforced the work ethic, it also drew energetic young men to its ranks because it provided them with the confidence that God would be on their side.[19]

In business it was also important to have Methodists on your side. A natural inclination to favor brothers in the faith while engaging in commercial activity was strengthened by specific directives in the Methodist *Discipline*, which admonished Methodists to buy from each other and to employ other Wesleyans when practical. Because, by 1810, approximately 21 percent of the peninsula's adult population—sixteen and over—were Methodists, Wesleyans represented a very significant sector of the buying and employing public. In short, there was considerable economic pressure on craftsmen, merchants, attorneys, and physicians to find truth in the Wesleyan persuasion. At the end of the eighteenth century, a Talbot County, critic of Methodism pointed out that businessmen and professionals "are apt to join in with those amongst whom they are most likely to succeed best."[20]

Poor Whites

To be poor—that is, to be a tenant farmer, laborer, or owner of a few acres—left one particularly receptive to "true religion." Francis Asbury shared this rather quixotic view with evangelists of many faiths. The acquisition of wealth, by contrast, sometimes caused men to "forget that they are Methodists."

On a nostalgic trip through the peninsula in 1810, Asbury admitted that the houses of some of the rich were open to him, but "O God, give us the poor." Lack of worldly success characterized many Methodists, but was not limited to just the rank and file of Peninsula Methodism. At Brown's Chapel on the Sussex-Caroline border, even some of the society's principal leaders "had not been successful." But then again, "had they prospered in their pursuits, perhaps they never would have sought God."

Without extant class records, it is impossible to give a precise estimate of the number and percentage of Peninsula Methodists who were of "the better sort," the "middling sort," or the "lower sort." But there is no doubt that on the peninsula as elsewhere, poor whites made up a significant percentage of the Methodist membership. On the Eastern Shore of Virginia in 1789, a concerned Francis Asbury lamented the difficulty Methodists had in raising money. "We have the poor but they have no money, and the worldly wicked rich we do not choose to ask."[21]

Asbury urged some of the peninsula's poor whites to move west where opportunities were greater. For those poor who remained behind, however, Methodism offered a value system and life-style that was a means for escaping economic destitution. The Methodist regimen called for rising before the sun, working hard and long, and showing little patience with idle conversation, amusements, drunkenness, and other forms of self-indulgence. The type of family that needed Methodism most to set its economic house in order was similar to the one found by Asbury in Delaware in 1781, "lying in bed until sunrise, and drinking a dram after they are up."

George Morgan lived in poverty in Northwest Fork Hundred, western Sussex County. His son, William Morgan, who later moved to Lewes, realized early on that his father's weakness for alcohol "made him poor and kept him poor indeed." Determined not to follow his father's path, young Morgan decided to avoid intemperance and gambling and to work hard at learning a trade. But to avoid his father's vices and thus his father's fate, William Morgan realized that he needed the support of a local Methodist society.[22]

Sometimes, the Methodist way wasn't enough to escape poverty. Illness or accident might kill or cripple breadwinners, leaving poor white families facing economic catastrophe. In such circumstances, belonging to a Methodist class meeting could be crucial economic insurance. In the class meeting, members aired their most private thoughts, and material concerns of an urgent nature were bound to surface. In the process, material sharing became a natural extension of spiritual sharing. At times, critical economic help might come from Methodists outside the local society. In 1796, for example, a sick member of the Georgetown, Delaware, society received donations from Methodists in other societies on the circuit.

Poor whites must have also valued the egalitarian way in which Methodists addressed each other. Certainly French revolutionaries were no more democratic in their demand that all Frenchmen be addressed as "citizen" than were Methodists who cheerfully called each other "brother" and "sister." Although most lay leadership positions were filled on the peninsula by the "middling" and "better sort," this still didn't detract from the heady feeling produced when a poor farmer heard himself called "brother" by a wealthy and esteemed member of the gentry.[23]

White Women

Like other institutions of that era, Peninsula Methodism was male dominated. All clerical and lay leadership positions were reserved for men. Women weren't even allowed to vote for church trustees and were segregated from men at Methodist worship services. While there is evidence that elsewhere a few Methodist women may have been exhorters, there is no evidence of this on the peninsula. Perhaps the closest was Mary White, wife of Judge Thomas White of Sussex County, Delaware, who occasionally led class meetings, religious exercises, and probably would have preached if Asbury had been more encouraging. Paradoxically, the same white women who had so little overt power probably represented a clear majority of Delmarva's white Methodists.[24]

In the face of their second-class status, it is difficult to explain why Methodism was particularly attractive to peninsula females. Of course there is the traditional explanation that women have a greater disposition than men for piety.

Moreover, the very real threat of death in childbirth must have increased the religious sensibilities of many women.

A second explanation rests on the socio-biological argument that genetic inheritance considerably influences the human personality. The father of socio-biology, Edward O. Wilson, maintains that females are predisposed, by modest genetic differences, to be more intimately sociable than men. The one institution that could meet these female social needs was the Methodist Church. Indeed, the propensity of women to gather at their segregated entrance for a bit of socializing after Sunday service brought such complaints from impatient husbands that the trustees at Asbury Church, Wilmington, did away with segregated entrances in 1832.[25] But like the greater disposition of women for piety, this explanation is impossible to substantiate.

A third explanation rests on the expectations of peninsula families for their daughters. While sons were trained to be breadwinners, daughters were groomed to be good mothers and wives. In many peninsula houses, an education in spiritual values was considered every bit as important as learning to cook and sew. Although Nancy Mitchell of Worcester County, was from a family of some means, her father decided against the frivolous education of a boarding school and for an education at home which included instruction on how to "behave herself in the house of God." Far to the northwest in Chestertown, Anna Matilda Moore was brought up "with a strict and scrupulous regard for her spiritual and eternal interests." A case in point was the first wife of Isaac Davis of Kent County, Delaware, who had a religious education, "wanted religion," and subsequently became a Methodist.[26]

But probably the most compelling reason why Methodism attracted more peninsula women than men was that Methodism met the female need for independence, self-esteem, and power. For men, this need could be fulfilled by simply playing out traditional male roles at home or in the commercial and political arena provided by the outside community. To most peninsula women, however, only the local Methodist society offered the same opportunity.

Unlike other decisions that concerned self and family, peninsula women—as the sexual imbalance in Wesleyan societies indicates—often acted independently of their husbands in deciding to become Methodists. This independent step and the resulting deep attachment to a movement beyond the control of non-Methodist husbands must have seemed a bit threatening to some men. Perhaps it was to keep an eye on this threat that some non-Methodist husbands accompanied their wives to chapel services.

Not surprisingly, some men objected to the greater religious intensity of their wives and, on at least one occasion, these objections led to a bizarre scene. In 1802 during a service at Green's Chapel, not far from Dover, a woman cried out for mercy and her enraged husband ordered her out of the chapel. Defiantly she insisted that first she would make her peace with her Maker. Although the irate husband quickly seized his wife and physically removed her from the chapel, she continued her monologue with God even while being dragged down the aisle and out the door. Despite meeting some resistence from their menfolk, women found that attendance at religious services and, particularly, at all-female class meetings not only conjured up a sense of female solidarity, but to some it also offered a respite from their husbands' direct control.

Although the Methodist sermon was delivered by men, it praised such idealized feminine traits as patience, love, gentleness, sensitivity, humility, and submissiveness, and rejected the competitive values of the male-dominated spheres of commerce, politics, and sport. One had only to look to the behavior of Freeborn Garrettson and other itinerants in the face of brutal persecution on the peninsula during the American Revolution for a compelling demonstration of the personality traits that Methodists considered Christlike.[27] By lifting up these so-called feminine traits for praise, circuit riders affirmed female self-esteem. In doing so the itinerants must also have softened resentment over the lack of overt female power in the Methodist polity.

But women did exercise considerable covert power, particularly over the itinerants. Because circuit riders were dependent on Methodist women for their room and board, quite naturally circuit riders did what they could to please their hostesses. Since the itinerants were usually young and single, older matrons often became surrogate mothers who provided circuit riders with sympathetic understanding, advice, and encouragement to go along with a bed and meals. While serving in Dorchester County, in 1800, a young and discouraged Henry Boehm considered abandoning the itinerancy after less than a year in the saddle. Sarah Ennalls, wife of Henry Ennalls, put an end to these thoughts by reminding Boehm that his eternal salvation might depend on the course he was about to take. Two years earlier, a second circuit rider's doubts about remaining in the itinerancy were also ended by Sarah Ennalls' counsel. Even the few older itinerants relied on feminine advice and encouragement. One example was Benjamin Abbott who was substituting on the Dover circuit for his son, when he reported that Mary White, wife of Judge Thomas White, "took me by the hand, exhorting me for some time. I felt very happy under her wholesome admonitions."[28]

Certainly women, who could exercise such influence over the itinerants, were a formidable force to contend with when displeased. Not only could Methodist women show their displeasure by refusing their moral support and by closing their homes to hard-pressed itinerants, they could also cut back on their financial contributions and persuade those husbands who were Methodists to do the same. This wouldn't be the first nor the last time that the power of the purse was used to drive home a message to a basically authoritarian institution.

Blacks

Free and enslaved blacks joined with white females in presenting, on the peninsula, the same interesting paradox. Despite being segregated and being denied voting rights and leadership roles in the Methodist polity, both groups were inordinately drawn to Methodism.

For the years 1787-1820, more than a third of all peninsula Methodists were black. Moreover, a higher percentage of blacks than whites became Methodists. In 1810, for example, about 25 percent of Delmarva's adult blacks were Methodists, while the figure for whites was slightly less than 20 percent.[29]

Although treated as third-class citizens, blacks were drawn to peninsula Methodism because, with the possible exception of the Quakers and Nicholites, no other religious body treated them better. The early Methodist itinerants on the peninsula were generally vigorous opponents of slavery. At first the English-born preachers such as Asbury led the anti-slavery struggle, but shortly peninsula-born itinerants such as Joseph Everett were leading the abolitionist charge. Everett not only preached against slavery, he also refused to eat with slaveholders until they freed their slaves. In 1797, an Episcopal rector in Talbot County, observed that the Methodist preachers "relish the manumitting subject as highly as the Quaker preachers and spread the evil far and wide." In Somerset County, in 1801, a circuit rider told his congregation to assume that "the clouds of vengeance are collecting over the heads of the inhabitants of this country for their cruelty to the poor distressed Africans."[30] During the early nineteenth century, peninsula Methodism began to back away from its clear stand against slavery. The gradual erosion of

black membership after 1810 probably reflected the fact that peninsula blacks no longer viewed Methodism as a vigorous enemy of slavery.

The emotional dimension of early Methodism seemed particularly compelling to blacks. While whites, including even "the better sort," demonstrated their commitment to religious emotionalism, it was often a black outburst from the galleries or from the back of the meeting that proved a godsend to peninsula preachers unable to stir lethargic whites. Indeed, at times black religious enthusiasm made many white Methodist uncomfortable.[31]

But it would be a mistake to see black Methodism as just a highly emotional variant of white Methodism. Some of the peninsula's blacks had been born in Africa while many, if not most of the rest, remembered or heard stories of parents, grandparents, and great-grandparents who had crossed the Atlantic in the holds of slave ships. Over the years most of the culture and language of Africa was lost, but some remnants of the African heritage did survive. It is easy to see, for example, a strong residue of African behavior patterns in the happy, unrestrained actions of blacks at religious services. Perhaps foremost was the positive celebration of life that characterized blacks in worship and led them to reject the sense of guilt which seemed to pervade white Methodism.

To be more specific, the black style of joyful, demonstrative responses during religious services—which seemed so alien and therefore, so threatening to many peninsula whites had its roots in the religious practices of the African village. As Albert J. Raboteau's study of slave religion has shown, among American slaves the gods of Africa soon gave way to the God of White Christianity, but the African style of worship didn't die. Rather, it found a home in Methodism and in some of the other evangelical faiths. And so it was that peninsula Methodism, as refracted by black sensibilities, preserved in its services the cultural shards of the African past. Put another way, peninsula Methodism provided a theater in which the sons and daughters of Africa could reaffirm, through joyful, emotional participation, just who they were.[32]

The Promise of Salvation

In Talbot County, Maryland, in 1782, Freeborn Garrettson found blacks "in vassalage" but happy in the consolations of Christianity. The central consolation offered by Methodism was the promise of a better life to come. Salvation was the primary focus of itinerants' sermons on the peninsula, and the subject of greatest interest to their listeners, black or white, rich or poor.[33]

In 1773, Samuel Keene, rector of St. Luke's Parish, Queen Anne's County, summed up the Anglican position on life after death. Keene said that he and other Christians only had "the hope" that they were saved, but no certainty. But Delmarvans wanted more than just "hope." They wanted "certainty" and the Methodists not only preached "certainty," they practiced it.

Typical was the way four Methodists met death. Sarah Coulter of Lewes, Delaware, had been delivered from "the bondage of sin and its consequences, the fear of Death and Hell . . ." soon after joining the Wesleyans. On her deathbed in 1789, she "cried out with a strong and distinct voice, 'Oh death where is thy sting, o grave where is thy victory.'" In the early nineteenth century, the wife of Isaac Davis of Smyrna, Delaware, just before dying, "audibly and distinctly said 'Here I go to Heaven' and died without a struggle or a groan." In 1813 in Queen Anne's County on Spaniard's Neck, west of Centerville, planter Robert Emory was on his deathbed. The dying man was asked by his son John, a circuit rider and future bishop, "Do you see your way clear to heaven?" Robert Emory answered, "Yes, I am as sure of it as that two and two make four." A few minutes later he "tranquilly breathed his last." The confidence with which these and other Methodists faced death caused non-Methodists to stand up and take notice.

But probably no death excited the interest of the general populace as did the death and funeral of John Laws. As a young man living in the St. Johnstown area just east of Greenwood in northwestern Sussex, Laws contracted a terminal illness and was subsequently visited and converted to Methodism by Asbury. Prior to dying in 1779, Laws spoke persuasively to his family and acquaintances of his newfound faith and how it enabled him to face death with confidence. A large number who heard Laws were moved "to reform their own lives and seek the Lord." Approximately a thousand people gathered at Law's funeral and heard a sermon preached by Asbury. That same year a Methodist society, inspired by Laws' words and example, was formed in St. Johnstown.[34]

Peninsula Methodism attracted gentry and slaves, yeomen cultivators and tenant farmers, storekeepers and watermen, men and women. Part of its message appealed to the sensibilities of particular socio-economic, racial, or sexual groups. But its central message, calling for a moral revolution and promising salvation, simultaneously appealed to the needs of all classes, both races and sexes. Because of the compelling nature of its message and the lack of serious competition from other religious groups, in the late eighteenth and early nineteenth centuries Methodism on the Delmarva Peninsula had a greater and more diverse following than in any other region of the United States.

NOTES

1. William Morgan, Memoir, 20, 21, Hall of Records, Dover, Del.
2. Statistics on blacks compiled from *First Census of the United States, 1790* (Philadelphia, 1791), passim.
3. Figures used in calculating Methodist percentages came from *Minutes of the Annual Conferences of the Methodist Episcopal Church, 1773-1828,* and *Fourth Census of the U.S., 1820* (Washington, 1820). Working on the assumption that very few Methodists were fifteen or under and finding that approximately one-half of the Peninsula's population was sixteen and over in 1820, I used the latter half to compute the percentage of adult Delmarvans who were Methodists. For an estimate of church membership across the U.S. in the first half of the nineteenth century, see Edwin S. Gaustud, *The Rise of Adventism, Religion, and Society in Mid-Nineteenth Century America* (New York, 1974), xiii.
4. Morgan, Memoir, 2, 101, 102; William Duke, *Observations on the Present State of Religion in Maryland* (Baltimore, 1795), 44; John Lednum, *A History of the Rise of Methodism in America* (Philadelphia, 1859), 418; Francis Asbury, *Journal and Letters,* I, 470, 471.
5. Isaac Davis, Autobiography, 1, typed copy in possession of Mrs. James McNeal of Bethany Beach, Del. Joseph Everett, "An Account of the Most Remarkable Occurrences in the Life of Joseph Everett," *Arminian Magazine* (1790), 505. Adam Wallace, *The Parson of the Islands* (Baltimore, 1906), 69, 88, 89; Thomas Smith, *The Experience and Ministerial Labors of the Rev. Thomas Smith* (New York, 1840), 72-78; Asbury, *Journal and Letters,* I, 387.
6. Lednum, *A History of the Rise of Methodism in America,* 417; Smith, *The Experience and Ministerial Labors of the Rev. Thomas Smith,* 105; James Mitchell, *The Life and Times of Levi Scott* (New York, 1885), 32; Nathan Bangs, *The Life of the Rev. Freeborn Garrettson* (New York, 1832), 74, 218; Andrew Manship, *Thirteen Years of Experience in the Itinerancy* (Philadelphia, 1881), 157; Asbury, *Journal and Letters,* I, 303, 496; Thomas Rankin, The Diary of the Rev. Thomas Rankin, 160, typed copy, Drew University, longhand at United Library, Garrett Theological Seminary, Evanston, Il.
7. *Laws of Delaware,* II, 1218; III, 155; IV, 495; Edmund deS. Brunner and Wilbur C. Hallenbeck, *American Society: Urban and Rural Patterns* (New York, 1955), 216; William Wade, *Sixteen Miles from Anywhere: A History of Georgetown, Delaware* (Georgetown, Del., 1976), 7, 11, 12: William H. Williams, *A History of Wesley United Methodist Church, 1779-1978* (Georgetown, Del., 1978), 7, 8.
8. Rev. Henry Davis to Bishop John Claggett, Annapolis, Md., June 3, 1816, Maryland Diocesan Archives, Maryland Historical Society, Baltimore, MD; Proposals offered to the parishioners of St. Peter's Parish [Easton, Md.] May, 1788, Maryland Diocesan Archives; Smith, *The Experience and Ministerial Labors of the Rev. Thomas Smith,* 74; Asbury, *Journal and Letters,* II, 633; I, 612; St. Stephen's Parish Vestry to Bishop James Kemp, Sassafras Neck, Cecil Co., Md., Nov. 1816, Maryland Diocesan Archives. For specific examples of Methodism pushing Episcopalianism out of most of Maryland's Eastern Shore, see Rev. Henry Davis to Bishop Claggett, May 16, 1808; Rev. William Wicks to Bishop Kemp, Princess

Anne, Md., Aug. 23, 1819; and Rev. Purnell Smith to Bishop Kemp, May 27, 1820; in Maryland Diocesan Archives.

9. Ethan Allen, *Clergy in Maryland of the Protestant Episcopal Church Since the Independence of 1783* (Baltimore, 1860), 5, 6; Kirk Mariner, *Revival's Children* (Salisbury, Md.), 83; Charles A. Silliman, *The Episcopal Church in Delaware, 1785-1954* (Wilmington, Del., 1982), 22; *Minutes of the Annual Conferences of the Methodist Episcopal Church 1773-1828* 285; Asbury, *Journal and Letters*, II, 633; Duke, *Observations on the Present State of Religion in Maryland*, 18-21; Thomas Coke, *Extracts of the Journals of the Rev. Dr. Coke's Five Visits to America* (London, 1793), 18; Morgan, Memoir, 15.

10. James H. Lappen, *Presbyterians on Delmarva, The History of the New Castle Presbytery*, 26; John W. Christie, "Presbyterianism in Delaware," H. Clay Reed, ed., *Delaware, A History of the First State*, II, 652.

11. Mariner, *Revival's Children*, 12-16, 28; Blanche Sydnor White, *History of the Baptists on the Eastern Shore of Virginia 1776-1959* (Baltimore, 1959), passim; Albert Henry Newman, *A History of the Baptist Church in the United* (New York, 1915), 273; Morgan Edwards, "Materials Towards a History of Baptists in Delaware State," *Mag. of Hist. and Bio.* IX (1885), 52. For Methodist responses to the Baptist challenge see Asbury, *Journals and Letters*, I, 305, 306, 344; Asbury to Ezekiel Cooper, Bolingbroke, Talbot Co., Md., Nov. 12, 1790, Ezekiel Cooper Collection, No. 16, United Library, Garrett Theological Seminary, Evanston, Il.

12. Nicholites were followers of Joseph Nichols (1730-1770) of Kent Co., Del. Believing in approximately the same principles as the Quakers, the Nicholites were numerous in southern Kent Co., and northern Sussex Co., Del., and in Caroline Co., Md. By the end of the eighteenth century, most of the Nicholites on Delmarva had migrated to North Carolina or were absorbed into nearby Quaker Meetings. For an overview of the Nicholites see Kenneth Carroll, *Joseph Nichols and the Nicholites* (Easton, Md., 1962). For examples of Methodist concern for the Deists and Catholics see William Colbert, *A Journal of the Travels of William Colbert*, II, 88, 89, typed copy, St. George's U.M. Church, Philadelphia; Robert Ayres Journal, Jan. 9, 1786, Hist. Soc. of Western Pa., Pittsburgh, Pa.

13. Wallace, *The Parson of the Islands*, 89.

14. The value system of eighteenth century Delmarva seems to have paralleled the value system found on Virginia's Western Shore by Rhys Isaac, "Evangelical Revolt: The Nature of the Baptist Challenge to the Traditional Order in Virginia, 1765-1775," *William and Mary Quarterly*, (July 9, 1974), 345-368. The sources for the generalization concerning Delmarva's value system and the rejection of that value system are far too numerous to list here. These sources will be individually cited in a detailed treatment in my forthcoming book, "The Methodist Revolution, The Delmarva Peninsula as a Case Study, 1769-1820."

15. Landed gentry of Maryland's Eastern Shore who became Methodist included: Benton Harris of Worcester Co., Henry Airey and Henry Ennalls of Dorchester Co., General James Benson, Thomas Harrison, William Hindman, and Henry Banning of Talbot Co., Capt. William Frazier, Phillip Harrington, and Henry Downes, of Caroline Co., Col. William Hopper, William Bruff, Robert Emory, and James Bradley of Queen Anne's Co. In Delaware, Methodist converts from the gentry included: Thomas White, Philip Barratt, and Allen McLane of Kent Co., David Nutter, Rhoads Shankland, John Wiltbank, and Lemuel Davis of Sussex Co. Peninsula attorneys and physicians who became Methodists included Richard Bassett of Dover, who also owned considerable land in Cecil Co., Md., Dr. Charles Ridgely of Dover, Dr. James Anderson of Chestertown, and Dr. Sluyter Bouchell of Cecil Co. Even on Virginia's Eastern Shore, the last sector of the Peninsula reached by circuit riders, Methodist converts of the "middling and lower sorts" were proud to note that their ranks had been joined by the likes of Col. Thomas Paramore of Northampton Co. and captains Thomas Burton and William Downing of Accomack Co. All but one of the early membership records (class meeting records) of Methodist societies on the Peninsula have been lost. Nevertheless, the Methodism of the above people has been established by the use of a number of sources including *Biographical Dictionary of Maryland Legislatures, 1635-1789*, I, passim; Trustees' Minutes Bethel Methodist Church, Cecil Co., Md; Barratt's Chapel Archives, Frederica, Del., 1, 3; Asbury's *Journal and Letters*, passim; Emerson Wilson, *Forgotten Heroes of Delaware* (Cambridge, MA, 1969), 167, 254-262, 416; Colbert, *Journal*, passim; as well as numerous other primary and secondary sources. For a short list of wealthy American Methodists who lived beyond the Peninsula see Lednum, *History of the Rise of Methodism in America*, 167.

16. John B. Boles, *The Great Revival, 1787-1805* (Lexington, Kentucky, 1972), 169, 170; and Frank Baker, *An Introduction to the History of New England Methodism, 1789-1839* (Durham, 1941), 16-19 indicate the lower-class nature of early Methodism beyond the Delmarva Peninsula.

17. For a brief introduction to "old Methodism" and Asbury's use of it to fight the schismatics see Asbury, *Journal and Letters*, I, 85, 346; *Minutes of the Methodist Conferences Annually Held in America, 1773-1813* (New York, 1813), 19, 25, 26, 28; James W. May, From Revival Movement to Denomination: A Re-Examination of the Beginnings of American Methodism, (Ph.D. dissertation, Columbia University, 1962), 105-112.

18. Asbury and his preachers got along particularly well with Anglican rectors Samuel Magaw of Dover, Del., Sydenham Thorne of Milford, Del., and Hugh Neill of Queen Anne's Co., Md. Once these three Anglican clerics became aware of the nature of "old Methodism," they became very friendly and even participated in Methodist services on the Peninsula. Asbury, *Journal and Letters*, I, 300, 310, 319, 341, 342, 345, 390; III, 28. By 1783, Methodism had spread to such singular Anglican families as Barratt, Bassett, Sipple and White in Kent Co., Del; Anderson in Kent Co., Md.; Bruff and Benson in Talbot Co.; Downes and Frazier in Caroline Co.; and Airey, Ennalls and Hooper in Dorchester Co. See Lednum, *A History of the Rise of Methodism*, 166, 167, passim; Asbury, *Journal and Letters*, I, passim; Freeborn Garrettson Collection, Drew University, Madison, N.J., passim; "Memoir of Mrs. Anna Matilda Moore," *Methodist Magazine* (New York, 1828), 136-137. For the impact of conversions among the gentry on the lower orders see Smith, *Experience and Ministerial Labors of the Rev. Thomas Smith*, 97; John Wesley Andros Elliott, [Septuagenarian] Unwritten History of Eastern Shore Methodism, #5 (Circa 1885-86), xeroxed copy in the possession of the Rev. Dr. Kirk Mariner, Vienna, Va.

19. Isaac Davis, Autobiography, 3, 6, 8-12; *Smyrna Times*, April 2, 1856.

20. *Discipline of the Methodist Episcopal Church*, fifth ed. (New York, 1789), 49; Ethan Allen, St. Peter's Parish in Talbot Co., III, 36, Hall of Records, Annapolis, Md.

21. Asbury, *Journal and Letters*, I, 651, 335, 497, 612; II, 635; Boles, *The Great Revival*, 166-169.

22. Asbury, *Journal and Letters*, I, 497, 397; Morgan, Memoir, 17-19, passim.

23. William Colbert, Journal, II, 111, (typed copy at St. George's U.M. Church, Philadelphia. Original is at United Library, Garrett Theological Seminary, Evanston, Il.). The use of the prefix "brother" and "sister" is too common in the primary source materials to cite.

24. State laws for the incorporation of individual church congregations limited voting rights to free, white adult males. These state laws reflected restrictions on women already in practice. See, for example, Dudley's Chapel Minutes of Board of Trustees, 1797-1900, 5, Hall of Records, Annapolis, Md. For examples of state mandat-

ed voting restrictions in Maryland see Trustee's Minutes, 1809-1847, Zion U.M. Church, 6, 7, Cambridge, Md. See Trustees' Book, 1807, Wesley U.M. Church, Georgetown, Del., for restrictions in Delaware. For a typical example of an all female class meeting led by a male, see Smith, *Experience and Ministerial Labors of Rev. Thomas Smith*, 27. *Discipline of the Methodist Episcopal Church*, fifth ed. (New York, 1789), 31; Charles Johnson, *The Frontier Camp Meeting* (Dallas, 1955), 46; John D.C. Hannah, ed., *The Centennial of Asbury Methodist Episcopal Church* (Wilmington, 1889), 140, 151; Frank C. Baker, Jr., *An Introduction to the History of Early New England Methodism 1789-1839* (Durham, N.C., 1941), 21; Lednum, *A History of the Rise of Methodism in America*, 270. Since early membership records for individual Methodist societies on the Peninsula—with the exception of Asbury Church, Wilmington—aren't exact, it is impossible to present a statistical breakdown of male vs. female members. However, Colbert, Journal, IV, 60; Ayres, Journal, 15 and passim; Records of Asbury M.E. Church, Wilmington, V, Hall of Records, Dover, Del; and a study by Terry David Bilhartz, "Urban Religion and the Second Great Awakening: A Religious History of Baltimore, Maryland, 1790-1830," Ph.D. dissertation (George Washington Univ., 1979), 62, indicates that Methodists, on the Peninsula and on the west side of the Chesapeake, were overwhelmingly female. In the case of Asbury Church, Wilmington, women outnumbered men almost two to one.

25. Jeffrey Savor, "Edward O. Wilson, Father of a New Science," *Science Digest* (May, 1982), 86; John D.C. Hanna, ed., *The Centennial Services of Asbury Methodist Episcopal Church*, 151.

26. Morgan, Memoir, 102; "Memoir of Mrs. Anna Matilda Moore," *Methodist Magazine* (New York, 1828), 135; Davis, Autobiography, 7.

27. Smith, *The Experience and Ministerial Labors of Rev. Thomas Smith*, 99. For the behavior of Garrettson and other itinerants in the face of persecution see William H. Williams, *The Garden of American Methodism: The Delmarva Peninsula, 1769-1820* (Wilmington, Del., 1984), chap. II. For particularly interesting views on why more women than men joined churches in New England during the eighteenth and early nineteenth century see Nancy F. Cott, *The Bonds of Womanhood: "Woman's Sphere" in New England, 1780-1835* (New Haven, Conn., 1977), 126-159; and Laurel Thatcher Ulrich, *Good Wives: Image and Reality in the Lives of Women in Northern New England, 1650-1750* (New York, 1982), 215-216.

28. Boehm, *Reminiscences*, 59-60; Smith, *The Experience and Ministerial Labors of Rev. Thomas Smith*, 30, 31; Abbott, *The Experience and Gospel Labours of The Rev. Benjamin Abbott*, 109. A real opportunity for female leadership in Methodism opened up with the sectarian development of the Sunday School in the 1830s. See Mariner, *Revival's Children*, 82.

29. Figures on black and white membership are drawn from *Minutes of the Annual Conferences of the Methodist Episcopal Church, 1773-1828*, passim; and the first four U.S. census returns.

30. Frank E. Maser ed., "Discovery," *Methodist History* (Jan., 1971), 35; Asbury, *Journal and Letters*, I, 273, 274, 582; Boehm, *Reminiscences, Historical and Biographical of Sixty-four Years in the Ministry* (New York, 1865), 26, 70; Allen, St. Peter's Parish in Talbot Co., III, 35; Colbert, Journal, II, 104, 126, 216, IV, 8, 41, 48.

31. For just a few examples of "the better sort" and the emotional side of Methodism see Rachel Bruff in Garrettson Collection, Drew University; Boehm, *Reminiscences*, 151, 152; John A. Munroe, *Louis McLane* (New Brunswick, N.J., 1973), 11, 12; Nathaniel Luff, *Journal of the Life of Nathaniel Luff, M.D.* (New York, 1848), 126, 127; Kirk Mariner, *Revival's Children*, 59. For black religious enthusiasm and white reaction see Colbert, Journal, IV, 49, 56, passim, III, 129; Asbury, *Journal and Letters*, I, 274, 655; R.W. Todd, *Methodism of the Peninsula* (Philadelphia, 1886), 183-185; A. Chandler, *A History of the Churches on the Delmar Circuit* (Wilmington, Del., 1886), 10; Minutes of Board of Trustees, Asbury M.E. Church, Wilmington, Del., June 9, 1805, Barratt's Chapel, Frederica, Del.; Barratt's Chapel Record Book, 7-9, Barratt's Chapel.

32. Did African culture and, in particular, African religion survive among American slaves? This has become a subject of considerable controversy among historians. Melville J. Herskovitz in *The Myth of the Negro Past* (Boston, 1958) argued that the African heritage survived among American blacks despite the trauma of slavery. E. Franklin Frazier in *The Negro Church in America* (New York, 1964), and in other works, maintains that the African in America was almost totally stripped of his culture by American slavery. A particularly stimulating treatment of the survival of African religious traits among American slaves can be found in Eugene D. Genovese, *Roll Jordan Roll: The World the Slaves Made* (New York, 1976), 161-284. I have found the most satisfactory study of African religious remnants in White Christianity in Albert J. Raboteau, *Slave Religion: The Invisible Institution in the Antebellum South* (New York, 1978), 43-92.

33. Daniel Blake Smith, *Inside the Great House: Planter Family Life in Eighteenth Century Chesapeake Society* (Ithaca, N.Y., 1980), 265-267; George A. Phoebus, *Beams of Light on Early Methodism* (New York, 1887), 12.

34. William Watters, *A Short Account of the Christian Experience of William Watters* (Alexandria, Va.) 38; Bishop James Kemp to Rev. William Duke, Baltimore, Sept. 19, 1815, Maryland Diocesan Archives (Kemp had observed Peninsula Methodism while Episcopal rector in Dorchester Co., for nineteen years.); Asbury, *Journal and Letters*, II, 388, I, 302; Davis, Autobiography, 2, 7, 8, 10, 14; Robert Emory, *The Life of the Rev. John Emory, D.D.* (New York, 1841), 12; William Coulter to Ezekiel Cooper, Dorchester Co., Md., March 29, 1800, Ezekiel Cooper Collection, United Library, Evanston, Il., Lednum, *A History of the Rise of Methodism in America*, 229.

African Methodisms and the Rise of Black Denominationalism

Will B. Gravely
University of Denver

At least since 1921, when Carter G. Woodson published his classic survey, *History of the Negro Church*, it has been commonplace to refer to religious separatism in the free black communities of the post-Revolutionary generation as "the independent church movement."[1] A quarter-century earlier, Bishop James W. Hood of the African Methodist Episcopal, Zion Church used a similar idiom to describe the origins of northern black congregations. Discounting denominational differences among antebellum black Protestants, Hood argued that a common racial bond made for "a general, grand, united and simultaneous Negro movement." Regretting the scarcity of early sources and the absence of comprehensive histories, the bishop declared, "there was more in it than what appears on the surface," for "it was a general exodus of colored members out of white churches."[2]

Contemporary historians have reinforced the implications of Woodson and Hood by treating the earliest institutionalization of black religion in the United States, as distinct from the "invisible institution" of slave religion, in terms of an incipient black nationalism.[3] Their interpretive perspective emphasizes the natural evolution of separate churches within the expanding Afro-American community life of northern urban centers in the late eighteenth century. The social forces that account for their emergence lie in the demography of black communities, the effects of migration and economic change on their composition, the presence of intra-religious competition and social dissent within them. Pre-eminently, black religious independence arose from communal initiative and a corporate ethnic consciousness that expressed "nationalist aspirations" at a pre-theoretical but practical, institutional level.[4] Simply put, black churches, as the first public institutions which black people controlled, provided the original context for what E. Franklin Frazier called "a nation within a nation" — the institutional equivalent to W. E. B. DuBois' insight about the dialectic of double-consciousness in black American experience and identity.[5]

Much of the proto-national orientation of the earliest black churches, to return to Bishop Hood's analogy, existed beneath the surface. Obviously, separate black churches served the needs of the black communities in which they resided. Insofar as these communities formed a separate culture, an implied "black nationality" was present from the beginning. By the 1830's, with a black press, an annual convention system and numerous voluntary associations alongside the churches, such an argument has strong force. But there were interlocking relationships between free African benevolent societies in Boston, Providence, Newport, New York, and Philadelphia as far back as the 1780's, with a coordinated effort to sponsor emigration.[6] Within the independent church movement, however, local developments with differing connections to biracial denominational structures were primary for a generation. Not until the appearance of separate black denominations with itinerating ministers was there a coordinated effort to create networks across and between black communities. Denominationalism, however, brought not only connections to other congregations elsewhere. It also meant schism and competition within black communities.

The nearest equivalent of a corporate linkage between the first separated congregations appears in Daniel Coker's pamphlet against slavery, published in 1810. In his appendix, the black Methodist preacher and schoolmaster used the early Christian images of "chosen generation," "royal priesthood," "holy nation" and "peculiar people" to demonstrate "what God [was] doing for Ethiopia's sons in the United States of America." His evidence was the African church movement, contained in a compilation of four lists, naming thirteen ordained black clergy (excluding himself), another eleven licensed Methodist local preachers, eight "descendants of the African race, who [had] given proofs of their talents" in public, and fifteen separated congregations. The churches represented four denominational traditions, all biracial at this date, and ten cities, including Charleston, South Carolina's ill-fated African Methodist congregation to which Denmark Vesey would belong. But Coker saw them all as "African churches," whose common characteristic lay in their nearly simultaneous emergence in less than two decades.[7]

Over the next twelve years following the appearance of Coker's booklet, a new institutional structure, black denominationalism, evolved within the African church movement. In that development, Coker was himself instrumental, becoming a separatist leader among black Methodists in Baltimore and merging his followers with other dissidents in the region, centering in Philadelphia, to form in 1816 the second of three African Methodist denominations. Three years earlier, in 1813, black Methodists in Wilmington, Delaware made the first denominational break with the Methodist Episcopal Church to create the African Union Church. In 1822, a third African Methodist denomination arose in New York City, culminating more than two decades of separate congregational existence of the Zion church.

This paper, as a retelling of a familiar history, has been motivated by three concerns. First, the renaissance of black history over the past two decades has surfaced new or forgotten sources which flesh out the basic story and make possible comparative analysis across denominational and community boundaries. Methodist developments in Philadelphia, Baltimore, Wilmington, and New York can be seen in a larger context of the independent church movement.[8]

Secondly, this study concentrates on the expansion, in the independent church movement, from congregational autonomy within patterns of interdependence with biracial denominational judicatories, to denominational autonomy. Since the three African Methodist denominations pioneered in this process, my question has been to ask how and why they took religious separatism to its fullest conclusion. In this way an assessment can begin of the implications of denominationalism within American church history generally.[9]

Finally, there are several pragmatic issues which white and black Methodists contested in the evolution of congregational autonomy and in the shift to Afro-American denominationalism. I draw particular attention to five factors indigenous to the organizational life of Christian churches: access to ordination, representation in denominational governance, consultation about pastoral appointments and services, the ownership and use of church property, and participation in congregational discipline. These same factors are present in Baptist, Presbyterian, and Protestant Episcopal settings where, as with Methodists, the maintenance of white control and the refusal to share power with black members triggered the rise of independent congregations. Black churchfolk refused to contain or segregate the sacred power which they experienced in Christian faith from these more mundane forms of power. They wanted to elect and to be elected to office, to ordain and be ordained, to discipline as well as be disciplined, to preach, exhort, pray, and administer sacraments — in sum, to have their gifts and graces acknowledged by the whole community. Where that acknowledgement was withheld, black Christians resisted and protested, organized and created new institutional alternatives for themselves.

I

"Our only design is to secure to our selves our rights and privileges, to regulate our affairs, temporal and spiritual, the same as if we were white people."—Richard Allen and the trustees of Bethel Church to the Philadelphia Conference of the Methodist Episcopal Church, April 8, 1807[10]

When Bishop Francis Asbury preached the dedicatory sermon on June 29, 1794, the first African Methodist church building, named Bethel, was available for black Methodists in Philadelphia.[11] That event ended eight years of struggle for Richard Allen, ex-slave and a local preacher in the Methodist society who formed a class of forty-two black members in 1786 and first proposed that a separate "place of worship" be erected "for the colored people." He was met with opposition both from the Methodist elder that year, Caleb Boyer, and by "the most respectable people of color in this city."[12] In November, 1787, Allen convened black members of "the Methodist Society of Philadelphia" to consider "the evils under which they laboured, arising from the unkind treatment of their white brethren." The meeting, apparently, followed the incident, told without date in Allen's autobiography, at St. George's church when white trustees pulled black worshippers from their knees during prayer.[13]

Between 1788 and 1791 Allen endured the threats of Richard Whatcoat and Lemuel Green, elders in Philadelphia, who tried, he recalled later, to "prevent us from going on" with an "African church" project.[14] During the same period he was censured and finally excluded from the Free African Society, which organization he helped found in April, 1787. As they banished Allen in June, 1789, his colleagues charged him with "attempting to sow division among us" and with "rashly calling or convening the members together." He had, according to his own account, continued to support the ideas of an African church, even though the Free African association took upon itself in 1791 the major responsibility to construct a building and work out "a plan of church government." When that plan turned out to be Protestant Episcopal in polity, due to Dr. Benjamin Rush's influence, Allen cooperated with the project but refused an invitation to be the church's first pastor. Intent on remaining Methodist, despite the difficulties he had experienced in the denomination, Allen, with a committee of ten others, turned to the community for subscriptions to his Bethel church. The campaign began in the spring of 1794, after the St. Thomas African Episcopal Church was under way. By summer a remodelled blacksmith shop frame had become a suitable building.[15]

If the dedication of the first Bethel building in June, 1794, closed one struggle for Richard Allen, his model for the congregation and its relationship with the Methodist Episcopal denomination insured that further difficulties awaited him. Officially, Allen was unordained but licensed as a local preacher with responsibilities under white elders assigned to St. George's church. His initiative had solved the first problem confronting black Methodists whose memories were still fresh of "many inconveniences" that resulted "from white people and people of color mixing together in public assemblys." Issuing a "public statement" in November, 1794, Allen and the Bethel trustees justified their need for "a convenient house to assemble in separate from our white brethren."

The Bethel proclamation contained ten articles and regulations that confirmed the intent to abide by "the Methodist Episcopal Church for our Church government and discipline and with her creeds and articles for our faith." Since the black congregation held the deed for the church property, however, a disclaimer was necessary to protect the "right and proprietory of our house" from denominational ownership. Moreover, the document asserted the goal of the Bethel founders to push for ordination of black "persons endowed with gifts and graces to speak for God." It also declared the "right" of the majority of voting (males in close communion) members of the congregation "to call any brother that appears to us adequate to the task to preach or exhort as a local preacher, without the interference of the Conference or any other person or persons whatsoever." Beyond that, the statement defined provisions for elections, limited membership to "descendants of the African race" while retaining "mutual fellowship" with "white brethren" as visitors "in Bands, classes

and Love Feasts," empowered trustees with "temporal concerns," and retained "matters of a spiritual nature concerning discipline" as "now in use in the Church."[16]

The "public statement" was an assertion of black religious independence, not a negotiated agreement with the Methodist Episcopal denomination. The posture of Allen and the Bethel trustees, who insisted on remaining Methodist while holding property for blacks to use and while refusing to go any more to St. George's church, must have been enigmatic to many whites. Allen was publicly committed to the denomination, had its bishop behind him, and opened the building to sympathetic white ministers in the Methodist conference. Yet he did not turn over the property to the denominational officials, and his congregation claimed an autonomy disallowable under Methodist standards. It was not surprising, therefore, in 1795 that "our warfare and troubles," Allen remembered later, "now began afresh." That year John McClaskey, whom Allen had faced down in 1792 over the fund-raising project for the first African church, returned to the St. George's appointment. Determined to respond vigorously to Bethel's autonomy, McClaskey found that it was necessary to turn to Ezekiel Cooper, on leave from the itinerant ministry and trustworthy to blacks because of a strong antislavery commitment, and request him to negotiate a compromise.[17]

It encompassed a charter of incorporation, dated September 12, 1796 and entitled "Articles of Association of the African Methodist Episcopal Church" in Philadelphia. The articles required loyalty to the denomination, but placed the Bethel property under a board of black trustees "for the religious use of the ministers and preachers of the Methodist Episcopal Church" and "likewise for our African brethren." They retained the stipulation from the "public statement" that members would always be "coloured persons." A similar provision protected defendants in cases of congregational discipline, allowing appeal beyond the white elder to a jury from Bethel church. At the same time, the black congregation conceded the right of the white elder to license and assign local preachers and to officiate sacramentally. It added, however, the qualification, "for the time being," after the recognition of the elder's authority over "spiritual concerns." Reiterating the forceful assertion of 1794, the leaders of Bethel anticipated a time when white supervision would end, when "coloured brethren shall graduate into holy orders," as the articles expressed it. Such expectations were established on reasonable grounds of comparison with another denomination since Absalom Jones, former Methodist and leader in the Free African Society, had already been consecrated deacon in the Protestant Episcopal ministry.[18]

Three years after the incorporation, the articles were made public and Bishop Asbury ordained Allen the first black deacon in the Methodist Episcopal Church. A few months later, the General Conference of 1800 approved Asbury's innovation and provided for other such ordinations, but there were still difficulties to be faced. The legislation was left out of the *Discipline*, thus making the office of black local deacon an anomaly in the Methodist system.[19] As it stood, Allen was not a member of the annual conference of travelling ministers, but remained under the supervision of the elder for Philadelphia. The unprecedented local nature of the office prevented him from celebrating the Lord's Supper or officiating otherwise at baptisms and weddings outside the appointment, or when the elder was available.[20]

The curb on Allen's ministerial authority did not hamper the growth of the Bethel congregation. Moreover, Allen's varied business activities kept him active beyond his pastoral duties. Black membership at Bethel, and at another black mission established in 1794 called Zoar, grew spectacularly, from 211 in 1799 to 738 in 1805.[21] In 1801, Allen published a hymnal for use in the church.[22] He maintained good relations with several of the white Methodist clergy who came to the city and who often stayed with him and Sarah Allen when they officiated at Bethel.[23]

The accommodation of 1796, however, only worked when the white elder in Philadelphia conceded a large measure of autonomy to Allen and the black trustees — an autonomy assumed in the public statement of 1794 and effectively guarded in the Articles of Agreement. When the Virginian, James Smith, came to St. George's in 1805, old controversies flared up over congregational discipline and the limits and powers of the white elder. After Smith threatened to lay claim to the Bethel property in behalf of the denomination, Allen was forced to admit how vulnerable the trustees were, depending on how the Articles were construed. Consulting a lawyer, he found a way to secure Bethel's interest. As a civil corporation, the congregation amended its charter by two-thirds vote of the members. The state supreme court approved such a document — "The African Supplement" — on March 16, 1807.[24]

The new legal measure addressed the perennial irritants — the ownership and use of property,

the powers of the trustees, and the absence of ordained black elders to function in the congregational life of Bethel church. In place of "the consent of the elder," its first article substituted a two-thirds ratification by the adult male members of "one year's standing" on all property transactions by the trustees. Three other major changes aimed at the power of the elder completed the revisions. The trustees could appoint "any other person, duly qualified" according to the Methodist *Discipline* to "preach and exhort" whenever the elder did preach, as was his right, "once every Sunday, and once during the course of the week." The alteration made the right into a demand and moved the power of determination fully into the hands of the trustees. Amendments also empowered the black local preachers at Bethel to hold quarterly meetings, love feasts, and trials of "disorderly members," when the elder neglected or refused to do so. Disciplinary cases where former members of Bethel who had been expelled had "been received as members of the Methodist Episcopal Church elsewhere" made another change imperative. Having vested the trustees with the right to open buildings to meetings, the Supplement backed them in maintaining excommunication by barring any who had been dismissed from Bethel church.[25]

The Supplement extended the autonomous authority of the Bethel congregation and challenged, again, the usual requirements of Methodist structure. It would not have been necessary, of course, had Allen or other black deacons been advanced to elder's orders or become members of the annual conference. As it was, the Philadelphia conference accepted Allen's notification, signed as "Pastor," that the Supplement had been legally obtained denying independence or separation as a goal, the statement, nonetheless, reasserted black autonomy. "Our only design," it read, "is to secure to our selves our rights and privileges, to regulate our affairs, temporal and spiritual, the same as if we were white people." On behalf of the conference, Bishop Asbury accepted the memorial, expressing confidence "that our African brethren" remained "Methodists according to our Discipline." The carefully worded response did not approve the Supplement, but received it insofar as it was "not contrary to the allowed usages, customs, and privileges of the Methodist Episcopal Church."[26] The two contradictory positions were fated to come face to face before some third party. Meanwhile, Allen had weathered another challenge to an African Methodism, while he remained, however tenuously, within the denominational structure.

The Supplement did not end Bethel's problems, but it did insure the congregation's ultimate protection and pave the way to denominational separation. Its passage went relatively unnoticed for four years, but in 1811 the Methodist conference went on the offensive. First, the trustees at St. George's church claimed that the Supplement was void because they had not approved it. The contention accompanied a move to reconnect Bethel to the appointment at St. George's. Secondly, the elder, Stephen G. Roszel, sought unsuccessfully to have the Bethel membership repeal the Supplement by the same means that it had been obtained in the first place. Neither tactic succeeded. In 1812, Bethel was made a stationed church and placed, with two other congregations, under Thomas G. Sergeant. When that plan was discontinued the next year, the old question, rooted in the refusal of Methodists to sanction black elders, emerged again. The Bethel congregation appealed to Bishop Asbury for assistance, but he refused to intervene.[27]

As an effort to curb Bethel's independence financially, a controversy smoldered during the next two years over the fee structure for sacramental services. When Bethel came under St. George's church, its elder and the black trustees disagreed over money. From his point of view, the black congregation ought to contribute funds to support the larger ministry of which it was a part. The issue was not fees charged for services performed, except in cases of conducting marriages.[28] From the point of view of Allen and the Bethel trustees, the one remaining limitation to autonomy was access to elder's orders and the sacramental authority it conferred. Until that could be had, they would pay for the necessary services. Their resistive position was calculated to force the denomination to become inclusive in its clerical orders or face continued aggravation from its black members.[29]

By this time blacks numbered more than 1300, or about two-fifths of the Methodist membership in Philadelphia. By far one of the largest congregations in the denomination, Bethel's success was viewed ambivalently by white officials. Moreover, within the denomination, significant changes had accompanied its rapid growth. Consistently from 1800, it backed away from its original antislavery standards for church membership and ordination. Had Allen been ordained elder, he would have had slaveowning ministerial colleagues in conferences on the border and in the South. Accommodation to proslavery sentiment was so necessary that Bishop Asbury and the General Conferences of 1804 and 1808 approved expurgated versions of the *Discipline* with the chapter on slavery omitted. Following the abortive effort to petition state legislatures in behalf of emancipation in 1800, the denomination withdrew from taking any official position on the social and political question of human bondage.[30] While these developments occurred without Allen's participation or direct comment, he could hardly have failed to notice them.

As a further complication, there may have been a breach between Allen and Bishop Asbury. Although he had sponsored the black diaconate and had earlier been a staunch opponent of slavery, Asbury had finally compromised about emancipation. His journal, in 1809, reflected the denomination's concessions, fatefully conceding that saving the souls of the Africans was more important than freeing their bodies. There is no direct evidence of an overt break with Allen, only Lorenzo Dow's retrospective suggestion, but Asbury made no mention of the black leader or Bethel church in his journal or letters during the last five years of his life. And, after ordaining eight additional black local deacons for New York and Philadelphia between 1806 and 1809, Asbury ceased the procedure.[31]

Two events in the summer of 1814 set in motion the actions that led in the next year and a half to a final break between Allen's Bethel congregation and Asbury's denomination. On July 7, the pastor of the Academy church in Philadelphia and future bishop, John Emory, issued a public letter disowning the Bethel membership as Methodist because the black trustees were exercising the spiritual discipline as outlined in the African Supplement. Later the same month, a legal challenge to their authority forced a showdown. In 1812, Robert Green was excommunicated by a disciplinary committee of ten officials at Bethel church for breach of rules. As a trustee himself, Green complained to the white elder, and then took the case to the state supreme court. His suit was argued on July 30, 1814. The following January, the judges overturned the church's action on procedural defects in the "manner this Committee was selected or appointed" for the disciplinary trial of Green.[32]

A few weeks later, just before the Philadelphia conference met in the spring, Robert R. Roberts, pastor at St. George's church, tested whether the court's action had discredited Allen's leadership or the power of the trustees. He announced his intention to preach at Bethel, as was his right by the original Articles of Agreement, but the trustees, not to be outdone, stood on the authority of the Supplement that it was their prerogative to choose preachers. When Roberts arrived, he found Jacob Tapisco in the pulpit. Rebuffed, he left the building, but further strife was predictable.[33] In a new effort to thwart Bethel's autonomy, the annual conference tried again to include the black church in the regular appointments. The new elder at St. George's, an Irishman named Robert Burch, would add Bethel to his pastorate for 1815.[34]

Green's lawsuit forced another challenge to the Supplement — the issue of local control of property. His victory forced a sheriff's sale of the land and building on June 12, 1815, at which Allen, as highest bidder, successfully retained possession.[35] But the tug-of-war was still not over. In December, Burch, following the example of Roberts, sought to preach at Bethel, using Green, the dissaffected trustee, as his host. On this occasion, the congregation blocked the aisles at the New Year's Eve service, preventing Burch from going to the front. That collective symbolic gesture brought the developments of nearly thirty years to full circle. In the early years of incipient black independence, white trustees and black members clashed in St. George's church. Now the shoe was on the other foot, when Bethel trustees and congregation physically prevented the St. George's minister from officiating in their building.[36]

Immediately, Burch petitioned the state supreme court for access to the pulpit as his legal right, but the judges refused to grant his claim. Instead, Bethel church, standing on the legality of the African Supplement, gained its independent status. Four months after the announcement of the court's decision, it joined representations from Baltimore, Salem (New Jersey), and Attleborough (Pennsylvania) to form the African Methodist Episcopal denomination. After waiting seventeen years, Allen was ordained elder, and made, after Daniel Coker became ineligible, the bishop of the new organization, serving in that capacity until his death in 1831.[37]

II

"Gone with Coker," the designation used in the membership records for the black Methodist societies of Baltimore to indicate those who had withdrawn to form Bethel church and join the African Methodist Episcopal denomination.

The beginning of an independent African Methodist church in Baltimore is difficult to substantiate with primary evidence, limited as are the early sources in specifying the stages that led to a final break for more than two hundred members, exhorters, and local preachers in the

black classes in 1815. Secondary sources, in the form of autobiographical recollections and undocumented histories, refer back to the roots of a separatist movement in 1787, the second year that the annual minutes of the Methodist Episcopal Church recorded membership by race. The tradition recounts black objections to seating arrangements in the gallery of the Light Street church, leading to separate classes and prayer meetings in houses and businesses like Caleb Hyland's boot-blacking cellar.[38] The degree of racial separation over the next decade, besides dividing black members into their own classes, which was apparent as early as 1786, is impossible to establish. Black Methodist membership in the city did grow from 111 in that year to 269 in 1788. The numbers seven years later were not substantially higher, with 282 members in the societies of the city and a separate circuit.[39]

In 1795, there was sufficient interest in forming "a distinct African, yet Methodist Church" that negotiations began with white officials like Bishop Asbury. No documents, like the Articles of Association used in Philadelphia and in revised form in New York, survive, but Asbury made clear that the same assertive posture that characterized the Bethel movement under Allen reappeared in Baltimore. In October, 1795, the proposals which had come to him asked that "in temporals" the African Methodists would be "under their own direction." Taken by surprise at the full implications of the plan, Asbury regarded the blacks as asking "greater privileges than the white stewards and trustees ever had a right to claim."[40] Twenty months later, he was still "trying to organize the African church," but by that time the project to obtain a building had already advanced.[41]

It is not clear whether Asbury's reference in 1797 was to a building which the African Academy first leased for black education by the American Convention for Promoting the Abolition of Slavery, or a short-lived effort to establish a second African church on Fish Street in rented quarters.[42] The Academy building, which became by deed in 1802 the Sharp Street church, was the single African meetinghouse listed in Baltimore's city directory that year and on a map in 1804.[43]

During the decade from 1801-1811, there were black trustees holding and selling land and obtaining title to the Academy building in behalf of the African Methodist Episcopal classes in Baltimore. A Bethel congregation, which traced its origins to the abortive Fish Street organization in 1797, may have continued to meet separately from other black Methodists in the Academy, since Daniel Coker's pamphlet of 1810 refers to two African Methodist churches in the city. If that were the case, however, there was still a common identity between all the black Methodist classes of Baltimore until 1815. By 1812, a separate Asbury African church was an additional meeting place for these classes, but it was not until there was a formal break, led by Coker, that the buildings can be said to have spawned identifiable congregations. The Sharp Street and Asbury congregations after 1815 remained loyal to the Methodist Episcopal Church, thus inheriting the property rights of the original African church of Baltimore even though they did not incorporate until 1832. The separatists, on the other hand, were forced to find new quarters, as Coker first rented a former Presbyterian building and then purchased the Fish Street property originally used in 1797.[44]

The date is not clear when white Methodists in Baltimore licensed the first black local preachers and exhorters, but in 1810 Coker, whom Asbury had ordained a local deacon in 1808, listed seven men in those roles. That pattern of leadership, to which black class leaders should be added, remained normative until the secession of 1815. Black classes met in locations over the city, worshipped in two African churches and depended on white elders for sacramental function and final disciplinary authority. There was a modicum of black independence in the system, for black trustees owned and controlled property, Coker was a local deacon, black local preachers gave congregational leadership, and black exhorters and class leaders functioned in customary fashion. The city's black population responded to the religious energies of the African Methodists, producing significant numerical growth from 637 in 1808 to 973 in 1813.[45] By March, 1814, the totals were indeed impressive: forty-one classes with 1552 members, eight black local preachers and ten black exhorters.[46]

Seeds of dissension were also present, however, as a negotiated agreement between the white elder and "the African Church in Baltimore" in 1814 recognized. The document, designed "to preserve the peace and union" of the black classes with the denomination, spelled out the pastoral expectations of the white elder. The black membership unquestionably felt slighted, so that it had to request that special attention be given to the visitation of the sick, the baptism of children, a regular pastoral conference with the classes at least quarterly, and the performance of funeral services, with sermons "if the deceased have been an aged upright official member, who died tryumphant [sic] in the Lord." In exchange,

"the African Society" agreed "to bear their part of the expense of the preacher."[47]

The agreement of 1814, as viewed by the more recent members and by the younger leaders, did not settle the real needs for black independence.[48] With Coker at the center, a group of dissidents met weekly, according to David Smith who belonged in the circle, preparing for full separation. By this time, developments in Philadelphia were well known to the Baltimore organizers, and Coker was coordinating his plans with Richard Allen. The "club," as Smith termed the group, agreed to make the break late in 1815, a few weeks prior to the final round of controversy in Philadelphia. More than two hundred members of the black classes kept to the agreement, leaving Methodist Episcopal authorities to strike their names from the rolls with the comment, "gone with Coker."[49] Over the next four years, the new Bethel congregation worked out problems of incorporation and obtained new property. In 1818, when the first session of the Baltimore annual conference of the new African Methodist Episcopal denomination convened, the number at Bethel church had jumped to 1096, and nine former local preachers and exhorters were ordained by Bishop Allen.[50]

The connection between Allen and Coker, the Philadelphia and the Baltimore movements for independence, was forcefully dramatized on January 23, 1816, when the Maryland African Methodists celebrated the Pennsylvania court decision which freed Bethel church. Preaching to a jubilant audience, Coker claimed that the court had vindicated religious liberty in the United States. The biblical archetype for the victory was the Jewish story of freedom from exile where the chosen people "were held against their will." Black Methodists had experienced ecclesiastical caste like the Jews had known Babylonian captivity. "Those Jews . . . had not equal privileges with the Babylonians," Coker asserted, "although they were governed by the same laws, and suffered the same penalties." The legal decision cleared the way for African Methodists to embrace "the opportunity that is now offered us of being free," as Coker put it in biblical idiom, "to sit down under our own vine to worship, and none shall make us afraid."[51]

If freedom was the major motif of Coker's sermon, his title insisted that the black seceders had "withdrawn from under the charge of Methodist Bishops and Conference, (BUT ARE STILL METHODISTS)." The convention of April, 1816, and the subsequent Discipline of the new denomination which appeared in 1817 proved as much. Virtually all features of Methodist Episcopal doctrine and polity were carried over to the new church, which added, appropriately, a strong condemnation of slavery to its standards. With ordination in the hands of the independent denomination and with black churchmen representing their own congregations, the last obstacles to equal power and full autonomy had been overcome.[52]

III

"Then that body of us who built the meeting house, could not see our way clear to give up all say." Peter Spencer and William Anderson describe the African independent church movement in Wilmington.[53]

An observer at the organizing convention of the Bethel Methodist connection, Peter Spencer of Wilmington had, with William Anderson, anticipated by three years the result of the movements for independence and denominational separation in Philadelphia and Baltimore. Failing to join with Allen, the African Union Church subsequently remained the smallest of the three black Methodist denominations, with a regional base in Delaware and Pennsylvania. Its route to independence, abbreviated to less than a decade, moved through two stages toward congregational, then denominational autonomy.

There were black members of the Asbury Methodist Episcopal Church in Wilmington from its founding in 1789, when nineteen of the original sixty-two persons in the church were classed as "colored." Between 1800 and 1802, these numbers climbed dramatically increasing two and a half times to reach 117, or eight less than the white total for the latter year. Even though black classes met separately, white officials began to complain of overcrowding and of damages to the main floor of the building. Hence, in June, 1805, they acted to force all black classes to meet in the gallery. The resolution instructed black class leaders to "govern themselves accordingly."[54]

Prior to these demands, there was already some interest, dating back to January, in building an "African Church."[55] An appeal for assistance to the general public became the more necessary when, in late June, Spencer and Anderson rebelled against the command of the trustees and led forty-one other secessionists from Asbury church. They met in private homes until the African Chapel, or Ezion Methodist Episcopal Church (named for the port of Ezion-geber where King Solomon kept a fleet of ships, I Kings 9.26), was dedicated.[56]

From the beginning, difficulties paralleling the conflicts in Philadelphia and Baltimore threatened the harmony of the black congregation. It had no local ordained deacons and was, thus, even more dependent on the white Methodist elder for pastoral attention. The founders of Ezion believed they could "refuse any that were not thought proper to preach," but they ran into stiff opposition in 1812 from white elder, James Bateman. When the charter members of Ezion resisted him that winter, Bateman summarily "turned out all the Trustees and class-leaders." The two sides ended in court, but Spencer's protesters lost the case. A minority of black members, siding with the white elder, retained the church property for t he denomination, while the remainder followed Spencer in a second schism within eight years in Wilmington Methodism.[57]

The separatists moved rapidly. Forming a board of seven trustees (four of whom were listed as "labourers" and two as blacksmiths in the city directory), they purchased a lot in July, 1813, and opened their building by fall. Incorporating under the Delaware law of 1787 which *authorized* religious bodies, the African Union Church drew up "articles of association" for itself, dated September 18, 1813. Forty charter members, six of whom were women, signed the document.[58]

By the end of the first year, the Wilmington church had linked up with a congregation in Pennsylvania and another in New York to begin denominational connections. In 1815 new churches began in Christiana and New Castle, Delaware. Following the death of "Father" Spencer in 1843, the church suffered fragmentation, but it survived to lay claim to the first black denominational break with the Methodist Episcopal Church.[59]

The African Union movement represented the sharpest fracture with the biracial denomination from which it withdrew. In contrast with both other African Methodist communions, the Unionists simplified their polity. They elected five laymen as ruling elders in each congregation, where power was vested for licensing local preachers and ordaining ministers. Rejecting both the presiding eldership and the episcopacy, the African Union church retained ordination of deacons, who could preach and baptize but not celebrate the Lord's Supper or administer church discipline, and of elder ministers who had full authority in these matters.[60]

The struggle for independence in Wilmington was essentially a lay movement, since neither Spencer nor Anderson were ordained clergy. It emphasized local autonomy more than connectionalism. By providing a skeletal structure as a small denomination, however, the African

Union church made it possible for other congregations to organize, to own their own property, and to participate in every level of church government in a congregational or "associated" polity. Insuring black control of local churches, the Unionists gained what had been prohibited them in the Methodist Episcopal Church.[61]

IV

"So long as we remain in that situation our Preachers would never be able to enjoy these privileges which the Discipline of the white Church holds out to all its Members that are called to preach, in consequence of the limited access our brethren had to those privileges, and particularly in consequence of the difference of color." Abraham Thompson, James Varick and William Miller state the source of the separation of Zion Methodism in their "Founder's Address" of 1820.[62]

A third black Methodist denomination began in an independent congregation which was originally part of the John Street church of New York city. Six black classes under white leaders existed as early as 1793, when there were 143 members.[63] In August, 1796, some of that number conferred with Bishop Asbury to request permission to meet separately with their own class leaders. In October, that group rented a house on Cross Street, where they gathered during the next four years for prayer meetings and preaching services. Three of their number, James Varick, Abraham Thompson, and June Scott were licensed by the John Street quarterly conference, which still maintained formal authority over the black society in behalf of the denomination.[64]

In 1799, the Zion society, as it was called, selected trustees and announced a "subscription" before the public to erect "an African church in the city." By July of the next year, the cornerstone was laid at a site on Leonard and Church streets. In September the structure was dedicated. During the next six months the trustees obtained a charter for the church and worked out, as instructed by the General Conference of 1800 to which they had appealed, "Articles of Agreement" with the denomination. Appropriately, John McClaskey, fresh from participating in the same process in Philadelphia, was pastor of the John Street church who acted as formal agent for the New York conference.[65]

There were two significant differences between what had been negotiated in Philadelphia and what transpired with the trustees of Zion church, led by Peter Williams, Sr. The document signed in 1801 in New York formed a board of black trustees, but limited their function to maintaining property for the denomination. In contrast to Philadelphia, these trustees had no authority in matters of church discipline. That restriction kept the Zion society more dependent on the denomination than the Bethel church was. Secondly, the agreement in New York defined the process by which local preachers could be granted ordination as local black deacons. Such authorization both promised a new level of inclusion and simultaneously restricted ordination to the ambiguous legislation of 1800 Any further advancement to elder's orders would require new general conference legislation, a procedure limited to the quadrennial sessions of that body.[66]

Over the next two decades, the Zion church avoided some of the bitter controversy with denominational officials which had erupted in Philadelphia, but it faced internal dissension over matters which remained unsettled in the Articles of Agreement. First, blacks had to wait five years before the first three of their local preachers were ordained local deacons by Asbury. In 1808 William Miller and Daniel Coker joined Varick, Thompson, and Scott, who had been made deacons in 1806, in that rank. Without a plan for rotating black preachers who did not belong to the conference's itinerant ministry, there was inevitable competition among five ordained deacons in one congregation. By 1810, Coker move to Baltimore. In 1812 Thompson and Scott joined the African Free Methodist Society, led by a former Quaker, John Edwards, but it soon disbanded. Thompson kept his standing in Zion church by returning apologetically, but Scott left for good. Two years later, in February, 1814, Miller founded, with Thomas Sipkins (a former trustee of Zion), a new black Methodist church named African Asbury. By the process of elimination, Varick became the central leader of Zion church, with Thompson as his assistant.[67]

Beginning in 1808, Zion church had become a community center for free blacks in New York City. It hosted five of the next six annual New Year's Day celebrations of the end of the African slave trade. The occasion was marked by parades which featured the city's black benevolent associations and by religious services with choral music and orations. The black preachers connected to Zion congregation figured prominently in the festivities. For 1810, William Miller was the orator, for example, while James Varick was the evening preacher for the first commemoration in 1808. George White, a local preacher, prayed in the ceremonies of 1810, as did Miller and Varick the next year. Abraham Thompson was the preacher on January 1, 1811.[68]

Proclaiming their public convictions about the evil of slavery and celebrating their own freedom, these Zion churchmen provoked the taunts and vandalism of white mobs, but their response was not passive acceptance. Rather they complained formally to the Common Council of New York on at least four occasions between 1807 and 1817, charging that the watchmen of the city were neglecting their duties. They asserted their rights to protection of church property and of religious assembly without interruption.[69]

The perennial goal of the Zionite movement, as it had been for the Bethel congregation in Philadelphia, was access to the regular ministry and conference membership for black preachers. For the entire period of its autonomous existence, from 1796 through 1822, the Zion church had white elders as senior pastors who rotated preaching and pastoral assignments throughout the city. Local black deacons, from 1806, and licensed preachers served under white direction. At the time the congregation began a new building to meet the demands of increased membership in 1818, that practice became a liability, especially after Richard Allen's denomination came to town to form new churches for this connection.[70]

Over the next four years, Zion's leaders petitioned and negotiated, waited and planned, all the while hoping to find a way to remain within or attached to the Methodist Episcopal Church. That possibility required what the General Conference since 1800 and the episcopal leaders of the denomination persistently refused to do—ordain blacks as elders and accept both deacons and elders into conference membership, or, create an "African conference" as part of the connection.

After deciding not to join the Bethel movement, the Zion congregation began to move on its own in the summer of 1820. With the backing of the white elder, William Stillwell, who was leaving the Methodist Episcopal ministry over differences of polity, the members printed a *Discipline* for themselves. In November, Varick and Thompson served their first communion on their own.[71] Meanwhile, they kept pressing for a way to obtain full ordination. Twenty-one months later, after being refused by three Methodist bishops, two annual conferences, and the Protestant Episcopal bishop of New York, the two deacons, with Leven Smith, were consecrated elder by three sympathetic white elders from the parent denomination.[72] A month afterward, Varick became the first superintendent of the

Zion denomination, which quickly attracted congregations on Long Island, New Haven, and Philadelphia.[73]

Some adherents to the new movement still hoped that sympathetic white Methodists would be able to convince the General Conference of 1824 to set up "an annual conference for our coloured preachers." That conference dashed those expectations, and continued the exclusive precedent until the Washington and Delaware colored conferences were formed in 1864.[74] Left to go its own way, the African Methodist Episcopal, Zion denomination, which rarely used the appendage "Zion" for much of the antebellum period, completed the institutionalization of racial separation by denomination among Methodists until these were renewed during the era of Reconstruction.[75]

V

"Your committee feel well satisfied from good authority, that it is not yet time to set off an annual conference, for our coloured preachers; and that such an act, would not at this time, be useful to them, or us; but dangerous to thiers [sic], and our common good." Report of the Committee to whom was referred the affairs of the people of colour, Methodist Episcopal General Conference, 1824.[76]

Though there were differences between the four case studies in this essay, black Methodists in each city faced a set of common circumstances. Their routes to congregational autonomy carried them through the processes of property ownership, church building and maintenance, black trusteeism, access to local preacher, exhorter and diaconal ranks of ministry, the control of congregational discipline and the question of denominational representation. In Philadelphia, where the refusal to grant full ordination was the most blatant, the Bethel congregation took the overwhelming majority of black Methodists into a new separated denomination. In Baltimore, the Bethel secessionists had no separate property claims, which remained with black loyalists who were in the majority and who remained the largest black congregations in episcopal Methodism until after the Civil War. Denial of elder's orders and hence of denominational representation lay behind the dissatisfaction of the separatists who refused to be pacified by the agreement of 1814 seeking to receive more attention from white pastors. In Wilmington, the Baltimore story had been foreshadowed when the loyalists at Ezion church maintained property for the Methodist Episcopal denomination. The African Union church was unable to protect any of its resources which its founder had possessed when active in the Asbury and Ezion congregations. Once again, conflicts with white elders triggered a schism. In New York the Zion church riveted its attention on the issue of ordination, remaining patient beyond any realistic expectation that the Methodist Episcopal Church would budge from its policies of the previous twenty years. When the plan for an African conference within the biracial denomination failed, a third denominational break was inevitable.

The anomaly of the black local deacon as episcopal Methodism's limit to black ministerial standing had no comparable precedent in the early African Baptist and African Presbyterian organizations in Boston (1805), New York (1808) and Philadelphia (1809, 1811). Biracial Baptist associations and presbyteries ordained blacks to the ministry and accepted them and their congregations into regular status in their judicatories. In contrast, the Methodist Episcopal legislation on the black diaconate was kept private, and all ordinations performed by Asbury were conducted apart from regular conference procedures. Without full ordination, there was no chance for direct denominational representation and participation in governance. Episcopal Methodism upheld that prohibition throughout the pre-Civil War period, symbolizing the same denial of political participation by blacks in civil government at national, state, and local levels. Only the Protestant Episcopal Church practiced a comparable discrimination. It granted priestly orders to its first African candidates, but diocesan leaders denied, first in Pennsylvania and then in New York, congregational representation to black churches and their ministers.[77]

The African Methodisms illustrate an important application of lay trusteeism, a movement pervasive in both white Protestant and Roman Catholic churches of the same period. If the black membership in the four Methodist societies considered in this paper had been unable to have black trustees, the economic basis for owning property and erecting church buildings would have been undermined. The St. Thomas African Episcopal Church pioneered the movement, and Allen and his Methodist associates were quick to emulate it. The Zion society in New York did not have as much power vested with the trustees, but their presence insured the grounds for a separate establishment. In Baltimore and Wilmington, where independence meant the loss of property, black trustees loyal to the Methodist Episcopal Church retained their power and forced new options upon those who seceded.

The Bethel congregation in Philadelphia made the most effective use of trusteeism for controlling pastoral assignments and for exercising congregational discipline and authority. In Baltimore and New York, the thrust for independence came from the ministerial leadership, black deacons, local preachers and exhorters, while in Wilmington the movement was based entirely in lay leadership. Pastoral and disciplinary issues did not hamper the independent developments among black Baptists and Presbyterians since their pastors had full ordination and equal ministerial standing and since matters of church discipline had no been racially divisive. The trustees and vestry of St. Thomas Episcopal church had comparable power to the trustees of Bethel church in Philadelphia, but they did not exercise it in ways that provoked controversy or forced decisions about denominational separation and reorganization.

Interpreters of black church history have often claimed that the evangelical fervor of the Second Great Awakening accounts for the fact that blacks gravitated to Methodist and Baptist churches rather than to more ritualistic or confessional denominations. Following Donald Mathews' revisionist interpretation of the early nineteenth century revivals, our study of the origins of three African Methodisms demonstrates that black Methodists participated in distinctive ways in the organizational revolution of American Protestantism which is the social meaning of the second awakening. They worked with the institutional innovations of the Methodist system to promote local, then connectional, autonomy. They moved into lay roles as trustees and class leaders. They became local preachers and exhorters. They sought ordination and got a partial resolution. They purchased property and built churches. When the logic of their developing autonomy failed to include conference membership for ministers, direct representation in the denomination and full ordination, the biracial association which existed for a generation broke down and complete independence brought black denominationalism.[78]

NOTES

1. Woodson, HISTORY OF THE NEGRO CHURCH (Washington: Associated Publishers, 1921). Recent examples of the concept occur in Carol V. R. George, SEGREGATED SABBATHS: RICHARD ALLEN AND THE RISE OF INDEPENDENT BLACK CHURCHES, 1760-1840 (New York: Oxford University Press, 1973) and Gayraud S. Wilmore, BLACK RELIGION AND BLACK RADICALISM (New York: Anchor, 1973).
2. SKETCH OF THE EARLY HISTORY OF THE AFRICAN METHODIST EPISCOPAL ZION CHURCH WITH JUBILEE SOUVENIR AND AN

APPENDIX (n.p., n.d.), 61-62; ONE HUNDRED YEARS OF THE AFRICAN METHODIST EPISCOPAL ZION CHURCH (New York: A. M. E. Zion Book Concern, 1895), 5-7.

3. John H. Bracey, Jr., August Meier, Elliott Hudwick, eds., BLACK NATIONALISM IN AMERICA (Indianapolis: Bobbs-Merrill, 1970), xxvi-xxvii, 3ff; Alain Rogers, "The African Methodist Episcopal Church: A Study in Black Nationalism," THE BLACK CHURCH, I (1972), 17-43.

4. For examples of this interpretive perspective, see Theodore Hershberg, "Free Blacks in Antebellum Philadelphia," JOURNAL OF SOCIAL HISTORY, 5 (1971-72), 183-209; Ira Berlin, "The Structure of the Free Negro Caste in the Antebellum United States," JOURNAL OF SOCIAL HISTORY, 9 (1975-76), 297-318 and "Time, Space, and the Evolution of Afro-American Society on British Mainland North America," AMERICAN HISTORICAL REVIEW, 85 (February, 1980), 44-78. More directly applicable to the black church are two exceptional essays, George A. Levesque, "Inherent Reformers—Inherited Orthodoxy: Black Baptists in Boston, 1800-1873," JOURNAL OF NEGRO HISTORY, 60 (October, 1975), 491-525 and Emma Jones Lapansky, " 'Since They Got Those Separate Churches': Afro-Americans and Racism in Jacksonian Philadelphia," AMERICAN QUARTERLY, 32 (Spring, 1980), 54-78. See also Gayraud S. Wilmore, "Reinterpretation in Black Church History," THE CHICAGO THEOLOGICAL SEMINARY REGISTER, 73 (Winter, 1983), 25-37, with the phrase "nationalist aspirations" quoted on p. 30.

5. E. Franklin Frazier, THE NEGRO CHURCH IN AMERICA (New York: Schocken, 1974 ed.), ch. 3 and W. E. B. DuBois, THE SOULS OF BLACK FOLK in THREE NEGRO CLASSICS, intro. by John Hope Franklin (New York: Avon Books, 1965), 215.

6. Floyd J. Miller, THE SEARCH FOR A BLACK NATIONALITY: BLACK COLONIZATION AND EMIGRATION (Urbana: University of Illinois Press, 1975), 6-15; Dorothy Sterling, ed., SPEAK OUT IN THUNDER TONES: LETTERS AND OTHER WRITINGS BY BLACK NORTHERNERS, 1787-1865 (Garden City: Doubleday, n.d.), 3-12. The manuscript records of the Free African Society of Newport show an entry for June 20, 1793 which notes a contribution by the Rhode Island organization to the African Church building project in Philadelphia, in the Newport Historical Society.

7. A DIALOGUE BETWEEN A VIRGINIAN AND AN AFRICAN MINISTER (Baltimore: Benjamin Edes for Joseph James, 1810), 37-42. This paper omits consideration of black Methodist churches on Long Island, in Salem, New Jersey, Annapolis, Maryland and West Chester, Pennsylvania which are on Coker's list. There was also an African Presbyterian church in Philadelphia which he did not include, and an African church in Wilmington, North Carolina in 1807, mentioned in THE JOURNAL AND LETTERS OF FRANCIS ASBURY, ed. Elmer T. Clark (Nashville: Abingdon Press, 1958), II, 556, n. 117.

8. The historiographical context of blacks within Methodism is ably demonstrated in Harry V. Richardson, DARK SALVATION (Garden City: Doubleday, 1976).

9. Russell E. Richey begins to raise the kind of questions of black denominationalism that American church historians have neglected. See his edited volume, DENOMINATIONALISM (Nashville: Abingdon, 1977), 207-09.

10. THE LETTERS OF FRANCIS ASBURY, 366-67.

11. Allen dates the opening in July, 1794, in THE LIFE EXPERIENCE AND GOSPEL LABORS OF THE RT. REV. RICHARD ALLEN (New York: Abingdon, 1960), 31. THE JOURNAL OF FRANCIS ASBURY, II, 18.

12. Allen, THE LIFE EXPERIENCE, 24 and MINUTES OF THE METHODIST CONFERENCES, HELD ANNUALLY IN AMERICA; FROM 1773 to 1813 (New York: Daniel Hitt and Thomas Ware, 1813), 60.

13. The first published reference to the incident is in the preface to THE DOCTRINES AND DISCIPLINE OF THE AFRICAN METHODIST EPISCOPAL CHURCH (Philadelphia: John H. Cunningham, 1817), 4. Milton Sernett has refuted the traditional date of 1787 on the basis of records showing that the first gallery at St. George's was constructed in 1792-93. Without denying that the event happened, he proposes a closer chronological connection to the dedication of the first building and the public statement of 1794 (see below, 7). See his BLACK RELIGION AND AMERICAN EVANGELICALISM (Metuchen: The Scarecrow Press, 1975), 116ff., 218ff. and Benjamin Tucker Tanner, AN OUTLINE OF OUR HISTORY AND GOVERNMENT FOR AFRICAN METHODIST CHURCHMEN, MINISTERIAL AND LAY (Philadelphia: A. M. E. Book Concern, 1884), 142-48. Allen's account in THE LIFE EXPERIENCE is undated, 25-26, but he attested to the veracity of the incident to answer a disaffected church member, Jonathan Tudas. See Trustees of Bethel and Wesley Churches, THE SWORD OF TRUTH (Philadelphia: J. H. Cunningham, 1823), 13.

14. Allen, THE LIFE EXPERIENCE, 24, and MINUTES OF THE METHODIST CONFERENCES, 1773-1813, 74, 93, 104.

15. William Douglass, ANNALS OF THE FIRST AFRICAN CHURCH IN THE UNITED STATES OF AMERICA (Philadelphia: King and Baird, 1862) 10-11, 15-22, 33-40, 45-46; L. H. Butterfield, LETTERS OF BENJAMIN RUSH (Princeton: Princeton University Press, 1951), I, 599-600, 602-03, 608-09, 716-17; II, 1071; George W. Corner, ed., THE AUTOBIOGRAPHY OF BENJAMIN RUSH (Princeton: Princeton University Press, 1948), 202-03, 221; Allen, THE LIFE EXPERIENCE, 29-30.

16. Tanner, AN OUTLINE, 142-48, contains this important document.

17. Allen, THE LIFE EXPERIENCE, 26-27, and MINUTES OF THE METHODIST CONFERENCES, 1773-1813, 116, 161. See also George A. Phoebus, ed., BEAMS OF LIGHT ON EARLY METHODISM IN AMERICA (New York: Phillips and Hunt, 1887), 217, 222-23.

18. ARTICLES OF ASSOCIATION OF THE AFRICAN METHODIST EPISCOPAL CHURCH, OF THE CITY OF PHILADELPHIA, IN THE COMMONWEALTH OF PENNSYLVANIA (Philadelphia: John Ormred, 1779; reprinted Philadelphia: Rhistoric Publications, n.d.), 3-4, 8, 10; Douglass, ANNALS, 104-06.

19. Jesse Lee, A SHORT HISTORY OF THE METHODISTS (Baltimore: Magill and Clime, 1810), 271-72; Reginald Hildebrand, "Methodist Episcopal Policy on the Ordination of Black Ministers, 1784-1864," METHODIST HISTORY, 20 (April, 1982), 125-26.

20. Hildebrand, 126-27.

21. MINUTES OF THE METHODIST CONFERENCES, for 1799, 223-26; for 1805, 343-47. J. R. Flanigen, METHODISM: OLD AND NEW (Philadelphia: J. B. Lippincott & Co., 1880), 51-52, 61-62. The building at Bethel was expanded in 1800. On Allen's secular employment, see George, SEGREGATED SABBATHS, 75, 90; Charles H. Wesley, RICHARD ALLEN: APOSTLE OF FREEDOM (Washington: Associated Publishers, 1935), 99-123; THE PHILADELPHIA DIRECTORY FOR 1798 (n.p., n.d.), 15.

22. A COLLECTION OF SPIRITUAL SONGS AND HYMNS SELECTED FROM VARIOUS AUTHORS BY RICHARD ALLEN, AFRICAN MINISTER (Philadelphia: John Ormred, 1801), with a second edition issued later the same year which added ten additional hymns. See Eileen Southern, THE MUSIC OF BLACK AMERICANS: A HISTORY (New York: W. W. Norton, 1971), 86ff., 517.

23. Phoebus, ed., BEAMS OF LIGHT, 252-54; THE JOURNAL OF FRANCIS ASBURY, 235, 432; Francis H. Tees, THE ANCIENT LANDMARK OF AMERI-

CAN METHODISM OR HISTORIC OLD ST. GEORGE'S (Philadelphia: Message Publishing Co., 1951), 94.

24. George, SEGREGATED SABBATHS, 66-69; Allen, THE LIFE EXPERIENCE, 32, 37-41 (for a text of the African Supplement).

25. Allen, THE LIFE EXPERIENCE, 37-41.

26. THE LETTERS OF FRANCIS ASBURY, 366-67.

27. MINUTES OF THE METHODIST CONFERENCES for 1812, 562. The reconstruction of these events comes from notes taken in the 1816 legal suit (see below, 15), in the Edward Carey Gardiner Collection, Pennsylvania Historical Society. Though there is no record in his LETTERS or JOURNAL, at least one conference was held with Asbury according to these notes and the A. M. E. DOCTRINES AND DISCIPLINE, 6.

28. J. Emory to "Sir," 6 April, 1815 in the Gardiner Collection articulated the logic of the white elders.

29. Allen, THE LIFE EXPERIENCE, 33-34; A. M. E. DOCTRINES AND DISCIPLINE, 5-6.

30. See my essay, "Early Methodism and Slavery: The Roots of a Tradition," THE DREW GATEWAY, 30 (Spring, 1964), 150-65. A copy of one of the expurgated versions of the Methodist Episcopal DISCIPLINE is in the Perkins Library Rare Book Room, Duke University. See also George, SEGREGATED SABBATHS, 77-80.

31. See the entry for 5 February 1809 in THE JOURNAL OF FRANCIS ASBURY, 591. Lorenzo Dow accused Asbury of being jealous of the rising power of Richard Allen, first in print in 1816. See HISTORY OF COSMOPOLITE (Cincinnati: H. M. Rulison, 1856), 545-48.

32. See notes of the legal suit of 1816 in the Gardiner Collection for confirmation of the public letter by Emory, also mentioned in Allen, THE EXPERIENCE, 33-34. For the case of Green v. African Church Called Bethel, see miscellaneous legal notes in the Yeates Papers, Pennsylvania Historical Society and Wesley, RICHARD ALLEN, 147-48.

33. Allen, THE LIFE EXPERIENCE, 34, and Robert Burch, 16 December 1815, in notes for the legal suit of 1816 in the Gardiner Collection.

34. MINUTES TAKEN AT THE SEVERAL ANNUAL CONFERENCES OF THE METHODIST EPISCOPAL CHURCH IN THE UNITED STATES OF AMERICAN FOR THE YEAR 1815 (New York: J. C. Totten, 1814), 36.

35. See notice of "Sheriff's sale," dated June 12, 1815 and a copy of the certificate of sale, stating that Allen had purchased the "brick meeting house and Lot of ground" for $9,600, plus two year rent charges amounting to $525. Wesley links the sale to the legal case of 1816, but it clearly belongs to the settlement involving Robert Green, for which see RICHARD ALLEN, 146.

36. Allen, THE LIFE EXPERIENCE, 34-35, and Richard Allen to Daniel Coker, 18 February 1816, as reprinted in Tanner, AN OUTLINE, 152-55. See also legal notes for the case of 1816 and Burch's letter of 16 December 1815, in the Gardiner Collection and Wesley, RICHARD ALLEN, 140-41.

37. A. M. E. DOCTRINES AND DISCIPLINE, 8-9; Daniel A. Payne, HISTORY OF THE AFRICAN METHODIST EPISCOPAL CHURCH (Nashville: A. M. E. Sunday School Union, 1891, reprinted by Arno Press, 1969), 13-14. Blacks in Philadelphia Methodism left to join the Bethel movement, dropping their number from 1371 in 1815 to seventy-five in 1816. See MINUTES for 1815, 21-29, and for 1816 (New York: J. C. Totten, 1816), 27-35.

38. James A. Handy, SCRAPS OF AFRICAN METHODIST EPISCOPAL HISTORY (Philadelphia: A. M. E. Book Concern, n.d.), 13-14.

39. MINUTES OF THE METHODIST CONFERENCES, 1773-1813, 60-61, 75, 154-56.

40. THE JOURNAL OF FRANCIS ASBURY, II, 51, 65.

41. Ibid., 129 and THE LETTERS OF FRANCIS ASBURY, 160.

42. Handy, SCRAPS, 14, 24, and James M. Wright, THE FREE NEGRO IN MARYLAND (New York: Columbia University, 1921), 216.

43. Bettye C. Thomas, "History of the Sharp Street Memorial Methodist Episcopal Church, 1787-1920," pamphlet (n.p., n.d.), unnumbered page 2; Cornelius William Stafford, THE BALTIMORE DIRECTORY, FOR 1802 (Baltimore: John W. Butler, n.d.), 64 and A. Hoen & Co., "Baltimore in 1804," Peale Museum, Baltimore, "Improved Plan of the City of Baltimore" in the Lovely Lane Museum and Methodist Historical Society, Baltimore; Wright, 213.

44. Thomas, unnumbered page 3; Wright, 213, 217-18, 222-23; Baltimore City Station Class Records, Lovely Lane Museum; BIOGRAPHY OF REV. DAVID SMITH, OF THE A.M. E. CHURCH (Lenia: Xenia Gazette Office, 1881), 28-29. Even after the separation of 1815, the loyalists continued to use the name "African Methodist Episcopal."

45. Coker, DIALOGUE, 41; MINUTES OF THE METHODIST CONFERENCES, 1773-1813, 420-25, 592-99.

46. Baltimore City Station Class Records.

47. Ibid.

48. Glen A. McAninch, "We'll Pray For You: Methodist Ethnocentrism in the Origins of the African Methodist Episcopal Church in Baltimore," M. A. thesis, University of North Carolina at Chapel Hill, 1973, 41, 50.

49. BIOGRAPHY OF REV. DAVID SMITH, 26-30. The Baltimore City Station Class Records show forty black classes with 1274 members after Coker's secession. I counted 217 names stricken from the lists.

50. McAninch, 73; Wright, 217-18, 222-23; MINUTES OF TWO CONFERENCES OF THE AFRICAN METHODIST PREACHERS HELD AT BALTIMORE AND PHILADELPHIA IN APRIL AND MAY, 1818 (Philadelphia: Richard Allen, 1818), 9, 14. There were 1322 black Methodists remaining with the Methodist Episcopal societies in 1818, see MINUTES OF THE METHODIST CONFERENCES for 1818, 22-31.

51. The only extant copy, apparently, of Coker's sermon in the New York Public Library's main branch was torn out of a bound volume of collected pamphlets. A summary of the sermon is in Wesley, RICHARD ALLEN, 141-42, 150, and an extract is in Herbert Aptheker, ed., A DOCUMENTARY HISTORY OF THE NEGRO PEOPLE OF THE UNITED STATES (New York: The Citadel Press, 1969, original ed., 1951), 67-69.

52. A. M. E. DOCTRINES AND DISCIPLINE, 1817, 190. The complete title of Coker's sermon is SERMON DELIVERED EXTEMPORE IN THE AFRICAN BETHEL CHURCH IN THE CITY OF BALTIMORE, ON THE 21ST OF JANUARY, 1816, TO A NUMEROUS CONCOURSE OF PEOPLE, ON ACCOUNT OF THE COLOURED PEOPLE GAINING THEIR CHURCH (BETHEL) IN THE SUPREME COURT OF THE STATE OF PENNSYLVANIA, BY THE REV. D. COKER, MINISTER OF THE SAID CHURCH, TO WHICH IS ANNEXED A LIST OF THE AFRICAN PREACHERS IN PHILADELPHIA, BALTIMORE &C WHO HAVE WITHDRAWN FROM UNDER THE CHARGE OF THE METHODIST BISHOPS AND CONFERENCE, (BUT ARE STILL METHODISTS), n.p., n.d.

53. THE DISCIPLINE OF THE AFRICAN UNION CHURCH OF THE UNITED STATES OF AMERICA, 3rd. ed. enlarged (Wilmington: Porter & Eckel, 1852), iv.

54. John D. C. Hanna, THE CENTENNIAL SERVICES OF ASBURY METHODIST EPISCOPAL CHURCH, WILMINGTON, DELAWARE. OCTOBER 13-20, 1889 (Wilmington: Delaware Printing Co., 1889), 146, 160.

55. See notice in MIRROR OF THE TIMES AND GENERAL ADVERTISER (Wilmington), 6 February 1805.

56. Asbury preached in "the African chapel in Wilmington" on May 2, 1810. THE JOURNAL OF FRANCIS ASBURY, 636.

57. Hanna, CENTENNIAL SERVICES, 160, and THE

DISCIPLINE OF THE AFRICAN UNION CHURCH, iii-v.

58. The "Articles of Association" are recorded in the Division of Historical and Cultural Affairs, Department of State, Hall of Records, Dover, Delaware. Typed versions are in the Historical Society of Delaware, Wilmington. A DIRECTORY AND REGISTER FOR THE YEAR 1814 . . . OF THE BOROUGH OF WILMINGTON AND BRANDYWINE (n.p.: R. Porter, 1814), as a typed copy in the Historical Society of Delaware, 45-52 shows home addresses and vocations for three-fourths of the charter members of the African Union church.

59. Union Church of Africans v. Ellis Sanders, Court of Errors and Appeals, June term, 1855, typed copy in Historical Society of Delaware, unnumbered page 4; Lewis V. Baldwin, 'Invisible Strands of African Methodism," Ph.D. dissertation, Northwestern University, 1980, 103-05, 118-22. There were 1263 members in four states in 1837.

60. Baldwin, 105-08.

61. Ibid., 87, and A DIRECTORY AND REGISTER FOR THE YEAR 1814, 45-52.

62. William J. Walls, THE AFRICAN METHODIST EPISCOPAL ZION CHURCH: REALITY OF THE BLACK CHURCH (Charlotte: A. M. E. Zion Publishing House, 1974), 49, quoting the first DISCIPLINE.

63. Samuel A. Seaman, ANNALS OF NEW YORK METHODISM (New York: Hunt & Eaton, 1892), 465.

64. Walls, THE A. M. E. ZION CHURCH, 47-48; THE JOURNAL OF FRANCIS ASBURY, 55, 95-96.

65. AMERICAN CITIZEN AND GENERAL ADVERTIZER (NEW YORK), 21 March 1800 as quoted in Walls, THE A. M. E. ZION CHURCH, 53; also 56-57 where the General Conference report instructed the Zion Society to model itself after the Bethel "Articles of Agreement" or to obtain a charter like white congregations within the New York Conference. MINUTES OF THE METHODIST CONFERENCES 1773-1813, 247 (for 1800).

66. ARTICLES OF AGREEMENT BETWEEN THE GENERAL CONFERENCE OF THE METHODIST EPISCOPAL CHURCH, AND THE TRUSTEES OF THE AFRICAN METHODIST EPISCOPAL CHURCH, IN THE CITY OF NEW YORK (Brooklyn: Thomas Kirk, 1801), 6-7; Walls, THE A. M. E. ZION CHURCH, 56-57.

67. THE JOURNAL OF FRANCIS ASBURY, 506, 568; Walls, THE A. M. E. ZION CHURCH, 65-69.

68. Dorothy Porter, ed., EARLY NEGRO WRITING 1760-1837 (Boston: Beacon Press, 1971), 343ff., 365ff., 374ff. for three orations. See also Adam Carman, ORATION DELIVERED AT THE FOURTH ANNIVERSARY OF THE ABOLITION OF THE SLAVE TRADE, IN THE METHODIST EPISCOPAL CHURCH, IN SECOND-STREET, NEW YORK, JANUARY 1, 1811 (New York: John C. Totten, 1811) and William Miller, A SERMON ON THE ABOLITION OF THE SLAVE TRADE: DELIVERED IN THE AFRICAN CHURCH, NEW YORK, ON THE FIRST OF JANUARY, 1810 (New York: John C. Totten, 1810).

69. David Henry Bradley, Sr., A HISTORY OF THE A. M. E. ZION CHURCH (Nashville: Parthenon Press, 1956), 65-66.

70. There were 963 members of Zion and Asbury churches in 1818. MINUTES TAKEN AT THE SEVERAL ANNUAL CONFERENCES OF THE METHODIST EPISCOPAL CHURCH IN THE UNITED STATES OF AMERICA. FOR THE YEAR 1818 (New York: John C. Totten, 1818), 28-37; Christopher Rush, A SHORT ACCOUNT OF THE RISE AND PROGRESS OF THE AFRICAN M. E. CHURCH IN AMERICA (New York: Christopher Rush, et al., 1866), 32ff.

71. John Jamison Moore, HISTORY OF THE A. M. E. ZION CHURCH IN AMERICA (York: Teachers' Journal Office, 1884), 59.

72. Walls, THE A. M. E. ZION CHURCH, 76-82.

73. Ibid., 83.

74. JOURNAL OF THE GENERAL CONFERENCE OF THE METHODIST EPISCOPAL CHURCH, 1824, 244, 246, 254 and Peter Cartwright et al., "Report of the committee to whom was referred the affairs of the people of colour," May 27, 1824, General Conference Papers, Drew University, Madison, New Jersey.

75. I have examined the beginnings of the fourth black Methodist denomination, "The Social, Political and Religious Significance of the Formation of the Colored Methodist Episcopal Church (1870)," METHODIST HISTORY, 18 (October, 1979), 3-25.

76. Cartwright, "Report of the committee," General Conference Papers.

77. These comparative conclusions come from my current research a version of which in unpublished form was presented to the Society for Historians of the Early American Republic, July, 1982 in Memphis under the title, "The Exodus: The Emergence of Independent Black Churches in the New Nation, 1787-1821."

78. Mathews, "The Second Great Awakening as an Organizing Process," AMERICAN QUARTERLY, 21 (1969), 23-43.

The People and the Preachers at St. George's:
An Anatomy of a Methodist Schism

by Dee Andrews
The Philadelphia Center for Early American Studies
and the University of Pennsylvania

When Thomas Coke and Francis Asbury wrote their "Explanatory Notes" to the 1798 edition of the *Doctrines and Discipline* of the Methodist Episcopal Church, one of the aspects of the Methodist movement they sought most to emphasize was the role that "the people" played in the affairs of the church. Responding in part to the republican character of American politics, and in part to Virginia preacher James O'Kelly's attacks on Asbury's authority, the bishops stressed the ways in which the rank and file of Methodist societies influenced the proceedings of the itinerant preachers in their conferences.[1]

Coke and Asbury were sensitive to the issue of the popular voice in Methodism since, in fact, Methodist members had little official influence on policy-making in the church in the 18th century. There were no lay representatives in either the annual or general conferences. The closest thing to a lay representative in the formal structure of the church was the class leader who took part in the regular quarterly meetings of the local circuits. But even these leaders were appointed by the preacher rather than elected by the congregation.[2] In most respects, the formally organized connection in America was run from the top down by preachers who were themselves appointed to or dismissed from circuits at the discretion of their bishops.

Political representation, however, was not the only measure that might be used to determine the nature of popular influence on a religious movement. In the event of a crisis, preachers might find that it was their authority that was tempered by the demands of local societies, rather than the other way around.

St. George's Church in Philadelphia was the first Methodist society in America to have official ties with the Wesleyan Connexion in England. In the 1790s it was one of four Methodist chapels in or near the city. Altogether these congregations comprised the "Philadelphia Society of the Methodist Episcopal Church," colloquially known by the name of the original chapel—St. George's.[3]

At the Philadelphia society, as at all Methodist societies, the line demarcating the role of the clergy from that of the laity was not always precise. In the offices of the class leader and local preacher, Methodism granted members a considerable amount of authority in the pastoral affairs of local churches. As Coke and Asbury wrote: "Our [class] leaders under God are the sinews of our society, and our revivals will ever, in a great measure, rise or fall with them."[4] Class leaders played a fundamental part in sustaining the evangelical character of the church. Leaders and local preachers furthermore might be individuals who did not possess much power in society at large, such as female or black members, or white members of humble social background. At St. George's in the 1790s the leaders included Mary Wilmer, a founding member of the society, John Dennis, a laborer turned cordwainer, Reiner Gilbert, a tailor, and Manly Smallwood, another cordwainer, or shoemaker. Smallwood was also a licensed local preacher.[5] Among the various tasks they performed at St. George's was to act as confessors for the class members under them, and as collectors of the quarterly donations that helped keep their chapels afloat. They were also potential sponsors for aspiring preachers who frequently performed their first public exhorting under the aegis of a class leader.[6]

Coke and Asbury stressed that class leaders and local preachers might themselves rise up through the ranks to become itinerant preachers: "From all that has been observed," they concluded, "it must be clear to every candid reader, that it is not the yearly conference *only*, or the bishops, or presiding elders *only*, in the intervals of the conferences, who choose the local or travelling preachers. On the contrary, *they* have no authority to choose at all, till the people, through their leaders, stewards, &c. recommend."[7] Clerical mobility, however, was a two-way street among Methodists. Itinerants might, and frequently did, quit the traveling connection in order to marry, or carry on a business or trade. The lure of Philadelphia's commercial life seems to have been strong for several itinerants, a number of whom settled there shortly after receiving their appointments to the city. John Dickins located in Philadelphia in order to work more fully for the church as its book agent, as did Ezekiel Cooper after Dickins's death in the yellow fever epidemic of 1798. But other itinerants were drawn to more worldly pursuits. Daniel Ruff opened a shoe warehouse, and Lemuel Green became a merchant. Thomas Haskins and Charles Cavender became grocers.[8] These ex-itinerants brought with them personal ties to the major figures in the church, as well as their own sense of authority. Although they were technically no longer a part of the church's conferences, they all continued as located preachers: Dickins, Green, and Cavender were local elders, and Ruff and Haskins, local deacons. In 1797, Dickins and Haskins also sat on the board of trustees of the society, Dickins as secretary and Haskins as treasurer.[9]

The interests of members and preachers were intermeshed in a third way in the activities of the trustees and the financial supervision of the chapel. The trustees at St. George's were empowered to purchase and sell, within certain limits, the real and personal property of the church, as well as to make use of any accruing interest. The trustees could not take from the stationed preacher the "religious use, benefit and enjoyment of the said Church."[10] Nevertheless, the maintenance and improvement of the chapel depended to a great extent on the money that the trustees were able to borrow or were themselves willing to lend. The influence of the Philadelphia trustees, furthermore, extended beyond the geographical scope of the city. In 1797, nine members of St. George's, seven of them trustees, were made managers of the Methodist Episcopal Church's pension fund, called the Chartered Fund. The purpose of this fund was distributing assistance to "superannuated" or "worn-out" itinerants and their families.[11]

The society at St. George's, then, was not composed of a simple hierarchy of laity, local preachers, and licensed and ordained itinerants. Rather, lay members carried out a number of pastoral offices in the church, administering to the needs of the great proportion of their fellow members; ex-itinerants performed the pastoral functions of local preachers and the secular functions of trustees; itinerants, furthermore, depended for their bread and butter on the philanthropic impulses and financial acumen of itinerants-turned-merchants and other local businessmen who acted as creditors and fiscal managers for the local society as well as the Methodist connection as a whole.

Hence, when a conflict arose at St. George's, any or all of these aspects—the popular, the personal, and the material—might be at issue. Such was the case in Philadelphia between the summer of 1800 and the summer of 1801. The conflict became so serious, in fact, that some of St. George's longest standing members seceded to form a new independent Methodist society. What happened?

I

The only specific evidence for the initial cause of the controversy is a remark that Asbury made in his journal some time after the conflict came out into the open. Asbury notes that charges of misconduct had been brought against Henry Manly, a trustee and a class leader. These charges had been dropped and Manly, readmitted into the society: with this, Asbury thought, the matter should have been at an end.[12] The charges against Manly are unknown. They may have been related to the extensive renovations that were being carried out at St. George's church during the spring, summer, and fall of 1800, though Manly was not the treasurer at the time; or they may have had to do with a personal quarrel between Manly and the stationed preacher, Lawrence McCombs.[13] At any rate, Manly's name does not appear in any of the other evidence relating to the conflict. Instead, the disagreement that autumn seemed to have developed over the appropriate procedures to be used by the stationed preacher in the quarterly meeting for the circuit. As Ezekiel Cooper recalled, McCombs responded to arguments by "breaking several class-leaders who differed with him in opinion." These leaders were Hugh Smith and David Lake, trustees as well as leaders, and William Sturgis. In their places McCombs named five new class leaders: Caleb North, a trustee, and Abel Mathias, John Higner, Thomas Kelly, and Robert Carr, none of whom as far as the records show had held offices in the society before.[14]

According to the *Discipline*, McCombs was within his rights in changing the leaders at the society. Nevertheless, he had to answer to a higher authority in the Methodist connection— the presiding elder. The purpose of the presiding elders, Coke and Asbury explained, was to act as "fathers in the gospel" to the people in their districts: "*These offices* in the church are peculiarly designed to meliorate the severity of the christian discipline, as far as they [sic] respect *the people*. In them the people have a refuge, an asylum to which they may fly on all occasions."[15]

In 1800, the presiding elder for Philadelphia was Joseph Everett, a 68-year-old itinerant who had been in the field since 1781. Apparently Smith, Lake, and Sturgis flew to him for restitution. Everett subsequently challenged McCombs' actions at St. George's, promptly reappointed Smith, Lake, and Sturgis, and removed North, Mathias, Higner, Kelly, and Carr from their briefly held positions. When McCombs objected to Everett's challenge, Everett reappointed him to another station in the district and appointed in his place Richard Sneath as the new stationed preacher.[16]

Sneath arrived at St. George's in November or December. McCombs, however, refused to leave, with the result that a large party of members, who had apparently approved of his dismissal of Smith, Lake, and Sturgis, formed around him as the church rapidly deteriorated in the winter and spring of 1801. The party of "malcontents," as Asbury was to call them, opposed all efforts at a compromise.[17] Consequently they ended up with the presiding elder and the new stationed preacher against them as well as most of the class leaders, seven of whom had been appointed by Sneath in January. Finally, the party petitioned the annual conference, meeting in Philadelphia in early June 1801, for redress of their grievances.[18]

Much to the disappointment of the petitioners, the conference responded by leaving the matter in Everett's hands, requesting that bishops Asbury and Richard Whatcoat address the Philadelphia society regarding the controversy.[19] This the bishops did in a published letter replete with scriptural allusions to the evils of dispute among brethren. They noted especially that "we lament that there has been a division of sentiment, either among the preachers or members; But as all men do not see alike, in matters of church discipline, we beseech you brethren, not to suffer a difference in opinions or views, to alienate your affections from your brethren, the church, or the cause of God." The Philadelphians had always been generous to the connection in the past, but there was necessary also the "soul-cheering *feast of love* and *union* among yourselves. . . . How can you expect your preachers to live and labour among you in the fire of contention," the bishops asked rhetorically, "and always to be wading through the waters of strife?"[20]

The bishops' address did nothing to assuage the anger of the McCombs party, nor did McCombs's own reconciliation with Everett at around the same time. Consequently, those who had allied themselves with McCombs began to move away from association with the connection. On June 8, Thomas Haskins, a new leader for the petitioners, requested that he not be reap-

pointed as local preacher at St. George's. "For me to *exercise* any Official functions in the Methodist Churches in *Philadelphia in the present Situation of its affairs*," he explained, "would be repugnant to those feelings, as well as a violation of that sense of propriety & duty which ought to activate every upright honest Man, *Sacrifices* which your enlightened & feeling hearts cannot expect me to make."[21]

Several days later, the group, including Haskins, recent itinerant Charles Cavender, founding member Lambert Wilmer, and trustees James Doughty and Samuel Harvey, addressed a letter to "The Methodist Connection in the City of Philadelphia" in which they declared that they were withdrawing from membership in the Methodist society there. The implication of the letter was that the aggrieved members would return if certain disruptive members at St. George's were expelled.[22]

This did not happen. Instead, the thirty-three men and thirty women who had withdrawn by August were forced to devise their own society and conference. Consequently they rented part of the building of the Academy of Philadelphia a block and a half south of St. George's, which had originally been constructed on the prompting of George Whitefield, the famous itinerant. It was probably in this place that they held their own conference on August 18.[23] This unorthodox Methodist meeting then drew up a discipline of their own, which they called the "Constitution" for the newly formed "United Societies of the People called Methodists (late in connection with the Methodist Episcopal Church)." The use of the plural "societies" in their name suggested that they hoped other members of Methodist churches would do as they had.[24]

Unlike the *Discipline* of the Methodist connection, the new society's constitution established a church run by its members. The articles delineating the power of the officers of the church followed closely parts of the act of incorporation for St. George's and of the Methodist Episcopal Church's *Discipline*. Its articles of faith and general rules were also copied in slightly abbreviated form from the *Discipline*. The longest section of the document was taken up with the actual wording of the various sacramental rites to be performed.[25] But members played a number of roles in the new society that were usually reserved for preachers. The president of the conference was Lambert Wilmer, a former class leader, licensed preacher, and trustee, but never an itinerant. The procedures for running the society, furthermore, were quite democratic compared with the Methodist connection. No one could be a class leader or licensed preacher without the consent of two-thirds of the class to which he belonged. The conference, furthermore, was required to review the grievances brought before it by members—a provision that was undoubtedly meant to address the Philadelphia conference's refusal to deal with the McCombs party's complaints that spring. And the constitution could be altered by the conference, but only with the consent of two-thirds of the male white members over the age of 21.[26]

Another major difference between the new society and the Methodist Episcopal Church, however, was that admission into the church at the Academy was more exclusive than it was at St. George's. A probationer could be admitted on trial at the Academy only if recommended by the leader of the class to which the person wished to belong, and could be admitted into full membership only on the approval of the whole conference rather than that of the preacher as in the Methodist Episcopal Church. "And in the Case of doubtful characters the Conference may extend the time of Trial, or lay them aside as they may Judge best."[27] Overall, the seceders had constituted a religious society in which they retained most of the authority for the lay members in pastoral as well as secular matters. But they also limited acceptance into the society to those already familiar with its members. In some respects, whom you knew mattered as much as what you had experienced in grace.

II

On the surface of it, the controversy at St. George's over the winter and summer of 1800 to 1801 had involved the interaction of preachers with preachers, and lay members with preachers. The spark for the conflict, after all, had come from McCombs's refusal to follow Everett's order. The conflict initially had become a matter for the church at large because a stationed preacher—McCombs—had rejected the authority of the presiding elder—Everett—and it had entailed many more issues than a recounting of events reveals. While the participants repeatedly invoked the formal structure of the M.E. Church to substantiate their arguments, the controversy seems in the final analysis to have arisen from problems not of church politics but of social class and personal influence.

St. George's had been undergoing major social changes in the late 1790s. Most significantly, its membership had been increasing year by year with revivals. In 1799, Ezekiel Cooper wrote to another preacher that "we had some stir among us here. About forty or fifty have joined society

in about two months past." Philip Bruce, stationed in Philadelphia the following summer, also noted that "we still have some little good a doing in the City [,] some Awakenings and Conversions." One reason why Asbury was reluctant to interfere with Everett's actions in Philadelphia in 1800 was because the revival there in the autumn was still going strong in December. "They had great congregations, great shoutings; and God was with them, and nearly one hundred had joined society. To all this what can we do but say, 'Well done, good and faithful servant' and servants!'"[28]

The register for the members admitted on trial to the Philadelphia society at the end of the 1790s corroborates these comments. In 1797, sixty-six white probationers were admitted to St. George's and Ebenezer; in 1798, seventy-nine were admitted; and in 1799, 104. Then the increase is remarkable: in 1800, 186 probationers joined classes run by the white churches, sixty-seven of them admitted in November by Richard Sneath. Before the end of May 1801, 263 more joined. In just three-and-one-half years, from October 1797 through May 1801, the total number of white probationers and members had risen from 363 to 669, many of them coming into the society in the midst of its controversy.[29]

The church was being transformed right before the eyes of its long-standing members from a moderate-sized organization in the early 1790s to a substantial-sized organization in 1800 with congregations at St. George's and Ebenezer alone divided into twenty-three different classes meeting throughout the city. The membership of the black chapels, furthermore, officially recorded in the conference minutes, increased from 257 in 1800 to 448 in 1801.[30] This great rise in membership from revivals meant that the nature of religious worship in the Philadelphia society was likely to move in the direction of increasing emotionality. But perhaps more importantly for St. George's, where members were at least ostensibly committed to evangelical worship, the revivals meant that the society would be open to increasingly diverse and popular attendance.

Indeed, Cooper thought that the major source for conflict at St. George's from 1800 to 1801 was social tension. As he wrote in his journal, the preacher McCombs "struck in with those who were considered the most wealthy and respectable members, but who were opposed to the poor, who had the majority of members on their side. Thus the wealthy and respectable minority were on one side, and the poor majority on the other. It became a very serious question which should prevail: wealth and worldly respectability on the one side, or the majority on the other?" Cooper had attempted to remain neutral in the quarrels, with the result that "the wealthy and respectable were surprised at me to take part with, what they called, the poor and ignorant part of the Society against them; and the others lamented and were surprised that I did not give them a more decided support in opposition to, what they considered, the overbearing measures of what they called 'the great men.'" The "respectable" party, furthermore, disapproved of the winter revival, "and endeavored to make it be believed that it was a delusion, etc."[31]

Cooper's neutrality was overturned by the McCombs party's insistence that they get their way in the affairs of the society. Several of the "great men," Cooper observed, "gave way to such bitterness of spirit, and to such an abusive practice of evil-speaking and persecution, that I, more than ever, was convinced their motives were not pure and that their designs were not good." When trustees Doughty, North, Baker, and Harvey withdrew from the church, furthermore, they left a debt of some $3000 for renovations done on the building at St. George's since the spring of 1800. "It was now supposed, and intimated by those who withdrew, that we should never be able to pay the debt, and that the church would be sold by the creditors, and that they would buy it." A stonecutter working on the building told Cooper that some of the Academy members had advised him to sue for his payments.[32]

In comparing the social status of the members of the Academy society with those remaining at St. George's, it is immediately apparent that Cooper was right to see great distinctions between the two groups. If the social profile of the members of the new society is compared with that of the other white Methodists in Philadelphia, a striking pattern emerges.[33] Thirty-eight men were now meeting at the Academy, including thirty-three who had withdrawn from St. George's and five who joined the new society from elsewhere. Of these, thirty were listed in the city directories during this time. Twelve of the men listed in the directories were merchants or retailers, thirteen were artisans or manufacturers. In other words, the proportion of merchants and artisans, 40% and 43% respectively, among the men whose occupations can be identified was about the same. Only one identifiable laborer and one mariner (who eventually returned to St. George's) belonged to the new society.

At St. George's, however, the breakdown of the occupations of the 207 men who remained is markedly different. First, fewer of these members, as compared with the Academy members, were listed in the city directories, suggesting that many of the men who chose to remain were journeymen, laborers, or other unskilled workers frequently not mentioned in the directories.[35] The likely proportion of unskilled workers in the Philadelphia society as a whole appears even higher if the black members at Bethel and Zoar are taken into consideration. Seven male members at St. George's can in fact be identified as laborers; another member was a mariner, and three more were carters.

Most striking of all, however, is the difference in the proportion of merchants and artisans to this group as a whole as compared with the new society. Of the eighty-seven men at St. George's whose occupations can be identified, the number of merchants and shopkeepers, fourteen in all, was nearly the same as the number meeting at the Academy. But at St. George's they comprised only 16% of the total as compared with 40% at the Academy. At the same time, 54 members at St. George's were artisans—62% of those whose occupations can be identified. While the proportion of merchants and artisans at the Academy were about equal, in other words, there remained at St. George's nearly four times as many artisans as there were merchants.

Among the artisans at the new society, furthermore, there were at least five men who may have been proprietors of large workshops: a house carpenter, a shipwright, a callicoe printer, a tin manufacturer, and a brass founder. At St. George's, however, while there were a number of artisans who may have owned large shops — a house carpenter, a coachmaker, a boot manufacturer, and a soap and candle manufacturer, as well as a number of tradesmen working for the shipping industry, namely, a wharf-builder, two shipwrights, a rope-maker, a mast-maker and a sail-maker—most of the artisans were in modest crafts normally requiring little capital investment, such as shoemaking, tailoring, and baking. Twenty-two of the artisans at St. George's, or 41%, were engaged specifically in one of these three occupations.

These social distinctions between the two societies hold for their officers as well. The leaders at the Academy church included grocers Cavender and Haskins, merchant Samuel Harvey, and shopkeeper John Gouge as local preachers; merchants Jacob Baker and Caleb North, grocer James Swain, and physician William Budd as stewards; and merchants Lambert Wilmer and James Doughty as class leaders. Only the class leaders John Hood and

John Hewson, Sr., among the officers at the Academy were artisans, the one a silk-and-stuff shoemaker, the other a callicoe printer.

By contrast, the officers of the Philadelphia society who chose to remain at St. George's included trustees Hugh Smith, a house carpenter, and David Lake, a shoemaker, two of the three class leaders who had been removed by McCombs the previous autumn, as well as Daniel Doughty, the wharf builder, Alexander Cook, the soap and candle manufacturer, and John Dennis, another shoemaker. Among the local preachers remaining were Pennel Beale, a cabinet maker, John Walker and Manly Smallwood, shoemakers, and David Abbott, a tailor. Smith and the class leaders Doughty, Cook, and Beale may well have been running large workshops.[38] Nevertheless, the prominence of artisans in the society at St. George's is unmistakable.

The different character of the two societies is further illustrated by their female membership. Four-hundred-and-twenty-nine women were probationers or members of St. George's and Ebenezer at the end of May 1801, or 64% of the total white membership of the Philadelphia society. Only thirty women left for the Academy, fourteen more joining from outside the Philadelphia society. Of the women who left St. George's, at least ten and perhaps as many as seventeen were married to men who left with them, including Hannah Baker, Elizabeth Haskins, Zibia Hewson, and Margaret Doughty, Sr.[39] Ten of the female members, or a third of those who left had been members of one of two classes led by John Hood at St. George's. Along with Wilmer and Baker, Hood had been one of the original members of the Philadelphia society, and undoubtedly inspired great loyalty among his class members.[40] The great majority of women, however, nearly 400 in number, remained at St. George's. Ann Hewson, a 20-year old daughter of Zibia and John, the callicoe printer, herself returned to the old society sometime after the summer of 1801.[41]

The leaders of Cooper's "respectable" party, then, tended to be men of the merchant class—importers, shopkeepers, grocers, dealers in retail and wholesale goods. His "poor" party was largely artisans—carpenters, shoemakers, and tailors. The events that led to the withdrawal of McCombs party from the old society take on a different aspect in light of this social anatomy. With the revivals at the end of the century, a growing majority of Philadelphia Methodists were what contemporaries called the "lower" and "middling" sorts—white and black laborers, artisans, young journeymen, as well as women.

At least two of the three class leaders removed by McCombs fitted this description, as did the officers who chose not to leave in the summer of 1801. Those who did leave were in many ways rejecting not only the authority of the preachers, but also the social character of the church. In its stead they established a society that minimized the role of preachers but also raised social barriers to admission. Thus the Methodist chapel in Philadelphia with the most "popular" involvement in its governance was also the wealthiest and the least revivalistic.

III

The question remains how the leaders of the Methodist Episcopal Church were to deal with the outcome of the course of events in Philadelphia. The major goal of the Methodist preachers, after all, as expressed in Asbury's first comments on the Philadelphia crisis, was to promote revivals. As the 1798 *Discipline* directed the preachers: "You have nothing to do but to save souls."[42] This mandate, however, was complicated by the personal friendships that preachers had with one another, and by their need and desire to maintain ties with the older, established adherents of the Methodist movement. Thomas Haskins, one of the major figures among the seceders, for example, had been an attending preacher at the 1784 Christmas Conference. In the summer of 1801, furthermore, amidst the turmoil in Philadelphia, he was editing Asbury's journals, and considering editing Richard Whatcoat's.[43] In July, after Haskins and his party had withdrawn from the old society, Asbury urged him to confer with Ezekiel Cooper in hopes of finding a solution among the various stationed and located preachers. The only matter that Haskins and Cooper seemed to have been able to discuss, however, was what Haskins-the-editor and Cooper-the-book-agent had in common, namely, Asbury's journals.[44]

Throughout the summer of 1801, Asbury continued to correspond confidentially with Haskins, suggesting ways in which a compromise might be reached. The letters are cordial and intimate. In June, Asbury wrote: "I wish it not to be made public that I have anything to do in the matter of advice. I confide in you and I know not that I could write to the body or any other person but yourself." He went on to suggest that Haskins and his party "must consider whether you keep your places in the church and with which property you can demand that satisfaction, and how improper, if not impossible, it might be for you to obtain it if withdrawn." Haskins wrote back in July apologizing for the formality of his letter which, he explained, discretion required.[45]

In contrast, the tone of Asbury's letters to Cooper was distant and frequently patronizing. "I hope the sword of contention will be sheathed to be drawn no more," he wrote to Cooper in August of 1801. "Order and discipline, I trust, will be attended to." He had been writing to Cooper in this way for several years. In a letter written in 1795 when Cooper was stationed in New York City, Asbury reprimanded him for his casual social habits among the New York members: "You have a house to eat in," Asbury wrote, "you need not go to feast with the Church of God. We ought to visit as doctors, or as persons to plead the cause of their souls; not as guests, to eat and drink, but as divines for souls." He concluded the letter saying, "We have had few city preachers but what have been spoiled for a poor man's preachers."[46]

The irony, of course, was that Cooper seemed to want to be a poor man's preacher. Asbury, however, continued to tolerate the seceders in Philadelphia despite their unwillingness to accept the authority of the presiding elder, the annual conference, and the bishops. Asbury's attitude can in part be attributed to his fidelity to old friends and acquaintances. But it is also possible that he was loath to alienate those among the trustees of the Chartered Fund who had joined the Academy, and it is also clear that he doubted whether the members remaining at St. George's in the summer of 1801 would be able to make it on their own, without the support of the wealthier members who had become increasingly indispensable to the survival of the church.

In the course of the dispute over the year, the Philadelphia society had indeed lost the assistance of most of their trustees. They were also faced with a sizeable debt. By the dint of canvassing, and the donations of two of the more prosperous members at St. George's, Cooper was able both to pay off the debts of the church and to complete the construction at Ebenezer.[47] He was aware, furthermore, of the skepticism of his fellow preachers. As he wrote in a statement regarding the payment of St. George's debt: "It was supposed, that our poverty, our want of skill in management, our small influence among those who were able to contribute to our relief, or that from some other cause, our house of worship must be sold to pay its debts, or otherwise mortgageded [sic] & incumbered to save it."[48] In addition to making the Philadelphia society financially solvent, that is, Cooper had had to rescue its credibility as a viable, if poor, society.

The credibility of the Academy as a Methodist society remained secure. Less than a year later, in May 1802, its members were received back into the Methodist connection with George Roberts, another friend of Asbury's, as their stationed preacher. The Academy was never reunited with St. George's. Instead it remained in the early nineteenth century a prosperous congregation distinguished from two poorer white and two black Methodist congregations in the city.[49]

This episode in the history of the Philadelphia Society illustrates the numerous aspects of clerical and lay relations that need to be taken into account in assessing the character of popular involvement in the Methodist movement in the eighteenth century. When challenged by members, the itinerants readily exerted their formally established authority. But they were willing also to "meliorate the severity of the christian discipline" for various considerations. Among these were their friendships with preachers who had returned to local societies, their unwillingness to alienate Methodism's prominent, long-standing members, their constant need to keep chapels, and their own connection, financially healthy. Lay members, meanwhile, asserted their not so clearly defined authority with apparently few qualms quite apart from the operations of church authority so methodically cataloged and meticulously glossed by Coke and Asbury in the Methodist *Discipline*.

Schisms in Methodist societies, then, particularly those in the cities where change was rapid and ways of life most sharply contrasted, arose as much from battles among the people themselves as from arguments between people and preachers. In Philadelphia in 1800 the conflict between the artisan party on the one side and the merchant party on the other divided the church. Their controversy underscores the social strains that had come to mark the Methodist movement by the end of its first generation.

NOTES

My thanks to Gary B. Nash for suggesting the topic of this paper, Kenneth Rowe and Louise Capron at the Methodist Archives, Drew University, and Brian McCloskey, St. George's United Methodist Church, Philadelphia.

1. [Methodist Episcopal Church], *The Doctrines and Discipline of the Methodist Episcopal Church in America With Explanatory Notes, by Thomas Coke and Franics Asbury*, 10th ed. (1798; reprint ed., Rutland, VT: 1979).
2. Ibid., p. 70.
3. I will use the names "St. George's" and the "Philadelphia Society" interchangeably except where the meaning suggests otherwise. The other societies were Ebenezer, a white congregation just south of the city; Bethel, a black

congregation in the southwestern part of the city; and Zoar, another black congregation north of the city in an area called Campington.

See also *The History of American Methodism*, ed. Emory Stevens Bucke, 3 vols. (New York: Abingdon Press, 1964), I, 82-5; Francis H. Tees, comp., "History of Old St. George's Methodist Episcopal Church" (Philadelphia: n. p. [1933], 53-5.

4. [MEC], *Discipline*, 1798, p. 147n.

5. [St. George's Methodist Episcopal Church], "The Names of the Officers, and Members of the Methodist Church in Philadelphia," [c. 1794]-1814, Historical Society of the Eastern Pennsylvania Conference of the United Methodist Church, St. George's United Methodist Church, Philadelphia [hereafter cited as HSEPC]. Smallwood was also a licensed local preacher [ibid.]; on Mary Wilmer, see John Lednum, *A History of the Rise of Methodism in America, Containing Sketches of Methodist Itinerant Preachers, From 1736 to 1785* (Philadelphia: 1859), pp. 41-42.

6. [MEC] *Discipline*, 1798, pp. 146-7.

7. Ibid., p. 67.

8. Jesse Lee, *A Short History of the Methodists in the United States of America from 1766 to 1809 to which is prefixed a brief account of their rise in England* (Baltimore: 1810), pp. 316-330; [St. George's MEC], "The Names of the Officers," Occupations have been identified in *The Prospect of Philadelphia and Check on the Next Directory*, ed. Edmund Hogan (Philadelphia: 1795); *The Philadelphia Directory for 1800*, ed. Cornelius William Stafford (Philadelphia: 1800); *The Philadelphia Directory, City and County Register, for 1802*, ed. James Robinson (Philadelphia: 1802).

9. [St. George's MEC], "The Names of the Officers."

10. *An Act for Incorporating the Methodist Episcopal Church, Known by the Name of Saint George's Church, In the City of Philadelphia, in the Commonwealth of Pennsylvania* (Philadelphia: 1789), pp. 6-7.

11. [St. George's MEC], "The Names of the Officers." The names of the trustees of the Chartered Fund are listed in *Articles of Association of the Trustees of the Fund for the Relief and Support of the Itinerant, Superannuated, and Worn-Out Ministers and Preachers of the Methodist Episcopal Church, In the United States of America, Their Wives and Children, Widows and Orphans* (Philadelphia: 1797), p. 4.

12. Francis Asbury, *The Journal and Letters of Francis Asbury*, eds. Elmer T. Clark, J. Manning Potts, and Jacob S. Payton, 3 vols. (London and Nashville: Epworth Press and Abingdon Press, 1958), 2:273.

13. See entries for April–December 1800 in [St. George's Methodist Episcopal Church], Receipt Book, 1795-1806, HSEPC.

14. Cooper is quoted in George A. Phoebus, comp., *Beams of Light on Early Methodism in America* (NY & Cincinnati: 1887), pp. 288-9. [St. George's MEC], "The Names of the Officers."

15. [MEC], *Discipline*, pp. 70, 52.

16. Lee, p. 318; [St. George's MEC], "The Names of the Officers"; Phoebus, comp., *Beams of Light*, pp. 288-89. Notes appearing to be in Sneath's hand are written after the date 7 November 1800 in [St. George's MEC], "The Names of the Officers"; Sneath's name appears in an entry for 5 December 1800 in [St. George's MEC], Receipt Book. For a discussion of Everett's career, see Lednum, *Rise of Methodism*, pp. 328-332.

17. Phoebus, comp., *Beams of Light*, p. 289, Asbury, *Journal and Letters*, 2:273.

18. The new class leaders are listed with the date 23 January 1801 in [St. George's MEC], "The Names of the Officers." Asbury, *Journal and Letters*, 3:206.

19. Phoebus, comp., *Beams of Light*, pp. 290-91. [Methodist Episcopal Church], *Minutes of the Methodist Conferences, Annually Held in America; from 1773 to 1813, Inclusive* (New York: 1813), p. 262.

20. Asbury, *Journal and Letters*, 3:207-10.

21. Phoebus, comp., *Beams of Light*, pp. 290-91; Haskins to Messrs. Swain & Coate 8 June 1801, HSEPC. James

Doughty's letter of resignation from his trusteeship is cited in *History of Ebenezer Methodist Episcopal Church of Southwark, Philadelphia*, comp. Centennial Publishing Committee (Philadelphia: 1890), p. 44.

22. [Lambert Wilmer, et.al.], to "The Methodist Connection in the City of Philadelphia," 12 June 1801, Ezediel Cooper Papers, The United Library, Garrett Evangelical/Seabury Western Evangelical Theological Seminaries, Evanston, IL [extracted in "Calendar of the Ezekiel Cooper collection of early American Methodist manuscripts, 1785-1839," Drew University Library, Madison, NJ]. On Wilmer, see Lednum, *Rise of Methodism*, pp. 41-42.

23. John F. Watson, *Annals of Philadelphia*, rev. ed., 3 vols. (Philadelphia: 1881), 3:274ff.

24. "[Constitution for the] United Societies 1801," HSEPC. "Societies" has been altered to read "Society" on the title page of the document.

25. Ibid., pp. 17-36.

26. Ibid., p. 4.

27. Ibid., p. 10.

28. Cooper to Daniel Fidler, 9 February 1799, Drew University Library; Bruce to Daniel Fidler, 9 August 1799, Drew University Library; Asbury, *Journals and Letters*, 2:273.

29. [St. George's MEC], "The Names of the Officers." The members for St. George's and Ebenezer are not distinguished in the register, except for two members admitted by McCombs in July 1800 under "A list of members received on trial at Ebennezer."

30. Ibid.,; the statistics for the black members are listed in [MEC], *Minutes of the Methodist Conferences, Annually Held in America; from 1773 to 1813, Inclusive*, pp. 241, 257.

31. Cooper quoted in Phoebus, comp., *Beams of Light*, pp. 287-288, 290.

32. Ibid., pp. 289-291; [St. George's MEC], Receipt Book.

33. The names of the members of the two societies are from [St. George's MEC], "The Names of the Officers," and [Union Methodist Episcopal Church], "Register of the Names of Official & Private Members of the Methodist Society meeting at the College," 1801-1811, HSEPC. Occupations have been identified from *The Philadelphia Directory for 1800; The Philadelphia Directory for 1801*, ed. Cornelius William Stafford (Philadelphia: 1801); and *The Philadelphia Directory, City and County Register, for 1802*. I have used the occupational categories outlined by Sharon V. Salinger in "Artsans, Journeymen, and the Transformation of Labor in Late Eighteenth-Century Philadelphia," *William and Mary Quarterly*, 3d ser., 40 (1983): 67. She in turn adapted these from Allan Kulikoff, "The Progress of Inequality in Revolutionary Boston," *William and Mary Quarterly*, 3d ser., 28 (1971): 375-412.

34. Of the three remaining men, one was an insurance clerk, another a physician, and the third a tax collector.

35. Ninety-four men are not listed in the directories for 1800 & 1802. Twenty-seven more have multiple entries that make identification uncertain.

36. There was also a smattering of government employees, professionals, and clerks remaining at the old society, including: the superintendent of roads, a clerk from the U.S. Registrar's Office, a teacher, and an accountant.

37. Artisans involved with the shipping industry included: a wharf-builder, two shipwrights, a rope-maker, a mast-maker, and a sail-maker. On the status of 18th-century artisans, see Richard B. Morris, *Government and Labor in Early America* (New York: 1947), pp. 35-44 and Billy G. Smith, "Struggles of the 'Lower Sort': The Lives of Philadelphia's Laboring People, 1750 to 1800" (Ph.D. diss., University of California at Los Angeles, 1981), chs. 3-5.

38. The names of the officers of St. George's discussed here are those remaining, by process of elimination, from the 1800 list of officers. No list of officers exists for 1801, but all these men appear as class leaders, local preachers or stewards in the class lists for 1802: see [St. George's

Methodist Episcopal Church], "A Register of the Names, of the Members of the Methodist Episcopal Church, In Philadelphia," 1802-1810, HSEPC. Pennel Beale had been a jorneyman cabinetmaker in 1791-2 (Salinger, "Artisans," p. 73).

39. [St. George's Methodist Episcopal Church], Register of Marriages, 1789-1817, HSEPC.

40. On John Hood, see Lednum, pp. 41-2.

41. [Union MEC], "Register"; [St. George's Methodist Episcopal Church], Register of Births and Baptisms, 1785-1817, HSEPC.

42. [MEC], *Discipline*, 1798, p. 59.

43. Asbury, *Journal and Letters*, 3:212, 216, 217.

44. Ibid., pp. 215, 223.

45. Ibid., pp. 212-2; Haskins to Asbury, 11 July 1801, photocopy at Drew University Library.

46. Asbury, *Journal and Letters*, 3:218; 132-3.

47. Phoebus, comp., *Beams of Light*, pp. 290-91. The two members were Alexander Cook and Daniel Doughty, who gave $125 and $150 respectively. Most donations were between $1 and $10. ([St. George's Methodist Episcopal Church], "Monies Received for the Church by E. Cooper and paid over to the Committee for the Dividend to Creditors," 3 November 1801, HSEPC).

48. [St. George's Methodist Episcopal Church], "General Statement of the Case and Situation of the E. Church Called St. George's," 14 November 1801, Ezekiel Cooper Papers, Drew University Library.

49. Asbury, *Journal and Letters*, 2:337; 3:239. In 1811 the heads of the Academy church built a chapel called St. Thomas's in 10th Street between Market and Chestnut: "This was much the best church edifice that the Methodists then had in the nation, and it was called by Mr. Asbury, who first preached in it in 1812, by way of eminence, 'The City Road,' after Mr. Wesley's London chapel.

"A number of the Academy members entertaining the notion that this fine church, as they called it, was built to accommodate a few of the most wealthy Methodist families, refused to worship in it; and, as we have been informed, started a prayer-meeting at the same hour that the preaching was at St. Thomas's, in the region of Thirteenth and Vine, which was the germ of Nazareth Church. As a congregation could not be raised for St. Thomas's to sustain it with free seats, and as the time for pews (which might have saved it) in a Methodist church in this city was not yet, the church was sold, and the Episcopalians bought it, and called it St. Stephen's" (Lednum, *Rise of Methodism*, p. 430).

Methodist Ministers and the Second Party System

Richard Carwardine
University of Sheffield

Amongst the most far-reaching of the many profound developments that marked American society in the first half of the nineteenth century was the establishment of a democratic political system, based on universal white manhood suffrage, tending towards two-party polarisation and recognisably the forerunner of the country's modern political forms. During the 1820s and 1830s a new breed of professional politician and party manager, typified by the 'Little Magician', Martin Van Buren, experimented with conventions and other forms of elaborate party discipline and machinery as a means of coming to terms with the broadened suffrage; by 1840 two competing and almost equally balanced parties, Whigs and Democrats, whose popular strength extended into virtually every corner of the union, dominated the political landscape. In the early and mid-1850s, with the disintegration of the Whig party, this so-called 'second party system' collapsed but its characteristic political practices survived into the new party alignments that superseded it.[1]

Contemporaneous with the emergence and maturing of this party system was a second process of profound importance for the shaping of America, the phenomenal growth of Methodism. Numbering only 73,000 members in 1800, the Methodist Episcopal Church [MEC] grew at a rate that terrified other religious bodies, reached a membership of a quarter of a million by 1820, doubled its members in the following decade, penetrated into every quarter of the country, including traditionally hostile New England, and became the largest denomination in America.[2]

Methodist advance and the emergence of mass political parties were not causally related, but neither were they wholly unconnected processes. Both were sustained by and helped foster a mood of growing egalitarianism in American society and a faith in the ability of the ordinary American to speak and act for himself. Methodist Arminianism, inclusive, democratic and optimistic, was just the faith for a society where traditional patterns of political deference were no longer secure. Methodist practices, too, contributed to the political forms and culture of the second party system. The style and fervour of

Methodist camp meetings and revival singing, for example, found their way explicitly into the often frenzied election meetings of the period, and party activists were quite capable of adopting the terminology of the Church. Whig campaigners in Tennessee in 1840 planned 'political Camp-meetings' in every county of the state, described their political hierarchy in ecclesiastical terms ('Bishops' for senators, 'presiding elders' for electors, 'local preachers' for party activists) and aimed 'to make war upon the heathern (sic)' through the 'preaching' of 'political salvation'.[3]

Curiously, we lack any sustained study of the political role of the Methodists in an era when they were increasing in social prominence and when political culture was changing so dramatically. This gap is all the more serious in view of the writings of the 'ethnocultural' school of political historians. These not only argue that in this period religious preference and ethnic attachment were of primary significance in determining voting behaviours, but seem to suggest a pivotal role for Methodists: Ronald Formisano concludes that it was a shift in Methodist partisan attachment that contributed to the political confusion and realignment of the 1850s.[4] This paper aims to help fill this historiographical hole by exploring the response of Methodist ministers to the new forms and practices of the second party system. What political and moral responsibilities did they consider themselves to lie under? What was their proper mode of political action? What partisan preferences did they hold? How did those preferences shift? And what political influence, if any, did they wield?

I

The early Methodist preachers were preeminently soul-savers and revivalists for whom election and other forms of political activity were subordinate and largely irrelevant to their primary purpose. 'From pure motives I have ignored politics, so far as parties are concerned', Heman Bangs reflected during the highly-charged campaign of 1860. 'Since I became a minister of Christ, my only business has been to save souls.' As a young circuit-rider in Kentucky, Thomas Eddy found no difficulty in dismissing the Clay-Polk struggle of 1844 and in focusing on his own advance towards entire sanctification and on the cultivation of a general revival: 'I could scarcely bear to labour all year, & see no outpouring of God's spirit.' Whether pursuing their own or the country's spiritual needs, ministers at times of high political excitement were swift to show that the language and themes of political discourse were more appropriately employed in a higher cause. Leonidas Hamline, attending the General Conference of 1840 in Baltimore during the great Log Cabin rallies in the city, protested that he scarcely gave politics a thought: 'I am myself a candidate, but it is for *eternal life*. I aspire to a throne, but I must have one which will not perish.' When later in the year the electorate went to the polls the editor of the *Pittsburgh Christian Advocate* reminded his readers that there could be only one successful candidate for the presidency 'but we may all be successful aspirants after the honor that comes from God . . .and all make our election sure . . . Our *souls* are at stake.' Daniel De Vinne succinctly summarized the views of his generation when he concluded that 'if I had another life to live over again, I had rather it should be that of a Methodist preacher, than that of the President of this Great Republic.'[5]

More to the point, political activity, especially electioneering, was regarded as positively harmful, since it hampered the individual's spiritual growth. Matthew Simpson, attempting to stiffen his moral resolve in the face of the distractions of the Log Cabin campaign, drafted a private memorandum enjoining tougher spiritual exercises: 'Converse no more on politics, unless in answer to a question propounded.' Many lacked Simpson's discipline. In Missouri William Patton concluded that during that election Christians 'suffered considerable loss in their own personal enjoyments', and echoed the words of a Pennsylvania colleague that 'in nine cases out of ten . . . religious politicians are generally the most inattentive to the means of grace.' Election campaigns were widely believed to extinguish, interrupt or delay revivals. Peter Cartwright's complaint that 'great *declensions* and many *backslidings*' resulted from the political 'tornado' of 1840 were reiterated across the country, and similar complaints of religious 'havoc' followed the later presidential elections, particularly the 'hurrah' campaigns of 1844 and 1856.[6] Local church revivals did not disappear entirely during election campaigns, as many ministers were anxious to explain: 'Never perhaps were more Camp M[eetings] held in this region,' Robert Emory wrote from Churchville, Maryland, in September 1840, '& never, perhaps, in spite of the political excitement were they more successful'; Joseph Fort recalled that despite the counter-attractions of the presidential election of 1852 'such was the general interest . . . shops, and stores, and even the hotel was closed at night' in New Providence, during one of the greatest revivals of his ministry.[7] Nonetheless the consensus amongst ministers was that political excitement when unchecked tended towards limiting church growth.

Scrutiny of the features and implications of the second party system served to reinforce Methodist disquiet. The church's spokesmen, sympathetic to the view widely held in the early years of the new republic that political parties were factional and unhealthy, regularly denounced what Bishop James Andrew described as 'the wild, blind, reckless partisanship' of the times. Parties had 'an awful tendency to engender strife, discord, division'—'denounced in the holy Book as crimes of no small import.' They could divide congregations, 'arraying father against son, and neighbor against neighbor, and alienating the affections of brethren from each other.' They artificially divided the wider community, whose natural unity, inspired by republicanism and Christian sentiment, was only able to blossom in brief moments of national tragedy, as after the deaths of William H. Harrison and Andrew Jackson, when political conflict momentarily ceased. Party antagonisms obstructed millennial advance, for only a 'nation of freemen, united in common support of a government established by common consent' could provide the necessary unity of effort that would spread 'true holiness in their own happy land, and abroad over the face of the whole earth.' Internal denominational acrimony over the slavery question, of course, heightened Methodists' sensitivity to the evils of party. The secessions from the church of abolitionist Methodists (regarded by regulars as shameless 'partisans' who set brother against brother) and the sectional schism of the 1840s, dramatically demonstrated what 'party spirit' could do.[8]

Parties were not necessarily evil, for as Francis Hemenway remarked, 'We know there may be an honest difference of principles.' But in the hands of party managers and professional politicians, for the great majority of whom politics were no longer a trust but a trade, political parties were used to promote individual self-interest and narrowly defined group interest, ahead of the needs of the nation as a whole: 'The government is administered, now by this party and now by that, for party purposes, and not for the good of the country. Laws are enacted not to promote justice, so much as to secure political power.' Such self-interest was but a step away from 'dishonesty, corruption, vice, chicanery, and political artifice and intrigue', 'Jesuitism in politics', 'sleight of hand measures'. To win and retain power unscrupulous demagogues manipulated the gullible amongst the native population and more especially amongst the ever-growing hordes of immigrants who, 'uncultivated in morals and mind' and 'intoxicated by a few inspirations of the air of liberty . . . gather around our ballot boxes . . . the inviting dupes of the designing.'[9] Consequently 'infidel, swearing, drunken black-legs', 'duelists, Sabbath-breakers, [and] profane persons' secured office by trampling down reason and free discussion in emotional election campaigns that degenerated into little more than 'bear shows', a sequence of 'disgraceful scenes' that endangered the morals of the community. The heated abuse and sharp invective of stump orators and propaganda sheets ensured the 'scalping and roasting alive' of political opponents; political friends were idolised and eulogised—Alfred Brunson grumpily dismissed Andrew Jackson's reception after his election to the presidency in 1828 as 'man worship'; flamboyant parades, and rallies of unprecedented size and passion discouraged careful private assessment of political issues; candidates and their supporters travelled and canvassed on the sabbath; the hard cider campaign was by no means the only one to witness the 'treating' of a liquor-loving electorate. Even tobacco consumption reached distressing levels, for as Robert Emory reported from Baltimore during the 1844 campaign animated groups of election-minded tobacco-chewers spat their juice 'in such quantities, that Market St. for several days, could not be promenaded with any safety to [the ladies'] dresses—the pavement was so flooded.'[10]

Such corruption of American democratic republicanism prompted a number of Methodists to follow Bishop Andrew's advice to 'avoid politics'. 'There has been an unusual degree of political excitement & and parading here, but it is all nothing to me, & really looks like vanity . . . to see human beings intoxicating themselves with delusive hopes and vain aspirings', Enoch Mudge reported from Massachusetts in 1844. 'I have not exchanged a word with . . . anyone here on the subject of politicks. I am not a voter.' Mudge's attitude and that of like-minded colleagues was not a prelude to a Garrisonian-style, anarchist crusade against all political institutions: the worst human government was better than none at all, since society could not exist without government. Nonetheless, Mudge's thinking was erected on a providentialist premise that ultimately only God could rescue American society from its ills, that undue faith in the political process represented an over-reliance on human instrumentality. 'I . . . abide the decisions of Providence, reposing on the arm that overrules & directs the storms in church & state, as in our physical world.' As James Bontecou of the Ohio Conference remarked, reflecting on the decline of moral standards in political life, 'if God don't come to our rescue, we are gone, I fear.'[11] For such men the death of William Henry Harrison in 1841, the first president to die in office, and that of Zachary Taylor a decade later served to confirm the folly of trusting in the political process: if men put too much faith in their leaders, God would remove them to teach the nation to trust in him alone.

The vast majority of Methodist ministers, however, for two broad reasons, did not opt out of political life, but instead sought to fashion their own code of proper political activity, often very different from the code of the non-devout, and often showing considerable variation from one minister to another. First, total political withdrawal would have set them swimming against the tide of American popular culture in an era when in so many other ways they found themselves flowing with it. Public interest in politics reached a new intensity in these years; turnout in the presidential elections of 1840, 1844 and 1856 far exceeded earlier levels and was rarely to be equalled in later contests. Methodist ministers found it difficult to resist the pressures brought directly to bear on them. H.H. Green recalled at the end of his life that in the 1840s and 1850s 'politics was the very breath of life, every man was a politician. They talked politics in the morning, they thought politics through the day, and they drank politics and fought politics around the corner grocery at night . . . The preacher was systematically scolded by one party because he preached politics and by the other party because he did not preach politics.' An exasperated correspondent of the New York *Christian Advocate and Journal* complained that '[p]ublic meetings teem with censure upon the preacher who will not enlist for' this party or that, a lament viewed with sympathy by the editor, Thomas Bond, who for a period in the 1840s refused to publish political news in consequence of the abuse he received alternately from Whigs and Democrats for alleged partisan bias.[12]

Secondly, it was argued that Methodist abstinence from politics left American democracy and republicanism vulnerable to the powers of darkness. Christians had a duty to God and their country to protect a system of government sanctioned by scripture, founded on Christian principles, defensive of religious liberties and designed by the Almighty to be a beacon to the rest of the world. Typically, Rezin Sapp of Michigan, for whom the Bible was a 'purely democratical' textbook, reminded Christians that God would 'hold them responsible for the non-performance of the duties which they owe as citizens of an elective government' destined to spread 'the principles of liberty and virtue in their highest forms throughout the globe.' Without Christian guardianship, republicanism—as in the classical world—would fail: "A republic is the body, Christianity is the soul."[13] The overturning of 'the purest and best of all human governments', democratic republicanism, made more likely by the recent political abuses of the second party system, could only be prevented by 'Christian patriotism', by members of the religious community vigorously exercising their political rights.[14] The sheer numerical strength of Methodism gave to both its lay members and its ministers a particular responsibility to throw their political influence 'on the side of good morals, equal rights, [the] Constitution, law and peace'. In Ohio, for example, where in the 1840s Charles Elliott calculated that about half the population were members or adherents of the MEC, the thousand or so local and travelling preachers were regarded, together with the rest of the membership, as particularly 'responsible to the state, the United States, and the world, for good government.'[15]

Those who shared in this attitude towards Methodist political activity were generally agreed that their principal political obligation was to engage in prayer for the country's rulers. Scriptural and other historical examples indicated that the Almighty was 'intimately concerned with the passing events of time' and would not hesitate to intervene to reward those who diligently sought him. As Abraham had interceded for the cities of the Plain, and Moses for the Jews, so God had graciously rewarded the prayers of the Pilgrim Fathers, the rebellious American colonies and the founders of the new nation. He would continue to assist the good and correct the wicked in response to Christian pleading.[16]

Yet prayer alone was insufficient. Just as their theology of revivals encouraged the use of a range of means extending beyond prayer—protracted meetings, sustained preaching, the call to the altar, and so on—so Methodists advocated various additional 'instrumentalities' in pursuit of Christian political ends, the most essential being 'a regular and conscientious exercise of the elective franchise.' 'Every man should feel himself *bound* to vote', every vote counts, 'Heaven has provided the ballot-box' were common pulpit refrains. Ministers practised what they preached, even though itinerants, and particularly bishops, complained that their travels tended practically to disfranchise them. David Lewis recalled how the business of the Ohio Annual Conference was hurried to a close in 1840 to allow members to get home in time to vote; writing to Bishop Simpson in 1860 Aaron Wood asked for a day's postponement of the Northwestern Conference to prevent a clash with the state election.[17] A confirmed voter, George Coles described his perseverance in a very close New York election in 1844: 'I tried three or four times to get a chance to put in my vote but the press was so great that I could not get to the door till between 3 & 4 P.M.'[18]

In preparation for voting, ministers recognised their obligation to scrutinise the issues and the candidates with great care; for instance, James Gilruth, as presiding elder in the Detroit district in the mid-1830s considered it his duty to chew over a mixed diet of Whig circulars and a biography of Andrew Jackson. Their aim in voting should be 'the glory of God' and, as James Finley urged, to promote 'the general good, . . . the good of [the] country' and not 'Individual or party purposes.' William Winans explained that consistency was not a virtue when it meant voting for a man solely because of his party attachment. The Methodist's priority in an era when standards of public morality appeared annually to be declining had to be 'to prevent improper incumbents from getting into office.' According to Leonidas Hamline, 'A Christian citizen ought sooner to thrust his hand into a burning furnace, than suffer it to place in the ballot box a ticket blurred with the name of an infidel, vicious condidate.' A contributor to the *Western Christian Advocate* began with a disclaimer—'We do not ask that those who claim our votes, should belong to this denomination or that, nor even that they should be *pious* men'— but continued: 'we fear that . . . wrath will come upon us . . . if we vote for those who treat with open scorn the Christian religion, whose characters are stained with *drunkenness, Sabbath-breaking, profaneness, gambling,* or *murder, (dueling).*' Public scrutiny of the private lives of political candidates—particularly unmarried men, notoriously the most vulnerable to moral decay—would eventually teach the political parties to nominate only moral men for office. Voting, then, was indisputably a moral act and 'bad voting', as Calvin Fairbanks termed it, a sin. 'I as much expect to give an account to God for the manner in which *I vote* as for the manner in which I pray,' explained Thomas Eddy, echoing Samuel Lewis' view that at the day of judgement men would have to answer individually for their votes and would not be able to hide behind the skirts of party.[19]

In their discussions to establish the boundaries of legitimate political activity, many ministers concluded that their active political responsibilities ceased after casting their votes and accepting the election result with equanimity. The American who said in the 1830s that clergymen were 'a sort of people between men and women' nicely represented their position, which fell short of the adult white male's unquestioned freedom to air his political opinions and participate fully in the processes of party politics, but which exceeded that of the unfranchised woman. It was widely agreed that ministers should not attend political meetings, preach on party political questions, stand for office, or in any way attempt to convert their congregations to their own political opinions. It would only encourage church members to 'speak evil of magistrates or ministers', expressly forbidden by the Methodist *Discipline*. It would also, as Charles Browne of Port Republic, Virginia, explained, 'lose [us] considerable influence with our people.' The provision of his state's constitution excluding clergymen from membership of the state legislature pleased those who argued that both scripture and good sense enjoined their ministers to stick to their task of spreading the gospel. Joshua Soule was all too aware of the problems that ministerial association with a particular party could cause when in 1840 he found his private eulogy of William Harrison incorporated into Whig propaganda; he consumed considerable time, energy and embarrassment attempting to explain away his gaffe. At Indiana Asbury University where it was said on the eve of the 1844 election that William Larrabee 'spends at least half his hour in the recitation room in teaching Locofocoism' Lucien Berry was terrified that the charge would weaken the institution's public standing at a critical period in its history.[20]

Similar concerns led the editors of Methodist newspapers to steer clear of party politics. Reflecting on a list of about fifty thousand subscribers to the four major publications, representing an estimated readership of a quarter of a million, Thomas Morris reminded Matthew Simpson, as he took over the editorship of one of them, the *Western Christian Advocate*, that his paper could 'accomplish more than the entire episcopal board' provided it took a conciliatory, non-controversial approach.[21] The New York *Christian Advocate* and its Pittsburgh namesake customarily disclaimed any desire to discuss the bank or tariff questions, deliberately avoided the issue of Texas annexation, and apologised for mischievous partisans who slipped separately printed political speeches into the paper at the point of distribution. 'There is not a vestige of party politics in our paper, on one side or the other', protested the editor of the *Pittsburgh Christian Advocate*, worried by those who had discontinued their subscriptions on the grounds that it had failed to carry the occasional messages of the state governor. Political self-denial equally characterised the formal proceedings of the Methodist annual and general conferences for the reason that many members would be alienated, and that any attempted control of Methodists' political action would be the first step towards turning the MEC into the established church of the United States: 'All political parties would pay court to our ministers, and from a spiritual Church we should be degraded to a mere government machine.'[22]

It nonetheless proved impossible in practice to purify the ministry of its compulsive partisans. Some, like David R. McAnally, edited campaign newspapers, or lent their moral authority to a particular candidate, as did William Barnes and Arthur Elliott to Harrison in 1840 by officiating at his meetings. Others, like Peter Cartwright and Alfred Brunson, even stood successfully for political office, as Illinois Democrat and Wisconsin Whig respectively. Colleagues might raise their eyebrows and even their voices at such goings-on but there was a clear logic to this public commitment to party, implicit in John Inskip's recognition that 'all political questions have a connection, more or less direct, with both morality and religion.'[23] If Methodists had a duty to God to promote righteousness and eliminate national sins—a principal theme of Methodist and other evangelical Protestant literature of the period—and if one particular party appeared to be more clearly identified than the other with those sins, then the public embracing of the lesser of two political evils had a clear moral justification. Of course, ministers often saw little morally to choose between the contending parties, whose divisions they regarded as factitious and unrelated to religious issues. But not all saw matters in this light, and as political questions of undoubted moral and religious significance began not only to intrude into but to dominate party politics in the 1840s and 1850s, so more and more Methodists saw no conflict between their religious profession and a highly visible political posture. They found it increasingly difficult to remain silent on matters relating to temperance, Roman Catholicism, the Mexican War, the spread of slavery and the future of the Union itself, despite the continuing opposition of 'non-political', 'quietest' Methodists, particularly in the South. This increasingly public political activity of Methodist ministers was closely related to significant shifts in their party attachments in the 1840s and 1850s. Both developments deserve a careful analysis not simply for what they reveal about the history of Methodism but as a means towards a fuller appreciation of the second party system and the process of its collapse.

II

The persecution of the early Methodists by the defenders of the ecclesiastical and social establishment, most particularly in New England, is a well-told story. Methodists were obliged to pay taxes to support the churches established by law; poor ministers incurred heavy fines for performing marriage ceremonies for their own members; hostile mobs destroyed meeting houses, intimidated worshippers and attacked itinerant preachers, whom they regarded as 'incarnate demons' and 'intruders into the land of steady habits.' Even where the early Methodists suffered no legal disabilities they experienced discrimination at the hands of socially entrenched Calvinists, as in the Western Reserve of Ohio where the informal Standing Order of Presbyterians and Congregationalists worked to deny them access to preaching places.[24] Part of Methodism's strategy of self-defence had been to take political refuge in the Jeffersonian Democratic-Republican party, whose ideas on religious freedom and on the separation of church and state drew succour from the Federal Constitution and stood in sharp contrast to those of the Federalists, generally regarded as the party of the Calvinist establishment and the socially well-to-do. Although Jefferson himself was perceived as at best a deist and by his Federalist enemies as an atheist of doubtful morals, Methodists very generally rallied to his party's standard. Many ministers could have described themselves, as did William Winans, as 'rather enthusiastic' Jeffersonians; a few, like Jeremiah Stocking of Connecticut and Dan Young of New Hampshire, even sought state political office as Republicans in order to fight for full disestablishment and for Methodist equality under the law.[25]

The forces that made most Methodists Jeffersonian Democrats under the first party system lured many of them into the ranks of Jacksonian Democracy during the second, particularly in its early years. Jacksonians were committed to a philosophy of *laissez-faire* not only in political economy and social legislation, but also in the area of religion and the legal enforcement of moral behaviour.[26] They seemed to offer a home to those Arminian Methodists who continued instinctively to define themselves politically as anti-Federalist, and who feared that John Quincy Adams' National Republicans and then nascent Whiggery represented the Calvinist establishment in new clothing. It was no accident that Solon Stocking adopted Democratic principles, as had his Jeffersonian father, when he found the full social weight of Connecticut's Standing Order pressing down on him as he tried to conduct Methodist revival services in the 1820s; Calvinist arrogance and bigotry, or the enduring memory of them, drove a number into the welcoming arms of the Jacksonians. Herein undoubtedly lies part of the reason for Methodist resistance to the charms of a Whig party which made markedly successful overtures to the membership of other evangelical denominations. Hugh McCulloch certainly exaggerated when he argued that up to the 1850s there were few exceptions to the rule of general Methodist identification with the Democratic party, but the evidence produced by Lee Benson, Ronald Formisano and other historians who have attempted to correlate party strength and church attachment makes it clear that in the heyday of the second party system Methodists maintained a considerable Jacksonian attachment, symbolised by the assertive loyalty of such luminaries as Edward R. Ames, Edmund S. Janes and Peter Cartwright.[27]

Yet, without necessarily calling into question the findings of the ethno-cultural historians in regard to the political loyalties of the mass of Methodists, it is clear from a careful reading of their published autobiographies and private papers that Methodist preachers were disproportionately Whig, not Democrat, during the second party system. Some showed their colours early on. George Peck might keep his hostility to Jackson private in the 1828 election, but William Winans, who had followed Henry Clay in his pilgrimage from anti-Federalism *via* National Republicanism to Whiggery, made no secret of his antipathy to Jackson. Winans' political sermons were a model of discretion, however, when compared with the prayers of 'a violent Anti-Jackson preacher' in the Baltimore Conference who, when visiting the White House in 1831 along with thirty or so of his colleagues, knelt and 'prayed that the Gen[eral] might be converted', 'which he did so loud, that he could be heard at the President's gate.' By the 1840s Whiggery had a firm grip on the Methodist leadership: Henry Bascom, James Andrew and John Emory upheld it in the South; Matthew Simpson and Chauncey Hobart, who had to swallow hard before preaching his sermon on Jackson's death, typified the party's ministerial supporters in the west, where it was claimed that most of the Indiana Conference was Whig in 1840; John Inskip, George Crooks, John McClintock and George Coles spoke for many in northeastern Methodism. When the English Wesleyan James Dixon visited America in 1848 to attend the General Conference, it was his clear impression that the vast majority of the Methodist ministers that he met on his extensive travels were firmly in that political camp.[28]

In a few instances Methodist ministers gravitated towards the Whigs out of despair over those Jacksonian economic policies that had helped give definition to the parties in the 1830s, particularly the attack on the Bank of the United States. Lorenzo Dow's admiration for Jackson evaporated, while George Brown held the Democrats morally responsible for the financial panic of 1837 and the economic distress that followed.[29] Most Methodists, however, did not move in a Whiggish direction for reasons of specific economic policy. They did so rather because the Democrats unabashedly embraced social groups and sub-cultures which increasingly appeared to threaten the influence and status of evangelical Protestantism in the culture as a whole, and because Whiggery seemed to offer the best means of sustaining Christian influence in public life.

The same liberal Jacksonian philosophy that attracted Methodist enemies of the informal Calvinist establishment also offered equality of treatment to Mormons, freethinkers and others out of step with the dominant Protestantism around them.[30] Most threatening of all the groups sheltered by the Democrats was the burgeoning Roman Catholic community—German and Irish immigrants whose alleged hard-drinking habits, disrespect for the Sabbath and obedience to dissolute priests not only offended evangelical sensibilities but undermined the Christian purpose of the nation. The full evangelical indictment of the Catholic Church needs no recapitulation here. What does deserve

emphasis is the close identification of that church with the Democratic party—by 1844 some 95 percent of New York's Irish Catholics were loyal Jacksonians—and the recognition of this alignment by fearful Methodists. If William Gannaway Brownlow was the most vitriolic of Methodist critics, charging Catholic immigrants with almost unanimous support for the Locofocos, denouncing Van Buren as a sycophantic flatterer of the Pope, and portraying Bishop John England as a Jacksonian propagandist, his was not the only pen to denounce the Democrats' furthering of Catholic ends. The *Christian Advocate and Journal* grew ever more angry at the efforts of the Catholic hierarchy in the early 1840s to secure state funding for their schools in New York and other cities: 'The school question is now made a political one in the city of New York with the Romanists claiming the aid of the Democrats, and the Whigs asking the help of Protestants . . . . The Protestants have not done this; . . . the Romanists are the aggressors.' Methodists grew similarly embittered—particularly those of Irish extraction like Charles Elliott—by the Democratic party's complicity in the efforts of the Irish Catholic community to secure the repeal of the Anglo-Irish Union of 1800.[31]

Although the Whigs did not adopt an unequivocally anti-Catholic posture, as William Seward's attempted wooing of the Catholic hierarchy in New York in the early 1840s made clear, they were nevertheless able to establish themselves as the best hope of thwarting Catholic political influence and on a number of occasions in the 1830s and 1840s successfully annexed embryonic nativist movements.[32] More generally, they worked with great energy to cultivate their image as the Christian party in politics, a mantle they took over from the Antimasonic party, whose members they had largely managed to absorb. Free-masonry was a sensitive issue for Methodists, both at the time of its emergence as a political issue in the 1820s and throughout the antebellum period: it was hated and feared by many individual Methodists and regarded with disfavour by some conferences, although the Church as a whole did not pass judgment, since too many Methodists were prominent in this and other secret societies. Whiggery undoubtedly benefited from Methodist animus against the order. It was also helped by its 'Christian' and paternalist stand on the Indian question, as compared with the 'sordid cupidity' of the Jacksonians' policy, which Methodists regarded as 'crooked and disgraceful', a distinct break with the traditional Republican policy from Jefferson to Adams. Whig anti-partyism, with its implications for the return of a cohesive Christian community, helped sustain their Puritan image, as did their much emphasised sympathy for sustaining overt Christian influence in government, symbolised by William Henry Harrison's invoking of religion in an inaugural address for the first time since Washington and in President John Tyler's reversing Jacksonian policy by calling for a day of national humiliation and prayer.[33]

Democrats, fearing a convergence of Methodism and evangelically-oriented Whiggery, stressed in their propaganda the 'Federalist' roots of the Whig party, and its threat to the separation of church and state, but to little avail. Whereas in the early years of the century the fear of Federalism and state-supported Calvinism had been powerful enough to hold within the Republican party both Methodism and, as Alfred Brunson recalled, 'the infidel portion of the community, though these classes were antipodes in all things pertaining to religion', by the 1830s very many Methodists were quite prepared to take their place in a party ideologically shaped in part by Calvinists. Concerned by the decline of religion in the public life of the nation—financial corruption and the evils of the 'spoils system', the threat to chaplaincies in Congress and the state legislatures, congressmen's continued resort to duelling to settle disputes, Sabbath-breaking and intemperance amongst public figures, for example—many Methodist ministers appear to have concluded that the Whigs, sympathetic to legislation to defend moral standards, offered a surer hope of a remedy than the Democrats and their principle of moral *laissez-faire*. During the 1830s and 1840s many Methodists abandoned their faith in moral suasion alone as a means of preserving a Christian social order and turned to the government for legislative support, whether to outlaw duelling, prohibit the liquor trade, forbid gambling, sustain the traditional Protestant Sabbath or protect camp meetings from the disturbances of liquor sellers and scoffers. For the benefit of those within and outside Methodism who worried that such measures represented a threat to the separation of church and state, Methodist spokesmen sought to distinguish between an improper sectarian establishment and an entirely proper exercising of Christian influence over legislation: 'No enlightened Christian wishes to see Church and State united in government; but if men [are] to do all things to the glory of God, they must be constantly governed by the moral law of God; and hence religious principle must be made the basis of political action.'[34]

Methodists' growing readiness to sit alongside Calvinist evangelicals in the same political party was encouraged by a developing harmony between the two groups as theological and socio-economic gaps narrowed. In the first place, the enormous popular appeal of democratic Arminianism during the Second Great Awakening imposed irresistible pressures on the Calvinist churches to modify their doctrines of human inability, election and limited atonement. Many Calvinist ministers either responded to pressure from below, as their congregations revolted against a strict creed, or were themselves the popularizers of a 'new divinity', the Arminianized Calvinism associated with Nathaniel Taylor, and practitioners of the 'new measures' adapted by Charles Finney from Methodist revivalism.[35] As the Second Great Awakening drew to a close both Methodists and Calvinists came to reassess their theological position and to recognise their near agreement on evangelical fundamentals in the face of threatening heterodoxies: Mormonism, Universalism and, most seriously, Roman Catholicism. '[T]he times call for unity of spirit and effort among the evangelical churches', announced the *Christian Advocate and Journal* in 1842, at the very time when all orthodox Protestant denominations were already involved in defending themselves against Catholic intrusions, through the American Protestant Union. At the Evangelical Alliance meetings in London in 1846, much applauded by American Methodists, George Peck, carried away by the occasion, could demand: 'Perish the Calvinistic and the Arminian controversy.' During the 1840s and 1850s many evangelical ministers took him at his word as they co-operated in interdenominational efforts for revival, often spurred by a common attachment to perfectionist doctrine.[36]

Secondly, some of the antipathy between Arminian and Calvinist melted as Methodists progressed from being a socially despised sect of the poor, 'the offscouring of all things', into a respected denomination of some power and influence in the community, able to throw off its inferiority complex and forget much of the suffering experienced at the hands of snobbish Presbyterians and Congregationalists. As Methodists grew wealthier and built larger, more ornate churches with organs, rented pews and steeples, as they demanded and secured a college-bred, more sophisticated and urbane ministry, as they preached before Presidents and respected statesmen and officiated as chaplains of the Senate and the House of Representatives, so they left their persecuted past behind.[37] When Selah Stocking transferred from the New England to the Oneida Conference in the 1830s he discovered that 'his church members were among the leading citizens of the place; and he soon found himself associated with families of wealth and refinement.' Similar reflections emanated from southern and western Methodists in that and later decades, and even in New England significant improvements in their wealth and social status occurred during the antebellum period. Methodist representation amongst the wealthiest and most influential in the community was the exception and not the rule, but by the 1850s Methodists were to be found in state governorships, in the United States Senate and in the Supreme Court.[38] By no means all Calvinists accepted Methodists' new status: a senior Ohio preacher complained to Matthew Simpson in 1850 of the Presbyterians continued 'vauntings and . . . thrusts at Methodism' and in Galesburg, Illinois, a few years later Milton Haney experienced 'persistent and bitter' opposition from a transplanted colony of New England Congregationalists. Yet, more tellingly, in the same decade George Coles could look back over his thirty years in America and conclude that '[o]ne thing is certain, the evangelical sects are more harmonious in their feelings toward each other than they were formerly'; while the elderly Nathan Bangs, addressing an interdenominational prayer meeting after the revival of 1857-58 confessed: 'I have been a man of war all my days almost. I have fought the Calvinists, the Hopkinsians, and the Protestant Episcopalians . . . but I have laid aside the polemic armour long since, and I felt it my duty to preach . . . upon brotherly love'; and the New Hampshire Congregationalist Nathaniel Bouton confirmed that '[t]here is now more liberality and charity among different denominations than formerly. If our fathers erred in being too exclusive and bigoted, we are in danger of the other extreme.'[39]

In 1840, at the very moment that Whigs were demonstrating that they had come of age, that they had an ideology and organisation sufficiently coherent to win them a national election, two issues that were eventually to destroy the party were already raising their heads: slavery and nativism. Methodists could ignore neither. Indeed, they and other evangelical Protestant denominations did much to force public discussion of issues whose moral implications they believed justified their active involvement in the political arena. As the leaders of Methodism came to define their positions and reconsider their Whiggery, they made their own particular contribution to the complex political configurations of the early and mid 1850s and to the collapse of the second party system.

A small minority of northern Methodist ministers of strong antislavery principles deserted the Whigs near the time of the election of 1840, most particularly the Ohio local preacher, Samuel Lewis, who was later to stand variously for state and national office as candidate of the Liberty party and the Free Soilers. Lewis' departure from a party whose position on economic issues he much admired was the result of what he regarded as its succumbing like the Democrats to the control of apologists for slavery, particularly once John Tyler had entered the White House. But most northern Methodists were not then ready to take his radical step of supporting 'independent nominations'—abolitionism in a political context, as it seemed. Typical of mainstream ministerial attitudes was that of the Pittsburgh Conference, which in 1841 according to Charles Elliott regarded abolitionism as 'a system of agitation— a political faction—a slandering of their Church—an injury to the colored race—a schism in the Church—an appeal to revolutionizing sentiments and feelings.' 'Ultras' like Lewis were regarded warily, sometimes excluded from churches, their status as preachers even in jeopardy at times. Abolitionist and third-party action threatened Methodist unity and the integrity of the Union, both of them essential to the fulfilment of America's religious destiny.[40]

However, during the 1840s antislavery sentiment deepened within the northern branch of the church at the same time that the vast majority of its members remained resistant to militant abolitionism. Already convinced that slavery was a great moral and social evil, they were increasingly persuaded that they faced an arrogant and aggressive southern leadership in both church and state anxious to strengthen the place of slavery not just in the south but in the nation as a whole. Despite the Plan of Separation established after the church schism, MEC ministers in the border conferences of Ohio, Baltimore and Philadelphia later in the 1840s suffered physical violence at the hands of mobs encouraged by Methodist editors and lay sympathisers. Moreover, southern magistrates regularly suppressed or burnt copies of the supposedly seditious *Christian Advocate and Journal* and the *Western Christian Advocate*. Some southern ministers were said to have engineered the breach in Methodism to encourage southern secession, the break up of the Union and an eventual civil war: Thomas Bond likened William A. Smith, president of Randolph Macon College, to Marat and Robespierre for his disunionist demagoguery. Against such a background it was little wonder that many northern Methodists who considered themselves moderates on the slavery question came to regard the annexation of Texas and the Mexican War as the product of a Slave Power bent on spreading its social and political influence within the Union. 'That 250,000 slaveholders should rule this great empire is a thing not to be endured', John McClintock told Stephen Olin, adding ominously: 'it can't be endured much longer.'[41]

By the time of the political crisis and settlement of 1850 many northern Methodists had taken up a free-soil stance of opposition to the expansion of slavery into all territories. Francis Hemenway, in his Independence Day celebration of American liberty and prosperity in 1851, could not avoid dwelling on the 'great moloch' of slavery: only the slave states had the power to challenge slavery within their borders, 'but we do claim', he said, 'that this odious God-defying . . . institution shall be divested of its nationality . . . and that our Federal Government - our nation shall cease to patronize & uphold it.' Thanks also to the demands of the new Fugitive Slave Law, men like Asa Kent, transformed from a harsh critic of antislavery Methodists into a moral and financial supporter of passengers on the underground railroad, were either drawn into the Free Soil party or sought free-soil commitments from the Whigs and Democrats. 'Think not that I am a "naked abolishionist [sic]" for I have always heretofore "went the regular nominee", but I now wish it distinctly understood that I'll do so no more, unless that nominee is an out & out Wilmot Proviso man', wrote a Methodist from Eaton, Ohio, to Matthew Simpson at the time when Simpson's free-soil editorials in the *Western Christian Advocate* had been causing a major political stir: 'Our preacher Bro. White is commending your course & articles *very highly*.'[42]

Antislavery Methodists were only prepared to go on voting Whig for as long as the party evidenced sympathy for free soil; in the early 1850s northern Whiggery appeared sufficiently true to the cause for its Methodist supporters to remain generally loyal. A number of southern Methodists, of course, were growing increasingly suspicious of the free-soil elements in Whiggery, their concern well epitomised by William G. Brownlow's desertion in 1852 of his party's regular presidential nominee, Winfield Scott, who it was feared would fall under the sway of Seward and northern radicals. But what most seriously threatened to cut the ties joining Methodism to Whiggery were the problems relating to immigration. The three million immigrants who entered the United States between the mid-1840s and the mid-1850s inevitably intensified existing Protestant fears

over Catholic influence, its threat to common-school education and democratic republicanism, and its encouragement of Sabbath-breaking, intemperance, crime and pauperism. Yet at the time when anti-Catholics and nativists turned for solutions to these problems towards their most natural political allies, the Whigs, a combination of tolerance, anti-nativism and careful political calculation was pushing that party into wooing the immigrants and Catholic community. William Seward's overtures to the Catholic hierarchy in New York state had been a straw in the wind: many Whig leaders, including Scott in 1852, spoke flatteringly to Catholic audiences, eulogising Daniel O'Connell, praising the Pope, and even commending their Irish brogue. Despite pressure on them to support temperance measures along the lines of the Maine Law, many Whigs sought to fudge the issue and to avoid a commitment for or against prohibition that would in one way or another lose them votes.[43]

In growing anger Methodist ministers, disgusted by the way the politicians of all parties temporised, spoke of igniting what Thomas Goodwin described as 'a flame of righteous indignation that will burn till all party bonds are consumed, and freemen will vote for good men who will not give the reins of power to the lawless and unprincipled.' William Simmons declared that he would never 'vote for any man, Whig or Democrat, for the legislature of Ohio, who is not a friend to the temperance cause.' If the regular parties would not put up sound candidates then Methodists, as Goodwin and his Indiana colleague B.F. Crary argued early in 1853, 'being now free from the yoke of party', would simply amputate the 'gangrened members on the body politic' and elect non-aligned and decent men. Francis Hemenway of Massachusetts and George Coles of New York were just two whose practice matched the prescriptions of their ministerial colleagues by voting the Maine Law ticket in state and local elections that year.[44] At the same time very many Methodist ministers, hypnotised by the glorious prospects held out to them by the nativist and anti-Catholic Know-Nothing party, cast off their traditional ties. A few like Mark Trafton of Massachusetts and W.H. Goodwin of New York even stood successfully for political office; very many more offered their votes, most dramatically in Indiana, where Joseph Wright, the state governor and himself a Methodist, complained that at least two-thirds of MEC ministers were connected with the secret organisation. By no means all Methodists approved of the intolerance, secrecy and proscription encouraged by the new party, but it drew quite enough support to destroy the informal alliance between the church's ministers and Whiggery.[45]

During these years, then, and particularly in 1854—when the repeal of the Missouri Compromise and the bursting forth of Know-Nothingism shattered political loyalties—disillusioned southern, pro-slavery Methodist preachers like Brownlow, northern free-soil ministers like Simpson and northern prohibitionists and anti-Catholics like Coles moved from Whiggery to new political attachments by a variety of routes. By the election of 1856, however, their destinations were becoming clear: the majority of northern Methodist ministers, if not their members, had moved into the Republican party, noisily anti-slavery, silently anti-Catholic, while southern Methodists either found their way into the Democratic party (from which not all had strayed anyway) or into Millard Fillmore's American party, Whiggish, anti-Democratic and mildly nativist. The alignments of the second party system were dead.

III

Methodist ministers, then, took their political duties seriously during the era of the second party system—so seriously that increasingly during the 1840s and 1850s they were attacked for interfering in political matters supposedly beyond their proper concern. When John Inskip publicly attacked the Polk administration for its involving America in a war with Mexico he was himself denounced as 'reverend stumper'; Matthew Simpson's editorial stand in the Western *Christian Advocate* on free soil and the 'higher law' during the crisis of 1850 called down the fury of hostile politicians; B.F. Crary's involvement in the politics of temperance evoked cries of 'meddling with politics' from what he regarded as canting, 'whiffling demagogues'. Whether or not Methodist ministers really were meddling in politics—and it could be argued that what increased was not simply their outspokenness, but the level of sensitivity of the issues raised, and the fragility of political parties—it is clear that their critics had a considerable respect for their potential political influence. Why else should they worry about what Methodist leaders said in their pulpits and wrote in their denominational newspapers? Why else were the eyes of the political world fixed on the quadrennial General Conferences of the church? Why else should politicians court her ministers and leading laymen? Typically, in 1840 Andrew Jackson encouraged Van Buren to offer a Tennessee postmastership to a Methodist minister who wielded considerable local influence, on the grounds that if he were deprived of the post on

President Harrison's taking office, the county would swing to the Democrats in protest. As Francis Hodgson complained in 1856, now that the church was so strong each political party was 'eager to make her its tool.'[46]

In fact, critics of Methodism in some ways worried too much about ministerial political influence. Methodist congregations were often so clearly divided on political issues that ministers hesitated to offer clear partisan directives: Joshua Soule explained that as an officer of a church that embraced 'citizens of different opinions in political matters, I conscientiously decline any interference . . . in the recommendation of my friends who are applicants for office.' Charles Browne was clear that '[a]s ministers, if we warmly espouse either side of [a] great political question, we will lose considerable influence with our people.' It was not unknown for church members to walk out of services—as sometimes happened when Samuel Lewis preached—or to join another congregation, to escape 'political preaching' of one kind or another. Ministers were less reluctant to exert partisan influence in private, however. Lucien Berry, confirmed Whig, wrote jubilantly to Matthew Simpson of the defeat of an Indiana opponent: 'The preachers done [*sic*] all they could privately & nearly the entire Methodist vote went against him.'[47]

Where Methodist ministers wielded greatest political influence, however, was less in demanding particular partisan allegiances, as in helping to sharpen the sensibilities of their church members on the moral issues that came to dominate political discourse in the 1840s and 1850s. By encouraging a public debate on the correct moral response to slavery, to the possibility of its expansion into new territories, to the Catholic influence in politics and education, to the social and moral threats posed by immigration, they encouraged their members to adopt positions that forced the major parties to respond. Thomas Bond, editor of the *Christian Advocate and Journal*, thought it was improper for him to consider the political aspects of the slavery question; yet he did remind his readers that 'as individual citizens we are bound by Christian duty to determine the moral obligations which our religious professions enjoin, in respect to it, and to act upon the sober conviction to which we may come in the exercise of our political rights and privileges.' He continued: 'no well-intentioned Christian can be justified before God in withholding whatever of political influence he may have, from the effort to ameliorate, and ultimately to abolish the whole system of slavery as it exists in the United States.'[48] By such means ordinary Methodists were encouraged, not to support a particular party, but to see slavery, intemperance, Catholic intrusions and so on as national sins whose elimination was essential for the moral and religious growth of God's chosen country and for the avoidance of God's wrath. The implications for party politics were profound. Moral absolutism challenged compromise and consensus as the controlling forces of political thought and action. Politics became sectionalized, and by April 1861 compromise and consensus had collapsed.

NOTES

1. See, in particular, M.J. Heale, *The Making of American Politics 1750-1850* (London, 1977), pp. 149-202; Lee Benson, *The Concept of Jacksonian Democracy: New York as a Test Case* (Princeton, 1961); Richard P. McCormick, *The Second American Party System: Party Formation in the Jacksonian Era* (Chapel Hill, 1966); Ronald P. Formisano, *The Birth of Mass Political Parties: Michigan, 1827-1861* (Princeton, N.J., 1971); Michael F. Holt, *The Political Crisis of 1850s* (New York, 1978).
2. Charles C. Goss, *Statistical History of the First Century of American Methodism* (New York, 1866), p.110.
3. Thomas B. Alexander, 'Presidential Election of 1840 in Tennessee', *Tennessee Historical Quarterly*, I (1942), 26-27, 34-36; Hugh McCulloch, *Men and Measures of Half a Century* (New York, 1888), pp. 54-56; *Western Christian Advocate* [Cincinnati], 7 Aug. 1840. For cross-fertilization from the world of politics to the churches, see the New York *Christian Advocate and Journal*, 29 Sept. 1841, which advocated the use of 'reclaiming committees' in pursuing backsliders.
4. Formisano, *Mass Political Parties*, pp. 153-55, 312-15. Seymour M. Lipset, 'Religion and Politics in the American Past and Present' in Robert Lee and Martin E. Marty, eds. *Religion and Social Conflict* (New York, 1964), pp. 69-126, is a suggestive essay.
5. Heman Bangs, *The Autobiography and Journal of Rev. Heman Bangs* . . . (New York, 1872), p. 316; T.M. Eddy to A. White, 9 Nov. 1844, 1 Mar. 1845, Thomas M. Eddy Papers, Garrett-Evangelical Theological Seminary Library; Walter C. Palmer, *Life and Letters of Leonidas L. Hamline* (New York, 1866), p. 88; *Pittsburgh Christian Advocate*, 11 Nov. 1840; Daniel Dorchester, 'Rev. Daniel De Vinne', New England Conference Collection, Boston University; Thomas B. Miller, *Original and Selected Thoughts on the Life and Times of Rev. Thomas Miller and Rev. Thomas Warburton* (Bethlehem, Pa., 1860), p. 17; *Christian Advocate and Journal*, 28 Oct. 1840; *Western Christian Advocate* 12 Feb. 1841.
6. George R. Crooks, *The Life of Bishop Matthew Simpson* (London, 1890), p. 168; *Pittsburgh Conference Journal*, 26 Mar. 1840; *Western Christian Advocate*, 30 Nov. 1840, 11 June 1841; *Christian Advocate and Journal*, 25 Sept. 1856, 20 Dec. 1860. Cf. *Southern Christian Advocate* [Charleston, S.C.], 23 Oct. 1856; David Lewis, *Recollections of a Superannuate; or, Sketches of Life, Labor and Experience in the Methodist Itinerancy* (Cincinnati, 1857), pp. 293-96; Bangs, *Journal and Autobiography*, p. 257.
7. R. Emory to J. McClintock, 14 Sept. 1840, and J.P. Fort, 'Reminiscences', p. 238, manuscript collection, Drew University; *Pittsburgh Christian Advocate*, 11 Nov.

1840. The impact of electoral campaigns on Methodist patterns of revival—as compared to the *supposed* impact, which is all that matters in the present context—deserves attention in its own right.
8. *Western Christian Advocate*, 10 July, 18 Dec. 1840, 30 July 1841; *Christian Advocate and Journal*, 2 Sept., 4 Nov. 1840; Chauncey Hobart, *Recollections of My Life: Fifty Years of Itinerancy in the Northwest* (Redwing, Minn., 1885), pp. 202-3; Benjamin F. Tefft, *The Republican Influences of Christianity: a discourse delivered on occasion of the death of William Henry Harrison* . . . (Bangor, Me., 1841), especially pp. 13-15; Alfred Brunson, *A Western Pioneer: or, Incidents of the Life and Times of Rev. Alfred Brunson, A.M., D.D., embracing a period of over seventy years*, 2 vols. (Cincinnati, 1880), 2: 136-37; La Roy Sunderland to E. Kibby, 9 Sept. 1835, and R.M. Burt to 'Mr. Cox', 20 June 1848, New England Conference Collection.
9. *Western Christian Advocate*, 30 Oct., 25 Dec. 1840, 17 Dec. 1841, 19 Aug., 16 Sept., 11 Nov. 1842; George Peck, *National Evils and Their Remedy: a discourse delivered on the occasion of the National Fast, May 14, 1841* . . . (New York, 1841), pp. 12-13; Matthew Simpson, 'Reasons for Building a Metropolitan Church in Washington', 3-4, manuscript collection, Drew University; *Christian Advocate and Journal*, 23 June 1841; Tefft, *Republican Influences of Christianity*, p p. 15-17.
10. *Western Christian Advocate*, 1 Jan., 21 May, 30 July, 17 Dec. 1841, 19 Aug., 14 Oct. 1842; George Peck, *The Life and Times of George Peck, D.D.* (New York, 1874), pp. 217-19; R. Emory to C.W. Emory, 9 Nov., 13 Nov. 1844, manuscript collection, Drew University; *Christian Advocate and Journal*, 23 Oct. 1856; Brunson, *Western Pioneer*, 1: 334-45; Dan Young, *Autobiography of Dan Young*, edited by W.P. Strickland (New York, 1860), pp. 273-75.
11. William Warren Sweet, *Religion on the American Frontier*, vol. IV: *The Methodists, 1783-1840* (Chicago, 1946), p. 455; E. Mudge to B. Pitman, 22 Oct. 1844, and J. Bontecou to S.L. Pease, 17 Aug. 1840, New England Conferences Collection; *Western Christian Advocate*, 17 July 1844. For Garrisonian anarchism, see especially, Lewis Perry, *Radical Abolitionism: Anarchy and the Government of God in Anti-slavery Thought* (Ithaca, 1973).
12. H.H. Green, *The Simple Life of a Commoner: An Autobiography* (Decorah, Iowa, 1911), pp. 51-52; *Christian Advocate and Journal*, 3 Aug. 1842. Cf. William E. Gienapp, "'Politics Seem to Enter into Everything': Political Culture in the North, 1840-1860", in Stephen E. Maizlish and John J. Kushma, eds. *Essays on American Antebellum Politics, 1840-1860* (Arlington, Texas, 1983).
13. *Western Christian Advocate*, 19, 26 Feb., 9 Apr. 1841; Tefft, *Republican Influences of Christianity*, p. 6 and passim.
14. See, for example, Leonidas Hamline's editorials on 'Christian Patriotism' in *Western Christian Advocate*, 31 July, 7 Aug. 1840.
15. *Ibid.*, 17 Dec. 1841, 22 Jan. 1842.
16. *Ibid.*, 7 Aug., 25 Sept. 1840, 24 Sept. 1841; Thomas O. Summers, *Christian Patriotism: a sermon preached in Cumberland-St.M.E.Church, Charleston, S.C., on Friday, Dec. 6, 1850* . . . (Charleston, S.C., 1850), passim.
17. *Christian Advocate and Journal*, 28 Oct. 1840, 30 Oct. 1856; *Western Christian Advocate*, 30 Oct. 1840, 26 Mar. 1841; William G.W. Lewis, *Biography of Samuel Lewis, first superintendent for common schools for the state of Ohio* (Cincinnati, 1857), p.369; Lewis, *Recollections of a Superannuate*, p. 294; A. Wood to L. Smith *et al.*, Aug. 1860, Matthew Simpson Papers, Library of Congress.
18. George Coles 'Journal', 5 Nov. 1844, manuscript collection, Drew University; cf. 5 Nov. 1854, where he condoned a 'harsh and vulgar' translation of a Pauline epistle since it was designed to drive home the Methodist's duty to vote.
19. Sweet, *The Methodists*, pp. 428, 436; newspaper cutting

from the *Madison Courier*, n.d., Eddy Papers, Garrett-Evangelical Theological Seminary Library; T.M. Eddy, 'Sermon on the Death of General Z. Taylor . . . July 1850' in *ibid.*; *Christian Advocate and Journal*, 28 Oct. 1840; *Western Christian Advocate*, 7 Aug., 30 Oct. 1840, 21 May, 4 June 1841, 9 Dec. 1842; *Pittsburgh Conference Journal*, 5 Sept. 1839, 17 Sept. 1840; Calvin Fairbank, *Rev. Calvin Fairbank during Slavery Times: How He "Fought the Good Fight" to Prepare "The Way"* (Chicago, 1890), p. 168; Lewis, *Samuel Lewis*, pp. 325, 343.

20. John F. Wright, *Sketches of the Life and Labors of James Quinn* (Cincinnati, 1851), pp. 188-89; W.J. Rorabaugh, *The Alcoholic Republic: An American Tradition* (New York, 1979), p. 220; *Christian Advocate and Journal*, 2 Sept. 1840, 3 Aug. 1842, 25 Sept., 30 Oct. 1856; *Western Christian Advocate*, 10 July, 4 Sept. 1840, 26 Mar. 1841; Sweet, *The Methodists*, p. 643; *Pittsburgh Conference Journal*, 21 Mar. 1840; Jacob B. Moore, *The Contrast: or, plain reasons why William Henry Harrison should be elected President of the United States . . .* (New York, 1840), p. 5; L.W. Berry to M. Simpson, 30 July, Simpson Papers, Library of Congress.

21. T.A. Morris to M. Simpson, 16 Aug. 1848, Simpson Papers, Library of Congress.

22. *Christian Advocate and Journal*, 19 Aug. 1840, 23, 30 June 1841, 13 July 1842, 21 Jan. 1846, 17 Jan. 1856; *Pittsburgh Christian Advocate*, 2 Apr. 1841; Enoch M. Marvin, *The Life of Rev. William Goff Caples of the Missouri Conference of the Methodist Episcopal Church, South* (St. Louis, 1871), pp. 258-59.

23. Frances M.B. Hilliard, *Stepping Stones to Glory: From Circuit Rider to Editor and the Years in Between: Life of David Rice McAnally, D.D. 1810-95* (Baltimore, 1975), pp. 55-61; *Ohio State Journal*, 14 Dec. 1839, 16 Sept. 1840; Brunson, *Western Pioneer*, 2: 212-13; Helen H. Grant, *Peter Cartwright: Pioneer* (New York, 1931), pp. 148-55; *Western Christian Advocate*, 10 July 1840; *Christian Advocate and Journal*, 2 Sept. 1840; William McDonald and John E. Searles, *The Life of Rev. John S. Inskip, President of the National Association for the Promotion of Holiness* (Chicago, 1885), p. 49. Joseph Creighton believed that it was his own Democratic political allegiance that spurred his Whig presiding elder to obstruct his entry into the travelling ministry. Joseph H. Creighton, *Life and Times of Joseph H. Creighton, A.M., of the Ohio Conference* (Cincinnati, 1899), pp. 24, 67.

24. George C. Baker, *An Introduction to the History of Early New England Methodism 1789-1839* (Durham, N.C., 1941); Brunson, *Western Pioneer*, 1: 27-30, 35-43, 171-73; A. Hunt, 'Reminiscences' 22 Mar. 1847: J.B. Thomas to A. Stevens, 8 Oct. 1860: DD. Kilburn, ms. recollections: G. Pickering to E. Kibby, 19 Dec. 1798: manuscript collection, Drew University; Daniel De Vinne, *Recollections of Fifty Years in the Ministry . . .* (New York, 1869), pp. 14-15, 31-32; *Christian Advocate and Journal*, 23 Oct. 1856. In Connecticut in the first decade of the century, '[t]he great mass, if not the entire, of the Methodist Church and her adherents were Republicans, and so were the entire infidel portion of the community . . . [E]very convert to Methodism . . . became a Republican, if he was not one before.' Brunson, *Western Pioneer*, 1: 43.

25. Ray Holder, *William Winans: Methodist Leader in Antebellum Mississippi* (Jackson, Miss., 1977), p. 36; Selah Stocking, 'A Brief Sketch of the History of the Rev. Jeremiah Stocking', New England Conference Collection; Young, *Autobiography*, pp. 4, 101-3, 278-90.

26. Arthur M. Schlesinger, Jr., *The Age of Jackson* (Boston, 1945), pp. 350-60; Benson, *Concept of Jacksonian Democracy*, pp. 86-109.

27. Septimus Stocking, 'A Brief Historical Sketch of the life of the Rev. Solon Stocking', New England Conference Collection; William Gordon, 'Autobiography', *ibid.*; McCulloch, *Men and Measures*, p. 75; Benson, *Concept of Jacksonian Democracy*, pp. 191-92; Formisano, *Birth of Mass Political Parties*, pp. 153-55; Donald B. Cole, 'The Presidential Election of 1832 in New Hampshire',

Historical New Hampshire 21 (1966), 40-42, 49; E.R. Ames to M. Simpson, 21 Jan. 1845, 5 Jan. 1849, Simpson Papers, Library of Congress; Thomas H. Pearne, *Sixty-One Years of Itinerant Christian Life in Church and State* (Cincinnati, 1898), p. 49.

28. S.D. Lewis to G. Peck, 3 Nov. 1828, George Peck Papers, Syracuse University Library; Holder, *William Winans*, pp. 76, 94, 99; William Winans, *A Funeral Discourse on Occasion of the Death of Hon. Henry Clay . . .* (Woodville, Miss., 1852), p. 9; R. Emory to J. Nicols, 11 Apr. 1831, G.R. Crooks to J. McClintock, 21 Oct. 1848, J. McClintock to R. Emory, 23 Jan. 1848, G. Coles to G. Cubitt, 21 Feb. 1845, manuscript collection, Drew University; Moses M. Henkle, *The Life of Henry Biddleman Bascom* (Nashville, Tenn., 1856), pp. 105-7, 281-85; George G. Smith, *The Life and Letters of James Osgood Andrew, Bishop of the Methodist Episcopal Church South* (Nashville, Tenn., 1883), p. 436; *Western Christian Advocate*, 5, 26 Mar. 1851; Hobart, *Recollections* pp. 200-02; W.W. Hibben, *Rev. James Havens* (Indianapolis, 1872), p. 182; McDonald and Searles, *Life of Inskip*, pp. 66-67, 75-76; James Dixon, *Personal Narrative of a Tour through a part of the United States and Canada: with notices of the History and Institutions of Methodism in America* (New York, 1849), p. 63.

29. George Brown, *Recollections of Itinerant Life: including early reminiscences*, 3d edition (Cincinnati, 1866), pp. 269-70; Brunson, *Western Pioneer*, 1: 138.

30. Leonard W. Levy, 'Satan's Last Apostle in Massachusetts', *American Quarterly* 5 (1953), 16-30; Benson, *Concept of Jacksonian Democracy*, pp. 193-97.

31. Benson, *Concept of Jacksonian Democracy*, p. 171; William G. Brownlow, *A Political Register, Setting forth the Principles of the Whig and Locofoco Parties in the United States, with the Life and Public Services of Henry Clay* (Jonesboro, Tenn., 1844), pp. 77, 109-11, 113-16; *Christian Advocate and Journal*, 27 Apr., 18 Nov. 1842; *Western Christian Advocate*, 12 Nov. 1841, 8 July 1842.

32. Glyndon G. Van Deusen, 'Seward and the School Question Reconsidered', *Journal of American History* 52 (1965), 313-19; Louis D. Scisco, *Political Nativism in New York State* (New York, 1901), pp. 29-38. For an examination of the Whigs as the 'Christian Party' in 1840, see Richard Carwardine, 'Evangelicals, Whigs and the Election of William Henry Harrison', *Journal of American Studies* 17 (1983).

33. J. Cutler Andrews, 'The Antimasonic Movement in Western Pennsylvania', *Western Pennsylvania Historical Magazine* 18 (1935), 255-66; Sweet, *The Methodists*, p. 284; T.J. Brown to M. Simpson, 13 Apr. 1850, Simpson Papers, Library of Congress; James Erwin, *Reminiscences of Early Circuit Life* (Toledo, Ohio, 1884), pp. 61-62; John Burgess, *Pleasant Recollections of Characters and Works of Noble Men . . .* (Cincinnati, 1887), pp. 211-13; Holder, *William Winans*, pp. 104, 108; Ronald Formisano, 'Political Character, Antipartyism and the Second Party System', *American Quarterly* 21 (1969), 683-709; *Western Christian Advocate*, 30 Apr. 1841.

34. Brunson, *Western Pioneer*, I: 43, 285-86; J. Copeland to D.P. Kidder, 20 Feb. 1839, Daniel P. Kidder Papers, Garrett-Evangelical Theological Seminary Library; *Pittsburgh Conference Journal*, 20 Feb. 1840; *Western Christian Advocate*, 3, 17, Jan., 27 Mar., 13 Nov. 1840, 29 Jan., 19, 26 Mar., 2, 30 Apr., 13 Aug., 15, 22 Oct., 24 Dec. 1841; Luther Lee, *Autobiography of the Rev. Luther Lee, D.D.* (New York, 1882), p. 233; *Ohio State Journal*, 5 Aug. 1840, 20 Feb., 3 Mar. 1841: *Christian Advocate and Journal*, 25 May 1842; Tefft, *Republican Influences of Christianity*, pp. 10-11.

35. William G. McLoughlin, Jr., *Modern Revivalism: Charles Grandison Finney to Billy Graham* (New York, 1959), pp. 4-165; Richard Carwardine, *Transatlantic Revivalism: Popular Evangelicalism in Britain and America, 1790-1865* (Westport, Conn., 1978), pp. 3-18.

36. *Western Christian Advocate*, 21 Feb., 6 Mar., 4 Sept. 1840, 27 Mar., 4 June, 9 July 1841; *Christian Advocate and Journal*, 14 Dec. 1842, 17, 31 Dec. 1845, 4 Nov. 1846,

24 Feb. 1847; Timothy L. Smith, *Revivalism and Social Reform in Mid-Nineteenth-Century America* (New York, 1957), pp. 103-147. Cf. Daniel Wise, *Popular Objections to Methodism Considered and Answered . . .* (Boston, 1856), p. 121 and passim.

37. William McDonald, *History of Methodism in Providence, Rhode Island from its Introduction in 1787 to 1867* (Boston, 1868), pp. 47-48, 53-54; Bertram Wyatt-Brown, 'Prelude to Abolitionism: Sabbatarian Politics and the Rise of the Second Party System', *Journal of American History* 58 (1971), 334; Stephen Parks, *Troy Conference Miscellany, containing a Historical Sketch of Methodism within the Bounds of the Troy Conference of the Methodist Episcopal Church* (Albany, 1854), p. 67. John Durbin, Henry Bascom, John Newland Maffit, George Cookman and William Daily, amongst others, kept the Methodist flag flying in Congress.

38. Stocking, 'Sketch of Selah Stocking', New England Conference Collection; Gordon, 'Autobiography', *ibid.*; *Christian Advocate and Journal*, 20 Oct. 1847; R. Emory to J. Nicols, 8 July 1833, manuscript collection, Drew University; George Peck, *The Past and the Present: a semi-centennial sermon . . .* (New York, 1866), pp. 10-22; A.G. Porter to M. Simpson, 26 Oct. 1844, Simpson Papers, Library of Congress.

39. J. Drummond to M. Simpson, 20 Apr. 1850, Simpson Papers, Library of Congress; Milton Haney, *The Story of My Life* (Normal, Ill., 1904), pp. 115-16; George Coles, *My First Seven Years in America* (New York, 1852); Talbot W. Chambers, *The Noon Prayer Meeting of the North Dutch Church, Fulton St., New York: Its Origin, Character and Progress* (New York, 1858), p. 247; *Christian Watchman and Reflector* [Boston], 24 Apr. 1856.

40. Lewis, *Samuel Lewis*, pp. 286-302, 318, and passim; *Western Christian Advocate*, 13 Aug. 1841.

41. Freeborn G. Hibbard, *Biography of Rev. Leonidas L. Hamline, D.D., late one of the Bishops of the Methodist Episcopal Church* (Cincinnati, 1880), pp. 190-222, 239-40; *Christian Advocate and Journal*, 5, 12 Oct., 11, 18, 25 Nov. 1846, 20, 27 Jan., 3, 10, 24 Feb., 6, 27 Oct., 3 Nov. 1847; McDonald and Searles *Life of Inskip*, pp. 66-67, 75-76; J. McClintock to S. Olin, 31 Oct. 1844, manuscript collection, D rew University.

42. F.D. Hemenway, 'Oration for July 4, 1851', Francis D. Hemenway Papers, Garrett-Evangelical Theological Seminary Library; William T. Worth, 'A Sketch of the Life and Labors of the Rev. Asa Kent, 1780-1860', pp. 28-29, New England Conference Collection; J.C. Chambers to M. Simpson, 2 May 1850, J. Drummond to M. Simpson, 8 May 1850, W. Ternell to M. Simpson, 20 Aug. 1851, Simpson Papers, Library of Congress; S.P. Chase to M. Simpson, 26 Apr. 1850, manuscript collection, Drew University.

43. E. Merton Coulter, *William G. Brownlow: Fighting Parson of the Southern Highlands* (Chapel Hill, N.C., 1937), p. 119; *Christian Advocate and Journal*, 22 Dec. 1847; David M. Potter, *The Impending Crisis 1848-1861* (New York, 1976), pp . 225-65.

44. *Western Christian Advocate*, 11 Aug., 29 Dec. 1852, 2 Feb., 30 Mar. 1853; Hemenway, 'Diary', 8 Feb. 1853, Garrett-Evangelical Theological Seminary; Coles, 'Journal', 8 Nov. 1853 [cf. entries for 27 June, 9 Sept., 5 and 7 Nov. 1854], manuscript collection, Drew University.

45. William H. Daniels, *Memorials of Gilbert Haven, Bishop of the Methodist Episcopal Church* (Boston, 1882), p. 55; *Western Christian Advocate*, 14 Feb. 1855; J.A. Wright to M. Simpson, 23 Oct. 1854, Simpson Papers, Library of Congress. For Methodist and other evangelical opposition to Know-Nothingism, see Lewis, *Samuel Lewis*, p. 373; Augustus B. Longstreet, *Know Nothingism Unveiled* (Washington, 1855); Richard Carwardine, 'The Know Nothing Party, The Protestant Evangelical Community and American National Identity', in Stuart Mews, ed., *Studies in Church History*, vol. 18: *Religion and National Identity* (Oxford, England, 1982), pp. 449-63.

46. McDonald and Searles, *Life of Inskip*, pp . 75-76; *Western Christian Advocate*, I, 15 May 1850; J.L. Smith to M. Simpson, 23 May 1850, B.F. Crary to M. Simpson, 31 May 1851, Simpson Papers, Library of Congress; *Correspondence of Andrew Jackson*, ed. John Spencer Bassett, 7 vols. (Washington, D.C., 1926-35), 6:84; *Christian Advocate and Journal*, 12 June 1856. Cf. Wesley Norton, *Religious Newspapers in the Old Northwest to 1861: A History, Bibliography, and Record of Opinion* (Athens, Ohio, 1977), p. 122.

47. *Western Christian Advocate*, 26 Mar. 1841; *Pittsburgh Christian Advocate*, 30 Apr. 1840; *Christian Advocate and Journal*, 2 Sept. 1840, 17 Nov. 1841; Lewis, *Samuel Lewis*, p. 318; L.W. Berry to M. Simpson, 9 Aug. 1849, Simpson Papers, Library of Congress.

48. *Christian Advocate and Journal*, 2 Sept. 1846.

The Emerging Voice of the Methodist Woman:
The Ladies' Repository, 1841-61

Joanna Bowen Gillespie
Center for Research on Women, Stanford University

At the end of its first American century, Methodism took time to congratulate itself on its success in using print as an instrument of salvation and evangelization. Paeans of praise flowed from Methodist pens in a volume titled *Methodism and Literature* (1883), published for the Methodist centennial. Methodist clergy lauded their own newspapers, "that great family of *Advocates*"; their own Sunday school literature—instruction books, question books, and Sunday school library books; and their own official literature—theology, history, and sermons, "a veritable stream of living waters." They also exalted Christian biography as the Christian's obligation because it "served to embalm the great and the good, perpetuating what otherwise might have passed away." Their once-prestigious magazine, *The Ladies' Repository and Gatherings of the West*, published monthly by the Methodist Publishing House in Cincinnati from 1841-78, was not mentioned in that celebratory volume.[1]

This fact is puzzling, since in its time *The Ladies' Repository* (*LR*) was an impressive denominational achievement. For thirty-five years a handsome professionally-published octavo-sized magazine, embellished with high-quality steel engravings, was sent out each month to a paid subscription list numbering as many as 40,000 during the 1850s—its numerical peak. Undoubtedly each issue was read by many more than such numbers indicate to us today, thanks to group subscriptions and copies passed from hand to hand. *The Ladies' Repository* intended to be the Methodist *Godey's Lady's Book* and to siphon off some of that emerging women's audience which magazines were helping to create in the second quarter of the 1800s. But *LR*'s numerical inferiority alone would not have daunted Methodist celebrators of publishing successes.[2]

Perhaps the Methodist evaluators of their print achievements did not view a "commercial" women's magazine as "serious" Methodist literature, although they had no trouble seeing their children's literature in that light. Or perhaps the demise of *LR* in the decade just preceding the publication of *Methodism and Literature* excused them from dealing with it. Perhaps it was assumed, if indeed it was consciously debated, that women Methodists would have read the same religious matter men Methodists did.

Whatever the reasons for not celebrating the *Ladies' Repository* in 1883, we in 1983 treasure it as a rich source of Methodist social history in the midnineteenth century.

From the vantage point of *two* hundred years of American Methodism, we can see that the crucial fact about *LR* was its readers; they were *the* educated women of midnineteenth century Protestant Christian evangelicalism. Methodist subscribers (many were from other denominations as well) tended to be those women who were ambitious, well-educated for their time, and would-be local leaders. It was these "new American women" that the successful Cincinnati Methodist layman Samuel Williams had in mind when he initiated the *LR* in 1839-40. He wanted to produce a magazine which would be more religiously appropriate for them, "less full of sentimental tales and fashions direct from France" than secular women's journals.[3] And Methodist women themselves eagerly welcomed their *own* Christian publication according to letters in the *Advocates*.[4]

For the better part of two centuries, the only published expression of a woman's interior experience available to Christian women was the genre of pious memoirs—since novels were strictly out of bounds and there were relatively few women authors of travel writings or history. From 1830–50, the "modern" American woman's consciousness began to be cultivated by and to surface in a stream of popular magazines. For the first time, ordinary women found their everyday lives visible in print. Even good evangelical Methodist women gave themselves religious permission to use their daily lives as subjects for literary expression. Reflections inspired by the daily routines of a frontier homestead or employment in a bakery shop began to be viewed through a kind of halo, thanks to vehicles such as *LR* in which females could "talk" with each other about such mundane but religiously-hallowed activities.

Up to the 1830s it was extremely rare for the average woman to have any visible public role, even if the rare Methodist woman had been testifying and exhorting along a wilderness circuit with her husband as early as 1815.[5] Large

numbers of evangelical girls and women had flocked to teaching in Sabbath schools during the second decade of the nineteenth century, but the mass movement of females into public school teaching was still in the future. Women were simply not welcome in public life, even that of their churches. And while the new phenomenon of a denominational magazine didn't make them any more welcome, it did whet the Methodist female's taste for a somewhat more visible place in the life of her church. *LR* provided a print "bridge" for the woman who wanted to reach beyond her domestic boundaries into some sort of modest public recognition, but also to remain safely within her religiously-prescribed identity.

Thus what *LR* did was to assist educated Methodist women, long before they would have articulated such a culturally-daring thought to themselves, to reach out from their own kitchen tables, to an authority—a public voice—to whom they felt the right of access: the editor of "their" magazine. For many evangelical women, a first entry into the public eye was via print, not directly. This paper traces the emergence of the voices of these ordinary midnineteenth century. evangelical women in their initial "public appearances" through letters to *LR*'s editors during its first two decades.

It is the letters themselves (and the readers who wrote them) that reveal the difference between a religious magazine such as *LR* and a popular, secular one such as *Godey's*. The magazines were not so different in their literary tone, although *Godey's* was filled with stories and *LR* eschewed fiction almost entirely until the 1860s.[6] But the topics about which women corresponded with the two magazines were totally contrasting. *Godey's* editorial and exchange department was full of practical household-management information: letters requested recipes, patterns, etiquette, and nutrition facts. *LR*, on the other hand, followed what it considered "the higher path." Articles and essays were never about such prosaic things as food or clothing, only about religion and woman's role, religiously defined. Articles on "concrete" topics were limited to biblical history, nature, religious family life, and various intellectual currents of the time, such as phrenology, spiritualism, or phonography.[7] But in *LR*'s pages, at least, women were allowed to experience and occasionally comment about essays in this male-defined intellectual field. *LR* implicitly encouraged women to "theologize," as well as poeticize, about their own inner experiences.

While other women's magazines of the period published other aspects of the American female's

life and thought, *LR* provided a major forum for women's abstract thinking. Evangelical women of the mid-1800s equated religious thought with abstract thought; they had no separate category of secular philosophical thinking, so participating in any kind of discussion about religion in a popular magazine was a significant new step for the average woman. *Godey's* fiction "feminized" its moral instruction, making it more palatable by disguising it, in fictional form. *LR* took an unabashed prescriptive stance for the better part of its first twenty years, and thus engaged its readers in thinking about and reacting to "male" topics of discourse.

By the end of the nineteenth century, a readership such as that nurtured by *LR* had interacted with its own print medium in such a way as to produce an entirely new consciousness. Even by the 1870s, the imaginations of increasingly self-confident Methodist women were no longer enthralled with male-prescriptive religious journalism; women were writing it themselves, as well as moving into other intellectual fields.

From the 1870s on, women authors within the religious community were developing, with their own specialized journals, new areas of Christian women's activism. These newer women's magazines focused specifically on temperance or on foreign missions.[8] But even the least-sophisticated Methodist women in the 1880s, whose daily lives remained very circumscribed, were no longer satisfied with the former didactic style of religious journalism. They too were blossoming into a broader range of interests including some where religion was only an overtone rather than the major tune. It is as if the *Repository's* own well-intentioned "preaching" to women had been subverted by its own success. *LR* readers had so absorbed its messages of women's spiritual autonomy and self-development that they had become able to move outside the mental perimeters of their Methodist subculture. They were thus ready to be "at home" in the wider world where the culture itself was fostering women's interest in themes of discovery, self-management, pragmatism, and achievement.

During its first two decades, the official public authoritative (male) voice of the *Ladies' Repository* was perceptibly weakened, while the female reader's private, increasingly-independent agenda, religiously authorized and encouraged by her own "in-house" print forum, became more and more audible. Pouring this bursting sense of self into letters, articles, and poetry, offering the bright sayings of her children to her own religious community, the "modern" midnineteenth century Methodist woman leaps from *LR*'s pages. We must wend our way through the same thickets of nineteenth-century religious rhetoric as did these females did in order to discern *LR*'s role in their religious, literary, and social-psychological evolution.

I

Midwestern boosterism was important in the Methodist venture of producing a women's magazine. Easterners who had become Ohio transplants wanted to prove that they were as civilized as their citified cousins, and that there was indeed a full-blown culture out on the banks of the Ohio River.[9] Besides wanting to make Cincinnati "the Athens of the West," midwestern Methodists prided themselves on being less awed by social rank and tradition than Easterners, and on being in the vanguard of education for the people. In spite of a backwoodsy, anti-intellectual stance consciously cultivated by some of their leaders, Methodists were as deeply committed to literacy as to salvation. This alliance had put them in the forefront of the Common School movement—Methodists were involved in founding all types of educational institutions designed to civilize the frontiers,[10] including the first women's college west of the Mississippi, MacMurray College, in Jacksonville, Illinois (founded 1848). And Methodism was, by their reckoning, a special gift to women: "The rise of Methodism, more than any preceding religious uprising since the apostolic days, has contributed to the *solution of the woman question* in its ecclesiastical relations"[11] (emphasis added). Such a grand claim was not generally held by the denomination as a whole, but Methodism was seen as a popular and progressive religious movement, including what it did specifically for women.

Built on John Wesley's systematized religious practice, Methodism offered a useful mode of living in a new expanding nation because it "adapted to crude masses of newcomers congregating in our new states and territories, from all nations. It takes hold of and reduces them to order, imparting life to their hearts and regularity to their conduct," as Bishop Morris wrote in the *LR* (1856).[12] Besides self-discipline and the channeling of ambition, Methodist religious experience gave spiritual self-empowerment to the everyday Christian. In its intensely personal impact, Methodism impelled an instinctive energy in its converts which had to find outlets in action, right there in local situations. This action often set them at odds with other Christians— protesting against a mill owner whose conscience was not troubled about doing business on Sunday, for example. Their activist tendency also fueled their eagerness for their *own* publications.

The Methodist version of Christianity often had a defensive ring, in prose and print: "If we had not our own [publishing house], our young would grow up in complete alienation from Methodism. . . . Our church lives in an atmosphere of polemic hostility.[13] And [in the competition for religious-print supremacy] the kingdom of printing ink must needs be taken by Methodist violence."[14]

Methodist self-definition and Methodist literature may have benefited from Methodist chauvinism, but Methodist numerical success undoubtedly had more to do with the organizing genius of its founder and the personal perfectionist energy created in its adherents. In each of the years between 1840 and 1844, Methodists documented an average gain of 107,724 members. "It is generally conceded that Methodism has been the most energetic religious element in the social development of the continent, if not *the* mightiest agent."[15]

From an aggregate membership in 1844, the last year before Northern and Southern Methodists divided over the issue of slavery, of 1,170,000 members and 4,600 travelling preachers, Methodism expanded to an astounding centennial count in 1884 of more than seven million members. As Abel Stevens exulted in his centennial history of Methodism, "we are more than one-fifth of this nation."[16]

Stevens named four factors as critical to this denominational success story: "We are a system of spiritual life, of evangelical liberalism, of apostolic propagandism. . . . But above all, we are a stupendous means of popular intelligence."[17] Intelligence for the people, not just the clergy—for women and children, too. Methodism was synonymous with education, the means of self-cultivation, instruction, and learning— due to "our magnificent press system, the admiration of all our sister churches."[18] Wherever Methodist preachers went ("and where did they *not* go?" Stevens trumpeted rhetorically!), they carried glad tidings of salvation on their lips and published the acceptable year of the Lord by means of their press. "What a mighty engine is the press! What an event when this engine was first set in motion! . . . Since then, what a revolution has been effected in the entire civilized world!"[19]

Allowing for centennial hyperbole, it is possible to see at least part of that revolution—that occurring in Methodist women's consciousness—in the fresh, highly individualistic voices of readers which were bubbling up around the edges of the conventional academic essays dominating *LR*'s pages. We can also trace the function of Methodist print as "a stupendous means of popular intelligence" by watching the interplay between the two voices "visible" in *LR*: that of the Methodist ministers who were the officially-appointed editors and writers, plus those few women sounding exactly like them who wrote similarly-didactic religious essays, *and* that of the reader, slowly becoming visible in dialogue with herself, her fellow readers, and the editor. During *LR*'s first two decades, we can almost see the ground slowly being washed away from the foundations of official prescriptive Methodism toward women—until, after the Civil War, the whole superstructure crumbled and was reformulated.

Today we see that the succession of Methodist minister-editors: The Revs. L.L. Hamiline, 1841–44; Edward Thomson, 1844–46; B.F. Tefft, 1846–52; William Clark Larrabee, 1852–53; David W. Clark, 1853–63; (and after the scope of this paper, Isaac William Wiley, 1864–72; E. Wentworth, 1872–76; and Daniel Curry, 1876), were confronted with an impossible task. They were to shape and direct the minds and aspirations of their readers according to an already-outmoded Second Great Awakening world view. But in order to build a paid constituency they also had to respond to what was becoming an ever-more-independent readership—something their magazine was helping to create. Response to readers may be one explanation for the increasing visibility of letters in *LR*. By printing more and more from the readers, the editors demonstrated their journal's popularity, reduced their own isolation, and unwittingly provided a print platform for the ambitious farm girl or young mother. Small wonder the *LR* editorial voice became less strident during the 1850s; it was being "seduced" into addressing a new type of reader who wanted less hortatory messages and in a different voice.

For *LR* readers, dramatic public activism in a crusade such as suffrage was still many years away. But numbers of them were in training for it, literarily speaking. Even in the modest forum of prayer groups or Sunday school classes, the development of a distinctive voice for women who were spilling across the boundaries of their "sphere" was seriously under way. "The Church today in Indiana, and everywhere, owes as much to the patient labors of *women* in their warfare upon sin, as to men, in many cases even more. In the nursery, in departments of charity and benevolence among the poor and lowly, in the aggressive temperance movement, in public schools, around altars of prayer, in the esthetical departments of social and religious society, hers is the creative genius."[20]

The contents of this church journal dedicated to these new women, judged by contemporary conventions of what is good literature, measure up surprisingly well—in spite of our mind-set that most nineteenth century evangelical literature falls outside our standards of intellectual respectability. Our ear for this type of popular religious writing has been deadened by a din of modern superiority and condescension. We have been unable to read nineteenth century women's writings with unarched eyebrows because of what we label as the "sentimentality" visible beneath a coating of quaint rhetoric, archaic scholarship, and dated religious concepts.

But if we set aside this cultural conditioning and scholarly bias, we begin to discern the situations from within which these women and their advisors wrote. We begin to empathize with their peculiar combination of civil powerlessness, personal dignity, and religious empowerment. We relinquish the luxury of condemning these midnineteenth century women for not being what we wish they had been, and stop denigrating their religious self-expression as merely "sentimental."

By tracing the ideas and language in the *Repository* to their location in the psyches and social experience of the writers, we begin to see and hear the emerging sense of personal importance, spiritual independence, and self which the midnineteenth century Methodist woman was developing, *within* her own subculture. If her writing in her own church magazine seems, at first, as a modern critic writes, "like a cluster of ostensibly private feelings which (unaccountably) attain public, conspicuous expression," we are finally able to see that the remarkable thing about it was its being published at all.[21]

Although it has been easy, in the past, to dismiss the ornate circumlocutions and flowery self-denigration of much nineteenth-century female writing as sentimentalism, that kind of scolding now seems historically inappropriate. For example, "Sentimentalism always and only exists in tandem with a failed political consciousness" and "has no content but exposure, while it invests that exposure with special significance."[22] Such judgment obliterates any awareness that for an ordinary, bright-but-unsophisticated village girl in midnineteenth century America, exposure in print was a necessary first step toward the development of what would eventually be called "political consciousness." Unpalatable as the terms of these women's self-discovery may seem to us today, we must realize that even such a minor experience as seeing their thoughts in public print in a church periodical was a crucial landmark in many women's psychological and religious history.

A second stumbling block is that few modern scholars can identify with the psychic strength that *LR* readers would have found in *their* religious experiences—in Methodism's affirmation of self and its assurance of salvation, its gift of an unassailable, inner confidence which was new. It is also doubtful if many historians today can make intuitive connections between evangelicalism in the nineteenth century and the emergence of midnineteenth century individualism in women.[23]

What is clear to us through the pages of *LR* is that its readers in the 1940s and 50s, emboldened by a religiously-engendered individualism (resulting from their evangelical conversion experience and given public nurture through a magazine encouraging their "conversation" about this "abstract" part of their lives), were forging an autonomous self and voice. They were allowing themselves to view this self-development as part of their Christian duty, rather than something egotistical or evil. For the educated midnineteenth century Methodist woman, expressing opinions in print could be considered almost a requirement in the living out of her own particular Christian calling.

II

The first issue of *The Ladies' Repository* exuded confidence in the competence and intellectual ability of its readers. (It struck me on first reading, as an 1840s equivalent of a top-flight feminist—non-religious, of course—journal today, such as *Signs*.) The articles were intelligent and demanding, displaying erudition. The initial essay, "Female Education," stated the standard nineteenth-century ambivalence about educated women, putting down "female fanatics" and elevating "the modest mien of true religion." But the magazine's credal statement was found in a long, stylish essay entitled "Female Influence," by the Rev. J. S. Tomlinson of Augusta (Georgia) Academy: "I have long felt that the amount of reading matter included in the Ladies' Departments of our periodicals [presumably he means the weekly newspapers, the various *Advocates* for each region of the country] was altogether inadequate."[24]

This brave beginning, which appeared to be heading toward a critique of the superficiality of much journalism, veers into a tangential argument about quantity (rather than the quality and rigor of articles aimed at women). Tomlinson spares a glance at the "modern fashionables" who would not enjoy his thesis, i.e., that women's major arena for influence is in the nurseries of the nation. Thus he enunciates *LR*'s central theme: religious domesticity. His argument is standard. If either sex is to be stinted in terms of literary nourishment, let it be the male. "There are no great men without strong-minded, sensible, well-informed women as mothers," he concludes with the highest praise he can use.

Forceful adjectives are the surprise in this essay, since they are words not usually associated with Victorian females—mostly portrayed as delicate, shrinking, and ethereal. The women Tomlinson conjures up as mothers of the future are frank, forthright, and strong. Naturally such new women will be free of "slavish" interest in worldly adornment, self-display, and (by implication) egotistical ambition.[25] The wasp-waisted gowns so appealingly pictured in *Godey's* outrage him because they "horribly compel women to pass through torture and agonies [differing from Indian suttee only in that the suffering caused by fashion] is far more protracted, and too often transmitted in all its terrible consequences to an innocent unfolding posterity."[26]

Recalling himself abruptly, Tomlinson admits, "I have wandered from my original point, [which is] the superior place that maternal influence has in the formation of individual and social character." To this Methodists now bring "all the additional aids afforded by periodical publication."[27] Mr. Tomlinson's object is to place before *LR* readers, in the most eloquent style at his command, the ideals for the evangelical woman of 1841. His essay carried the clarion call of authoritativeness right into the parlors and kitchens of *LR* readers—right into their own "sphere."

The editors never doubted their prescriptions for women—Christian mothers first, then as wives or daughters, teachers or missionaries. Any self-doubt expressed in *LR* came more from Ohio-based defensiveness or regional pride. Two contradictory impulses were often side by side in an issue: sophisticated elitist essays promoting "self-elevation," and populist midwestern egalitarianism expressed in blunt, flat-footed prose.

The intention of making the *Repository* a journal of high literary quality was often tempered by demographic as well as religious considerations. Methodists were bound to see that grace was as generously bestowed on the humblest farmer's daughter as on the new graduate of their academies or colleges. In a belief-community where each person's experience of salvation was as valuable as the next one's, on what grounds could an "in-house" editor reject the spiritual musings of a country girl and accept only the more elaborate poetry of a college graduate? A Methodist minister attempting a high-brow literary task risked being thought un-Christian for such decisions. He was a captive of his own Arminianism, and of midnineteenth-century midwest egalitarianism.

By late 1842, at the end of the second volume of *LR*, the editor's struggle to maintain an elevated standard through "good sense in the tone of the articles" and "high literary and artistic merit" had begun to weigh heavily. The year's last editorial contained an aggrieved note: "We have tried to keep the *Ladies' Repository* as pure, and as entertaining as could comport with purity . . . but some readers seem to find the best articles least entertaining. What do they want, *experiences and 'such like'*?' "[28] (emphasis in original).

Regional boosterism sometimes evoked regional envy. A Midwesterner's review of a new volume of the *Lowell Offering* in 1844 expressed both:

> Verily New England beats everything. We admire the land of the Pilgrims for its granite hills and its granite intellects, its cold ice and its cold calculations, its scaly fishes and its scaly notions, its stormy oceans and its restless independent spirit. . . . We would like to look at these "factory girls." We shake hands with them in our hearts across the mountains and hope that the *Lowell Offering* will be a blessing both to readers and contributors.[29]

Until the last sentence of the review, the reader is uncertain as to which will prevail, admiration or resentment. Even as late as 1849, the editor (and by extension, Midwestern Methodists generally) could be stung by the Eastern disdain in a letter "marvelling" at the idea of "an elaborate ladies' monthly by the Methodists of the Midwest!" The editor took revenge by characterizing this correspondent "from Yankeedoodledum" as "waxing puffatory" "over the presumption of Porkdom."[30] Eastern condescension was met with an elaborate bumptiousness, as close as a Methodist editor could come to verbal fisticuffs.

After five years in publication, the second editor, Edward Thomson, was driven to lament: "Within the limited walk assigned to *LR*, it is exceedingly difficult to find attractive themes."[31]

This is the first hint at a discrepancy between the official public voice and what people might rather be reading about privately. He added wistfully, "Could we enter the arena of politics or religious warfare . . . it would be much more interesting."[32] Editorializing over the flood of Roman Catholic immigrants into the countryside or beating the drums for abolition would have appealed to many *LR* subscribers and writers, but would definitely have crossed editorial boundaries the official church magazine was constrained to honor.

Although *LR* had been brought into being to compete with *Godey's*, the editor at the end of its first decade cautioned readers *not* to compare their magazine with commercial ones. Rather the readers should focus on the higher spiritual and intellectual standards adhered to by *LR*'s official stance. "It is not the design of this work to descend to the low degree of the world around us, but to bring that world up to the true standards of good sense, sound knowledge, correct taste, and pure religion."[33]

But in bringing the rest of the world up to *LR*'s standards, a first major accommodation to the world was made. In 1853, what would have been a humor column in a secular magazine made its first appearance, titled "The Mirror of Wit, Apothegm, Repartee, and Anecdote." In 1856, editor Clark could proudly report: "We have never believed that only 'light literature' was good for a ladies' magazine. . . . We are happy to report that to the honor and intelligence and *mind* of the ladies of this country, some of the most elaborate and profound articles in the *Repository* last year were among the most popular, that is, elicited the most remarks and attracted the most attention."[34]

Even as he wrote, Clark may have subconsciously realized that this was the apotheosis of the official prescriptive voice for Methodist women. His readers were ready to take those good minds into other, greener pastures. Bright students at the midwestern Methodist MacMurray College, in Illinois, would eagerly greet the *Repository* as it arrived each month—but they would take from it what they liked and ignore the rest. They were no longer looking to their church's magazine for wisdom and authentication, because they were discovering it in other dimensions of self-cultivation.

III

The readers' voices appear initially in offhand mention only; the first, 1842, is when the editor refers to a letter from a poetry contributor whose latest submission has been delayed due to an injury sustained in a fall from her horse. Next we see a few long letters treated as mini-essays on public issues; e.g., one in 1850 on women's property rights, another on the presumption of visitors who overstay their welcome in ministers' homes. Eventually, a column appeared which was totally composed of letters from readers—and they were about the readers' children.

By the 1850s, *LR* readers used two main topics as excuses for seeing their writing in print (other than articles and poems): death and children. "Memorializing" the death of a friend, spouse, or child was sufficient sanction; many letters state frankly the writer's hope to preserve the dear one's name in print, thus obtaining print immortality for them. ("Letters are tiny tributes to dead friends . . . and achieve immortality while still here on earth." Vol. VII #3, March 1847.)

But crowding out death as a topic, by 1855, was the reporting of childrens' bright sayings. Here the newer voice of the Methodist mother becomes apparent. The women who write proudly about their children's amusing way with words have enough sense of self and of language to enjoy a child's verbal mistakes. We also observe the instant blossoming of parental competition. "I have been fond of glancing over your 'Sideboard for Children.' I have been much amused with instances of precocity and early natural genius with which it is sometimes laden. It strikes me that I have a little fellow who in this respect will suffer but little in comparison with any of them . . . he is little beyond his second year."[35]

And another mother writes, "As you occasionally treat your readers to specimens of children's talk, and as the race of *smart* children has not entirely died out, I submit a few scraps."[36]

The noted Hartford, Connecticut, poet and author, Lydia Huntley Sigourney, may have spoken for the entire class of educated evangelical, midnineteenth century mothers when she introduced an article titled "Words of the Little People" in August 1856. "It would sometimes seem as if the wit and pathos of the present world were with the children. Their unsophisticated minds and simplicity of heart give such force to every original idea that it is a pity their sayings should so often be forgotten."[37]

Here was a summary of a change in evangelical women's perspective, from the 1840s to near-Civil War times. Like other formerly-struggling folk, some Methodist women had achieved an emotional and intellectual perspective which allowed them to appreciate, and even boast

about, their children's experiments with language. They also had a religiously sanctioned vehicle in which to experiment with their new literary self-expression. They could unapologetically own their children's forwardness ("I'm tired of always being your child, let's pretend *I'm* the mother") and dignify baby-talk by recording it. For example,

Preach Small. "Mother," said a little seven-year-old, "I could not understand our minister today, he said so many hard words. I wish he would preach so that little girls could understand him. Won't he, mother?" (Mother replies yes, if we ask him.) Soon after, her father saw her tripping away. "Where are you going, Emma?" "I'm going over to the minister's house, to ask him to preach small."[38]

And

The Moon and her Babies, we read this: " 'Mamma, mamma,' cried a little one whose early hour of retirement had not permitted much study of the starry heavens, "here is the moon come, and brought a sight of little babies with her.' "[39]

The popular exchange of children's "wisdom" became an acceptable topic for the mother who had no other reason to write, women who were perhaps the majority of *LR* readers.

Those women who dared correspond about something more self-centered than children simply poured out personal feelings: "I love the *Repository*; it embalms the memories of loved ones who have joined the song of the redeemed in the upper sanctuary. In this wild west its regular visits are esteemed like those of a familiar friend."[40]

In 1846, a questing voice appeared for the first time, in a letter to the editor written for no reason other than "the prompting of my own heart to send a few lines to the *Repository*."[41] The letter is arresting in its eagerness. The writer uses cliches which she assumes will communicate more than their literal meaning; i.e., describing homesickness for her Missouri homeland, "my spirit as a caged bird longed to soar to its native mountains."[42] At the age of twenty-two, she has had little exposure to the wider world, but she idealizes her "plain little village" as "free of affectation or refinement." Her highest praise is couched in midwestern scorn for "ceremonies of fashion, dress, or manners." "If things are neat and becoming, they have reached the popular standard [prevailed here]; the height of our ambition seems to be to encourage everything calculated to elevate the mind and improve the heart."[43]

But then she reveals that she is a normal young woman after all (instead of a moralizing middle-aged minister): "Many young couples are here, who having plighted their faith in a far distant land and left parents and friends, have cast their lot among us. In the fate of such I always feel intense *interest*."[44]

As is often characteristic of first appearances in print, the writer must append a self-deprecating comment and justification: "I find I must close. I am aware that what I have written is exceedingly desultory; and I would not have written at all had I not noticed that there is seldom if ever anything sent you from Missouri, [signed] Mary."[45]

This letter, printed without comment or explanation by the editor, shows Mary-the-reader striving to be part of a public dialogue, displaying a literate if not altogether accurate vocabulary, and feeling proprietary about *LR*. She felt at ease writing about nothing in particular except her own limited observations of a limited horizon. In effect she was saying, "Look, world, here I am!" This vivid testimony to the private idiosyncratic effect of print (as compared with oral) communication was arming a population of Methodist women all across the land with a means of psychic mobility while they sat at their own kitchen tables.

More often, women wrote the editor to check up on a poem or manuscript, and to obtain some sort of verification of their talents. "Just as two years ago I peeped between your leaves at my neighbor's and espied, with many blushes, my first saucy little note to the editor."[46] Or, as another woman wrote, "Burn it if you like, but do read it first. Criticize it and *me*; poke fun at it if you like, but do *notice* it."[47]

Letters served some women as a preprofessional correspondence school: "I don't send my contributions because I consider them worthy, by any means, but it is something of pleasure to see my rhymes in print. It comes so natural for me to scribble I oft find myself poetizing before I know it."[48]

One correspondent used military metaphor (the only indication of the impending Civil War in *LR*, 1861) to elicit a response from the editor about her manuscript: "In times of war, one feels an aversion to neutrality, to being nowhere, and if my articles do not pass muster, say so and relieve me of my long-endured suspense. I had rather go forth at once to execution . . . than remain in the prison of my anxiety any longer."[49] However, she closed by assuring the editor of her deep loyalty to the *Repository*: "I shall not secede from my valued and well-tried friend, the *Repository*, even for rejection of anything I write."[50]

An example of the new Methodist female voice appears in rather self-assertive images that occasionally surface, as in a poem about a young woman leaving home, titled "Going Forth," by Augusta Moore. The sixth stanza reads (emphasis in original):

So I strove to strangle fear and sorrow,
  And to nerve my heart for coming strife;
And I vowed I would not flinch or falter,
  Tho' through *fire* led on my path of life—
    Dare the strife,
Dash ahead and *force* a way through life.

The final stanza ends with the motto: "Face the danger—it will flee away."[51] These verbs are surprisingly harsh for a women's poetic contribution to a religious journal.

However, the most astonishing example of the new female literary boldness appeared in a response to an earlier letter to the editor by Jesse Brumbler (obviously a pseudonym). He had waxed nostalgic about the "good old days" of Methodism and was judgmental about the current Methodist clergy and their wives. The scorn with which his suggestions were rejected by a woman who was not a clergy wife indicates both the way midnineteenth century Methodists had come to view themselves and their place in the scheme of things, and the self-confidence a formerly-submissive Methodist female could now display in arguing for progress. Her letter mandates extensive quoting: "From the religion which produces no liberality of views, no enlargement of heart, Good Lord, deliver us."

[In answer to his complaint against expensive church edifices] . . . The elegance of our churches has by no means kept pace with our means as a denomination. This is a shame when Christians live in elegance and continue to worship God in unsightly, mean, and repulsive buildings. Nine times out of ten this results *not* from love of "old-fashioned Methodism" but from lack of refinement or of feeling and manners . . . or from miserliness and meanness. There is no religion or love of God in it!

[Rejecting the correspondent out of hand]
Such persons make religion repulsive, and dishonor Methodism. If we were poor, unable to do otherwise, it would be right that we should worship in log houses.

[About ministers wanting to be settled in one location for a term] Your mean notion that preachers ought to work through the week like other people, on the land, so as not to be a burden to others. . . . You are right, that the minister ought to work—on sermons, study, and visiting his flock. [You are] the type of person who is always first to grumble if [you] find out the minister has a little property. . . . This attitude, meanness and dishonesty will drive the best men out of the itinerancy. . . .

[About ministers' wives taking in sewing or washing to supplement the minister's income, one of his suggestions in the earlier letter] Mr. Grumbler, that is an argument which defies reply. One can only sit in the silent admiration of your lofty views.

Throwing all restraint to the wind, her closing peroration veers into attack and an unfortunate lapse of grammar: "If God don't send leanness into your soul—we fear it is already nothing but leanness now—and if your children are not ruined by the miserable pelf you are robbing God in order to hoard, I shall be greatly mistaken. So farewell!"[52]

The writer was confident that *LR* readers shared her indignation, since most of them would also be in favor of modern, full-time, salaried clergy living in parsonages and conducting a professional ministry rather than itinerating and preaching under the elms. These new ideals were the product of ambitious and educated Methodist Christian women, those poised on the forward edge of Methodist subculture, headed inexorably into the mainstream of middle-class sophistication. Their daughters would undoubtedly become the club-women of the 1880s.

Sophronia Naylor Grubb, a member of the first MacMurray College graduating class (1852), was one of those forthright midwestern college women who was far beyond the idea of education for mere survival, even if she was not quite ready to contemplate entering the male profession of medicine, as Mrs. Sarah Josepha Hale (of *Godey's*) had been urging in a letter to college women including students at MacMurray.

We had no dream beyond being homemakers as our mothers had been before us; the girl who wished to prepare herself for a career, who had a definite ambition to do original or creative work in music, art, or literature had not been born . . . but, the acquisition of that . . . education . . . to which we were giving our best energies, was to fit us more perfectly for homemaking, to render us dispensers of a more graceful hospitality, and to add a glory, all its own, to the common life.[53]

Mrs. Hale's phrase, "to add a glory . . . to the common life," epitomized the changed focus of Methodist women's inner experience from 1840 to 1860. Education and print media such as *LR* had breached the domestic sphere, beckoning them toward more than just basic self-improvement. "Girls from small towns or rural communities with a restricted social and intellectual background who were eager to learn how to add a glory to the common life," wrote Clarissa Keplinger Rinaker, also MacMurray Class of 1852, longed for a mental world more congruent with that of the secular world.[54]

Of course the world outside their Methodist college wouldn't let them choose the avenues they thought they were preparing themselves for, "inspired with the belief that we were expected to accomplish something for ourselves and for humanity. . . ."[55] But education and internal strength, religiously sponsored, had unleashed an energy which was beginning to defy external shaping. Methodist women were ready to run their own foreign mission study and fund-raising programs. No wonder *The Ladies' Repository* was shortly to become irrelevant to them.

IV

Methodist popular literature, that "stupendous means of popular intelligence" in the midnineteenth century, had included a women's religious journal in an effort to sound one voice —official and prescriptive—in the lives of its women. But readers of the *LR* used it to shape an unforeseen expansion of themselves and had in turn been shaped by their interaction with it. The occasional naivete in some of the letters of the first two decades must be seen for what it was: evidence of an emerging independent perception of self in relation to church, community, and the larger world.

A century later, several questions about *LR* remain with us. Why did the Methodists, so eminently practical in every aspect of religion and life, choose to exclude the practical side of women's lives from their magazine? How could the editors avert their gaze from the arena of daily household minutiae to which they were high-mindedly directing women's religious efforts? Also, with their ambition for a "quality publication," why did they eschew illustration and a more readable layout, leaving that to secular journals such as *Godey's*? And why were they so committed to a bland, non-partisan official voice, in contrast to their individual Christian commitment against such evils as slavery? (Similarly, *Godey's* editor for nearly fifty years, Mrs. Sarah Hale, worked privately for abolition but never alluded to it in her editorials.) Apparently, *LR*'s evasion of controversial topics was not unusual in its time, nor is it unknown in ours.

We may thank those hard-pressed *LR* editors for maintaining a print vehicle which became the instrument of self-expression for a midnineteenth century population of Christian women, preserving a picture of their thoughts and motives for us. For historical Methodism, *LR* is a revealing record of the commonplace, from time to time brightly illuminating a particular segment of life in its era.

LR's first two decades offer us exemplary cultural data about the midnineteenth century evangelical Methodist women who evolved from viewing themselves as part of a subgroup in American culture into claiming part of the mainstream as their location. *LR* was part of the new "information-culture" of the mid-1800s which ushered in and developed the new consciousness of American women, interacting with its readers as a significant factor in the social landscape of their everyday lives. It helped readers understand and articulate their own times and provided a literary bridge from the earlier genre of popular religious literature— pious memoirs—to the specialized women's religious journals of the post-Civil War era.

The Ladies' Repository was one of the means by which the religious and social authority in official Methodist literature accommodated to the changing social environment, as it shaped itself to the readers' market it had helped cultivate. That *LR* readers outgrew their own magazine in 35 years or less is one kind of testimony to its effectiveness.

NOTES

1. *Methodism and Literature, A Series of Articles from Several Writers on the Literary Enterprise and Achievements of the Methodist Episcopal Church.* Frederick A. Archibald, Editor. Cincinnati: Walden and Stove, 1883, p. 267, p. 264, p. 82. The magazine was titled *The Ladies' Repository and Gatherings of the West* from 1841-48, after which the latter phrase was dropped.
2. Frank Luther Mott, *The History of American Magazines*, Vol. I, 1741-1850. Cambridge: Harvard University Press, 1957, p. 388.
3. Lee Soltow and Edward Stevens, *The Rise of Literacy and the Common School in the United States: A Socioeconomic Analysis to 1870.* Chicago, Illinois: The University of Chicago Press, 1981, p. 78; Mott, *History of American Magazines*, p. 388.
4. James Penn Pilkington, *The Methodist Publishing House: A History*, Vol. I. Nashville: Abingdon, 1968, 276–79.
5. E.g., *Memoirs of Fanny Newell (1793–1824) Written by Herself; and Published at her Particular Request and the Desire of Numerous Friends.* Hallowell, Maine: 1824.
6. As early as Vol. II (1842), one parodistic story, "The Faulty Mistress," was published, with characters such as Paul Censor and Mrs. M. B. Fretful—but it was intended to be above the label "fiction," more a cautionary parable. Vol. V (1845) had one story in it by a bishop's wife. Vol. VI (1846) produced a story, "The Exile," plus an editorial defense of its conclusion on the grounds that it was *history*. Evidently this hardly silenced opponents of fiction because in 1847, Vol VII, No. 4, the editor expostulated: "My readers know I don't write fiction and have often spoken against it." And again in 1849, a feverish editorial denial of any stance favorable to printing fiction (Vol. IX, No. 7, p. 191): "I never wrote a line of fiction in my life and never knowingly put any in the *Repository*, unless I was deceived by contributors." Nevertheless the antifiction policy was quietly eroded during the 1850s, and much weakened by 1860.
7. In Vol. XVI, No. 1, January 1856, there is a long scholarly article "Phonography and Phonotypy" by the Rev. D. D. Whedon, recommending it as a variety of what we now call shorthand or phonetic symbol writing (pp. 30–32).
8. The Methodist women's magazine *The Heathen Woman's Friend* (1869-1940) was immensely popular and influential, and undoubtedly drew much of the readership away from *LR* in its later years. See Joan Jacobs Brumberg, "Zenanas & Girlless Villages: The Ethology of American Evangelical Women, 1870–1910," in *Journal of American History* 69, No. 2 (Sept. 1982) 347–371.
9. Mott, *History of American Magazines*, p. 388.
10. David Tyack, in "The Kingdom of God and the Common School: Protestant Ministers and the Educational Awakening in the West," *Harvard Education Review*, 36, No. 4 (Fall, 1966), 447–469. His phrase "Protestant paideia" describes the institution-building repeated in community after community across the nation—family, church, and school reinforcing one another. In "From Social Movement to Professional Management: An Inquiry into the Changing Character of Leadership in Public Education" (with Elizabeth Hansot), *American Journal of Education*, 88 (May 1980), 291–310, Tyack points out the contribution of evangelical religion to the spread of common schools.
11. Maggie Newton Van Cott, *The Harvest and the Reaper; Reminiscenses of Revival Work.* New York: N. Tibbals & Son, 1876. Introduction, Bishop Haven, p. xxxvii.
12. *Ladies' Repository*, XVI, No. 1 (January 1856), p. 19.
13. "Sunday School Literature" (unsigned), *Methodist Quarterly Review*, 1850, p. 283.
14. Archibald, *Methodism and Literature*, p. 51.
15. Abel Stevens, *The Centenary of American Methodism: A Sketch of its History, Theology, Practical System and Success.* N.Y.: Carlton & Porter, 1865, p. 126.
16. Stevens, *The Centenary of Methodism*, p. 107.
17. *Ibid.*, pp. 145, 162. Obviously the central concept for Prof. Stevens was the word "system" which he uses positively throughout.
18. Archibald, *op. cit.*, p. 54.
19. Nathan Bangs, *A History of the Methodist Episcopal Church.* Vol. IV: 1829-40. New York: Lane & Sanford for the Methodist Episcopal Church, p. 452.
20. J. C. Smith, *Early Methodism in Indiana: Biographical Sketches.* Indianapolis: J. M. Olcott, 1879, p. 75. Jed Dannenbaum, "The Origin of Temperance Activism and Militancy Among American Women," *Journal of Social History* 15, No. 2 (Winter, 1891), 236–252, connects the perception of women in the temperance movement as "aggressive" with their usurping the public platform, otherwise still culturally proscribed for women.
21. Ann Douglas, *The Feminization of American Culture.* New York: A. A. Knopf, 1977, p. 254.
22. *Ibid.*, p. 254.
23. Carl N. Degler, *At Odds.* New York: Oxford University

Press, 1980, pp. 191–194. Although he gives religion some credit for helping women discover individualism, he is apparently unaware that evangelicalism was the key to it for American women not in elite circumstances or sophisticated circles. The only place he deals with evangelical religion is in the chapter on domestic reform, Ch. XIII, "The World Is Only a Large Home."

24. "Female Influence," *Ladies' Repository* Vol. I, No. 1 (Jan. 1841), p. 29.
25. *Ibid.*, p. 29.
26. *Ibid.*, p. 29.
27. *Ibid.*, p. 29.
28. *Ladies' Respository* II, No. 12 (Dec. 1842).
29. *Ladies' Repository* IV, No. 6 (June 1844), p. 286.
30. *Ladies' Repository* IX, No. 1 (Jan. 1849), p. 48.
31. *Ladies' Repository* VI, No. 7 (July 1846), p. 222.
32. *Ibid.*, p. 222.
33. *Ladies' Repository* X, No. 10 (October 1850), p. 380.
34. *Ladies Repository* XVI, No. 1 (Jan. 1856), p. 63.
35. *Ladies' Repository* XVI, No. 11 (Nov. 1856), p. 704.
36. *Ibid.*, p. 704.
37. *Ladies' Repository* XVI, No. 8 (August 1856), p. 511. Two secondary references provide an understanding of the general change in America regarding childrearing, toward more permissive and less authoritarian parental stance: Bernard Wish, *The Child and the Republic* (Philadelphia: University of Pennsylvania Press, 1968), and Joseph F. Kett, *Rites of Passage* (N.Y.: Basic Books, 1977). They draw on such midnineteenth century religious and parental advice books as Horace Bushnell's *Views of Christian Nurture* (1847) and Lyman Cobb's *The Evil Tendencies of Corporal Punishment* (1847). "Mother's love replaced father's discipline as the central gesture of the nuclear family." (William G. McLoughlin, *Revivals, Awakenings, and Reforms* (Chicago: University of Chicago Press, 1978), p. 124).
38. *Ladies' Repository* XVI, No. 1 (Jan. 1856), p. 64.
39. *Ladies' Repository* XVI, No. 3 (March 1856), p. 192.
40. *Ibid.*, p. 192.
41. *Ladies' Repository* VI (1846), p. 192.
42. *Ibid.*, p. 192.
43. *Ibid.*, p. 192.
44. *Ibid.*, p. 192.
45. *Ibid.*, p. 192.
46. *Ladies' Repository* XVI, No. 2, p. 128.
47. *Ladies' Repository* XVI, No. 3 (March 1856), p. 192.
48. *Ladies' Repository* XVI, No. 2, p. 128.
49. *Ladies' Repository* XXI, No. 7 (July 1861), p. 447.
50. *Ibid.*, p. 447.
51. *Ladies' Repository* XVI, No. 11 (Nov. 1856), p. 647.
52. *Ladies' Repository* XVI, No. 2 (Feb. 1856), p. 114.
53. Mary Watters, *The First Hundred Years of MacMurray College* (Springfield, Illinois: Williamson Printing and Publishing Co., 1947), p. 49.
54. *Ibid.*, p. 66.
55. *Ibid.*, p. 59-60.

Rich Methodists: The Rise and Consequences of Lay Philanthropy in the Mid-19th Century

Donald B. Marti
Indiana University at South Bend

Silas Lapham had real-life counterparts in the middle and late 19th century. Real Laphams were rising from modest beginnings to great affluence. They made an awkward new elite, sometimes, hardly knowing how to enjoy their fortunes, but they had at least one definite idea about the use of money. Just as Lapham "gave with both hands" to his unspecified church and its charities, so his actual counterparts gave abundantly to churches which, not infrequently, were Methodist Episcopal. Their philanthropies enriched Methodist institutions; their consequent influence with ministers and their rising confidence produced a new kind of lay participation in Methodist polity. The church fully shared the advantages and hazards of their new fortunes.[1]

The idea that Methodists might be rich was novel in the middle third of the 19th century. Methodists had always been characterized, in and out of their fellowship, as very ordinary people. A Maryland Episcopalian, in 1798, described them as "for the most part persons of the lower classes of life, and distinguished by that ignorance upon which the Jacobin" (read Jeffersonian Republican) "chiefs work so successfully." Methodists themselves agreed that their denomination had first grown among poor folk. The Reverend Gilbert Haven of the New England Conference, later a bishop in post-Civil War South Carolina, thought that some of the denomination's special virtue arose from that fact. Poor folk, if they were also decently independent, had a wholesome radical tendency. It was good to be economically and socially unprepossessing. It did no moral harm to be looked down upon by more respectable elements. Francis Asbury made the same point when he criticized Quakers for having become "respectable." He said: "There is death in that word."[2]

After the middle of the 19th century Methodists spoke of their lowly origins with a new kind of pride. They began to congratulate themselves on how far they had risen. William Claflin, for example, told the 1890 Centennial Convention of the New England Conference that only the "common people" had responded when Jesse Lee first brought Methodism to Boston, that the good man had preached standing on a table provided by some anonymous layman because there was no better pulpit for him. But now, Claflin observed, the "conveniences for our meetings are somewhat increased." He did not have to add that laypeople were making better provision for their preachers because some of them were richer and less anonymous than they had been in Jesse Lee's time. Claflin exemplified all of that obviously enough. He was an ex-Governor of Massachusetts, a wealthy manufacturer of boots and leather, and one of the first laymen to serve in the General Conference of the denomination. Several hundred thousand dollars stood between him and his modest origin. He was part of the change that his speech described.[3]

Ministers understood that the rise of some considerable fortunes among the laity was changing the denomination. Matthew Simpson, who became a bishop in 1852, was notably sensitive to its implications. Since 1839, when he became president of Indiana Asbury University (later DePauw), he had been learning to cultivate brethren with money and political influence. Such laymen were distressingly few in Indiana when Simpson first went there, but they became more numerous and really useful as his career flourished and took him to other places. He thought that was the great social change affecting American Methodists. The Lord was rewarding his common people for their diligence, and they were sharing their success with the church. They were also sharing it with ministers, particularly Matthew Simpson. Their hospitality, lecture fees, and business advice gave him some first-hand knowledge of how much better it was to be rich than poor. At the height of his career Bishop Simpson was markedly different from the plain-living circuit rider he had been in his youth.[4]

Rich Methodists changed Simpson. He was delighted to observe that they were also changing the church. In 1855, for example, he encouraged some of the wealthier brethren in Pittsburgh to erect Christ Church, the first American Methodist church built in the Gothic Revival style. Previous Methodist chapels had been deliberately modest, as John Wesley decreed; they made no great show beside the architectural splendors of other denominations. When Christ Church and other grand edifices arose, Methodists discovered that their new churches needed formal pews, rather than the plain benches to which they had been accustomed. They called for liturgical embellishments as well. Simpson welcomed all of that. Certainly men who had earned fine homes and "social refinement" had the right to expect similar graces in their churches. The fact that they were willing to pay for them made their claim all the stronger.[5]

Simpson's appreciation of rich Methodists, and the importance that he attributed to their impact on the denomination, had a particularly detailed expression in 1878. He then published the first edition of his *Cyclopaedia of Methodism*, which purported to describe all of the branches of Methodism throughout the world. In fact it concentrated on the Methodist Episcopal Church in the northern United States, with only a little attention to other Methodist bodies there and abroad. Nearly sixteen hundred entries describe individual people, mostly Simpson's contemporaries. They suggest who, and what sorts of people, were most important to Simpson's church.[6]

More than eleven hundred of the entries describe ministers; thirty-two concern women, mostly the wives of ministers. The remainder describe laymen, including 347 members of the Methodist Episcopal Church (North). A few of those laymen were included for achievements in music; one was a reformed drunkard become temperance lecturer. But the vast majority were listed because of their achievements in medicine, law, politics, education, or some kind of business. Twenty-two were physicians or dentists, primarily; thirty-seven were chiefly notable for their political and military attainments; forty-six were primarily attorneys; fifty-two were educators, mostly college professors; and one hundred and forty-eight were businessmen. None were chiefly known as farmers. A few had a little farm experience, usually early in life, but nobody was listed because of his achievements on the land. And only one man, an engraver for the United States Mint, was recognized for craftsmanship. Simpson's lay elite was professional and commercial.[7]

Simpson's capsule biographies are often more fulsome than specifically informative. His descriptions of business careers are only occasionally circumstantial; sometimes they merely note that the subject was a "merchant" or a "skillful businessman." Of Daniel Drew's business life it

was enough to say that he had started as a cattle drover and had gone on to steamboats, railroads, and "heavy stock operations in the New York market." Readers of the newly published *Chapters of Erie* might have thought that "heavy," though an appropriate adjective, was not enough. Certainly later writers found Drew a more colorful subject than he appears to be in Simpson's account. Similarly, the bishop swept briefly over other careers that were important in less controversial ways. He reports, for example, that the Harper brothers had a considerable publishing house. The important point, about the Harpers and Drew alike, was that they were successful and Methodist. Simpson had seen enough of snobbish attitudes toward his denomination; he meant to prove that Methodists could be men of mark.[8]

The bishop's descriptions of the rich men's gifts to the church, and their various works on its behalf, range from vague to quantitatively explicit. He reports that Oliver Archer, a railroad man, was a "generous giver" and that Charles Rowland, an "extensive manufacturer in Cincinnati," was "largely identified" with church interests. At the same time, he wrote that Daniel Drew had committed $500,000 for the seminary that bears his name. He also knew that George Jackson Ferry, a trustee of both Drew and of Wesleyan universities, had divided $25,000 between the two institutions. Simpson could be very specific about such numbers. He was also specific about laymen's membership on church boards and societies that were intended to promote sunday schools, missions, church extension, and other good works.[9]

Simpson's references to particular philanthropies show that laymen had a broad range of interests, but that one kind of benevolence was especially popular. Lewis Miller, an Ohio farm implement manufacturer, was the principal source of money behind the Chautauqua movement; Joseph H. Thornley, a Philadelphia dry goods merchant, was one of several rich men who financed camp meeting associations; Abel Minard, a New York banker, established a home for the daughters of foreign missionaries. But rich Methodists gave most frequently for church buildings, missions, Sunday schools, and—above all—colleges and seminaries. Seventeen of the good works that Simpson specifies benefited Sunday schools, which were about as popular as church construction and missions. He specifies fifty-seven benefactions to colleges and seminaries.[10]

Of course Simpson himself was especially interested in education. He had been a college president. He was sensitive to the imputation that Methodists were educationally inferior to other denominations. Not surprisingly, gifts to Indiana Asbury, Drew, Wesleyan, Northwestern, Syracuse, and other new Methodist institutions of the period got his particular attention. Colleges and seminaries were also, pretty clearly, of special interest to the rich men he described. The middle of the 19th century was the denomination's great period of college founding; from 1830 to the Civil War various groups of Methodists "founded thirty-four permanent schools of higher learning." A few others, such as Boston University, began immediately after the war. Colleges and seminaries, above all else, were the monuments that rich Methodists left to mark their success and their impact on the church. The pastor who encouraged Drew to found a seminary said that it "will live when you are dead." Many such institutions preserve the memory of Drew's contemporaries, though not usually their names.[11]

Methodist colleges and seminaries drew groups of rich men together in local or regional clusters. John Evans, Orrington Lunt and other rich men in Chicago came together around Northwestern University; prominent New York and New Jersey Methodists focused on Drew; western New Yorkers combined to build Syracuse University; Michigan had Albion; Pittsburgh made originally Presbyterian Allegheny College into a Methodist institution. All over the country clusters of rich men made colleges and seminaries their principal means of embellishing their church.[12]

One such cluster flourished in Boston. Its principal members were Lee Claflin, Isaac Rich, and Jacob Sleeper. All three received substantial notices in Simpson's *Cyclopaedia*, though the bishop is characteristically general about their commercial lives. Considered in more detail, the Bostonians exhibit common characteristics which suggest ways of thinking about rich 19th century Methodists generally.[13]

All three were highly successful businessmen; none left a detailed account of his working life. They were tight-lipped about business. Perhaps, as Edward Chase Kirkland suggests of even richer businessmen in the period, they were diffident about their success, considering that it "occupied a low priority in any absolute scheme of values." The best-documented of the three was Lee Claflin, whose family papers, including some of his own diaries and correspondence, have been preserved.[14]

Lee Claflin was born in 1792, tenth of eleven children in a poor Hopkinton, Massachusetts,

family. Orphaned at age five, he spent the next several years in the home of a farmer who took care to exact enough labor to pay for the child's board. Claflin left for an apprenticeship in the tanning trade at the earliest possible moment, probably not long after his tenth birthday. He joined the Methodist Episcopal Church during his apprenticeship, and remained loyal to it until he died in 1872.

Claflin had his own tannery at Milford, close to Hopkinton, by the early 1810s. It was a small business, as tanneries generally were at the time. It grew because of a thousand dollar dowry obtained, with other gifts, from his bride's family, in 1815. Loans from trusting fellow Methodists also helped him to expand the tannery, and begin some modest vertical integration. By 1825 he was putting out leather to neighborhood shoemakers for conversion into heavy men's boots. He first marketed his boots in Providence. Then, in the early 1830s, he began to ship to New Orleans and St. Louis, where he also bought hides for his several tanneries and for others' as well.

Claflin abandoned the putting out system in 1840. He then concentrated his bootmaking in a factory at Hopkinton. He was one of the first entrepreneurs to do that. At the same time, he concentrated his personal attention increasingly on marketing and a complex of investments in land, coal, shipping, and banking. He found it convenient to do all of that from an office in Boston. Country boy made good, he had come to the metropolis. He resembled Silas Lapham in that, but the parallel is not perfect. Hopkinton was near Boston, so he kept his home there, lived plainly in the style of that place, and avoided the social agonies that Lapham had to confront in fashionable Boston.[15]

Less is known about Isaac Rich, but his acquaintances agreed on a few facts and some traditions. He was born on a poor Cape Cod farm in 1801, then came to Boston at age fourteen. After working in an oyster shop, he began to sell fish on his own account from a wheelbarrow. He prospered, admirers believed, because of extraordinary diligence and religious inspiration. The inspiration came to him through Wilbur Fisk, then a minister at Charlestown, later president of Wesleyan University, who met the poor young peddler pushing his wheelbarrow across the Charlestown bridge. Fisk invited Rich to attend his church; Rich came and joined the denomination a few years later. The religion it gave him included assurance that God was good to hard-working young men. That made him fearless. Late in life he said that he had "never doubted . . . that I should succeed, never was discouraged." In fact he did succeed, in both fish and real estate.[16]

Jacob Sleeper also began in a country place, New Castle, Maine, where he was born in 1802. Apparently his family was somewhat more prosperous than the Claflins and Richs; at least it gave him an academy education, but such advantages were abruptly lost when his father died. Then fourteen years old, Sleeper went to work at an uncle's store in Belfast, Maine. He joined the church in his Belfast period, which ended when he left for Boston in 1825. Starting his city career as a bookkeeper, Sleeper formed a partnership with a clothing dealer ten years later. The firm prospered by selling clothes to the navy. Sleeper further increased his fortune by shrewd investments in real estate, banking, and insurance. He rose from more advantageous beginnings than Claflin and Rich could claim, but he certainly rose.[17]

Claflin, Rich, and Sleeper all experienced a great deal of mobility, both economic and geographic. Oscar Handlin suggests that they were uprooted, in their own fortunate way, from their class and local backgrounds. They were "internal immigrants" who could neither identify completely with older elites nor accept an entirely separate identity with the foreign immigrants of the day. Handlin guesses that they resolved that dilemma by "continual emphasis upon their Protestantism and their Yankee heritage," which certified that they were not like the Irish, and by insisting on the special character of their Protestantism, which was evangelical and not some attenuated ghost of Puritanism such as the Brahmins espoused. Being Methodist defined their status in a secure and satisfying way, Handlin thinks.[18]

In any case, being Methodist was obviously important to them. Among other things, it guided their use of money. Money, they said in various ways, was for doing good. While Rich and Sleeper lived well, and studiously plain Lee Claflin enabled his children to live very well indeed, they all reserved large parts of their fortunes for good works, mostly within the church. Sleeper, for example, gave altogether a half million dollars to one Methodist cause, Boston University. He had retired from active business with less than that, and though he surely increased his estate by later investments, his gifts must have been a substantial proportion of the whole. When he thought that he had enough, he began to give the bulk of his additional income to good works. Similarly, Lee Claflin is estimated to have given as much as a half million dollars to a variety of causes, mostly within the church. When he began to keep a systematic record of his giving, in 1849, he said that he had enough and would devote his "increase" to benevolence. Finally, Rich devoted the great bulk of his estate to the church. What he did not give in life was assigned to Boston and Wesleyan universities in his will. He had little else to do with his money; all seven of his children died before he did.[19]

Claflin, Rich, and Sleeper were serious philanthropists. They gave abundantly and with studied intent. Claflin, especially, made the mindfulness of giving explicit. Usually taciturn, he produced one long, private letter to his son William, on the subject of stewardship, in 1845. It was an important topic, so much so that he asked William to keep the letter and refer to it from time-to-time. Its point was that a real Christian had to practice a kind of asceticism. "If you are a Christian," Lee Claflin wrote, "you have forsaken all for Christ. Our saviour says if any man will be my disciple let him forsake all that he hath and follow me." Clearly Lee did not want William to forsake his boots and leather, but he did want him to do all of his work as Christ's steward. He especially wanted his son to remember the "saying of the great Wesley—I get all I can, I save all I can, I give all I can. "[20]

Claflin had obviously read or heard John Wesley 's 1744 sermon on "The Use of Money." It was an appropriate text for him. Wesley wrote it at a time when humble English Methodists were rising economically, making him fear that they would become "lovers of the present world." Wesley had to exhort them not to use their money self-indulgently, but to live modestly, preserving a surplus to "do good to them that are of the household of faith." If an "overplus remained, they ought to do good outside the household. Lee Claflin understood all of that, and acted on it. And if his friends spent more than he did on their own pleasures, they at least honored Wesley's injunction not to "stint" in doing good. They also followed Wesley in concentrating their gifts within "the household of faith."[21]

The results of their philanthropy were impressive, especially for educational institutions. The Wesleyan Academy at Wilbraham, Massachusetts, for example, which was New England's first enduring Methodist school, survived because of their gifts. Begun in 1825, it struggled through a generation with donations as small as ten cents each solicited from the laity in general. In 1850 Lee Claflin enrolled his younger son, Wilbur Fisk Claflin, accepted election to its boards of trustees and examiners, and began to give money. His presence was critically important in 1857, when the academy had a disastrous fire. Then a committee of eleven clergy and laymen, including Claflin, Rich, and Sleeper, more than replaced the losses. A brick boarding house was named for Rich, who gave more than $38,000.

The three also gave substantially to Wesleyan University at Middletown, Connecticut. Begun in 1831, the first Methodist college in New England, it received large donations from Claflin, Rich, and Sleeper, all of whom served on its board of trustees. Rich alone gave $40,000 to the library that bears his name, and $100,000 to the university's endowment. Similarly, all three contributed to the Biblical Institute that began at Concord, New Hampshire, in 1847. The institute was the cornerstone of their largest venture in education.[22]

It assumed that importance in 1867 when its trustees, of whom Lee Claflin was president, decided to move the institute to Boston. That was expected to increase the interest and generosity of Boston Methodists, who had no educational institution belonging to the denomination in their city. Then some individuals began to urge that an ambitious university be organized around the Institute. The Reverend William F. Warren, later president of Boston University, attributed the idea to Lee Claflin; the Reverend J. H. Twombly, later president of the University of Wisconsin, claimed the credit for himself. Twombly thought that a university would improve the "inferior" intellectual and professional status of Boston Methodists. He later recalled that Sleeper was the first important layman to encourage the project, and that Lee Claflin also gave it early support. Sleeper and Claflin together recruited Rich, who felt some initial reluctance to divert any large part of his money from Wesleyan University.[23]

Rich, Sleeper, and Claflin gave to other causes as well, but educational institutions were their clear favorites, just as they were the clear favorites of the men listed in Simpson's *Cyclopaedia*. Handlin suggests that they favored education because they identified it with social advancement; it was a means of assuring their children's status. However that may have been, it is more obvious that they deeply respected education because they revered the clergy. Education, certainly college education, had become the special qualification and perquisite of ministers.

By one account, Isaac Rich wanted to be a minister. But he felt that "God didn't give me a call; I prayed for one, but it didn't come." So he was a businessman who kept a portrait of the Rev. Wilbur Fisk in his office for daily inspiration, and put his money where it would be used to train more such godly men. So, too, Lee Claflin revered Fisk, for whom he named a son, and viewed education as a means of getting more such learned clergymen. Son William was removed from Brown University when it became clear that he had no calling to preach; a man God did not want for a preacher would do better to learn the boot trade than to spend useless years in college.[24]

For Rich and Claflin, at least, support of education was most fundamentally a way of supporting the clergy. Claflin also did that through his contributions to the Preachers' Aid Society, which he served as president, and his gifts to individual ministers and their families. He also had a marked tendency to find his friends among clergymen. Son William showed the same preference; a business associate once complained that William was more attached to "smooth tongued flattering politicians and priests" than he was to his business associates. Rich and Sleeper also enjoyed clerical society. It had a gravity and glamor not to be found among bootmakers and fish venders.[25]

If simple businessmen, painfully modest about their merely commercial accomplishments, revered the clergy, ministers also professed some strong feelings for the businessmen. They were grateful for gifts that improved their personal and professional lives. And they admired the businessmen's sheer practical competence. Ministers had their high callings, and occasionally some learning, but they were not esteemed for their worldly competence. Ann Douglas suggests that some of them—she does not refer to Methodists in particular—were set apart with the ladies, given a vague kind of influence in place of real power. Men in that position respected the businessmen for their practical accomplishments. A writer in *Zion's Herald*, for example, conceded that "we preachers are undeniably not the best financiers in the world," and advised the church to take advantage of businessmen's practical expertise. Similarly, J. H. Twombly argued that the New England Conference could benefit from the "counsels of men of extensive practical business." The ministerial members of the conference presumably lacked practical experience.[26]

Twombly made that point as part of an 1857 report to the New England Conference from a special committee appointed to consider the wisdom of lay representation in the conference. He argued that the church's growing educational

163

and philanthropic enterprises required practical management, something businessmen were best able to provide. Further, he guessed that the laymen would become even more generous when they had a voice in governing church affairs; "men have more interest in an enterprise when they help to control it, than when they do not." Finally, Twombly thought that the "preeminence of the clerical over the lay element" was the one really dangerous source of dissension in the church. Methodists had never fought over doctrine, but they had occasionally experienced divisions about lay representation in conferences.[27]

Twombly was observing some very polite dissension on that point when he wrote his report. All through the 1850's the conference newspaper, *Zion's Herald*, had been reporting innovations favoring lay representation in other places, and creating echoes in New England. It reported, for example, that the Virginia and South Carolina conferences allowed lay members of their boards of stewards to speak on all financial issues that arose in the conference meetings. The *Herald* endorsed that because it was a way of harnessing the laity's practical competence without diluting essential clerical authority. In 1855 the New England Conference tried to achieve the same result by allowing its committees on financial, educational, and philanthropic matters to select lay members. Only the committee on education chose to do that. Lee Claflin, Rich, and Sleeper served with three other laymen and seven ministers.[28]

Lay participation in the New England Conference expanded again in 1858. The previous year's session adopted Twombly's report on lay representation which required the stewards in each of the conference's four districts to choose five lay delegates to the 1858 meeting. The lay delegates were to have voice and vote on benevolent and educational matters; everything else has for ministerial delegates only. Lee Claflin and Jacob Sleeper were among the first twenty lay delegates; Isaac Rich served two years later. They were also among the lay delegates who actually attended conferences. Some of the people selected as lay delegates did not. When the system was allowed to lapse in 1871, it was thought that laymen had lost interest because the conference gave them too little to do.[29]

At the same time, laymen in other places were showing a great deal of interest in being represented in general conferences. In 1852 Philadelphia laymen began an ultimately successful twenty-year campaign for that reform by holding a national lay convention in their city.

The convention was less national than its sponsors hoped that it would be; New Englanders, in particular, held back because they suspected the convention organizers of southern sympathies. One of the two delegates from Massachusetts, a minister, gave some credence to that suspicion by arguing that the church would never have been allowed to divide over slavery if only laymen had been represented in the critical general conferences of the previous decade. Despite its limitations, the convention produced a petition to the General Conference of 1852 which was seriously received. The conference even took time to hear laymen sent as spokesmen for the convention.[30]

The convention had some claim to be treated seriously, pro-Southern or not. Its leaders were substantial characters. One of the spokesmen dispatched to the general conference was Francis H. Root, a Buffalo, New York, manufacturer of stoves and iron castings who was a principal mover behind the foundation of Syracuse University. Men of such weight had to be heard. So the conference listened, and formed a special committee to examine the petition. The committee decided that lay representation was "inexpedient" for the time being, but it said nothing to prejudice future discussion of the issue. In fact, its chairman would become the principal advocate among the clergy, of lay representation. He was the newly-elected bishop, and long-time admirer of successful laymen, Matthew Simpson.[31]

Lay representation gathered increasing support over the next decade. The General Conference of 1860 tried to settle the issue by a vote of adult, male church members, but the result was both negative and inconclusive. Lay conventions continued to meet; Bishop Simpson addressed one in New York in 1863, arguing that lay representation would increase lay philanthropy. "Laymen, bring your money," he urged. The assembled laymen cheered: "God bless the Bishop." A year later Lee Claflin chaired a convention in Boston which declared that Methodism without lay representation was undemocratic, and all too nearly Roman. Two weeks later he went with others, including son William, to a national lay convention in Philadelphia. A report of the general conference of that year approvingly noted that the lay convention included "the best business talent in the country,."[32]

The campaign for lay representation continued through the General Conference of 1868. Boston, for example, had an 1867 lay convention chaired by William Claflin. Then Lt. Gov. Claflin praised the church for its ready adaptation to change, and made very clear that the next year's general conference should decide the issue. In fact the conference did call for another vote. It was affirmative. Two lay delegates from each annual conference were received in the General Conference of 1872.[33]

It would be all too easy to exaggerate the importance of lay representation in the general conferences. In the long view of Frederick Norwood's general history, the proportion of lay delegates in the general conference was small; equal representation waited for the next century. Arguably laymen were actually losing ground in the denomination because the old offices of lay preacher and class leader were becoming less important as ministers were increasingly available to do the work that had belonged to such officers early in the century. Laymen were not necessarily more important than they had been. But some laymen had assumed a new role in church polity.[34]

Ministers who attended the 1872 General Conference said that those laymen were an impressive sight. Bishop Simpson was predictably approving, and Andrew Endsley of Pittsburgh Conference enthused that the "one hundred and twenty-nine laymen here are in the main men of note in their respective localities." They were successful merchants and manufacturers, leading politicians, and distinguished attorneys. In fact they were all of those things and more. Simpson listed ninety-two of the lay delegates in his *Cyclopaedia*, including five governors, a dozen congressmen, at least fourteen college trustees, and one professor. Almost all of the delegates enjoyed business or professional success, though there were a few men who worked for the Book Concern and one black farmer whose moment of political prominence had ended with Reconstruction. He was exceptional. In 1872 the church was recognizing its "men of note."[35]

That seemed appropriate. After all, the diligent, upwardly mobile laymen had shared their success with the church. They had brought their money, as Simpson and other clerical promoters of education, benevolence, and good architecture had asked. Thanks to the embellishments they provided, Methodists no longer had to feel themselves inferior to Episcopalians, or at least Presbyterians. Whatever Asbury or Wesley might have thought of the fact, they had become respectable.

NOTES

1. William Dean Howells, *The Rise of Silas Lapham* (Boston: Houghton Mifflin Co., Riverside Editions, 1957), p. 21.

Howells mentions Lapham's philanthropies in a single sentence. The hazards of wealth are bemoaned in Wade Crawford Barclay, *History of Methodist Missions*, Vol. 3 (New York: The Board of Missions of the Methodist Church, 1957), pp. 49-50, which draws upon William Warren Sweet, *Methodism in American History* (NY: The Methodist Book Concern, 1933). Sweet and Barclay perceive a generalized softening of moral fiber following from the denomination's growing prosperity. This essay intends to be concrete about some of the results of that prosperity. It is obviously a very general sketch of a topic that might be treated in much greater detail. Sidney Ahlstrom has recommended attention to the philanthropies of evangelical laymen, and that might well include detailed study of rich Methodists.

2. Henry F. May, *The Enlightenment in America* (New York: Oxford University Press, 1976), pp. 271-2; *Zion's Herald*, 7 January 1869; George Claude Baker, Jr., *An Introduction to the History of Early New England Methodism* (Durham: Duke University Press, 1941), p. 18.

3. George A. Crawford, *The Centennial of New England Methodism* (Boston: Crawford Bros., 1891), pp. 47-8.

4. Robert D. Clark, *The Life of Matthew Simpson* (New York: The Macmillan Co., 1956), pp. 85 - 193, 276.

5. *Ibid.*, p. 192; Matthew Simpson, *A Hundred Years of Methodism* (New York: Phillips and Hunt, 1876), p. 165; earlier Methodist thinking about church buildings is explained in James Porter, *The Revised Compendium of Methodism* (New York: Nelson and Phillips, 1875), p. 108.

6. Matthew Simpson, *Cyclopaedia of Methodism* (Philadelphia: Everts and Steward, 1878).

7. *Ibid.*, see especially pp. 504 and 545. Apart from a few farm implement manufacturers, the only people in Simpson's book who were principally identified with agriculture were a black Louisiana farmer, Pierre Laudry, who had participated in politics during Reconstruction (p. 527) and Orange Judd, editor of the *American Agriculturist* and a publisher of agricultural books (p. 504).

8. *Ibid.*, pp. 311-12. The DAB portrays Drew as "sharp-witted, grasping, and unscrupulous," adding that "his trickiness was combined with a sanctimonious devotion to Methodism." Ezra Squier Tipple, *Drew Theological Seminary, 1867-1917* (New York: Methodist Book Concern, 1917), p. 21 takes a more appreciative view, quoting a contemporary who considered Drew "one of the pleasantest figures in the New York Methodism of that period . . . ."

9. Simpson, *Cyclopaedia*, pp. 48, 768, 357.

10. *Ibid.*, pp. 612, 860-61, 849, 613.

11. Clark, *The Life of Matthew Simpson*, pp. 72-3 reports the bigotry Indiana Methodists of Simpson's time had to confront. A Presbyterian legislator pronounced them too ignorant to conduct a college; Tipple, *Drew Theological Seminary*, pp. 23-4n; Harold F. Williamson and Payson S. Wild, *Northwestern University: A History, 1850-1975* (Evanston: Northwestern University Press, 1976), p. 2; Frederick A. Norwood, *The Story of Methodism* (Nashville: Abingdon, 1974), pp . 217-20.

12. Williamson and Wild, *Northwestern University*, pp. 2-4; Simpson, *Cyclopaedia*, references throughout the volume.

13. Simpson, *Cyclopaedia*, pp. 220, 754-5, 808; Oscar Handlin, *Boston's Immigrants, A Study in Acculturation* (Cambridge: Harvard University Press, 1959), pp. 219-20 offers some suggestive generalizations about the three.

14. Edward Chase Kirkland, *Dream and Thought in the Business Community, 1860-1900* (Chicago: Quadrangle Paperbacks, 1964), p. 3; Donald B. Marti, "Laymen, Bring Your Money: Lee Claflin, Methodist Philanthropist, 1791-1871" *Methodist History* XIV (April, 1976), 165-185.

15. Marti, "Laymen, Bring Your Money."

16. *Wesleyan Argus*, 31 January 1872; James Mudge, *History of the New England Conference of the Methodist Episcopal Church* (Boston: The Conference, 1910), pp. 263-4; *DAB*; Mary B. Claflin, *Real Happenings* (New York: Thomas Y.

Crowell and Co., 1890), pp. 14-22; *Harper's Weekly*, 17 February 1872.

17. *Boston Journal*, 1 April 1869; *DAB*; Mudge, *History of the New England Conference*, p. 265.

18. Handlin, *Boston's Immigrants*, pp. 219-20.

19. Sleeper entry in *DAB; Zion's Herald*, 2 March 1871; Lee Claflin's Sunday Journal, August 12, 18, in Claflin Collection, Rutherford B. Hayes Library; *Wesleyan Argus*, 31 January 1872; Mudge, *History of the New England Conference*, p. 264.

20. Lee Claflin to William Claflin, n.p., February 2, 1845, Claflin Collection, Hayes Library.

21. Albert C. Outler, ed., *John Wesley* (New York: Oxford University Press, 1964), pp. 238 - 50.

22. Marti, "Laymen, Bring Your Money," pp. 173-7; Mudge, *History of the New England Conference*, p. 329.

23. Marti, "Laymen, Bring Your Money," pp. 177-8; William F. Warren, "The Origin of Boston University," *Bostonia* IV (October, 1903), 20.

24. *Wesleyan Argus*, 31 January 1872, p. 118; *Zion's Herald*, 31 August 1871.

25. James A. Woolson, otherwise unidentified letter written in 1892 or soon after, with friendlier letters in Claflin Papers, Hayes Library.

26. Ann Douglas, *The Feminization of American Culture* (New York: Alfred A. Knopf, 1977), especially chapters two and three. Douglas' analysis does not purport to include evangelical clergy, but may have fit Methodists reasonably well by the mid-19th century; *Zion's Herald*, 5 May 1858; 11 February 1852.

27. *Zion's Herald*, 5 May 1858.

28. *Ibid.*, 11 February 1852; 18 April 1855; Mudge, *History of the New England Conference*, pp. 242-3.

29. Mudge, *History of the New England Conference*, pp. 243-4; *Zion's Herald*, 16 March 1859.

30. *Zion's Herald*, 4 February 1852; 10 March 1852.

31. Simpson, *Cyclopaedia*, p. 766; Simpson, *A Hundred Years of Methodism*, p. 174.

32. Simpson, *A Hundred Years of Methodism*, p. 175; Mudge, *History of the New England Conference*, p. 245; *Zion's Herald*, 3 June 1863; 18 May 1864; 25 May 1864.

33. *Zion's Herald*, supplement to 28 November 1867; Simpson, *A Hundred Years of Methodism*, pp. 187-8.

34. Norwood, *The Story of Methodism*, pp. 257-8.

35. Barclay, *History of Methodist Missions*, Vol. 4, p. 46n; Simpson, *Cyclopaedia*, especially p. 527.

The Role of Auxiliary Ministries in Late Nineteenth-Century Methodism

William McGuire King
University of Virginia

Everyone knows that the post-Civil War era was a time of rapid social and cultural change, which transformed the way middle-class Americans saw themselves and their world. Recent American religious historians, such as Paul Carter, Robert Handy, Ernest Sandeen, William Hutchison, George Marsden, and Ferenc Szasz, have begun paying more attention to the changes occurring in American religious life during these decades, recognizing that in many respects the religious developments and controversies of late Victorian America served as the fountainhead of our contemporary religious situation.[1] Most of these discussions, however, have focussed on changes in theological modes of thought or changes in social assumptions and values. Relatively little attention has been paid, by contrast, to changes occurring in popular denominational life and ministry or to new patterns of middle-class religious behavior. It is too easy simply to assume that we know what was going on within the mainline Protestant churches in this period.

The thesis of this paper is that one finds within Methodist and other evangelical denominations of the late nineteenth century an increasing dissatisfaction with older, revivalistic modes of ministerial work and a search for new patterns of religious self-perception and commitment within evangelical congregations. The most obvious evidence for this kind of alteration in religious attitude is provided by Charles Sheldon's novel *In His Steps*.[2] Its instant popularity for a broad spectrum of evangelicals attests to the fact that it had touched a nerve in popular religious sentiment. Although the minister in Sheldon's novel, Henry Maxwell, continues to patronize and support the revivalistic services taking place in the mythical town of Raymond, the real point of the novel is that Maxwell is dissatisfied with an exclusively revivalistic conception of the church's ministry. Two themes within the novel bear upon this dissatisfaction. In the first place, Maxwell believes that the ministerial work of the church must operate on the basis of a new model of ministry, a more inclusive and participatory model. Thus Maxwell challenges all the members of his congregation to see themselves as engaged in the ministerial work of the church. In the second place, the message of the novel is that this inclusive ministry must reach out into secular culture, to assimilate that culture to its own ideals. This new understanding of the relationship between ministry and culture eventually leads Maxwell himself to become disenchanted with traditional forms of ministry and to leave his congregation for settlement work in the inner city of Chicago.

The popularity of *In His Steps* suggests that a reexamination of the nature of ministry and of appropriate models for ministry were becoming prevalent within evangelical denominations, including the Methodist denominations. Ministry was no longer restricted to the vocation of the itinerant minister or to the promotion of revivals and conversion experiences. Nor was ministry seen any longer as simply a confrontation between religious ideals and worldly values but rather as an *assimilation* of social and cultural life to religious ideals.[3] Religion and culture intermingled as evangelicals increasingly found themselves experiencing religious self-fulfillment through a fuller intercourse with the powers of this world. "Americans of the late nineteenth century," according to Donald H. Meyer, "like other Victorians, longed to feel at home in the universe."[4] This Victorian yearning for sense of "at-homeness" in the world may have helped to reshape the goals of ministry into ones that extended beyond the confines of religious boundaries to embrace the entire realm of human culture. Ministry was increasingly being redefined as a "service vocation," as a service *to* the world and *on behalf* of the world, not in opposition to the world. At the same time, once this redefinition took place, ministry would no longer be viewed as the prerogative of the professional clergy alone; the concept of ministry would itself be democratized. Ministry was a service of the entire church to meet personal, social, and cultural needs; and as a service activity, ministry would become the responsibility of all church members, lay and clerical alike.

Such a redefinition of ministry was particularly useful in meeting certain structural needs of the denomination after the Civil War. Starting in the 1870s, the denominations underwent a tremendous growth both statistically, in terms of membership and financial resources, and organizationally. Organizational expansion and consolidation within the Methodist Episcopal Church began in 1872, when the General Conference (which was also the first general conference to accept lay delegates) assumed full control over the older benevolent societies of the denomination and turned these societies into official "boards." Such boards were now to function as program arms of the general conference.[5] The new boards welcomed the service-oriented model of ministry for it provided an ideal way to strengthen the commitment of the laity to the work of the boards and it generated a sense of corporate denominational identity. The ministry of the church now assumed a multidimensional character in which the religious devotion of the laity could be channelled to support the service opportunities provided by the denominational apparatus.

How these changes affected the work of the local pastor will not be explored in this paper, although that is a question that needs investigation. This paper will focus instead on the rise of auxiliary sorts of ministries within Methodism. The characteristic of auxiliary ministries is that they began as semi-official service agencies of the denomination; they were neither a part of the board structure of the denomination nor part of the regular duties of the itinerant ministry. Most of the auxiliary ministries were aimed at mobilizing lay talent in an effort to supplement the work of the local pastoral ministry. It was not unusual, however, for the auxiliary ministries, such as the Deaconess Movement and the Epworth League, to become absorbed later into the official board structure of the denomination.

Although the late nineteenth-century auxiliary ministries bore some similarities to the work of the benevolent societies of the earlier nineteenth century, they existed for quite a different purpose. The benevolent societies had been created in order to raise and distribute funds, and their work was always somewhat remote from the concerns of the local congregations. By contrast, the auxiliary ministries that were established after the Civil War were directly concerned with training lay workers and with building lay commitment to the overall religious and social ministries of the local congregation. Such ministries therefore altered the ways in which local congregations operated and changed the nature of the relationship between church and society.

Several auxiliary ministries are especially worthy of note: the Sunday School/Chautauqua movement (that is, the religious education movement), the Epworth League (that is, the youth movement), the Deaconess Movement (or female religious worker movement), and the National City Evangelization Union (or the institutional church movement). Each played an important role in redefining the function of the laity in the overall ministry of the church and in forging a stronger bond between local congregations and denominational structures.

One of the key figures in the development of auxiliary ministries in the Methodist Episcopal Church after the Civil War was John Heyl Vincent, who was elected to the episcopacy in 1888. Vincent had an immense confidence in the power and importance of education and teacher training. Vincent was openly critical of the emotionalism and sentimentality of the older revivalism. In his book *The Revival and After the Revival* (1882), he criticized revivalistic techniques for their limited usefulness in church work and felt that the ministry of the church must no longer rely so exclusively upon revivalistic methods and models. Not surprisingly, his thought was in part shaped by the writings of Horace Bushnell and Frederick Denison Maurice.[6] Vincent wanted the denomination to adopt the highest standards of education, both in seminaries and in local congregations, and to devote more of its resources to the training of lay workers as professional religious educators.

John Vincent became corresponding secretary of the Methodist Sunday-School Union in 1868; and in this capacity, he soon became, along with B. F. Jacobs, a key figure in the creation of the International Sunday-School Lessons. These lessons played an important role in the life of the late Victorian Protestant churches, for they provided a uniform and systematic course of biblical instruction that cut across denominational lines and drew upon the scholarly resources of the entire Protestant community. What was closest to Vincent's heart, however, was the actual training of Sunday-school teachers. He wanted them to have the same level of expertise as their public school counterparts. He thus organized a number of Training Institutes and "Normal Schools" for the purpose of professionalizing Sunday-school work. According to his biographer, Vincent viewed the local church itself "as a school with many departments, each well equipped and well officered, all working in harmony. From the pastor in the pulpit to the parent in the home the adults were nothing less than members of a faculty. Their business was to instruct, and they should know the best way of going about that business."[7]

Although Vincent placed tremendous emphasis on Bible study, especially study that focussed on biblical geography and history, his educational aims were far broader. He believed that through religious education "we may acquire skill in awakening and stimulating intellectual activity, educating the conscience, strengthening faith and developing will power." Education would produce students who would be "interested in other people, in works of beneficence and in the promotion of good will among all classes of society."[8] The end result of religious education, therefore, would be the production of Christian character and social citizenship.[9] Vincent's writings, such as *Sunday School Institutes and Normal Classes* (1870), *The Modern Sunday School* (1887), and *A Study in Pedagogy* (1890) reiterated the need for professional and "scientific" methods in the church's educational programs.

Vincent's arguments and practical reforms were well received by Victorian Methodists. In part, this reception was a result of the cult of professionalism that was coming to dominate the middle-class Victorian outlook in America. According to Burton J. Bledstein, in his recent study of *The Culture of Professionalism* in Victorian America, "by the 1860s . . . ambitious middle-class persons were seeking a professional basis for an institutional order."[10] The word "amateur" now often took on a pejorative connotation, whereas education and the school diploma were the primary means "with which an individual sought entry into the respectability and rewards of a profession."[11] Education, however, was conceived in largely practical terms as a way of building personal character and acquiring the skills necessary to engage in significant "service" to one's society and culture.[12]

This stress on education is indicative of the increasing merger of religious and cultural values in popular Victorian evangelical culture, and it was becoming more pronounced in the latter part of the nineteenth century. The old revivalistic antagonism between religion and culture was breaking down. Sacred and secular realms were no longer viewed in mutually exclusive terms. Vincent himself revealed the pervasive sense of "at-homeness" with the world when he wrote that "things secular are under God's guidance and are full of divine meanings . . . All things are sublime . . . Flowers, fossils, microscopic dust, foul soil, things that crawl and things that soar . . . all are divine in origin and nature."[13]

The Vincent philosophy that stressed an educational model for ministry came to full fruition in the creation of the Chautauqua Institute, which he founded with Lewis Miller in 1874. Vincent wanted to make sure that the Chautauqua Assembly, as it was at first called, would not be confused with a camp meeting assembly. It was not to be a revivalistic type of movement. "The Assembly was totally unlike the camp-meeting," he said; "we did our best to make it so."[14] The initial purpose of Chautauqua was strictly educational—to train Sunday-school teachers—although a more social emphasis gradually took over. "The heart of the Assembly was the Normal Class, at which was pursued a systematic course of Bible study and of modern methods of conducting a Sunday-school."[15] Later, a school of foreign languages was added, in which Sunday-school teachers could learn the rudiments of Hebrew, Greek, or Latin. The director of this school was William Rainey Harper, who later became the first president of the University of Chicago. Harper was assisted by Vincent's son, George, who went on to become a prominent sociologist and Dean of the Faculty at the University of Chicago. Chautauqua thus offered church workers a high quality, intensive six-week training session in religious education.

The work of Chautauqua quickly expanded to encompass general lay education as well. Prominent public speakers gave addresses in the Chautauqua Amphitheater, which was built to accommodate several thousand guests. Among the better known speakers were Frances Willard, who first came to national attention from the Chautauqua platform, Washington Gladden, Lyman Abbott, Andrew Fairburn, Francis Peabody, Stanley Hall, and Henry Drummond. This list of speakers indicates the generally liberal and culturally open outlook of Chautauqua. All sorts of issues—religious, philosophical, scientific, historical, political, and social—were addressed by Chautauqua speakers. Particularly effective speakers were liable to receive the "Chautauqua salute," which involved the waving of white handkerchiefs.

Not the least important of Chautauqua's contributions to religious education was the creation of the Chautauqua Literary and Scientific Circle in 1878. Through the agency of Chautauqua, reading circles were established in churches and civic institutions throughout the country, providing hundreds of small towns and villages with the benefits of adult education. By 1891, approximately 180,000 readers had participated in the Chautauqua program and 20,000 readers a year were being "graduated" from Chautauqua's extension school. Chautauqua's contribution to popular adult education and to middle-class culture prompted the critic, Charles

Eliot Norton, to remark, "I regard Chautauqua as the most significant and hopeful fact in American life at the present time."[16]

A blend of cultural uplift and liberal religious enthusiasm marked the spirit of Chautauqua and helped to change the religious outlook of middle-class evangelicals. Religious education and lay training were now popular themes covered by the denominational press. Vincent's belief that religious piety was improved by exposure to literature and scholarship became a commonplace assumption, as is evident by the sort of articles that now appeared in denominational papers and journals. Evangelicalism had become genteel. And with the gentility came a definition of the religious life in terms of personal and cultural uplift, sacrificial service on behalf of others, and usefulness to society.

Both the Epworth League and the Deaconess Movement of the late nineteenth century owed a large debt to the sort of spirit reflected in the Chautauqua philosophy. In 1884, John Vincent organized a national youth organization called the Oxford League, on the model of the eighteenth-century Methodist Holy Club at Oxford. The goals of Vincent's Oxford League were the promotion of biblical and literary studies, building religious piety and moral character, and "training of its members in works of mercy and help."[17] George Vincent and James Joy, the later editor of the *Christian Advocate*, served as editors for the Oxford League's magazine, *Our Youth*. In 1889, in Cleveland, Ohio, the Oxford League merged with several other competing Methodist youth organizations to form the Epworth League of the Methodist Episcopal Church. A year later, the southern church organized its own Epworth League along similar lines. By 1896, over 16,000 local chapters had been established in the northern denomination.

The Epworth League served a very interesting function in the ministry of the local church. An early pamphlet of the League explained that one of the League's specific goals was to generate a sense of denominational loyalty among Methodist youth by having them read "distinctively Methodist literature" and by reinforcing commitments to the work of the local congregation.[18] Early League handbooks were quite explicit in stating that denominational loyalty would be reinforced through the training of Methodist youth "in Church life and teaching; their employment in works of charity and social service, the inculcation of missionary ideals . . . [and] their direction to lives of service at home and abroad."[19] Under the auspices of

what was called the "Department of Mercy and Help," terminology that Vincent himself had made current, Epworth Leaguers were expected to participate in the pastoral and social service work of the local congregation and to assist the local pastor. It was assumed that this training would produce a lifelong commitment to Christian service, lay ministries, and denominational objectives. Such commitment would result in a general program of Christian citizenship and reform, for the ministry of the League would be a " 'stimulus and direction to general Christian culture.' "[20]

The organization of the Deaconess Movement and the creation of religious training schools for lay workers in the late nineteenth century also provided a new way of supplementing and strengthening the ministry of the local church. The training schools, such as the Chicago Training School for City, Home and Foreign Missions; the New England Deaconess Home and Training School; and the Scarritt Bible and Training School, were all founded to train lay workers, especially young women, in church work. According to Virginia Brereton, the schools concentrated their efforts on "Bible pedagogy, the modern Sunday school, teacher training, organization of church work with young people and youth, child study and storytelling, and the principles and history of religious education."[21] It was no coincidence that Lucy Rider Meyer, the foundress of the training school idea and the head of the Chicago Training School, began her career working in the Sunday-school movement and was inspired by the writings and example of John H. Vincent.[22]

Many of the women who were graduated from the training schools became deaconesses. The deaconesses served in many ways as a bridge between the ministry of the local churches and the needs of the wider social environs. The General Conference of 1888, in granting formal recognition to the Deaconess Movement, explained that "the duties of the deaconess shall be to minister to the poor, care for the sick, provide for the orphan, comfort the sorrowing, seek the wandering, save the sinning."[23] The deaconesses engaged in an extensive program of home visitation and relief and, as a leading deaconess explained, "there was a tendency to annex her to the church as a sort of an assistant pastor, church visitor—what you will—a servant of the church."[24]

The success of the Deaconess Movement revealed another important function of the auxiliary ministries in late Victorian Methodism. Many middle-class youth, not the least of whom were women, suffered from severe vocational anxieties. The question of "life work" was a vital personal and spiritual concern of earnest Victorian youth. Victorians basically viewed one's occupation as an extension and expression of one's own character.[25] A career decision was therefore very much a decision about who one was. It was assumed that every one had been given a central purpose in life, a purpose tinged with religious as well as moral meaning. This vocational anxiety was heightened by the fact that Victorian society was one in which professional opportunities were expanding and one in which service vocations were opening up with increasing rapidity. The problem of vocational choice was a new problem for many American families. As Burton Bledstein has noted, there was in late Victorian America "a proliferating number of specialized services and novel tasks which a progressive civilization defined as essential and which the middle-class person himself viewed as previously nonexistent opportunities."[26] Middle-class youth no longer were expected to pursue predetermined and traditional vocational routes; instead they were under pressure to pursue a "significant" career, one which expressed their inner character and moral ideals. Under these circumstances, the question of vocation was one that generated considerable inner tension and anxiety among upwardly mobile youth. Frances Willard, the great temperance reformer and suffragette, probably articulated the sentiment and perplexities of many religiously trained youth: " 'I shall be twenty years old in September [1859] and I have as yet been of no use in the world. When I recover [from her illness], when I possess once more a "sound mind in a sound body," I will earn my own living; "pay my own way," and try to be of use in the world.' "[27] To be of use in the world: that was the chief thing.

The auxiliary ministries of the church helped the youth and young adults in the churches to discover ways to be "of use in the world." By stressing education, professionalism, lay training, and a ministry of service to the world, they reinforced middle-class cultural aspirations and offered concrete outlets for middle-class idealism. They also benefitted the denomination because they wrought new bonds between the laity and the work of the church, integrating the concerns of the laity into the ministry of the church and generating a sympathetic regard for the program goals of the denominational agencies. Being a Methodist was no longer simply defined as membership in a religious society; it was defined in terms of Methodist programs and participation in Methodist service.

The auxiliary ministries thus helped to solve a problem that had long vexed American Methodism: the problem of connectionalism. American Methodists had always had to struggle with the question of what bound local Methodist societies to one another. Where did the source of unity in Methodism lie, given its somewhat flexible theological and doctrinal positions? Although often unspoken, this question has haunted Methodism from the beginning. In the early nineteenth century, it was largely answered—as Asbury answered it—in terms of the itinerant ministry. The itinerancy was the chief link connecting local societies to the larger denominational family. Even the benevolent societies were linked to the denomination through the itinerancy. By the time of the Civil War, however, the professional Methodist ministry was becoming less itinerant and more "settled"; and thus the itinerant system itself could no longer serve as an adequate vehicle of connectional unity. The answer to the problem of connectionalism was now sought, on the one hand, through an expansion and centralization of the benevolent work of the denomination[28] and, on the other hand, through a redefinition of the conception of ministry. This redefinition democratized the meaning of ministry and broadened its cultural orientation. Through the work of auxiliary ministries—in cooperation with denominational boards and local congregations—connectional ties could be strengthened and an affinity with the national work of the denomination could be fashioned.

In retrospect, there were still other long-range historical and cultural contributions made by the work of the auxiliary ministries. Their historical and cultural significance was probably twofold. In the first place, their general emphasis on professionalism, education, vocation, and social service helped to break down the older revivalistic separation between religion and the world. Sacred and secular were now seen as parts of one grand system of divinity, a system that could easily be labelled Christian civilization. That this religious reorientation was occurring on the popular religious level was surely important, for it helps to explain why theological liberalism found such a ready reception within the mainline Protestant churches and seminaries in the late nineteenth century and early twentieth century. Indeed, more work needs to be done in American religious history on the generation of popular—as opposed to formal—liberal sentiment within the denominations.

In the second place, this popular liberalism

prepared the way for the general acceptance of the social gospel in the early twentieth century. By 1920, denominational agencies were thoroughly staffed by men and women of a social gospel persuasion. What is curious is how many of these individuals became interested in religious vocations and church work through their participation in the auxiliary ministries of the late Victorian church. Out of the ranks of the Sunday-school movement and the Epworth League, for example, came later social gospel advocates like James Joy, George Vincent, Dan Brummitt, S. Earl Taylor, Herbert Welch, Paul Hutchinson, Blaine Kirkpatrick, Owen Geer, and many others. Out of the training schools and Deaconess Movement came Winifred Chappell, Grace Scribner, Isabelle Horton, and Bertha Fowler. Mention should also be made of another auxiliary ministerial agency, the National City Evangelization Union. Between 1892 and 1912, the NCEU coordinated the work of denominational city missions and promoted the concept that city churches should be institutional churches, ministering to the total social and cultural needs of inner city residents and employing large staffs of specially trained lay workers.[29] From the NCEU came future leaders of the Methodist Federation for Social Service: Frank Mason North, George Mains, J. W. Magruder, and Harry Ward.

The auxiliary ministries were not themselves social gospel agencies; they had a different rationale and purpose. But they did provide the cultural and religious viewpoint and training and the social exposure that helped to make many of their participants and leaders warmly receptive to the new social message of the social gospel. As Dan Brummitt remarked in his book on *The Efficient Epworthian*:

Mercy and Help work [as it was called in the old Epworth League] had forced us to broaden and deepen our conception of what was expected of young Christians in their relation to their fellows . . . Mercy and Help had much to do with the kindling of the new spirit of service . . . Its goal is social salvation, the deliverance of human society from disease, poverty, crime, and misery; the development and perfection of the institutions of man's associated life, and the construction of a social order that is the city of God on earth.[30]

Not only did the service work of the auxiliary agencies generate a new social spirit, but their emphasis on Christian vocation, professionalism, and denominational loyalty did much to shape the peculiar character of the American version of the social gospel and to guarantee its institutional footing within the denomination.

NOTES

[1] Paul A. Carter, *The Spiritual Crisis of the Gilded Age* (Dekalb: Northern Illinois University Press, 1971); Robert Handy, *A Christian America* (New York: Oxford University Press, 1971); Ernest Sandeen, *The Roots of Fundamentalism* (Chicago: University of Chicago Press, 1970); William R. Hutchison, *The Modernist Impulse* (Cambridge: Harvard University Press, 1976); George Marsden *Fundamentalism and American Culture* (New York: Oxford University Press, 1980); Ferenc Morton Szasz, *The Divided Mind of Protestant America, 1880-1930* (University, Alabama: The University of Alabama Press, 1982).

2. For an interesting discussion of related themes, see Paul Boyer, "*In His Steps*: A Reappraisal," *American Quarterly* 23 (Spring 1971): 60-78.

3. For the distinction between assimilative versus coercive reform, see Joseph Gusfield, *Symbolic Crusade* (Urbana: University of Illinois Press, 1963).

4. Donald H. Meyer, "American Intellectuals and the Victorian Crisis of Faith," *American Quarterly* 27 (December 1975):595.

5. See William McGuire King, "Denominational Modernization and Religious Identity: The Case of the Methodist Episcopal Church," *Methodist History* 20 (January 1982), 75-89.

6. Leon H. Vincent, *John Heyl Vincent* (NewYork: The Macmillan Company, 1925), p. 264.

7. *Ibid.*, p. 82.

8. John H. Vincent, "A Forward Look for the Sunday-school," in *The Development of the Sunday-School, 1780-1905* (Boston: Executive Committee of the International Sunday-School Association, 1905), p. 170.

9. *Ibid.*, p. 169.

10. Burton J. Bledstein, *The Culture of Professionalism* (New York: W. W. Norton & Company, Inc., 1976), p. 31.

11. *Ibid.*, p. 33.

12. *Ibid.*, p. 34.

13. Quoted in Theodore Morrison, *Chautauqua: A Center for Education, Religion, and the Arts in America* (Chicago: University of Chicago Press, 1974), p. 47.

14. Quoted in *ibid.*, p. 33.

15. Leon Vincent, p. 121.

16. Quoted in *ibid.*, p. 157.

17. Paul Hutchinson, *The Story of the Epworth League* (New York: The Methodist Book Concern, 1927), p. 18.

18. *Ibid.*, p. 34.

19. *Epworth League Handbook* (Nashville: Publishing House of the M. E. Church, South, 1915), p. 10.

20. Hutchinson, p. 56.

21. "Preparing Women for the Lord's Work," in *Women in New Worlds*, edited by Hilah F. Thomas and Rosemary Skinner Keller (Nashville: Abingdon Press, 1981), p. 188.

22. Louis F. W. Lesemann, "Our Founder," in *In Memoriam* (Chicago: The Chicago Training School, 1922), p. 15.

23. Quoted in Isabelle Horton," The Deaconess in Social Settlement Work," in *The Socialized Church*, edited by Worth M. Tippy (New York: Eaton & Mains, 1909), p. 152.

24. *Ibid.*, p. 153.

25. Bledstein, p. 146; see also James B. Gilbert, *Work Without Salvation* (Baltimore: The Johns Hopkins University Press, 1977).

26. Bledstein, p. 39.

27. Quoted in Mary Earhart, *Frances Willard: From Prayers to Politics* (Chicago: University of Chicago Press, 1944), p. 48.

28. See King, *op. cit.*

29. On North, see Creighton Lacy, *Frank Mason North* (New York: Abingdon Press, 1967); for the work of the NCEU, see issues of the *Christian City*, edited by North.

30. Dan B. Brummitt, *The Efficient Epworthian* (New York: The Methodist Book Concern, 1914), pp. 210-211.

III. AGENDA

Lost in the Ocean of Love:
The Spiritual Writings of
Catherine Livingston Garrettson

Diane Lobody Zaragoza
Ph.D. Candidate, Drew University

In one of his riotous stories about life on Cape Cod during the late nineteenth century, Joseph C. Lincoln describes an encounter between a sea captain and a local carpenter:

When Captain Darius, grown purse-proud and vain-glorious, expressed a desire for a hen house with a mansard roof and a cupola, the latter embellishments to match those surmounting his own dwelling, Simon was set aback with his canvas flapping. At the end of a week he had not driven a nail. "Godfrey's mighty!" he is reported to have exclaimed. "I don't know whether to build the average cupola and trust to a hen's fittin' it, or take an average hen and build a cupola round her. Maybe I'll be all right after I get started, but it's where to start that beats me."[1]

Historians are faced with much the same dilemma whenever unsuspected source material floats to the surface of the discipline. It is always difficult to decide what to do with heretofore unknown facts or writings or people. Some of us prefer to fit this new information into one of our own imposing interpretive structures because we have spent so much time building a particular way of looking at history. And yet the iconoclasts among us enjoy nothing so much as the opportunity to create a new interpretation carefully measured to accommodate the newest and most exciting historical resources. Catherine Livingston Garrettson is one of the new hens confronting the Methodist coop. We have in her unexplored writings a remarkably detailed record of the spiritual life of an early American Methodist. While Garrettson is not likely to turn Methodist historiography upside down, her life and her words do insist that we look at evangelical spirituality in a different way. At the very least the Garrettson manuscripts argue for a richer appreciation of the mystical stream in American piety. At the most, Garrettson's writings present us with the splendid opportunity to describe and analyze with great care the intricate movements of the evangelical experience at the very beginning of Methodism in America. In either case, our understanding of Methodist spirituality, and particularly women's spirituali-ty, will be adjusted and enhanced because of the wonderful treasure that Garrettson has left for us.

Catherine Livingston Garrettson was a rather ordinary woman who left an extraordinary collection of unpublished and private writings. Born in 1752, Garrettson was one of the New York Livingstons. As a daughter in this politically active and wealthy family, she was a belle of Hudson River society. Her life satisfied the expectations of her family's position: she danced at balls, read enlightenment philosophy, summered in Rhinebeck and wintered in New York City, and spent leisurely days visiting and receiving company. Above all she showed a flair for writing. She dissected the characters of her acquaintances in deliciously gossipy letters, and evidenced the pungent wit so characteristic of eighteenth-century style.

The family's religious background was unexceptional, and by no means evangelical. The firm Calvinism of her mother, the pleasant deism of her brothers, and the cultural Christianity of her sisters were hardly likely to produce deep religiosity. Indeed, she was thirty-two years old before she took religion very seriously. As she looked back over the course of her early years in her autobiography, it is clear that Garrettson saw her conversion in 1787 not as a single and surprising moment of transformation, but as the culmination of a longer process of religious change.

The year 1782 I spent a Winter in Philadelphia at my Brothers, who was there Minister of Foreign Affairs, and highly respectable in that department. And if the smiles of the World and pleasures of it could have bestowed happiness I should constantly have enjoyed it, but No, there was something wanting, and a dear Friend who was also an inmate in this same dwelling, and myself would sit up after returning from brilliant Balls, and gay parties, and Moralize on their emptiness. . . [2]

From vague dissatisfaction with the glittering scene, Garrettson moved to a more intentional concern with spiritual matters. She retreated often to her room for reading and meditation, and in 1785 had an experience in which "my heart was melted, and many tears flowed from my eyes. I determined to give myself to this Jesus."[33]

The peace which accompanied this experience was not long-lived. The exuberant social obligations of her family overwhelmed her new religious principles.

> Cards went out from my sister Lewises for a private Ball. My particular Friends and favorites were asked. Good Manners I thought demanded my presence. Other inducements I had none, and I was so innocent on the subject of my new attainment that I saw not the gulph into which I was about to precipitate myself.[4]

Much to her despair, she danced away her peace and plunged into darkness. The deaths of two close friends shortly thereafter deepened her distress. She entered upon a period of careful introspection, and on October 13, 1787, the day before her thirty-fifth birthday, Garrettson was utterly and inalterably converted. Alone in her room, as she read over the church service, she prayed:

> "By thine agony and Bloody sweat, by thy Cross and passion; by thy glorious Resurrection and Ascension and the coming of the Holy Ghost." Scarce had I pronounced those words, when I was received, and made unspeakably happy. A song of praise and thanksgiving was put in my mouth—my sins were pardoned my state was changed; My soul was happy—In a transport of Joy I sprang from knees and happening to see myself as I passed the Glass I could not but look with surprize at the change in my countenance all things were become new.[5]

Garrettson was introduced to Methodism shortly thereafter by one of the servants in her mother's household.

Given the religious experience and background of the Livingston family, it comes as no surprise to us that the family was horrified when Garrettson became a Methodist. During this period in Rhinebeck there were woefully few Methodists, none of whom had the status or the wealth of the Livingston family. The family was even more appalled when she had the singularly poor taste to fall in love with the Methodist circuit rider, Freeborn Garrettson. Her mother's vehement opposition prevented their marriage for nearly five years, but Catherine prevailed and they were married in 1793. Freeborn Garrettson was a major figure in the formation of American Methodism, and Catherine entered very happily into the life and ministry of the clergy wife, sometimes traveling with Freeborn, but more often assuming leadership in her church and community in Rhinebeck. The Garrettsons built a home for themselves which was open to any Methodist minister or other Christian for extended rest and refreshment after the Lord's labors. Catherine was deeply involved in the affairs of her community, caring for the sick and poor, working with the infant school movement, participating in prayer meetings, engaging in evangelism among the wealthy families of New York, and functioning as a spiritual director in a network of evangelical women.

In some ways Garrettson does not sound very ordinary. She was well-educated and well-to-do, married to a prominent Methodist and traveling in the circles of the New York aristocracy. But she was not a preacher or a professional evangelist or a missionary; she did not write books or begin a new religious movement or agitate for social reform on a national scale. She was not at all famous except insofar as she was Freeborn Garrettson's wife, or Judge Livingston's daughter, or Robert Livingston's sister. She was very simply an ordinary woman who was converted at the beginning of the evangelical era, who embraced evangelical religion and lived according to its piety until her death in 1849.

Catherine Garrettson is most extraordinary, though, in her scrupulous attention to her religious experience. The vast manuscript collection which records her spiritual life is a remarkable wealth of material, including more than four hundred letters, fifteen journal books, an autobiography, a dream journal, a series of memoirs of family and friends, and a variety of miscellaneous writings. In these hundreds of unpublished pages we have before us the splendid reality of one women's spiritual life over the course of seventy years, a precious documentation of her journey of faith. Garrettson's writings can begin to unfold for us the nature of American evangelical experience among laywomen of the early national period. All of these materials are religious in tone and content, expressions of a highly charged evangelical piety in which Garrettson looks with infinite care into her life, seeking the activity within herself and the will of God for herself.

The journals will be the focus of this essay. In one sense these writings are by no means useful autobiography. These are not charming, chatty, informative diaries. We look in vain in the journals (and indeed in all of the rest of the writings) for tales of Freeborn's adventures on the road or juicy anecdotes about the marvelous Methodists who stayed in the Garrettson's home. Nor is this in any way a systematic theology, although she does occasionally comment on matters of theology. This is pre-eminently devotional literature, consisting of the reflections of a woman growing in faith. Garrettson sets the boundaries in the first paragraph of the first journal. It is almost a prologue to the whole, and she never changes her focus.

> Having dedicated myself, my time, my Heart, my Wishes to that Great Power whose I am, and whose I desire most ardently to be, I begin this Book for the sole purpose of seeing, What advances I make in the divine life; that by comparing one day with another, I may be enabled by the Grace of God, to find that I have each day gain'd and lost. Gained some emanation of light from my Redeemer; lost some of the Corruptions of my own Heart, foil'd some of the Temptations of my Adversary.[6]

Garrettson's Wesleyan theology called for a faith that progressed; her journals are the introspective measurements of her movement toward sanctification and perfection. The daily entries concern themselves with her prayer, her reading, her meditations. She tells of her sins, her feelings, the current state of her relationship with God. She pours out descriptions of the hideous times, the dull times, the rapturous times. She seeks to express the fullness of her religious experiences, that she might know herself better and love God more completely. The journals are a massive work of confession, both the confession of her sin and the confession of her faith. The journals of the first six years after her conversion, which will be the center of our study, are particularly rich and complex, for they open before us the special journey of the Christian toward mystical union with God.

Jorge Luis Borges, in his inevitably provocative way, comments that "it may be that universal history is the history of the different intonations given a handful of metaphors."[7] Throughout her journey toward mystical union, Garrettson lays out before us symbols and movements which resonate throughout the Christian mystical tradition. She describes the common mystical experiences of purgation, or the humbling awareness and repentance of sin; illumination, or darts of knowledge of God and acute desire to live a holy life; and mystical union, the experience of union with God, or the immediate presence or knowledge of God. These three stages are not necessarily consecutive, and indeed Garrettson moved from one to the other, sometimes gracefully and sometimes suddenly. Certain themes present themselves again and again from the very beginning of the journals. She yearns for union with God; she is grievously

sensitive to her own failures and needs; she sees herself as passive before God's mercy and judgment, and active in her own desire and sin; she wants to serve God in some meaningful way; she sees the providence of God working within her life, and she knows that God sees her as she truly is, and loves her through and through. Despite the repetitive nature of the journal entries, though, there is a very clear process at work. Garrettson does not leap into the ecstasies of mystical union without preparation. There is in the journals a sense of appropriate transition and genuine growth in faith.

Garrettson's autobiography describes the early days after her conversion as "a state of constant communion with God."[8] The journals indicate that such communion was not always sweet. The earliest entries follow a fairly standard pattern: a description of how she slept, in what mood she awoke, how she prayed, whether she did or did not feel God's presence, what she read, whether she sinned, and what interesting insights or experiences had illumined her knowledge of God. For the first few weeks after her conversion, Garrettson lived in an atmosphere which was almost dream-like in quality.

This was not a time of delerious emotion; ferocious heights and depths were yet to come. There is, rather, a sense of calm euphoria in the entries:

> Arose some time before the Sun, and found unspeakable delight in pouring out my Soul, in prayer. I sought my God in his Word, and found him every where present. Wrote to my Sisters, and endeavored to make them sensible of the goodness of my Divine Redeemer: but Eloquence here, must fail; tis to be enjoyed, not described![9]

While the undercurrent of delight in her new life with God did last, we begin also to see the development of a serious examination of her sinful self. Her sense of personal sin ought not to be surprising to us. Her life was radically altered by the conversion, and Garrettson began to engage in a fierce struggle between the familiar expectations of worldly activity and the rigorous demands of evangelical Christianity. The corruption of her sinful nature could not withstand the discernment of the pure eye of God, and Garrettson propelled herself into a scathing, searing examination of her life and conduct. Unless we see this experience as a part of the humiliation and mortification of the purgative state in mystical experience, it is virtually impossible for us to understand why she berates herself for such seemingly unimportant sins, and further, why she believes that God withdraws from her when she sins. She writes of one of her besetting sins, oversleeping:

> Instead of rising as I ought to have done to thank and praise I with the Sluggard said a little more slumber, a little more Sleep, and by and by Lord I will thank thee. . . . I awoke some time after, but my Beloved was withdrawn. I called but He was not near, He did not absolutely refuse to hear, but He would not comfort, chear, and enliven as he was wont to do; I however waited upon him, and wished to receive my punishment with submission.[10]

The smallest sins were paradigms of deep faithlessness and unworthiness. Garrettson had experienced, and continued to experience, the presence of God. "O! that Language was given me adequate to the Sublimity of the Subject," she writes, "that I might acknowledge, how Gracious, how tender; how like a God he acts with his Servants."[11] But she yearned to maintain this new relationship, and the prerequisite to its continuance was the creation of a new identity as a child of God, one in which sin was eradicated and the barriers between herself and God torn down. The most insignificant sin was enough to keep God from her. Garrettson was determined to ferret these wrongs out of herself, to accept God's punishment for them, to repent of them, and to change her life accordingly. Garrettson took this self-examination and reconstruction of character very seriously, and fully expected that God would leave her to her own grief until she had duly repented and learned from the experience of God's removal. Garrettson adored her God, and the very idea of God's withdrawal was dreadful. Worse yet was the experience of being utterly abandoned by God.

It is important that we not take too lightly Garrettson's search for the sin in herself and the devastatingly humiliating results of that search. This was a crucial issue for Garrettson, and more serious yet was the attendant terror on seeing herself separated from God. Early in her evangelical life she asks God to let her see exactly who she is as a sinful creature, and the experience is horrifying, not least because of God's withdrawal:

> I examined my own Heart, and found there the seeds of that vanity and selfishness that had so often on former occasions burst out upon me, and plunged me in guilt before an Eye of infinite purity. Instead of praying to that Great Power, Whose Hand is ever near to help those who confide in Him, I prayed that He would lay me low, low in the Dust before Him, that He would shew me myself, and encrease my dependence on Him. Presumtuous Wretch!—How bold, how daring was the

request—I pressed it upon my Heavenly Master. Unwillingly and by degrees, He complied. He was withdrawing Himself from me the Whole Day.[12]

Nothing abated this withdrawal, and Garrettson found no solace in her isolation. She indeed saw herself without God, and could find no comfort in meditation, prayer, or Scripture. She experienced with vivid pain the reality of a life without God, the result of a life in sin.

The process of purgation, though, was not merely a period of torment. Underlying the grief of her sin was a confidence in a "prayer hearing sin forgiving God." There were gleams of ecstatic vision, warm receptions of the love and peace of God, and a persistent sensitivity to the tenderness and protection of her "master." The purgative way was an alternation of pain and pleasure. By detaching herself from the expectations of the world, Garrettson was purified and trained into a new identity and a close relationship with God. The punishment she suffered was the sense of being abandoned by God, unable to reach God and call God back by any of the means ordinarily available to her:

> Towards Bed time, my sorrow and Heaviness encreased upon me I took Gods Holy Word and ought to have found Consolation in the first Chap. that the Book opened in, the XLth in Isaiah. But I was not to be comforted, but by the Light of my Life, the presence of my God; He hid his Face, and my Soul plung'd in darkness and refused comfort from any other Hand than His; I was greatly Afflicted; and entreated my Gracious Master would not make my tryal to heavy for me.[13]

But abandonment was never a permanent condition. Again and again Garrettson reiterates her nearness to God and her happiness in God. For all that she saw herself as an unworthy, cold-hearted, stupid and mistrustful child—and indeed her descriptions of herself are consistently caustic—God yet stayed near to her:

> My affections have been in Heaven all this day. And I have been enabled to bless God with my whole heart. I lay me down in his love, who has supported me all the day in hopes that wether life or death be my Lot ere tomorrows Sun I may enjoy Him who is my only portion and my only Bliss.[14]

The euphoria that characterized this early stage was not itself a state of union with God in the classical mystical sense. She began to have sharp darts of longing for a deeper sense of the presence of God, and moved gracefully into a period of mystical illumination. None of this was very easy for Garrettson, not least because of the opposition of her family. Yearning for God's presence was accompanied by a more profound awareness of her own inadequacy and despair. These apparently wild swings of emotion from heady delight to abysmal depression seem to have risen in proportion to her family's critical assessment and total incomprehension of her newly-found evangelical fervor. It is difficult to judge whether the opposition fueled the intensity, or her preoccupation with religion created the family's disapproval. In any event, repression was on the rise. "I am," she wrote to her sister, "so unfortunate as to have no companion in my own Family, and have often compared myself to the 'Pelican in the Wilderness' to the sparrow on the house top.' "[15]

Garrettson's conversion caused an already difficult relationship with her mother to deteriorate rapidly. Garrettson had adored her father; her autobiography spends considerable time enumerating his strong and lovely qualities. Her mother rates but one description, strained praise at that: "my Mother was a good Woman and very much respected and I doubt not experienced religion."[16] Margaret Beekman Livingston was a grand matriarch who firmly governed the family after her husband's death in 1775. Garrettson continued to live at home, as befitted an unmarried daughter, and it is very clear from all of her writings that her revolutionary change of heart did not go unnoticed.

Garrettson found little support for her religion amongst her family, none of whom could appreciate the ardent evangelicalism of their "dear Kitty." (Indeed, after 1787 never again did she refer to herself as Kitty; her transfigured vision of herself was reflected as she claimed her full name.) Her life at home became more and more unbearable. Her rapid and blatant changes of mood had to have been unsettling to her mother. Garrettson spent hours in solitude, praying and reading, and it may not be coincidental that shortly after one episode of terrifying despair and near hallucination, her room was taken from her:

I am now on the point of being deprived of the greatest happiness I have on Eart[h], which is this room; in which I have spent so many happy, and so many miserable hours. I shall now have no Corner to serve my God; this is so Afflictive, that my soul is weighed down with grief, and my Eyes have been drown[ed] with tears at the mere prospect. This was my last remaining consolation, but this also I must be deprived of. O my God! my only refuge! and my only hope leave me not; tis now that I shall require a double portion of thy grace.[17]

Without doubt it cannot have been easy to live with Garrettson, who one day would be tramping through the woods delighting in God's good creation, and the next day—or even the next hour—would be writing in paroxysms of misery;

I now fell into a great Agony, and prayed to know why my heavenly Master treated me thus. I supposed it was to humble me; and I desired to be most humble; I threw myself on the floor and bemoan'd my Redeemer's absence, with tears, and great anguish. . . . I said in haste that this day should be a day of fast and retirement, that I would taste no food; and my Face should wear no Smiles, till the Lord would shew peace to my sorrow.[18]

The rapid transitions evidenced in Garrettson's journal are not at all unusual in the Christian mystical tradition. The illuminative stage is characterized by an increasing desire, often not satisfied, to see God and feel God's presence. Full union with God is not a part of illumination, but shining moments that suggest such union are intrinsic to the nature of this experience. And so it was for Garrettson. Even as she felt the depth of her own sinfulness, she also found herself in rare and precious moments carried into wordless prayer, stunned by the glory of God:

I was carried out of myself in speechless Wonnder, love, and praise. This Manifestation of Gods condescending love lasted as nearly as I can tell ten or fifteen minutes. . . . Would, I could have been, perfectly willing at that moment to quit this life: it appeared to me, if I could have said in sincerity, Lord, now receive me to thy Self; my request would have been heard.[19]

This stage was most difficult for Garrettson to describe. Like many Christian mystics, she was forced to use metaphorical language, and spoke of tasting, touching, or seeing God in those all too brief experiences of God's presence as she prayed. But her use of such language does give us an idea of the immediacy of her experience. Garrettson was not talking about the everyday Christian awareness that God is somehow near and active in our lives in a general way. She was writing quite explicitly of the vivid consciousness of God's presence here and now, in this place and this time. There is nothing vague about these descriptions. Nevertheless the duration of such an experience was inevitably brief, temporary, and ultimately dissatisfying. Garrettson was given a taste, but no more, and a deep desire for its repetition.

In this period, which lasted from 1788 to 1791, Garrettson became increasingly assured of God's providential intention for the events of her life. The disapproval of her family, along with their disruption of her hopes for marriage, were painful and difficult to bear, and she perceived her life as filled with persecution. Indeed, at one point in this period she dreamed that she was being crucified. Her mother's distress over Catherine's sudden religious fanaticism was certainly exacerbated by the relationship between Catherine and Freeborn. Margaret Livingston was convinced that Freeborn was a fortune hunter, and could not understand why Catherine refused to find a more suitable husband, as her sisters had done. Matters became intolerable, and Catherine was forced to leave her mother's home and move in with a sympathetic sister, Margaret Tillotson. In all of this oppression, Garrettson continued to see God's providential work, and was certain that God's intention for her life would be fulfilled. Here passivity before the purpose of God becomes a dominant theme in the journals, and appears to have alleviated her anxieties. She was also confident that these tribulations would serve to sanctify and perfect her, and she spoke most deliberately about her submission to God's will as she lived through these adversities.

This illuminative period carried with it feelings of uselessness and a strong desire to be doing something to encourage God's work in the world. Garrettson, as was noted earlier, was a daughter in a prominent and wealthy family. Being useful was simply not expected of a woman in her position. The journal entries give a fairly thorough description of this upper class woman's life: she sewed, she read, she visited friends and neighbors, she stayed out of the way when her room was being cleaned, she travelled, she wrote letters. This was hardly the kind of life to commend itself to a woman eager to serve God and work for the coming of the kingdom. There were marvelous advantages to living a life of leisure, though. Garrettson had great quantities of time available to be used for concentrated religious thought and activity. Every day was conducted according to a strict pattern. Upon arising from bed, Garrettson immediately poured herself into prayer. After breakfast, she examined her actions during the previous day, prayed that she might discover more about God and herself on the basis of that day, and then described these discoveries in her journal. She then read in the Scriptures or in some commendable Christian book, and wrestled with theological issues. After lunch she rested again, then read and prayed and wrote letters, and

performed whatever duties were incumbent upon her—usually sewing or visiting a neighbor. After supper she attended family worship, which she did not always find agreeable, and then retired to her room for the evening. The night times were most productive in terms of her spiritual life; she prayed for hours on end, and went to sleep only to have striking dreams which she thought were sent by God or by her adversary, Satan.

We need to take care lest we condemn Garrettson's life as indolent. She was not in this period living up to our understanding of the active Christian life, but she did create for herself a structure which lent itself to an internal spiritual discipline. All of that reading and thinking and praying kept worldly activity from interfering with the development of a rich spiritual life. Her experiences of purgation, illumination, and mystical union would not have been as intense or as productive had she not given herself to a life entirely built around prayer and meditation. Other activities would have cluttered her mind and distracted her soul from the primary desire, which was to be united to God. Indeed, after she married Freeborn she entered upon an extremely active life, and the experiences of mystical union vanished.

Nonetheless, Garrettson yearned for a task. She wrote of her longing for a call to holy work: "make use of me I entreat, I emplore thee. . . . set me upon some work. I long to be doing something."[20] She prayed that she might be useful to God, and as the years of this period passed, she began a vigorous evangelism campaign, sparing no effort in badgering and cajoling and threatening and persuading friends and family and perfect strangers in her often successful attempts to convert them. Concommitantly she strived to live virtuously and charitably, not out of fear, but out of longing desire to please and serve God.

This period of illumination, then, was characterized by a joyful sense of God's power, brief visions of God, confidence in God's providential care, a general sense of passivity or waiting before God, and a profound hope that God would set Garrettson upon a useful vocation. But all is not pleasant in the life of every Christian; most particularly, Christian mystics sink into terrible times of agony. The usual term for these times is the dark night of the soul, and this, no less than the delightful moments of divine love, is a significant part of the period of illumination. Evelyn Underhill's description is valuable:

The 'Dark Night of the Soul,' once fully established, is seldom lit by visions or made homely by voices. It is of the essence of its miseries that the once-possessed power of orison or contemplation now seems wholly lost. The self is tossed back from its hard-won point of vantage. Impotence, blankness, solitude are the epithets by which those immersed in this dark fire of purification describe their pains.[21]

In the spring of 1788, Garrettson began to experience the constant absence of God. It is important that we not imagine that this absence was caused by a waning of Garrettson's energy or desire. She did not simply give up on God and go on to more interesting things. Rather, at the very time when her religious life was issuing forth in a mature and rich faith, God suddenly withdrew. This absence continued for months; Garrettson called it her banishment from God, and her descriptions are heartbreaking:

I seek the light of my Sun, but tis obscured, tis hidden from me, and I droop, and tho' not hopeless, I am almost miserable! Ah my dear redeemer! My advocate! My God! Thou knowest with what ardour I love thee!—O! do not take the light of thy countenance from me. . . . I walked, I have read, I have written, but I am no nearer thee; I know there is no merit in them; but I will go on because it is my duty and the only pleasure left me. I went to bed with my mind on the rack. I hope all things, but possess nothing. All is dark, is double darkness.[22]

Garrettson was not completely abandoned; occasionally there were sudden, gracious, and poignant reminders of the presence of God. "God's visitations are so short," she writes, "I have scarcely time to Hail, before they are gone and my Bright Sun is obscured by dark, thick clouds, which my feeble sight cannot penetrate."[23] Mostly, though, these many months gave rise to painful and groaning prayers. "Seven months I have wandered in a strange land! I have been afflicted! tormented! disappointed! deluded! I have been bewildered and almost distracted!" Garrettson did not lose her faith. In the same passage she reiterates her confidence in the grace and faithfulness of God. "In all this I have never for a moment turned my eyes from that God who governs every event of my life. I have never for one moment ceased to believe that he will Bless, if I continue faithful."[24]

Garrettson never perceived this dark night of the soul as punishment for particular sins. She quite straightforwardly acknowledged that she could find no reason for it. It did not imply that she had lost her faith, nor that God's absence was a permanent state. She passively awaited the return of the sweet graces of God, and when they did not come, she simply continued her customary pattern of reading, prayer, and meditation. There is no doubt, though, that she was deeply affected and almost frantic during this period, which lasted until 1790. A part of the agony of the time evidenced itself in her inability to keep the journal; she discontinued writing until 1791, and was certain that God had made her unable to write.

Garrettson was able to bear the strain. She clearly saw this dark night as a purification of the deep sin of her nature. She took comfort in the promises of Scripture, and continued to wait for God's return. She was not left entirely in isolation. During the months in which she ceased to write in her journal, Garrettson chose to note God's wonderful treatment of her in dreams. Convinced that the dreams were consolations sent to her by God, she wrote them out and occasionally engaged in their interpretation. While this is not the place to examine the dreams and analyze their content, it is illuminating for us at the very least to hear at least one dream narrative, for the dreams cast light on our understanding of Garrettson's interior struggle. In August 1789 she "dreamed I was in much distress and suffering the reproach of unjust suspicions; borne down with shame; and unsupported. I was giving myself up to the most gloomy reflections; when a little bird flew into the window and took refuge in my Bosom. I was in an instant comforted."[25]

The period of the dark night served a number of functions. In one sense it can be seen as an exhausted reaction to several years of religious intensity. However painfully, it served to complete much of the necessary purification and concommitant change of perspective on the Christian life. Underhill suggests that the dark night is directed toward an act of utter surrender to God, and the experiences which were to follow certainly indicate that this was true for Garrettson. Finally, and by no means insignificantly, this was a dark night not only in relation to God but in the whole of Garrettson's life. She fell in love at this time only to have her family refuse to countenance the marriage. She was thrown out of her mother's home and left without a room of her own. The persecution of many family members reached its height in these months. Yet under all of this strain, all of this separation from Freeborn and family and home, Catherine was able to maintain her faith and confirm her commitment. If the absence of God and the interruption of her relationships could not destroy her, then she was surely called to a special kind of spirituality. This calling evidenced itself at long last. Garrettson describes an extraordinary vision, in which she sees a reason for renewed confidence and affirmation:

> My Bed stood beside the east Window. It was a Moon light Night. And I suddenly awoke and directed my eyes to the east as I looked a bright beautiful Starr shot thro' the casement across the foot of my bed to the opposite side of the Wall, and then turned back thro' the same Window and disappeared. Instantly a diadem of Stars bright but not dazling took the same direction, and on its return was thrown over the Looking Glass between the two east Windows where it remained while I contemplated its indiscribable beauty and could distinguish every bright star of which it was composed, with astonishment, and with delight, as my future Crown if faithful unto death. By degrees it faded away till I could see it no more. I was cheared, encouraged, and set out anew in my heavenly race.[26]

As quickly as it came, Garrettson's dark night vanished. It is perhaps no coincidence that the darkness of her personal life lifted at the same time. She became involved in a wider network of Methodist women, and found extensive support from them. Her evangelical efforts among family members were beginning to bear fruit, and the opposition of her brothers and sisters to her relationship with Freeborn abated. Family pressure encouraged Garrettson's mother to reconsider her stance on the marriage, and in 1793 a date for the wedding was set. Life circumstances were no longer oppressive, and the joy and relief she experienced, while still tentative, shines in her journal. She resumed keeping her diary in April 1791, when she was motivated to do so by the death of her "father in Christ," John Wesley. And it was in this period, over the next two years of her life, that she experienced the fulfillment of mystical union.

Such experiences did not burst upon her in any sudden way. All throughout her evangelical life, Garrettson had felt, to some degree, the presence of God. She embarked on Methodism with a feeling for God's particular concern for her. During the illuminative phase, she had felt moments of sharp longing for God, and occasionally was swept up into wordless prayer and adoration for brief periods of time. From 1791 to 1793 a radically different kind of encounter with God took place. Garrettson came to know in these years an absolute union with God: she saw God; she saw Christ. And in this time the journal entries became hymns to the glory of God, sung in the language of the Christian mystic.

She began this period by realizing the movement of God breaking in on her soul during prayer and by having constant communion with God for hours on end. But by 1792 these more common occurrences were replaced by a more exact, concrete, mystical union. She writes that she

> went to my private devotions, and after prayer found a quiet waiting upon God. I leaned myself against the post of Bed, and found my soul swallowed up in God, as I have never before experienced. Oh! what moments were these! A Divine sweetness thrilled thro' my whole Frame. I can compare myself to nothing more aptly than a blank sheet of paper, not a thought, not an idea that I can trace passed through my mind. . . . Perhaps an half hour I was there waiting upon God in speechless adoration. . . . I never before experienced any thing like this. I have felt Joy; my soul has been melted with gratitude.[27]

Over and again Garrettson was swept up into the intimate, passionate union with God. Although the experiences themselves were ineffable, she attempted to describe them, often using metaphors of dissolution or of being lost in the being of God. She reached for a language sufficient to evoke the powerful reality of being with God:

> I felt for some moments as if my heart was drinking in holiness—And then followed such a shedding abroad the love of God in my soul, that it appeared to me I was all light, life, and power.[28]

> I was made acquainted with the love of the Father—I gazed at uncreated love, love in its original source! Here was nothing sublime—nothing aweful. It was exstacy! The highest Felicity a Mortal could taste—accompanied with peace, sweetness indiscribable, wonder love and praise. I sank as it were into the Bosom of the Father.[29]

> I could cry out, I am the temple of the holy Ghost. I am espoused to Jesus, and in him united to the Glorious Trinity. His visits were not short, for hours I could say his left hand is under me, and the right hand of his power is over me. . . . I was lost. I found myself a drop in the Ocean of love.[30]

These extraordinary experiences encouraged Garrettson to resign herself perfectly to the will of God. She was utterly passive when God came to her and filled her being, and she was able to articulate that unity often by resorting to metaphors of the senses. "Divine sweetness penetrated my soul, and made the tears of gratitude and love abundantly flow down my Cheeks."[31] Garrettson was aware that her language was insufficient. She exclaims again and again that no words can describe what she has felt. She was most adamant that these experiences were real and not hallucinatory, and that her words were barely adequate. "With my bodily Eye I saw nothing all was presented to my mind. And what I then saw, no pen, or tongue can ever discribe."[32]

Her reception of mystical union, however, did not carry with it a blending of her essence with that of God. She did not identify herself with God, but was always careful to maintain the radical distinction between a mere creature and the glorious Creator. She sees God; she is not herself God. During one remarkable night Garrettson requested most humbly that she see God's glory. God responded by displaying both the glory of the Father and the glory of the Son:

I could plainly distinguish the love of the Father and the love of the Son. The one was a thing that created wonder: and to be gazed at with astonishment and admiration not to be discribed. Tis a vast Object held up to the void; and the rapture it inspires is from the contemplation of it—But the Love of Jesus is a well of water springing up within us. . . . We feel that God is intimately nigh, and the enraptured mind breaks out in praises. In the other case, speech is useless.[33]

The visions were not limited to the sight of God alone. Garrettson saw, among other things, the whole history of human redemption from Adam to the present, the crucifixion of Jesus Christ, and the events of the millennium yet to come. Her descriptions of these experiences are nearly overpowering. She notes with acute attention to detail not only the content of the mystical rapture itself, but also its effect on her mind. She remained during this period deeply sensitive to her own spiritual movement, and profoundly aware that these were very rare and gracious moments in her life. While able to be bold in her requests of God, nevertheless Garrettson did not presume upon God, knowing that the gift of God's immediate presence—the lifting of the veil between creature and Creator, as she put it—could be withdrawn at any time, and would only come in God's good time. That was an important lesson to learn. The mystical visions increased in intensity and frequency as Garrettson drew closer to the time of her marriage. Indeed, when the date for the wedding was set, the visions reached rapturous heights. The relationship between the two events did not go unnoticed. Writing to a friend, Garrettson observed that "ever since I have consented, and agreed to a time for my union with the best of men: more or less I have been happy with God."[34] But once Catherine married Freeborn, these intense and overwhelming ecstasies vanished.

As Garrettson's circumstances changed with her marriage, so also did the dynamics of her spiritual life. Her position and responsibilities as wife, mother, and active participant in Freeborn's ministry did not allow Catherine the time to devote to the contemplative life of the earlier years. She had finally found a way to serve God. For the first time she ran her own household, with a daughter to raise. She traveled with Freeborn and kept house for visitors. She cared for the sick and the dying, met regularly for prayer with groups of women, built a church with Freeborn, and organized a Sunday School.

This explosion of activity and concern for others shifted her religious focus from the life of contemplation to the life of active service. This is reflected in both the quantity and content of the journals. Six of the volumes were written between 1787 and 1793, while only three volumes cover the thirty-five years of marriage. And while Garrettson continued to be concerned about the state of her life in Christ, she no longer had either the dreadful depths of despair or the soaring heights of mystical union. Her highs were lower and her lows were higher. Her great lament through these years was her deadness, dullness, and insensibility in spiritual matters.

But Garrettson did not lament the loss of her visionary days while she was married. Only her widowhood recalled those days of ecstasy. Freeborn died in 1828, and Catherine never recovered from the blow. She loved Freeborn with exquisite tenderness and passion, and her mourning mingled with a renewed sense of the absence of God. Her faith did not falter, but God seemed hidden. Her six volumes of journal entries during her widowhood cry out with a yearning to recall the visions, and were filled with grief and unfulfilled desire. Catherine died in 1849 without ever receiving the full sanctification, assurance, and perfection for which she longed. Life without Freeborn was also a life without the affirmation of her worthiness and the presence of the living God.

It is difficult at this stage of research in women's history to determine the extent to which Garrettson's evangelical experience was normative. Garrettson's spiritual life was certainly intense, but it may be that the fundamental movements of her experience were not out of the ordinary. Most evangelical Christians were not called to a life of mystical union. But while most evangelical people may not have gone through mystical states of purgation, they did examine their lives, repent their wrongdoing, and strive to drive sin out of themselves. They may not have had illuminative periods, but they did have moments when they knew the presence of God acting in and through the events of their lives. They may not have attained visions of God, but they did yearn to love God and to have their God touch their lives and transform them into new people. Garrettson's experiences were, perhaps, unusually striking, but the path that she walked was by no means alien to the path that every evangelical Christian walked. Perhaps the very intensity of her life before God will serve to enlighten our appreciation for the subtleties and intricacies of early nineteenth-century American evangelical spirituality.

NOTES

1. Joseph C. Lincoln, *Kent Knowles: Quahaug* (New York: A.L. Burt Company, 1914), pp. 3-4.
2. Catherine Livingston Garrettson, Autobiography (unpublished manuscript, 1817-1832), pp. 3-4.
3. *Ibid.*, p. 5.
4. *Ibid.*, pp. 6-7.
5. *Ibid.*, p. 11.
6. Catherine Livingston Garrettson, Journal, vol. I unpublished manuscript), introduction.
7. Jorge Luis Borges, *Labyrinths*, edited by Donald A. Yates and James E. Irby (New York: New Dimensions Pub., 1964), p. 193.
8. Autobiography, p. 13.
9. Journal, vol. I, November 28, 1787.
10. Journal, vol. I, December 5, 1787.
11. Journal, vol. I, November 17, 1787.
12. Journal, vol. I, December 12, 1787.
13. Journal, vol. I, December 4, 1787.
14. Journal, vol. I, January 2, 1788.
15. Catherine Livingston Garrettson, unpublished letter to Janet Montgomery, November 25, 1791.
16. Autobiography, p. 1.
17. Journal, vol. III, April 29, 1788.
18. Journal, vol. II, February 21, 1788.
19. Journal, vol. III, March 22, 1788.
20. Journal, vol. V, June 8, 1791.
21. Evelyn Underhill, *Mysticism*, eleventh edition (New York: E.P. Dutton and Co., Inc., 1961), p. 381.
22. Journal, vol. IV, May 16, 1788.
23. Journal, vol. V, December 23, 1790.
24. Journal vol. IV, December 14, 1788.
25. Catherine Livingston Garrettson, Exercise Book (unpublished manuscript), pp. 15-16.
26. Autobiography, pp. 13-14.
27. Journal, vol. V, June 3, 1792.
28. Journal, vol. VI, n.d. (1792).
29. Journal, vol. VI, March 11, 1793.
30. Journal, vol. VI, March 10, 1793.
31. Journal, vol. VI, March 7, 1793.
32. Journal, vol. VI, March 10, 1793.
33. Journal, vol. VI, March 14, 1793.
34. Catherine Livingston Garrettson, unpublished letter to Catherine Rutsen, March 11, 1793.

New Directions for the Study of Blacks in Methodism

Lewis V. Baldwin
Vanderbilt University

More than a decade ago the Methodist scholar Frederick A. Norwood reminded us that the Methodist tradition is incomprehensible apart from the significant and unique contributions made by black Methodists.[1] Indeed, people of African descent and Methodism have had a long-standing relationship, dating as far back as 1737 when John Wesley, Methodism's founder, sought to instruct Africans he met in South Carolina in the fundamentals of the Christian faith. For more than two centuries, the black/ Methodism relationship has been mutually enriching and durable, notwithstanding the organizational schisms and divisions which have characterized it. And today there are at least six million black Methodists in the United States, Canada, Africa, the West Indies, South America, and other parts of the world. These black Methodists fall under several denominational banners, such as United Methodist (U.M.), African Methodist Episcopal (A.M.E.), African Methodist Episcopal Zion (A.M.E.Z.), African Union Methodist Protestant (A.U.M.P.), Christian Methodist Episcopal (C.M.E.), Reformed Zion Union Apostolic Methodist (R.Z.U.A.M.), Reformed Methodist Union Episcopal (R.M.U.E.), and Union American Methodist Episcopal (U.A.M.E.).[2]

Despite the long historical association between black people and Methodism, there is still the need to include blacks more fully in the accounts related to the Methodist Episcopal tradition. This need has been strongly emphasized in Frederick Norwood's *The Story of American Methodism* (1974). This work recognizes the importance of ethnic and racial varieties in Methodism not merely for the sake of historical accuracy and integrity, but also because they are indicative of the diversity which has long marked and enriched Methodist history.[3]

The story of black people and Methodism has been isolated from the records concerning the Methodist tradition for so long by scholars that, despite some important work completed in this area, many possible topics remain to be researched. It should be made clear at the outset that topics focusing on the relationship between blacks and Methodism should not be explored without taking into consideration the ways in which people of African descent have influenced the shaping of the Methodist tradition and in turn have been influenced. With this in mind, I want to suggest some areas where historical (or any other) scholarship needs to be applied before we get anything like a full picture of the importance of black people in the understanding of the Methodist heritage.[4]

The initial task of the scholar who would assign blacks their proper place in the history and tradition of Methodism is perhaps to study the relationships between John Wesley and peoples of African backgrounds. A study of this nature would constitute a new approach, since major studies have been done on virtually all aspects of Wesley's life and thought *except* those that concern Africa and African peoples. The professional historian, theologian, or sociologist of religion who accepts this challenge should search Wesley's letters and journal and study those numerous scattered references to his encounters with and ideas about Africans. Of equal significance is Wesley's *Thoughts Upon Slavery* (1774), which affords an amazingly positive and sympathetic image of Africa and of African peoples. Other works by Wesley which merit attention for what they reveal about his attitude toward Africans include his *Seasonable Address to the Inhabitants of Great Britain* (1776), which is a rousing denunciation of slavery, and the substantive passage in his *The Imperfections of Human Knowledge*, where he used the Hottentots as examples of human nature in its fallen state.[5] The eighteenth century Quaker leader Anthony Benezet had a profound impact on Wesley's views regarding African slavery, and any creditable study of Wesley's vision of Africa and Africans would have to take into account Benezet's *An Historical Account of Guinea* (1771). All of these sources should be studied in conjunction with important secondary sources concerning Wesley's thoughts on Africa and African peoples, such as the ones provided by Frank Baker, Richard M. Cameron, and Donald G. Mathews.[6] Other suggestions for a study of this kind are provided in Lewis V. Baldwin, "Sources and Ideas for the Study of John Wesley and Africa," *The A.M.E. Zion Quarterly Review*, XCVI, 2 (July, 1984), 24-26.

Careful studies of the contributions that black people have made to the Methodist style and ethos from the time of Wesley to the present should be undertaken. Much has been written about the Methodist influence on black people, but what about the black influence on Methodism? The mere presence of black Methodists has historically been a factor in the shaping of Methodism's social witness and policies, as even a casual examination of that denomination's struggle with slavery and racism will prove. Furthermore, thorough research on the Methodist revivals and camp meetings of the eighteenth and nineteenth centuries will undoubtedly show that much of the preaching, shouting, singing, and religious dance which took place were inspired in the white Methodists through contact with their African converts. W.E.B. DuBois, Melville J. Herskovits, Lawrence W. Levine, and Frederick A. Norwood are among the very few scholars who have admitted that the style and ethos of Methodism owe much to black thought and methods.[7] Indeed, black people have been involved in every major turning point in American Methodist history. Scholars of American religion and theology must begin to take seriously the often silent but potent influence that millions of black Methodists have had and continue to have on Methodism in America and in other parts of the world.

We could use more serious treatments of the lives and activities of early African Methodist leaders such as Morris Brown, Daniel Coker, Harry "Black Harry" Hosier, Peter Spencer, John Steward, and James Varick. Even if we cannot have full-length biographies of these men, the sources are sufficient to write articles on them. Hagiographies will not satisfy this need. We need critical studies similar to David L. Lewis' work on Martin Luther King, Jr.[8] We especially need to know more about lesser known but pivotal figures like Spencer, Stewart, and Varick. This author has already begun intense research on Spencer. The memoirs of John Stewart, said to be among the holdings of the Union Theological Seminary in New York, would be vital to a study of his impressive missionary work among the Wyandot Indians in Ohio in the early years of the nineteenth century. Bishop William J. Walls' book on the history of the A.M.E. Zion Church would be quite useful in evaluating the life and contributions of Varick.[9]

A book that establishes a comparative context with the different branches of African Methodism would teach us a great deal. Scholars who explore this subject might compare and contrast the A.M.E., the A.M.E. Zion, and the C.M.E Churches with smaller and less popular branches of African Methodism, such as the A.U.M.P., the U.A.M.E, the First Colored Methodist Protestant, the Independent African Methodist Episcopal, the Reformed Methodist Union Episcopal, and the Reformed Zion Union Apostolic Methodist Churches.

The range of possible focuses for studies of this type is broad. First, consideration could be given to the kind of social and theological forces which gave rise to various African Methodist churches. It is evident that all African Methodist churches came into being because of racism, but the record shows that the founding of the Union Church of Africans, the A.M.E Church, and the A.M.E. Zion Church in the north in the pre-Civil War years was in some ways different from the establishment of the C.M.E Church, the Reformed Methodist Union Episcopal Church, and the Reformed Zion Union Apostolic Methodist Church in the south during Reconstruction. The African Methodist churches in the north began in bitter conflict with whites, and their leaders had to engage in intense legal battles before gaining their unconditional independence from white Methodism. The African Methodist churches began in the south because both blacks and whites, for the most part, realized that the social changes wrought by the Emancipation Proclamation called for new ecclesiastical arrangements. More investigative work on the origins of branches of African Methodist will most likely suggest other important differences.[10]

Second, the similarities and dissimilarities in the tenets and disciplines of African Methodist bodies, and their somewhat different structures and modes of managing church affairs, would be a rewarding study. We know that all branches of African Methodism have remained essentially Methodistic with articles of religion, general rules, disciplines, and polities based largely, though not exclusively, on the Wesleyan and Methodist model. But this does not tell the whole story. For example, the structure of the early A.M.E. Church with its bishops, deacons, traveling preachers, and strong connectional system was quite unlike the early Union Church of Africans with its elder ministers, lay elders, deacons, stationed pastorate, and weak connectional system. Perhaps this difference in structure resulted in part from the fact that the Union Church of Africans, which started under the leadership of Peter Spencer in Delaware in 1813, began as a lay movement.[11] Another example of structural differences is that the A.U.M.P. Church, unlike most African Methodist Churches with roots in the nineteenth century, did not embrace the episcopal structure until

1967. Even today one can detect slight differences in structures and styles among branches of African Methodism. The available books of *Discipline* of various African Methodist Churches, issued in the nineteenth and twentieth centuries, would have to be carefully studied for information along these lines.[12]

Third, works that focus on how African Methodist bodies have differed in terms of size, growth patterns, and extent of influence would prove fruitful. The regional significance of the A.U.M.P., U.A.M.E., and other small African Methodist groups could be studied over against the national prominence of the A.M.E., A.M.E. Zion, and C.M.E. churches. Studies of this variety would have to be guided by many probing and perplexing questions: Why did the early Union Church of Africans, out of which developed the A.U.M.P. and U.A.M.E. churches, experience such slow growth during the pre-Civil War era? Why have the A.U.M.P. and U.A.M.E. denominations—which claim antiquity on a level with the A.M.E. and A.M.E. Zion bodies—remained so small and regional throughout their histories? How can we explain the drastic decline of the A.U.M.P. Church, the U.A.M.E. Church, the Independent African Methodist Episcopal Church, the Reformed Methodist Union Episcopal Church, the Reformed U.A.M.E. Church, the Reformed Zion Union Apostolic Methodist Church, and the Colored Methodist Protestant Church in the twentieth century? Why do black people know practically nothing about these small branches of African Methodism? Why have they gone virtually unnoticed by both black and white professional church historians, theologians, and sociologists of religion? Are the small and regional African Methodist churches significant in the understanding of the African Methodist tradition? Should they be included in the accounts related to the Wesleyan and Methodist tradition generally? How are we to understand the alternating patterns of growth and decline which have characterized the A.M.E., A.M.E. Zion, and C.M.E. denominations in the twentieth century? Answers to these questions will further enlighten us as to the vitality and variety endemic to African Methodism.

Finally, comparative studies of African Methodist denominations should not overlook the extent to which these churches have found a special or unique expression. While it is true that denominations composed largely of black Methodists have always had much in common with the Wesleyan and Methodist tradition generally, this should not obscure the fact that African Methodist Churches have traditionally been something more and something less than white Methodist Churches. This diversity should not be surprising, given that black people have customarily been cut off from most areas of American institutional life. Because of the strange circumstances under which the black experience developed in America, African Methodist denominations—and black religious institutions generally—have had to accommodate a multiplicity of needs which extend beyond the strictly *spiritual* or *ecclesiastical*.[13] To an extent they have been expressions of black power or nationalism, thereby providing a context for self-help, expression, recognition, leadership, and group identity and solidarity. This expression has not been entirely different for those blacks who have traditionally remained within white Methodist Churches. By their very existence, African Methodist bodies have stood as a testimony to the conviction that slavery and racism are inconsistent with God and the dignity and worth of persons.[14] Moreover, African Methodism has had and continues to have a distinctive life of its own as far as worship style and tradition are concerned. The worship of African Methodists has featured a variety of liturgical innovations shaped by the African background the the experience of oppression—innovations which encourage group involvement. The present writer's recent award-winning study of the A.U.M.P. and U.A.M.C. churches recognizes unique features such as these as being essential to an understanding of the African Methodist heritage, and it is something of a pioneer effort to establish a comparative context with the various branches of African Methodism.[15]

A solid historical study of union negotiations and of schisms within the ranks of African Methodists has yet to be written. Any worthwhile examination of this subject would have to begin with the organizing convention of the A.M.E. Church in April, 1816, when there was a determined but unsuccessful effort to bring all African Methodist churches together to form a large and powerful connection.[16] Dennis C. Dickerson, Frederick A. Norwood, and Roy W. Trueblood have written about union talks between African Methodist denominations, but they deal only with the A.M.E., A.M.E. Zion, and C.M.E. Churches. This author's work on the A.U.M.P. and U.A.M.E. Churches discusses union negotiations between these bodies. The scholar who is interested in doing further research in this area should check the sources mentioned in my book and in the treatments by Dickerson, Norwood, and Trueblood.[17] For information on schisms, one should look at relevant and available court cases, accounts afforded by the Bureau of Census of the United States Department of Commerce on Religious Bodies, and works by this author, Carter G. Woodson, and Frederick Norwood.[18] An in-depth study of union efforts and of schisms among African Methodists should emphasize those barriers which have historically prevented mergers, such as personality conflicts, the willingness to maintain separate identities, and differences in polity and style.

The involvement of African Methodists in foreign mission efforts deserves to be studied more seriously. Since the early years of the nineteenth century, black Methodists have directed their modest foreign mission programs to Canada, the Caribbean Islands, and to Africa.[19] A.M.E. foreign missionary work has been discussed in books by Lewellyn L. Berry and Eunice Griffin, and Howard D. Gregg's *History of the A.M.E. Church* makes important references to A.M.E. congregations in places like Africa, South America, and the West Indies.[20] Information on A.M.E. Zion foreign mission activities is available in Bishop William J. Walls' excellent work on that denomination. But there is a need for a lengthy and critical examination of foreign missions as conducted by the A.M.E., the A.M.E.Z., the C.M.E., the A.U.M.P., and the U.A.M.E. churches. Such a study should evaluate the theology of missions as advanced by these denominations, and it should not ignore their contemporary work in parts of the so-called Third World. It should also address the following questions: Have the institutional forms of African Methodist missions differed significantly from those of white Methodist churches? Will the need for foreign missionary services diminish as the independent African Church movements become more established, and as independent African and Caribbean countries preempt these areas of responsibility for the state?[21] Scholars who explore foreign mission efforts on the part of African Methodist churches might find much that would be of theoretical use in writings on African missions among black Americans by Sylva M. Jacobs and Walter L. Williams.[22]

Studies that give proper emphasis to the significant roles played by black women in the history of Methodism are long overdue. We very much need to know more about Methodism and black women not simply because of the current widespread interest in women's studies, but, more importantly, because black women have left their mark on the Wesleyan and Methodist tradition. John Wesley offered spiritual advice to African women as early as 1737, and one of the first two African slaves he baptized in 1758 was a woman.[23] Black women have been active in American Methodism from the appearance of a servant named Betty at a society meeting at the New York home of Philip Embury in 1766 to the election in 1984 of Reverend Leontine T.C. Kelly to the episcopacy of The United Methodist Church. They have traditionally filled roles as deaconesses, missionaries, church organizers, preachers, revival subjects and leaders, social reformers, Sunday School teachers, and as strong spiritual forces in the black community.[24] Considering the wide range of contributions made by black women in the history of Methodism, it is disturbing that Methodist scholars have virtually ignored them for so long.

A small number of works have appeared recently which cover certain aspects of black female participation in the history of the (United) Methodist Church.[25] However, nothing is presently available which does justice to the tremendous importance of Amanda Berry Smith, Ida B. Wells, Mary McLeod Bethune, Leontine T.C. Kelly, and others. Amanda B. Smith, Mary M. Bethune, and Leontine Kelly easily merit individual treatment by scholars. Aside from their personal memoirs, a number of other sources are accessible for studying their lives and activities.[26] On the African Methodist side, there is a pressing need for research on black women in the A.M.E. Church, the A.M.E. Zion Church, the A.U.M.P. Church, the C.M.E. Church, the U.A.M.E. Church, the Reformed U.A.M.E. Church, the Reformed Methodist Union Episcopal Church, the Reformed Zion Union Apostolic Methodist Church, the Independent A.M.E. Church, and the Colored Methodist Protestant Church. Scholars like Jualynne E. Dodson and Jacquelyn Grant are presently writing about women in the A.M.E. Church, and they are also performing a valuable service in compelling the contemporary black theology movement to take the historic roles and perspectives of black women seriously. The life of Jarena Lee, a preacher in the A.M.E. Church in the early nineteenth century, is briefly discussed in a work by Rosemary R. Ruether and Rosemary S. Keller. The Reverend Mrs. Lee's autobiography is also available, and so are writings about A.M.E. women such as Sarah Allen, Fanny J. Coppin, and Rosa Parks.[27] Biographical sketches of powerful figures like Sojourner Truth and Harriet Tubman of the A.M.E. Zion Church have been completed, but they do not center enough on these women's deep religious faith and on the full scope of their contributions as members of their church. Sojourner Truth left a narrative of her life which cannot be disregarded if one is to capture the spirit of this phenomenal personality.[28] For important information on women's roles in A.U.M.P. and U.A.M.E. history, one should examine articles by the present author.[29] Virtually nothing exists that sheds light on black female involvement in the other branches of African Methodism. The difficulties in the way of research in these areas are monumental due to the sheer scarcity of sources.

More studies are needed that focus on African Methodism during the Civil War and Reconstruction. Israel L. Butt, Bishop John Wesley Gains, and Bishop Daniel A. Payne did write books on the A.M.E. Church for that period, but their works lack the critical focus and depth of scholarship that are so essential to a first rate study.[30] A careful sifting of the periodicals, minutes, and books of *Discipline* of African Methodist churches would tell us something about the social and political behavior of these churches, as well as about the nature of their missionary outreach to the newly-freed black men and women in the south. We have been led to believe that African Methodist denominations experienced tremendous growth in the four decades after the Civil War, and that they worked alongside the white Methodists in establishing educational institutions and other programs designed to uplift ex-slaves. But this is not borne out by this writer's book on the A.U.M.P. and U.A.M.E. churches, and by Clarence E. Walker's recent work on the A.M.E. Church during the Civil War and Reconstruction. The writer's study suggests that although the A.M.E., A.M.E. Zion, and C.M.E. churches exploded in both size and geographical extent between 1865 and 1900, the A.U.M.P. and U.A.M.E. bodies remained small and regional. Walker has demonstrated that shocking tensions, conflicts, and even hostilities existed between the A.M.E. Church, the A.M.E. Zion Church, the C.M.E. Church, and the two white Methodist churches.[31] Such findings clearly illustrate the need to reexamine African Methodism in the late nineteenth century.

Special attention should be devoted to finding out more about those branches of African Methodism that were organized in the late nineteenth and early twentieth centuries. The C.M.E. Church, which developed out of the M.E. Church, South in 1870, has been discussed at length in works by C.H. Phillips, Joseph A. Johnson, and Othal Lakey.[32] However, we could benefit from a critical study of this denomination and its development. Very little is known about the Reformed Zion Union Apostolic Methodist Church, which was started by black Methodists in Boydton, Virginia in 1869. The same applies in the case of the Reformed Methodist Union Episcopal Church, which resulted from a split within the A.M.E. Church in Georgetown, South Carolina in 1884. The Independent A.M.E. Church, which was also born out of a schism within the A.M.E. Church between 1897 and 1908, is listed in *The Yearbooks of American Churches* up to the 1960s. The Reformed Zion Union Apostolic Methodist Church and the Reformed Methodist Union Episcopal Church are mentioned in this same source for the years 1900 to 1972, and since 1973 information on them has been included in all editions of *The Yearbooks of American and Canadian Churches*. Most of the congregations of the First Colored Methodist Protestant Church, founded around 1840, merged with the Union Church of Africans to form the A.U.M.P. Church in 1866, but we have no idea as to what happened to that small number of congregations which continued as the Colored Methodist Protestant Church. Bits of information on this church can be found in various twentieth century sources prepared by the United States Bureau of Census on Religious Bodies, and it is mentioned in some of *The Yearbooks of American Churches*.[33] Most of the available documents concerning the Reformed U.A.M.E. Church, which emerged out of a split within the U.A.M.E. Church in Wilmington, Delaware, around 1935, are housed at the Delaware Division of Historical and Cultural Affairs, Bureau of Archives and Records, Hall of Records, in Dover, Delaware. Unless we move swiftly to discover more about these small and relatively unknown branches of African Methodism, an important chapter in the history of African Methodism will be lost.[34]

One way of understanding more about African Methodism in the four decades after the Civil War is to focus on some of its outstanding leaders for that period. These inquiries will require serious studies of outstanding personalities like Daniel A. Payne and Henry McNeal Turner of the A.M.E. Church; Frederick Douglass, J. W. Hood, and Alexander Walters of the A.M.E. Zion Church; Isaac Lane and William H. Miles of the C.M.E. Church; Edward Chippey, Gaylord Peterson, and Daniel J. Russell, Sr. of the A.U.M.P. Church; and John C. Ramsey, Lorenzo Dow Blackson, and Edward Williams of the U.A.M.E. Church. More investigative work will have to be finished before we can identify strong and important leaders in the other small African Methodist denominations.[35]

More time and energy could be devoted to studies of blacks who were affiliates with white Methodist churches in the late nineteenth and early twentieth centuries. We know that the Methodist Episcopal Churches, north and South, moved during this period to segregate their black members, but many questions remain largely unanswered: Why did both M.E. Churches follow similar courses in dealing with their black memberships? Were they influenced in their actions by social pressures for segregation? How were white Methodists able to reconcile segregation with Christian ideals? What percentage of the blacks in the M.E. Churches, North and South, actually desired separate ecclesiastical arrangements for themselves? Why did they desire such arrangements? What percentage preferred to remain with the white Methodist churches? How did important black leaders like Hiram Revels respond to the practice of racism and segregation in the M.E. Churches? What social and theological issues were involved in the creation of the all-black Central Jurisdiction in The Methodist Church in 1939? How did white Methodists deal with the Central Jurisdiction after 1939? For direction in answering these questions, one would have to turn to books and articles by Methodist churchmen and scholars such as Jim Lawson, Frederick A. Norwood, Robert L. Wilson, Douglas Wingeier, and J. Philip Wogaman.[36]

The story of blacks in Methodism in the twentieth century generally has not been fully told. Scholars especially need to reexamine the activities of black Methodists during the so-called "dark ages" because previous research has been based largely on the presupposition that black churches were essentially otherworldly and accommodationist in character. This view suggests that black Methodists, and all other black denominations for that matter, were not socially and politically active in the five decades before the emergence of Martin Luther King, Jr. and the beginnings of the civil rights and black power campaigns. Scholars could go a long way in challenging this perception by giving proper attention to the positive contributions made by black Methodists in the first half of this century. The significant roles played by black Methodists like Walter Brooks, Reverdy C. Ransom, and Alexander Walters in the organization of the Niagara Movement (1905) and the National Association for the Advancement of Colored People (1909) could be stressed more forcefully. More emphasis could also be placed on the relationship between various Methodist groups and the development of the National Urban League (1910) and the Congress of Racial Equality (1943).[37] Furthermore, Methodist scholars need to focus more attention on the positive and productive ways in which blacks in various Methodist churches responded to the issues of black oppression, urbanization and industrialization, the depression, and the migrations. When the necessary research has been completed, we may realize that black Methodists were far more active in furthering the cause of black liberation and survival than is usually known or imagined.

Black Methodist involvement in the civil rights and black power movements of the 1950s and 60s has not been sufficiently assessed in extant studies of American Methodism. The great contribution of the A.M.E. deaconess Rosa Parks, commonly called "the Mother of the Civil Rights Movement," is scarcely mentioned even in histories of the A.M.E. Church. We need to know more about the extent of involvement in these movements on the part of black bishops in the (United) Methodist Church and in the predominantly black Methodist denominations. The civil rights activities of Bishop George F. Brown of the A.U.M.P. Church and Bishop David E. Hackett of the U.A.M.E. Church have already been documented in the present writer's work on these bodies.[38] Information on the involvements of other black Methodist preachers and bishops can be obtain through oral sources and through a careful examination of documents such as *The Black Power Statement of the National Committee of Negro Churchmen*, which was signed by black bishops from the A.M.E., A.M.E. Zion, C.M.E., and (United) Methodist Churches in July, 1966.[39] Interestingly enough, the leaders of the A.U.M.P. Church, the U.A.M.E. Church, and other small black Methodist denominations did not sign this statement. The rise of the Black Methodists for Church Renewal as a caucus in The United Methodist Church in 1968 is another example of how black Methodists responded to the forces unleashed by the civil rights and black power crusades.[40] Scholars who write about the history of American Methodism should take such developments more seriously.

The responses of black Methodists to the contemporary black theology movement would make for an interesting study. James H. Cone, the major spokesman for this movement, came out of the A.M.E. Church. But A.M.E. churchmen generally, like many black Methodists, have been slow in accepting and supporting black theology. Cone has expressed disappointment with this lack of acceptance in some of his more recent writings.[41] We would profit considerably from studies which answer the following questions: Why has Cone been excluded from participating freely as a theologian in the A.M.E. Church and in other black Methodist churches? Why is there seemingly such a chasm between what black theologians are saying and what many black Methodists, clergy and laity, believe? Is it possible that black theology will be more appealing to black Methodists and black church persons generally in the future as more young, trained black ministers and theologians become pastors of black churches? What does James Cone say in his most recent writings about the relationship between black Methodists and black theology in the future? To my knowledge, no scholar has seriously addressed these questions in a work on American Methodism. Of course, time will be the most important element in answering some of them.

Finally, we do not have a good, solid study of the participation of black Methodists in ecumenical concerns in this century. The need for a historical account of union negotiations between black Methodists was raised previously, but what about studies that deal with black Methodists and ecumenical concerns on a broader scale? We need to know why the smaller and lesser known branches of African Methodism—unlike the A.M.E., the A.M.E.Z., the C.M.E., and blacks in The United Methodist Church—have not participated in major ecumenical ventures like the World Council of Churches, the National Council of Churches, the World Methodist Council, the Consultation on Church Union, and the National Committee of Black Christians. Is this indicative of how the A.U.M.P. Church, the U.A.M.E. Church, and other small and regional African churches have languished in the backwaters of American Methodism? Is it possible that these churches will become more active in ecumenical concerns in the future? It is necessary for us to find answers to these questions.

Other directions could be given for studies of black people in Methodism, but this is enough for now. The work that ought to be done may never be completed, but if scholars seriously apply themselves to the task we will gain a greater understanding of the role and importance of black people in the Wesleyan and Methodist tradition.

NOTES

1. Frederick A. Norwood, *The Story of American Methodism: A History of the United Methodists and Their Relations* (Nashville, 1974), pp. 10, 273, and 432-436.
2. Nehemiah Curnock, ed., *The Journal of the Rev. John Wesley, A.M.*, 8 vols. (London, 1938), I, pp. 350-353; and Larry Murphy, "Methodism: An Evaluation from Within and Without," *Explor: A Journal of Theology*, Vol. 5, No. 1 (Spring, 1979), p. 55.
3. Norwood, *The Story of American Methodism*, pp. 10, 273, and 432-436.
4. Lewis V. Baldwin, *"Invisible" Strands in African Methodism: A History of the African Union Methodist Protestant and Union American Methodist Episcopal Churches, 1805-1980* (Metuchen, N.J., 1983), pp. 256-275.
5. Ibid., p. 12.
6. Frank Baker, "The Origins, Character, And Influence Of John Wesley's Thoughts Upon Slavery," *Methodist History*, Vol. XXII, No. 2 (January, 1984), pp. 75-86; Richard M. Cameron, *Methodism and Society in Historical Perspective*, 2 vols. (Nashville, 1961), I, pp. 53 ff.; and Donald G. Mathews, *Slavery and Methodism: A Chapter in American Morality, 1780-1845* (Princeton, N.J., 1965), pp. 5-6.
7. See John Hope Franklin, ed., *The Souls of Black Folk in Three Negro Classics* (New York, 1965), pp. 339-340; Melville J. Herskovits, *The Myth of the Negro Past* (Boston, 1958), Chapter VII; Lawrence W. Levine, *Black Culture and Black Consciousness: Afro-American Folk Thought from Slavery to Freedom* (New York, 1977) Chapter I; Norwood, *The Story of American Methodism*, pp. 273 and 432-436; and Albert J. Raboteau, *Slave Religion: The "Invisible Institution" in the Antebellum South* (New York, 1978), Chapters II-III.
8. See David L. Lewis, *King: A Critical Biography* (New York, 1970). For a recent contribution toward filling this gap in scholarship, see Warren T. Smith, *Harry Hosier: Circuit Rider* (Nashville, 1981).
9. See Lewis V. Baldwin, "Father Peter Spencer: Portrait Of An Unknown Pioneer African Methodist Leader," *The Journal of the Interdenominational Theological Center*, Vol. IX, No. 1 (Fall, 1981), pp. 31-43; and William J. Walls, *The African Methodist Episcopal Zion Church: Reality of the Black Church* (Charlotte, N.C., 1974), Chapter VIII. The Baldwin piece is not a good critical evaluation of Spencer, and more recent findings indicate that the final two paragraphs, which cover a schism in the Spencer movement, are not entirely correct. For the correct account, see Baldwin, *"Invisible" Strands in African Methodism*, Chapter III.
10. Harry V. Richardson, *Dark Salvation: A Story of Methodism As It Developed Among Blacks in America* (New York, 1976), pp. 224-225; and *The United States Department of Commerce, Bureau of Census, Religious Bodies: Statistics, Doctrine, Organization, and Work, 1926* (Washington, D.C., 1929), pp. 995-1047.
11. Baldwin, *"Invisible" Strands in African Methodism*, Chapter II.
12. Ibid., pp. 168-173 and 256-275.
13. Ibid., Chapters II-VIII.
14. Ibid., Chapters II-VII; Norwood, *The Story of American Methodism*, pp. 171 and 272-273; Alain Rogers, "The African Methodist Episcopal Church: A Study in Black Nationalism," *The Black Church*, Vol. I (1972), pp. 17-43; and Sterling Stuckey, ed., *The Ideological Origins of Black Nationalism* (Boston, 1972) pp. 1-5.
15. Baldwin, *"Invisible" Strands in African Methodism*, Chapters V and VII; and Winthrop S. Hudson, *Religion in America: An Historical Account of the Development of American Religious Life* (New York, 1965), p. 225.
16. *Colored American* (Oct. 21, 1837), p. 2; and Baldwin, *"Invisible" Strands in African Methodism*, pp. 50-55.
17. Dennis C. Dickerson, "Black Ecumenism: Efforts to Establish a United Methodist Episcopal Church, 1918-1932," *Church History*, Vol. 52, No. 4 (Dec., 1983), pp. 479-491; Norwood, *The Story of American Methodism*, pp. 280-281; Baldwin, *"Invisible" Strands in African Methodism*, pp. 199-200, 253-255, and 268-270; and Roy W. Trueblood, "Union Negotiations Between Black Methodists in America," *Methodist History*, Vol. VIII, No. 4 (July, 1970), pp. 18-29.

18. *The United States Department of Commerce, Bureau of Census, Religious Bodies, 1926*, pp. 995-1046; Baldwin, *"Invisible" Strands in African Methodism*, Chapters II-III and VI; Carter G. Woodson, *The History of the Negro Church* (Washington, D.C., 1921), Chapter IV; and Norwood, *The Story of American Methodism*, Chapters XV-XXXIV.

19. Lawrence N. Jones, "The Black Churches: A New Agenda," *The Christian Century* (April 18, 1979), p. 434.

20. Lewellyn L. Berry, *A Century of Missions of the A.M.E. Church, 1840-1940* (New York, 1942); Eunice Griffin, *The Rise of American Missions, The African Methodist Episcopal Church* (New York, 1960); and Howard D. Gregg, *History of the A.M.E. Church: The Black Church in Action* (Nashville, 1980).

21. Walls, *The African Methodist Episcopal Zion Church*, pp. 228-406.

22. Sylvia M. Jacobs, ed., *Black Americans and the Missionary Movement in Africa* (Westport, Conn., 1982); and Walter L. Williams, *Black Americans and the Evangelization of Africa, 1877-1900* (Madison, Wis., 1982).

23. Curnock, ed., *The Journal of Rev. John Wesley*, I, pp. 350-353; and IV, p. 29.

24. Baldwin, *"Invisible" Strands in African Methodism*, p. 16; W.A. Reed, "Methodists Consecrate 1st Black Woman Bishop," *The [Nashville] Tennessean* (July 21, 1984), p. 1-B; and Rosemary R. Ruether and Rosemary S. Keller, *Women and Religion in America: The Nineteenth Century* (San Francisco, 1981) p. xiii. We really need more information concerning how black Methodists have responded historically to black female preachers. For references to how A.M.E.s, A.U.M.P.s, and U.A.M.E.s have responded to female preachers in their denominations, see Clarence E. Walker, *A Rock in a Weary Land: The African Methodist Episcopal Church During the Civil War and Reconstruction* (Baton Rouge, 1982), pp. 25-26; Lewis V. Baldwin, "Black Women and African Union Methodism, 1813-1983," *Methodist History*, Vol. XXI, No. 4 (July 1983), pp. 225-237; Baldwin, *"Invisible" Strands in African Methodism*, pp. 62-63, 94, 105-107, 174-177, 194-196, and 266-268; Baldwin, "Women in A.U.M.P. Church History," *August Quarterly '84: An Afro-American Celebration of Roots and Reunion Since 1813* (August 26, 1984), pp.4-5; and Bill Frank, "Blacks Should Present United Front," *The Morning News*, Wilmington, Delaware (August 27, 1984), pp. 1ff.

25. Ruether and Keller, *Women and Religion in America*, pp. 4-5, 10, 18-23, 249, and 267; John T. King and Marcet H. King, *Mary McLeod Bethune: A Woman of Vision and Distinction* (Lake Junaluska, N.C., 1977); and *To A Higher Glory: The Growth and Development of Black Women Organized for Mission in the Methodist Church, 1940-1968* (Cincinnati, 1978).

26. Ruether and Keller, *Women and Religion in America*, pp. 4-5, 10, 18-23, 249, and 267; Alfreda M. Duster, ed., *Crusade for Justice: The Autobiography of Ida B. Wells* (Chicago, 1970); King and King, *Mary McLeod Bethune*; Reed, "Methodists Consecrate 1st Black Woman Bishop," p. 1-B; and Lynn Norment, "In The Male Domain Of Pastoring: Women Find Success In The Pulpit," *Ebony* (Nov., 1981), pp. 99-104. The Ruether and Keller book refers to other sources of Amanda Berry Smith and Ida B. Wells.

27. Doris E. Saunders, "Black Women as Clergy and the Black Experience," *The Crisis* (June-July, 1983), p. 16; Jacquelyn Grant, "The African Methodist Episcopal Church and Women," *A.M.E. Working Papers II* (New Orleans, 1980), pp. III-13–III-22; "Empowerment of the Daughters: An African Methodist Mandate," *A.M.E. Working Papers I* (Atlanta, 1980), pp. IX-1–IX-4; Gayraud S. Wilmore and James H. Cone, *Black Theology: A Documentary History, 1966-1979* (New York, 1979), pp. 361-442; Ruether and Keller, *Women and Religion in America*, pp. 194-195 and 212-214; Horace Tolbert, *The Sons of Allen* (Xenia, Ohio, 1906); Levi J. Coppin, *The A.M.E. Church and South Africa: Observations of Persons and Things in South Africa, 1900-1904* (Philadelphia, n.d.); and Martin Luther King, Jr., *Stride Toward Freedom: The Montgomery Story* (New York, 1958), pp. 43-47, 55, 61, 63, 69, and 110. For very recent studies of black women and the black church by a major black theologian, see James H. Cone, *My Soul Looks Back* (Nashville, 1982), Chapter V; and Cone, *For My People: Black Theology and the Black Church* (New York, 1984), Chapter VI.

28. Olive Gilbert, *Narrative of Sojourner Truth: A Bondswoman of Olden Times* (Boston, 1875); Ruether and Keller, *Women and Religion in America*, pp. 5, 11, and 25-27; Earl Conrad, *Harriet Tubman* (New York, 1969); and Sarah Bradford, *Harriet Tubman: The Moses of Her People* (New York, 1961).

29. Baldwin, "Women and African Union Methodism, 1813-1983," pp. 225-237; and Baldwin, "Women in A.U.M.P. Church History," pp. 4-5.

30. Israel L. Butt, *History of African Methodism in Virginia, or Four Decades in the Old Dominion* (Hampton, Va., 1908); John Wesley Gains, *African Methodism in the South or Twenty-five Years of Freedom* (Atlanta, 1890); Daniel A. Payne, *History of the African Methodist Episcopal Church* (Nashville, 1891); Payne, *Recollections of Seventy Years* (New York: 1968); and Payne, *The Semi-Centenary and the Retrospection of the A.M.E. Church* (Baltimore, 1866).

31. Baldwin, *"Invisible" Strands in African Methodist Methodism*, Chapter IV; and Walker, *A Rock in a Weary Land*, Chapters IV-V.

32. Charles H. Phillips, *The History of the Colored Methodist Episcopal Church in America; Comprising its Organization, Subsequent Development, and Present Status* (Jackson, Tenn., 1898); Joseph A. Johnson, *Our Faith, Heritage and Church* (Privately published, 1975); and Othal H. Lakey, *The Rise of "Colored Methodism": A Study of the Background and the Beginnings of the Christian Methodist Episcopal Church* (Dallas, 1972).

33. *The United States Department of Commerce, Bureau of Census, Religious Bodies, 1926*, pp. 1035-1046. This source indicates that the Independent African Methodist Episcopal Church was started in 1897, but the founding date has been set at 1907 by Benson Y. Landis, *The Yearbook of American Churches* (New York, 1965), p. 80. Also see *The Doctrine and Discipline of the African Union First Colored Methodist Protestant Church of America, or Elsewhere*, First Revised Edition (Wilmington, Del., 1867), pp. 3-14; Daniel J. Russell, Jr., *History of the African Union Methodist Protestant Church* (Philadelphia, 1920), p. 20; Baldwin, *"Invisible" Strands in African Methodism*, Chapter IV; and Norwood, *The Story of American Methodism*, p. 174. Dr. Norwood claims that the African Union First Colored Methodist Protestant Church, more commonly known as the African Union Methodist Protestant Church, split in 1875 and "brought into existence the present denomination." My findings do not bear out this claim. A schism did occur within the Union Church of Africans or the African Union Church between 1851 and 1856, eventually resulting in the A.U.M.P. and U.A.M.E. denominations. However, it is possible that several congregations from the A.U.M.P. Church broke away in 1875 and continued as the Colored Methodist Protestant Church. More research will have to be done before we can substantiate this.

34. Baldwin, *"Invisible" Strands in African Methodism*, p. 188.

35. Daniel A. Payne, *The African Methodist Episcopal Church in Its Relations to the Freedmen: An Address* (Xenia, Ohio, 1868); Payne, *Recollections of Seventy Years*; Edwin S. Redkey, *Respect Black: The Writings and Speeches of Henry McNeal Turner* (New York, 1971); Frederick Douglass, *Narrative of the Life of Frederick Douglass: An American Slave* (Cambridge, Mass., 1960; originally published in 1845); Philip S. Foner, ed., *The Life and Writings of Frederick Douglass*, 5 Vols. (New York, 1975); James W. Hood, *Sermons by J.W. Hood*, 2 Vols. (York, Pa., n.d.); Alexander Walters, *My Life and Work* (Chicago, 1917); Isaac Lane, *Autobiography of Bishop Isaac Lane, D.D.* (Nashville, 1916); Phillips, *The History of the Colored Methodist Episcopal Church*; Russell, *History of the African Union Methodist*

Protestant Church; and Baldwin, *"Invisible" Strands in African Methodism*, Chapter IV.

36. Jim Lawson, *Methodists for Church Renewal: Where We Begin* (Privately published, n.d.); Norwood, *The Story of American Methodism*, Chapter XXIV; Robert L. Wilson, *The Effect of Racially Changing Communities on Methodist Churches in 32 Cities in the Southeast* (New York, 1968); Douglas Wingeier, *The Treatment of Negro-White Relations in the Curriculum Materials of the Methodist Church, 1941-1960* (Boston, 1962); and J. Philip Wogaman, *Methodism's Challenge in Race Relations: A Study Strategy* (Washington, D.C., 1980).

37. Gayraud S. Wilmore, *Black Religion and Black Radicalism: An Examination of the Black Experience in Religion* (New York, 1972), Chapter VI; and Baldwin, *"Invisible" Strands in African Methodism*, Chapter VI.

38. Baldwin, *"Invisible" Strands in African Methodism*, Chapter VI.

39. See C. Eric Lincoln, *The Black Church Since Frazier* (New York, 1977), pp. 169-178.

40. Ibid., pp. 194-196.

41. James H. Cone, *My Soul Looks Back*, Chapters I-III. Cone makes it clear, however, that some black churchpersons, including Methodists, have been supportive of his work.

Mercersburg's Quarrel with Methodism

Charles Yrigoyen, Jr.
General Commission on Archives and History
The United Methodist Church

Introduction

The first half of the nineteenth century was a fascinating and exciting period in the history of American religious life. It was the time of the Second Great Awakening, that unusual wave of revivalism which swept back and forth across the nation for at least fifty years after 1800. There is little doubt that this Awakening left a significant mark on the nation's social and religious life long after its excitement was apparently spent.

Like the Great Awakening of almost a century earlier, the Second Awakening emphasized a religious experience of salvation. Unlike its predecessor, however, it had two distinctive features: the camp meeting and the use of techniques, known as the New Measures, to bring the wayward to their rebirth. Camp meetings were not only particularly important for frontier social and religious life, but they also became popular means for evangelizing in areas where the population was not as widely scattered. The New Measures were revivalistic means used by pastors and evangelists to provoke sinners to conversion. If not invented by the famous Presbyterian evangelist Charles Grandison Finney (1792-1875) they were certainly popularized by him. The New Measures included intense revival campaigns sometimes called "protracted meetings," public mention of the unconverted by name, meetings of inquiry to determine a person's state of salvation, and, perhaps most controversial, the use of the "anxious bench," seats to which were brought during a revival service those anxious for their salvation experience.[1]

It is not surprising that Methodists, very sympathetic to experiential religion, were much involved in the Second Great Awakening. They were ardent supporters of the camp meeting and effectively employed the New Measures.[2] During the course of the Awakening, Methodism realized large numerical growth. Between 1800 and 1850 the membership of the Methodist Episcopal Church and the Methodist Episcopal Church, South rose from 65,000 to over 1.4 million.[3]

Other Protestant denominations in America were also affected by the pervasive influence of the Second Great Awakening. Presbyterians, Congregationalists, Lutherans, the Dutch Reformed and the German Reformed churches, to name a few, felt its effects.

The Second Great Awakening did not go without challenge. It was opposed by those who were convinced that its religion was too superficial and emotional. Some opponents felt it was not sufficiently rational. Others claimed that its methods, especially the New Measures, were dangerously innovative and manipulative. In some churches there developed pro-Awakening and anti-Awakening parties. One denomination which was caught up in internal debate about the Awakening and the New Measures was the German Reformed Church.

The Mercersburg Theology

New Measures revivalism had become an important force in the early 1840s in the German Reformed Church, a comparatively small denomination in America. While its excesses were not as keenly visible in the German Reformed Church as in Lutheranism, this form of revival spirit was present. Many German Reformed congregations were conducting protracted meetings regularly. The prestigious Race Street German Reformed Church in Philadelphia invited Charles G. Finney to hold a New Measures crusade in their building as early as 1828. Through the next two decades this type of religious excitement spread into every quarter of the denomination.[4]

Many German Reformed Church leaders were skeptical about the consequences of the New Measures. They believed that this approach to the Christian faith was a betrayal of the Reformed tradition upon which the denomination was historically founded. Furthermore, revivalism was blamed for two schisms in the church, both led by German Reformed pastors whose religious experiences and sympathies for revivalism resulted in the creation of new churches. Philip William Otterbein (1726-1813) had founded the Church of the United Brethren in Christ. John Winebrenner (1797-1860), alleged to have been one of the first pastors in the denomination to utilize the New Measures, had organized the Church of God.[5]

Opposition to revivalism, especially of the New Measures variety, came to be centered at the Theological Seminary of the German Reformed Church located at Mercersburg, a little town in southcentral Pennsylvania. This small institution gave birth to one of the most celebrated theological movements in American Protestantism. The movement is generally referred to as the Mercersburg Theology.[6]

The Theological Seminary was originally located at Carlisle, Pennsylvania. In 1829 it was moved to York and in 1837 it was relocated at Mercersburg where it was situated with Marshall College, another educational institution of the German Reformed Church. By modern standards the Theological Seminary was tiny. The student body was never large and two professors comprised the faculty. Despite its size, however, the Theological Seminary, as might be expected, was an important force in the life of the denomination.

In the 1840s and 1850s two exceptionally gifted individuals occupied the faculty chairs at Mercersburg. They were John Williamson Nevin (1803-1886) and Philip Schaff (1819-1893). More than any other persons, these two men may be considered the progenitors of the Mercersburg Theology. Their sermons and public statements, their writings, and their leadership in denominational committees and organizations defined the main thrust of the movement.

John Williamson Nevin was born and raised in a Scotch-Irish family in the Cumberland Valley of Pennsylvania. He was a graduate of Union College near Schenectady, New York, and Princeton Theological Seminary from which he received a degree in 1826. Nevin was licensed to preach by the Carlisle (Pennsylvania) Presbytery in 1828. From 1829 to 1839 he taught at the Western Theological Seminary (Presbyterian) near Pittsburgh, Pennsylvania. In 1839 he was elected Professor of Theology at the Theological Seminary of the German Reformed Church at Mercersburg. He had become well versed in the tradition of the German Reformed Church and highly respected the life and thought of the German people. Nevin arrived in Mercersburg in the spring of 1840 prepared to take up his teaching duties.

When Nevin began his professorship at Mercersburg he became alarmed at the drift of the German Reformed Church and American Protestantism away from genuinely biblical faith, the spirit of the early church, and the insights of the Reformation. Much of the blame for this departure from authentic Christian belief and practice rested with revivalism, especially New Measures revivalism which he characterized as false religion and "quackery." In his first major work, The Anxious Bench (1843),[7] and in subsequent books and pamphlets such as The Mystical Presence (1846),[8] The Church (1847),[9] Antichrist, or the Spirit of Sect and Schism (1848),[10] and The Apostles' Creed (1849),[11] Nevin set forth his analysis of the malaise of American Protestantism and the German Reformed Church and offered correctives. His views were also circulated in a large number of essays and articles published in the Reformed Church Messenger and the Mercersburg Review.

The second principal figure, Philip Schaff, was a native of Switzerland. He was educated at the universities in Tübingen, Halle, and Berlin. While serving as an instructor at the university in Berlin, Schaff was visited by two clergymen from the United States who were authorized to issue him a call to teach in the Theological Seminary at Mercersburg. He had been recommended for the post by German church leaders and several of the professors at Halle and Berlin. Schaff accepted the call probably hoping "to bring German scholarship and theology to an America lacking in intellectual and theological depth."[12] He arrived in Mercersburg in 1844 and immediately found in John Williamson Nevin an amiable associate who shared his high regard for continental historical and theological ideas.

Like his colleague, Schaff was horrified at the state of American Protestantism. He was particularly disturbed by its anti-intellectualism, its lack of understanding concerning the historical development of Christianity and the widespread "sectarianism" which plagued American religion. Schaff expressed his distress and proposed reform in The Principle of Protestantism (1845),[13] What is Church History? (1846),[14] History of the Apostolic Church (1853),[15] and America: A Sketch of the Political, Social, and Religious Character of the United States of North America (1855).[16] From 1848 to 1853 he also served as the editor of Der Deutsche Kirchenfreund, the first American theological journal in the German language. Schaff published a large number of articles in other journals including the Mercersburg Review. He left the Mercersburg school in 1863. His distinguished career continued later in New York where he served as Secretary of the New York Sabbath Association and subsequently as a professor at Union Theological Seminary. Schaff was the premier church historian in America in the nineteenth century.

The Mercersburg professors' criticism of

American Protestantism, including the German Reformed Church, was composed of three basic accusations.

First, they complained that American Protestantism was *unchristological*. Both Nevin and Schaff were convinced that a faulty Christology was abroad in the churches. It tended to concentrate either on Jesus' ethical teachings or his vicarious death. Although Jesus' words are important, Nevin claimed, his mission was not simply to point people to salvation by correct instruction.[17] People cannot be brought to God through doctrine or example. Likewise, Jesus' death, offered in obedience to God, was not the singularly important event in his life. James H. Nichols observes that Nevin "laid his emphasis on the Person rather than the work of Christ, the Incarnation rather than the atoning death, and thus ran counter to prevailing evangelical theology."[18] Sound Christology emphasized the Incarnation, which Nevin said was "the key that unlocks the sense of all God's works, and brings to light the true meaning of the universe."[19]

Nevin drew on the Pauline concepts of the first Adam and the Second Adam (I Corinthians 15) to make clear the significance of the Incarnation. The whole human race was included in the life of the first Adam. His posterity were born into his fallen nature and participate in it. Estrangement from God results. The answer to this predicament is the incarnate Christ, the Second Adam, who assumed human nature in order to take upon himself the burden of sin, to conquer sin and death, and to lift the fallen nature of the human into eternal union with God.[20] The true meaning of Christ is to be found in the whole of his incarnate life which encompasses his birth, ministry, death, descent, resurrection, ascension, and glorification.

Christianity is participation in the divine-human life of the Second Adam, a mystical union between the incarnate Christ and his people. The work of the Holy Spirit complemented by the believer's faith creates the mystical union by which God and the person are united in Christ.

Second, Nevin and Schaff charged that American Protestantism was *unchurchly*. It was permeated by a revivalism which emphasized the salvation of the individual. In their ecclesiology American Protestants, especially of the Reformed tradition, had surrendered to "Puritan and Methodistic modes of thought."[21] The church was not a human creation nor was it incidental to Christianity in Nevin's estimation. Salvation didn't lie beyond the church and outside it, but directly in its bosom. In his landmark sermon, "The Church," preached in

1846, Nevin stated, "Out of the Church . . . , or as separated from the general life of Christ in his people, there can be no true Christian character and no Christian salvation. Christianity and the Church are identical. . . ."[22] George H. Bricker summarized Nevin's view of the church as follows:

> He saw the Church not as a gathering of converted individuals but was a holy mother who imparts the new life of Christ to all her children. Salvation comes through his divine institution whose spiritual and sacramental resources mediate the new life of Christ. Christ lives in the Church and the particular members receive Christ through her. . . . What he saw in American Protestantism of his day, and especially in revivalism, was a denial of this position, which he considered fundamental in the New Testament.[23]

The Mercersburg professors were persuaded that the weak ecclesiology of most American Protestants was, at least in part, due either to their neglect or misunderstanding of the church's historical development. Schaff proposed that the history of the church be viewed organically. Each of its epochs had a place if its total life was to be apprehended. In each period God was at work governing and guiding the church according to His wisdom. Protestants should, therefore, cast aside that notion of church history which assumed there was no genuine Christianity between the early church and the Reformation.

Nevin and Schaff abhorred the multiplicity of religious "sects" in America. They denounced the subjectivistic religious experiences of persons such as Jacob Albright, Philip William Otterbein and John Winebrenner which were the foundations upon which new "sects" were established. This sectarianism divided the Body of Christ. Nevin and Schaff, on the other hand, counselled the outward and visible unity of the church. They envisioned an "evangelical Catholicism."[24]

The New Measures promoted a very weak understanding of the church. In *The Anxious Bench* Nevin fired his initial blast at the New Measures which he referred to as "the system of the bench." It was an inferior, shallow, and superficial approach to Christianity as compared to "the system of the catechism" which included sound Christian instruction, pastoral visitation and nurture, order, discipline, and the sacraments.[25]

Third, Schaff and Nevin denounced American Protestantism for being *unsacramental*. They were exceedingly distressed by interpretations which made the sacraments "mere outward signs, in the case of which all proper efficacy is supposed to be previously at hand in the inward state of the subject by whom they are received."[26] The sacraments were more than empty signs or ceremonies. They were objective transactions in which "a real spiritual energy" was conveyed to the recipient, the benefits of which are appropriated by him/her through faith.[27] The sacraments, instituted by Christ, were the chief means by which he conveyed his life and benefits to his people. They were crucial to the life of the church and to the life of the believer.

Nevin attributed the defective understanding of the sacraments to the sect system. He wrote, "Our sect system must be considered in its very nature, unfavorable to all proper respects for the sacraments. This may be taken, indeed as a just criterion of the spirit of sect, as distinguished from the true spirit of the Christian church."[28] The sects undervalued the "sacramental and objective in religion" in favor of the subjective element. Nevin was especially concerned about the Lord's Supper. If the essence of Christianity was the vital mystical union between Christ and his people, the Lord's Supper strengthened and invigorated that union. The Lord's Supper made possible a real participation in the vitality of Christ's life. Concern for the Lord's Supper was an important consideration in the formulation of a liturgy for the German Reformed Church in which Nevin and Schaff had a significant role.[29] They "championed the renewal of corporate worship to make it less subjective, less privatized, more objective, more communal, and more sacramental."[30]

Mercersburg's Quarrel With Methodism

The Mercersburg professors were not reluctant to identify one of the culprits which had led American Protestantism astray. It was Methodism. In fact, they asserted that Methodism may well have been the chief offender in the deterioration of Protestant church life in America, at least in the first half of the nineteenth century. Therefore, in various places in their writings they levelled their criticisms against the Methodists and two "sects" to which Methodism had given life, i.e., the followers of Philip William Otterbein and those of Jacob Albright. Nevin stated, "Already the *life* of Methodism, in this country, is actively at work among other sects, [for example, the United Brethren and the Evangelical Association] which owe no fellowship with it in form."[31]

Nevin and Schaff had reservations about John Wesley, the founder of Methodism. Both of them felt that Wesley was not much of a theologian. In contrast to the giants of the Reformation he was a theological lightweight. Nevin mentioned one Reformation leader alongside of whom Methodism's founder appeared grossly inferior. He wrote, "Wesley was a small man as compared with Melanchthon."[32] Schaff was not inclined to be more complimentary concerning John Wesley's theological skills. Compared to German Pietism, Methodism was deficient in spiritual depth and lacked a vigorous, fruitful and profound theology. Undoubtedly, Wesley was responsible for this situation. Schaff described him as "a pungent preacher," "a legislative genius," and "an exceedingly shrewd, skillful business man." When assessing spiritual vitality and reflection, however, Charles Wesley was more gifted than his older brother in Schaff's opinion.[33]

The Mercersburg theologians considered Methodism "the chief author and promoter of *revivals*" and camp meetings.[34] Methodism's energy and organization were devoted to this work, even to proselytizing among other churches, "thinking that it alone [could] really convert."[35] For sometime this revivalistic approach prompted the Methodists to disparage education for its preachers. Schaff observed:

> appealing to the apostles and evangelists of the primitive church, [Methodism] used to condemn learning and theology from principle, as dangerous to practical piety; and to boast, that its preachers had "never rubbed their backs against the walls of a college," and yet knew the better how to catch fish in the net of the kingdom of God.[36]

Schaff admitted, however, that Methodism had begun to change by the early 1850s and had established colleges, seminaries and periodicals to encourage its clergy to be more cultured. Parenthetically, he wondered, "whether they will not thus lose more in their peculiar character and influence with the masses, than they will gain in the more cultivated circles."[37]

Of course, a principal criticism of Methodism was its employment of the New Measures. Schaff wrote:

> In worship, Methodism is not satisfied with the usual divinely ordained means of grace. It really little understands the use of the Sacraments, though it adheres traditionally to infant baptism, and four times a year celebrates the Lord's Supper, as a simple commemoration. It has far more confidence in subjective means and exciting impressions, than in the more quiet and unobserved but surer work of the old church system of educational religion. The main point with it is always effect on the sinner by special efforts of the

preacher; and with this view it has invented and perfected, especially in America, a machinery for the purpose, altogether foreign to [German] Pietism—the system of what is called *new measures*.[38]

Schaff then listed the main features of these New Measures:

This includes not only prayer-meetings—an institution as old, by the way, as Christianity, and only invested by Methodism with a peculiar meaning and importance; but also and especially camp-meetings, commonly held in forests or under tents, often for weeks together in a good season of the year; protracted meetings, which may be held also in the church and in the winter season, and are designed to compensate for the regularly returning church festivals rejected by the Methodists, as by the Puritans; class-meetings, anxious or inquiry meetings on appointed week days for the interchange of religious experience, and a special personal conversation with anxious sinners (a kind of substitute for the Roman Catholic confessional); and finally, the anxious-bench, a genuine modern American invention, i.e., a seat before the pulpit, to which after sermon the penitent hearers are invited, and where they are pressed with special exhortations, and wrought up to the most intense nervous excitement, till the new life "breaks through," and then the sense of forgiving grace often vents itself in a jubilee of ecstacy, as boisterous as the violent lamentations, groans, and not rarely convulsions, in which the sense of sin had just before found utterance.[39]

While these New Measures may have proven themselves to be powerful means to awaken sinners and promote religious life, Schaff claimed that

in reality very much that is human and impure, mingles itself in, and these new measures have led to the most injurious outbreaks of religious fanaticism; above all they have nourished a dangerous distrust of the ordinary means of grace, the calm preaching of the Word, the sacraments, and catechetical instruction. The Methodists reject not only confirmation, as a useless or hypocritical form, but also the idea of objective baptismal grace; and they often dreadfully neglect all religious training of children, in the vain, presumptuous expectation that some exciting revival-sermon in a camp meeting or a few hours on the anxious-bench, will answer the purpose of the tedious process of parental discipline and care, and regular pastoral visitation. No wonder that, under such influences, and that in many districts where the quick straw fire of Methodistic revivals has burned brightly, it has left a complete desolation, with frivolous mockery of all religion.[40]

John Williamson Nevin's appraisal of the New Measures was virtually the same as Schaff's. The "system of the bench" was "neither Calvinism nor Lutheranism, but Wesleyan *Methodism*."[41] It was vastly inferior to the "system of the catechism" which possessed a much better comprehension of salvation, the Christian life, and the church.

Writing in 1855 Schaff acknowledged that New Measures revivalism was declining. He said,

The flourishing period of new measures is now, in general, pretty much past, and even among the Methodists the swollen stream of religious excitement seems to be again seeking its natural, fixed channels, especially in the more cultivated city congregations, which have never really approved those unwholesome excesses.[42]

Whether or not New Measures revivalism had created, it had already spawned a "sect system" which contradicted the unity of the church and supported unsound religion. In addition to Winebrenner's Church of God, Nevin and Schaff often cited two "sects" which had been conceived in the womb of Methodism, the Church of the United Brethren in Christ and the Evangelical Association, two of the denominations now incorporated into The United Methodist Church. Schaff reported:

The influence of Methodism on the Lutheran and German Reformed Church at the close of the last and beginning of the present century, produced several new sects, in doctrine, government, and worship entirely conformed to the Methodist Episcopal model. Such are the United Brethren in Christ, founded about 1800, by William Otterbein, a pious Reformed Minister from Germany; [and the] Evangelical Communion (Evangelische Gemeinschaft), commonly called the Albrecht Brethren, founded somewhat later by Jacob Albrecht, a Lutheran layman of Pennsylvania. . . .[43]

For the Mercersburg theologians a "sect" was a religious group which had been founded mainly on the subjective religious experience of one or more individuals. They objected to sects on the grounds that they were "unchurchly, unhistorical and untraditional." Schaff cynically described the founding of a sect as follows:

Anyone who has, or fancies that he has, some inward experience and a ready tongue, may persuade himself that he is called to be a reformer; and so proceed at once, in his spiritual vanity and pride, to a revolutionary rupture with the historical life of the church, to which he holds himself immeasurably superior. He builds himself of a night accordingly a new chapel, in which now for the first time since the age of the apostles a pure congregation is to be formed; baptizes his followers with his own name, to which he thus secures an immortality, unenviable it is true, but such as is always flattering to the natural heart; rails and screams with full throat against all that refuses to do homage to his standard; and with all this though utterly unprepared to understand a single book, is not ashamed to appeal continually to the Scriptures, as having been sealed entirely, or in large part, to the understanding of eighteen centuries, and even to the view of our Reformers themselves, till now at last God has been pleased to kindle the true light in an obscure corner of the New World! Thus the deceived multitude, having no power to discern spirits, is converted not to Christ and his truth, but to the arbitrary fancies and baseless opinions of an individual, who is only of yesterday. Such *conversion* is of a truth only *perversion*; such *theology*, *neology*; such *exposition* of the Bible, wretched *imposition*. What is built is no church, but a chapel, to whose erection Satan himself have made the most liberal contribution.[44]

Nevin's examination of the "sect system" in America in which the churches founded by Albright and Otterbein were frequently cited as "sect" examples, was equally as condemning as Schaff's. Nevin outlined his views in *Antichrist, or the Spirit of Sect and Schism* (1848) and in two articles published in the *Mercersburg Review* in 1849. According to Nevin the sects claimed no creed but the plain meaning of the Bible. But, if the Bible is so clear, why were there so many sects with substantially different theologies? The sects asserted the right of private judgment and theological freedom for the individual, but in reality each sect had a system of doctrine and practiced an intolerance which made a mockery of this declaration. The sects had no regard for history; each held that it was "self-sprung from the Bible, or through the Bible from the skies." The sect

> hates church tradition; will hear of no binding force in church history; but straightway manufactures a log chain of authority in the very same form, out of the little yesterday of its own life, which it binds mercilessly on the neck of all its subjects. It will have no saints or fathers; but forthwith offers us instead its own founders and leaders and makes it well nigh blasphemy to speak a word in their dispraise.[45]

The sect splits the Body of Christ. The sect spirit was theologically unstable, subject to the whims of its leaders, and unfriendly to the cultivation of theology "as a science." It was a plague of unchurchly and unsacramental religion. It had no place for sacramental grace or for the biblical concept of the holy catholic church. The sect system carried in itself only the principle of "endless disintegration."[46]

The Mercersburg theologians had a quarrel with Methodism. They charged that Methodism was responsible for much of the malaise they detected in American Protestantism prior to the Civil War. New Measures revivalism and rabid sectarianism were evidence of the unchristological, unchurchly and unsacramental nature of Methodist theology and practice.

Statements From The Defense

It is difficult to measure the effects of the Mercersburg critique within Methodism itself. The least we can observe about it is that it was not completely ignored. *The Methodist Quarterly Review*, the primary theological journal of the Methodist Episcopal Church, dealt with some of the issues raised by Nevin and Schaff in reviews of two of their books.

Nevin's *Antichrist: or the Spirit of Sect and Schism* was reviewed in *The Methodist Quarterly Review* in 1848. Unfortunately, the review is brief and tantalizing. It reads:

> That we differ from Dr. Nevin almost *toto coelo* in regard to church questions, is no reason why we should not acknowledge him as a profound thinker and an earnest man. He grapples with great questions vigorously and directly: he is no trimmer, no juste-milieu man, but an able, thoughtful, honest, and fearless Christian teacher. We hope to be able to give a general and careful review of his writings hereafter, and shall feel, in doing it, that we are dealing with a *man* and a scholar.[47]

Regrettably, the promised "careful review" never appeared.

Schaff's views were treated with more than the passing mention shown Nevin. Before examining the responses to Schaff's thoughts on Methodism, however, it should be pointed out that at least the editor of *The Methodist Quarterly Review* was not totally alienated by his remarks about his church. Between 1849 and 1858 five articles by Schaff appeared in its pages. All of them were devoted to church history and were not polemics against the denomination.[48]

The Methodist Quarterly Review carried two major articles which sought to answer the criticisms of Methodism made by Philip Schaff. The first was an extensive book review of Schaff's *America*. It was written by B.H. Nadal, a professor at Indiana Asbury University.[49] Nadal claimed that Schaff either deliberately misrepresented Methodism or sadly misunderstood it.

Nadal, first of all, dealt with Schaff's accusation that Methodism exerted great influence over the lower classes, particularly among blacks, and that in its zeal it exercised "impure motives of proselytism." The reviewer held the former criticism to be a compliment. It was "a great pity that every church [was] not fitted for the work of saving the poor and unlettered."[50] Was not Christ especially concerned for them! The charge of proselytizing, however, was reckless, false and slanderous. Methodism had simply tried to preach the Gospel and nurture the committed in places where the Christian faith was not present or where it was languishing. Methodism had "ever scorned to decoy Christians of other communions into their own. Indeed, [Methodists] have suffered more from proselytism than any other Church in the land: thousands converted among us and formerly belonging to us are now members of other Churches," he wrote.[51]

Concerning Schaff's complaint that Methodism condemned learning and theology as impairing practical piety, Nadal was startled. How could anyone familiar with the Wesleys or Methodist history make such a statement? From the beginning Wesley urged his preachers to read and learn. The first *Discipline* directed the preachers to spend at least five hours each day in study. Coke, Asbury, Emory, Hedding and Bangs were hardly leaders with a dislike for education and theology. And how could one account for the birth of Cokesbury College among a group of people so hostile to education? Nadal concluded that Methodism had "always insisted with equal earnestness, that those who are called to the work of the ministry are bound to do their utmost to cultivate their minds and to acquire knowledge, especially that which pertains to their holy calling."[52] Furthermore, contrary to Schaff's allegations, Methodist clergy were no more prone to conceit and vanity when they acquired "a little learning" than the clergy of other churches. Not conceit and vanity, but "earnestness and simplicity" were the characteristics which qualified a person for the Methodist ministry.[53]

Next Nadal took up Schaff's disparagement of the Methodist emphasis on "experimental Christianity." Nadal's comment was brief:

We do indeed, with Jesus and the apostles, insist on experimental Christianity, repentance and the new birth; we labour to bring on the battle of repentance, and rejoice in the pangs of the spiritual birth, but we teach nothing in regard to the specific amount of any kind of feeling whatever—just the reverse indeed—we pretend to have no mystical

thermometer by which to determine the spiritual temperature either of the renewed or the penitential state.[54]

Schaff had distorted Methodist attitudes toward the "ordinary means of grace." Methodists, Nadal replied, revered baptism and the Lord's Supper, even if they had not shown their " 'practical religious respect for Rome' and Mercersburg, by adopting the doctrines of baptismal regeneration and the *real spiritual presence*."[55] Methodists used no means of grace which was substantially new. Camp meetings, prayer meetings and class meetings simply employed the ancient practices of preaching, praying, singing and counseling. Even the mourner's bench was merely a place to sing, to pray and to point the struggling sinner to the Savior. Nadal said,

Substantially, then, the Methodists use the means of grace instituted by Christ, and *them only*; and the objections brought against them in this connexion, relate exclusively to non-essential circumstances, such as, that the preaching, the praying, the singing, etc., are done in a grove, in a private house, or at a certain bench or altar, or on a weekday. Concerning these circumstances the apostles and the private Christians of their day were as little careful as the Methodists. . . .[56]

Likewise, counter to Schaff's assertion, the Methodists did not neglect the religious education of the young. Their preachers were required by the *Discipline* to instruct the children, to organize Sunday schools wherever possible, to catechize, and to counsel youth on "experimental and practical godliness."[57]

In his review Nadal was not content merely to defend Methodism from Schaff's attack. His response also contained a few caustic comments about the Mercersburg Theology which Nadal described as "mystical and metaphysical." He noted that the clergy of the German Reformed Church were having difficulty mastering "this new system." He said,

most of her ministers seem to move like a man bearing about him a concealed treasure, of which he knows neither the value nor the exact whereabouts, though he is pretty sure he had it somewhere. The general impression is, that however clearly Drs. Nevin and Schaff may be able to see in this newly-imported, hazy, German, doctrinal atmosphere, the great body of their ministers are befogged by their "too little learning;" and hence with a discretion scarcely to be expected in this country of independent thought, they have mostly yielded themselves in unreasoning and dutiful silence to the guidance of authority, and by tacit consent have left both the promulgation and defence of the new theology to their two great leaders. But while with the majority the effect of the new teaching has been thus repressive and sedative, with a considerable number who think they see bottom through the deep or muddy waters, it has been far otherwise; and where a learned professor might have presented to his audience a body of smoke in a robe of moonshine, and supplied by rhetorical and metaphysical gymnastics what was lacking in solid doctrine, these poor fellows only grope and flounder.[58]

Nadal's review stirred a published response by John McClintock, former editor of *The Methodist Quarterly Review*. McClintock reproved Nadal for misjudging Schaff's interpretation of Methodism. Schaff did not mean to vilify Methodism as Nadal had charged.[59] In reply to McClintock, however, Nadal reiterated his persuasion that Schaff's description of Methodism in *America* was intentionally designed to injure his church.[60]

A second article which appeared in *The Methodist Quarterly Review* was written by William Nast (1807-1889), prominent Methodist and editor of *Der Christliche Apologete*, a German language Methodist publication. Nast was troubled by Schaff's "repeated assaults upon German Methodism," particularly in *Der Deutsche Kirchenfreund*.[61] He resented the injurious and unfair comments about Methodism which Schaff permitted to be printed in this theological monthly. Nast complained that Schaff had unjustly made two attacks on Methodism.

First, Schaff had singled out German Methodists as an example of "barbarous Christianity." Schaff alleged that their worship was "fanatical and chaotic," especially at camp meetings. Furthermore, the German Methodists were characterized in Schaff's words as,

an opposition to culture of mind and learning, an opposition which springs not from humility, but mostly from an overbearing contempt of others, and from intellectual imbecility, and which results too often in the ruin of a practical religious life, and trains up a wild, unrestrained youth; then the uncharitable anathematizing of the denominations, as if there was no piety at all to be found in them, because they have not adopted the new measures; again the perversion of justification by faith into a justification by feeling; in short, the one-sided conception of Christianity as an indistinct matter of feeling, while true Christianity aims to pervade equally and harmoniously the *whole* man and all the faculties of the soul; the extravagant importance put upon self-invented means of conversion, and a conscious or unconscious depreciation of the regular, divinely ordained means of grace, especially of the sacraments, which in their

system become empty signs and ceremonies; finally, the doctrine of the attainability in this life of a moral perfection, which rests on a Pelagian basis ignoring the deep abyss of sin and nourishing the most dangerous kind of pride, spiritual vanity, [and] pharisaism.[62]

Second, Schaff had personally assailed Nast and *Der Christliche Apologete* in his *Kirchenfreund*. Schaff referred to Nast and his publication as "a spiritless (insipid) paper, full of unsalted piety and vain praises of camp meetings and awakenings, . . . ignoble and Jesuitical in his polemics, robbing his colleagues frequently of articles without giving credit, but otherwise caring little for what takes place in Christendom, except where it suits his purpose."[63]

Nast's reply to Schaff's charges asserted that by Schaff's admission he had little first-hand knowledge of German Methodism. Schaff's caricature was misleading. Citing one Methodist doctrine which Schaff had mentioned, Nast wrote,

How much more worthy of a theological professor and of the editor of a learned theological periodical would it have been, if Professor Schaff, instead of making groundless and ignominious charges against the Methodists, had thoroughly reviewed, examined, and refuted that Methodistical doctrine of Christian perfection, which appears to him so unsound and dangerous, . . . or, indeed, any of our doctrines and usages, as they are set forth in our books and tracts.[64]

Nast judged that Nadal's critical review of Schaff's *America* was a fair assessment of Schaff's bias against Methodism. Although Schaff was a man of great learning, Nast lamented his misinformation about Methodism and his distorted judgments of it.[65]

The charges of the Mercersburg theologians were not unnoticed and unanswered. A few Methodist writers issued responses, but their replies did not result in any further apparent theological argument between Methodism and Mercersburg. Perhaps one reason for this was the Mercersburg professors' preoccupation with addressing attacks on their views within their own church. Their christological, ecclesiological, liturgical and sacramental ideas stirred considerable controversy within the German Reformed Church.[66]

Conclusion

There is no question that there was a real quarrel between the Mercersburg theologians and Methodism. Nevin and Schaff were the proponents of views which were much different from those of American Methodists, especially with regard to ecclesiology and evangelism.

Recent history has proven that the judgments which Nevin and Schaff made regarding Methodism and the sect system, especially Methodism's spawning the Evangelical Association and the United Brethren in Christ, may have been too severe. The Evangelical United Brethren union of 1946 and the United Methodist union of 1968 are but two testimonies of an ecumenical spirit which they did not foresee. They were wrong in some other opinions as well such as their sweeping and incorrect condemnation of Methodism as uninterested in education for its clergy or laity. The early and sustained activities of Methodism in this area are well documented.

There is at least one major question to be raised about the Mercersburg quarrel with Methodism. There are hints of it in the Methodist replies to Schaff. How well did Nevin and Schaff know Wesley's theology? There is little, if any, evidence that they were acquainted with his writings. It seems, rather, that their judgments about Methodism were formed on their observations of American Methodist practices and, even then, perhaps on a limited sampling of Methodist customs. Had they a deeper knowledge of Wesley they might have been somewhat appeased by his love and respect for the early church fathers which they too shared, his understanding of the sacraments as more than "empty signs and ceremonies," and his high regard for liturgy. Their criticism of American Methodism may have included another dimension, i.e., the manner in which American Methodism had strayed from the theology of its founder.

NOTES

(This essay also appeared in *Methodist History* and is published here with permission.)

1. Winthrop Hudson, *Religion in America* (New York: Charles Scribner's Sons, 1965), 141-145.
2. Richard Carwardine, "The Second Great Awakening in the Urban Centers: An Examination of Methodism and the New Measures," *The Journal of American History*, LIX (September, 1972), 327-340.
3. *Encyclopedia of World Methodism* (Nashville: The United Methodist Publishing House, 1974), II, 2712.
4. Bard Thompson, *et al.*, *Essays on The Heidelberg Catechism* (Philadelphia: United Church Press, 1963), 54-55.
5. For more about Winebrenner see Richard Kern, *John Winebrenner: 19th Century Reformer* (Harrisburg, PA: Central Publishing House, 1974).
6. There have been a number of works published over the past 25 years which describe the Mercersburg Theology and contain representative writings of its major figures. E.g., James Hastings Nichols, *Romanticism in American Theology* (Chicago: The University of Chicago Press, 1961), James Hastings Nichols, editor, *The Mercersburg Theology* (New York: Oxford University Press, 1966),

Philip Schaff, *The Principle of Protestantism*, edited by Bard Thompson and George H. Bricker (Philadelphia: United Church Press, 1964), John Williamson Nevin, *The Mystical Presence and Other Writings on the Eucharist*, edited by Bard Thompson and George H. Bricker (Philadelphia: United Church Press, 1966), Charles Yrigoyen, Jr. and George H. Bricker, editors, *Catholic and Reformed: Selected Theological Writings of John Williamson Nevin* (Pittsburgh: Pickwick Press, 1978), and Charles Yrigoyen, Jr. and George H. Bricker, editors, *Reformed and Catholic: Selected Historical and Theological Writings of Philip Schaff* (Pittsburgh: Pickwick Press, 1979).
7. See especially the second edition (Chambersburg, PA: Publication Office of the German Reformed Church, 1844).
8. (Philadelphia: Lippincott, 1846).
9. (Chambersburg: Publication Office of the German Reformed Church, 1847).
10. (New York: Taylor, 1848).
11. Mercersburg: Mish, 1849).
12. John B. Payne, "Philip Schaff: Christian Scholar, Historian and Ecumenist," *Christian Intelligencer*, II (Fall, 1982), 17.
13. (Chambersburg: Publication Office of the German Reformed Church, 1845).
14. (Philadelphia: Lippincott, 1846).
15. (New York: Scribner, 1853).
16. (New York: Scribner, 1855). Hereafter referred to as *America*.
17. Nevin, *The Mystical Presence and Other Writings on the Eucharist*, 214-215. Hereafter referred to as *The Mystical Presence*.
18. *The Mercersburg Theology*, 78.
19. Nevin, *The Mystical Presence*, 201.
20. Nevin, *The Mystical Presence*, 214-215.
21. Emanuel V. Gerhart, "The German Reformed Church," *Bibliotheca Sacra and Biblical Repository*, XX (January, 1863), 33.
22. Nichols, *The Mercersburg Theology*, 60.
23. *A Brief History of the Mercersburg Movement* (Lancaster: Lancaster Theological Seminary, 1982), 13.
24. Bricker, *A Brief History of the Mercersburg Movement*, 14. Schaff used the term "Protestant Catholicism" in *The Principle of Protestantism*. 230.
25. Yrigoyen and Bricker, *Catholic and Reformed*, 89-126.
26. Nevin, *The Mystical Presence*, 92.
27. Nevin, *The Mystical Presence*, 108.
28. Nevin, *The Mystical Presence*, 92.
29. See Jack Maxwell, *Worship and Reformed Theology: The Liturgical Lessons of Mercersburg* (Pittsburgh: Pickwick Press, 1976).
30. Payne, "Philip Schaff: Christian Scholar, Historian and Ecumenist," 18.
31. Yrigoyen and Bricker, *Catholic and Reformed*, 13.
32. Yrigoyen and Bricker, *Catholic and Reformed*, 13.
33. Schaff, *America*, 170.
34. Schaff, *America*, 166-167.
35. Schaff, *America*, 167.
36. Schaff, *America*, 167-168.
37. Schaff, *America*, 168.
38. Schaff, *America*, 173.
39. Schaff, *America*, 173-174.
40. Schaff, *America*, 175.
41. Yrigoyen and Bricker, *Catholic and Reformed*, 12.
42. Schaff, *America*, 176.
43. Schaff, *America*, 204.
44. Schaff, *The Principle of Protestantism*, 149-150.
45. Yrigoyen and Bricker, *Catholic and Reformed*, 164-165.
46. Yrigoyen and Bricker, *Catholic and Reformed*, 173.
47. *The Methodist Quarterly Review*, VIII (October, 1848), 638.
48. The articles were "The Preparation For Christianity in the History of the World, A Proof of its Divine Origin," XXXII (July, 1849), 429-447 and (October, 1849), 542-552; "The Government and Discipline of the Apostolic Church," XXXIII (July 1851), 429-445 and (October, 1851), 574-600; and "The Oldest Opposition to Christianity, and Its Defense," XL (October, 1858),

605-624.

49. B. H. Nadal, "Schaff on America," *The Methodist Quarterly Review*, XVI (January, 1856), 122-144.
50. Nadal, "Schaff on America," 132.
51. Nadal, "Schaff on America," 134-135.
52. Nadal, "Schaff on America," 136-137.
53. Nadal, "Schaff on America," 139.
54. Nadal, "Schaff on America," 139-40.
55. Nadal, "Schaff on America," 141.
56. Nadal, "Schaff on America," 141-142.
57. Nadal, "Schaff on America," 142-143.
58. Nadal, "Schaff on America," 138.
59. Letter from John McClintock, *The Methodist Quarterly Review*, XVII (January, 1857), 125-126.
60. Letter from B. H. Nadal, *The Methodist Quarterly Review*. XVII (April, 1857), 296-298.
61. William Nast, "Dr. Schaff on Methodism," *The Methodist Quarterly Review*, XVII (July, 1857), 428.
62. Nast, "Dr. Schaff on Methodism," 431.
63. Nast, "Dr. Schaff on Methodism," 432.
64. Nast, "Dr. Schaff on Methodism," 434.
65. Nast, "Dr. Schaff on Methodism," 435-436.
66. See Nichols, *Romanticism in American Theology,* for a description of the debate.

Samantha and her Sisters: Images of Women in the Writings of Marietta Holley

Phyllis Tholin
National Women's Caucus, The United Methodist Church

Nineteenth-century women involved in the ferment over women's rights approached the issue from widely divergent perspectives of woman's nature, woman's sphere, woman's role, and the suitability of particular forms of education for women. Most of these perspectives were informed by understandings of Christian or Judaic concepts of creation, personhood, and social responsibility. Proponents of woman suffrage, as well as the opponents, called upon their religious faith to provide the ammunition for the fight.

One strong proponent of woman's rights was Marietta Holley. Her name is rarely recognized today, but her writings, under the pseudonymn of "Josiah Allen's Wife," were a well-known aspect of popular culture from about 1870-1920. Her humorous narrative sketches appeared in *Peterson's* and later in the *Ladies' Home Journal, Leslie's Weekly*, Will Carleton's *Every Where, The Christian Herald*, and others, and her books were widely sold by traveling book agents who carried them into remote rural as well as urban areas. Holley was a member of the Methodist Episcopal Church and a strong advocate of woman suffrage, temperance, and other reform movements of the late ninteenth century. Her ability to write appealingly about ordinary people and situations and to carry on her crusades in a popular form of dialect humor endeared her to a wide range of readers.

But Holley differed from many of the popular humorists who preceded her or were her contemporaries in that she had a cause, and she used her humor as a weapon to fight for that cause. The best introduction to Marietta Holley and her cause is her own writings. The following excerpt is taken from *Samantha Among the Brethren* written in 1890 to express her disagreement with the M.E. Church position on the role of women. In it the controversy of 1888 over the seating of women as lay delegates to the General Conference goes on in the context of the Jonesville Meetin' House where women provide the physical energy and financial support that keep the church alive while the "male deacons" bicker among themselves and withhold their contributions.

It (the General Conference) begin to set in New York the very day we tackled the meetin' in Jonesville with a extra grip.

So's I can truly say, the Meetin' House was on me day and night. For workin' on it es I did, all day long, and Josiah a-talkin' abut it till bed time, and I a-dreamin' abut it a sight, that, and the Conference.

Truly, if I couldn't set on the Conference, the Conference sot on me, from mornin' till night, and from night till mornin' . . . .

Josiah would set with the *World* and other papers in his hand, a-perusin' of 'em, while I would be a-washin' up my dishes, and the very minute I would get 'em done and my sleeves rolled down, he would tackle me, and often he wouldn't wait for me to get my work done up, or even supper got, but would begin on me es I filled up my teakettle, and keep up a stiddy drizzle of argument till bed time, and es I say, when he left off, the nite mairs would begin.

I suffered beyond tellin' almost.

The secent night of my arjeus labors on the meetin' house, he began wild and eloquent about wimmen bein' on Conferences and mountin' rostrums. And sez he, "That is suthin' that we Methodist men can't stand."

And I, havin' stood up on a barell all day a-scrapin' the ceilin', and not bein' recuperated yet from the skairtness and dizziness of my day's work, I sez to him:

"Is rostrums much higher than them barells we have to stand on to the meetin' house?"

And Josiah said, "it was suthin altogether diffrunt." And he assured me agin,

"That in any modest unpretendin' way the Methodist Church was willin' to accept wimmen's work. It wasn't aginst the Discipline. And that is why," sez he, "that wimmen have all through the ages been allowed to do most all the hard work on the church—such as raisin' money for church work—earnin' money in all sorts of ways to carry on different kinds of charity work connected with it—teachin' the children, nursin' the sick, carryin' on hospital work, etc .etc. But" sez he, "this is far, far different from gettin' up on a rostrum, or tryin' to set on a Conference. Why," sez he, in a haughty tone, "I should think they'd know without havin' to be told that laymen don't mean women."

Sez I, "Then many laymen that are tryin' to keep wimmen out of the Conference wouldn't have got in themselves if it hadn't been for wimmen's votes.

If they can legally vote for men to get in, why can't men vote for them?"

"That is the pint," sez Josiah, "that is the very pint I have been tryin' to explain to you. Wimmen can help men to office, but men can't help wimmen; that is the law, that is statesmanship. I have been a-tryin' to explain it to you that the word laymen *always* means woman when she can help men in any way, but *not* when he can help her, or in any other sense."

Sez I, "It seemed to mean wimmen when Metilda Henn wuz turned out of the meetin' house."

"Oh, yes," sez Josiah in a reasonin' tone, "the word laymen always means wimmen when it is used in a punishin' and condemnatory sense, or in the case of work, and so fourth, but when it comes to settin' up in high places, or drawin' sallerys, or anything else difficult, it alweys means men."

Sez I, in a very dry axent, "Then the word man, when it is used in church matters, always means wimmen, so far es scrubbin' is concerned, and drowdgin' around?"

"Yes," sez Josiah haughtily. "And it always means men on the higher and more difficult matters of decidin' questions, drawin' sallerys, settin' on Conferences, etc. It has long been settled to be so," sez he.

"Who settled it?" sez I.

"Why the men, of course," sez he. "The men have always made the rules of the churches, and translated the Bibles, and everything else that is difficult," sez he. Sez I, in fearful dry axents, almost pesky ones, "It seems to take quite a knack to know jest when the word laymen means men and when it means wimmen."

"That is so," sez Josiah. "It takes a man's mind to grapple with it; wimmen's minds are too weak to tackle it. It is jest es it is with the word 'men' in the Declaration of Independence. Now that word 'men' in that Declaration, means men some of the time, and some of the time men and wimmen both. It means both sexes when it relates to punishment, taxin' property, obeyin' laws strictly, etc., etc., and then it goes right on the very next minute and means men only, as to wit, namely, votin', takin' charge of public matters, makin' laws, etc.

"I tell you it takes deep minds to foller on and see jest to a hair where the division is made. It takes statesmanship.

"Now take the claws, 'All men are born free and equal.'

"Now half of that means men, and the other half men and wimmen. Now to understand them words perfect you have got to divide the sex. 'Men are born.' That means men and wimmen both—men and wimmen are both born, nobody can dispute that. Then comes the next claws, 'Free and equal.' Now that means men only—anybody with one eye can see that.

"Then the claws, 'True government consists.' That means men and wimmen both—consists—of course the government consists of men and

wimmen, 'twould be a fool who would dispute that. 'In the consent of the governed.' That means men alone. Do you see, Samantha?" sez he.

I kep' my eye fixed on the tea kettle, fer I stood with my tea-pot in hand waitin' for it to bile—"I see a great deal, Josiah Allen."[1]

Holley's memoirs, published serially after her death in her hometown newspaper, provide scant information about her early life. She was the youngest of seven children born to a pioneer farm family in upstate New York. The farm near Pierrepont Manor, just east of Lake Ontario and south of the St. Lawrence, was her home from her birth in 1836 to her death in 1926. Her formal schooling ended at age fourteen when she began to earn some money for her family by giving piano lessons. She continued to read when she could, borrowing books from a neighbor's library, and tried her hand at writing poetry. Her early poems, signed "Jemima" were published in the local newspaper. In 1867 she began to write for *Peterson's* and in 1871 her first sketch under the name "Josiah Allen's Wife" was published there.

She then submitted three sketches to the publisher Elijah Bliss, president of the American Publishing Company which was then publishing the works of Mark Twain, Bret Harte, Josh Billings, Joaquin Miller, and other popular writers, and asked him if he wanted her to write a book. Much to her surprise and dismay he chose the Samantha format. Holley would have preferred a more conventional romance or a book of poetry, and was convinved that no one would buy or read Samantha. But encouraged by Bliss, she wrote *My Opinions and Betsey Bobbett's*. This book, published in 1873, was enthusiastically received. She continued to write sketches for *Peterson's*, incorporating most of them in her later books.

With the proceeds from her early writing she was able to make much needed improvements in the family "cottage," a matter she reports later with pride. As her writing brought fame and financial success, she was able to build a grand new home with elaborate gardens near the original farmhouse. She often spent time in New York City, and cultivated a select group of literary friends, among them Rose Cleveland, Ella Wheeler Wilcox, Mrs. Frank Leslie, Clara Barton, and the Will Carletons. Her memoirs, however, give us few hints as to the genesis of her strong feminist consciousness or the social awareness and sensitivity that characterized her writings. Nor does she refer to her conversion to her Methodist faith (her father, at least, was a Unitarian) except to remark that her extreme shyness in public, a trait that continued with her throughout her life, made the required public testimony when she joined the church a painful experience.

But if Marietta Holley was extraordinarily shy, she was an able student of human nature. Through Samantha Allen she was able to project her insights into the foibles of men and women and to preach her sermons to the world. That she chose humor and caricature as her media made the sermonizing more acceptable to her audience. That she used "Josiah Allen's Wife" to deliver her message, made her a more credible proponent of woman's rights. She reflects in her memoirs:

I might have thought my comments would be received more graciously and it would soften somewhat the edge of unwelcome argument to have the writer meekly claim to be the wife of Josiah Allen, and so to stand in the shadow of a man's personality. . . . The plain common sense woman devoted to her home and home duties, was still desirous of claiming all the just rights belonging to our common humanity, while in Betsey Bobbett was portrayed the lackadaisical romantic female who, in an endeavor to please the forever masculine, professed herself willing to not have any rights at all.[2]

Holley's alter ego may *claim* to stand meekly behind her husband, but there is nothing meek nor overshadowed in the portrayal of Samantha. Yet in the preface and dedication of her first book, Josiah Allen's Wife establishes her credentials as a loyal, loving and responsible wife. The book is dedicated to "My own lawful Pardner, Josiah, Whom, (although I have been his consort for a little upwards of 14 years) I still love with a Cast-Iron Devotedness." Further credentials are spelled out in the preface:

In the first days of our married life, I strained nearly every nerve to help my companion along and take care of his children by his former consort, the subject of black African slavery also wearin' on me, and a mortgage of 200 and 50 dollars on the farm. But as we prospered and the mortgage was cleared, and the children were off to school, the black African also bein' liberated about the same time of the mortgage, then my mind bein' free from these cares—the great subject of Wimmen's Rites kept a-goarin' me, and a voice kept a sayin' inside of me,
"Josiah Allen's Wife, write a book givin' your views on the great subject of Wimmen's Rites."[3]

She is, then, established as faithful wife and dutiful mother. Her own child, we later learn, has died, but she has done her duty by her two step-children and loves them as her own. The grandchildren who appear in subsequent volumes she adores and idealizes as grandparents traditionally do. But it is against the figure of Josiah that Samantha's ideas become credible, and their relationship embodies the complex traditions of marriage. They are often antagonists: she a supporter of women's rights, he very much the male chauvinist; she sensible and rational, he sentimental and filled with wild ideas which he romantically clings to; she "equinomical" but generous, he stingy ("clost") but often foolishly spending money on a project rooted in his own vanity. She often manipulates him, softening him with food and flattery (since she can't vote she has no other means for accomplishing her ends) and he readily falls into her carefully planned traps.

It is from these polarizations that Holley derives much of her humor, but she is always careful to show the bond of love between the two "pardners". Samantha's loyalty to Josiah is firm and her love for him is genuine, the more so because he so rarely deserves it. Sentimental idealizations of the married state by single or married persons are often the targets of Samantha's common sense sermonizing, and the ups and downs of every-day married life provide many humorous scenes, but Samantha takes her marriage and her husband seriously and she loves Josiah in spite of his silly chauvinism because that is the nature of " pardners."

Samantha's credibility is further established as an excellent cook and an efficient and hard-working household manager. Early in *My Opinions* Holley establishes a bond between Samantha and the harried housewives of the day who were among her readers. In this passage, Samantha chats with Betsy Bobbett and looks after a neighbor's twin toddlers while attending to her Monday morning chores: Betsy Bobbett is speaking as we listen to the dialogue.

I have always felt that it was women's highest speah, her only mission to soothe, to cling, to smile, to coo. I have always felt it, and for yeah's back it has been a growin' on me. I feel that you do not feel as I do in this matter, you do not feel that it is woman's greatest privilege, her crowning blessing, to soothe lacerations, to be a sort of a poultice to the noble, manly breast when it is torn with the cares of life."

This was too much in the agitated frame of mind I then was.
"Am I a poultice, Betsy Bobbett, do I look like one?—am I in the condition to be one?" I cried turnin' my face, red and drippin' with prespiration towards her, and then attacked one of Josiah's shirt sleeves agin. "What has my sect done" says I, as I

wildly rubbed his shirt sleeves, "That they have got to be lacerator soothers when they have got everything else under the sun to do?" Here I stirred down the preserves that was a runnin' over, and turned a pail ful of syrup into the sugar kettle. "Everybody says that men are stronger than women, and why should they be treated as if they was glass china, liable to break all to pieces if they haint handled careful. And if they have got to be soothed," says I in an agitated tone, caused by my emotions (and by pumpin' 6 pails of water to fill up the biler), "Why don't they get men to sooth' em? They have as much agin time as wimmen have; evenin's they don't have anything else to do, they might jest as well be a soothin' each other as to be hangin' round grocery stores or settin' by the fire whittlin'."

I see I was frightenin' her by my delerious tone and I continued more mildly, as I stirred down the strugglin' sugar with one hand—removed a cake from the oven with the other—watched my apple preserves with a eagle vision, and listened intently to the voice of the twins, who was playin' in the woodhouse.

"I had jest as soon soothe lacerations as not, Betsey, if I hadn't anything else to do. I had jest as lives set down and smile at Josiah by the hour, but who would fry him nutcakes? I could smoothe down his bald head affectionately, but who would do off this batch of sugar? I could coo at him day in and day out, but who would skim milk—wash pans—get vittles—wash and iron—and patch and scour—and darn and fry—and make and mend—and bake and bile while I was a cooin', tell me?" says I . . .

A pause enshued durin' which I bent over the washtub and rubbed with all my might on Josiah's shirt sleeve. I had got one sleeve so I could see streaks of white in it, . . . and I lifted up my face and continued in still more reasonable tones, as I took out my rice puddin' and cleaned out the bottom of the oven. . . .

"Now Josiah Allen will go out into that lot," says I, glancin' out of the north window "and plow right straight along, furrow after furrow, no sweat of mind about it at all; his mind is in that free calm state that he could write poetry."

. . . "Now I, a workin' jest as hard as he accordin' to my strength, and havin' to look 40 ways to once, and 40 different strains on my mind, now tell me candidly, Betsey Bobbett, which is in the best condition for cooin', Josiah Allen or me? but it haint expected of him," says I in agitated tones, "I am expected to do all the smilin' and cooin' there is done, though you know," says I sternly, "that I haint no time for it."[4]

In the pragmatic concerns of day to day existence Samantha is the realist, winning her arguments with a sane and rational presentation of evidence, while Josiah is the impractical visionary. In matters of the spirit, however, it is Samantha whose faith in the unseen is stronger, while Josiah is the skeptic, often disputing the supernatural phenomena of the spiritual realm which she accepts.[5] Both are members of the Methodist Meetin' House and Josiah is a deacon (a largely ceremonial position) but it is Samantha who continually tends to his morals as well as her own and whenever she is able, she assumes the responsibility of guarding him from temptation. Josiah's Biblical interpretations are usually mis-interpretations (e.g. his sermon on sensible giving based on the story of the widow's "mit")[6] but Samantha knows the "skriptur" well and quotes it frequently to substantiate her positions. Whether she is arguing with Josiah or with Horace Greeley or with a Washington senator, her use of scripture is reminiscent of Elizabeth Cady Stanton and her Revising Committee.

But if Samantha is a faithful Methodist, she is also an ecumenist, and this undoubtedly strengthens her appeal to a broad readership. At one point in *Saratoga* she preaches to Josiah that the ways to heaven may lead by "blue Presbyterian paths, or Methodist pasters, or by the Baptist boat, or the Episcopalian high way or the Catholic covered way, or Unitarian Broadway, or the Shadow road of Spiritualism. . . ."[7] She is vehemently anti-Mormon and directs a more good-natured criticism at a sect resembling the Millerites, but accepts the spectrum of mainline Christian experience as both valid and valuable.

Samantha's crusading zeal does not end with women's rights, but embraces a wide range of 19th century reforms. Temperance is a major cause for her and she clearly sees it as a woman's issue related to voting and property rights for women. She expounds freely on the South and its treatment of blacks in the post Civil War period and reaches the conclusion that, since southern whites will not change their attitudes, the best hope for peace and dignity for blacks lies in government financed African colonization for those who wish to return. She is a proponent of better treatment for Native Americans, better housing for the immigrant poor, safety standards for public transportation, and economic justice for workers. Through it all runs the assumption, popular among the 19th century suffrage movement, that if women could vote they would immediately address all the ills and inequities of society.

However ardent her crusading spirit, Samantha takes pride in being "mejum." By this she means medium or moderate, as well as sensible and calm. The term is never meant to imply that she is half-hearted in her convictions nor in her efforts, but rather that her means are reasonable and her demeanor dignified. While she is sometimes carried away by her own enthusiasm and oratory ("soarin'" or "episodin" she calls it), she soon recalls herself to a sober and practical course.

Holley was often invited to readings of her material given by elocutionists. She rarely approved of their dramatizations of Samantha, since they usually failed to understand this one aspect of her character. Holley perceived Samantha as neither tragic nor bizarre, but "a combination of earnestness, commonsense and calmness." In fact it was and is her constant endeavor to be "mejum" herself and influence her excitable partner to be also.[8]

While Josiah is the primary figure against which Samantha's ideas are set, Holley also portrays a number of women who represent traditional ideas of woman's role. Betsey Bobbett especially is such a prototype. Betsey is silly, sentimental, and romantic, an unattractive spinster who is constantly bemoaning her single state and shamelessly pursuing every widower and bachelor in sight. She sees woman's worth measured only through her man, and her only worthwhile role as a "clinging vine" who must have an oak to cling to. When Betsey finally snares an aged widower, poor, shiftless and ailing, with thirteen children, her life becomes one of pain and drudgery. Not only must she care for her husband and stepchildren, but she also "works out" at housework to earn a bit of money to feed and clothe them all. Yet she maintains the fantasy that the honor of being "Mrs." is worth it all.

Betsey considers herself a poet, and her atrocious verse frequently appears in one of the local newspapers. Sometime after her marriage she expresses her misery in one of her poems:

> I count it true from spring to fall,
> 'Tis better to be wed, and groan,
> Than never to be wed at all.
> I'd work my hands down to the bone
> Rather than rest a maiden lone.

Further on she seems to find a solution:

> And sweeter yet, oh blessed lot!
> O state most dignified and blest!
> To be a widder calmly sot,
> And have both dignity and rest.[9]

Holley makes Betsey both a tragic and comic figure, but the attitudes she mirrors are no less real. Samantha's conversations with her provide many opportunities for little sermons about women's rights or women's roles.[10]

There are a number of other women who personify these same attitudes. Among them are the "auntys" who actively oppose woman suffrage. One is Drusilla Sypher, who is so "dretfully fond" of her husband, the deacon, that she monograms her linens MDS for Miss Deacon Sypher. Another is the Wider Doodle who spends months weeping and mourning the death of her last husband until she finds a new widower to comfort. That the widow's past life does not seem so idyllic to Samantha is apparent in the following account of her early morning conversation with the deceased (as passed on to us by Samantha).

"... he would say:
"'Dolly, I love to dream about you.'
"'Do you, Mr. Doodle?' says I.
"'Yes,' says he, 'and it seems jest as if I want to go to sleep and have another nap, jest a purpose to dream about you.'
"And so I would git up and cut the kindlin' wood, and build the fire, and feed the cows, and go round the house a gettin' breakfast, as still as a mice so's not to disturb him, and he'd lay and sleep til I got the coffee turned out, then he'd git up and tell me his dream. It would be all about how pretty I was, and how much he loved me and how he would die for my sake any time to keep the wind for blowin' too hard onto me. And he would eat jest as hearty and enjoy himself dretfully. Oh! we took a sight of comfort together me and Mr. Doodle did. And I can't never forget him."[11]

Holley also finds targets for her humor among women who are slaves to fashion. Much of *Saratoga* is devoted to what she calls "racin' after fashion," a pun on the fashionable horse-racing, water-cure set at Saratoga Springs. This volume, illustrated by Opper, was probably her most popular and least political book. In it she satirizes women who lavish attention on their lap dogs and turn their children over to nursemaids, as well as those who squeeze themselves into unhealthful corsets, uncomfortable shoes, and hobble skirts for the sake of fashion. She also extends her satire to women who take on the strenuous social life of the resort as a "rest" and some of the fashionable conventions such as flirting.

But all of Holley's characters are not caricatures. Both in *Sweet Cicely* and in *Samantha on the Race Problem* we find a woman who is not a comic character but who is pictured as having all the desirable attributes of womanhood and who is also a leader and reformer. Cicely is described as "prettier and purer and sweeter than any posy that ever grew... and she knew so much too, and was so womanly and quiet and deep." And later, "She would give all, dare all, endure all for them she loved."[12] As a mother she devotes all of her energy and means to the well-being of her son, and she works tirelessly to assure a future society in which he can live without the temptations of alcohol. Like Frances Willard, she sees alcohol as a systemic and economic evil to be conquered through political means, and prohibition as a way to save the family. While Holley seems to have no interest in drawing explicit parallels between Cicely and Willard, she presents Cicely as the personification, in a frail feminine form, of Willard's motto "For God and Home and Native Land."

Genieve heroine of *Samantha on the Race Problem*, is depicted with a similar womanliness and beauty, and with the same bravery and dedication, willing, as was Cicely, to devote her life and fortune to her cause. Her vision is one of safety and dignity for her people through a return to their African homeland. When her fiance is killed by a Klan bullet, she goes on to establish a community and sees her dream actualized. Both of these portrayals are somewhat sentimentalized, but compared to the emotional extravagance of much 19th century fiction, and especially to the dramatic language of temperance fiction of the time, they seem "mejum" indeed.

Sweet Cicely is also the book in which Holley defines most clearly the injustices of the law in relation to women. Here woman is shown as victim, helpless to save herself against the evils of greed and power used by men. A family of women is pictured in a variety of desperate predicaments as a result of discriminatory laws. Their property is taken from them by scheming, shiftless, or drunken husbands; their children are willed to the custody of relatives; they are taxed higher than their male colleagues; they are not allowed to defend themselves in court; they are beaten by husbands, imprisoned in their homes, denied control of their own property. But the predominant oppression is alcohol-related. Woman is victim of the self-serving economic and political interests that protect the whiskey trade. Though she is morally the stronger sex, she suffers inordinately because man is weak and easily tempted. In order to protect themselves and their children from poverty and abuse, women must structure a world in which men are shielded from the temptation to drink.

Holley's analysis of the role of women in society is consistent throughout her writings, but it is most clearly demonstrated in *Samantha Among the Brethren*. Here she takes on the role of women in the church. Though women may be the victims of society, in *Brethren* they are also the backbone of the social structure. In one of the most moving passages of all her books, she describes the sisters gathering to bring what contributions each can for the church fair. They need to raise $300 for the preacher's salary which is in arrears because the deacons have had a disagreement and refuse to pay. These women who must earn for themselves the few bits of pocket money that they control, give with sacrificial generosity. One brings twenty cents earned by picking ten geese at two cents each, another fifty cents she received for making three pairs of overalls, another has not put a ruffle on the bottom of her new dress and brings the thirty-two cents she has saved. One brings her only black mourning dress, another the last piece of her mother's antique china. One of the more prosperous women has sold a bit of butter without her husband's knowledge. Some of the sisters are reluctant to accept the proceeds of that sale until someone points out that the farm and all the cows were hers before she was married and the butter rightfully is hers.

The difference in roles between men and women is summed up in a dialogue between the deacons and their wives about the new position of deaconess created by the General Conference. The women are hard at work scrubbing the meetin' house and making items for the fair when the deacons come, directly from the post office, to bring them the latest news from the Conference. Deacon Sypher informs his wife that,

"... you women have got the privilege now, if you are single, of workin' your days at church work under the direction of us men."

"Then I could work at the Deacon trade under you," sez she admirin'ly, "I could work jest like you—pass round the bread and wine and contribution box on Sundays?"

But the Deacon hastens to remind her that is male deacons' work. "Wimmen deacons have other fields of labor, such as relievin' the wants of the sick and sufferin', sittin' up nights with small-pox patients, takin' care of the sufferin' poor, etc., etc." He goes on to assure her there is no way he and she could do the same kinds of church work, since he would not wish to "curtail the holy rights of wimmen" nor "stand in her way and keep her from doin' all this modest, unpretendin' work, for which her weaker frame and less hefty brain hez fitted her."

The deacons continue to talk about how it would weaken the church to have women "set" on the Conference (since "every woman you would admit would keep out a man") while the women move the heavy benches and scrub the floor. Finally Samantha reminds the deacons that all the women need to get back to their own housework and suggests that "seein' you men are all here, can't you lay holt and help carry out the benches?" But the deacons all have important work to do at home and depart hurriedly, leaving Samantha to speculate on how many of them are going off to play checkers.[13]

Is it possible today to assess the impact of Marietta Holley's writing? To what extent did she influence public opinion in favor of the causes she championed? In order to answer these questions, it is essential to look at the available publishing data relating to her writings, some of the opinions of her contemporaries and the style in which she presented her material.

We know that her prolific pen addressed a large audience. The newspaper introduction to her serialized autobiography reports that "My Opinions and Betsey Bobbett's sold in excess of Edward Egglestons' 'Hoosier Schoolmaster' and the total sales of 'Samantha at the Centennial' reached over 1,000,000 copies." It further states: "During the height of her popularity few American authors were better known."[14] Another newspaper article declares: "Her greatest popularity was perhaps in the Eighties and Nineties, when it is estimated she was as widely read as Mark Twain and even achieved a considerable audience in foreign countries."[15]

Peterson's National Ladies' Magazine boasted that it was the "Best and Cheapest" of the Lady's Books in 1876 with a circulation of 150,000.[16] It was then featuring her sketches several times a year. *The Ladies' Home Journal* grew from a "little paper" with a circulation of 200,000 in 1884 when she began to contribute to its pages, to a significant magazine with a circulation of 400,-000 in 1886,[17] a fact for which Holley herself modestly claimed at least a small share of the credit.[18] Publishing data for many of her books are difficult to find, but is is clear from publication dates in existing volumes of her books that some of them were in print for from ten to twenty years. *Brethren* was published in 1890 and 1892, and a paperback version was issued in 1897.

That many of Holley's contemporaries held her influence in high esteem is evidenced by their letters. Susan B. Anthony and Frances Willard invited her to their conventions or encouraged her to send a written word of greeting. Both fed her material for her books and encouraged her to write about particular situations. Anthony sent the legal material for *Sweet Cicely* and both a false teeth story and a broken hip story which were used in the book.[19] Willard wrote after reading *Brethren*, "I wish you'd tackle Bellamy's Heaven—that would sell like honey-comb & do lots of good." She adds, "You've lifted for us Methodist Wimmens and I thank and love you."[20] Will Carleton even suggested that she gently chide the British on the Boer War and enclosed an article by W.T. Stead from the *Review of Reviews* for background material.[21]

From among all of the reviews that must have been written of her books, Holley quotes from two of her favorites in her memoirs. One is by Senator Blair, who was an active supporter of the temperance movement. He wrote: "Her works are full of wit and humor, and yet are among the most logical, eloquent, pathetic and instructive productions of our time."[22] The other was by her friend Bishop Newman who wrote of *Saratoga*, "She stands alone in her own chosen sphere. The world would be a blank without her."[23] Perhaps one of the great compliments she reports also wounded her pride a bit. She tells of hearing Frances Willard lecture and use, without giving her credit, a line which Holley herself had written some years before in *Samantha at the Centennial*, "What was the Crusade to the Holy Land to compare with it (the warfare of the Temperance hosts)? That was to protect the sepulchre where the body of our Lord had once lain, but this was to protect the living Christ, the God in man."[24]

The success of any popular movement is largely dependent on a wide range of leadership which emerges in various aspects of political and cultural life. This was true of the Temperance Movement, the struggle for woman suffrage, and the fight for lay and clergy rights for women in the church. These movements produced leaders who organized political campaigns, lectured from public platforms declared their candidacy for public office, sought and received ordination, knelt to pray in saloons or poured out the demon rum in the gutters. Marietta Holley did none of these things, but her own unique contribution has assured her a place of honor among the many who have provided leadership in the struggle for women's rights.

Holley's use of humor and caricature not only charmed her readers but impressed her images more firmly upon them. Many women chuckled with Samantha and identified with her episodes of daily life. And the images were remembered. Samantha became, for at least a generation of women, a household word. She lifted their spirits and their self-images in ways that would have been far less likely with a more sober medium.

Samantha provided a significant alternative to the cultural stereotypes of women. By holding up the dignity of woman *in her own right* she brought a new sense of self-worth to both married and single women. Her rational common sense approach left women with the knowledge that they were capable of making wise decisions, though they did not have the actual power to implement those decisions. She solidified their belief in themselves and in the appropriateness of their participation in the struggle to gain personal, legal, and political recognition. By assigning the sentimental and chauvinistic attitudes to Betsey and Josiah, Holley was able to help women—and men—to laugh at those attitudes and identify with the sensible rational support of woman's rights. And she brought to women in the church a sense of their own importance within that structure and of the dignity and significance of their contributions.

Perhaps Frances Willard's praise of Holley was a bit extravagant, but it was not undeserved. "Brave, sweet spirit," she wrote, in her large, nearly illegible scrawl, "you don't know how much we all love you, no woman has more grandly helped the woman's cause."[25]

NOTES

1. Marietta Holley, *Samantha Among the Brethren* (New York: Funk & Wagnalls, 1890), pp. 251-257. This book includes a publisher's appendix with 6 speeches from the General Conference debate, three for and three against the seating of women delegates.
2. Holley, "The Story of My Life," *Watertown (N.Y.) Times.* Published serially beginning Feb. 5, 1931. Chapter 4.
3. Holley, *My Opinions and Betsey Bobbett's* (Hartford: American Publishing Co., 1873), p. v.
4. Holley, *My Opinions*, pp. 62-65.
5. See Holley, *Samantha Vs. Josiah* (New York: Funk & Wagnalls, 1906), for a book-length treatment of this dialogue.
6. Holley, *Brethren*, p. 349-352.
7. Holley, *Samantha at Saratoga* (Philadelphia: Hubbard Bros., Publishers, 1887), p. 516.
8. Holley, "Life," Chapter 13.
9. Holley, *My Wayward Pardner* (Hartford: American Publishing Co. 1880), p. 360.
10. E.g. Holley *Opinions*, p. 416. The sermon here compares marriage without love with prostitution.
11. Holley, *Samantha at the Centennial* (Hartford: American Publishing Co., 1877), pp. 63-64.
12. Holley, *Sweet Cicely* (New York: Funk & Wagnalls, 1885), pp. 1, 3, & 4.
13. Holley, *Brethren*, pp. 265-270.
14. "Miss Marietta Holley—An Autobiography" (article), *Watertown Times*, Feb. 4, 1931.
15. Rudolph Ojensness, "Centenary of Samantha" (article), *The New York Times*, July 19, 1936.
16. *Peterson's National Ladies' Magazine*, April 1876.
17. Letters to Marietta Holley from C.H.K. Curtis dated Sept. 20, 1884 and Sept. 25, 1886. Archives of the Watertown Historical Society, Watertown, N.Y.
18. Holley, "Life," Chapter 11
19. Letter to Holley from Susan B. Anthony, Jan. 21, 1885. Watertown Historical Society.
20. Letter to Holley from Frances Willard, Nov. 26, 1890. Watertown Historical Society.
21. Letter to Holley from Will Carleton, Nov. 8, 1899. Watertown Historical Society
22. Holley, "Life," Chapter 4.
23. Holley, "Life," Chapter 13.
24. Holley, "Life," Chapter 6.
25. Holley, "Life," Chapter 4.

BOOKS BY MARIETTA HOLLEY

1873 *My Opinions and Betsey Bobbett's*
1877 *Samantha at the Centennial*
1880 *My Wayward Pardner*
1880 *The Mormon Wife* (illustrated poem)
1883 *Miss Richard's Boy* (not in dialect)
1885 *Sweet Cicely*
1886 *Poems*
1887 *Samantha at Saratoga*
1890 *Samantha among the Brethren*
1892 *Samantha on the Race Problem* (later titled *Among the Colored Folks*)
1893 *Samantha at the World's Fair*
1895 *Samantha in Europe*
1899 *Around the World with Josiah Allen's Wife*
1904 *Samantha at the St. Louis Exposition*
1906 *The Borrowed Automobile* (Samantha vs. Josiah)
1909 *Samantha on Children's Rights*
1910 *"Who Was to Blame?"* (a booklet)
1911 *Samantha at Coney Island and 1000 Other Islands*
1913 *Samantha on the Woman Question*
1914 *Josiah Allen on the Woman Question*

Social Ministry and Surveillance: Harry F. Ward and the Federal Bureau of Investigation

By George D. McClain
Methodist Federation for Social Action

The Federal Bureau of Investigation has functioned throughout most of this century as a political police with the mission of monitoring intimidating and neutralizing political dissent.[1]

Persons and organizations engaged in the prophetic social ministry of the church frequently have become targets of FBI surveillance as they have articulated political positions dissenting from the general norm.

Thanks to documents obtained under the Freedom of Information Act (FOIA), it is known, for instance, that Martin Luther King, Jr., was one such target. William C. Sullivan, head of the FBI's Domestic Intelligence Division, said of King: "We must mark him now, if we have not done so before, as the most dangerous Negro for the future of the Nation from the standpoint of Communism, the Negro and national security."[2] King's FBI dossier reveals that the Bureau actually sought to replace him as head of the civil rights movement with another black leader.[3]

FBI files released in February, 1983, under the FOIA document that the Rev. Dr. Harry F. Ward, a prominent Methodist social activist whose remarkable career spanned nearly the first seven decades of this century, was the target of FBI surveillance over two periods, one of four years and another of 25 years.

Ward's social ministry within the church included his work as principal author of the original Methodist Social Creed,[4] co-founder and long-time executive of the Methodist Federation for Social Service, and a renowned and popular professor of ethics at Union Theological Seminary (N.Y.). His ministry in the society at large included serving as the initial president of the American Civil Liberties Union (ACLU), a post he held from 1920 to 1940, as leader of the American League Against War and Facism, and as a participant and leader in numerous causes associated with the political left.

The First Investigation: 1922-1925

In 1922 Harry F. Ward was first targeted for surveillance by the U.S. Justice Department's Bureau of Investigation, soon to be renamed the Federal Bureau of Investigation. At that time the Bureau was headed by William J. Burns, who before taking this position controlled the world's largest detective agency. As Bureau director, he acted as the chief red-baiter in the Harding administration, used his position to fight labor union activities (sometimes in cooperation with detectives of the Burns Agency), and regularly passed on material from Bureau files to right-wing organizations.[5]

To justify his ongoing repression of civil liberties and his continuing harassment of political dissenters, Burns testified before the U.S. House Appropriations Committee, apparently in early 1922, that the nation continued to be faced with a serious problem of widespread radical political activity.

Ward, most likely in his role as ACLU president, addressed an open letter to Burns, sharply criticizing his greatly exaggerated claims about the extent of radical political activity, stating that since 1919 widespread government repressive tactics against political dissenters, including those of Burns himself, had substantially reduced such activity. Only two years before the Bureau had carried out the so-called Palmer Raids, in which 10,000 suspected political radicals were illegally arrested.

Burns, piqued by this criticism, replied in a long defensive letter to the chair of the Appropriations Committee, seeking to discredit Ward and those with whom he collaborated in the defense of civil liberties. With this letter he also opened a secret investigative file on Ward.[6]

In the letter Burns claimed that Ward was "one of [the Soviet government's] prominent, though unofficial, assistants." Contending that Ward was "not so well known in circles where he should be known," Burns proposed to "set forth a few facts with regard to him" which would explain the motives for Ward's criticism.

He charged Ward with a "positive sympathy for bolshevism, as exemplified in Russia," a contention that was partly correct, in that Ward had an open and hopeful attitude toward the Russian Revolution, together with a somewhat cautionary and critical stance.[7] Burns claimed it was "largely due to the personal efforts of Mr. Ward" that a New York State legislative committee had classed Union Theological Seminary as "one of the two dangerous centers of revolutionary socialist teaching of a university type in ecclesiastical institutions."

"It could have been expected that the Methodist Church would not tolerate his activities," wrote Burns, referring, among other things, to his editorship of what Burns termed "the so-called Social Service Bulletin of the Methodist Federation for Social Service."

In perhaps his most sarcastic section Burns stated:

> To our knowledge the Rev. Mr. Ward has not been invited by Lenine [sic] to accept a chair in one of the theological seminaries of Russia. If he would transfer his operations to the city of Moscow, he would possibly be pushing a broom over the streets—certainly a more honest calling than using the church and the Scriptures for the spread of the doctrine of bolshevism and anti-Americanism.

Ward and his colleagues in ACLU, including Roger Baldwin and subsequent Supreme Court justice Felix Frankfurter, were identified by Burns as "prominent in the movement directed in favor of anarchists, 'conscientious objectors', 'pacifists', and the horde of otherwise inconspicuous entities who use radicalism as a means of subsistence or publicity." Burns caustically concluded:

> Examine the entire record of the life work Mr. Ward—an alien evidently — (there is no known record to indicate otherwise) who, like so many of them, has come as our national guest, in a vocation where, above all others, he has abundant opportunity to exercise all the privileges which it is possible to confer; whose vocation is or should be, the saving of souls, and whose paths should be 'the way of peace', but who, while our guest, reviles our sanctuary, pollutes the temple, and spreads from the very sanctum itself the seeds of discord, envy and strife:

This first entry in Ward's dossier well illustrates some of the general characteristics of the 593 pages concerning Ward which have thus far been released under the Freedom of Information Act.[8] These include:

a. The fierce hostility and personal contempt of high Bureau officials toward Ward. In January, 1924, shortly before he was to become head of the Bureau of Investigation, J. Edgar Hoover concluded a brief memo to Burns, his immediate superior, with these words: "Of course you know the general character and standing of *this creature*." (emphasis added)[9]

b. An image of Ward as having enormous influence. A 1925 report from the American Consul-General in Shanghai to the Secretary of State regarding Ward's visit to China ascribes "much of the pro-Soviet tendency in Nanking to Dr. Ward's remarks."[10]

c. The hope that church authorities would censor or expel Ward. Considerable wishful thinking of this sort was accepted as fact in Bureau reports, e.g., the false contention that Ward was expelled from his teaching position at Boston University School of Theology "because of his denying that he was present at an anti-draft meeting in New York City, which he actually addressed, counseling non-complaince with the Selective Service Law."[11]

d. A view of Ward based on an extreme anti-communism. An FBI memo charged that around 1920 his political views changed "from pale pink to dangerous red." Another informer reported, "Ward possesses a trend of thought more radical than the Communist Party ever had."[12]

e. Uncritical acceptance of allegations of Communist Party connections, from whatever source, be they paid informers, private individuals, vigilante organizations, or the reckless charges of investigating committees such as HUAC.

This initial FBI investigation of Ward, covering the period from 1922 to 1925, resulted in only a small dossier of 24 pages. The reason for the abrupt end to the investigation lay in reforms made in the Department of Justice as a result of the Teapot Dome scandal and the revelation of Bureau spying on Congressional representatives.

Harlan F. Stone was appointed attorney general in 1924 and within months terminated spying on the political beliefs and affiliations of American citizens. On May 24, 1924, he stated:

> There is always the possibility that a secret police may become a menace to free government and free institutions because it carries with it the possibility of abuses of power which are not always quickly apprehended or understood. . . . It is important that [the Bureau's] activities be strictly limited to those functions for which it was created and that its agents themselves be not above the law or beyond its reach . . . The Bureau of Investigation is not concerned with political or other opinions of individuals. It is concerned only with their conduct and then only with such conduct as is forbidden by the laws of the United States. When a police system passes beyond these limits, it is dangerous to the

proper administration of justice and to human liberty, which it should be our first concern to cherish.[13]

Stone shut down the FBI's anti-radical division and severed its links with private detective agencies. He also ended its dissemination of anti-radical propaganda, its spying into labor and political groups, and its illegal searches, seizures, and wiretappings.

Ironically as part of his reform and house cleaning operation, Attorney General Stone replaced FBI head Burns with one J. Edgar Hoover.

The Second Investigation: 1941-1965

In the late 1930s growing international tensions and the onset of an economic recession-within-a-depression helped create a rapidly escalating climate of hysteria about internal security which J. Edgar Hoover adroitly manipulated in order to resume the campaign Attorney General Stone had forced him to leave off in 1924 and to make spying on political activities a central fact of American political life. President Franklin D. Roosevelt himself contributed greatly to this enhanced repression by giving license and encouragement to FBI surveillance activities, beginning in the mid-30s. By 1940 he was sending J. Edgar Hoover the names and addresses of hundreds of persons who had written him messages of opposition to his foreign policy.[14]

A singular element in fostering the new climate of repression was the creation in 1938 of the House Un-American Activities Committee (Dies Committee or HUAC). Under chairman Martin Dies the committee mounted a wholesale vendetta against the political left, seeking to portray the New Deal, including Eleanor Roosevelt herself, as part of an enormous communist conspiracy. One writer contends that "Martin Dies named more names in one single year than Joe McCarthy did in a lifetime."[15]

By 1940 Hoover had so maneuvered the growing repression that

> the Bureau was permitted to monitor and harass individuals solely because of their opinions, expressions, and associations, even though they were fully protected by the First Amendment and light-years removed from espionage, sabotage, and law violations of any kind.[16]

The way was clear for Hoover, unfettered by any constitutional limitations, to fight what Frank Donner calls a "secret war" against political dissent.[17]

The centerpiece of J. Edgar Hoover's surveillance war was his clandestine plan for custodial detention of individuals "whose presence at liberty in this country, in time of war or national emergency, would constitute a menace to the public peace and safety of the United States Government."[18] Under this concentration camp program, instituted in 1939, the names of potential prisoners were indexed and filed on cards. Frequent checks were made of their current addresses to facilitate a quick roundup. When in 1943 Attorney General Francis Biddle ordered Hoover to terminate the custodial detention program for lacking justification, Hoover simply continued it under a new name, the Security Index.

In 1941, as Hoover was expanding his secret war on dissent, the FBI opened a second security investigation of Harry F. Ward. At the time Ward was 67 years old; the investigation would continue until he died at age 91.

As with the first FBI investigation of Ward, the opening of this second one was occasioned by Ward's criticism of the FBI and its director, this time in a speech in Baltimore about which an informer phoned in "a friendly tip" to J. Edgar Hoover.[19]

Bureau memoranda and reports of this second investigation continued to betray a personal hostility to Ward. For instance, the opening line of a long surveillance memorandum of 1941 refers to Ward as having "the dubious designation of 'Reverend'."[20]

The information entered in Ward's file was often based on the flimsiest of sources and sometimes simply mistaken. For some time FBI reports continued to repeat a mistaken entry that Ward began his affiliation with the Methodist Federation for Social Service (MFSS) in 1941, upon retirement from Union Seminary, when in fact he was a co-founder in 1907 and executive since 1911.[21] Another entry illustrates how the Bureau's anti-communist paranoia could lead it into gross factual error: "It is reported from a reliable source that the Social Service Bulletins [the publications of MFSS which Ward co-edited] were largely subscribed to by well known Communists."[22]

A remarkable admission of the flimsy sources of surveillance is contained in an FBI agent's report that Ward

> was said to be a suspicious character and deserved watching. (Name deleted) could not furnish any information that he himself knew the subject was suspicious, or in any way subversive, but advised that he had secured the information from someone whose name he could not recall.[2]

In May 1943, Hoover placed Ward on his custodial detention list and thus marked him for imprisonment in the event of a national emergency.[24] By September, 1943, Hoover had replaced the custodial detention listing with the Security Index; and Ward was listed on it from that time on.[25] From 1943 to 1949 Ward was tabbed—literally with a special tab on his Security Index card—for high priority apprehension in a national emergency.[26] This highest priority category for detention was referred to as "Detcom," an abbreviation for "Detention of Communists."

The FBI indicated great interest in Ward's citizenship status, apparently searching for grounds for deporting him, and pursued the matter until it was discovered that the English-born Ward had been a bona fide naturalized citizen since 1898. Even so, major Bureau reports were routinely forwarded to the Immigration and Naturalization Service.

Dossier information on Ward was collected from a variety of sources including:

1) "Pretext phone calls", seeking information under a phony pretext, especially from Union Theological Seminary.

2) Interception of mail from the Soviet Union to his summer home in Canada.[27]

3) Unofficial witch-hunting groups within Methodism, including Circuit Riders, Inc., the Committee to Preserve Methodism, and Methodist Laymen of North Hollywood.

4) Professional informers such as Elizabeth Bentley and Louis Budenz, who made a lucrative career out of false accusations.

5) U.S. Army and Navy intelligence agencies.

6) Government investigative agencies, such as HUAC, the Senate Subcommittee on Internal Security, and the California Committee on Un-American Activities.

7) Private communication from the Hearst press.[28]

8) First-hand reports by FBI agents attending public meetings.

An additional and most repugnant form of spying on Ward was the interrogation of his neighbors in Palisade, New Jersey. Regular questioning of the neighbors never yielded any evidence of unlawful or Communist Party activity. It did, however, result in file entries regarding his personal and family life. Most of this material appears to have been deleted from the FBI dossier in the form in which it was released; but certain examples, such as the following entry well illustrate the consequent inappropriateness and invasion of privacy.[29]

On June 5, 1958, (name deleted) advised that the subject was then residing at 1116 Arcadian Way, Palisade, New Jersey, and was then occupied as an author and retired minister. (Name deleted) stated that Ward Nursery School, which the subject's daughter operated at 1116 Arcadian Way prior to her death, continues to function on week day mornings having an enrollment of approximately forty children. (Name deleted) added that the subject spends a great deal of his time working in the gardens around his home.

(Name deleted) advised that he believed that the subject would go to Rural Route 1, Echo Bay, Ontario, Canada, for a portion of the summer as he has been doing over the past few summers.

This surveillance memo also offered a description of the 85-year-old man, including these characteristics: "Wears glasses; walks with cane; has English accent; usually wears cap." In another entry an informer passed on information that Ward "was listed in the personal address book of CORLISS LAMONT, National Chairman of the American Council for Soviet Relations."[30]

As might be expected, the Bureau showed supreme interest in the question of whether Ward was a member of the Communist Party. The FBI dossier itself contains an internally contradictory picture. Professional informer Louis Budenz claimed Ward was one of 400 "concealed Communists" he knew.[31] A labor union-connected informer claimed Ward was a Communist in 1940 and knew many Communists well.[32] The Chicago FBI field division claimed Ward was a Communist but did not carry a card.[33] On the other hand, the New Jersey State Police reported that he was "not a Communist, but he defends their rights."[34] Another informer reported on a Moscow restaurant conversation in which Ward was classified as one among some "fellow-travelers who didn't have the guts to join the party."[35] Regular FBI investigative reports repeatedly indicated that no evidence of activity in the Communist Party could be found, and it was apparently because of this that in 1949 he was removed from "Detcom" tabbing and placed in the second rank of Security Index listings slated for custodial detention.

In actual fact, membership in the Communist Party was precluded for Ward for two reasons. First of all, he believed throughout his entire ministry that grounding his judgment and actions on "the basic ethical principles of the religion of Jesus of which [he was] minister and teacher . . . required complete independence from all political parties."[36] Furthermore, the

Communist Party supported the Soviet Union and from his ethical perspective he had some significant disagreements about its policies and ideology.

Despite its faults, however, he believed the Soviet Union had made an historic step forward in its organization of a new economic system and he continued to have a deep appreciation and hope for the future of that nation. He sincerely believed that any public statement of his reservations about Soviet Communism might fall into the hands of those who only wanted to destroy the U.S.S.R. and therefore refrained from such statements.[37] This stance left him especially vulnerable to erroneous charges of Communist Party membership.

Ward's dossier repeatedly links him with a wide array of so-called communist fronts. For example, a 1957 investigative summary listed these: Jefferson School of Social Science, Methodist Federation of [sic] Social Action, National Council of American-Soviet Friendship, World Fellowship of Faith, American Committee for the Protection of Foreign Born, Joint Anti-Fascist Refugee Committee, Citizens Emergency Defense Conference, China Welfare Appeal, Inc., Committee for a Democratic Far Eastern Policy, and Families of Smith Act Victims.[38]

The FBI files show that the Bureau had considerable respect for Ward and his abilities and feared the damage he could do to the FBI. An informer advising J. Edgar Hoover said Ward had a "nasty tongue and pen" and urged Hoover to stay clear of controversy with him.[39] Another memorandum calls him "an author and speaker of no mean ability."[40] In 1958 it was recommended that Ward not be interviewed by the FBI, as it "could result in embarrassment to the Bureau inasmuch as subject [Ward] is an author and retired minister,"[41] A concern that was frequently repeated in subsequent internal FBI memoranda.

Part of the FBI's fear of Ward clearly lay in his position as a prominent clergyman. The informer who urged J. Edgar Hoover not to get into any controversy with Ward also noted that "the fact that Ward is a minister makes him all the more dangerous."

Overall, one is overwhelmed by the great time and resources employed, all at public expense, to spy upon a citizen about whom not a single violation of law was ever alleged. The files represent the endless repetition of stale data, occasionally updated. Much of the effort expended was to discover the obvious, such as that Ward retired from Union Seminary in 1941, a fact which the Bureau could have readily gleaned from the *Social Service Bulletin* if they had bothered to consult it.

The Function of Surveillance

The uses to which the information gathered in Ward's dossier was put are not altogether clear. Of course, the dossier served as Hoover's justification for including Ward on his custodial detention list and Security Index. If information or disinformation was leaked to right wing vigilante groups or if stories to discredit were planted in the press, evidence for such would likely have been deleted before release of the dossier. We do know that dossier material was shared with the army, navy, and air force intelligence agencies, the Office of the Secretary of Defense (an unusually highly placed recipient of surveillance memoranda), the U.S. Information Agency (presumably to assure that none of Ward's books were retained in USIA libraries abroad), and the Immigration and Naturalization Service.

Although Ward seemed to have been aware that his activities were under surveillance, there is no evidence that this exceptionally strong-willed person was deterred by it. But the surveillance must surely have exacted a psychic price from Ward and others engaged in prophetic social witness. There would always be the question as to what aspects of one's life would end up in an FBI dossier and through the FBI perhaps eventually appear in the press or in some right-wing vigilante tract. Ward's file itself documents that such fears were well-grounded. The FBI noted in someone's file that the person had in 1938 submitted the name of Ward, the person's former teacher, as a reference on an application for employment in the Richmond, Virginia, welfare department.[42] A history professor at Reed College was reported for supporting such speakers as Harry Ward on campus.[43] The Office of Naval Intelligence reported to the FBI that a particular couple had been married by Ward, adding that at least one of them "allegedly was sympathetic to the radical views of Dr. Ward."[44]

The very fact of secret monitoring of individuals' activities served as an effective weapon in the war to insure political conformity and to neutralize effective dissent. Donner explains:

The relatively open character of our society is psychologically disarming and makes the average subject highly vulnerable to fear when his or her politics are secretly monitored by the FBI—the national symbol of our identification of dissent with subversion. The undercover character of the investigation, the benighted standards of the informer, the assumed guilt of the subject, the denial of an opportunity to answer any charges and confront the accuser, can all be shattering. Because it is such an efficient instrument of repression, the informer system has been transformed from a mere investigative means into an end in itself. It is not the information furnished by the spy that makes him a prized Bureau asset but the fact that he is there: a concealed hostile presence to instill fear.[45]

Targeting of Other Religious Leaders

The Ward dossier serves to document that other leading church figures were also targets of the FBI's secret surveillance war against dissent and prophetic ministry.

One target was Georgia Harkness, a leading Methodist theologian, seminary professor, mystic, and social activist, especially on issues of peace.[46] Information in Ward's dossier indicates that Louis Budenz, a leading professional informer, "advised that Dr. Georgia Elma Harkness . . . was closely associated with the CP and subsequently agreed to join." He also stated that she was a member of "perhaps ten" Communist Party fronts from 1943 to 1945, a period when she was on the faculty of Garrett Biblical Institute. Budenz contended that it was under the influence of Dr. Ward that she became associated with the front groups.[47]

This entry on Georgia Harkness is included in the Ward dossier because of her alleged connection to him, but in view of the allegation made of Communist Party membership it is very likely that Harkness herself was also the subject of an FBI investigation.

Another prominent church leader under attack was Edler Hawkins, a long-time pastor at St. Augustine Presbyterian Church in the Bronx, a member of the faculty at Princeton Theological Seminary, and the first black moderator of the United Presbyterian Church. The three entries on Hawkins in Ward's dossier were occasioned by the fact that Hawkins was one of the sponsors of the 90th birthday celebration honoring Ward in 1962. One entry refers to a 1971 issue of "The Fiery Cross," a publication of the United Klans of America, Inc., Knights of the Ku Klux Klan. The article reported that Hawkins had been named professor of practical theology and coordinator of black studies at Princeton Seminary and that, while studying for the ministry, he was a student of Ward's at Union Theological Seminary.[48] Two other entries referred to his giving the invocation at Ward's 90th birthday celebration and in both instances Hawkins was cited as a member of the

state executive committee of the American Labor Party, an alleged communist front.[49]

Other references suggest that there were surveillance files on Henry Hitt Crane, a pacifist leader in Methodism; Methodist Central Jurisdiction Bishop Edgar Love, who also served a term as MFSA president; Louise Pettibone Smith, professor of religion at Wellesley College and the only woman contributor to *The Interpreter's Bible*; and Episcopalian social action leader William B. Spofford, editor of *The Witness*.[50]

The Ward FBI files also indicate that among the religious organizations spied upon during the 40s and 50s were the United Christian Council for Democracy, among whose leaders were Reinhold Niebuhr and Harry F. Ward, the Episcopal League for Social Action, the Religious Freedom Committee, and the Methodist Federation for Social Action.

Taken together, the evidence from the Ward dossier alone is sufficient to demonstrate that the FBI's "secret war" against lawful dissent also included an attack upon the free exercise of the church's social ministry.

In view of current concern about present-day surveillance of church activities by the FBI and CIA, it is important that the full history of this official attack on the church's social ministry be documented and analyzed. A first important step to be taken is for qualified researchers to use the Freedom of Information Act to obtain and analyze the FBI dossiers on such persons as Georgia Harkness, Henry Hitt Crane, Bishop Edgar Love, Bishop Francis J. McConnell, Bishop G. Bromley Oxnam, Thelma Stevens, and other religious leaders and social action organizations whom there is reason to believe have been under surveillance.[51]

The Attack on Prophetic Witness:
Then and Now

Ward himself made a useful distinction between three religious perspectives: institutional religion (i.e., dogmatism and fundamentalism), liberal religion, and prophetic religion. He described the roles of each in this way:

In the crisis before us, institutional (i.e., dogmatic) religion will serve as chaplain to the forces of reaction, blessing its program, justifying its repressions. It always has; it always will . . . Liberal religion will pass resolutions against both fascism and communism, affirm moral generalities and defend free speech. Prophetic religion . . . will recognize itself as one of the forces for social change. It will bring them hope and courage, sharing the dangers and persecutions that are the lot of those who break new paths in the social order. In that experience it will find new life for itself.[52]

Ward himself was a leading exponent of "prophetic religion," which today we would call the prophetic witness of the church. Although "the standard histories of the social gospel movement either ignore Ward entirely or treat him as an extreme and therefore irrelevant case," he was very much a participant in the social gospel movement. He was, for instance, a close friend of Walter Rauschenbush.[53]

What distinguished Ward from most of his social gospel contemporaries, however, was his concentration on economic analysis rather than sociology or political science, his avoidance of the idealism and individualism of the main-line social gospel, and his global perspective.[54] These distinguishing perspectives led Ward to the forefront of the ranks of what William King appropriately terms "social gospel radicalism."

In bringing Christian ethical principles to bear upon the presuppositions of the economic order, Ward focused on the profit system which underlay capitalism. He concluded that the profit motive functioned in capitalism in a way that was not only inefficient but also destructive of human values and human resources. To him the capitalist system was the gospel of mammon, inimical to the gospel of Jesus. He advocated, therefore, a process of non-violent revolutionary reform which would be accomplished by changing the nature and direction of capitalism, a task in which he saw a central role for Christianity.[55]

There is enormous pressure in our capitalist system for religious institutions and their leaders to provide ideological support for capitalism, at least in the form of appearing neutral and not acting overtly to challenge the prevailing underlying power arrangements. When a prominent church ethicist and social activist such as Harry Ward begins to wield influence over an important attitude-forming constituency such as mainline Protestant clergy and leaders and to generate organizational centers of dissent such as the Methodist Federation for Social Service, ACLU, the American League Against War and Fascism and myriad other groups, he or she becomes a danger to the powers that be; and one can expect that they will fight back with the means at their disposal.

The ethics of Georgia Harkness, too, included a sharp criticism of the capitalist system. She reviewed it as impersonal, mechanistic, and degrading to human personality, and as the root of economic imperialism.[56] That she, another social gospel radical who occupied influential

teaching posts, was also the object of the FBI's secret war on dissent should come as no surprise.

Similarly, today, when institutions, such as the National Council of Churches, the World Council of Churches, or the United Methodist Board of Global Ministries, threaten, however timidly, a U.S. foreign policy based not so much on human rights or the self-determination of peoples as on insuring the prerogatives of a U.S.-dominated market capitalism, we should not be surprised that those in the church, in the media, and in the government who see themselves as guardians of the existing order will fight hard, using any means available, to discredit and eliminate prophetic utterance and action.

Attacks in 1982-83 on the churches in *Reader's Digest* and the CBS "60 Minutes" television program should be seen in this light, as should the closely-related barrage of criticism from the Institute for Religion and Democracy. As for the role of government itself, the new guidelines regulating FBI domestic security investigations issued March 7, 1983, by Attorney General William French Smith mark a dramatic revival, after only seven years of restraint, of authorization for the FBI to open files on lawful political activities and to infiltrate dissenting organizations. These refurbished weapons for the secret surveillance war will surely be employed once again against church organizations and leaders who articulate an alternative vision for America.

In short, harassment and surveillance of prophetic religious leaders and organizations by a government committed to maintenance of an exploitative status quo should be expected at the same time as it is resisted. Such treatment was accorded "the prophets which were before you," said Jesus. It has long been so, it is presently so, and it will in the future be so — wherever and whenever the prophetic stance of Jesus Christ and the prophets is reproduced in relation to present-day systemic injustice.

In December, 1982, a number of denominational executives gathered to consider current U.S. government surveillance of the churches. At that gathering Rev. William Howard, past president of the National Council of Churches, gave a meditation which includes words which serve as a fitting commentary upon the "secret war" of intelligence agencies against Harry F. Ward and other prophetic religious leaders of the past, as well as the most probably secret and not-so-secret war today against the prophetic witness of churches and Christians:

If we stand with those for whom Jesus' ministry had particular focus and meaning, that is, the poor, the

218

powerless, the alone, then we will collide with the principalities and powers. Somehow we will be at odds with the status quo. Not because we seek conflict, but because the needs of the marginalized and the victimized will not be met without destabilizing the status quo, and the "powers-that-be" will concede nothing meaningful and fundamental, voluntarily. This is not true because you or I want it to be true, but it is important for us not to delude ourselves and deny the way things are . . . . This is the cross we must bear for standing with those who are without conventional power. And the intimidation we may feel in our bureaucracies on occasion is but a slight example of what the poor and unpopular feel as a matter of course.

Seen in this way, and understood in this way, we can confront whatever the future may hold with the resilience and determination that the journey requires; we can walk and not get weary, we can run and not get tired.[57]

NOTES

1. For a thorough articulation of this theme, see Frank J. Donner, *The Age of Surveillance: The Aims and Methods of America's Political Intelligence System* (Alfred E. Knopf, New York, 1980).
2. Donner, *Age of Surveillance*, p. 143.
3. Evan Hendricks, *Former Secrets: Government Records Made Public Through the Freedom of Information Act* (published by Campaign for Political Rights, Washington, D.C., 1982), p. 156.
4. William McGuire King, *The Emergence of Social Gospel Radicalism in American Methodism* (unpublished Ph. D. thesis, Harvard University, 1977), pp. 197ff.
5. Robert Justin Goldstein, *Political Repression in Modern America: From 1870 to the Present* (Cambridge MA/New York: Shenkman Publishing Co., 1978), pp. 174-5.
6. FBI Dossier of Harry F. Ward, FBI file #100-29509, pp. IX-4X, letter from William J. Burns to Martin B. Madden, 4/7/22.
7. For a discussion of Ward's attitude toward the Soviet Union, see Robert H. Craig, "An Introduction to the Life and Thought of Harry F. Ward," a 1976 reprint by Church Research and Information Projects of an article in *Union Seminary Quarterly Review*, Vol. XXIV, No. 4 (Summer 1969), pp. 4-5; and King, *Social Gospel Radicalism*, pp. 271-278.
8. The FBI states that there are approximately 800 pages in Ward's file.
9. Ward Dossier, p. 6X, memo from J. Edgar Hoover to William J. Burns, 1/3/24.
10. Ward Dossier, pp. 17X-18X, letter from J. V. A. McMurray to the Secretary of State, 9/10/25.
11. Ward Dossier, p. 23, internal memo, 7/10/41.
12. Ward Dossier, pp. 24, 37, internal memo, 7/10/41.
13. Goldstein, *Political Repression*, p. 176.
14. Goldstein, *Political Repression*, p. 250.
15. Goldstein, *Political Repression*, pp. 242-244.
16. Donner, *Age of Surveillance*, p. 64.
17. Donner, *Age of Surveillance*, pp. xii, 64.
18. Donner, *Age of Surveillance*, p. 163.
19. Ward Dossier, telephone message from deleted source to J. Edgar Hoover, pp. 19-20, 5/24/41.
20. Ward Dossier, p. 22, internal memo, 7/10/41.
21. Ward Dossier, p. 92, internal memo, 2/13/45.
22. Ward Dossier, p. 26, internal memo, 7/10/41.
23. Ward Dossier, p. 46, internal memo, 5/18/43.
24. Ward Dossier, p. 46, internal memo, 5/18/43.
25. Ward Dossier, p. 54, internal memo, 11/19/43.
26. Ward Dossier, p. 171, internal memo, 6/14/49.
27. Ward Dossier, p. 263, internal memo, 3/31/54.
28. Ward Dossier, p. 353, internal memo, 7/27/59.
29. Ward Dossier, p. 341, internal memo, 7/1/58.
30. Ward Dossier, p. 67, internal memo, 6/19/44.
31. Ward Dossier, p. 184, internal memo, 8/8/50.
32. Ward Dossier, p. 178, internal memo, 6/30/50.
33. Ward Dossier, p. 34, internal memo, 7/14/41.
34. Ward Dossier, p. 47, internal memo, 5/18/43.
35. Ward Dossier, p. 56, letter from K. R. McIntyre to Mr. Welch, 11/24/43.
36. Craig, "Introduction," p. 9.
37. Craig, "Introduction," p. 10.
38. Ward Dossier, pp. 314-322, internal memo, 6/6/57.
39. Ward Dossier, pp. 1-2, internal memo, 5/24/41.
40. Ward Dossier, p. 41, internal memo, 7/10/41.
41. Ward Dossier, p . 344, internal memo, 7/1/58.
42. Ward Dossier, p. 449, correlation summary, 1/3/75.
43. Ward Dossier, p. 450, correlation summary, 1/3/75.
44. Ward Dossier, p. 471, correlation summary, 1/3/75.
45. Donner, *Age of Surveillance*, p. 136.
46. Martha L. Scott, "Georgia Harkness, Social Activist and/or Mystic," in *Women in New Worlds: Historical Perspectives on the Wesleyan Tradition*, edited by Hilah F. Thomas and Rosemary Skinner Keller (Abingdon, Nashville, 1980), pp. 117-140.
47. Ward Dossier, p. 462, correlation summary, 1/3/75.
48. Ward Dossier, p. 513, correlation summary, 1/3/75.
49. FBI file on Harry F. Ward 90th Birthday Celebration, FBI file #100-440969, pp. 17a, 43a, 53a, 10/16/63, 11/6/63.
50. 90th Birthday File, pp. 43a, 46a, 48a, 51a, 10/16/63, 11/6/63.
51. An excellent guide in this endeavor is: Ann Mari Buitrago and Leon Andrew Immerman, *Are You Now or Have You Ever Been in the FBI Files: How to Secure and Interpret Your FBI Files* (Grove Press, New York, 1981).
52. Quoted in Alan Thomson, "Prophetic Religion and the Democratic Front: The Mission of Harry F. Ward," *Radical Religion*, Vol. V, No. 1, 1980. p. 32.
53. Heidi Vardeman-Hilf, *Harry F. Ward and the Social Gospel*, (unpublished M. Div. thesis, Union Theological Seminary [N.Y.], 1980), pp. 39ff.; Thomson, "Prophetic Religion," p. 29.
54. Vardeman-Hilf, *Ward and the Social Gospel*, p. 45; Thomson, "Prophetic Religion," pp. 29, 31.
55. Craig, "Life and Thought," p. 6.
56. Scott, "Georgia Harkness," p. 125.
57. William Howard, "Viewpoint: On Government Surveillance of the Churches," *Human Rights Perspectives*, Winter, 1983 (published by the Human Rights Office, Division of Overseas Ministries, National Council of Churches/USA), pp. 1-2.

Towards an Inclusive Church:
South Carolina Methodism and Race, 1972-1982

Charles H. Lippy
Clemson University

When the Methodist Protestant Church, the Methodist Episcopal Church, and the Methodist Episcopal Church, South united in 1939, the creation of the Central Jurisdiction institutionalized racial separation in the new denomination. While white annual conferences were grouped into geographic jurisdictions, black annual conferences, regardless of location, were placed into the Central Jurisdiction. This structure resulted from compromise.[1] Racial prejudice and discrimination in the nation as well as in American Methodism made racial separation expedient if union were to be achieved.[2]

From the start, the existence of the Central Jurisdiction was a source of black dismay.[3] Defeat of the Plan of Union in seventeen of the nineteen black annual conferences signalled this discontent, although these conferences did join the union.[4] In 1944, the Central Jurisdiction bishops declared:

> We entered the work of the new quadrennium in 1940 under a new arrangement in the new church which had in it many forebodings and much uncertainty. It was an administrative arrangement against which many of us had voted . . . We hope in the near future our Methodism may become sufficiently Christian in character and maturity to find a more excellent way.[5]

In 1948, the Central Jurisdictional Conference appointed a committee to study the matter of the racial structure, but its report four years later did not call for any change. A new committee in its 1956 report likewise made no recommendation for change.[6]

That same year, the General Conference adopted Amendment IX to the denomination's constitution. Becoming effective in mid-1958, it provided for the gradual abolition of the Central Jurisdiction by voluntary transfer of local churches from Central Jurisdiction annual conferences to those within the regional jurisdictions.[7] This General Conference also established a commission to study the problem, but in 1960 it simply urged continued use of Amendment IX procedures on the grounds that the effectiveness of that process had not yet received a fair test.[8]

However, the 1960 General Conference did create a Commission of 36, six from each jurisdiction, to continue study.

In its first report in 1961, the commission suggested realignment of annual conferences of the Central Jurisdiction to allow for entire episcopal areas to join regional jurisdictions.[9] At that point, though, the commission had not conferred with the Central Jurisdiction Study Committee, popularly known as the Committee of Five, authorized by the 1960 Central Jurisdictional Conference to aid in the abolition of the jurisdiction. In 1962 the two groups began to co-ordinate their work. The final report of the Commission of 36, overwhelmingly approved by the 1964 General Conference with minor revisions, drew heavily on recommendations from the Committee of Five.

The goal became the establishment of an "inclusive church." Specifically, the adopted report urged clarification of the procedures for voluntary merger, proposed legislation to transfer bishops from the Central Jurisdiction to geographic jurisdictions, and set up a temporary fund to augment pension rates in the Central Jurisdiction annual conferences. It also called for immediate realignment of Central Jurisdiction Conference boundaries, provided for retention of Central Jurisdiction representation on national boards and agencies until dissolution was complete, and suggested means of ensuring financial support for colleges, hospitals, and homes subsidized by the Central Jurisdiction or its churches. Finally, the report authorized creation of a twenty-four member commission to oversee implementation of these proposals and to report to the 1966 special session of the General Conference on progress. If progress were unsatisfactory, that special session was to set up a timetable for carrying out the recommendations.[10] As commentators noted, these actions refrained "from putting an end forthwith to the entity which publicly symbolizes racial segregation within the Methodist Church" and provided only for eventual administrative integration, not "actual" integration.[11]

One move of the 1964 General Conference did

spark hope that the plan of action was more than lip-service.[12] By a small margin the conference deleted any reference to the Central Jurisdiction in the legal documents which would constitute the denomination formed by union with the Evangelical United Brethren Church.[13] The General Conference which met to discuss that union in 1966 noted progress towards merger in the North Central and Northeastern Jurisdictions, initial steps towards merger in the South Central Jurisdiction, and interracial discussions in the Southeastern Jurisdiction. The conference did express determination "to do everything possible to bring about the elimination of any structural organization in the Methodist Church based on race at the earliest possible date and not later than the close of the Jurisdictional Conferences of 1972."[14]

But was 1972 a final date or a target date? The Judicial Council later ruled that the new constitution would not be in effect until the twelve-year transition implementing the Methodist-EUB union was over.[15] Since union began in 1968, transition would not end until 1980. Hence while conferences had to initiate merger by 1972, they did not have to complete it until 1980. However, as 1972 approached, there was a sense that the General Conference would impose plans of merger on those conferences which had not developed at least tentative procedures. And indeed that General Conference, meeting in Atlanta, set July 1, 1973, as a deadline for the dissolution of all remaining segregated conferences.[16]

South Carolina Methodists, black and white, took keen interest in all these deliberations for the Central Jurisdiction's South Carolina Conference (the '66 Conference) boasted the largest membership of any black conference—slightly in excess of 45,000.[17] While the white South Carolina Conference (the '85 Conference) was also numerically large—just under 195,000 members—the sheer number of black Methodists in the state made merger awesome. Most black Methodists at the time of the 1939 reunion were part of the Methodist Episcopal Church,[18] for during the Reconstruction era, virtually all black members of the Methodist Episcopal Church, South had left the denomination.[19] Records indicate that at the close of Reconstruction (1877), just 224 blacks retained membership in the Methodist Episcopal Church, South.[20]

The '66 Conference had gone on record favoring abolition of the Central Jurisdiction in both 1962 and 1963 while the Commission of 36 and the Committee of Five were formulating proposals for General Conference action. Nearly all the opposition to merger in South Carolina was expected to come from within the '85 Conference. In 1964, under the episcopal guidance of Bishop C.F. Golden, leaders of the '66 Conference began conversations about merger with Paul Hardin, bishop of the '85 Conference.[21] By 1966-67, committees to study merger were at work in both conferences. But it was not until the 1968-72 quadrennium, when both conferences came under the episcopal leadership of Bishop Hardin, that attention turned to drafting a formal merger document. In that quadrennium, the two conferences also began sponsoring joint pastors' schools.

Within the '85 Conference, the weekly South Carolina United Methodist Advocate, under the adroit editorship of A. McKay Brabham, consciously attempted to educate Methodists in the '85 Conference about merger as well as about the history of the '66 Conference. This step was much needed, for as John Curry has written, "It is no secret that before the merger of the jurisdictions there was little or no communication between members of the Central Jurisdiction and those of the Southeastern Jurisdiction, especially on the local level."[22] Soon the Advocate contained frequent articles and/or editorials on racism, special events in the '66 Conference, and the merger negotiations. In the minds of many, the Advocate was the instrument most responsible for defusing fear of merger among South Carolina's white Methodists.[23]

Yet from their first joint meeting in 1969, the merger committees recognized that issues operated on two levels. Most obvious was the practical and explicit, which focused on mechanics: pension and minimum salary schedules; representation on boards and agencies; support for, employment in, and access to the institutions of both conferences; determining district boundaries and district leadership; developing a formula for apportionments; and maintaining a genuine itineracy. These topics demanded resolution since there were, for example, inequities in pension rates and a proportionately larger number of part-time pastoral appointments in the '66 Conference. In addition, there was considerable apprehension over the extent to which white Methodists would support black institutions, particularly Claflin College, which had long symbolized the integrity of black Methodism in South Carolina.

But members of both committees realized that more serious issues were implicit, often unstated, or discussed off the record. Widespread racism, primarily among the whites, surfaced in a fear of cross-racial clerical appointments. Another current of opposition stemmed from resentment that the General Conference had mandated merger, making it seem imposed by a body unappreciative of the delicacy associated with questions of race in the South. Such repugnance is not surprising in a state proud of a history as a bastion of states' rights and local autonomy in the political sector. Among South Carolina's black Methodists qualms existed over precisely how "inclusive" a new conference would be. Given the numerical domination of whites and a *de facto* white supremacy mentality, would merger not mean absorption into white Methodism and consequent loss of both effective power and opportunities to shape the ministry of the denomination? Then, too, lurked the long-standing apprehension that merger would bring only administrative integration to South Carolina Methodism, not change in local church separatism.

The merger committees, of course, could formally address only the explicit, technical issues. By January 1970, a special task force drafted a preamble, and by May that year, the joint committees approved a preliminary plan of merger submitted to both conferences for a year of study before voting at their 1971 sessions.[24] The tentative plan called for separate nominating committees in each conference to submit names for membership on boards and agencies, with 75% coming from the '85 Conference and 25% from the '66 Conference. The same ration would apply to conference employment as well as to a conference board of trustees. Fifteen districts would comprise the conference, with eleven superintendents drawn from the '85 Conference and four from the '66 Conference for at least twelve years. Indeed, the racial ratio and other provisions would be guaranteed for twelve years. The document also devised a system to fund apportionments and, with financial support expected from a Temporary Relief Fund set up by the General Conference, adopted the higher equitable salary and pension rates plus the life and health insurance programs of the '85 Conference. Finally, the plan requested the bishop to appoint a continuing committee on merger to oversee transition and deal with unanticipated situations.[25]

The year of study witnessed countless open meetings throughout the state, with members of the merger committees available to answer questions. The '85 Conference's *Advocate* kept the issues before its readership through numerous articles and a heated exchange of letters to the editor. Bishop Hardin and the cabinets of both conferences labored vigorously to promote acceptance of the plan. Before the proposal came

to the floor, only one major alteration was made: the number of districts was reduced from fifteen to twelve, with three superintendents coming from the '66 Conference and nine from the '85 Conference.

The '66 Conference session in 1971 preceded that of the '85 Conference. Meeting at Claflin College May 26, 1971, delegates voted 241-9 (with nine abstentions) to accept the plan. Rhett Jackson, a layman from the '85 Conference who served on the national Commission on Religion and Race and who had visited every conference in the country where merger occurred, noted that the overwhelming majority dispelled all doubts that black Methodists were, when the chips were down, opposed to merger.[26] Two weeks later, in what Bishop Hardin termed "an hour of decision we cannot avoid," the '85 Conference defeated the plan 528-432 (with five abstentions).[27] Those speaking with the press after the tally designated anticipated costs in raising minimum salaries and pension rates, the twelve year guarantee of proportional representation, and the specter of cross-racial appointments as major reasons for the negative vote.[28]

Neither conference could ignore the directive of the General Conference. Hence Bishop Hardin appointed special Committees of Six in each conference to draft an alternative.[29] An open letter from the '85 committee in August 1971 attempted both to summarize and dispel white opposition.[30] The letter identified hostility to the principle of inclusiveness, the twelve year quota system, the number of proposed districts, and the cost factor as leading to defeat. It also reminded white Methodists that conference merger did not require local churches to merge nor would it affect the racial composition of local church membership or result in immediate cross-racial pastoral appointments. In addition, the committee acknowledged that merger would bring black superintendents to predominantly white districts and, perhaps as a word of caution to congregations contemplating secession from the denomination if merger were effected, noted that the General Conference legally owned local church property. The tone was clear: merger would occur whether or not the rank and file supported it.

By fall, the contours of a new plan which left many details for later consideration were in order. The '85 Conference met in special session in September and, after defeating one other proposal, approved in amended form this plan, 505-367 (with five abstentions). But black reservations about the amended plan surfaced quickly. The plan reduced the time for guaranteed black representation from twelve to eight years, called for an 80-20 ratio of membership on boards and agencies, structured the new conference into twelve districts without specifying how many superintendents should be designated from each race,[31] and appeared to weaken the intent of racial ratios by declaring that voting for board and agency members would be by conscience rather than fixed quotas.[32] Thus three weeks after the '85 Conference endorsed the plan, the '66 Conference, in the words of the *Columbia State*, defeated the plan "almost unanimously."[33] But time was running out. The General Conference would meet within the year and, as noted above, might take more direct action where merger lagged.

The two Committees of Six worked feverishly to prepare yet another plan. One senses, though, that this time persons from both conference knew a plan would pass if only to avoid direct General Conference meddling in South Carolina Methodist affairs. A month before a joint special session of both conferences, set for January 1972, the Committees of Six released their combined report. In essence, the plan retained the features of the one rejected the previous September, but sought greater clarity in detail. The plan called for:

1. Members of boards and agencies to reflect the ratio between black and white members for eight years, with delegates following their consciences on secret ballots to maintain the balance.
2. Each district to have one lay leader and two associate lay leaders, one from each of the former conferences.
3. Delegates from each conference elected to the General and Jurisdictional conferences in 1971 to continue to be the official representatives.
4. Nominations to boards and agencies to come from the combined nominating committees until the new conference had its own standing rules.
5. Boards to elect chairpersons on the basis of merit, not racial quotas.
6. The Women's Society of Christian Service (now the United Methodist Women) of both conferences to use the principles of this merger in working out their own merger.
7. Racial inclusiveness to mark election to boards and employment of conference staff, observing the approximate membership ratio at merger.
8. Twelve districts to comprise the conference by 1974.
9. The bishop to exercise his *Disciplinary* discretion in appointing superintendents, guided by the racial ratio of conference membership.
10. The conference program council to contain equal racial representation in its *ex officio* members, with the remainder chosen on a 75-25 white-black ratio.
11. The new conference to adopt its own standing rules, with the understanding that no rule could contravene the plan of merger for eight years.
12. Apportionments to reflect local church membership, previous giving, and the like.
13. Equitable salaries, pension rates, and insurance programs to be those of the '85 Conference with assistance requested from the General Conference Temporary Relief Fund to cover the additional costs.
14. Conference homes and institutions to be inclusive in both services and employment, with the new conference determining their means of support.[34]

On January 27, 1972, the two conferences met together in special session, but ballotted separately. Both conferences adopted the merger plan by substantial margins.[35] June brought a uniting conference, with Bishop Hardin and Bishop James S. Thomas, once a member of the '66 Conference, presiding at the uniting services. June also brought many sighs of relief, for many believed merger had been achieved. But many others wondered whether this merger would transform South Carolina Methodism into an inclusive church.

The first two years after merger witnessed a concerted effort by both blacks and whites to construct the machinery which would allow the new conference to function.[36] Experiments in biracial youth ministry abounded, only to be abandoned as participation declined. The Continuing Committee on Merger, until it was disbanded, held periodic hearings across the conference to assess whether the plan of union was being properly implemented. Reorganization came to all boards and agencies. Initially the matter of black representation and leadership received careful attention, although occasional episcopal prodding by the new resident bishop, Edward L. Tullis, was necessary to assure that blacks obtained positions of responsibility. In his five year report on merger in 1977, Bishop Tullis noted that blacks chaired nine of twenty-six conference boards and agencies and accounted for 40% of all board and agency officers for the 1976-80 quadrennium. These numbers suggest that for a time black Methodists exerted greater influence than the unofficial ratio system would warrant. But the proportion of black leadership declined in the 1980-84 quadrennium, giving birth to the fear that black presence will continue to erode.

Somewhat greater success has marked the redistricting of the conference, completed in 1974. Both Bishop Tullis and his successor, Bishop Roy Clark, have appointed cabinets in such a fashion as always to have at least three black superintendents. Both have adhered to the principle that no district should have a second black superintendent until each had had one. By and large, black superintendents have been well received wherever appointed; so, too, with white superintendents in districts with large black constituencies. To some extent, however, the success in this area may reflect the personalities and the individual character of the persons appointed rather than any widespread commitment to the principle of inclusiveness.

On paper at least, adherence to merger guidelines has also marked employment of conference staff. In 1977, for example, Bishop Tullis could report that two of five conference council on ministries staff members were black. Today, one of three is black. A reduction in staff led to the release of one black, an action many still see as having prompted in part by racism, although others argue that different considerations lay behind the move. Staff at conference-owned or supported institutions presents a more complex picture. As might be expected, blacks constitute a majority of faculty and staff at Claflin College; at the other educational institutions, the record is dismal. Agencies such as the Bethlehem Centers, which historically serve a clientele more black than white, reflect a better ratio, but those such as the Epworth Home or the Orangeburg Methodist Home, which continue to have a predominantly white clientele, do not—outside of service occupation areas.

Perhaps the strongest reminder of inclusiveness has been the *South Carolina United Methodist Advocate*. Although the *Advocate* played a major role in interpreting merger and paving the way for its acceptance in the former '85 Conference and although it became the communications organ of the new conference, the *Advocate* was slow at first to feature stories about black Methodist activity in its pages. But within five years of merger, the *Advocate* included many more articles and photographs relating to black Methodists. In 1973, for example, there was a total of twenty-nine stories and photos concerning black Methodism in South Carolina and the nation. By 1979, there were sixty-three such stories and photos. In addition, the *Advocate* has conscientiously attempted to hire a black or other ethnic minority person the last two times a staff vacancy occurred.

Another positive sign that merger may be creating a new Methodism in South Carolina centers around Claflin College. In many ways, Claflin was the heart of the former '66 Conference, training many of its clergy, repeatedly hosting annual conference sessions, and symbolizing in bricks and mortar both educational achievement and black independence of white struc tures. The schools of the '85 Conference—Wofford College, Spartanburg Methodist College, Columbia College, and, at one time, Lander College—never encapsulated white Methodist identity the way Claflin did and does black Methodist identity. In 1977, the South Carolina Annual Conference launched a $2 million fund drive for Claflin. The success of the drive, with 98.9% of the goal pledged by May 1977, signals recognition that Claflin's educational ministry is central to the work of the new conference and not just a token of black presence. As Claflin President Hubert Manning noted, "This program has done much to cement the bonds of merger."[37] Over the years, too, pastors' associations from each district have met at Claflin, in part so that its adopted white sons and daughters might come to know its work.

The relationship and status of another predominantly black educational institution in South Carolina—Boylan-Haven-Mather Academy in Camden—is more problematic and less sanguine. Operating as an agency of the General Board of Global Ministries, the academy has not been under the direct aegis of the conference and consequently has never evoked the devotion of South Carolina Methodists, black or white, as other schools have. Conference financial support has remained modest. Nevertheless, following merger, the *Advocate* began sporadic reporting of items of interest about Boylan-Haven-Mather and gave wide coverage to its ninetieth anniversary celebration in 1979. However, the Board of Global Ministries announced that declining enrollments and rising costs would necessitate closing the academy at the end of the of the 1982-83 school year. Its demise has not as yet cause an uproar among South Carolina black Methodists nor has it been seen as an anti-black move. Rather, as alternate educational opportunities for blacks emerged in the South, fewer needed Boylan-Haven-Mather in order to obtain a respectable secondary education. Hence its closing seems more like the burial of an institution whose purpose has ended than a racist assault on black Methodists.

Even though there have been black superintendents, board chairpersons, and conference staff and even though there has been support for institutions such as Claflin, black clergy and laity are quick to point out that representation and support are far from synonymous with effective power. Statistics aside, there is the perception that numerical domination of whites means that black concerns remain muted. This disparity between symbolic presence and real participation may have its roots in complacency among both blacks and whites. When merger did not split South Carolina Methodism and the fears of opponents failed to materialize, blacks and whites alike increasingly went about business as usual. There is also the matter of changing leadership. Several of those most active in merger have died or retired. A new generation, not necessarily less committed to inclusiveness but less alert to its nuances and subtleties, is assuming responsibility. Then, too, there continues the unstated conviction, shared by both whites and blacks, that many whites really did view merger as absorption of the '66 Conference into the '85 Conference and still operate as if white-initiated and white-oriented programs are the norm. But there is a more awkward dilemma. A hidden racism which assumes that there is or should be a "black" position or a single "black" voice on every issue frequently overtakes some whites who by persuasion and action support inclusiveness. Even well-intentioned whites frequently express frustration at their inability to ascertain what "they" want. But the range of views among black Methodists in South Carolina and the diversity of black ministries within the conference mean that there cannot be a uniform black perspective on any issue. Yet the variety of views expressed by black leaders all too often allows the white majority, if it adopts one position, to go its own way. The simple fact that roughly two-thirds of the numerical growth in South Carolina Methodism in the past decade has come from black congregations should intensify the need for augmenting effective black participation in the work of the conference. Racial ratios may remain implicitly intact and blacks and whites serve together on conference boards and agencies, but inclusiveness does not necessarily result.

In a more blatant fashion, however, a color barrier still divides South Carolina Methodists. In his five year report, Bishop Tullis noted that there were precious few signs of inclusiveness on the local level. A decade after merger, only a handful of racially-mixed congregations dots the map, and there is no concerted effort to change the status quo. Residual prejudice still lurks at the grass roots. Six years ago, Bishop Tullis noted the presence of some congregations which refused access to facilities for meetings to conference and district boards and the like because their composition was biracial. Merger on the conference level, where annual conference sessions are still numbered by the founding date of the former '85 Conference, is one matter; its implementation locally another.

But perhaps the most conspicuous sign that South Carolina Methodism remains racially separated is the prevailing policy regarding pastoral appointments. No cross-racial appointment has been made, and little has yet been accomplished to prepare for carrying out the *Disciplinary* mandate (par. 527) that appointments be made without regard to race, ethnic origin, or color. In a pastoral letter dated January 3, 198[3], Bishop Clark reminded all congregations that the conference had not begun to make cross-racial appointments. Hence the ideal of an open itineracy as a visible sign of an inclusive church has not been achieved.

The matter of itineracy is linked to the recruitment of black clergy.[38] In the starkest terms, without open itineracy any annual conference can admit only the number of black clergy candidates each year equal to the number needed to replace those vacating appointments. Hence there is a built-in inertia which impedes active recruitment of black clergy which may be expressed in a simple question: what would a conference do if it had more black clergy than black appointments? But the problem is more complex. In South Carolina, as elsewhere particularly in the Southeastern Jurisdiction, a higher proportion of black charges are at minimum or near-minimum salary, and a higher proportion are multiple church circuits rather than station charges than among white appointments. Before merger, in many cases this situation meant that even full members of the '66 Conference often had to seek outside employment for supplementary income. Frequently a spouse's income was essential to maintaining a household. The proportion of pastors who changed appointments each year in the '66 Conference was consequently lower than that in the '85 Conference.

This pattern has at least three critical ramifications for the conference created in 1972. First, it challenges the principle that appointments reflect a matching of a pastor's "gifts and graces" with the needs of specific local churches. Those who for economic reasons cannot move are restricted in opportunities for greater service. Second, the dearth of black appointments which have salaries in the upper quartile of all appointments in the conference minimizes the attractiveness of the ordained ministry as a career to younger black men and women. Avenues of service to humanity other than the ordained ministry draw on the same "gifts and graces" and provide greater economic security. Third, since transformations in the broader culture in the last two decades have made alternative professions more viable for black women and men, the South Carolina Annual Conference, as others, has realized that it requires its strongest black clergy for its strongest black churches and cannot spare them for experiments in cross-racial appointments.

But an even more compelling phenomenon shrouds the ideals of open itineracy and genuine inclusiveness. Reference has already been made to shifts within American society since the 1964 General Conference laid the groundwork for eliminating at least structural segregation in American Methodism. One such shift is the positive valuation given to ethnic consciousness. No longer, it seems to me, is the tone of American culture one which assumes all folk will conform to a WASP model or any other single model. Rather, a new appreciation of the unique heritage and peculiar contributions of every ethnic group has come to the fore. Inclusiveness as it was conceived twenty years ago may no longer be a valid ideal if its end is an amalgamation of both black and white religious styles, for such a move would extinguish what church and society have come to cherish. The case might be different if both groups were roughly equal numerically. But when one dominates, there remains the likelihood that the majority group will, wittingly or unwittingly, make only token acknowledgment of the presence of the minority. Neither extinction of a religious heritage nor an occasional nod to a minority is in keeping with a contemporary vision of an inclusive church. For the moment, then, there may be a case for maintaining a creative separatism, one in which both white and black churches draw on the strengths of the other, celebrate the expression of Methodism each encapsulates and labor together in a shared ministry. The few attempts at co-operative parishes in the South Carolina Annual Conference which have included both black and white congregations offer one possibility for translating this approach from the abstract to the concrete; yoking local churches together may provide another.

The South Carolina Annual Conference has had opportunities to nurture the spirit of inclusiveness in other ways. One might expect, for example, that the Ethnic Minority Local Church Priority mandated by the General Conference would keep the implications of merger before South Carolina Methodists. However, because the parameters of the Ethnic Minority Local Church Priority encompass all ethnic minority churches, some blacks feel that it has diluted progress towards inclusiveness because it permits recalcitrant white Methodists to push aside black concerns, ostensibly to advance more general ethnic minority matters which have little direct bearing on the South Carolina situation. Hence the general church's stress on ethnic minorities has not necessarily advanced the goals of merger.

Another effort to assess where South Carolina stands in implementing both the spirit and fact of merger came in a consultation held at Trinity United Methodist Church, Orangeburg, in the fall of 1981.[39] While some two hundred plus persons attended the consultation, its results were ambiguous at best. For many, the occasion became one where grievances were aired and frustrations expressed. Little came of the gathering by way of formulating specific programs or plans to enhance inclusiveness. But the fact of the consultation and a follow-up meeting just over a year later may be more significant than its content. While the first years after merger saw many biracial gatherings for dialogue and countless preliminary attempts to think through the implications of merger, the last five years have seen virtually none. If merger is, in Bishop Clark's words, "a journey toward a destination no one had yet achieved,"[40] then more such consultations need to be held throughout the conference on a regular basis. It is only through continued sharing of aspirations and goals, frustrations and fears, that South Carolina Methodism will progress on its journey. In this vein, a strong Black Methodists for Church Renewal group within the conference could stand as a beacon to highlight the work which remains to be done.

On balance, then, one must say that the merger of the '66 Conference and the '85 Conference has not as yet given birth to an "inclusive church." On a conference level, there has been administrative merger, but the white majority remains dominant. On a local church level, inclusiveness is more elusive, for there the impact of merger is scarcely felt. Apart from involvement in conference programs or reading about black and white congregations and activities in the *South Carolina United Methodist Advocate*, individual Methodists—black and white— may go about their religious affairs much as they did prior to merger and continue to stand aloof from the vision of inclusiveness. Until unresolved issues such as how to inaugurate open itineracy without sacrificing distinctive heritages and how to establish and perpetuate effective black leadership are continually before both clergy and laity, inclusiveness will remain a dream rather than a reality.

NOTES

1. Dwight W. Culver, *Negro Segregation in the Methodist Church* (New Haven: Yale University Press, 1953), pp. 60-78; Willis J. King, "The Central Jurisdiction," *The History of American Methodism*, 3 vols., ed. Emory S. Bucke (New York: Abingdon Press, 1964), 3:488.
2. "Methodists Vote Four Year Integration," *Christian Century*, 81 (May 13, 1964): 630.
3. Philip Wogaman, "Focus on the Central Jurisdiction," *Christian Century*, 80 (October 23, 1963): 1296.
4. "Report and Plan of Action for the Elimination of the Central Jurisdiction to the General Conference of The Methodist Church, Pittsburgh, Pennsylvania, April 26-May 8, 1964, by the Commission on Interjurisdictional Relations" (January 3, 1964), p. 5.
5. *Journal of the Central Jurisdictional Conference of The Methodist Church, 1944* (New York: Abingdon-Cokesbury, 1944), p. 112.
6. Commission on Interjurisdictional Relations report, p. 6.
7. *Ibid.*, p. 7; also see *Central Jurisdiction Speaks* (n.p., 1962), p. 4.
8. Commission on Interjurisdictional Relations report, pp. 7-8.
9. "First Report of the Commission on Inter-Jurisdictional Relations, The Methodist Church" (n.p., April 29, 1961), p. 3.
10. Committee on Interjurisdictional Relations report, pp. 24-31.
11. Margaret Frakes, "Methodists at Pittsburgh: I," *Christian Century*, 81 (May 20, 1964): 663-64.
12. "Beyond Lip Service," *Time*, 83 (May 15, 1964): 53.
13. See J. Claude Evans, "Methodist Merger Maneuvers," *Christian Century*, 82 (October 13, 1965): 1246-47.
14. *The Constitution for The United Methodist Church with Enabling Legislation and Other Historic Documents* (New York: Abingdon Press, 1967), p. 52.
15. Methodists for Church Renewal, "Changes in the Plan of Union . . . while Time Remains" (n.p., April 15, 1967), p. 6.
16. Merger plans were needed for four black and seven white annual conferences.
17. *Columbia State*, May 27, 1971.
18. My understanding of the story of the '66 Conference relies heavily on John Curry, *Passionate Journey: History of the 1866 South Carolina Annual Conference* (St. Mathews, SC: Bill Wise Printers, 1980), and Warren M. Jenkins, *Steps Along the Way: The Origin and Development of the South Carolina Conference of the Central Jurisdiction of the Methodist Church* (Columbia: Socamead Press, 1967).
19. Black members of the Methodist Episcopal Church, South tended first to join the African Methodist Episcopal, African Methodist Episcopal Zion, and Methodist Episcopal Churches and then the Colored Methodist Episcopal (now Christian Methodist Episcopal) Church when it was organized with the help of the Methodist Episcopal Church, South in 1870.
20. Albert D. Betts, *History of South Carolina Methodism* (Columbia: The Advocate Press, 1952), p. 390.
21. Jenkins p. 49.
22. Curry, p. 73.
23. Here and elsewhere I draw on materials gleaned from interviews with A. McKay Brabham (October 29, 1982), Allen Code (January 6, 1983), John Curry (September 27, 1982), Ernest Etheredge (October 1 3, 1982), A.V. Huff (September 29, 1982), Rhett Jackson (October 30, 1982), Harry R. Kent (February 26, 1983), C.J. Lupo (September 10, 1982), Hawley Lynn (September 24, 1982), I. DeQuincey Newman (January 17, 1983), Fred Reese, Jr. (January 17, 1983), and Eben Taylor (September 1, 1982). I am also grateful to the Wesley Foundation, Clemson, SC, for sponsoring a symposium on an earlier form of this paper, held February 26, 1983, and to the panel which responded to it: John Curry, Marian Jones, Harry Kent, and Eben Taylor.
24. Proposals for changes were to be sent to the committees by the end of 1970.
25. The text was printed in the *South Carolina United Methodist Advocate* (June 4, 1970), pp. 8-13.
26. *Columbia State*, May 27, 1971.
27. *Ibid.*, June 10, 1971.
28. *Ibid.*, June 10, 1971, and June 11, 1971.
29. *Ibid.*, October 26, 1971. The '66 Committee was named in the fall.
30. Mimeographed copy in the Wofford College Archives. I am indebted to Mr. Herbert Hucks, Jr., archivist at Wofford College where the archives of the South Carolina Annual Conference are located, for his gracious assistance during my many visits to the library to examine materials relating to merger.
31. One dilemma in designating quotas for appointment of superintendents was the *Book of Discipline's* provision that the bishop has sole authority to name superintendents.
32. *Columbia State*, September 24, 1971, and September 25, 1971.
33. *Ibid.*, October 17, 1971.
34. Mimeographed letter from the '85 Committee of Six, December 28, 1971, in the Wofford College Archives.
35. *Columbia State*, January 28, 1972, and *Spartanburg Herald*, January 28, 1972, reported the details. The two Committees of Six became the Continuing Committee on Merger to oversee transition.
36. The remainder of the paper draws heavily on notes from the interviews documented above, an undated mimeographed paper entitled "Signposts of 'Lack of Inclusiveness' in the South Carolina Conference of the United Mehodist [sic] Church ," every article relating to merger or black activities appearing in the *South Carolina United Methodist Advocate*. Advocate from 1970 through 1981, and Bishop Edward L. Tullis's five-year report on merger reprinted in the *Advocate* (May 12, 1977), p. 4.
37. *South Carolina United Methodist Advocate* (May 12, 1977): 4.
38. Helpful background is provided in Julian Austin Watson, "Challenging Black College Students to Explore the Ordained Ministry in the United Methodist Church as a Profession" (unpublished D.Min. dissertation, Candler School of Theology, Emory University, 1980).
39. *South Carolina United Methodist Advocate* (October 8, 1981): 2, 4-5, provided articles and commentary on the convocation. The February 10, 1983 issue reported on the follow-up meeting.
40. *South Carolina United Methodist Advocate*, p. 4.

Organizational Patterns of Korean-American Methodist Churches: Denominationalism and Personal Community

Illsoo Kim
Drew University

Introduction

A Korean "Great Awakening" has occurred in large metropolitan areas in both South Korea and the United States. Membership of mainline Protestant churches in South Korea increased from 3.76 million in 1978 to 5.85 million in 1980 with an annual average growth rate of 20 percent.[1] In 1982, the Presbyterians numbered some 5 million; the Methodists, some 800,000; the Baptists, some 300,000.[2] (Membership of the Korean Roman Catholic Church stood at 1.5 million in 1982.) South Korea has undergone "an explosive growth of Christianity unequaled in Asian history since the conversion of the Philippines in the colonial era by Roman Catholic Spain."[3]

A more explosive expansion of Korean Christianity can be found among Korean immigrants in the United States. Korean immigrant Protestant churches have increased in number from less than 20 in 1970 to more than 1,500 in 1983. As of 1983, there are some 170 Korean Methodist churches connected directly or indirectly with The United Methodist Church; some 230 Korean Presbyterian churches affiliated with United Presbyterian Church in the U.S.A.; some 250 Korean Baptist churches linked to Southern Baptist Convention. The remaining Korean churches are largely made up of Korean Presbyterian churches loosely affiliated with Korean Presbyterian denominations in Korea; independent churches, mostly Presbyterian, without any affiliation with either Korean or American denominations; Korean indigenous churches such as Unification churches and Full Gospel churches; and numerous, unofficial "home church" gatherings.

The religious density of Korean immigrants in the United States is much higher than that of their homeland Koreans. In 1982 Christians in South Korea constituted some 25 percent of the total population of 39 million; whereas Korean Christians, mostly Protestants, accounted for 65 percent of some 700,000 Korean immigrants[4] most of whom have entered the United States since the passage of the Immigration Act of 1965. The religious propensity of Korean immigrants to establish new churches is well expressed in a Korean anecdote: "When two Japanese meet, they set up a business firm; when two Chinese meet, they open a Chinese restaurant, and when two Koreans meet, they establish a church."

In this paper we would like to identify basic organizational characteristics of Korean Methodist churches in the New York Metropolitan area by presenting and exploring the historical factors underlying the explosive growth of Korean Protestant churches in both South Korea and the United States. In light of the fact that American missionaries introduced Koreans to the Protestantism of late 19th century America, Korean immigrants are in a unique position of re-transplanting their version of American Protestantism to so-called "post-industrial" American society. Given this historical context, we must examine how traditional Korean organizations have contributed to Korean receptivity to the American Protestantism.

Factors Conducive to the Korean Acceptance of Christianity

The following factors contributed to the successful propagation of Christianity in Korea. First, like ancient Jews in Judea, Koreans suffered foreign conquests, invasions, and interventions throughout their history. Japanese annexation of Korea in 1910 provided impetus for religious change. Under the political threat of losing national sovereignty to the Japanese, many Koreans sought Messianic deliverance by converting to a new religion—the American Protestantism.[5] For Koreans, as for ancient Jews, "the suffering of a people's community, rather than the suffering of an individual became the object of hope for religious salvation."[6] To cite a more contemporary example, the superpowers' division of the Korean peninsula into North and South Korea had a devastating psychological effect on Koreans, enhancing the need for Messianic salvation and concomitantly for the growth of Korean Christianity in South Korea.

Second, unlike missionaries from other western countries who were instrumental in expanding the colonial interests of their own countries, American missionaries in Korea as a whole had nothing to do with colonialism and imperialism there.[7] In fact, many Korean intellectuals accepted Christianity as a political means for gaining national independence from the Japanese colonialism even though American missionaries, deeply imbued with evangelism and pietism, tenaciously opposed the politicization of Korean churches.[8] Reflecting their own ideological biases, these missionaries argued that separation of church and state should be maintained.[9]

Third, because Christianity was accompanied by Western scientific knowledge and thought, Koreans called it the *soehag* (Western learning) movement. A number of Korean literati turned to Protestantism in order to learn Western knowledge and English at the modern schools founded and administered by American, especially Methodist, missionaries. During the Japanese rule over Korea (1910-1945), many Koreans achieved an upward social mobility through the modern education at the missionary schools.[10] Because of this long association of Christianity with social mobility, many contemporary Koreans have approached Christianity with a preconceived perception of it as something "Modern and Western," "made in U.S.A.," and "culturally sophisticated and desirable." Many contemporary Koreans have accepted Christianity, especially Protestantism, as a crucial component of modern, Western, culture which they zealously sought to emulate.

Fourth, it was the inhabitants of what we now call North Korea who, en masse, enthusiastically embraced Christianity at the turn of the century as an alternative to the corrupt state bureaucracy of the Yi dynasty (1392-1910) and to the ruling Confucian ideology. (During the Yi dynasty, the government discriminated against North Koreans when appointing the literati to preferred positions in the state bureaucracy.) In a continuation of this pattern, contemporary South Korean democrats including alienated intellectuals, students, and industrial workers have embraced Christian ideals as an alternative to the Korean tradition of what Karl Wittfogel called "Oriental Despotism."[11] The Korean version of the "Oriental Despotism" continues in the forms of fascist government in South Korea and of totalitarian communistic government in North Korea.

Fifth, an affinity between Christianity and Korean traditional religions such as Confucianism and shamanism is another factor that has contributed to the rapid growth of Korean Christianity.[12] This idea is well supported by an American missionary report published in 1907:

Many of the religious characteristics of the Korean people mark them for discipleship in the Christian faith. Believing as they do in the universal presence of spirits, it is not difficult for them to accept the doctrines of the spiritual nature of God. Confucianism with its age-long insistence on the fact that man is a moral being and must obey moral laws, prepares them to sincerely exemplify Christian ethics in their life.[13]

This religious affinity has effected such theological characteristics of Korean Protestantism as Confucian-style conservatism and shamanistic utilitarianism.

Sixth, the violent social changes that have swept over South Korean society since 1965 are another relevant factor for the mass conversion. Korean urbanites, most of whom are migrants from rural areas, seek a new religion—Christianity—in their search for a spiritual security and a new meaning of life in a turbulent urban society.[14]

All the aforementioned causal factors, which are well known to any serious students of history of Korean Protestant church, however, do not sufficiently explain the dramatic upsurge of Korean Protestant churches in the United States although such factors as "the religious affinity" and "the effect of the social changes" have some effect on the expansion. Therefore, we would like to examine another factor for the growth of Korean Protestantism, i.e., the traditional propensity of Koreans to create "personal community." The term "personal community" does not refer to a specific geographic area but to a set of personal networks through which persons or members exchange help, affection, loyalty, status symbol, material resources and flattery.[15] The effect of the personal community on the differential growth rates of Korean Methodism and Presbyterianism in both Korea and the United States will be analyzed from a historical perspective.

Different Missionary Policies of Methodism and Presbyterianism

Four Presbyterian groups from northern and southern U.S.A., Canada, and Australia began to undertake missions in Korea between 1884 and 1898. In 1907 the four missionary groups were merged to establish the Presbyterian Church of Korea. Two American Methodist groups—The Methodist Episcopal Church and the Methodist Episcopal Church, South—arrived in Korea in

1884 and 1896 respectively and cooperated with each other for their common mission. In 1930, long before the merger of the two groups in the United States, the two groups in Korea united to form the independent Korean Methodist Church whose unity still continues by overcoming two schisms of 1946 and 1950.[16] Several American Baptist missionaries came to Korea in the decade of 1890's. But they were so ill-financed and ill-supported by the Baptist Foreign Missionary Society that in 1900 they virtually gave up their missionary works in Korea. This led to a sluggish growth of Korean Baptist churches in Korea.

Although the two Protestant denominations—Methodism and Presbyterianism—began to recruit new members at the same time, the effectiveness of their missionary work differed substantially. As we have noted, as of 1982, Korean Presbyterian churches claimed some 5 million adherents whereas the Korean Methodist Church embraced some 800,000; in the United States, Korean Presbyterians also overwhelmingly outnumber their Methodist counterparts. This difference in numerical strength is quite striking in light of the fact that, in 1980 in the U.S., Methodists outnumbered Presbyterians by a margin of 3 to 1.[17]

A popular explanation for the difference in membership strength between the two denominations is that Presbyterian missionaries concentrated their efforts on the establishment of local churches partly through the education of village youth to assume church leadership in their local churches; whereas Methodist missionaries focused their energies and resources on the foundation of modern schools, which played an important role in the modernization of Korea.[18] This popular explanation does not provide us with a full picture. In fact, Methodist missionaries, like their Presbyterian fellows, endeavored to build local churches by resorting to such Methodist institutions as "circuit riders," "class meetings," and "revival services."[19]

A fundamental reason for the differential membership strength can be attributed to policy differences. Presbyterian missionaries adopted the widely praised Nevius Plan as their missionary strategy while Methodist missionaries did not accept the plan for a reason unknown to Korean church historians.[20] It is our assumption that American Methodist missionaries rejected the Nevius Plan, which was constructed by John L. Nevius, a Presbyterian missionary in China, because it was not compatible with the episcopal, connectional system of Methodism. The Nevius Plan is based upon the three principles of self-propagation, self-government, and self-support:

Self-propagation. Every Christian was expected to teach the faith to others, not as a professional evangelist but while carrying on his normal occupation.

Self-government. Groups of believers selected from among themselves their own unpaid "leaders," these groups were organized into circuits served by paid "helpers," preferably but not necessarily supported by the groups themselves.

Self-support. Each group was expected to build its own church and call and support its own pastor. Until they were thus self-supporting, they met in Christian homes and shared the services of a circuit evangelist.[21]

The Nevius Plan was designed to overcome the traditional method of carrying missions relying upon missionary funds to hire native converts in establishing and running the church. The plan, which was aimed at toughening converts by making them free from the foreign funds, was uniquely successful in Korea.[22] In view of the achievement oriented, individualistic character of Koreans, it opened a Pauline opportunity for a true believer to set up a "frontier" church upon which he depended for livelihood. More importantly, the Nevius Plan allowed local villagers to incorporate Protestantism into their traditional organizational patterns. Koreans were very responsive to the plan partly because the social structure of their villages coincided with the organizational principles of the plan.

Traditional Social Structure as It Fits into Presbyterian Form of Government

First of all, we must note that traditional Korean villages maintained an unofficial self-government.[23] The government of the Yi dynasty adopted a laissez-faire posture toward villages with the exception of such central controls as taxation and conscription of corvee labor. Shannon McCune observed:

From the court there spread down in the Confucian tradition a bureaucracy through the provinces and counties (or magistracies) to the towns. Villages were largely neglected except as a source of taxes and labor. In the village an unofficial type of democracy prevailed with local maintenance of law and order and with the carrying out of local public works. Contacts with town and county officials and adjudication of minor disputes or disruption of peace and order was the responsibility of the village elders, the male heads of the leading families. Usually on a rotating basis, one person was selected as the headman of the village.[24]

In the village, peasants organized their life activities on the basis of the *kye* association which has an organizational affinity with the Nevius Plan in particular and Presbyterianism in general. The *kye* association is a traditional cooperative that is designed to promote mutual assistance, friendship, good will, and common belief system. During the Yi dynasty of Korea, the cooperatives called *kye* became a dominant civic, economic, and religious institution which peasants organized to combat the exploitations by the central government.[25] The essential characteristics of the *kye* are described as follows:

An important form of mutual assistance was the *kye*, a form of unpaid group cooperation. Some *kye* were formed of small groups of villagers of the same age, sex, and social status. In other cases the entire community would form itself into a *kye* for the purpose of improving general living conditions. *Kye* composed of small, socially homogeneous groups were often created for a specific purpose, such as recreational or religious activities, community school maintenance, or guarding forest resources. Communitywide *kye* looked after village needs and could be expected to help in the event of death, sickness, and disaster. Groups of neighbors would also cooperate in maintaining roads and bridges and thatching and building houses.[26]

The traditional spirit of forming a small group association for a specific purpose was instrumental to the rise of the church. Here is an example:

A Korean village is generally composed of a number of closely related families. If the first man converted in the village happened to be influential, his conversion might result in the mass conversion of the village . . . Again, when the majority of a village turned to the new religion, the minority either conformed or withdrew. There was a fellowship among converts that was attractive to an outsider. The Christians were sympathetic toward each other and stood together in sorrow and joy.[27]

In addition to the Korean penchant for small units of self-government, Confucianism generated another behavioral pattern which affected the hierarchical social relationships in the church. Social relationships of traditional Korean society were based upon the so-called "five cardinal relations" which were defined and promoted by Confucianism as an intrinsic part of the social order. The "five cardinal relations" are relations between ruler and subject, father and son, husband and wife, brothers, and friends. Confucianism specified a moral code of conduct governing each of the relations. For instance, rulers must show benevolence toward subjects,

subjects must be loyal to their rulers. All realtionships, except those between friends, are hierarchical. A leading Korean novelist observed this Confucian hierarchical order permeates the Korean church:

The relation between pastor or elders and the lay believers is something like that between rulers and subjects . . . Pastors and elders always try to stand above the laity while the latter accept their ruling and interference as a matter of course . . . Pastors and elders of the Korean Church today stand above their lay brethren, trying to enjoy superior privileges in all things.[28]

In addition, the "five relations" express an interpersonal particularism, for they do not pertain to other interactions such as those between strangers, between villages, between cities, and between nations. The devotion of ethical reciprocity would not apply beyond the boundary of the "five relations." This ethical boundary set up a "community of blood" in contrast to the Puritan "community of faith" where a common ethical way of life was extended beyond the boundaries of kinship, village, city, and nation.[29] The "five relations" embody a Confucian personalism which is expressed in dealing with others in terms of primary group contacts. Weber noted the Confucian personalism in the context of China:

Chinese ethic developed its strongest motives in the circle of naturally grown, personalist associations or associations affiliated with or modeled after them. This contrasts sharply with the Puritan ethic which amounts to an objectification of man's duties as a creature of God. The religious duty towards the hidden and supra-mundane God caused the Puritan to appraise all human relations—including those naturally nearest in life—as mere means and expression of a mentality reaching beyond the organic relations of life. The religious duty of the pious Chinese, in contrast, enjoined him to develop himself within the organically given, personal relations.[30]

As we shall discuss later, Korean Protestants in both South Korea and the United States have carried this Confucian personalism into church community, thereby diluting the Christian ideal of universal brotherhood. Again, we would like to point out that the Confucian personalism has strengthened the Presbyterian pattern in Korean Protestant churches of almost all denominations. Presbyterianism in a Korean context embodies the Confucian hierarchical order in church community. It also provides a local autonomy necessary for constructing a delicate web of human networks expressing the Confucian personalism.

The Personal Community and Church Schism

We have so far discussed three such traditional institutions as unofficial self-government of village, *kye* association, and Confucian personalism to the extent to which they account for the prevalence of Presbyterianism in Korea. Needless to say, all the traditional institutions have been weakened and transformed by the forces of South Korean industrialization, urbanization, and modernization. However, weakening and transformation do not signal disappearance. The traditional Korean propensity for forming and running "primary" groups or associations, formal or informal, designed to relate oneself to others in concrete and personal terms has survived the forces of bureaucratization and urbanization of South Korean society. In the face of urban anomie, competition, and impersonality, South Korean urbanites have created and relied upon an "infinite" number of small, informal, and "primary" groups.[51] This leads us to construct the concept of Korean "personal community" in an ideal, typical sense.

When the "personal community" involves a small number of persons as in the cases of informal alumni meetings and *kye* associations, it exhibits the characteristics similar to those of what Charles Horton Cooley calls "primary groups." "By primary groups I mean those characterized by intimate face-to-face association and cooperation. . . . The most important spheres of this intimate association and cooperation—though by no means the only ones—are the family, the play group of children, and the neighborhood or community group of elders. These are practically universal, belonging to all times and all stages of development; and are accordingly a chief basis for what is universal in human ideals."[52] As the primary group can be located within large corporate organizations in Western societies (Bensman and Rosenberg, 1963: 82-83), so Korean personal community develops and exists in large organizations such as political parties, churches, military institutions, and business corporations.[53]

Since personal community expresses neither a territorial nor an ideological bond, it is more likely to foster factionalism in such voluntary organizations as churches, political parties, and professional associations. Moffett observed the Korean tradition of schisms:

> But ever since the war in 1950, the Korean church has been struck with the plague of virulent schisms

that have hurt her far more than any Communist invasion. Presbyterians have split into four rival factions. The Methodists have divided twice, but are successfully reunited again. Both the Baptists and the Holiness Church have been pulled apart by factional disputes. Some excuse these schisms as only natural in Korea where division is a national tradition. Buddhists have split into open warfare between married priests and unmarried priests. The sedate Confucianists are split in two fighting over roles in the temple. Factionalism in Korea's political parties has weakened the nation for centuries. Even the Seoul Symphony Orchestra split recently in a dispute over directors.[54]

As a result of continuous schisms and subschisms within both individual churches and denominational bodies, Korean Protestantism as of 1978, consisted of a total of 188 denominational bodies.[55] As of 1981, Korean Presbyterianism alone was divided into 45 denominational bodies.[56] This schismatic phenomenon has prompted Korean journalists to coin and use a new terminology—*gae gyohoe jueui* which roughly means "individual churchism." It refers to a fortress mentality of Korean Christians; they are concerned only with their own church. For better or worse, these religious schisms in Korea stimulate the growth of church membership partly because a splintered church or a group of splintered churches struggles to increase its membership. This partly explains the substantial proliferation of Presbyterian churches. Ironically, the lack of schisms in the Korean Methodist Church partly accounts for the low growth rates of its church membership.

The Emergence of Korean Protestant Churches in the New York Metropolitan Area

Korean Protestant churches in the New York metropolitan area have increased in number from six in 1971 to some one hundred fifty in 1983, reflecting not only the dramatic increase of Korean immigrants since 1970 but also a "Great Awakening" among Koreans in the new land. In the New York metropolitan area where some 100,000 Koreans reside, there is one Protestant church per 700 Koreans.[57] Of the one hundred fifty churches, thirty one are Methodist churches affiliated directly or indirectly with The United Methodist Church.

The dramatic surge of Korean Protestant churches is attributed to several factors. First of all, Korean immigrants are blessed with a sufficient supply of their own ministers. This puts them in contrast with other ethnic minorities who suffer a shortage of ministers. A large number of Korean ministers and theological students have entered the United States to seek economic, ministerial, and educational opportunities. Their influx has been facilitated by the United States immigration law which grants permanent residentship to a qualified ethnic minister. In addition, Korean-run theological schools with an educational affiliation with American seminaries have emerged in the United States and produced ethnic ministers without a strict "quality control."

An organizational connection between a Korean denominational church and its American counterpart should also be noted as a factor for the sufficient supply of ministers. For instance, the Korean Methodist Church in South Korea can send its missioners or ministers to the United States to establish "mission" churches under an arrangement with The United Methodist Church. A statement of agreement between the two churches reads: "The rapid growth of Korean population and congregations in the United States has naturally drawn our missional attention. With a deep feeling of Christian responsibility for our pastoral care and educational nurture of these congregations, both the Korean Methodist Church and The United Methodist Church affirm their joint missional task. For this specific task we have agreed to launch a missionary program between the Korean Methodist Church and The United Methodist Church by establishing mission churches in the United States of America."[38]

The abundant supply of Korean ministers has affected "a sprouting of Korean Churches on every block of New York City." A pioneering spirit of the minister is one of the key factors behind this upsurge:

Simply because a church provides its minister with his means of livelihood and the same high prestige his profession enjoys in the home country, the minister's personal ambition plays a dominant role in the emergence as well as the functioning of churches. Most ministers intend to reside permanently in the United States. For most, their professional training, generally acquired in the homeland, could not be transferred to any other occupation in the labor market of the larger society. Thus the meaning of each minister's existence in both an idealistic and a materialistic sense is directed toward creating and leading his own ethnic church. This is one of the most important causes of the rapid increase in the number of Korean churches. . . . [39]

The achievement ethic of the minister leads to fierce interchurch competition in recruiting church members. A Korean Methodist minister confessed: "There is no Christian spirit in our Methodist churches (other Korean Methodist churches located within the distance of 20 minutes' driving from his church). They resort to all kinds of subtle means to take away lambs (his congregation)." Each Korean church tends to be insular, with little contact or cooperation with other Korean churches. The Korean church community is atomized and individualized; it indeed fits into the Korean concept of "individual churchism." A Korean Presbyterian minister, who has established a new church, lamented, "They (other neighboring Korean churches) have never helped us. They think we're the enemy." And yet, there is a deep sense of "weness" and belonging within an individual church. The Korean quest for community in the new land is another key factor accounting for the rapid increase in the number of Korean Protestant churches.

The Korean Church Community in the New York Metropolitan Area

Given their socio-economic marginal status, Korean immigrants have selected and reinforced kinds of Korean cultural patterns which are conducive to their survival and success in a "hostile" and "alien" environment of urban America. They have accentuated the homeland pattern of the personal community. They have expressed their traditional propensity for personal community by forming a variety of small, voluntary associations.[40] Of all the informal or formal associations that provide them with a stage for the personal community, the Protestant churches are the most important beachhead in their struggle for the American dream. This largely explains the massive conversion of Korean immigrants into Protestantism. In spite of or because of their marginal status in a new land, they reaffirm or affirm Protestantism and feel a sense of pride, mission, and identity. A Korean Methodist minister stated:

They are lonely; they are discriminated against; they are oppressed by the system; they are underemployed, exploited and helpless in the new land . . . Korean-American United Methodists bring with them diverse gifts which their ethnic heritage endowed. They will bring with them the living faith tempered by the suffering; tested by the oppressions and persecutions; and nurtured by the hunger, poverty and hardship. They will bring with them the evangelical fervor once John Wesley had embraced and the disciplined life-style that is not foreign to the discipleship of Christ.[41]

233

However, Korean Protestant churches are much more than simple sites for religious services and salvation. In the absence of a territorial base for an ethnic community, Korean immigrants self-consciously organize church activities in order to build personal communities. The following are the basic characteristics of Korean Protestant churches in the New York metropolitan area:

First, by opening membership to all segments of the population, the churches provide a grass-roots base for communal action. At least for members, the churches provide some degree of integration and coordination for divergent life activities, an integration that does not exist in nonreligious organizations.

Second, as a nonterritorial base for community action, the churches provide members with a "family atmosphere," in which everyone knows everyone else and everyone else's business—a core characteristic of the personal community.

Third, by serving as a surrogate for the extended family, churches have become a focus for strengthening the immigrants' psychological defenses against the dominant institutions and culture of the larger society. A Korean Methodist minister defended a Korean linguistic subculture. " . . . Much is lost when you worship in language other than your own. No wonder that ethnic people naturally seek to attend the ethnic church where their own language is spoken. . . . Jesus was a Jew, spoke Aramaic language, the language of the time and the culture."[42]

Fourth, the most important task that the minister is expected to perform is to create a "family atmosphere" essential to the formulation of a "hot church." In order to accomplish the task, the minister must play multiple secular roles that are not defined by church polity: "The Korean pastor finds himself with many different responsibilities. He is a social worker who must help his people find jobs and apartments, who gives rides, buys cars, shops, translates, interprets, gets drivers' licenses and is responsible for the educating of the children."[43] In order to play the mundane roles effectively, the minister must become a well-rounded person capable of having a good rapport with all the church members. The minister, who neglects to play the secular roles but acts like a professional, time-conscious, and task-oriented American minister, will be judged negatively by the congregation: "He is too selfish." "He leans upon the American hierarchy (The United Methodist Church)."

By performing the multiple, secular functions, the minister actualizes the Confucian persona-lism the expressive primary group relationships upon which the personal community of church members is built. Since the minister and the congregation are inclined to "concretize" their loyalties and interests through the interpersonal interactions in the church at the expense of abstract, transcendental ideals and values, the church is inherently vulnerable to division and schism. Many Korean Protestant churches in the New York metropolitan area, like their counterparts in Korea, have been plagued by schisms and sub-schisms. The schisms have taken place for a variety of "personal" reasons including intrachurch factionalism over church leadership, church affairs, and the minister's personality and life style. A Korean theological student seriously said: "Many Korean ministers have been forced to resign because they cannot bear church members' innuendos against their wives. This is a big problem facing Korean churches." It is interesting to note that church schisms over the minister's theological position have been few in number.

As in South Korea, church schisms and divisions are most pronounced among Korean Presbyterian churches. This is so mainly because, for better or worse, the Presbyterian form of government in a Korean context is a breeding ground for a democratic and dynamic factionalism. In addition, the founding minister of a Presbyterian church tends to try to exercise an absolute control over church affairs in order to ensure his lifelong tenure. In doing this, he allies himself with a faction of the members loyal to him. A Presbyterian minister shouted to a dissenting group in a church dispute: "This church is my church. If you do not agree with me, please leave this church." In a positive sense, the schisms endemic to Presbyterian Korean churches contribute to a rapid increase in the number of Presbyterian churches in the United States.

Church as a Status Community

Because of the Confucian tradition of hierarchical order, Koreans in both South Korea and the United States accord high esteem and status to church leaders such as elders and deacons or deaconesses. As we shall see later, Korean Methodist churches in both South Korea and the United States have similar lay positions. In the context of the Confucian ideal of moral perfectability, the Koreans word *jangno* (or elder) evokes positive moral connotations: sobriety, benevolence, and responsibility. A Korean Methodist minister preached: "You should have your first son to be a minister; the second son to be an elder." Since the congregation is very responsive to this kind of veneration of elders, many Koreans strive to acquire that position. The marginal status of Korea intensifies the struggle for the status building in the church.[44] Here is a detailed description of it:

> . . . Church lay leaders are heavily drawn from among well-established and successful professionals and business men, most of whom are proud of their long experience in the United States. Far fewer businessmen than professionals are church members, all successful Koreans in these occupational classes have deeper status anxiety than do new arrivals struggling for everyday economic gains, because economic success allows more time for leisure activities and hence for status building. Even successful professionals cannot get along with their American colleagues in pursuing American lifestyles, for money alone does not guarantee successful businessmen and professionals a commensurate status recognition in the larger society. This sense of status alienation causes many successful professionals and businessmen to commit themselves deeply to church affairs as to other community activities. In these activities they can enjoy the prestige, granted by their fellow countrymen, that is denied them by their occupational or professional peers.[45]

The presbytery form of church government allows an ideal state for the status recognition and competition. This partly explains why the organizational structure of the lay leadership in almost all of the Korean Protestant churches in both South Korea and the United States is derived from the American Presbyterian church. Trustees, deacons or deaconesses, and elders who are selected by popular vote, constitute the lay leadership. In Korean Protestant churches, elders are elected for a life term—a major difference from the American Presbyterian church in which elders are elected every three years. The Korean Methodist Church in South Korea has a similar structure of lay leadership centered around the administrative board largely consisting of *jango* (elders), *gweonsa* (exhorting deacons), and *jibsa* (deacons). Although the Korean Methodist "elders" do not perform the same administrative functions as their Presbyterian counterparts, they are the most influential lay leaders in church government. They have their own nationwide organization called the National Council of Elders through which they exert a great influence on the politics of the Korean Methodist Church in South Korea.[46]

Korean Methodists in the United States had a serious problem with a structure of lay leadership, for the United Methodist Churches are free from a "presbyterization," i.e., do not have Presbyterian ranking positions of lay leaders. The position entitled lay leaders within American Methodists does not entail a body of lay leaders with the power, "high" status and religious sanctity that Presbyterian elders or Baptist deacons possess. Under the circumstance, Korean Methodists recommended and proposed to The United Methodist Church that they be allowed to apply the leadership ranking system of the Korean Methodist Church to Korean Methodist churches in the United States. Their proposal was approved at the 1978 General Conference in Chicago. Most of the Korean Methodist churches in the New York area have adopted and operated the system in the manner of Korean Presbyterian churches even though the National Association of Korean American United Methodist Churches stipulates that such positions as "elder steward," "exhorting steward," and "steward" are strictly honorific without administrative power.

This "presbyterization" of Korean Methodist churches has provided powerful internal dynamics to church organization.[47] It has activated the traditional Korean "instincts" for status recognition through Confucian hierarchical social relationships, in which certain responsibilities, obligations, and honors are arranged according to stratified statuses. A Korean Methodist minister said: 'Of course, they are a honorific position; but they are very important to us. We must reward those who have deeply committed themselves to the church for a long period of time. Otherwise, they would be bored with church life."

Conclusion

We have analysed the effect of the Korean traditional organizations and Confucian ethos on the rapid expansion of Korean Protestant churches in both Korea and the United States and the differential growth rates of Presbyterian and Methodist churches. Traditional organizations of Korea have an institutional affinity with Presbyterian organization. The tradition of local self-rule as expressed by the village structure and the cooperatives called *kye* coupled with the Confucian ethos of personalism created an atmosphere which was conducive to the adoption of American Presbyterianism. The traditional behavioral patterns of Koreans are well suited to the presbytery form of church government. Perhaps, this is the key factor in the success of the Nevius Plan in Korea.

The fact that Koreans have a penchant for small, autonomous groups or associations in which they relate themselves to others in concrete and personal terms has worked against a centralized Methodist government. In addition, Koreans tend to be suspicious of any form of central government, for they were exploited, harassed, and oppressed by the central bureaucracy of Yi dynasty. However, because of the Korean propensity for small groups, Methodist's "class meetings" have been successfully transplanted into Korean soil. Almost all of the Protestant churches, including Presbyterian denominations in both South Korea and the United States, have heavily relied upon that Methodist institution. For the same reason, Korean Methodist Church, in both South Korea and the United States have undergone a "presbyterization" in response to local needs.

In spite of or because of the tremendous social changes in South Korea, generated by recent economic development and urbanization, urban Koreans express their traditional inclination for clublike cells, and small groups or associations in which they exchange mutual assistances, loyalties, and affections. This is what we call Korean personal community. Confronted with a political uncertain urban anomie, and dog-eat-dog competition of South Korea, a large number of Koreans attempt to locate a spiritual security as well as a personal community in Christian churches. This has led to an unprecedented upsurge of Korean Protestantism.

Korean immigrants in the United States, many of whom experienced the "Great Awakening" of South Korea, have reinforced their cultural patterns of the personal community in order to defend themselves from the "hostile" and "alien" forces of the larger society. Of all the small, voluntary associations which provide a stage for the personal community, the Protestant churches play the most important role by becoming an effective substitute for an ethnic territorial community. Mainly because the personal community constructed in the church puts personal and concrete interests and loyalties ahead of Christian ideals of transcendental unity and brotherhood, Korean Protestant churches subscribe to the "individual churchism" which results in division and schism.[48]

Largely owing to the episcopal, connectional system of American Methodism, the Korean Methodist churches are far less prone to the "individual churchism" than other Korean Protestant churches in the United States. The central, administrative authority embedded in the connectional system of the United Methodist Church greatly helps Korean Methodist churches stave off church schisms over congre-

gational frictions with the pastor. However, from a Korean congregational point of view, the centralized form of Methodist governance causes many Korean Methodist ministers to develop a sort of "welfare mentality" which leads them to "lean on the Methodist bureaucracy," and which makes them ignore the congregational demand for ministerial devotion and attention to "personal" church affairs. Generally speaking, in a pure quantitative sense, Methodist governance moderates the numerical growth of Korean Methodist churches by depriving Korean congregations of local autonomy—the most important condition for an explosive church expansion in a Korean context.

NOTES

1. Byong Suh Kim, "Hangug gyohoe eui sinhag-jeog ihae" [Theological Understanding of the Korean Church], *The Korean Christian Review*, June 1982, p. 20.
2. Henry Scott Stokes, "Korea's Church Militant," *The New York Times Magazine*, November 28, 1982, p. 69.
3. Ibid., p. 68.
4. *The Dong-A Daily News*, Feb. 10, 1983.
5. See Samuel Hugh Moffett, *The Christians of Korea* (New York: Friendship Press, 1962), pp. 49-54; Spencer J. Palmer, "Western Religion and Korean Culture," in *Korea's Response to the West*, ed. Yung Hwan Jo (Kalamazoo, Michigan: The Korean Research and Publications, Inc., 1969), pp. 99-100.
6. *From Max Weber: Essays in Sociology*, trans. and eds. H.H. Gerth and C. Wright Mills (New York: Oxford University Press, 1958), p. 273.
7. Palmer, "Western Religion and Korean Culture," pp. 102-104.
8. Kyung Bae Min, *Hangug gidog-gyohoesa* [History of the Korean Church], (Seoul, Korea: The Christian Literature Society of Korea, 1972), pp. 180-194.
9. Kyung Bae Min, *Hangug minjog gyohoe hyeong-seong saron*]History of the Formation of Korean National Churches], (Seoul, Korea: Yonsei University Press, 1974), pp. 35-54.
10. Gregory Henderson, *Korea: The Politics of the Vortex* (Cambridge: Harvard University Press, 1968), pp. 207-208.
11. Karl A. Wittfogel, *Oriental Despotism: Comparative Studies of Total Power* (New Haven: Yale University Press, 1957).
12. Sung Bum Yun, *Gidog-gyo wa hangug sasang* [Christianity and Korean Thought], (Seoul, Korea: The Christian Literature Society of Korea, 1961), pp. 159-184; Myong Kwan Ji, *Hangug-in gwa gidog-gyo* [Koreans and Christianity], Seoul, Korea: Korean Christian Council of Education, 1969), pp. 144-155.
13. George Herber Jones, *Korea: The Land, People and Customs* (Cincinnati: Jennings and Graham, 1907), p. 64.
14. Kim, "Hangug gyohoe," p. 20; Stokes, "Korea's Church Militant, " p. 68.
15. For a different definition, see Elliot Liebow, *Tally's Corner, a Study of Negro Streetcorner Men* (Boston: Little, Brown and Company, 1967), p. 162.
16. Moffett, *The Christians of Korea*, pp. 112-114.
17. *New York Times*, June 15, 1982.
18. Rev. Henry G. Appenzeller, a graduate of Drew Theological Seminary, arrived in Korea in 1885 to "break the bonds that bind the people and bring them to the light and liberty of God's children." He played a pioneering role in the establishment of Western educational institutions. See Min, *Hangug gidog*, pp. 84-88.

19. Ibid., pp. 163-164; D. Allen Clark, *Hangug gyohoesa* [History of the Korean Church], (Seoul, Korea: The Christian Literature Society of Korea, 1961), pp. 84-88.
20. Min, *Hangug gidog*, p. 161.
21. Moffett, *The Christians of Korea*, p. 60.
22. There were regional variations in the success of the Nevius Plan. For instance, the Koreans in the southern part of Korea, especially, Seoul area, closely associated with the Confucian moral and political establishment of Yi dynasty, were not as responsive to the plan as those of the Northwestern provinces—those who were historically alienated from the Confucian establishment. In the northwest we can observe a striking difference in missionary success between Methodists and Presbyterians: "The Methodists working in the same area (the northwest) were reported by William Hunt in 1909 to be using American funds for building and for paying helpers. But he reports that this use of American church funds caused troubles of all kinds. The Methodist Church could grow only as fast as the money for buildings and pastors' salaries could be provided by the missionaries, while the adjacent Presbyterian Church, free of foreign control and funds but with plenty of working assistance from dedicated foreigners, grew rapidly." Roy E. Shearer, "The Evangelistic Missionary's Role in Church Growth in Korea," *International Review of Mission*, vol. 54 (1965), p. 466.
23. As for traditional Chinese village, see Max Weber, *The Religion of China: Confucianism and Taoism*, trans. and ed. Hans H. Gerth (New York: The Free Press, 1951) pp. 91-95.
24. Shannon McCune, *Korea: Land of Broken Calm*, (Princeton: D. Van Nostrand Co., Inc., 1966), p. 41.
25. G. Back Lee, *Hangugsa sinron* [New Theory of Korean History], (Seoul, Korea: Iljogak, 1967), p. 281.
26. Nena Vreeland et al., *Area Handbook for Korea* (Washington, D.C.: U.S. Government Printing Office, 1975), pp. 89-90.
27. L. George Paik, *The History of Protestant Missions in Korea 1832-1910* (Korea: Pyeng Yang Union Christian College Press, 1929), p. 284.
28. Kwang Su Yi, "Defects of the Korean Church Today," *The Korea Mission Field*, vol. 14 (1916), p. 253.
29. Weber, *The Religion of China*, Chapter 8.
30. Ibid., p. 236.
31. *The Dong-A Daily News*, March 9, 1983.
32. Charles Horton Cooley, *Social Organization* (New York: Scribner, 1909), pp. 23-24.
33. In this context, it must be noted that South Korean President Chun Doo Hwan masterminded a successful military coup in 1979 with the active supports of less than ten junior generals, all of whom were once classmates at the Korean Military Academy.
34. Moffett, *The Christians of Korea*, p. 27.
35. *World Christian Encyclopedia: A Comparative Study of Churches and Religion in the Modern World AD 1900-2000* (New York: Oxford University Press, 1982), p. 444. This figure includes indigenous churches.
36. *The Korea Gospel Weekly*, Jan. 31, 1981.
37. Hae Jong Kim, *Korean-American Ministries* (Madison, N.J.: Multi-Ethnic Center for Ministry, Drew University, 1980), p. 9.
38. *Korean-American United Methodist Reporter* (National Association of Korean American United Methodist Church), Spring, 1982, p. 2.
39. Illsoo Kim, *New Urban Immigrants: the Korean Community in New York* (Princeton: Princeton University Press, 1981), p. 198.
40. Ibid., pp. 208-225.
41. Kim, *Korean-American Ministries*, pp. 6-19.
42. Ibid., p. 5.
43. Sang Mo Kim, *A Process of Growth in Christian Experience Through Small Group Sharing and Searching: For Constituent Members of a Korean-American Congregation*. A dissertation for Doctor of Ministry (Drew University, 1979), p. 1.
44. See also J. Allen Williams, Jr. *et al.*, "Voluntary Associations and Minority Status: A Comparative Analysis of Anglo, Black, and Mexican Americans," *American Sociological Review*, vol. 38 (1973), pp. 637-646.
45. Kim, *New Urban Immigrants*, p. 204.
46. The Korean strength of presbytery rule is demonstrated by the fact that most of Christian signers of the Declaration of Independence, issued on the occasion of the Independence Movement of 1919 against Japanese rule, were local lay leaders representing local church communities. See Henderson, *Korea*, p. 82.
47. Another form of "presbyterization" took place in the Korean Methodist Church in South Korea. The 1976 General Conference passed a proposal aimed at a decentralization of the Korean Methodist Church. The administrative power of bishops, for instance, was severely curtailed in favor of the autonomy of local churches. The Korean Methodist Church is nicknamed a "Methodist Presbyterian Church."
48. The analysis of the effects of Korean shamanism, Buddhism, and Confucianism on the theological characteristics of Korean Protestantism would further clarify this problem of the schismatic church community.